AutoCAD 2027 for the Interior Designer

AutoCAD for MAC and PC

Dean Muccio

SDC PUBLICATIONS

SDC Publications
P.O. Box 1334
Mission, KS 66222
913-262-2664
www.SDCpublications.com
Publisher: Stephen Schroff

ISBN-13: 978-1-63057-815-2
ISBN-10: 1-63057-815-0

Printed and bound in the United States of America.

Acknowledgements

This version includes AutoCAD 2027 for both the PC and the Mac. Many more students are utilizing the Mac. The 2027 version for the Mac is close to resembling the PC version; however, there are still enough differences between the PC version and the Mac version that it warrants inclusion of those instructions.

This book is dedicated in loving memory to my son Matthew Muccio.

About the Author

Dean Muccio teaches AutoCAD as an online course for the Interior Design program as an adjunct Assistant Professor for Fairfield University, Fairfield, CT. He has also taught a variety of Engineering Graphics and Computer Aided Design and Manufacturing courses.

Dean is a retired Project Engineer from Sikorsky Aircraft Corporation in West Palm Beach, FL. He holds a B.S. degree in Mechanical Engineering from Norwich University, and an M.S. degree in Mechanical Engineering from Yale University.

Dean is a DIY homeowner who has tackled many remodeling projects. He has applied his engineering knowledge to refine his woodworking skills and to develop creative design solutions for space planning. The remodeling projects have provided a practical insight into what an Interior Designer must deal with when creating a design.

Table of Contents

Chapter 15 Miscellaneous – Techniques, Commands, and Options

Chapter 1

Getting Comfortable with AutoCAD

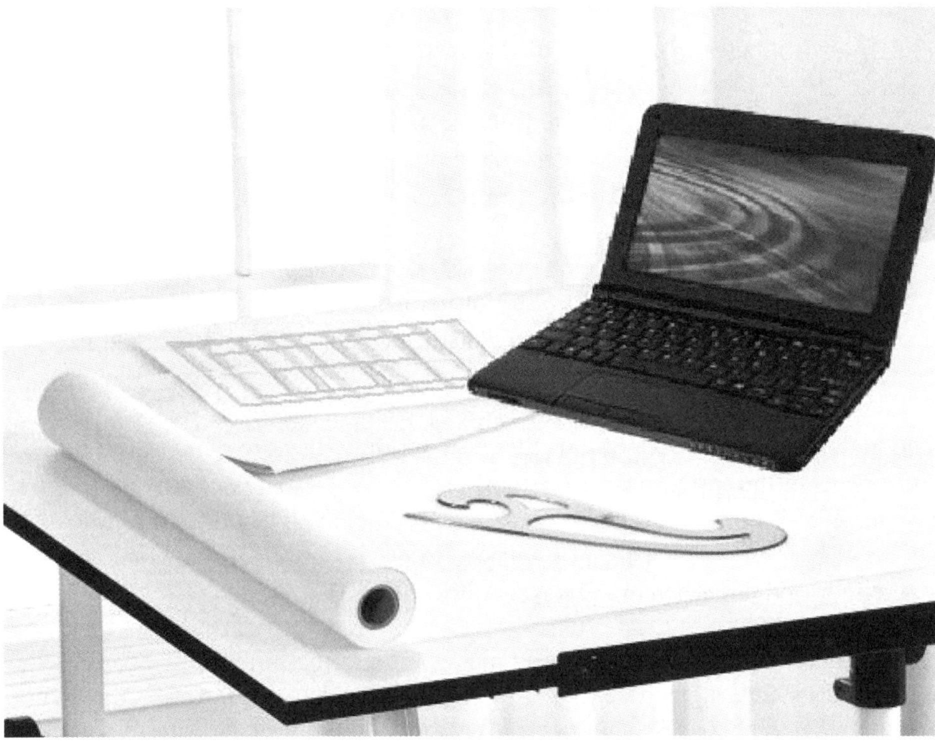

Learning Objectives:

- **Going from drafting to CAD – Ground rules of using AutoCAD**
- **Getting familiar with the AutoCAD Workspace screens**
- **Understanding AutoCAD Toolbars**
- **Getting AutoCAD Help**
- **Customizing your screen appearance and right mouse button**
- **Using a Flash Drive**
- **Opening and Saving drawings**

Introduction to AutoCAD

Congratulations on your decision to use the computer to draw your interior designs. AutoCAD is an excellent product that is very popular. Having your designs in AutoCAD format allows you to make changes easily, and it also allows you to integrate your interior design with the architect's design. In fact, if an architectural drawing is already available on AutoCAD, you can use that to build upon for your interior design.

There are many advantages to using AutoCAD instead of drawing by hand:

- Drawings are done full size and scaled only for printing.
- Working with a design team is easier with AutoCAD.
- You draw fixtures, furniture, appliances, etc. only one time and re-use them for other drawings.
- You can use items drawn by other designers; you no longer need to trace.
- You can have a library of items for re-use.
- You can use layers to visualize selected items one at a time.
- You can create/erase construction lines, etc. without the mess.

A major advantage to using AutoCAD is that all your drawings are done in full scale. For example, if the measurements of the room you are designing are 20′ x 20′, you actually draw the room as 20′ x 20′. If you have been doing your drawings by hand, you have been drawing to scale. Perhaps you have been drawing to ¼″ = 1′. This required you to use an architect scale or a calculator. You do not have to use either of these when drawing on AutoCAD.

Not only does this save you time, but it also makes integrating other drawings into your design very simple. Since it is standard practice to do drawings full scale on AutoCAD, the architectural drawing, and any available drawings such as furniture, appliances, etc. are readily available for your use. Sharing your designs with other designers and vice versa is made easy by drawing to full scale. In fact, there are several internet sites that have pre-drawn AutoCAD items such as furniture, plants, appliances, etc. Some are available for free; others are available for a small charge.

The AutoCAD LT version is for 2D drafting, and it is all the Interior Designer needs to complete floor plan and elevation type drawings. It is more economical than buying the complete AutoCAD version, which includes 3D. Either version works the same in the 2D mode (there is some advanced functionality that is not included in the LT version but is not a necessity for the Interior Designer).

The AutoCAD program has been upgraded over the years to include many enhancements. Most improvements were in the appearance of some command dialog boxes and right mouse-click functionality. There may be some differences in the look of things, but the basic procedures and functions have remained the same. The designer can easily adapt to these differences without the need for a completely new course or text.

Hand Drawing vs. AutoCAD

Using the computer to create your drawings may seem intimidating. This may be true especially if you have not done it before and only use a computer for social media, e-mail, family photos, and shopping. Perhaps you have used it to touch up some photographs using one of the many programs available.

You may be surprised at first that AutoCAD does not treat drawings the same as touching up photos. That is because AutoCAD recognizes the items on your drawing screen as specific objects such as lines, circles, arcs, etc. This is like how a word processing program recognizes the characters on the screen as letters, numbers, etc. – especially when you are using a spellchecker.

When you create your designs using drafting techniques, you strive for accuracy. This is necessary because items must fit properly. It can be discouraging (and expensive) when the carpenter tells you that the cabinets don't fit properly (or any other item) and to make up for it you must revise the design. Had your measurements and drafting been accurate in the first place, this mistake could have been avoided. Although AutoCAD cannot help you in measuring your client's rooms correctly, once you have the measurements, they are accurately reflected on the computer.

Accuracy in AutoCAD is achieved by the fact that it uses X and Y coordinates to determine exactly where lines, circles, arcs, etc. are on the drawing. Fortunately, we do not have to burden ourselves with this fact, and we can create our designs in confidence knowing that AutoCAD is working to keep it precise.

Throughout this book, we will do our best to avoid using X and Y coordinates; of course, there will be instances when it cannot be avoided. Instead, the intention is to keep the method of drawing as similar as possible to how you are currently creating drawings using your drafting equipment.

For example:

- We will draw lines longer than needed and trim them as required
    - Trimming will be like using your erasing shield to remove the excess line and have a clean intersection
- We will use circles and trim them to become arcs
    - Just like when you use a circle template or compass, sometimes you draw an arc bigger than needed and have to clean it up with your erasing shield

The best part is that we will not have eraser debris all over the place!

Clarifications and Ground Rules

Before we begin, it is best to clarify how to interact with the computer so that AutoCAD interprets your intentions correctly. Because it is a computer, it is looking at specific ways in which you communicate with it. You will be primarily using your mouse to pick locations on your drawing and selecting commands via icons or pull-down menus. You will also use your keyboard to key in specific values, and also for command shortcuts.

The following may help you throughout this book and with using AutoCAD. Some of the rules will be needed as we progress, so you may wish to refer to them, as we get further along.

Clarifications:

1. The words Pick, or Select, are meant to indicate that you must use your mouse/cursor and left click. For instances where a right mouse click is needed, it will be specifically stated to right-click.
2. Whenever it is required to type in a value or option letter, this must be followed by pressing the ↵ Enter key. AutoCAD will not recognize what you have typed on the command line until the ↵ Enter key is pressed.

AutoCAD Ground Rules:

1. AutoCAD is based on an X-Y coordinate system. The horizontal direction, starting from left and going right, is the positive X direction. Starting from right and going left is the negative X direction. The vertical direction, starting from the bottom of the screen and moving up, is the positive Y direction. Starting from the top of the screen and moving down is the negative Y direction. This book will attempt to avoid referring to X and Y directions; instead, it will refer to horizontal and vertical directions.

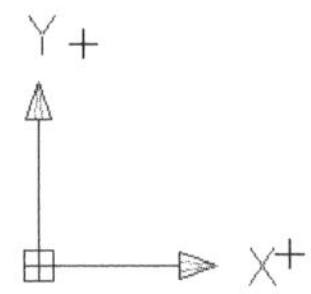

2. Positive angles are measured by starting from the positive X-axis and rotating in a counterclockwise direction. Note that you can use negative angles. For example, -90° is the same as 270°.

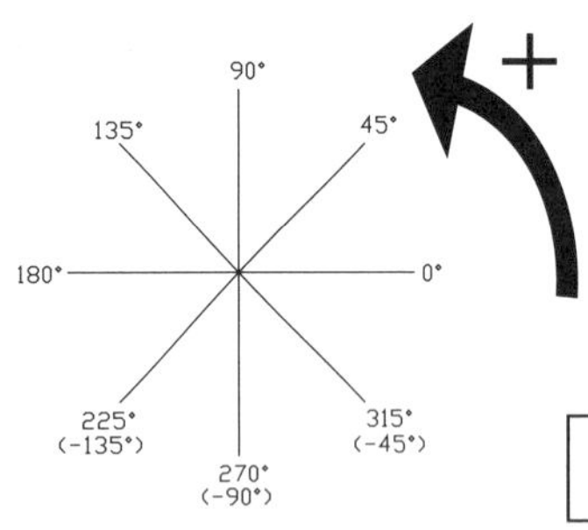

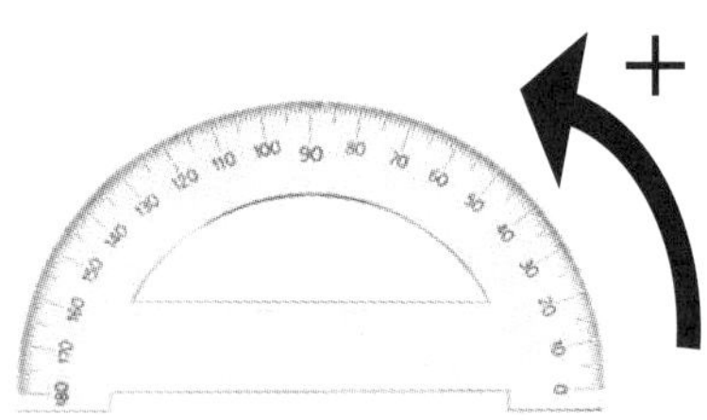

Angles are measured counterclockwise

3. To exit a command, press the ↵ Enter key or space bar. The Escape key (Esc) can also be used, but sometimes the Escape key will not work (depending on the command).
4. To repeat the previous command you used, press the ↵ Enter key. This comes in handy for fillets and offsets.
5. The default measurement is inches. When keying in distance values for feet, remember to use the foot symbol.
6. Standard practice is to draw everything full scale.
7. If you select objects with no command in the command line, AutoCAD will show grips on that object (little blue boxes). Grips can be removed by pressing the Escape key.

The AutoCAD Screen

When you start the AutoCAD program, the AutoCAD Start screen will appear. It will allow you to start a new drawing, open a drawing, or choose a recently opened drawing. It will also show notifications and connectivity to the internet to allow you to save your work beyond your own computer (this option is not covered in this text).

The Start screen is always available and is shown as a file-folder style tab at the top of the drawing screen. The command ribbon and standard icons are grayed out on the start screen.

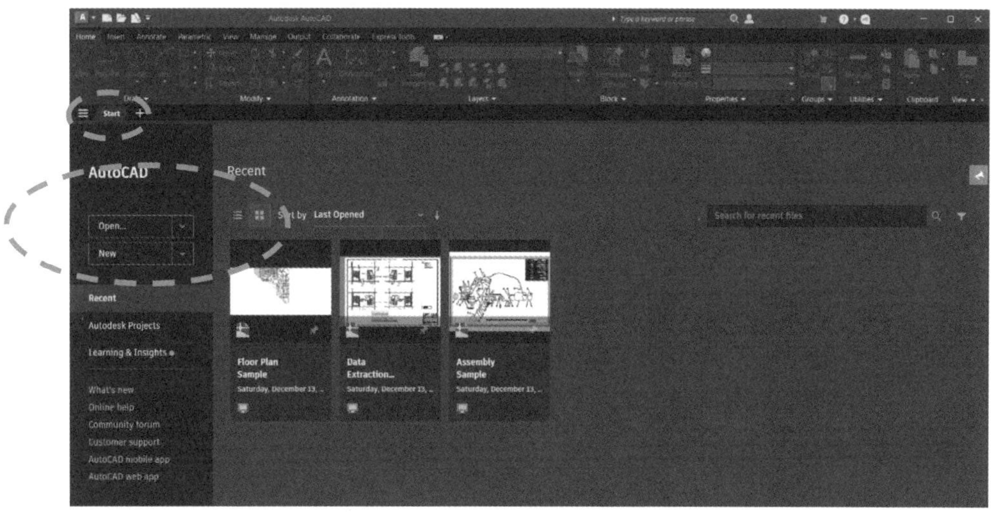

PC Start Screen

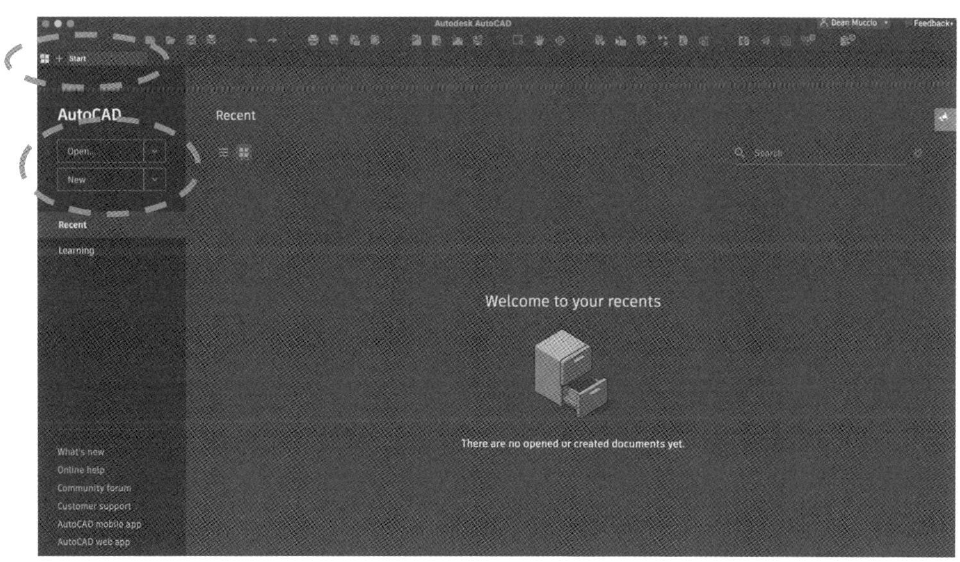

Mac Start Screen

By selecting the New icon, a new drawing is started using the default template, or you can use the pull-down menu and select a template. Once selected, a new tab is created. The new tab shows the name of the drawing (initially AutoCAD assigns the name of Drawing1). The new drawing name can be changed when you save it – more on this later. Also, later we will learn to create and use templates.
To help guide you through learning AutoCAD, it is a good idea to get familiar with the AutoCAD screen. Various toolbars, menus, and screen areas are mentioned throughout this text. The following figure will help you get familiar with the names of these items.

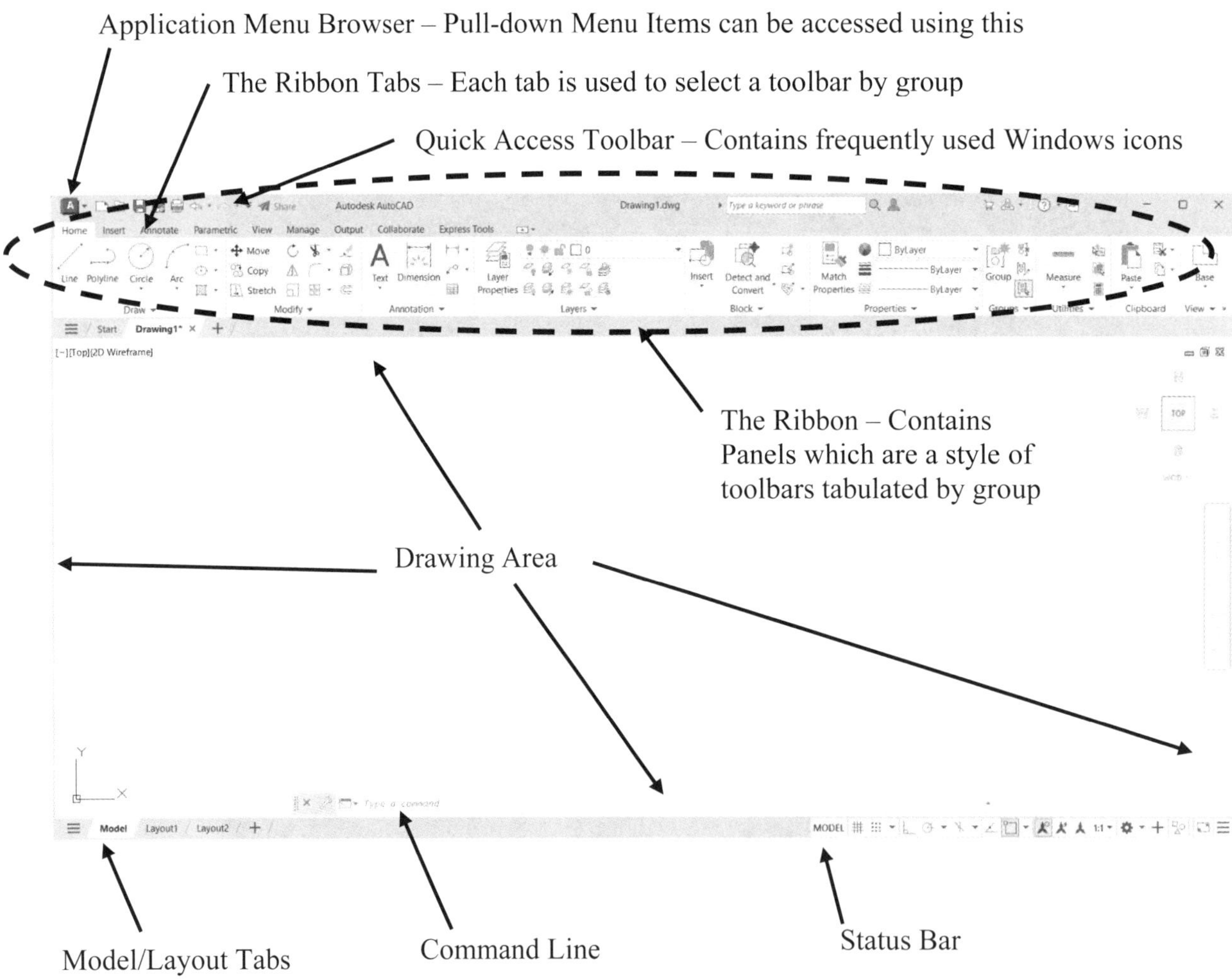

Default Drafting & Annotation AutoCAD screen

AutoCAD on the Mac

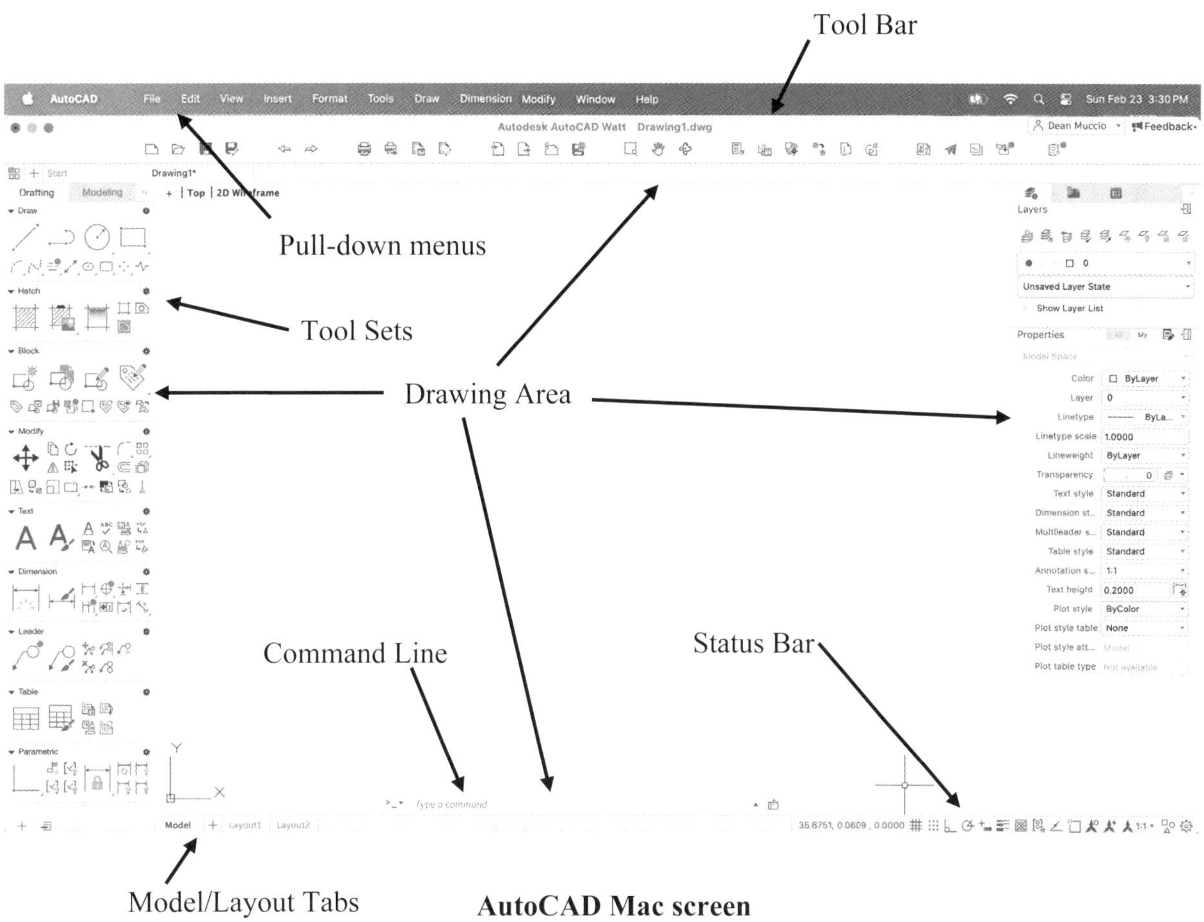

AutoCAD Mac screen

Status Bar icons

Before we begin drawing, let’s turn off the icons on the left side of the status bar. These are like switches – left click once to turn on, left click again to turn off. When they are turned on, they appear blue, when off, they are gray. The only icon to leave on is the Object Snap. We will discuss this more in later chapters.

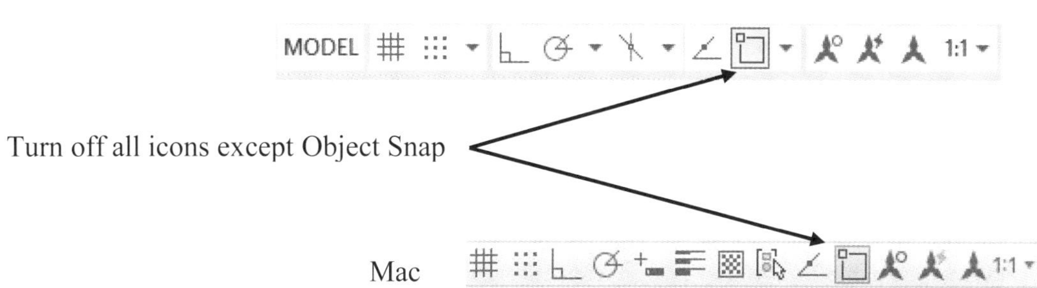

Toolbars

AutoCAD has numerous toolbars on the Ribbon, but not all toolbars are shown on your screen.

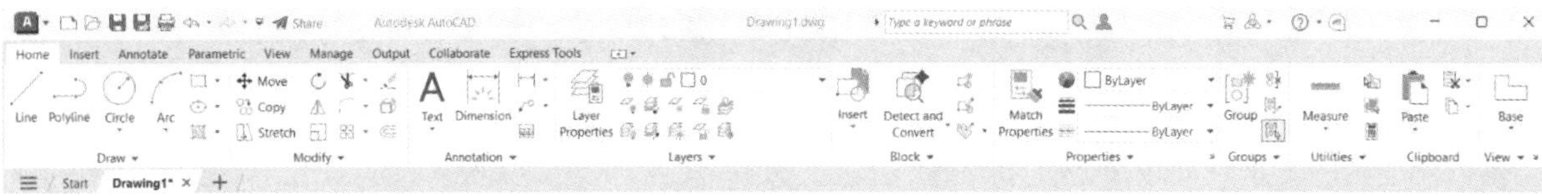

Tools are categorized by function and are accessed by selecting each tab. Each tab contains Panels. The Home tab contains the basic commands and will be the most used tab.

Toolbars on Mac

You can choose the list of toolbars from the selection choices by using tabs at the top of the toolbars:

The Drafting tools include icons to draw objects, modify objects, and gather information on objects. We will not be using the Modeling tools because they are primarily for 3D Modeling.

Command Line

AutoCAD utilizes a command line to display which command is selected and to prompt the designer for additional steps needed to complete the command. The command line is located near the bottom of the drawing space screen.

Mac:

The command line can be relocated on the screen by dragging from the left edge. It can also be re-sized by moving your cursor near the right edge of the outline until it changes to a split-arrow cursor. Select the right edge and drag right or left to re-size the command line.

When a command is selected, AutoCAD automatically enters the command text into the command line. When applicable, the command icon is also displayed in the command line, replacing the command prompt.

The following will appear in the command line when the LINE command is selected:

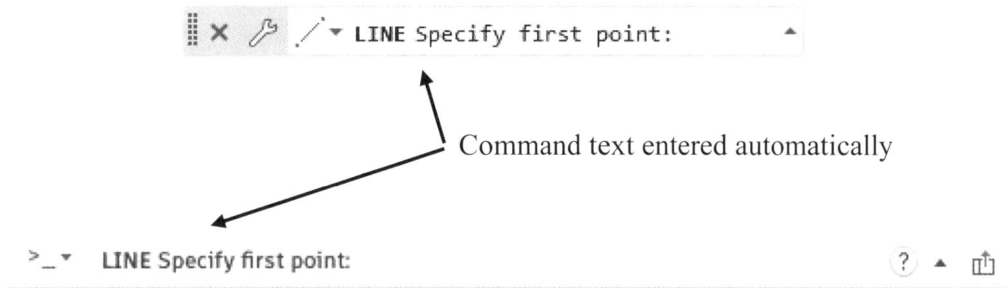

Mac:

Commands can be entered directly into the command line if desired. Some commands have “hot keys” that will allow a single character to represent the whole command. This saves typing.

During the command, you may be prompted for additional information or action. Each time the command line changes information, the previous text is displayed above the outline. Up to three lines are displayed with transparent text that will disappear from the screen after several seconds.

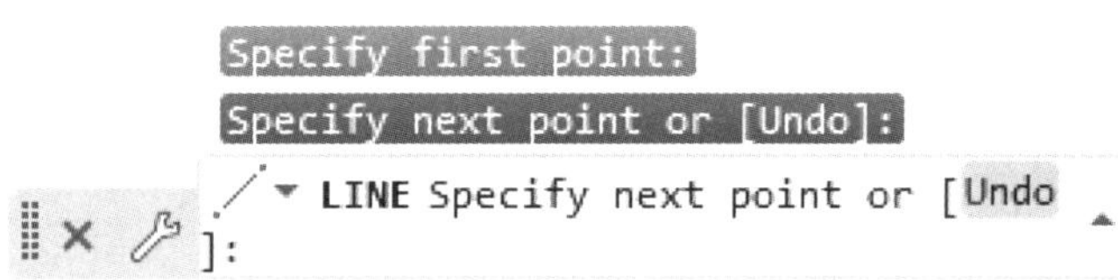

A longer list of previously displayed command line text can be viewed by selecting the arrow on the right-hand side of the outline.

Mac:

The command line can be docked by picking it on the end and moving it to where you want it. Here it is shown docked above the Model/Layout tabs.

Pick this end
to move the
command line

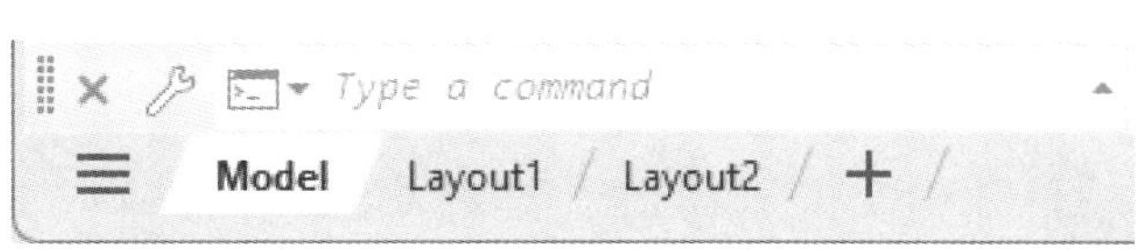

Options – Screen Color & Right-Click

When you start up AutoCAD for the first time, you will notice that the background is black with white gridlines. If you like this look, then you won't need to review this section. If you would like to change the background to a different color, such as white, then the following information will help you achieve that.

Customizing Screen Background Color

To change your drawing space background color, pick the Application Menu Browser button at the top-left of the screen and select Options.

The Options dialog box will pop up. Make sure the Display tab near the top of the dialog box is selected. You can change the color scheme from dark to light by using the pull-down selection. Select the Colors button.

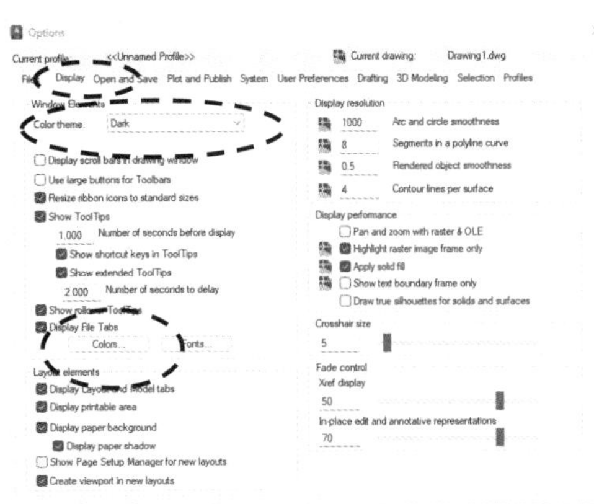

The Drawing Window Colors dialog box pops up. Use the pull-down selection for 2D model space. Change the color of the Uniform background to White by using the pull-down selection under Color. If you plan to change other colors, the color changes need to be done for each Interface element individually.
When done, select Apply & Close button. Pick the OK button to close the Options dialog box.

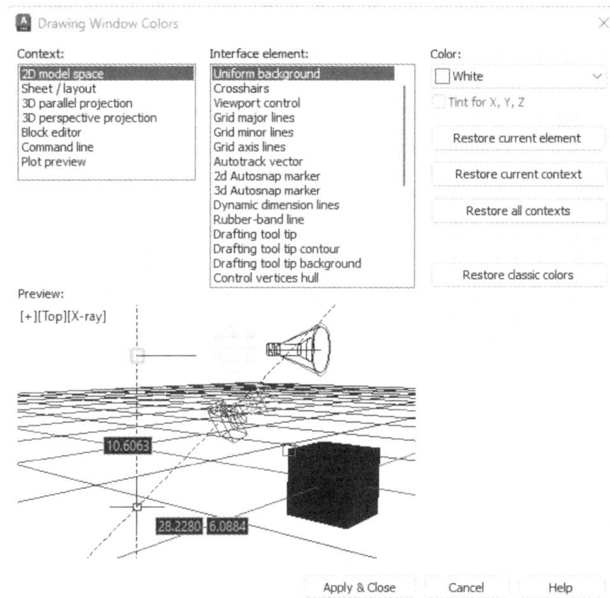

After you exit the dialog box, you will now have a white screen background. Of course, if you prefer a different color, the steps to make the changes are the same as described.

Customizing Screen Background Color for Mac

To change your drawing space background color, click on "**AutoCAD**" located at the top left of the screen to get a menu of choices. Alternatively, right-click in the drawing space. When the menu of choices is displayed select Settings… or Preferences (depending which method you chose):

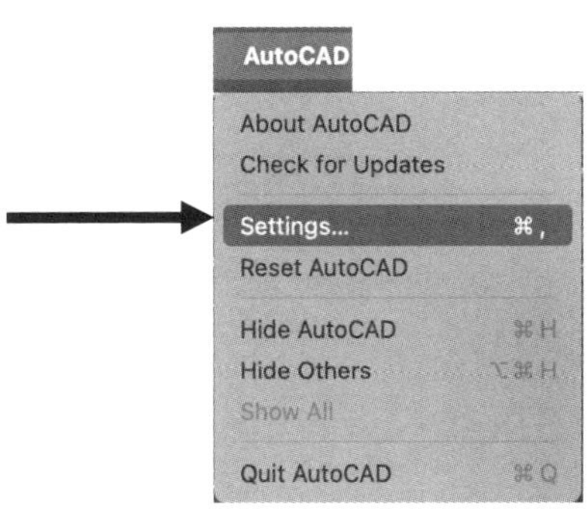

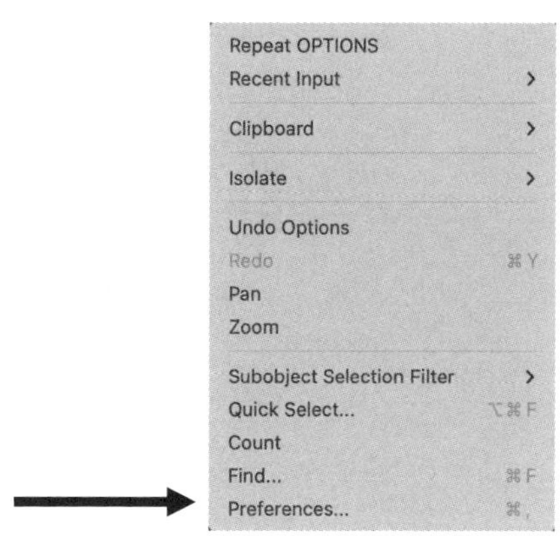

The Application Preferences dialog box will appear:

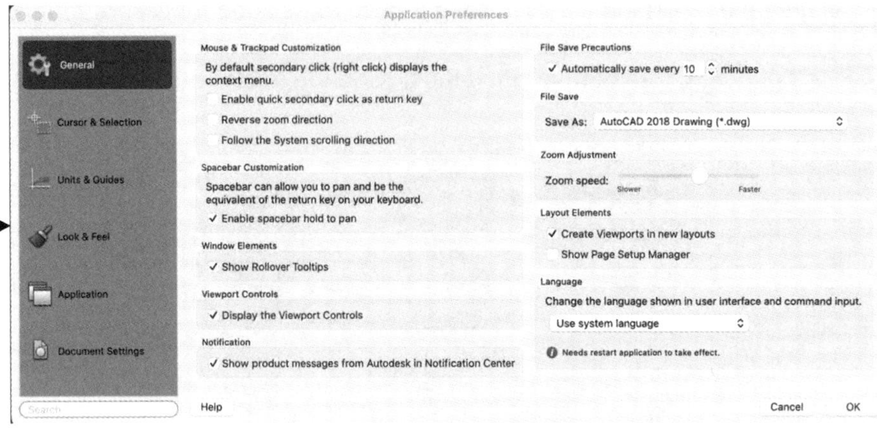

Select the Look & Feel option on the left panel.

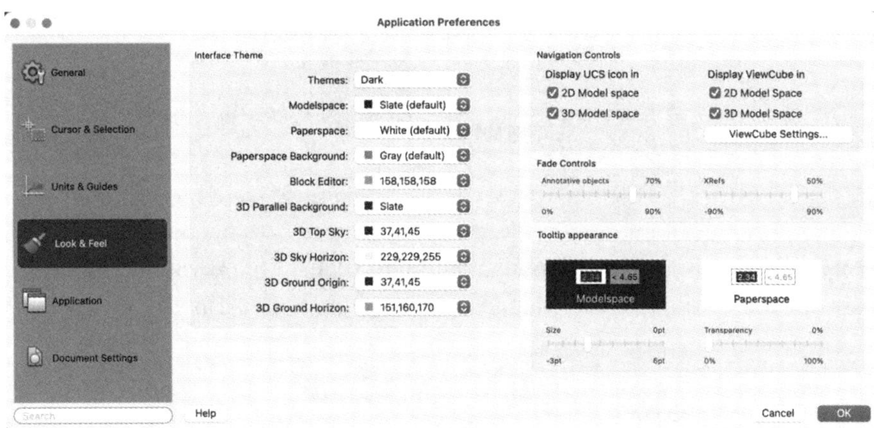

In the Interface Theme section in the upper left side, use the scroll arrows to select a color for Model space, and choose your color choice. This example shows white chosen:

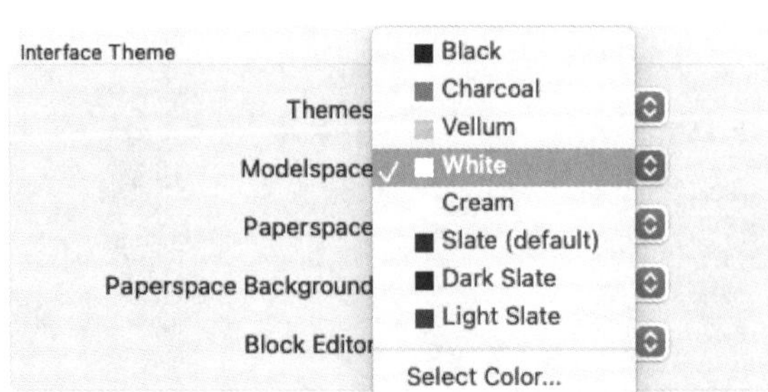

In addition to the background color, you can change the color of the menu icons from dark to light by using the selection arrows in the Interface Theme section in the upper left:

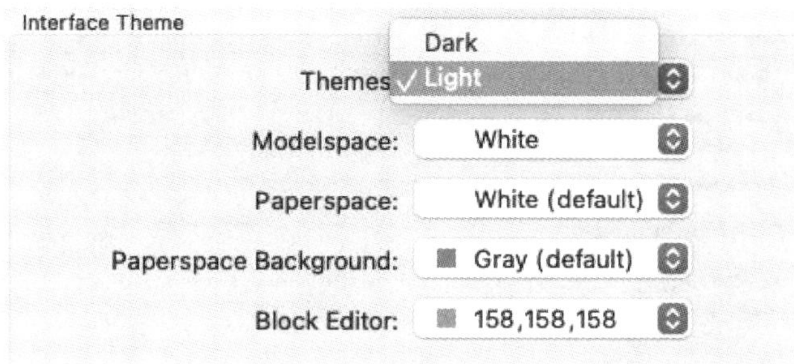

The dialog box can be closed by selecting the OK button. However, because we want to change more items, leave it open for now.

Customizing Right-Click

The default setting for AutoCAD Right-Click (in the drawing space) is to bring up the shortcut menu. Since repeating the previous command by pressing the ↲ Enter key requires a keyboard operation, it can be more convenient to use the right mouse button to repeat the previous command instead.

Shortcut menu is default setting

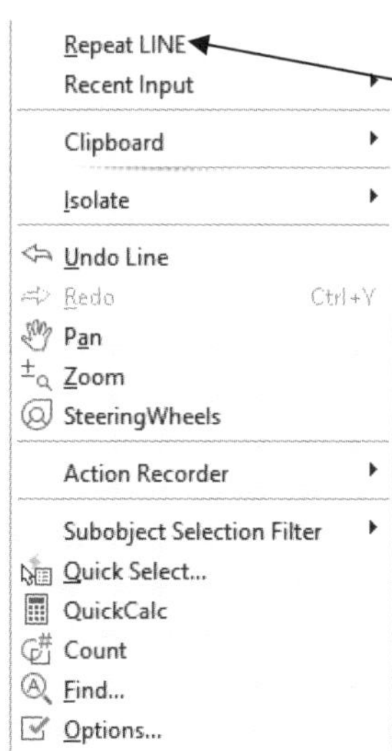

To repeat the previous command (for this example the previous command was Line), highlight and either left or right click.

The function of the right mouse button can be customized by using Options. Pick the User Preferences tab near the top of the dialog box. Select the Right-click Customization button.

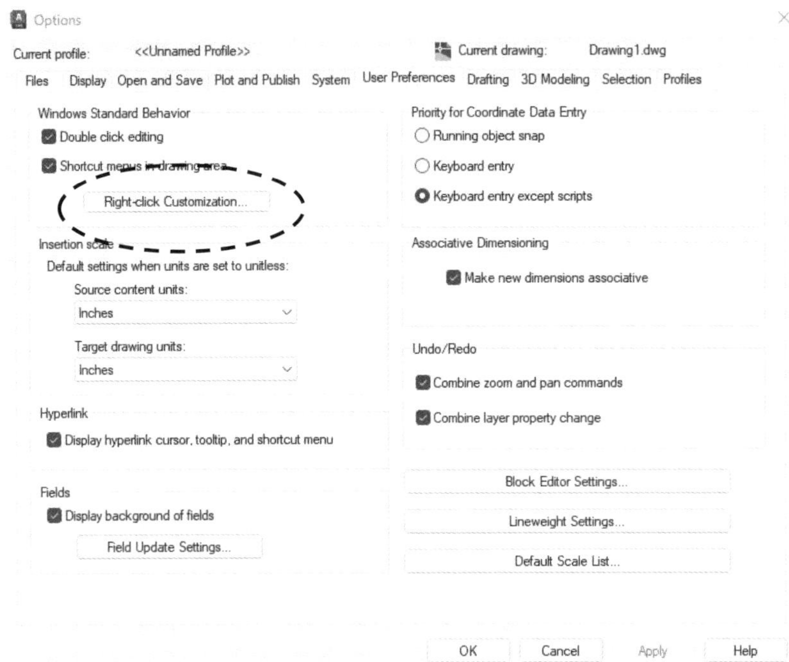

The Right-Click Customization dialog box pops up. Pick to place a checkmark to turn on time-sensitive right-click. When done, select the Apply & Close button. Pick the OK button to close the Options dialog box.

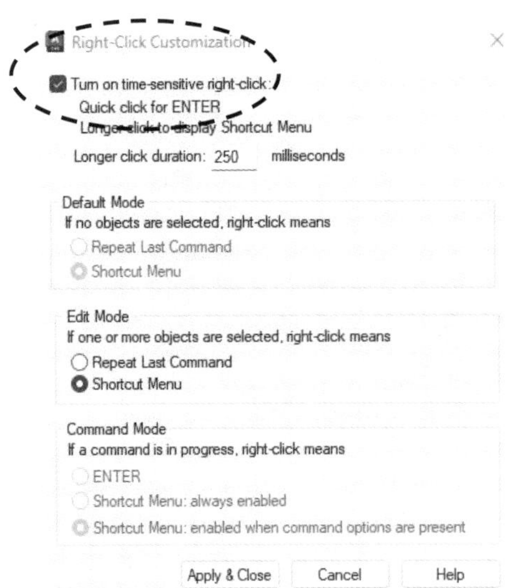

This option allows you to use the right mouse button to repeat the last command without bringing up the shortcut menu, unless you press and hold the button for a longer period of time.

Customizing Right-Click for Mac

Pick the General option on the left panel of the Application Preferences dialog box. Under the Mouse & Trackpad Customization section on the upper left, place a check-mark to Enable quick secondary click as return key.

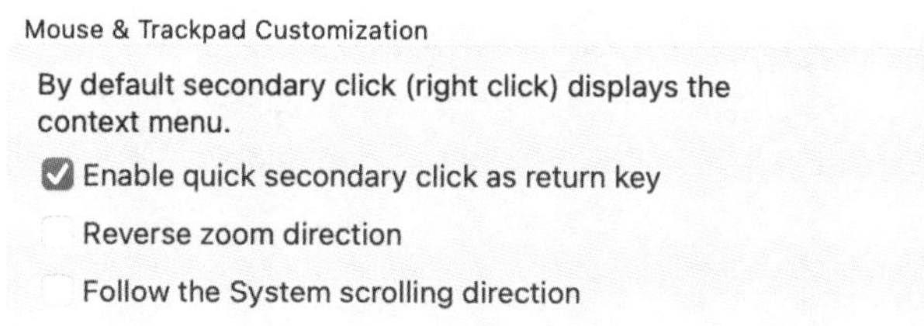

Navigation Controls: UCS icon, Navigation Bar, and View Cube

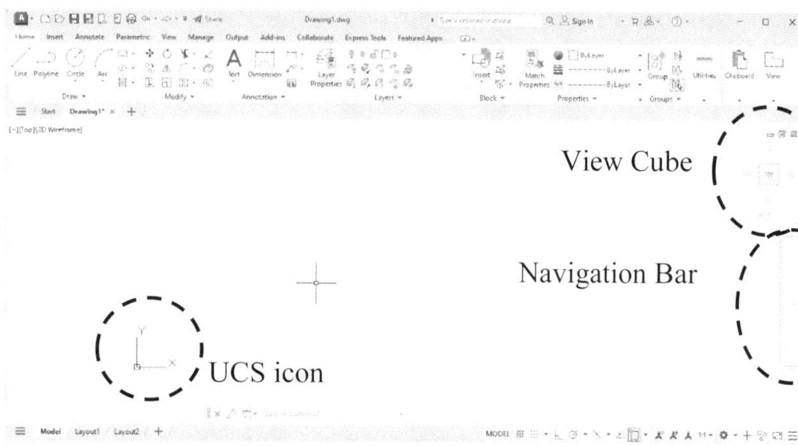

Additional display changes you may desire to make are to eliminate the X-Y axis (which is called the UCS icon), the Navigation Bar, and the View Cube. You eliminate the View Cube and Navigation Bar by using the View Tab on the Ribbon, and clicking to turn them off. They will no longer be blue when they are turned off.

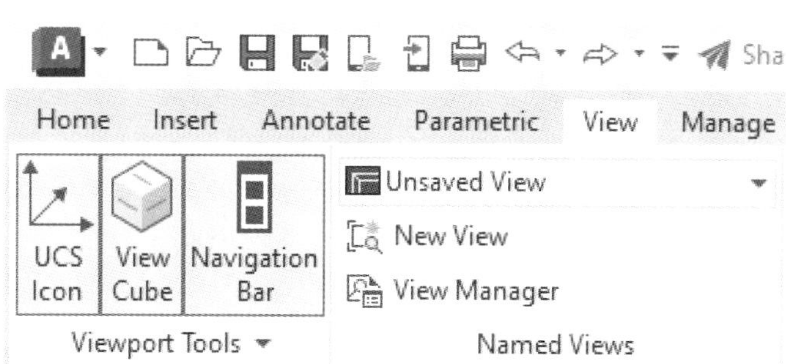

Navigation Controls on the Mac

Under the Look & Feel option of the Application Preferences dialog box, un-check the 2D Model Space display of the UCS icon and View Cube of the Navigation Controls section:

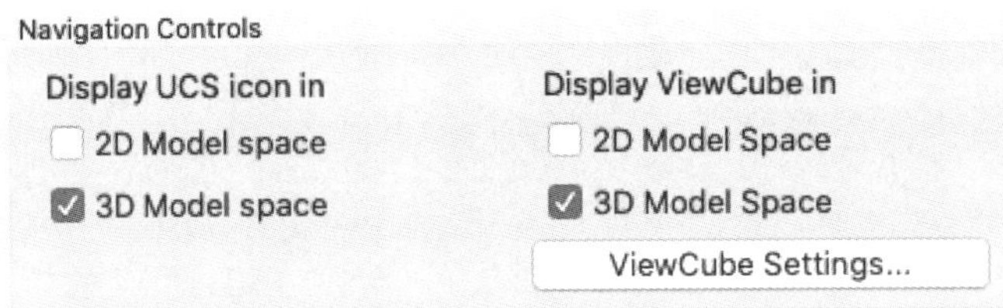

Because this text will not cover 3D, there is no need to uncheck the 3D items.

AutoCAD Help

The intention of this book is not to cover every command in complete detail. Instead, it will provide enough information for the new user to be productive using AutoCAD as quickly as possible. There are some textbooks available that attempt to provide a comprehensive instructional guide on how to use AutoCAD, and in those, there may still be some things that are not covered. You can refer to other texts if you may be seeking a different explanation of how a command works. Or, as an alternative, you can use the Help feature within the program. Fortunately, AutoCAD has provided a very good Help menu, which can be searched by topic. Like most other AutoCAD functions, there are several ways to access the Help screen. You can use the Help icon or pull-down, or simply press the F1 key. (Mac: use Command key with forward slash /)(⌘ /)

Using any of these methods will get you to the Help screen. You can explore commands and additional features. It is user-friendly, and self-explanatory. When you want to check features in more detail, this is the best way to do that.

Opening and Saving Drawings

Before beginning, it is recommended that you understand how to save your work. In addition, knowing how to manage files using Windows is very helpful. If you already know how to do that, this section will be a review for you.

Using Pull-Down Menu

You can use the Application Menu Browser to open or save your drawing.

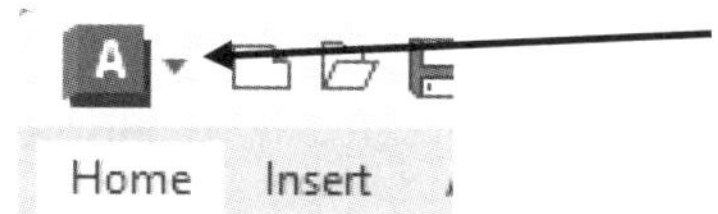

Click here to access the Browser

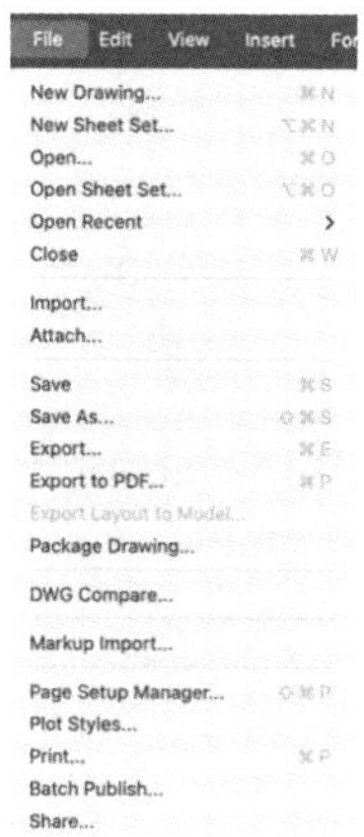

For Mac, use File pull-down menu at the top of your screen.

The functions are the same as described below, except use New Drawing instead of New Project.

The following selections will be the ones we are initially interested in:

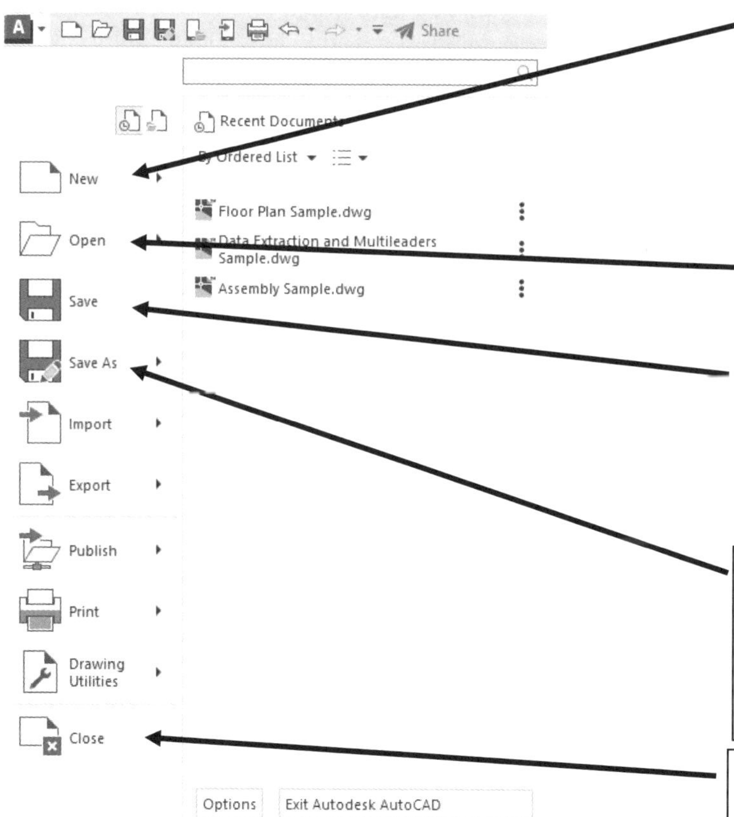

New… – Allows you to create a new drawing. You choose an existing template to begin your drawing, or use the default template. *Note: Template drawings will be covered later.*

Open – Allows you to open an existing drawing.

Save – Allows you to save the drawing you are currently working on. If this is the first time you are saving the drawing, it will work the same as the **Save As…** command.

Save As… – Allows you to save the current drawing under a new name and/or to a new memory location (hard drive, different folder, flash drive, etc.)

Close – Allows you to close drawings, but does not shut down the AutoCAD program.

Selecting New…

When you select the New… option, AutoCAD displays a Select template dialog box. The default location that it will look in is the template folder which is part of the AutoCAD software package installed on the computer. AutoCAD will pre-select a default template, which is a blank drawing. Otherwise, you can choose many of the other available templates. You can scroll through the list to see the many templates AutoCAD already has available to you. You can highlight (single left-click) any of them. As you do so, the Preview pane in the upper right side of the dialog box will show you a thumbnail view of the template.

Once you determine which template drawing you wish to use, either double-left-click on that template, or, once that template is highlighted, pick the Open button. 

Template drawings are helpful in that you start with a drawing that has all the customization included. For example, the drawing border and title block can already be included in the template. Later, you will learn how to create your own template drawing.

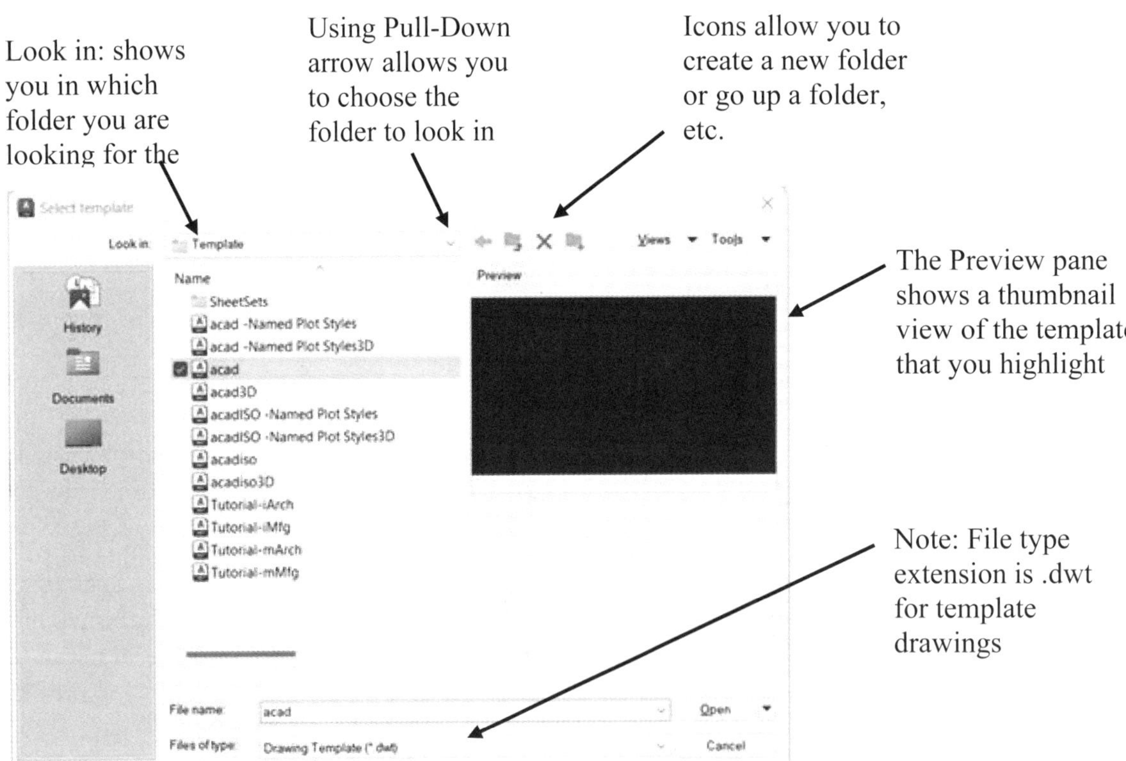

Mac:

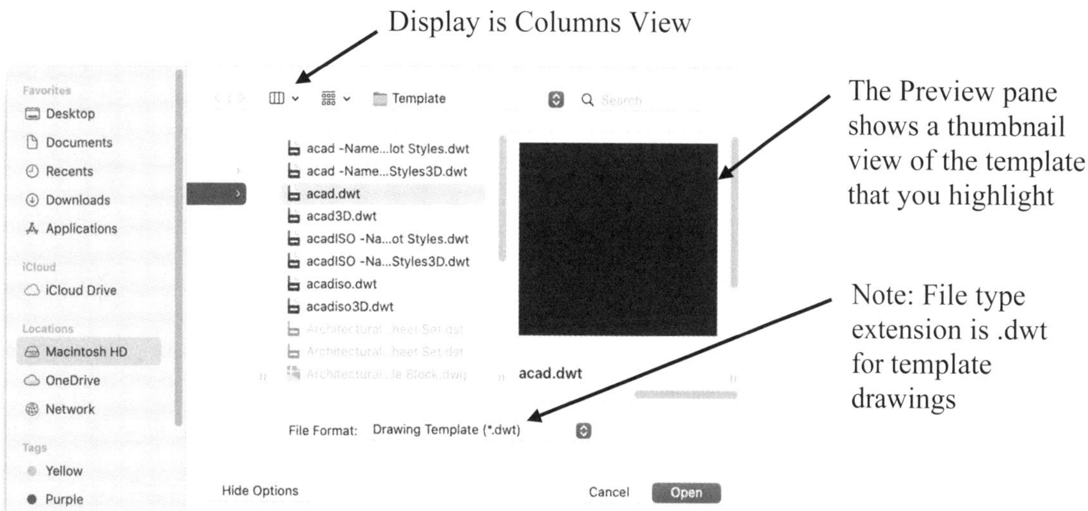

Selecting Open

Selecting Open is very similar to selecting New… because AutoCAD will be looking for an existing drawing. But instead of looking for a template drawing, which has a .dwt file extension, it will be looking for an AutoCAD drawing with a .dwg file extension. You can change the file type extension that you wish to open by using the pull-down arrow in the “Files of type:” box.

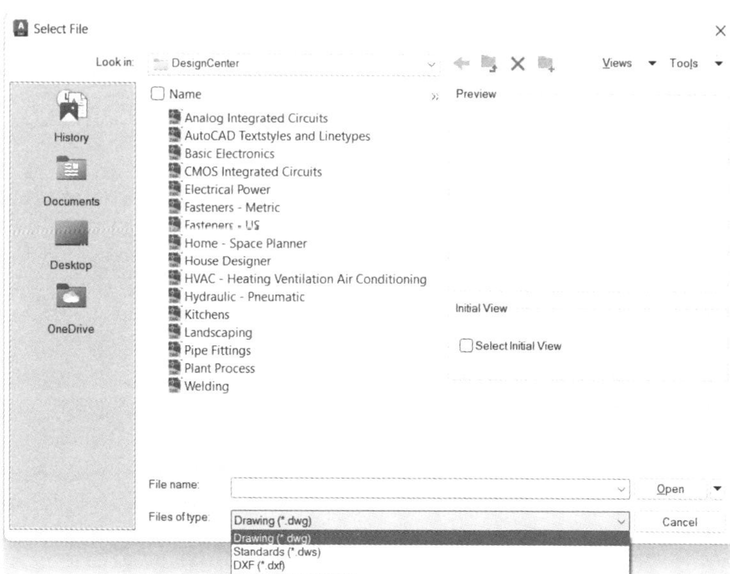

File types

.dwg is the standard extension used for an AutoCAD drawing

.dxf is a universal Drawing eXchange File type that allows drawings created by a non-AutoCAD program, that were saved as a .dxf file type, to be usable by AutoCAD

.dwt is the standard extension used for an AutoCAD template drawing

Mac:

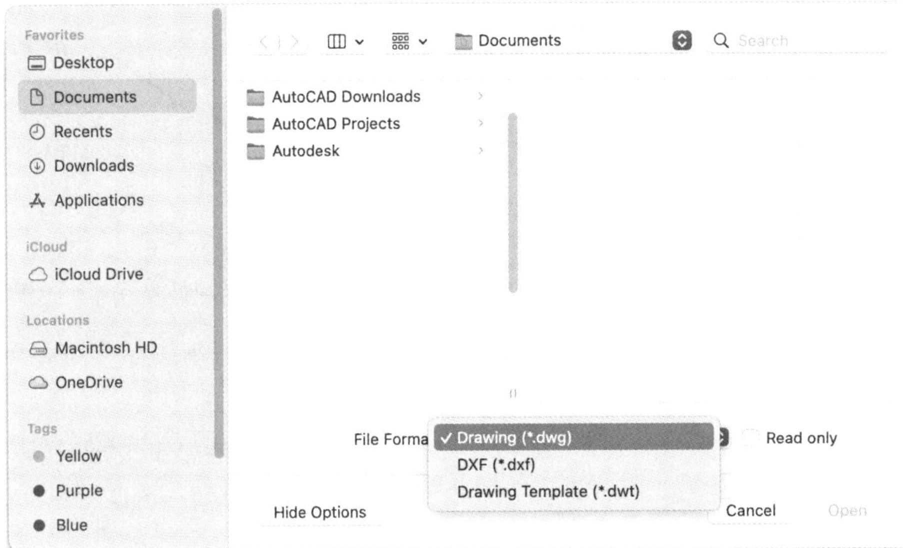

Selecting Close

When you select Close, you will be given a choice to close the current drawing or close all drawings.

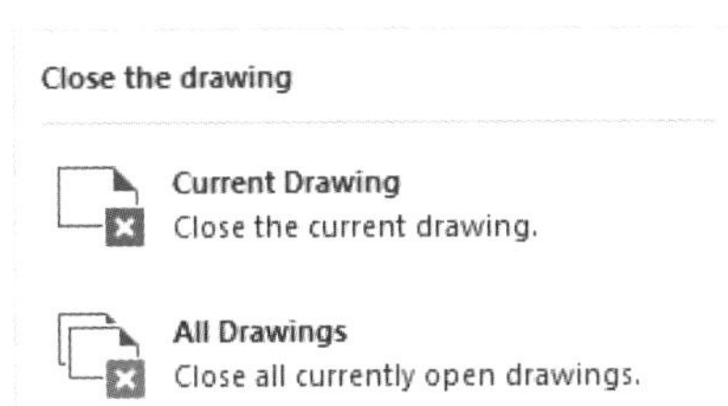

For the Mac, an Alert box will appear as follows:

Mac:

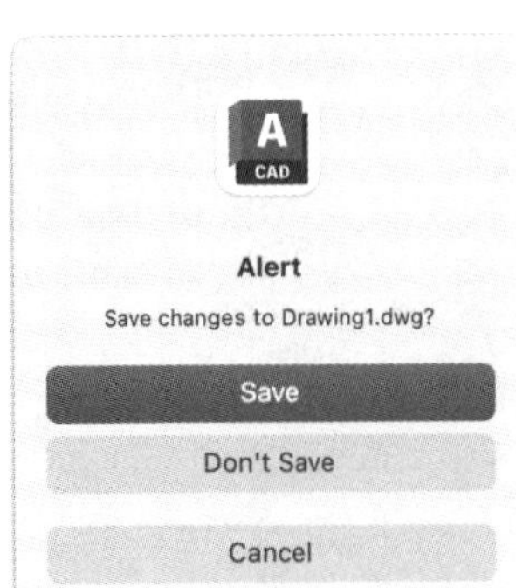

Selecting Save

When you select **Save**, a dialog box will appear if this is the first time you are saving your drawing, and the command works the same as the **Save As...** command. This is because a new drawing is given a default name by AutoCAD, such as Drawing1.dwg, and it is likely you would not want to save it under that name.

If this is not the first time saving the drawing, selecting **Save** will replace the existing version that was saved previously with the current version. In that case, no dialog box will appear, but the command line will show _Qsave. This is what AutoCAD refers to as a Quick Save.

Selecting Save As...

Use Save As... to save your drawing under a new name or to save it in a different location. This is useful if you wish to modify a drawing, but still want to preserve the original version. It is also useful if you want to save a duplicate copy to a separate folder or to a Flash Drive.

A Save As... dialog box will appear when this is chosen.

File types

You can choose to save your drawing as the current or earlier version of AutoCAD as a .dwg, .dwt, or .dxf. We will be primarily saving our drawings as a .dwg type. In later chapters, we will create our own template, which is a .dwt type. We will not be using the .dxf type. This type is used to enable other non-AutoCAD programs to read an AutoCAD drawing.

Saving your drawing as an earlier version allows sharing your files with other AutoCAD users that are using an older version of AutoCAD.

Look in:/Save in: and Favorites/Where: for Mac

The "Look in:", "Save in:", "Favorites", and "Where" work the same way. Understanding where your drawing is being saved, or where the drawing is located so that you can open it, is very important. You want to be able to locate your drawing later to make changes, etc. The pull-down arrow and the Icons help you manage that.

When opening a drawing, the top of the dialog box has a "Look in:" prompt:

Mac:

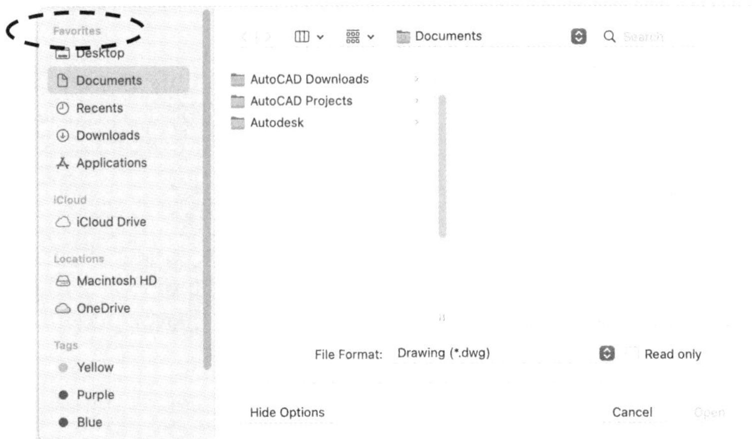

When saving a drawing, the top of the dialog box has a "Save in:" prompt:

Mac:

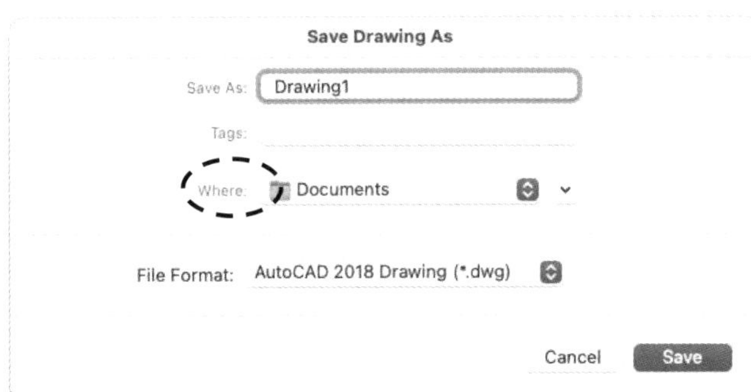

Summary

The topics covered in this chapter are meant to be an introduction to the AutoCAD working environment. The goal is to help you feel more comfortable creating drawings on the computer. When you have completed this chapter, you should now have an understanding of the following:

- Differences between drawing by hand vs. using AutoCAD
- Different ways of selecting AutoCAD commands
- Toolbars – using the Ribbon
- Using the Help feature
- Customize your screen colors and your right mouse button
- Opening, and saving your drawings

Review Questions

1. What are the advantages of using AutoCAD instead of drawing by hand?

2. Why do you always draw full scale in AutoCAD?

3. Which direction are angles measured in AutoCAD?

4. How do you access the Help feature?

5. Which pull-down menu and option do you use to change the screen color and customize the right mouse button?

6. How do you open and save AutoCAD drawings?

7. Why would you want to save your drawing as an earlier version of AutoCAD?

Chapter 2

Setting-up and Intro to AutoCAD

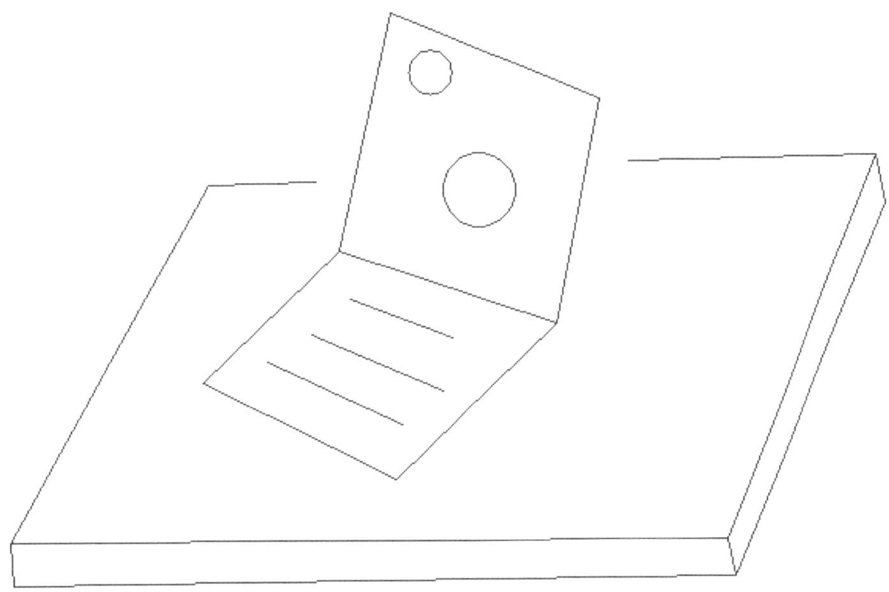

Learning Objectives:

- **Changing from Decimal to Architectural Units**
- **Three basic commands to get started**
    - **Line**
    - **Circle**
    - **Erase**
- **Methods of selecting objects**
- **Getting around your drawing by using Zoom and Pan**

Units

The Units command allows you to set the unit of measure for your drawing. For Interior Design, we want units of Feet and Inches. AutoCAD names this style of units Architectural. The default style is Decimal, with a precision of 4 decimal places, so you will need to change it to Architectural.

Procedure:

Pick (left click): **Application Menu Browser,** select **Drawing Utilities,** and select **Units**

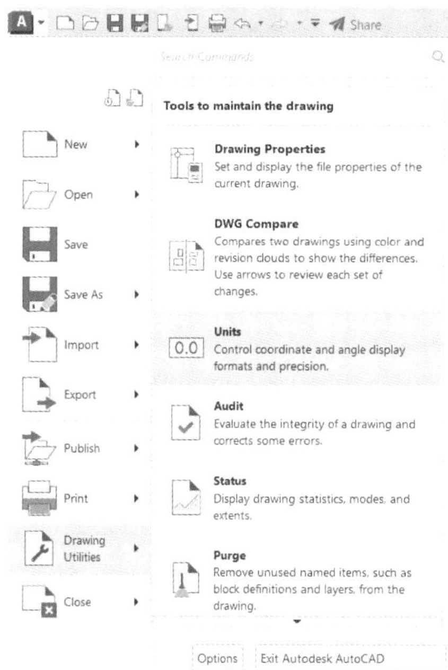

For Mac: Use pull-down menu **Format** and select **Units…**

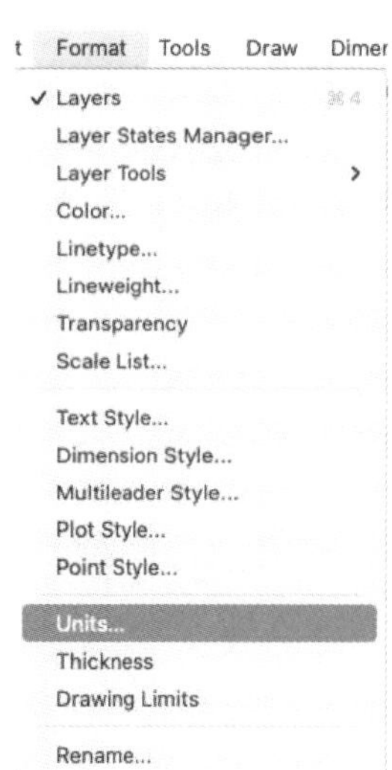

A dialog box will appear:

Mac:

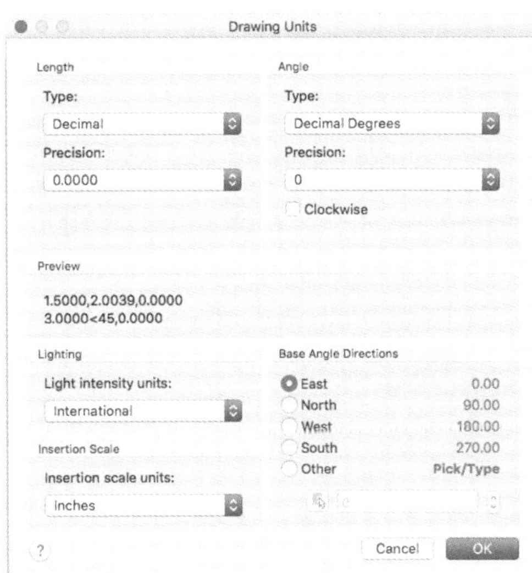

The dialog box contains pull-down selections for Length, Angle, and Insertion scale. We will not change the insertion scale. Within Length and Angle choices, there are also pull-down selections for Precision. Changing the precision only affects the displayed values of the coordinates and values shown when using Distance or List Commands (both to be discussed in later chapters). It does not change the true value of the object, which is stored in the AutoCAD model at a very high precision.

Change the units for Length to Architectural:

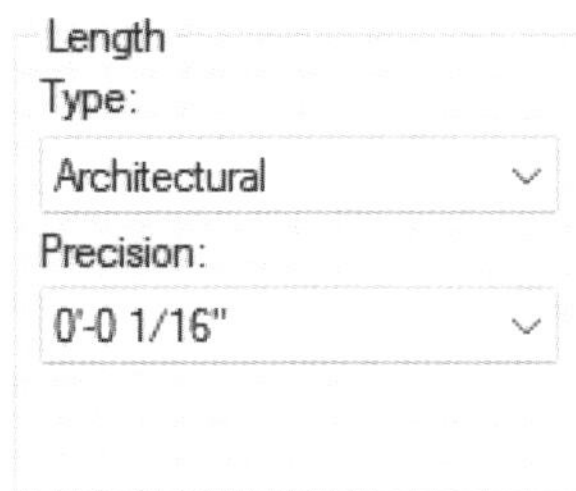

The Precision will automatically change to fraction style. Ensure that 1/16" is the precision. If not, use the pull-down selection to change it.

Leave the default values for Angle at Decimal Degrees with 0 Precision, with the Clockwise check box unchecked. Note that the default direction for angles is counterclockwise. We will leave this alone.

Feel free to explore different styles and precisions. When you are done exploring, set the values to those shown in the above figure.

Dynamic Input

In addition to the command line, information can also be displayed on your screen. This happens when Dynamic Input is turned on. When displayed, it can be found on the Status Bar. If it is not displayed, it can be added by picking the customization switch at the far-right end of the Status Bar and selecting it from the pick list. Once selected, it will now be displayed on the Status Bar. When it is turned on, it will be shaded blue.

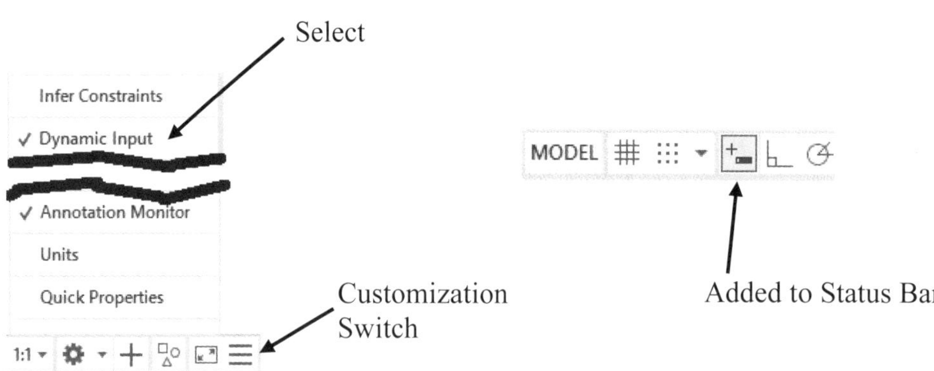

For now, turn Dynamic Input off. We will return to using it in a later chapter.

Three Easy Commands to Help Get You Started

Line

The Line command creates a point-to-point line. AutoCAD allows you to create multiple point-to-point lines within the single command. The Line command is a very basic AutoCAD command.

Procedure:

Pick (left click): **Line icon** from the Draw Panel of the Home Tab.

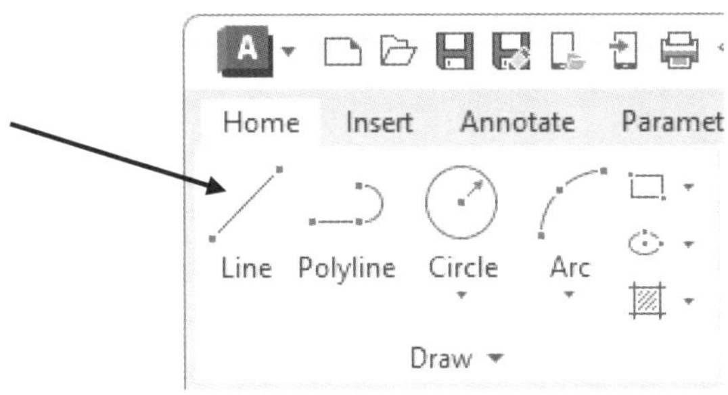

Mac

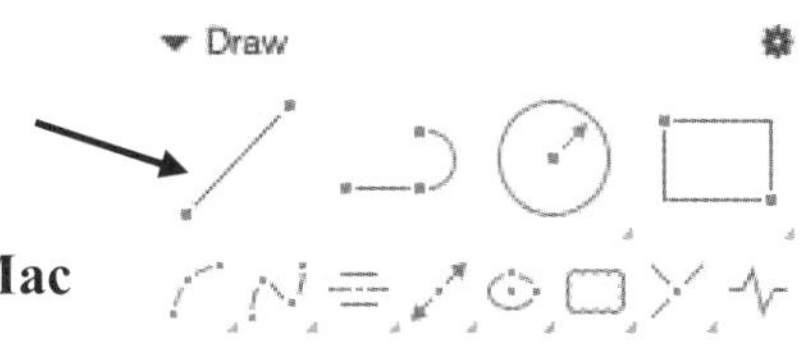

The command line prompts you with the following:

LINE Specify first point:

Pick anywhere on your screen to begin to draw a line.

After you specify the first point, the line will appear on the screen, anchored at the point you just picked, and will "rubber-band" to follow your cursor. The command line prompts you with the following:

Specify next point or [Undo]:

Left click on the screen again and a line will be created. A second line will start, anchored at the second point you just picked, and will "rubber-band" again to follow your cursor. Because AutoCAD does not know how many lines you intend to draw, the command line will continue to prompt you with the following:

Specify next point or [Undo]:

When you are done drawing lines, press the ↵ Enter key to exit the Line command.

AutoCAD will exit the Line command and display a command prompt.

Although other methods of putting lines on your drawing exist, they will not be covered here. You can explore these on your own using the help menu.

Recommendation:

The Line command has limited use. It is recommended to use this command when you want to draw lines between two existing points (such as endpoints of existing lines). Otherwise, using the Construction Line command and trimming is a much more intuitive approach. The Construction Line and Trim commands will be covered in the next chapter.

Try it:

Draw 3 lines to form the letter 'Z'.

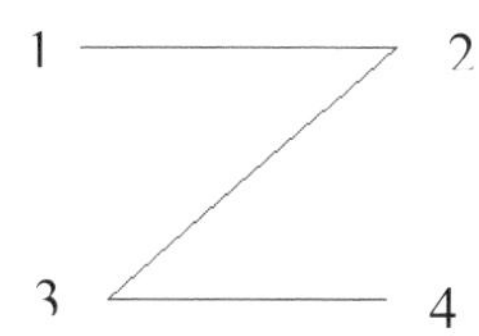

(Pick the Line icon)

LINE Specify first point: ***(Pick a point on the screen at location 1)***
Specify next point or [Undo]: ***(Pick a point on the screen at location 2)***
Specify next point or [Undo]: ***(Pick a point on the screen at location 3)***
Specify next point or [Close/Undo]: ***(Pick a point on the screen at location 4)***
Specify next point or [Close/Undo]: ↵

Remember, for the Line command, AutoCAD does not know when you are done drawing lines until you exit the command by pressing the ↵ Enter key.

Circle

The Circle command creates a circle. Creating a circle and trimming it can be an easy way to create an arc. A circle can be defined in multiple ways. The default method of creating a circle using the icon is to define the center and the radius.

Procedure:

Pick (left click): **Circle icon** from the Draw Panel of the Home Tab.

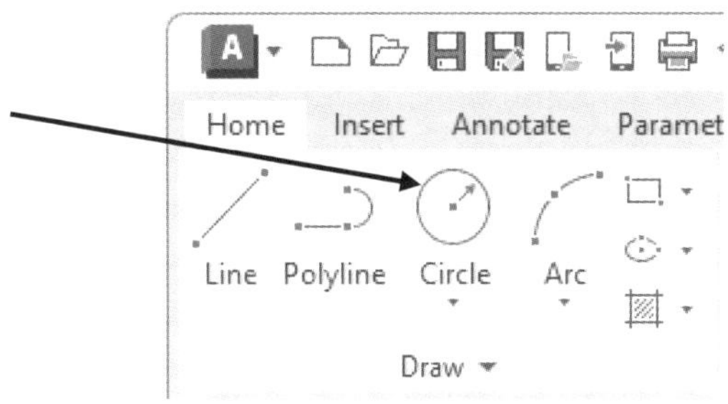

Mac

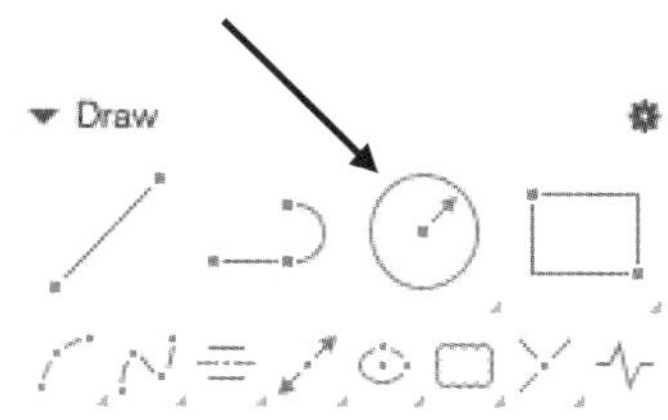

The command line prompts you with the following:
CIRCLE Specify center point for circle or [3P/2P/Ttr (tan tan radius)]:

For a simple circle, pick a location for the center point:

(Pick anywhere on the screen to define the center of the circle)

After you specify the center point, the command line prompts you with the following:
Specify radius of circle or [Diameter]:

You can specify the radius of the circle by typing a value (followed by the ↵ Enter key) or by picking a second point on the screen.

If you prefer to specify the diameter instead of the radius, select the Diameter option using your cursor, or type the letter **"d"** (followed by the ↵ Enter key) which is for the diameter option. You do not need to click in the command line to enter the letter; simply type and the letter will be entered in the command line. After doing so, the command line will prompt you with the following:

Specify diameter of circle:

After you define the radius (or diameter, if that option was used), a circle will be created and AutoCAD will exit the Circle command and display a command prompt.

Recommendation:

The Circle command is a very useful, easy to use tool. Circles can be used as an alternative to arcs, especially when the center point and radius are known, because a circle will become an arc after it is trimmed.

Although using circles with trimming may actually take more steps than drawing arcs using exact starting and ending points, it allows the designer not to have to think in terms of starting and ending points. After some practice, it can actually be quicker to draw this way, since less thought is involved.

Try it:

Draw a 1″ radius circle to the right of the lines you just created.

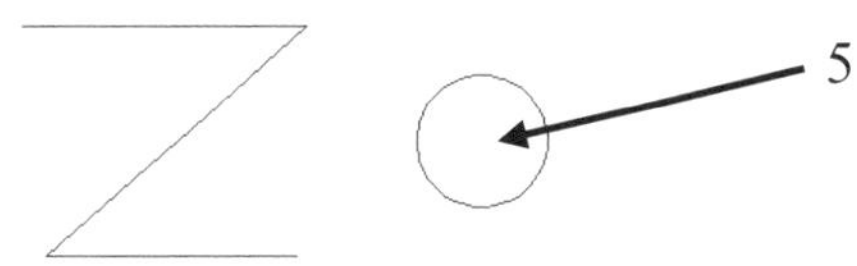

CIRCLE Specify center point for circle or [3P/2P/Ttr (tan tan radius)]: ***(Pick a point on the screen at location 5)***

Specify radius of circle or [Diameter]: **1↵ (Key in the value 1 and press the ↵ Enter key)**

AutoCAD will automatically end the Circle command.

Erase

The Erase command allows you to eliminate an object from your drawing.

Procedure:

Pick (left click): **Erase icon** from the Modify Panel of the Home Tab.

For Mac: Use pull-down menu **Modify** and select **Erase**

Mac

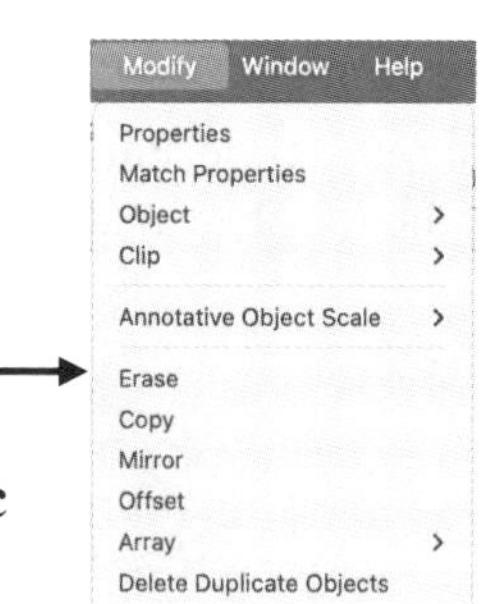

The command line prompts you with the following:

ERASE Select objects:

Select the object you want to erase by moving your cursor over the object and left-clicking the mouse to pick the object.

After you pick the first object, your command line will look like the following:

Select objects: 1 found
Select objects:

> As you pick objects to be erased, the line color changes to gray

AutoCAD will continue to prompt you for more objects to erase. When you are done selecting objects to erase, press the ↵ Enter key to exit the command.

Try it:

Erase the lines and circle you just created.

(Pick the Erase icon)
ERASE Select objects: ***(Pick one of the lines)****1 found*
Select objects: ***(Pick another line)*** *1 found, 2 total*
Select objects: ***(Pick the last line)****1 found, 3 total*
Select objects: ***(Pick the circle)*** *1 found, 4 total*
Select objects: ↵

> The information of how many objects found and the total is displayed above the command line

Your screen will no longer have the lines and circle on it.

When using the Erase command, you can select objects individually or you can use either a Selection Window or a Crossing Window to select multiple objects. The following section describes the different methods of selecting objects.

Methods of Selecting Objects

Objects can be selected individually by picking them (using the left mouse button), or by using either a Selection Window or a Crossing Window. A Selection or Crossing Window allows you to select objects by picking opposite corners of a "window" around the objects you want to select. The direction in which the opposite corners are chosen determines whether you are using a Selection Window or a Crossing Window.

> After you pick the first corner of the Window, make sure to release the mouse button before picking the second corner. If you drag your mouse without releasing the button, then a Selection Lasso will begin. A Window Lasso is left to right and Crossing Lasso is right to left. The Lasso feature has limited use. It is left to the student to explore the Selection Lasso.

Selection Window (LEFT to RIGHT)

A Selection Window is used during a command and the direction of picking the opposite corners is Left to Right. When a Selection Window is used, only those objects that are completely bounded by the window are selected. If only a portion of an object is in the window, it will not be part of the selection set.
The following example of selecting one of two lines to be erased illustrates this. The area inside the Selection Window will be shaded. Only the line that is completely bounded by the window will be selected. Picking on the screen in the order shown will result in the following:

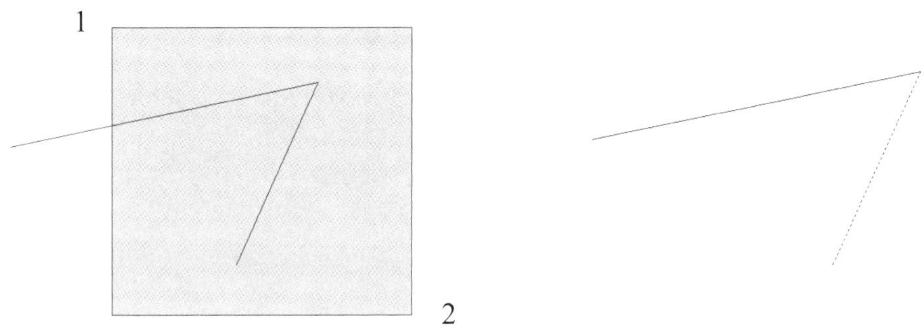

After the second Pick Point, the line selected will appear faded.

Crossing Window (RIGHT to LEFT)

A Crossing Window is used during a command and the direction of picking the opposite corners is Right to Left. When a Crossing Window is used, objects that are bounded by the window are selected, including those that only a portion of which crosses the window.

The following example of selecting two lines to be erased illustrates this. The area inside the Crossing Window will be shaded. Although only a portion of one line is completely bounded by the window, a portion of it will be selected. Picking on the screen in the order shown will result in the following:

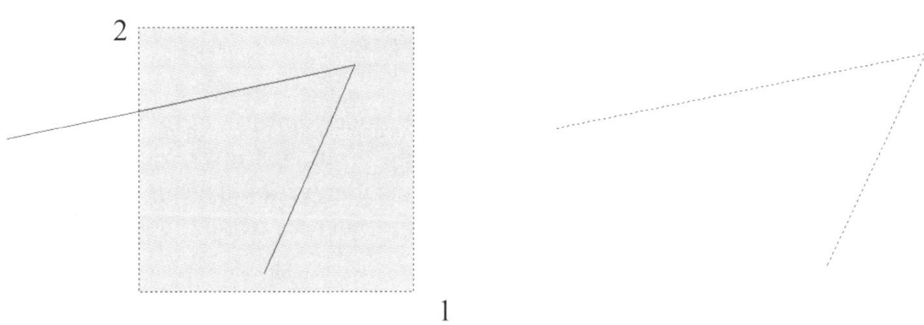

After the second Pick Point, both lines selected will appear faded.

Notice that the Selection Window boundary is shown as a solid line and a Crossing Window boundary is shown as a dashed line. In addition, the color of the area inside the Crossing Window is different from the color of the Selection Window.

Removing Objects from the Selection Set

When selecting multiple objects, you may have selected more objects than was intended. To remove objects from the selection set, simply hold the shift key and select the objects to remove. The selection method is the same: individual, selection window, or crossing window.

Using the same example as above (both lines were selected with Crossing Window during the Erase command), we can remove one of the two lines selected before completing the command. The following is the command line sequence:

ERASE Select objects:

Use a Crossing Window to select both lines

Specify opposite corner: 2 found

Once the 2 lines are selected, hold the shift key and pick the line you want to remove from the selection set.

Select objects: 1 found, 1 removed, 1 total

Select objects: ↵

Pressing the ↵ Enter key completes the Erase command.

Grips

While trying out AutoCAD, you may occasionally notice that your objects are highlighted and have little blue squares attached to them. Or you may have moved your cursor on the screen and found that AutoCAD appears to be drawing a rectangle (it isn't).

This can occur when you do not have a command in the command line and you left-click somewhere on your screen. After you do this, your command line will prompt you to specify the opposite corner. AutoCAD is attempting to create a selection window or a crossing window. If there are objects selected without a command in the command line, the grips will appear.

Picking objects without having an active command will place grips on them

Grips can be used to change object locations and sizes. For example, a line will have three grips attached to it: one at each end, and one at the mid-point. Picking the grip at the midpoint will allow you to relocate the line on your screen. Picking either end grip will allow you to change the length and angle of the line – this occurs because you are moving only one endpoint while the other endpoint stays fixed.

If you have no intention of using grips and you accidentally get them on your screen, simply press the Escape (Esc) key to make them go away.

Pressing the Esc key will remove the grips from your objects

Zoom and Pan

The Zoom and Pan features within AutoCAD allow you to view the drawing you are creating at different sizes and locations. Imagine that the drawing you are creating is similar to the paper on a drawing board and you are viewing your drawing through a camera lens. The Zoom feature allows you to get a close-up look at an area or get a wider view, depending on whether you zoom in on a specific area or zoom out. The Pan feature moves the camera side-to-side or top-to-bottom.

There are several methods to Zoom and Pan around your drawing. One of the easiest methods of zooming in and out and panning is to use the wheel on the wheel mouse.

Zoom and Pan Using the Wheel Mouse

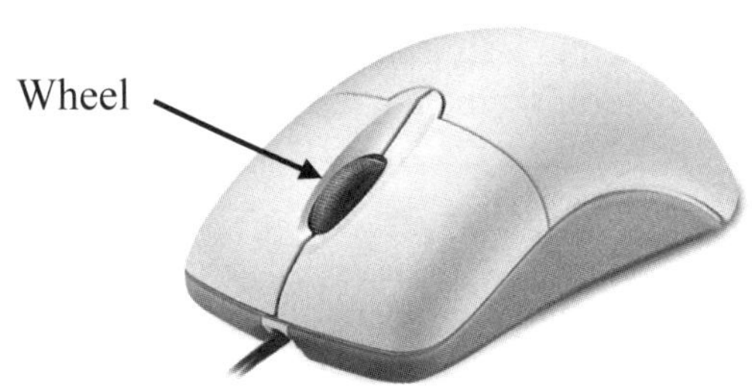

Wheel Mouse

Rolling the wheel forward and aft allows you to zoom in and out of the drawing. Pressing the wheel down will change the cursor from a pointer to a hand. Moving the mouse around, while pressing the wheel down, allows you to "pan" around your drawing. This feature can come in handy because you do not need to select an icon or key in a command. In addition, you can zoom and pan using the wheel while you are in the middle of a command.

You can also fill your drawing screen with all the objects you have drawn by double-clicking the wheel on the mouse. This is referred to as Zoom Extents.

Typing the Zoom Command

One method of zooming is to type the command. Typing the letter "z" is the shortcut for the zoom command.

>_ z ↵

Because the prompt is lengthy, some of it appears above the active section of the command line

ZOOM
Specify corner of window, enter a scale factor (nX or nXP), or
ZOOM [All/Center/Dynamic/Extents/Previous/Scale/Window/Object] <real time>:

AutoCAD will default to a Zoom Window command. A Zoom Window allows you to pick opposite corners of a selected area on your drawing to enlarge that area to fill your screen.

You can choose one of the multiple options shown in the square brackets. For instance, if you wanted to zoom the entire drawing, type the letter "a" for All. Each option is the same as previously explained.

Example of Zoom Window:

If you had the following items on your screen and you want to zoom in on just the circles, select the Zoom command by typing the letter "z" and then pressing the ↵ Enter key. This will begin the Zoom command. Now simply pick opposite corners around the circles (shown here at locations 1 and 2):

As you move your cursor from location 1 to location 2, you will notice what looks like a rectangle growing on the screen as it follows your cursor. That is the Zoom Window. You must left-click point 2 to complete the Zoom Window. After the second point is selected, the command will end. Only those items in that window will now fill the screen. Depending on the shape of the Zoom Window, some additional pieces of other items may also appear on your screen.

Recommendation:

I have found that using the wheel mouse is the easiest way to zoom and pan around the drawing. In addition, double-clicking the wheel mouse is the easiest way to see the extent of everything you have drawn.

Summary

In this chapter you have learned to:

- Change the units from decimal to feet and inches
- Create lines and circles
- Erase objects
- Select objects or remove objects from a selection set
- Get grips and make them disappear
- Navigate through your drawing using the Zoom command and mouse wheel

Review Questions

1. How do you change the units from decimal to feet and inches?
2. How does the line command end?
3. How does the circle command end?
4. When you erase objects, how do you know they were selected?
5. What is the difference between a crossing window and a selection window?
6. What are the blue squares called and how did they get there?
7. How do you get rid of the blue squares if you get them?
8. How do you use the wheel on your mouse to move around the drawing?
9. What is the shortcut key for the Zoom command?
10. What is a Zoom Window?

Exercises

1. Draw the star. Do not concern yourself with size or location.

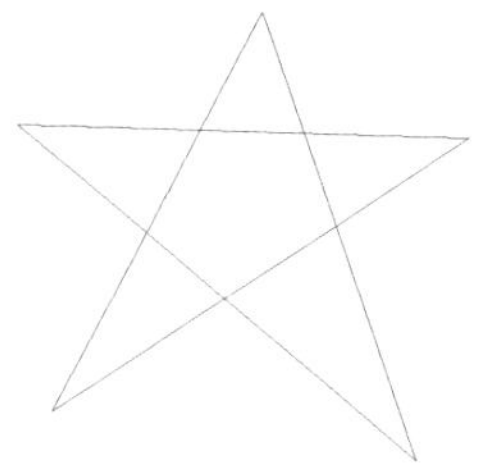

2. Draw the patch. Do not concern yourself with size or location.

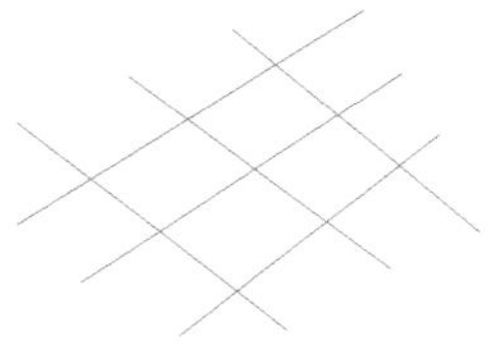

3. Draw the circles. Do not concern yourself with size or location.

4. Draw the lines and circle. Do not concern yourself with size or location.

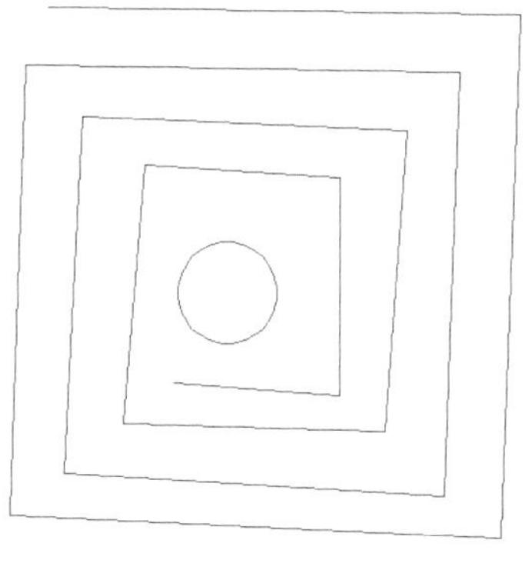

Chapter 3

Commands – Set 1: Drawing Construction - Getting Started

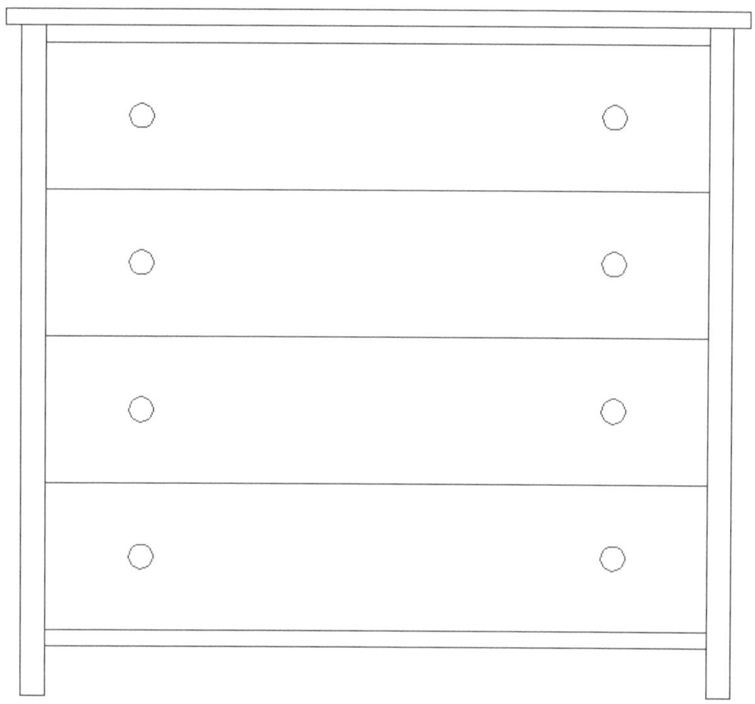

Learning Objectives:

- A familiar shape: Rectangle
- Change rectangles to lines by using Explode
- Creating parallel or concentric objects using Offset
- Creating Horizontal, Vertical, Angled, and Offset Construction Lines
- Changing the object limits using Trim, Extend, and Lengthen
- Improving drawing accuracy using Object Snap

In Chapter 2 we learned two basic Drawing commands and one Modify command to help us get started drawing: Line, Circle, and Erase. Not enough information was given in that chapter to allow you to create a drawing with accuracy. In this chapter we will learn more commands that will help us create an accurate drawing. We will also learn AutoCAD construction techniques that will help you to make drawings quickly.

We will start with the shape that is most familiar to us: the rectangle. From there, we will move on to creating infinitely long lines, known as construction lines. The nice part about construction lines is that you can make them horizontal, vertical or at a specific angle. This can also be done with the line command; however, I have found that the construction lines are much easier to work with.

Of course, infinitely long lines are not what we want as the final product. We will learn how to trim those lines. In addition, if a line is too short, we will learn how to extend it.

And finally, there are times when we need to connect a line or a circle to an endpoint, or maybe draw a line through a center of the circle. Using the Object Snap feature of AutoCAD will allow us to create drawings with complete accuracy.

Rectangle

The Rectangle command has several options: Chamfer, Elevation, Fillet, Thickness, and Width, as well as a prompt for the corners of the rectangle. These options allow you to manipulate the appearance and the placement of the rectangle before it is drawn. Chamfer and Fillet are options that change the corners of the rectangle. These options are described in a later chapter. We will not be using the other options.

Procedure:

Pick (left click): **Rectangle icon** from the Draw Panel of the Home Tab.

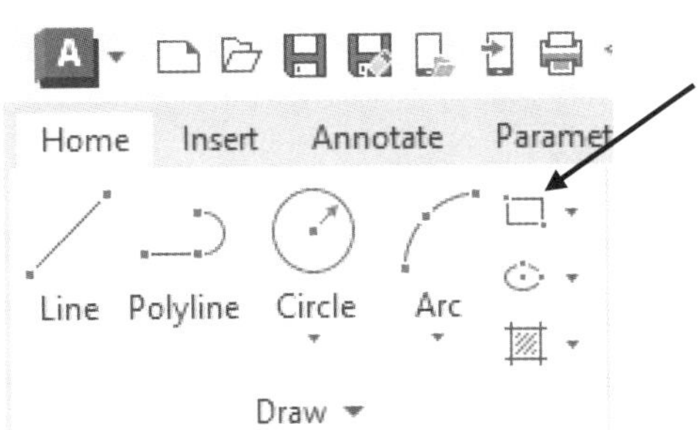

Mac

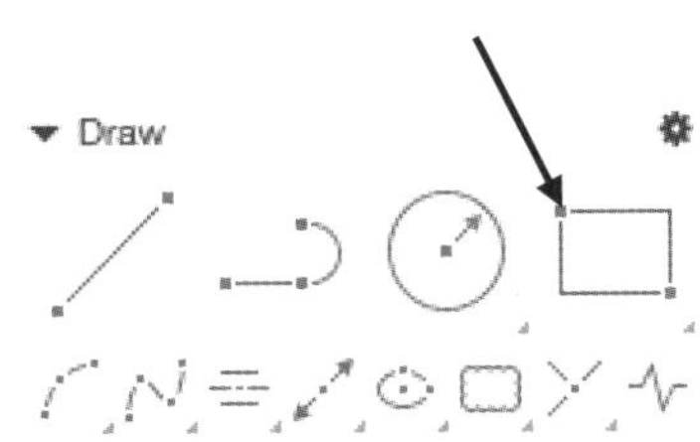

The command line prompts you with the following:

RECTANG *Specify first corner point or [Chamfer/Elevation/Fillet/Thickness/Width]:*

For a simple rectangle, anchor the first corner by picking anywhere on the screen or by picking a point on an existing object (must have OSNAP turned on or select an object snap override before picking – more about this later).

After you specify the first corner point, the command line prompts you with the following:

Specify other corner point or [Area/Dimensions/Rotation]:

You can specify the second corner by simply picking a second point on the screen. Of course, this will not let you know the size of the rectangle that was created.

A recommended method to create a rectangle of a specific size is to use your cursor to select *Dimensions*, or type "d" for *Dimensions* followed by pressing the ↵ Enter key. In the command line, AutoCAD will prompt you for the size of the rectangle in two steps. The first prompt is for the horizontal direction. The second prompt is for the vertical direction. Unfortunately, the wording of the prompts can be confusing.

Length is the AutoCAD prompt word for horizontal direction *Width* is the AutoCAD prompt word for vertical direction

AutoCAD prompts for the horizontal direction as follows:

Specify length for rectangles <X'-X">: Note: *X'-X"* represents any number
At this prompt type in the distance for the rectangle in the horizontal direction and press the ↵ Enter key.

AutoCAD prompts for the vertical direction as follows:

Specify width for rectangles <Y'-Y">: Note: Y'-*Y"* represents any number
At this prompt type in the distance for the rectangle in the vertical direction and press the ↵ Enter key.

AutoCAD has one more prompt. Because we have specified the location of one corner and the size of the rectangle, there remain 4 choices for the opposite corner. The prompt is as follows:

Specify other corner point or [Area/Dimensions/Rotation]:

Using your cursor, pick the location of the second corner of the rectangle. Note that there are four locations that can be picked (upper right, upper left, lower left, lower right). As you move your cursor around, the rectangle will follow for each location.

After you pick the second corner point, the rectangle command is complete, and you are back to the command prompt.

The rectangle is treated as a single object, and as such can be erased completely by picking anywhere on the rectangle.

Recommendation:

Use rectangles for the start of the room walls, drawing format borders, furniture or other rectangular shaped objects. The advantage of using rectangles is that they can be offset by using a single Offset command (more info on Offset appears later in this chapter). All four sides will be offset and trimmed at once. This is a time saver for walls. For ease of drawing, use the dimension option for the second corner. Doing it this way allows the designer not to have to think in X-Y coordinates.

If you use rectangles, it is recommended that you then convert them to lines (after you are done offsetting them). This is done by using the Explode command. Lines are then treated as individual objects and are easier to modify.

Try it:

Draw an 8′ x 16′ rectangle. Make sure you have Units set to Architectural before you start.

(Pick the Rectangle icon)
RECTANG *Specify first corner point or [Chamfer/Elevation/Fillet/Thickness/Width]:*
(Pick a point on the screen at location 1)

Specify other corner point or [Area/Dimensions/Rotation]: **d↵**
(Type the letter "d" and press the ↵ Enter key or pick *Dimensions* with your cursor)

Although it is prompting for length, AutoCAD is looking for the value for the horizontal direction:
Specify length for rectangles <8'-0">: **16′↵ (Type 16′ and press the ↵ Enter key)**

Although it is prompting for width, AutoCAD is looking for the value for the vertical direction
Specify width for rectangles <16'-0">: **8′↵ (Type 8′ and press the ↵ Enter key)**

Specify other corner point or [Area/Dimensions/Rotation]: ***(Pick a point on the screen at location 2)***

AutoCAD ends the command, and your rectangle is on the screen.

Explode

The Explode command allows you to break down a compound object to its basic components. As an example, a rectangle is made up of 4 lines. However, AutoCAD treats a rectangle as a single object. If you explode a rectangle, it will still appear as a rectangle on your screen, but AutoCAD now treats it as 4 separate lines.

Procedure:

Pick (left click): **Explode icon** from the Modify Panel of the Home Tab.

Mac

The command line prompts you with the following:

EXPLODE *Select objects:*

Select the object to explode by moving your cursor over the object and left-clicking the mouse to pick the object.

After you pick the first object, your command lines will look like the following:

Select objects: 1 found
Select objects:

AutoCAD will continue to prompt you for more objects to explode. When you are done selecting objects to Explode, press the ↵ Enter key to exit the command.

Recommendation:

Typically used for converting rectangles to lines. If you use rectangles, it is recommended that you then convert them to lines (after you are done offsetting them). This is done by using the Explode command. Lines are then treated as individual objects and are easier to modify.

Explode is also useful for converting Blocks to individual objects. Blocks will be covered in a later chapter.

Try it:

Hold your cursor over the rectangle that you just created. The rectangle will be highlighted and become bold lines and a tip will pop up identifying this object as a Polyline. A Polyline is what AutoCAD names the rectangle.

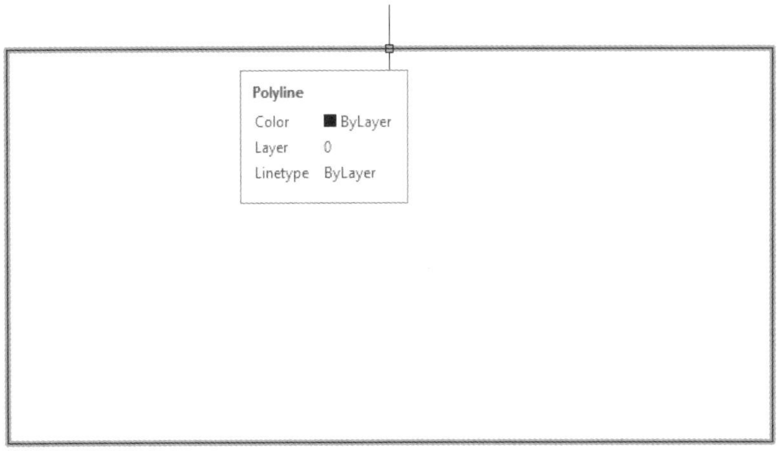

Now let's break down the rectangle into 4 separate lines by using the Explode command.

(Pick the Explode icon)

EXPLODE *Select objects:* ***(Pick the rectangle)*** *1 found*
Select objects: ↵
Pressing the ↵ Enter key exits the command and the command prompt returns.

Now hold your cursor over any of the lines of the rectangle and your pop-up tip will tell you that it found a line. The line will be highlighted, not the whole rectangle.

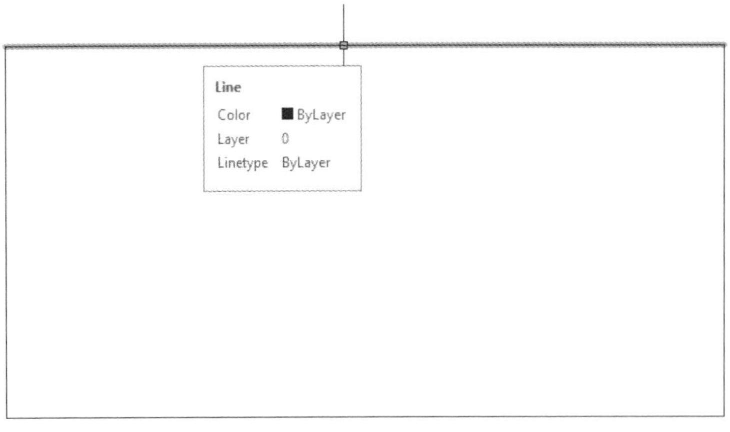

Offset

The Offset command creates parallel lines or curves, and concentric circles or rectangles/polygons, a specified distance away or through a specified point. This is used to create new objects from existing ones.

Procedure:

Pick (left click): **Offset icon** from the Modify Panel of the Home Tab.

Mac

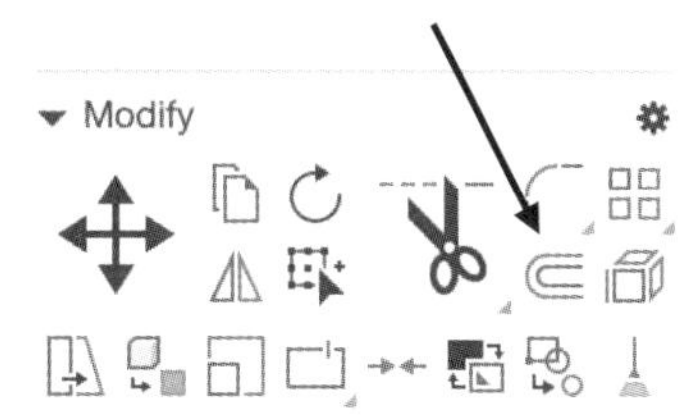

The command line prompts you with the following:

OFFSET *Specify offset distance or [Through/Erase/Layer] <X'-XX">:*

Key in a specified distance you wish to offset, followed by pressing the ↵ Enter key.
You can also accept the default of *<X'-XX">* by pressing the ↵ Enter key.

Note that the value inside the brackets is the value that was previously used in an Offset command. If this is the first time the Offset command is used for the drawing, the value would be *Through.*

After specifying the distance, the command line prompts you with the following:

Select object to offset or [Exit/Undo] <Exit>:
Select the object by left-clicking the mouse when the cursor is over the object you wish to select.

After selecting the object you wish to offset, the command line prompts you with the following:

Specify point of side to offset or [Exit/Multiple/Undo] <Exit>:

For specifying the point of side to offset, there are two choices that can be made here. As an example, a vertical line can be offset to the left or to the right. A circle, rectangle, or polygon can be offset inside or outside. To specify which side to offset, left-click the mouse when the cursor is on the side of the object you wish to offset.

If you want to offset multiple times, you can use the *Multiple* option by either selecting the word *Multiple* in the command line or typing the letter “m” followed by pressing the ↵ Enter key.

AutoCAD will continue to prompt for more objects to offset:
Select object to offset or [Exit/Undo] <Exit>:

To exit the command, press the ↵ Enter key.

When using the *Multiple* option, the distance away from the original object is displayed. For example, a single line offset by1″ multiple times will show the following on the screen:

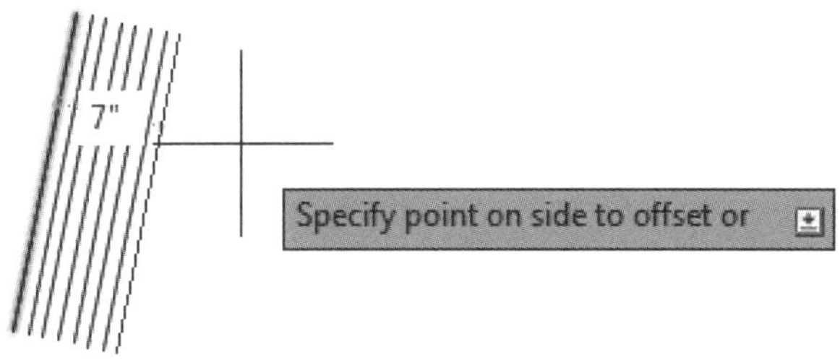

Recommendation:

The Offset command is a very useful tool, and likely the most used command. If you have lines on the drawing to offset, but they are not as long as you would like them to be after they are offset, then it is more convenient to use the Construction Line command (next topic) with the Offset option. An example would be if you had the interior walls drawn and want to construct the exterior walls. Using Offset would leave a gap at the corners. Trimming/Extending cannot be used. You can use Fillet with a Radius=0 (Fillet command will be covered in the next chapter) to close them; however, it is easier to avoid this situation by using a Construction Line Offset instead.

Try it:

Anywhere on your screen, draw a line, a circle, and a rectangle. All objects are an arbitrary size, but should at least be about 12″ in size. We will then offset each of these objects by 2″.

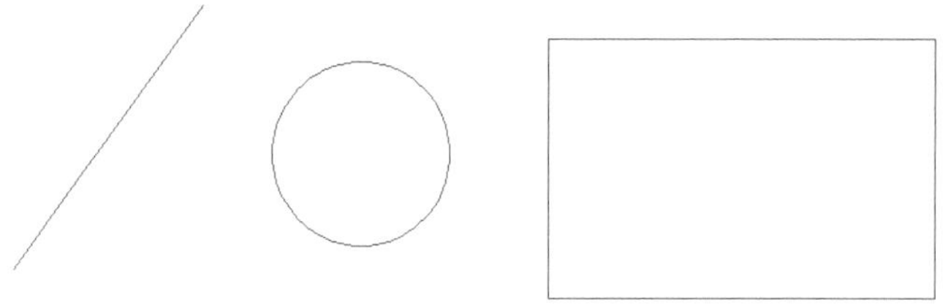

(Pick the Offset icon)

OFFSET *Current settings: Erase source=No Layer=Source OFFSETGAPTYPE=0*
Specify offset distance or [Through/Erase/Layer] <Through>: **2↵**
(Type "2" and press the ↵ Enter key)

Select object to offset or [Exit/Undo] <Exit>: ***(Pick the line)***
Specify point on side to offset or [Exit/Multiple/Undo] <Exit>: ***(Pick to the right of the line)***
Select object to offset or [Exit/Undo] <Exit>: ***(Pick the circle)***

Specify point on side to offset or [Exit/Multiple/Undo] <Exit>: ***(Pick outside the circle)***

Select object to offset or [Exit/Undo] <Exit>: ***(Pick the rectangle)***
Specify point on side to offset or [Exit/Multiple/Undo] <Exit>: ***(Pick outside the rectangle)***

Select object to offset or [Exit/Undo] <Exit>: **↵ (Press the ↵ Enter key to exit the command)**

When you are done, your drawing will look like this:

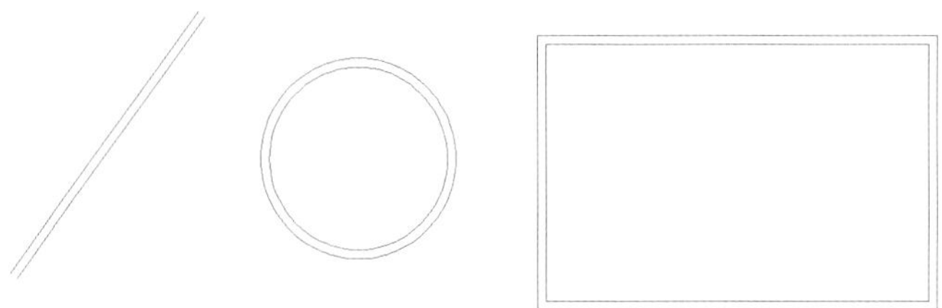

Construction Line

The Construction Line command creates a line (through a point that you select) that extends infinitely in both directions from the first point selected. You can select options at the command prompt to draw a horizontal, vertical, or angled construction line, or to offset the construction line by a distance from the object that you specify.

Procedure:

Pick (left click): Pick the pull-down arrow to expand the Draw Panel of the Home Tab. Pick the **Construction Line icon**.

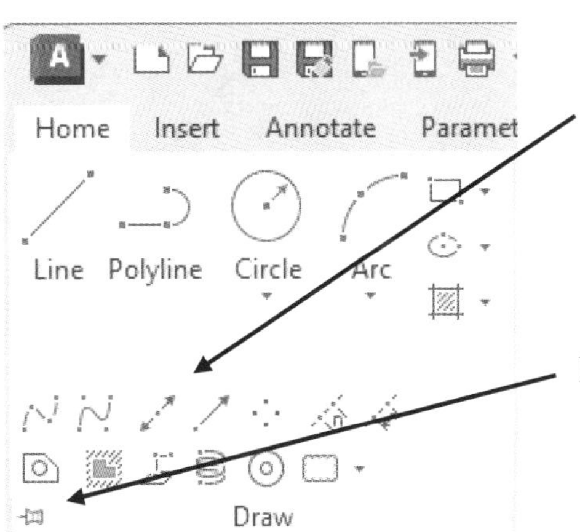

Push-Pin

Because the Construction Line icon is not displayed in the first row, the Draw Panel needs to be expanded by using the down arrow. The Draw Panel can remain expanded if you desire by selecting the Push-Pin. When selected, its appearance will change: 

To unpin it, pick it again.

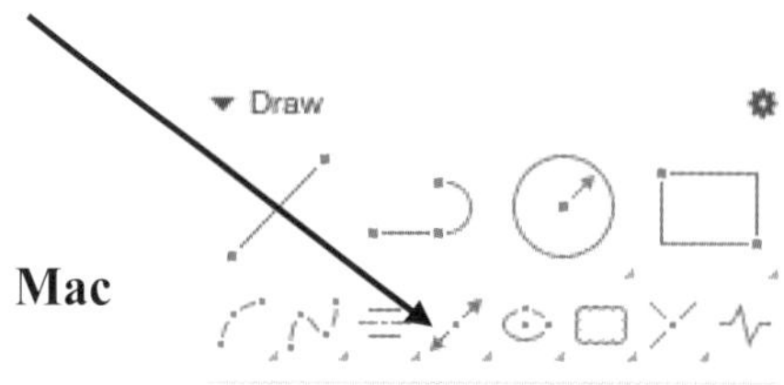

The command line prompts you with the following:
XLINE *Specify a point or [Hor/Ver/Ang/Bisect/Offset]:*

For a simple construction line, anchor the first point by either picking anywhere on the screen (with or without grid/snap turned on), or picking a point on existing object (must have OSNAP turned on or select an object snap override, which is covered later, before picking).

After you specify the first point, the command line prompts you with the following:
Specify through point:
You can specify the second point, or "through point" by picking anywhere on the screen or picking a specific point on an existing object.

After you select the "through point", the construction line will be created and another one will follow your cursor, coming from the same first point. AutoCAD will continue prompting for more "through points":
Specify through point:

When you are finished with putting construction lines on your drawing, press the ↵ Enter key to exit the Construction Line command.

Construction Line Options

Horizontal and Vertical Construction Lines

For a horizontal or vertical construction line, type the letter "v" or "h" at the Construction Line prompt and then press the ↵ Enter key. Alternatively, use your cursor to select either *Ver* or *Hor* from the options in the command line.

Note that the construction line will appear on your screen and will follow your cursor and prompt you with the following:

Specify through point:

The methods of specifying the "through point" are the same as previously described.

After you select the "through point", the construction line will be created, and another one will follow your cursor. AutoCAD will continue prompting for more "through points":

When you are finished with putting construction lines on your drawing, press the ↵ Enter key to exit the Construction Line command.

Angled Construction Lines

For an angled construction line, type the letter "a" at the construction line prompt and then press the ↵ Enter key. Alternatively, use your cursor to select *Ang* from the options in the command line. The command line prompts you with the following:

Enter angle of xline (0) or [Reference]:

Type in the desired angle of the construction line and then press the ↵ Enter key. The command line prompts you with the following:

Specify through point:

From here on, the command acts the same as the horizontal or vertical line options.

Offset Option

This option works the same as the Offset command, only it puts construction lines in. You must key in the distance and select the direction to offset.

Recommendation:

The Construction Line command is a very useful tool. Horizontal, vertical, and angled lines are the most commonly used options. The Offset option can also be very useful. The Bisect option is rarely used and is not described here. It is left to the student to explore this option if so desired.

After construction lines are put on the drawing, it is necessary to trim them using the Trim command (discussed in the next section).

Although using construction lines and trimming may actually take more steps than drawing lines exactly where you want them by using X-Y coordinates, it allows the designer not to have to think in terms of X-Y coordinates. After some practice, it can actually be quicker to draw this way, since less thought is involved.

Try it:

1. **Draw 5 horizontal lines anywhere on your screen.**

(Pick the Construction Line icon)

XLINE *Specify a point or [Hor/Ver/Ang/Bisect/Offset]:* **h↲**
(Type "h" and press the ↲ Enter key or pick *Hor* with your cursor)

Specify through point: ***(Pick a location anywhere on your screen)***
Specify through point: ***(Pick a location anywhere on your screen)***
Specify through point: ***(Pick a location anywhere on your screen)***
Specify through point: ***(Pick a location anywhere on your screen)***
Specify through point: ***(Pick a location anywhere on your screen)***
Specify through point: ↲ **(Press the ↲ Enter key to exit the command)**

2. **Draw 5 vertical lines anywhere on your screen.**

(Pick the Construction Line icon)

XLINE *Specify a point or [Hor/Ver/Ang/Bisect/Offset]:* **v↲**
(Type "v" and press the ↲ Enter key or pick *Ver* with your cursor)

Specify through point: ***(Pick a location anywhere on your screen)***

Specify through point: ***(Pick a location anywhere on your screen)***
Specify through point: ***(Pick a location anywhere on your screen)***
Specify through point: ***(Pick a location anywhere on your screen)***
Specify through point: ***(Pick a location anywhere on your screen)***
Specify through point: ↵ **(Press the ↵ Enter key to exit the command)**

3. Draw a 45° angled line anywhere on your screen.

(Pick the Construction Line icon)

XLINE *Specify a point or [Hor/Ver/Ang/Bisect/Offset]:* **a↵**
(Type "a" and press the ↵ Enter key or pick *Ang* with your cursor)

Enter angle of xline (0) or [Reference]: **45↵**
(Type "45" and press the ↵ Enter key)

Specify through point: ***(Pick a location on the screen for your line)***
Specify through point: ↵ **(Press the ↵ Enter key to exit the command)**

4. Draw a 4" Construction Line offset.

Draw a line anywhere on your screen. The length and angle are arbitrary.

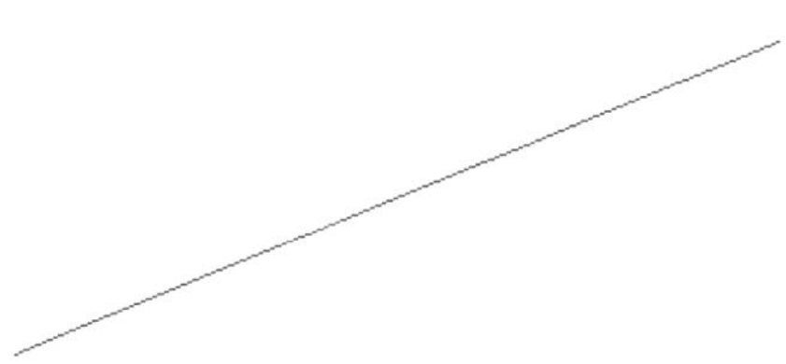

Now we will create an infinitely long line parallel to this one.
(Pick the Construction Line icon)

XLINE *Specify a point or [Hor/Ver/Ang/Bisect/Offset]:* **o↵**
(Type "o" and press the ↵ Enter key or pick *Offset* with your cursor)
Specify offset distance or [Through] <0'-2">: **4↵**

(Type "4" and press the ↵ Enter key)

Select a line object: ***(Pick the line)***
Specify side to offset: ***(Pick to the right of the line)***
Select a line object: ↵ **(Press the ↵ Enter key to exit the command)**

When you are done, your drawing will look like this:

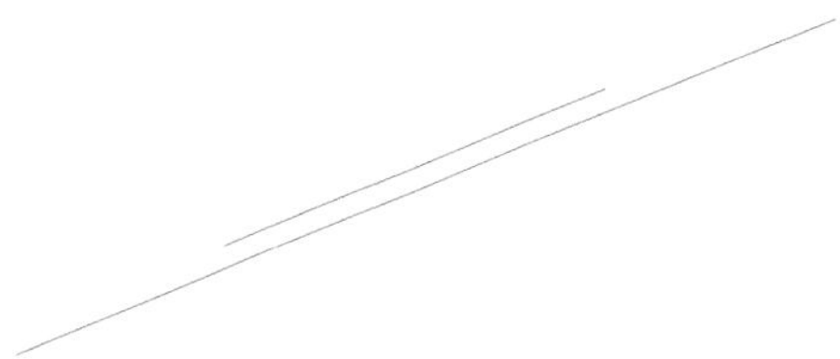

Changing Object Limits

The Trim command and the Extend command allow you to change the limits of existing objects. Trimming will shorten or cut out a section of an object. Extending will allow you to increase the length of an object (within the limits of the object's definition). One command can be used to perform the same as the other by holding the shift key during the object selection process. Both commands require specific cutting or boundary edges to define the endpoint location.

Lengthen allows you to drag an endpoint of a line or arc to lengthen or shorten it, without requiring you to define a specific cutting edge or boundary edge.

Trim

AutoCAD has two modes for trimming objects: Quick mode and Standard mode. The default mode is the Quick mode. Only this mode will be covered.

In the Quick mode, simply select the objects to be trimmed. As you move your cursor over the object, the portion that will be trimmed is displayed as a light gray color. That portion is defined by the nearest boundary, which is any objects that cross it. The objects that cross it are considered to be cutting edges. You can think of a cutting edge as a knife that will slice through the object you plan to trim. If the full-length of an object is between cutting edges, it cannot be trimmed; instead, AutoCAD will delete the object.

Multiple objects can be trimmed at once by dragging the cursor to define a freehand selection path, or by picking two points to define a line that will act as a crossing Fence.

Procedure:

Pick (left click): **Trim icon** from the Modify Panel of the Home Tab.

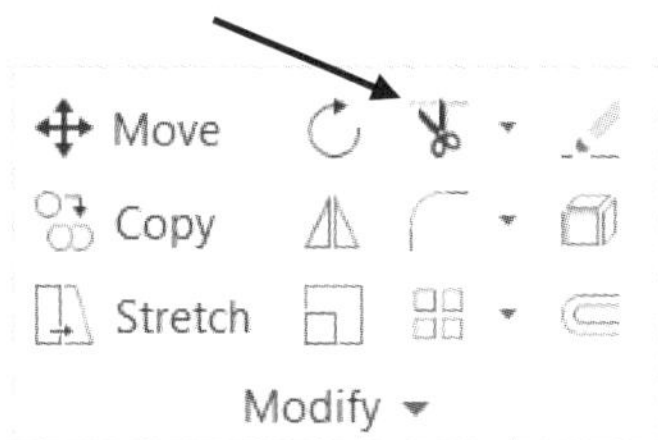

Mac

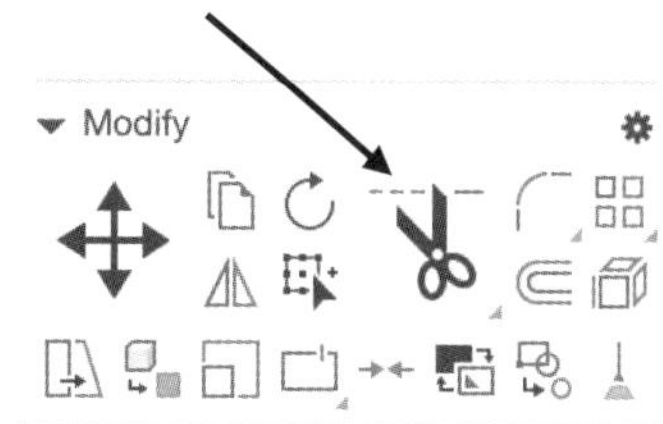

The command line prompts you with the following:

Current settings: Projection=UCS, Edge=None, Mode=Quick
Select object to trim or shift-select to extend or

TRIM *[cuTting edges/Crossing/mOde/Project/eRase/Undo]:*

To select the object to trim, move the cursor to the object you wish to trim, on the portion of the object you want to eliminate, and use the left mouse button to pick that object.

Example

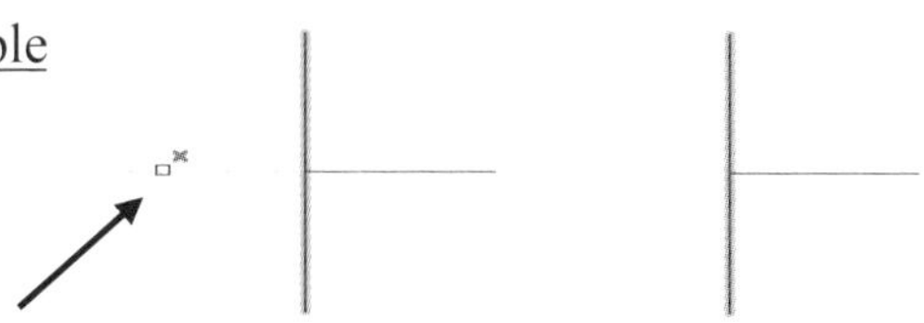

Selecting here Results in this

OR

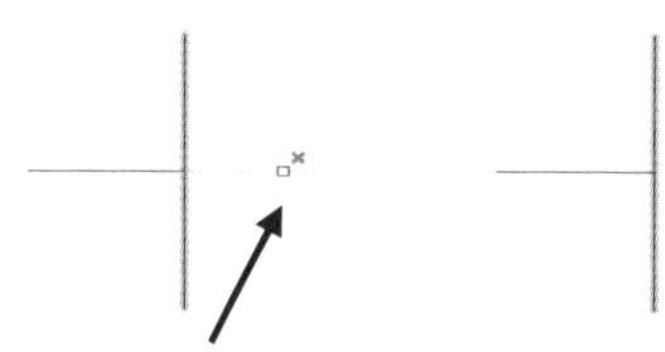

Selecting here Results in this

You can also select a portion of an object to trim that is between two cutting edges:

Example:

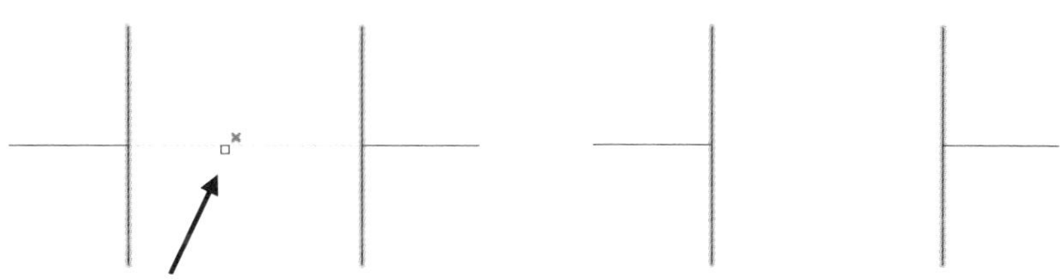

Selecting here Results in this

If an object was trimmed in error, use the Undo option: [*Undo*]. This must be done after an object was trimmed and while you are still in the command. Simply type the letter "u" followed by the ↵ Enter key or pick ***Undo*** with your cursor.

Select object to trim or shift-select to extend or
[cuTting edges/Crossing/mOde/Project/eRase/Undo]: **u** ↵

Try it:

Draw any size rectangle anywhere on your screen. Draw a horizontal construction line passing through the rectangle.

Now we will use the Trim command to trim the construction line to the rectangle.
(Pick the Trim icon)

Current settings: Projection=UCS, Edge=None, Mode=Quick
Select object to trim or shift-select to extend or
TRIM *[cuTting edges/Crossing/mOde/Project/eRase/Undo]:* ***(Pick the Construction Line near point 1)***

Select object to trim or shift-select to extend or
[cuTting edges/Crossing/mOde/Project/eRase/Undo]: ***(Pick the Construction Line near point 2)***

Select object to trim or shift-select to extend or
[cuTting edges/Crossing/mOde/Project/eRase/Undo]: ↵ **(Press the ↵ Enter key to exit the command)**

When you are done, your drawing will look like this:

Try it:

Let's try this again. Our new goal is to remove the portion of the construction line that passes through the rectangle.

Draw any size rectangle anywhere on your screen. Draw a horizontal construction line passing through the rectangle.

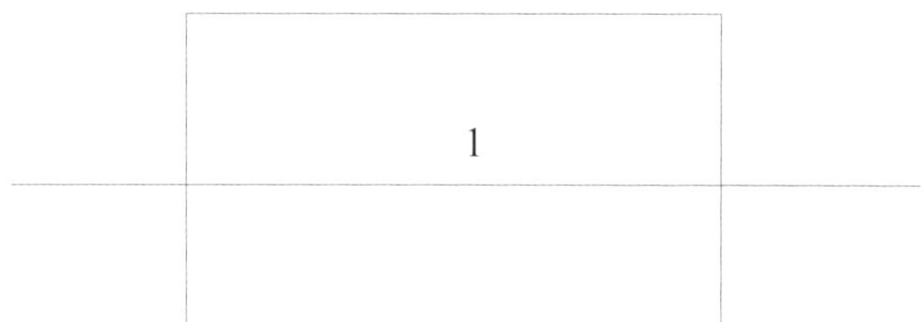

Now we will use the Trim command to trim away the construction line from inside the rectangle.

(Pick the Trim icon)

Current settings: Projection=UCS, Edge=None, Mode=Quick
Select object to trim or shift-select to extend or
TRIM *[cuTting edges/Crossing/mOde/Project/eRase/Undo]:* ***(Pick the Construction Line near point 1)***

Select object to trim or shift-select to extend or
[cuTting edges/Crossing/mOde/Project/eRase/Undo]: ↵ **(Press the ↵ Enter key to exit the command)**

When you are done, your drawing will look like this:

Extend

AutoCAD has two modes for extending objects: Quick mode and Standard mode. The default mode is the Quick mode. Only this mode will be covered.

In the Quick mode, simply select the objects to be extended. As you move your cursor over the object, the portion that will be extended is highlighted with a blue color with a preview of the extension. That portion is defined by the nearest boundary, which is any objects that are in the path of the extension. The objects that are in that path are known as boundary edges. You can think of a boundary edge as a wall that will stop the object from extending beyond. The Extend command can also perform as a Trim command by holding the shift key down while picking the object to trim (it will treat the boundary edge as a cutting edge instead).

Multiple objects can be extended at once by dragging the cursor to define a freehand selection path, or by picking two points to define a line that will act as a crossing Fence.

Procedure:

Pick (left click): Pick the pull-down arrow next to the Trim Command in the Modify Panel of the Home Tab. Pick the **Extend icon**.

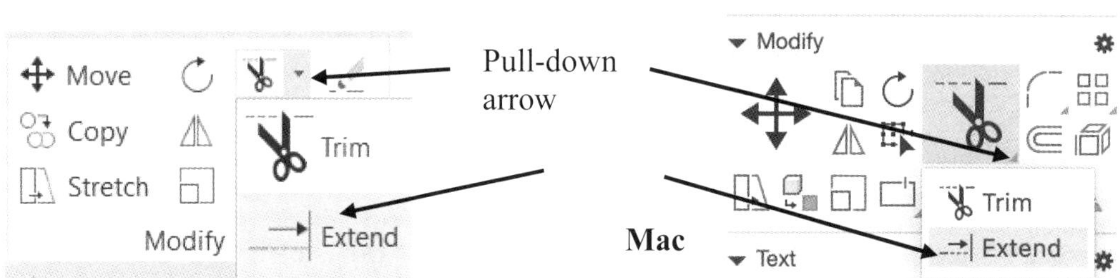

The command line prompts you with the following:

Current settings: Projection=UCS, Edge=None, Mode=Quick
Select object to extend or shift-select to trim or
EXTEND *[Boundary edges/Crossing/mOde/Project/Undo]:*

To select the object to extend, move the cursor to the object you wish to extend, on the portion of the object you want to increase in length, and use the left mouse button to pick that object.

Example:

Selecting here   Results in this

If an object was extended in error, use the Undo option: [*Undo*]. This must be done after an object was extended and while you are still in the command. Simply type the letter "u" followed by the ↵ Enter key or select ***Undo*** with your cursor.

Select object to extend or shift-select to trim or
[Boundary edges/Crossing/mOde/Project/Undo]: **u ↵**

Try it:

Draw two lines on your screen like these:

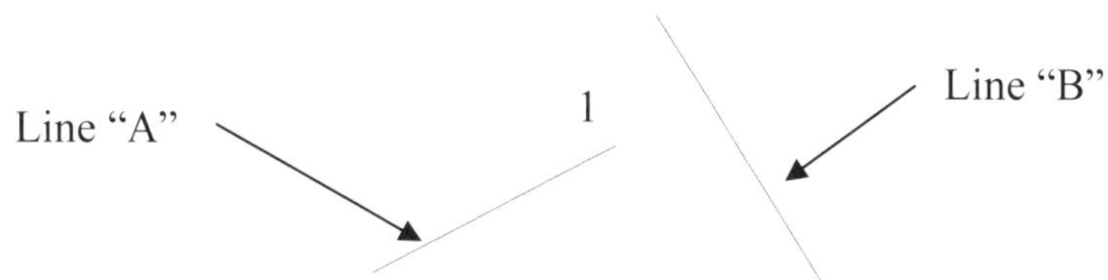

Now extend Line "A" to Line "B"

(Pick the Extend icon)

Current settings: Projection=UCS, Edge=None, Mode=Quick
Select object to extend or shift-select to trim or
EXTEND *[Boundary edges/Crossing/mOde/Project/Undo]:* ***(Pick Line "A" near the endpoint marked 1)***

Select object to extend or shift-select to trim or
[Boundary edges/Crossing/mOde/Project/Undo]: **↵ (Pressing the ↵ Enter key will end the command)**

When you are done, your drawing will look like this:

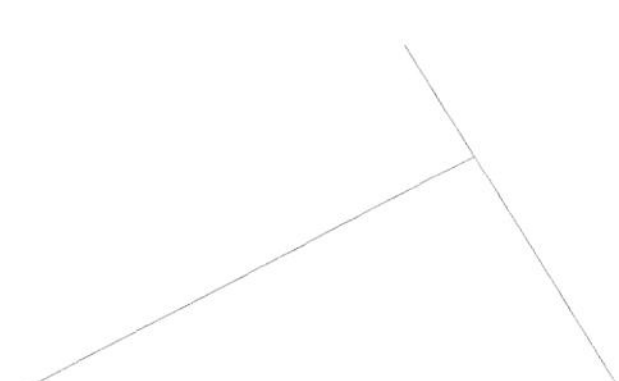

Lengthen

Lengthen can be used as an alternative to Trim and Extend. There are several options available for the Lengthen command, but only the Dynamic option will be covered. This option supplements the Trim and Extend commands (rather than be an alternative). It allows you to drag an endpoint of a line or arc to lengthen or shorten it, without requiring you to define a specific cutting edge or boundary edge.

Procedure:

Pick (left click): Pick the pull-down arrow to expand the Modify Panel of the Home Tab. Pick the **Lengthen icon**.

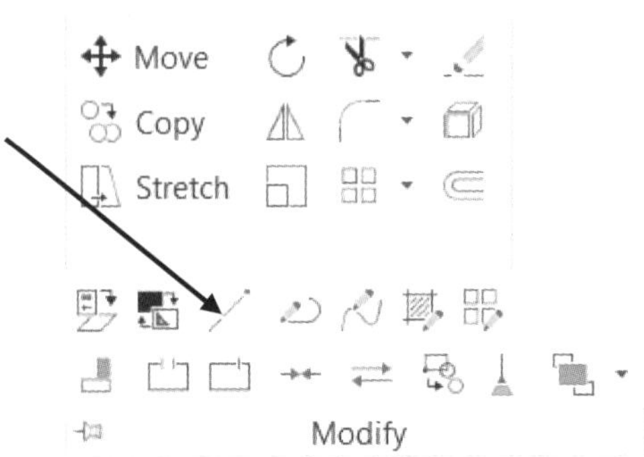

Customize Panel Icon

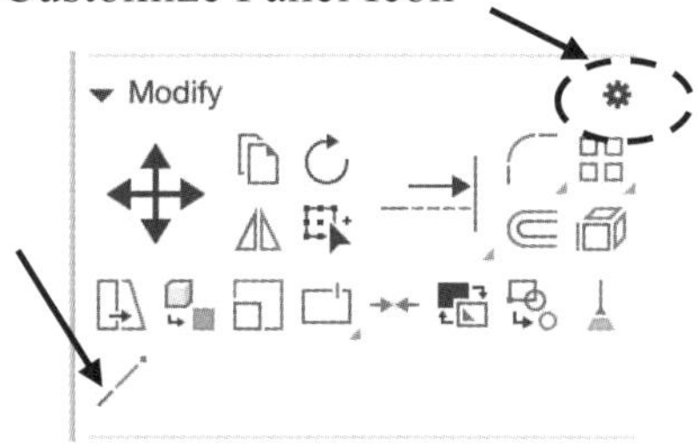

Mac

The Lengthen icon on the Mac can be displayed by selecting the Customize Panel icon and selecting it from the list.

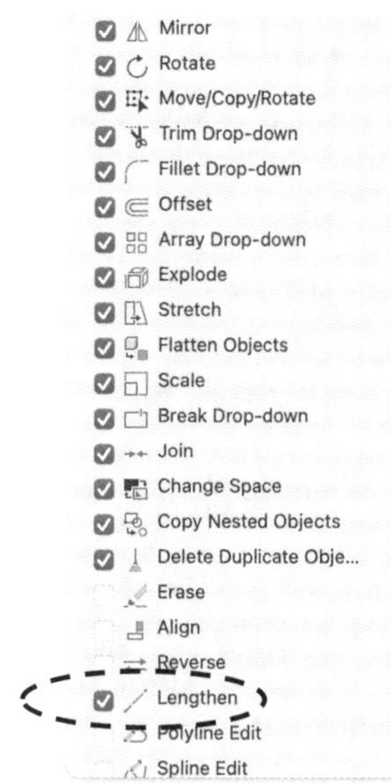

The command line prompts you with the following:

LENGTHEN *Select an object or [DElta/Percent/Total/DYnamic]:* **dy↵**
(Type "dy" and press the ↵ Enter key or pick *DYnamic* with your cursor)

Select an object to change or [Undo]
(Pick either a line or an arc near the endpoint you want changed)

Specify new end point:
(Pick a location on the drawing space to define the location of the new endpoint)

AutoCAD will continue to prompt for more objects to change:
Select an object to change or [Undo]:

To exit the command, press the ↵ Enter key.

Try it:

Draw three lines anywhere on your screen.

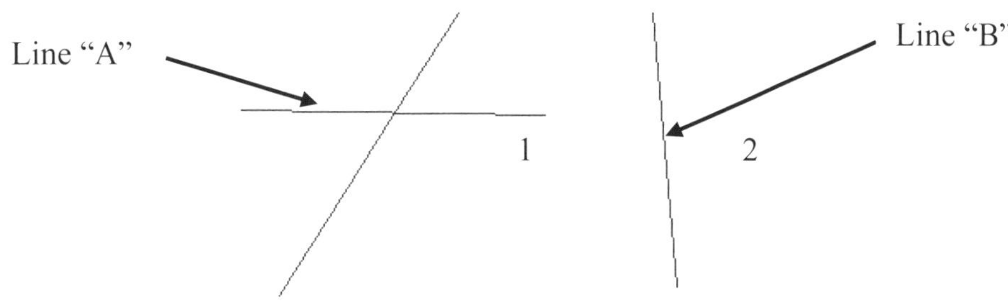

Now we will use the Lengthen command to extend line A beyond line B.

(Pick the Lengthen icon)

LENGTHEN *Select an object or [DElta/Percent/Total/DYnamic]:* **dy↵**
(Type "dy" and press the ↵ Enter key or pick *DYnamic* with your cursor)
Select an object to change or [Undo]: ***(Pick Line "A" near the endpoint marked 1)***
Specify new end point: ***(Pick near location 2)***
Select an object to change or [Undo]: ↵ **(Pressing the ↵ Enter key will end the command)**

When you are done, your drawing will look like this:

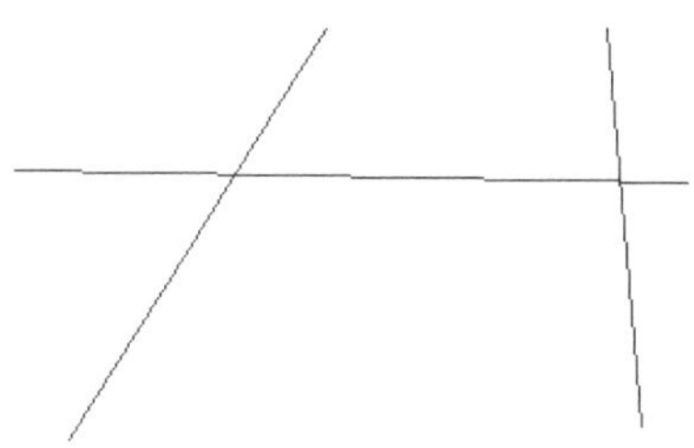

This command works the same way with arcs. Later in the book you will learn about arcs. Once you have an arc on your screen, you can try this command again.

Object Snap – OSNAP

A major advantage of using AutoCAD, or most Computer Aided Design programs, is the precision with which you can draw. To place objects in a precise location, such as the end of a line, the center of a circle, etc., AutoCAD provides two methods: OSNAP and Object Snap. OSNAP is an abbreviation for Object Snap. When it is turned on, it can be thought of as a Running OSNAP.

OSNAP icon

On the lower part of your screen, you will see the following:

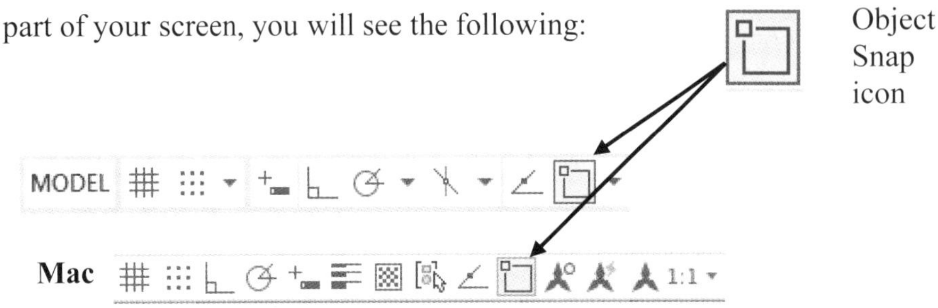

The Object Snap icon is a button that can be turned on and off. Move your cursor over the Object Snap icon and left-click to turn on the OSNAP feature. When OSNAP is turned on, the button will appear shaded blue-green.

There are many settings within OSNAP that can be turned on. To change those settings, hold your cursor over the OSNAP button and right-click, or pick the pull-down arrow. A pop-up box will appear by your cursor:

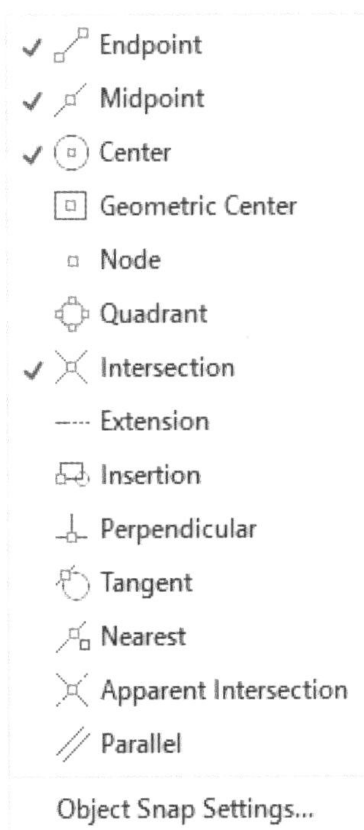

Mac

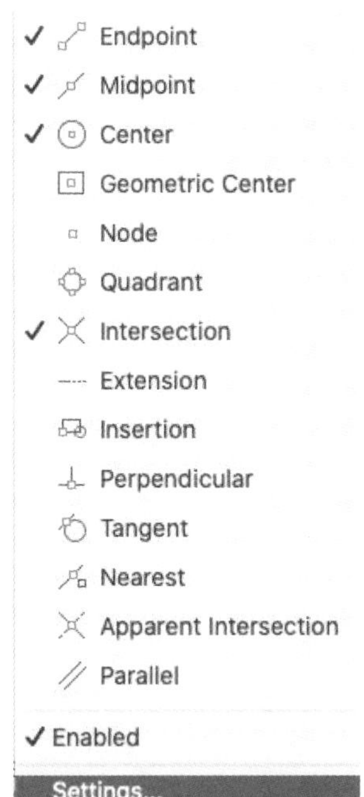

Each choice has an icon to the left of it. If the icon has a check mark next to it, that choice is selected. In this example, Endpoint, Midpoint, Center, and Intersection are selected. To select or de-select, pick on the icon. These are done one at a time.

An alternate method of selecting which Object Snap choices you want is to pick Object Snap Settings… (or Settings… on the Mac). A Drafting Settings dialog box will appear. You can individually select your choice by picking the check box so that a check mark appears. Pick the OK button to exit the dialog box.

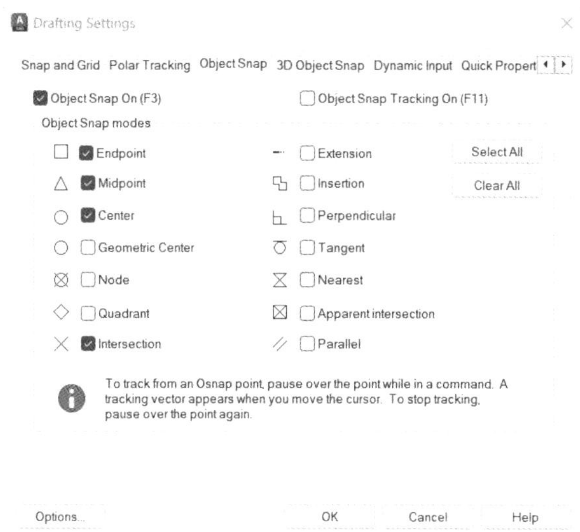

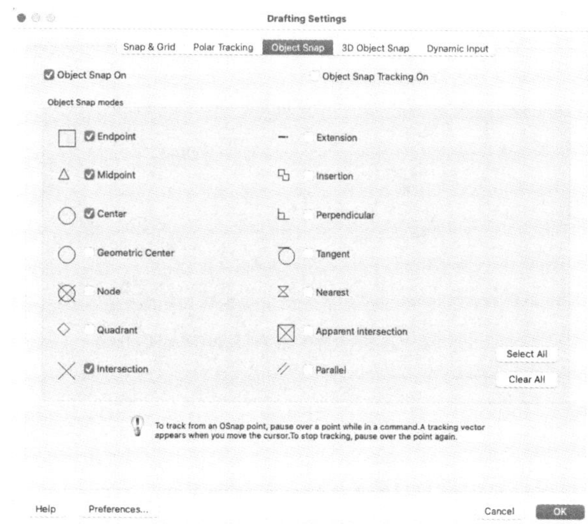

Mac

Using the OSNAP feature

Example 1. - Endpoint

In this example, let's place the center of a circle at the lowest end of the right vertical line of the three lines shown:

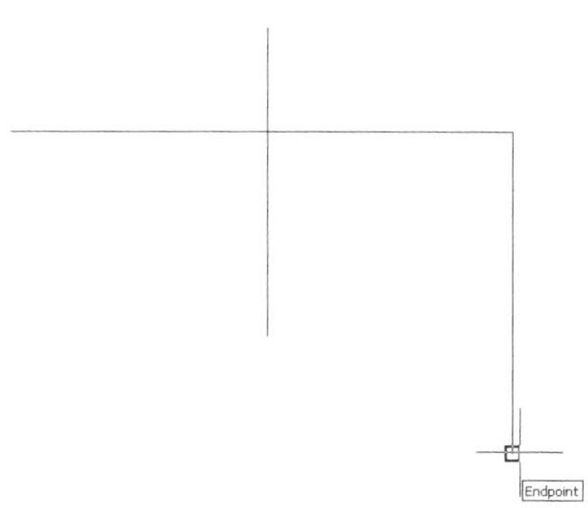

Notice that as the cursor gets near the endpoint of the line, an AutoSnap marker will appear at the end of the line, and a "tip" will indicate "Endpoint". Once the AutoSnap marker appears, left-click to pick the end of the line.

Pick anywhere away from that endpoint to complete the circle.

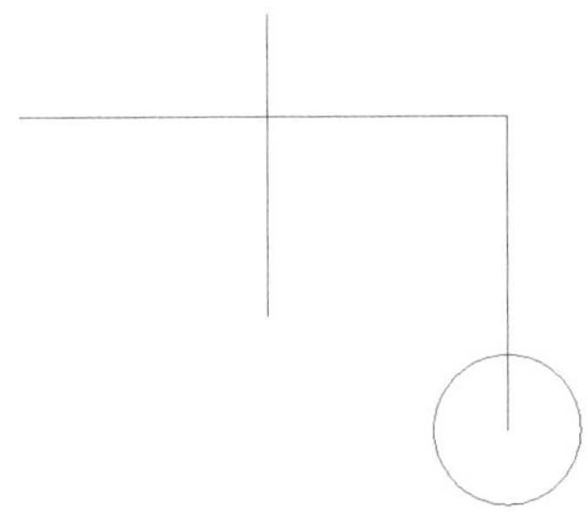

Example 2. – Intersection

Now let's place the center of a circle at the intersection of the left vertical line and the horizontal line:

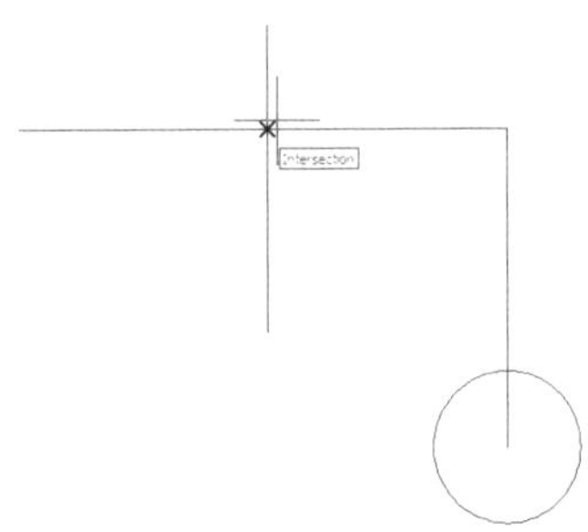

Notice that as the cursor gets near the intersection of the two lines, an AutoSnap marker will appear at the intersection, and a "tip" will indicate "Intersection". Once the AutoSnap marker appears, left-click to pick the intersection.

Pick anywhere away from that endpoint to complete the circle.

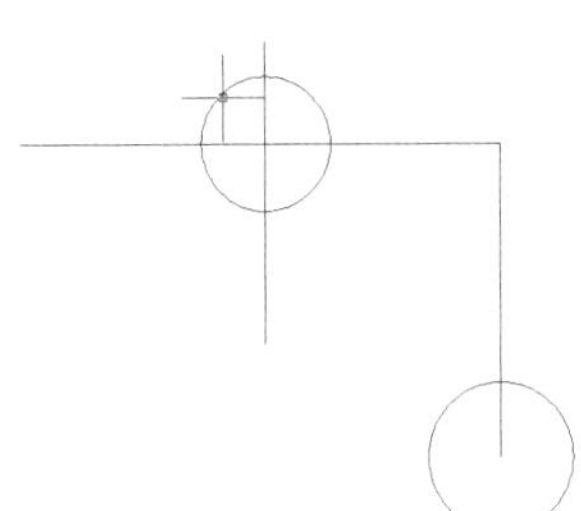

Object Snaps – Override

Object Snaps work very similar to OSNAP, except that these are one-time use overrides. Use Object Snaps when you are in the middle of a particular command to make your selection snap to a particular portion of an object. This can be done with OSNAP turned off or on. If OSNAP is turned on, you can override the OSNAP selection by typing a particular Object Snap command alias.

Object Snap Command Alias

You can type in the desired Object Snap in the command line. The command alias is the same whether you are using a PC or a Mac. To use an alias, type it in the command line, while in the middle of a command, followed by the ↵ Enter key.

The following aliases are for the most commonly used Object Snaps.

Object Snap	alias	Object Snap	alias
Center	cen ↵	Endpoint	end
Intersection	int ↵	Midpoint	mid ↵
Ouadrant	qua	Tangent	tan ↵
Perpendicular	per ↵	Nod	nod ↵

Example 3. – Midpoint

Let's add another circle to the horizontal line, but we need to add it to the midpoint of the line. Note that the midpoint of the line is very close to the intersection of the lines where the circle was created in example 2. If we leave OSNAP turned on, AutoCAD will try to find the intersection of the two lines as the cursor gets near the intersection. We can override this by selecting the Snap to Midpoint icon from the Object Snap toolbar while we are in the middle of the *Circle* command.

CIRCLE *Specify center point for circle or [3P/2P/Ttr (tan tan radius)]:* ***mid*** ↵

CIRCLE *Specify center point for circle or [3P/2P/Ttr (tan tan radius)]: _mid of* ***(Pick the midpoint of the horizontal line)***

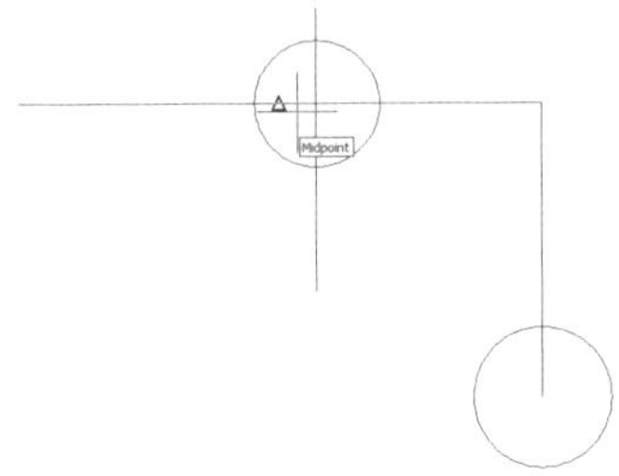

Notice that as the cursor gets near the midpoint of the line, an AutoSnap marker will appear at the intersection, and a "tip" will indicate "Midpoint". Once the AutoSnap marker appears, left-click to pick the midpoint.

Pick anywhere away from the midpoint to complete the circle.

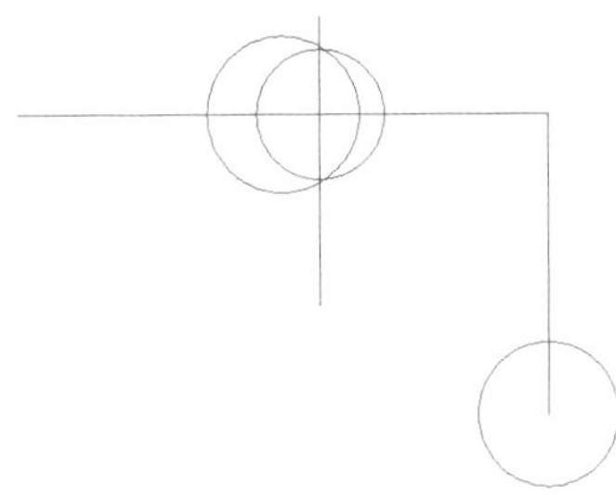

Try it:

Locate the circle inside the rectangle by using Construction Line Offset:

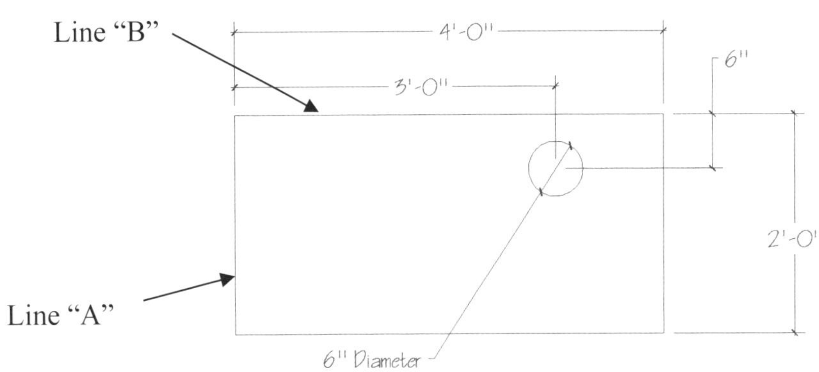

Before beginning, make sure that Object Snap icon on your Status Bar is turned on and that Intersection is selected. Ignore the default values shown.

(Pick the Rectangle icon)

RECTANG *Specify first corner point or [Chamfer/Elevation/Fillet/Thickness/Width]:*
Specify other corner point or [Area/Dimensions/Rotation]: **d↵**
(Type "d" and press the ↵ Enter key or pick *Dimensions* with your cursor)

Specify length for rectangles <16'-0">: **4'↵**
Specify width for rectangles <8'-0">: **2'↵**
Specify other corner point or [Area/Dimensions/Rotation]: ***(Pick for the opposite corner location)***

(Pick the Construction Line icon)

XLINE *Specify a point or [Hor/Ver/Ang/Bisect/Offset]:* **o↵**
(Type "o" and press the ↵ Enter key or pick *Offset* with your cursor)

Specify offset distance or [Through] <0'-4">: **3'↵**
Select a line object: ***(Pick the rectangle line "A")***
Specify side to offset: ***(Pick to the right of the selected line)***
Select a line object: ↵

Press the ↵ Enter key to repeat the Construction Line command

XLINE *Specify a point or [Hor/Ver/Ang/Bisect/Offset]:* **o↵**
(Type "o" and press the ↵ Enter key or pick *Offset* with your cursor)

Specify offset distance or [Through] <3'-0">: **6↵**
Select a line object: ***(Pick the rectangle line "B")***
Specify side to offset: ***(Pick below the selected line)***
Select a line object: ↵

We now have intersecting construction lines that define the center of the circle. With OSNAP turned on and set to look for Intersections, we can proceed to put the circle in the exact location.

(Pick the Circle icon)

CIRCLE *Specify center point for circle or [3P/2P/Ttr (tan tan radius)]:*
(Pick the Intersection of the Construction Lines)

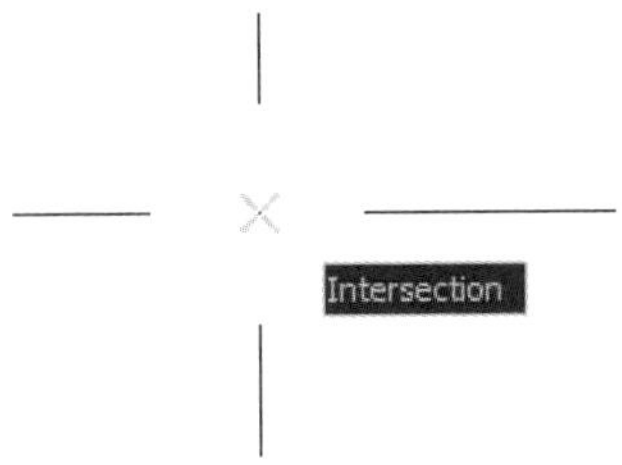

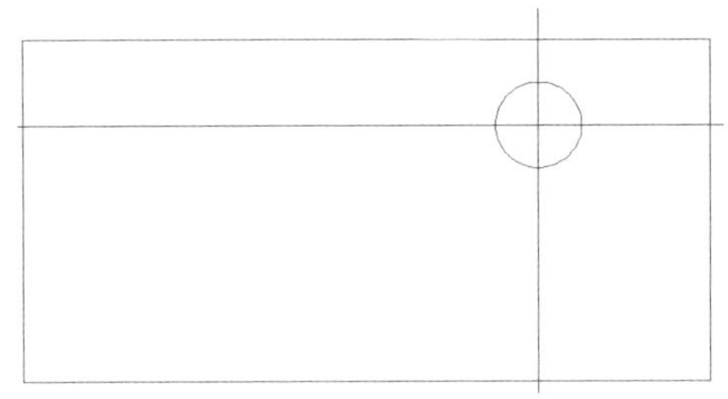

Specify radius of circle or [Diameter] <0'-3">: **d↵**
(Type "d" and press the ↵ Enter key or pick *Diameter* with your cursor)

Specify diameter of circle <0'-6">: **6↵**

The circle is now drawn exactly 6″ diameter exactly located in the rectangle. All we need to do now is to eliminate the construction lines to complete the drawing. Use the Erase command to do this.

(Pick Erase icon)

ERASE Select objects: ***(Pick the vertical construction line)*** 1 found
Select objects: ***(Pick the horizontal construction line)*** *1 found, 2 total*
Select objects: ↵

When you are done, your drawing will look like this:

Summary

In this chapter you have learned to:

- Create rectangles of specific size
- Change the rectangle object to individual lines using Explode
- Create parallel lines and concentric rectangles or circles using Offset
- Create infinitely long lines that are horizontal, vertical, or at a specific angle
- Create an infinitely long line parallel to an existing line object using the Offset option of the Construction line command
- Change the length of lines using either Trim, Extend, or Lengthen
- Place your objects at precise locations using the OSNAP or Object Snap override.

Review Questions

1. What is the option in the Rectangle command that allows you to create a rectangle of a specific size?

2. After you type in the size of the rectangle, what is the final step needed to complete the Rectangle command?

3. What command do you use to convert a rectangle into 4 separate lines?

4. What command is used to create a line parallel to another line?

5. How do you create an infinitely long parallel line?

6. How many steps are involved with creating an Offset?

7. How do you create horizontal, vertical, or angled lines that are infinitely long?

8. To change the length of a line, which commands can be used?

9. Which icon on the Status Bar must be turned on to draw accurately?

Exercises

1. Draw the Mirror

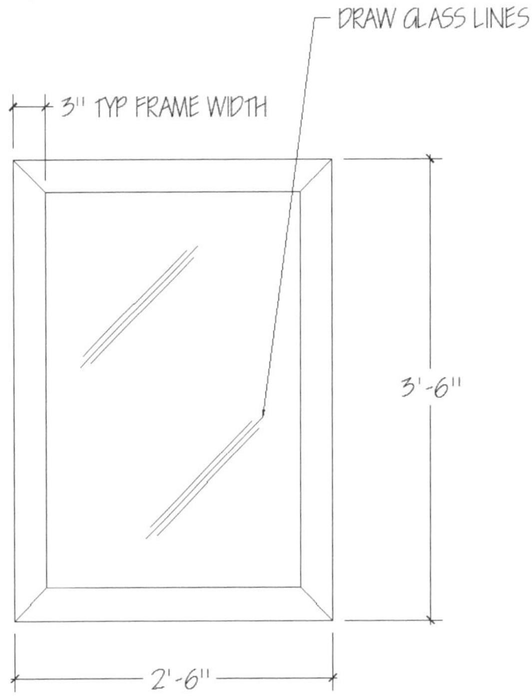

2. Draw the Luggage Rack (Use Offset or Construction Line Offset, with OSNAP turned on to locate each feature)

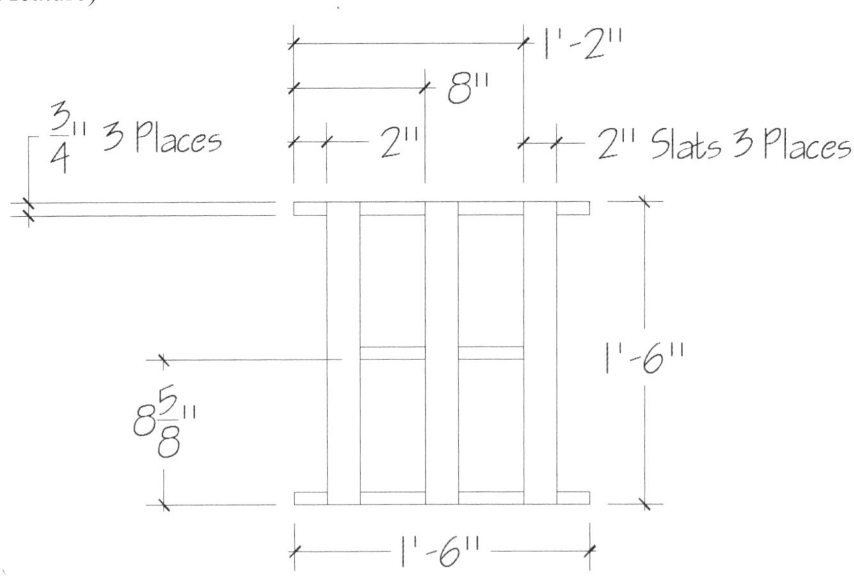

3. Draw the Floor Lamp – 1/4″ Spokes start at 45° and are 90° apart. Hint: Use angled construction lines and offset them 1/8″ each side for the spokes.

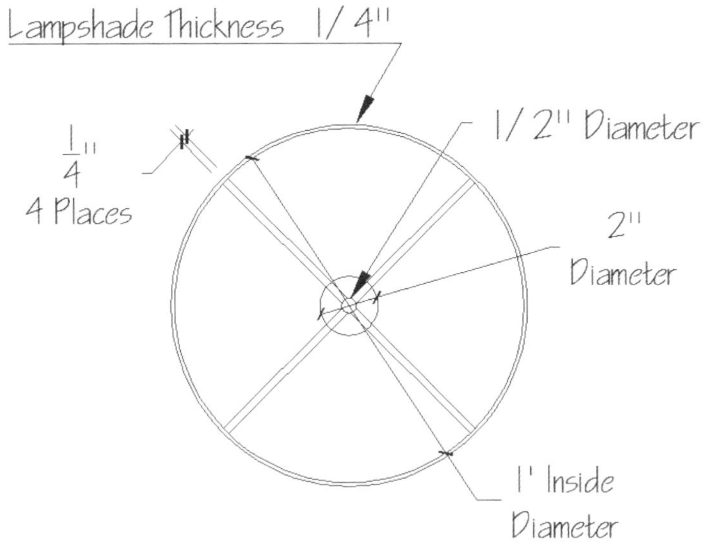

4. Draw the Dresser – Knobs are located the same for each drawer (Use Offset or Construction Line Offset, with OSNAP turned on to locate each feature)

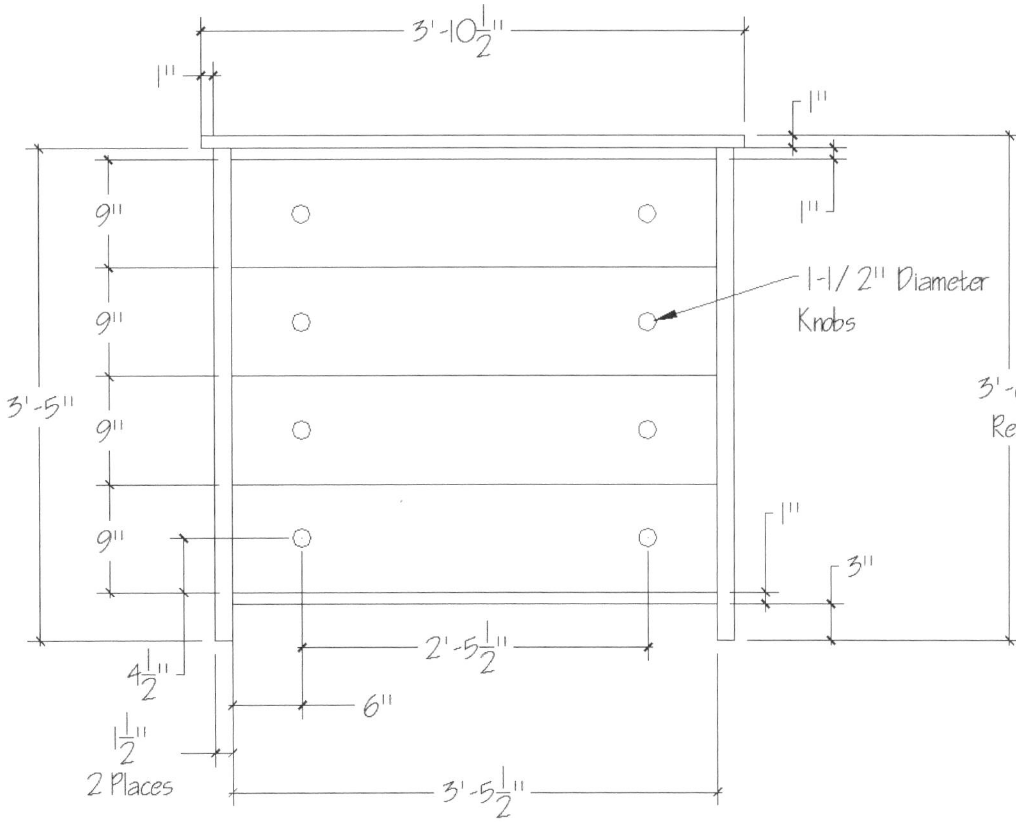

Chapter 4
Hotel Suite Project – Tutorial 1

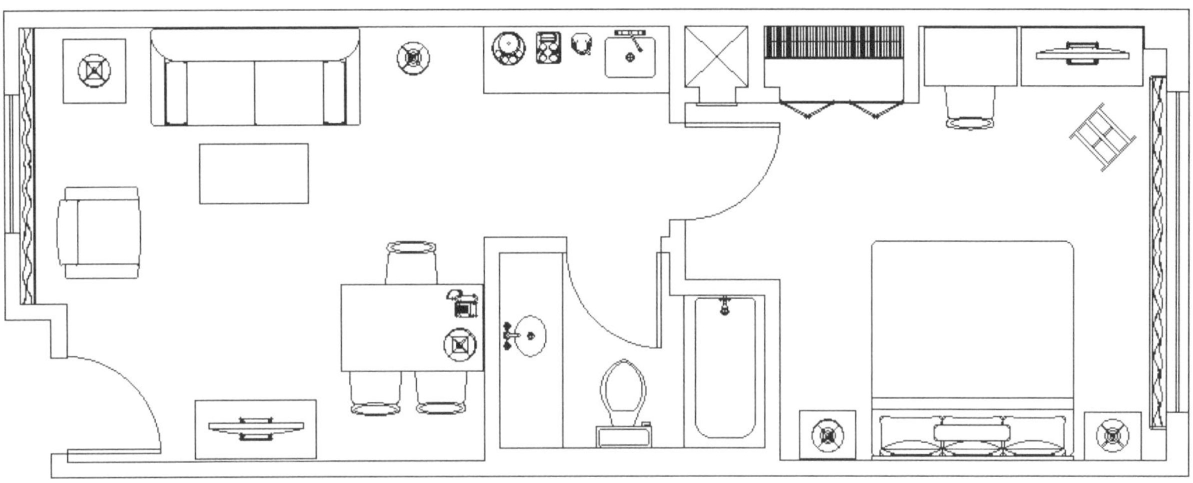

Learning Objectives:

- **To create a drawing of a real-world application using AutoCAD**
  - **Create the plan view of the outside walls of the hotel suite**
- **To utilize and reinforce the use of the AutoCAD commands learned in the previous chapters**

Hotel Suite Project

For our project, we will draw a hotel suite that will include a bedroom, bathroom, and a living room area. This project will utilize the majority of commands that will be covered throughout this book. The project will be broken down into multiple tutorials and each tutorial emphasizes commands covered in the preceding chapter.

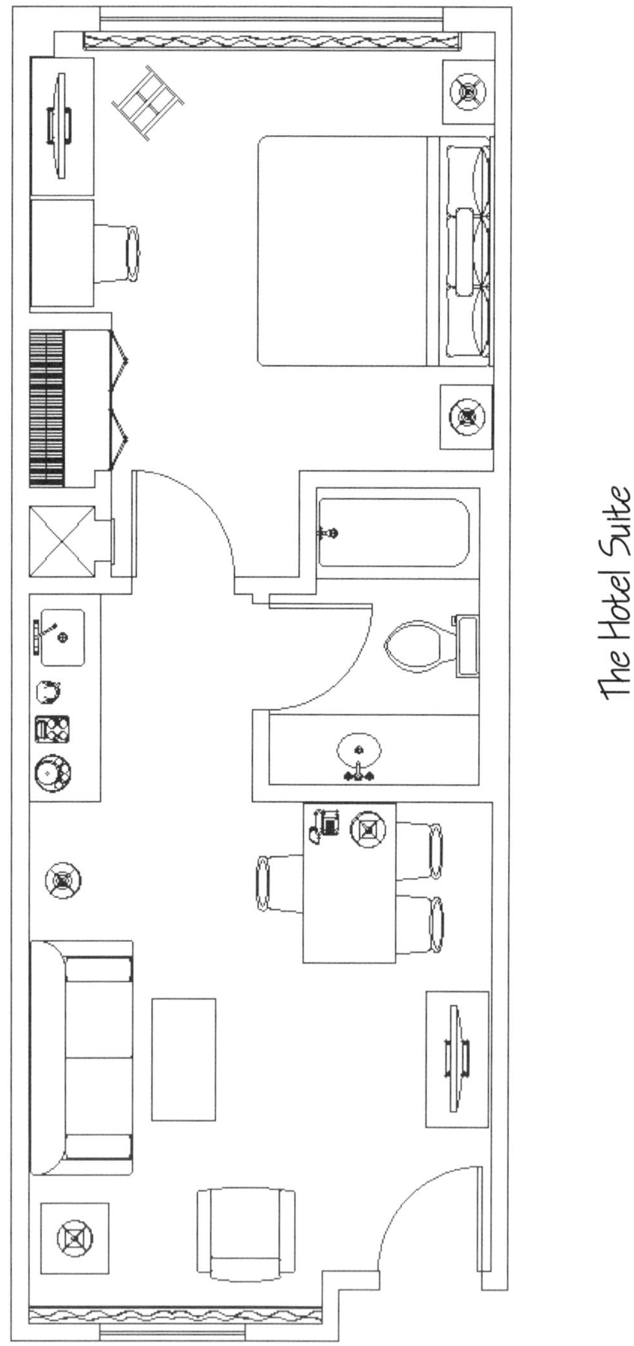

This tutorial covers the creation of the floor plan view of the hotel suite outside walls.

Commands & Techniques:

- Starting a new drawing
- Units
- Zoom - All
- Rectangle
- Offset
- Explode
- Construction Line – Offset
- Trim
- Extend
- Repeating commands by using the ↵ Enter key
- Erase
- Save

To help guide you through these tutorials, the following method is used to represent mouse and keyboard operations:

Bold font represents a keyboard operation.

Bold/Italic font in parentheses represents a mouse operation.

Italic font represents AutoCAD generated command line text.

Because the majority of the steps are repetitive, after the first several steps, the tutorial will not repeat every detail and prompt. When a new command is used, then the details will be given.

If you have already set up your mouse for customized right-click, everywhere the tutorial instructs you to press the ↵ Enter key, you can substitute that instruction with "right mouse-click".

For command options, where the text instructs you to type a letter or letters to use the option, you can use the cursor to select the option instead.

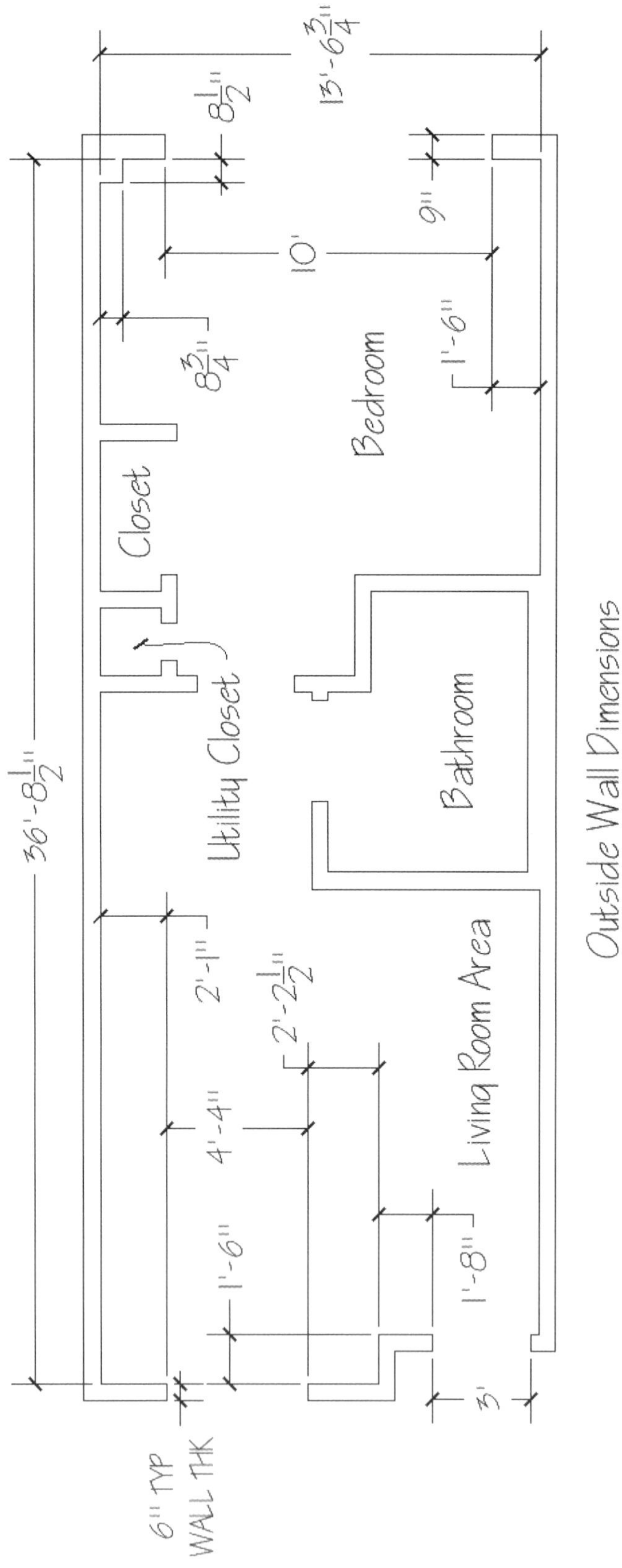
13'-6 3/4"
8 1/2"
9"
10'
8 3/4"
1'-6"
Bedroom
Closet
Utility Closet
Bathroom
36'-8 1/2"
2'-1"
2'-2 1/2"
Living Room Area
4'-4"
1'-6"
1'-8"
3'
6" TYP
WALL THK
Outside Wall Dimensions

Create the basic shell of the suite

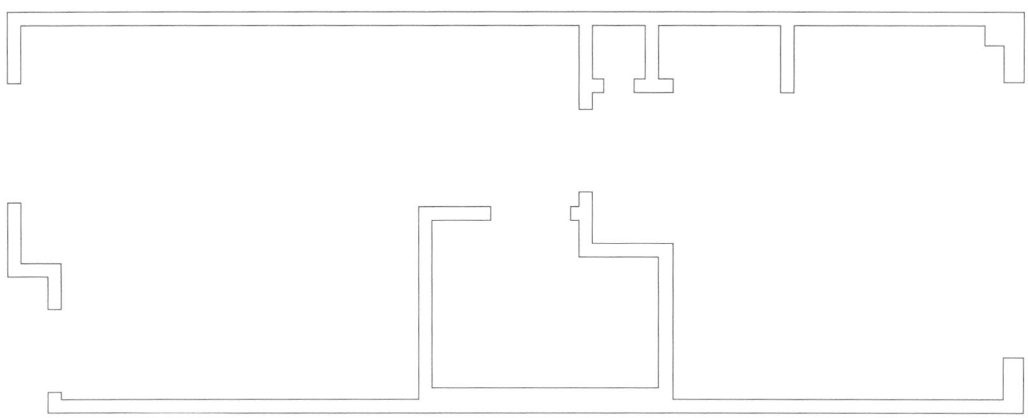

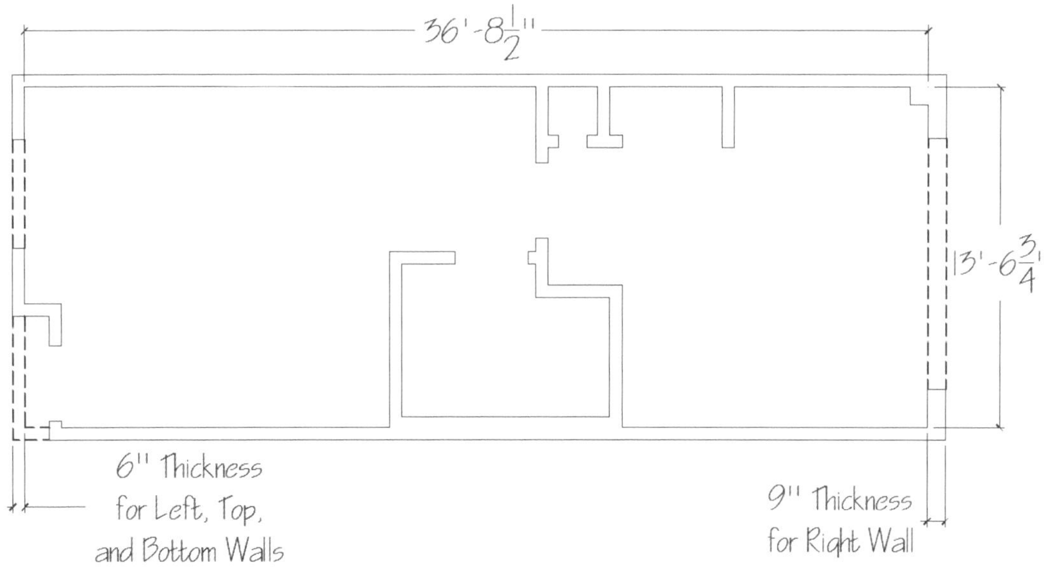

Basic Shell Dimensions

The dashed lines are shown to illustrate that we can start this drawing by using rectangles.

- Before beginning, start up a new drawing, use the Application Menu Browser to select Drawing Utilities, and change the Units to **Architectural.**
    - For Mac users, use the Format pull-down menu to change the Units to **Architectural.**

1. Change the units from decimal to feet-inches:

(Pick the Application Menu Browser, Pick Drawing Utilities, and Pick Units)
Mac: (Select pull-down menu Format, Units)

(Change to Architectural Units in the Length Type: (upper left portion) pull-down arrow in the dialog box)

(Pick OK to exit the dialog box)

2. Create the inside walls using Rectangle:

(Pick Rectangle icon)

RECTANG *Specify first corner point or [Chamfer/Elevation/Fillet/Thickness/Width]:* ***(Pick a point on the screen, below and to the left of the center)***

Use the Dimensions option to define the 36′8-1/2″ width and the 13′6-3/4″ height. AutoCAD uses confusing definitions for length and width: "length" = Horizontal direction, "width" = Vertical direction.

Note: when specifying Rectangle dimensions: - Length is the horizontal direction - Width is the vertical direction

Specify other corner point or [Area/Dimensions/Rotation]: **d↵**
(or pick *Dimensions* with your cursor*)*
Specify length for rectangles <0'-10">: **36'8-1/2 ↵**
Specify width for rectangles <0'-10">: **13'6-3/4 ↵**
Specify other corner point or [Area/Dimensions/Rotation]: ***(Pick to the upper right of the 4 choices given)***

As you move your cursor around the first corner point, four locations are available to choose. Pick the upper right location for the rectangle.

(AutoCAD will automatically end the Rectangle command)

When done, you will be left with only one rectangle; however, it will not be seen in its entirety. That is because it is too big for the size of the view.

3. Change the screen zoom so that the entire drawing space is on the screen:

>_ **z** ↵
ZOOM
Specify corner of window, enter a scale factor (nX or nXP), or
ZOOM *[All/Center/Dynamic/Extents/Previous/Scale/Window/Object] <real time>:* **a** ↵
Regenerating model.
(AutoCAD will automatically end the Zoom command)

When done, you will now be able to see the entire rectangle on your screen.

4. Use the Mouse Wheel to zoom out even further.

Your rectangle will appear even smaller. This will allow us to view more drawing space for when we offset the walls toward the outside.

5. Use the offset command to draw the outside walls:

(Pick Offset icon)

OFFSET Current settings: Erase source=No Layer=Source OFFSETGAPTYPE=0
Specify offset distance or [Through] <Through>: **6** ↵

Specify point on side to offset or [Exit/Multiple/Undo] <Exit>: ***(Pick the rectangle)***
Select object to offset or [Exit/Undo] <Exit>: ***(Pick to the outside of the rectangle)***

Since no more offset lines are required, pressing the ↵ Enter key will end the Offset command.

Select object to offset or <exit>: ↵

When completed, your drawing will look like this.

In Step 6b, we will erase this line

6. Draw the 9″ outside wall on the right side:

Our plan is to explode the rectangles first so that they become individual lines that we can work with. We will then be able to construct the thicker right wall.

6a. Prepare to draw the right outside wall by using the Explode command to convert the rectangles to lines:

(Pick the Explode icon)

EXPLODE *Select objects:* ***(Pick one of the rectangles)*** *1 found:*
Select objects: ***(Pick the other rectangle)*** *1 found, 2 total*

Since no more objects are to be exploded, pressing the ↵ Enter key will end the Explode command.

Select objects: ↵

6b. Erase the furthest right vertical line:

(Pick the Erase icon)

ERASE *Select objects:* ***(Pick the right vertical line)*** *1 found*

Since no more objects are being erased, pressing the ↵ Enter key will end the Erase command.

Select objects: ↵

When completed, your drawing will look like this.

In step 6c, we will create a construction line offset from this vertical line

6c. Construct the new right outside wall line for the 9″ thick wall:

(Pick the Construction Line icon)

XLINE *Specify a point or [Hor/Ver/Ang/Bisect/Offset]:* **o ↵**
(or pick *Offset* with your cursor)
Specify offset distance or [Through] <0'-6">: **9 ↵**
Select a line object: ***(Pick the right vertical line)***
Specify side to offset: ***(Pick anywhere to the right of the line you just selected)***

Since no more offset construction lines are required, pressing the ↵ Enter key will end the Offset command.

Select a line object: ↵

When you are done, your drawing should now look like this:

6d. Extend the horizontal lines to the new wall:

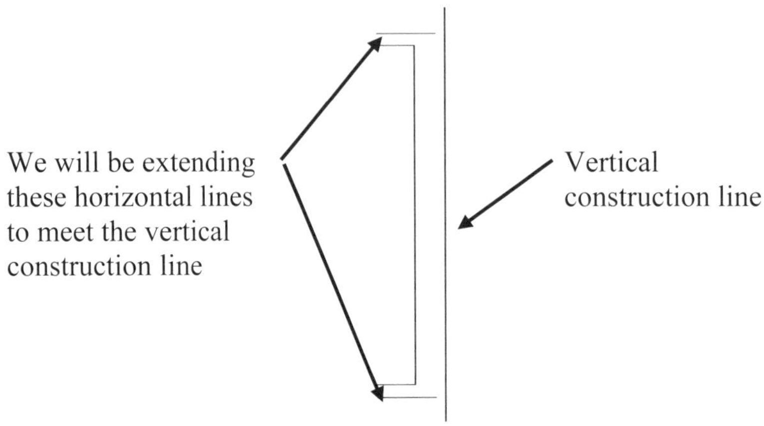

(Pick the Extend icon)

Current settings: Projection=UCS, Edge=None, Mode=Quick
Select object to extend or shift-select to trim or
EXTEND *[Boundary edges/Crossing/mOde/Project/Undo]:*

(Pick the top horizontal line)
(Pick the bottom horizontal line)

Note: the order in which you pick the lines to extend does not matter.

Since there are no more lines that need to be extended, pressing the ↵ Enter key will end the Extend command.

Select object to extend or shift-select to trim or
[Boundary edges/Crossing/mOde/Project/Undo]: ↵

When done, this portion of your drawing should look like this:

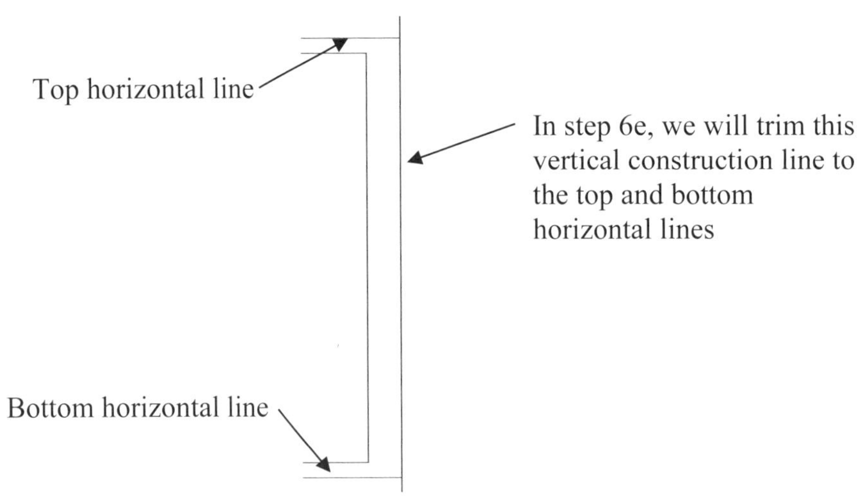

6e. Trim the vertical construction line of the new wall to the top and bottom walls:

Since we just used the Extend command, the icon for the Extend command is now shown in the panel, and to access the Trim command, the pull-down arrow must be selected.

(Pick the Trim icon)

Current settings: Projection=UCS, Edge=None, Mode=Quick
Select object to trim or shift-select to extend or
TRIM *[cuTting edges/Crossing/mOde/Project/eRase/Undo]:*

(Pick the construction line in a location above the top horizontal line)
(Pick the construction line in a location below the bottom horizontal line)

Note: the order in which you pick the location or lines to trim does not matter.

Since no more trimming is required, pressing the ↵ Enter key will end the Trim command.

Select object to trim or shift-select to extend or
[cuTting edges/Crossing/mOde/Project/eRase/Undo]: ↵

When you are done, your drawing should look like this:

7. Create the window opening in the bedroom.

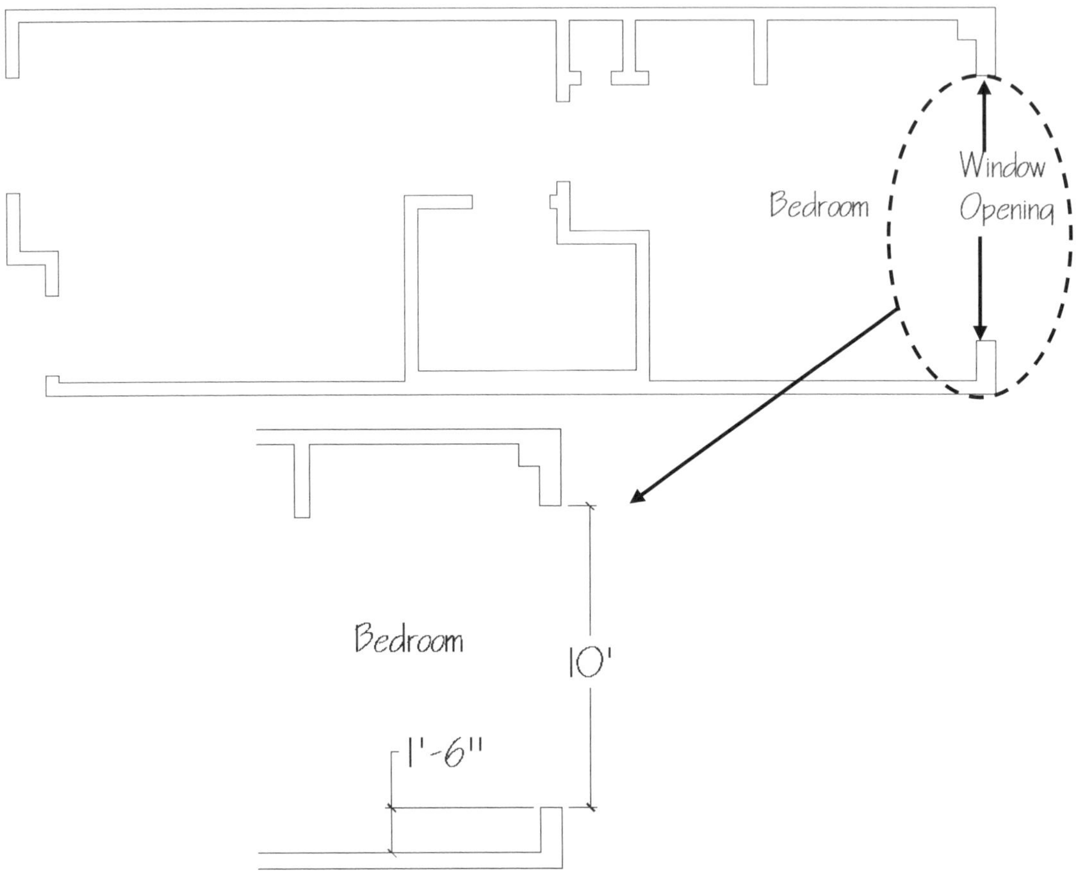

Our plan is to use both the **Construction Line – Offset** command and the **Offset** command to define the window opening. We will then trim the lines (and construction lines) to complete the window opening.

7a. Create a construction line offset from the bottom inside horizontal wall:

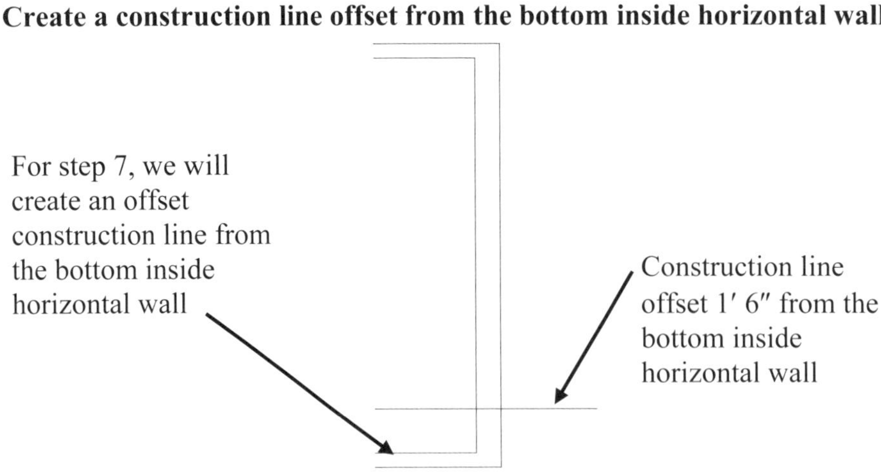

(Pick the Construction Line icon)

XLINE *Specify a point or [Hor/Ver/Ang/Bisect/Offset]:* **o↵**
(or pick *Offset* with your cursor)
Specify offset distance or [Through] <Through>: **1'6↵**
Select a line object: ***(Pick the bottom inside horizontal line)***
Specify side to offset: ***(Pick a location above the line you just selected)***

Since we are not offsetting any more construction lines at this distance, pressing the ↵ Enter key will end the command.

Select a line object: ↵
Command:

7b. Offset the new construction line to define the window size.

(Pick the Offset icon)

Current settings: Erase source=No Layer=Source OFFSETGAPTYPE=0
OFFSET *Specify offset distance or [Through/Erase/Layer] <1'-6">:* **10'↵**

Note that the default value for the offset distance is the last value used for either the Offset command or the Construction Line Offset command

Select object to offset or [Exit/Undo] <Exit>: ***(Pick the horizontal construction line that you just created in step 7a)***

Specify point on side to offset or [Exit/Multiple/Undo] <Exit>: ***(Pick a point anywhere above the horizontal construction line)***

Since there are no more objects that we plan to offset, pressing the ↵ Enter key will end the command.

Select object to offset or [Exit/Undo] <Exit>: ↵

When you are done, your drawing should look like this:

In step 7c, we will trim the lines and construction lines to create the window opening

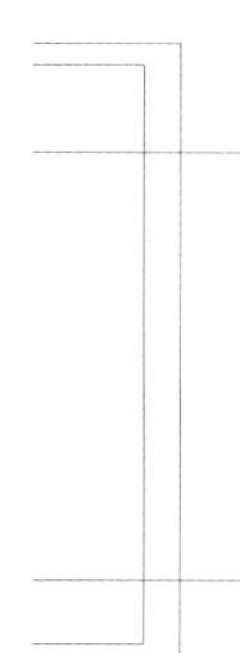

7c. Use the Trim command to trim the lines and construction lines:

(Pick the Trim icon)

Current settings: Projection=UCS, Edge=None, Mode=Quick
Select object to trim or shift-select to extend or
TRIM *[cuTting edges/Crossing/mOde/Project/eRase/Undo]:*

(Pick the objects to be trimmed in the appropriate locations shown (1-6). The order of selection does not matter)

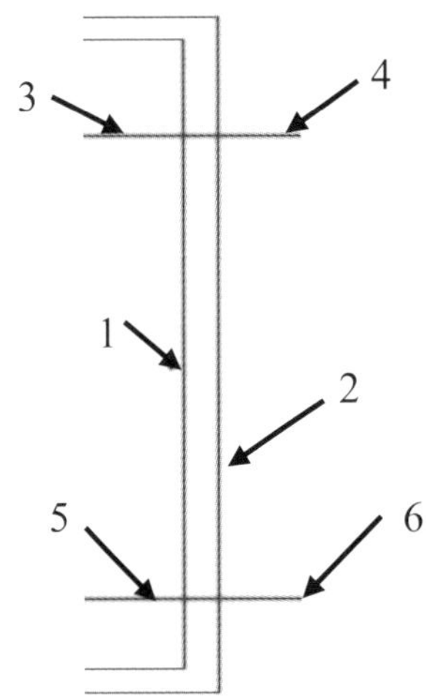

Since no more trimming is required, pressing the ↵ Enter key will end the Trim command.

Select object to trim or shift-select to extend or
[Fence/Crossing/Project/Edge/eRase/Undo]: ↵

The select object prompt will repeat until you press the ↵ Enter key to end the command

When you are done trimming, your window opening will be complete

8. Create the upper right corner of the bedroom.

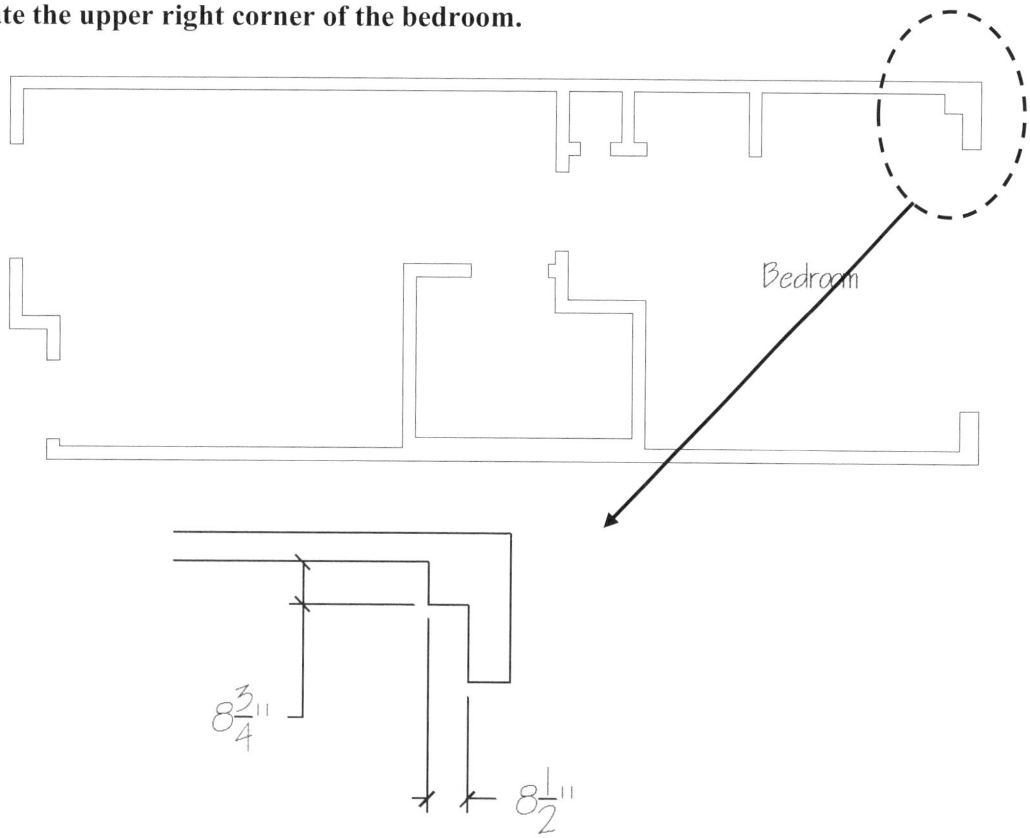

The upper right corner of the bedroom has a bump-out into the room because there is a structural column supporting the outside wall of the building. Our plan is to draw this bump-out by using the Offset and Trim commands.

Before beginning, you may want to use Zoom and Pan (using your mouse-wheel) to get a larger view of the upper right corner.

8a. Use the Offset command to offset the right inside wall line.

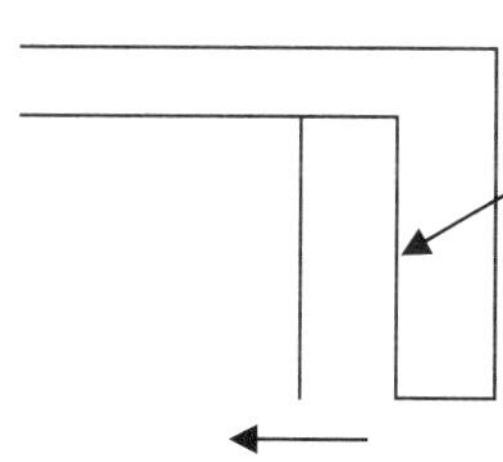

Offset this line
8-1/2″ to the left

8b. Press the ↵ Enter key to repeat the Offset command to offset the top inside wall line.

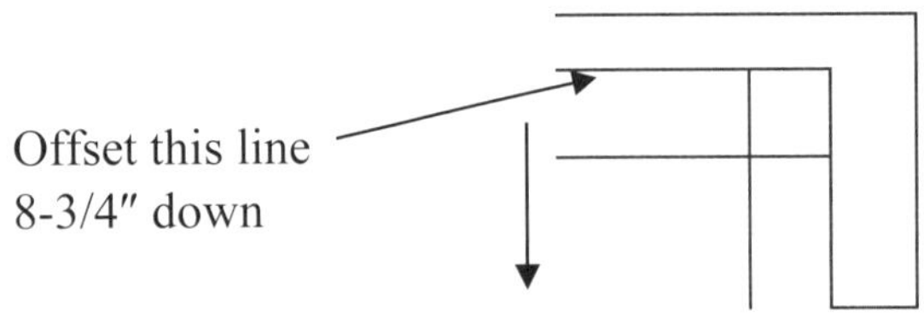

8c. Use the trim command to complete the corner.

Select the lines to be trimmed at the locations shown:

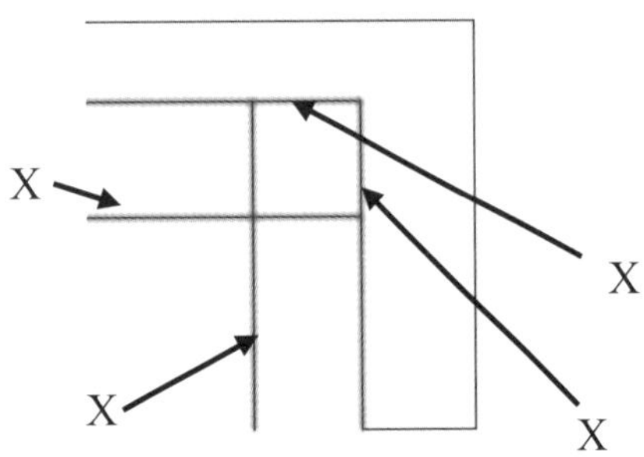

After trimming, the corner should look like this

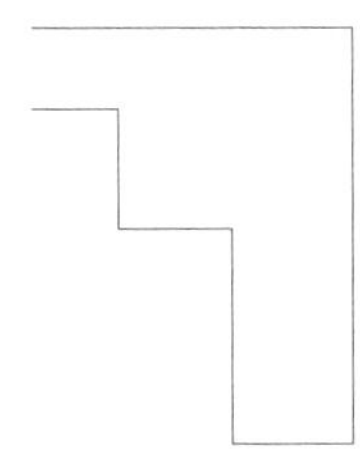

8d. Use Zoom with the Extents option to view all your objects:

>_ **z**↵
ZOOM
Specify corner of window, enter a scale factor (nX or nXP), or
ZOOM *[All/Center/Dynamic/Extents/Previous/Scale/Window/Object] <real time>:* **e**↵

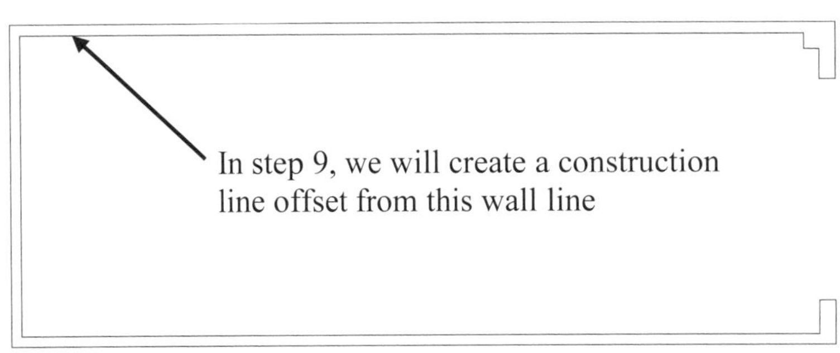

9. Create the window opening in the living room area:

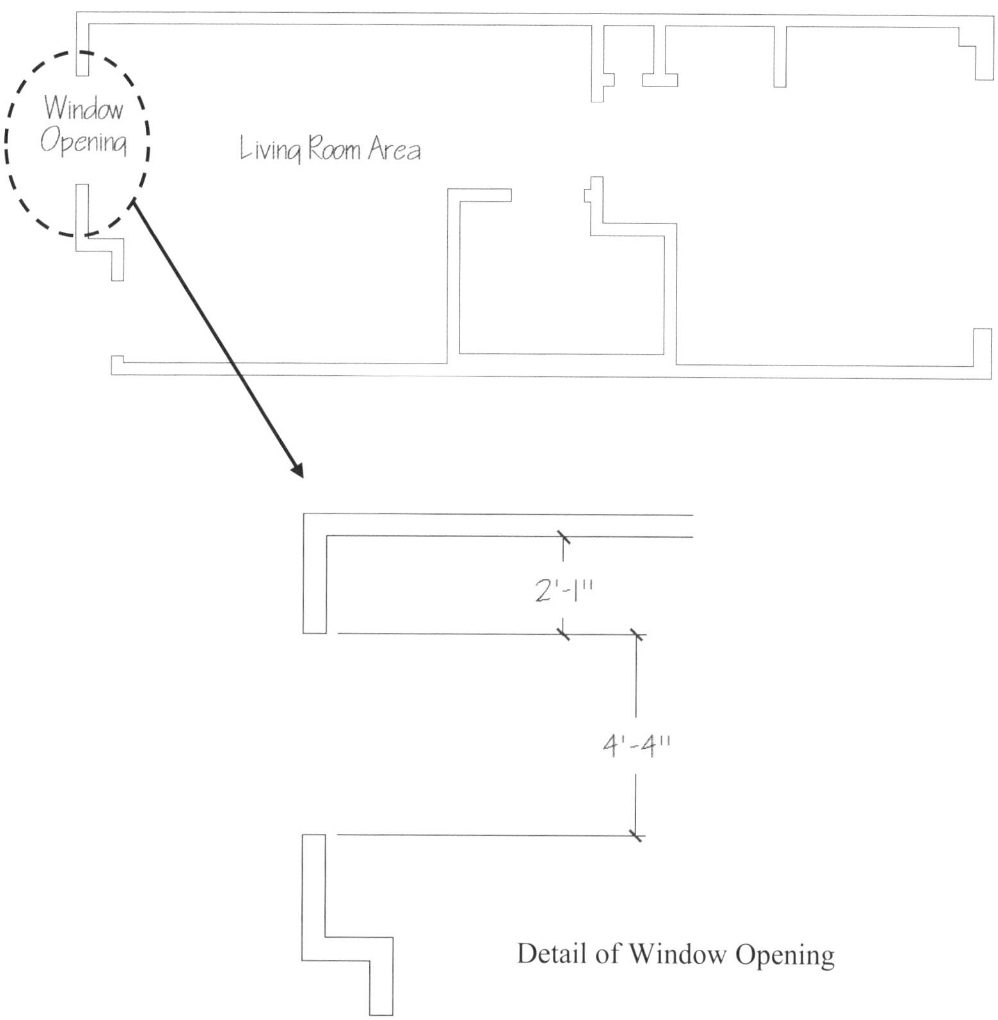

The steps required to create this window opening are very similar to the steps needed to create the bedroom window opening of step 7.

Our plan is to use both the Construction Line – Offset command and the Offset command to define the window opening. We will then trim the lines (and construction lines) to complete the window opening.

Before beginning, use the wheel mouse to zoom and pan to get a closer view of the window opening area that we will be working on.

9a. Create a Construction Line Offset 2′1″ from the upper inside wall

9b. Offset the construction line of step 9a 4′4″ down

9c. Use the Trim command to complete the window opening

When you are done trimming, your window will be complete

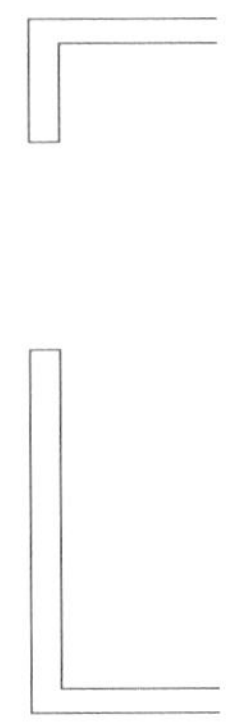

10. Create the entryway indentation into the living room area

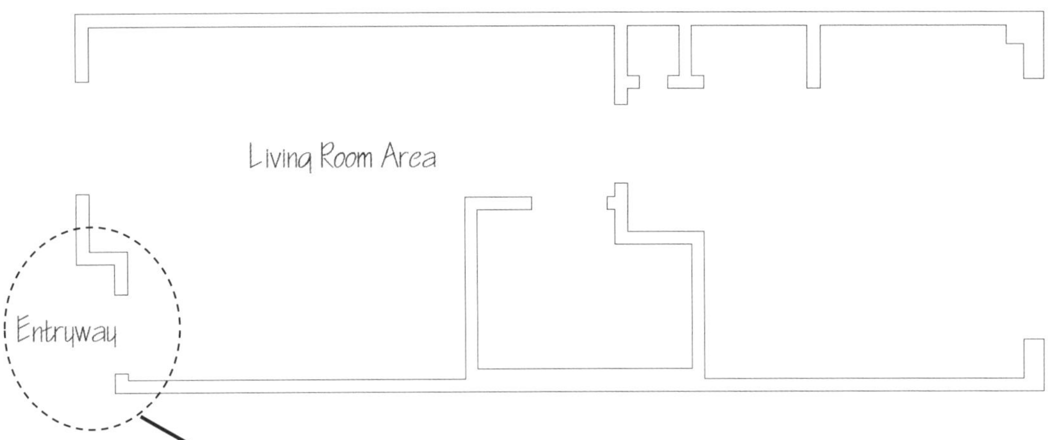

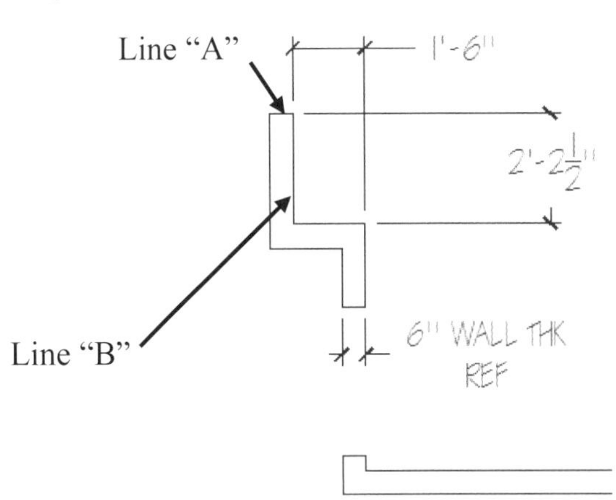

10a. Create a Construction Line Offset 2′2-1/2″ down from line "A"

10b. Create a Construction Line Offset 1′6″ to the right of line "B"

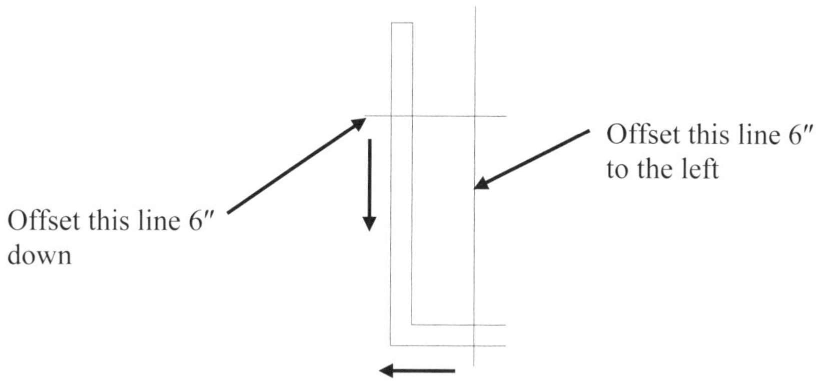

10c. Use the Offset command to Offset both construction lines 6″ each.

After this step, this part of your drawing should look like this:

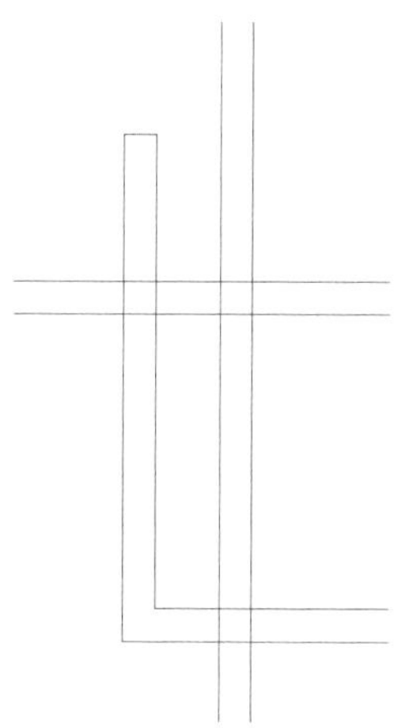

10d. Use the Trim command to trim construction lines.

10e. Use the Erase command (if needed) to eliminate any extra lines.

Depending on the order and location of the lines you picked during trimming, you may have some extra lines left over. Use the Erase command to eliminate them.

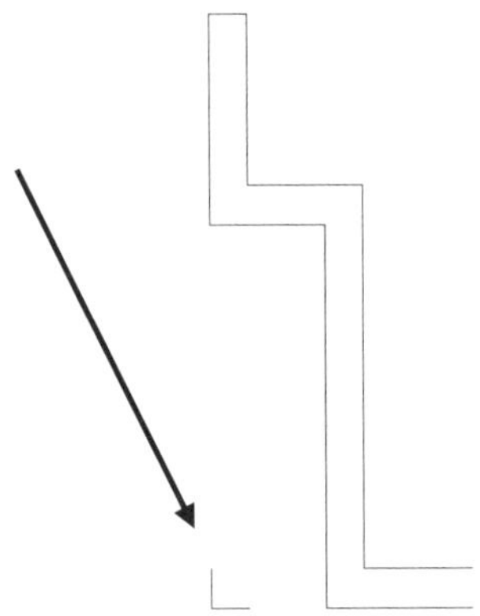

This is how much you have created so far! – Almost done!

11. Create the doorway opening into the living room area.

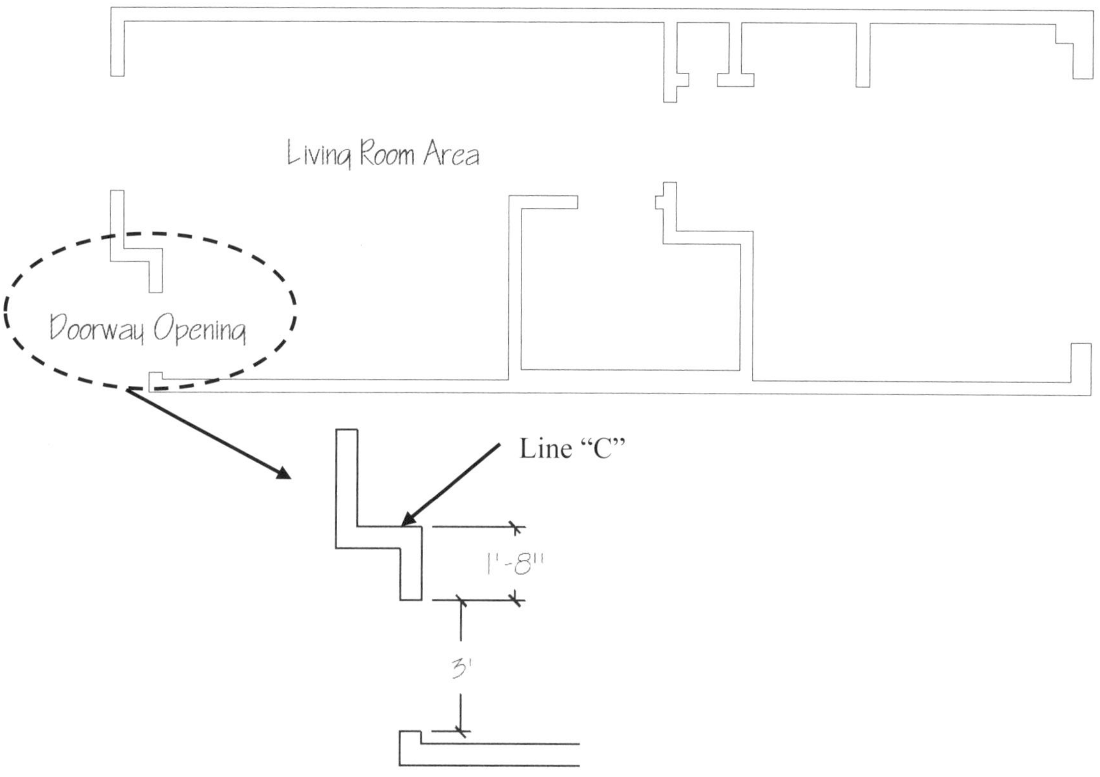

11a. Offset line "C" 1′8″ down.

11b. Offset the line created in step 11a 3′ down.

11c. Use the Trim command to complete the doorway opening.

Congratulations! You have now completed the basic shell of the hotel suite outside walls. Make sure to save your drawing so all that hard work won't be wasted!

12. Save the drawing.

(Pick the Save icon)
After picking the Save icon, a dialog box will appear. If this is the first time saving, it will look similar to this:

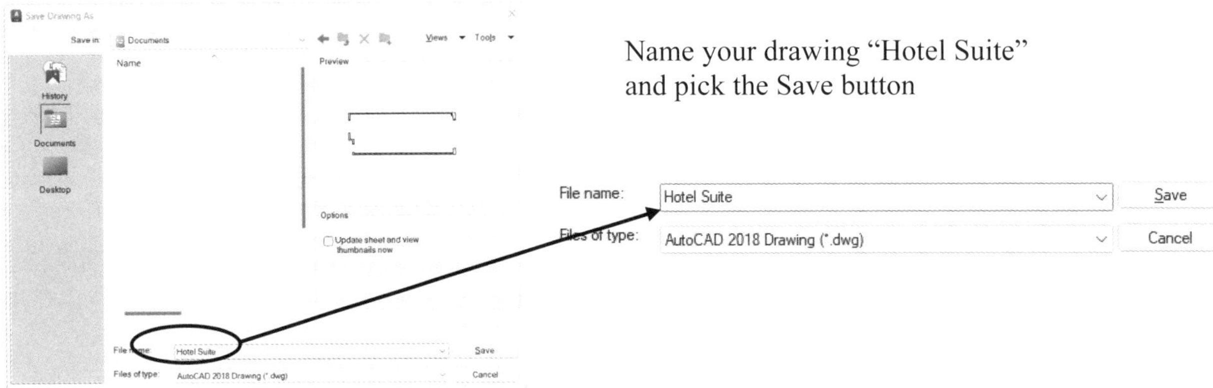

Name your drawing "Hotel Suite" and pick the Save button

Mac:

(Use the pull-down menu File and pick Save)
After picking Save, a dialog box will appear. If this is the first time saving, it will look similar to this:

Name your drawing "Hotel Suite" and pick the Save button

Chapter 5

Commands – Set 2: Working with Your Drawing

Learning Objectives:

- Measure distances and angles between objects
- Measure the radius of an arc or a circle
- Obtain information about an object
- Create round, beveled or sharp corners
- Move, copy, rotate, and make a mirror image of objects
- Use the Array command to perform a 2-direction Copy for a Rectangular Array
- Use the Array command to perform a simultaneous Rotate and Copy for a Polar Array

We are now able to draw basic objects very accurately. After you draw them, you may want to be able to verify that what you have drawn is as accurate as you believe you have drawn them. Fortunately, AutoCAD has tools for getting information about the objects on your drawing.

Getting Information from Your Drawing

Two methods of getting information about the objects on your drawing are Measure and List. These commands can be found on the Home Tab. The Measure command is under the Utilities Panel and the List Command is under the Properties Panel. On the Mac, the List command and measuring is on the pull-down Tools under Inquiry.

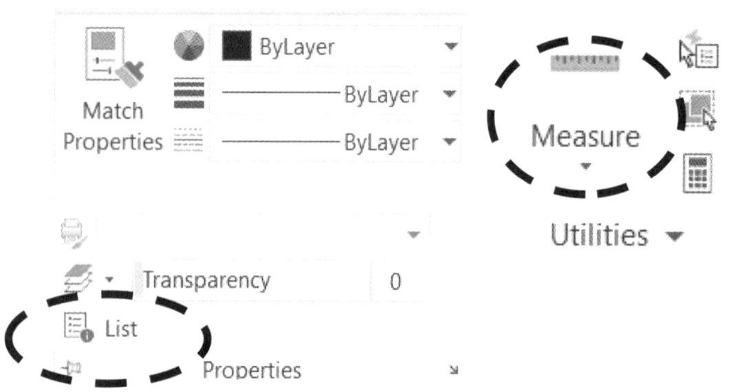

Measure

The Measure command allows you to measure distance between points, the radius of a circular object, the angle between lines, and the area bounded by an object or shape defined by selected points. It can also measure the volume of a 3D object, but only 2D is covered in this text.
The icon is a fly-out type of icon, with distance as the default icon on top. If you select something other than the distance icon on the fly-out, that icon will now be displayed instead.

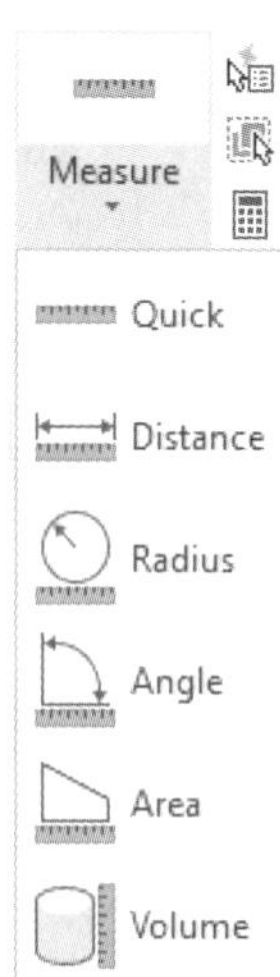

Distance

The Distance command is used to find the distance between two points, such as the endpoints of lines, center point of circle, etc. For accurate measurements, make sure you have OSNAP turned on.

Procedure:

Pick (left click): **Distance icon** from the Utilities Panel of the Home Tab. 

Mac users: Use the pull-down **Tools, Inquiry, Distance**

The command line prompts you with the following:

Enter an option [Distance/Radius/Angle/ARea/Volume] <Distance>: _distance
MEASUREGEOM *Specify first point:*

Select the first point of the two points you wish to find the distance between. For this example, pick point "A".

Example:

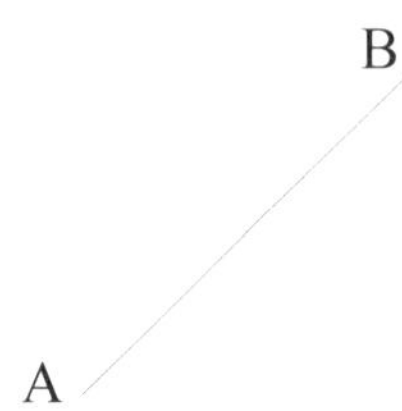

In this example, the line is 5″ long at a 45° angle

After you pick the first point, your command lines will look like the following:

Specify second point or [Multiple points]:

After you select the second point (point "B"), the requested information will be displayed above the active command line:

Distance = 0'-5", Angle in XY Plane = 45, Angle from XY Plane = 0
Delta X = 0'-3 9/16", Delta Y = 0'-3 9/16", Delta Z = 0'-0"

The command line will then prompt you to enter an option or continue to find distances:

Enter an option [Distance/Radius/Angle/ARea/Volume/eXit] <Distance>:

The command line will continue to prompt for more distance measurements, and allows you to choose other Measure Geometry options. If you have no more distances to measure, exit the command using the Escape key or typing **x** ↵ for eXit or pick ***eXit*** with your cursor.

In addition to the command line, the information can also be displayed on your screen. This happens when Dynamic Input is turned on. Dynamic Input switch is located on the Status Bar on the bottom of your screen. We added this to the Status Bar in Chapter 2. Turn on Dynamic Input by selecting the switch. It will be shaded blue when it is turned on.

Mac

Turn on Dynamic Input

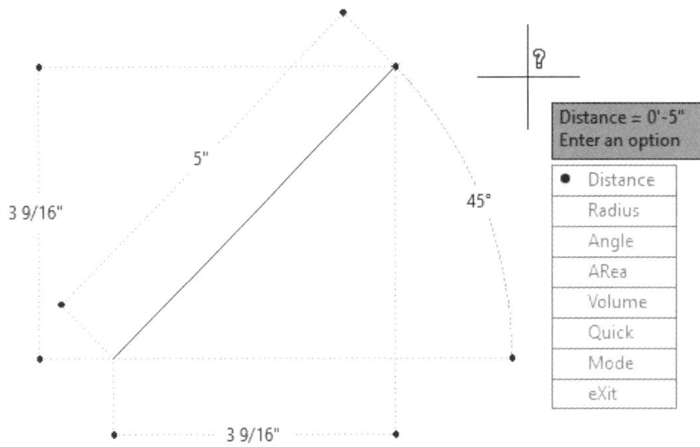

This info/option box can be relocated on your drawing - while still in the command, pick a new location on your screen. The box will relocate, but the info will remain.

The information provided will give the distance between points, regardless of the angle between them. It will also give you the angle that would exist if a line were drawn between those points. Remember, angles are measured in a counterclockwise direction from the positive X-axis (Horizontal axis to the right of the origin). The order in which you select the points will make a difference in the angle given. For this example, point A was below point B. If the point B were selected first, the information would be as follows:

Distance = 0'-5", Angle in XY Plane = 225, Angle from XY Plane = 0
Delta X = -0'-3 9/16", Delta Y = -0'-3 9/16", Delta Z = 0'-0"

Notice that the angle of 225° is 180° more than 45° (45+180=225).

In addition to giving the direct distance between points, AutoCAD also gives the distance from the first point to the second point in the X and Y (horizontal and vertical) directions (known as Delta X and Delta Y). Ignore the Z distance; this will always remain 0′-0″ since we are drawing in 2-D.

Note that in the first example (with the 45° angle) the X & Y values are positive because the direction from the first point to the second was to the right (+X) and up (+Y). For the second example (with the 225° angle) the X & Y values are negative because the direction from the first point to the second was to the left (-X) and down (-Y).

Radius

The Radius option allows you to measure the radius and diameter of an arc or circle.

Procedure:

Pick (left click): **Radius icon** from the Utilities Panel of the Home Tab.
Mac users: Use the pull-down **Tools, Inquiry, Radius**

Note that if the icon is not on the top of the Measure Fly-out list,
Pick the black triangle, and then move down the icon list to select the Radius icon.

The command line prompts you with the following:

Enter an option [Distance/Radius/Angle/ARea/Volume] <Distance>: _radius
MEASUREGEOM *Select arc or circle:*

Pick the arc or circle you are interested in. For this example, pick the arc:

Example:

Radius = 0'-3 9/16"
Diameter = 0'-7 1/8"

Both the radius and diameter of the selected object are displayed on the command line and on the screen:

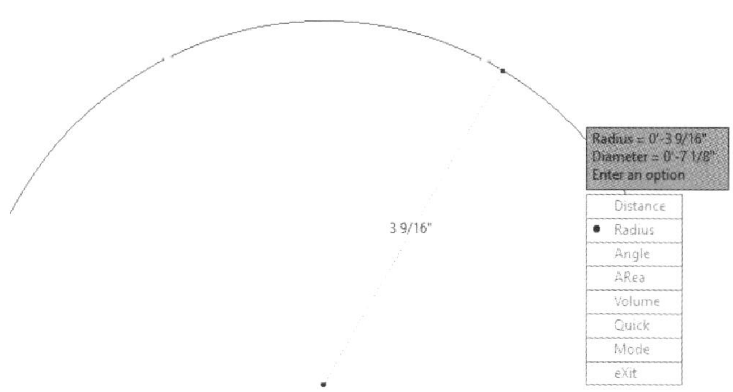

The command line will continue to prompt for more radial measurements, and allows you to choose other Measure Geometry options. If you have no more radii to measure, exit the command using the Escape key.

*Enter an option [Distance/Radius/Angle/ARea/Volume/eXit] <Radius>: *Cancel**

Angle

The Angle option allows you to measure the angle between lines, and between arc endpoints.

Procedure:

Pick (left click): **Angle icon** from the Utilities Panel of the Home Tab.
Mac users: Use the pull-down **Tools, Inquiry, Angle**

Note that if the icon is not on the top of the Measure Fly-out list, Pick the black triangle, and then move down the icon list to select the Angle icon.

The command line prompts you with the following:

Enter an option [Distance/Radius/Angle/ARea/Volume] <Distance>: _angle
MEASUREGEOM *Select arc, circle, line, or <Specify vertex>:*

Select the first line of the two lines you wish to find the angle between.
For this example, pick "Line 1".

Example:

Measuring angle between 2 lines

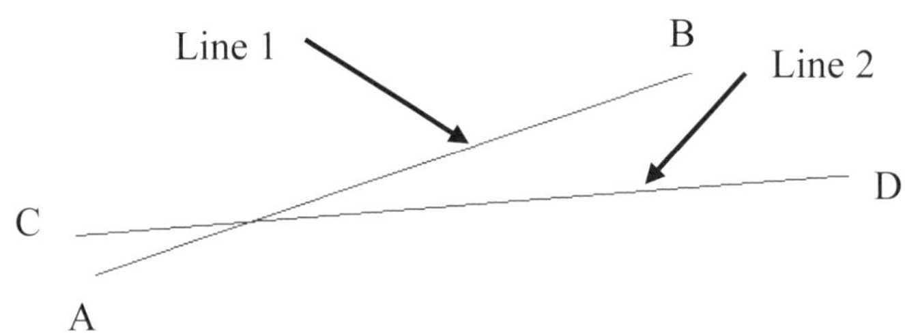

After you pick the first line, your command lines will look like the following:

Select second line:

After you select the second line ("Line 2"), the requested information will be displayed above the active command line:

Angle = 14°

The command line will prompt you to enter an option or continue to find angles:

Enter an option [Distance/Radius/Angle/ARea/Volume/eXit] <Angle>:

The command line will continue to prompt for more angle measurements, and allows you to choose other Measure Geometry options. If you have no more distances to measure, exit the command using the Escape key.

In addition to the command line, the information is also displayed on your screen if Dynamic Input is turned on:

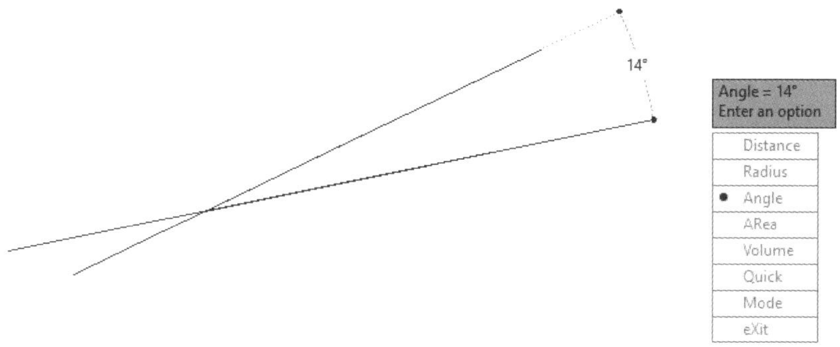

The angle that is measured may not have been the angle you desired. If you wanted the larger angle between the two, you could subtract the angle found from 180°. Alternatively, you could use the Vertex option. The vertex of an angle is the point where the two lines intersect.

Notice in the command line prompt, the vertex option is available:

Select arc, circle, line, or <Specify vertex>:

Simply press the ↵ Enter key to select this option. AutoCAD will then prompt you with the following:

Specify angle vertex: ***(Pick the intersection of the two lines)***
Specify first angle endpoint: ***(Pick endpoint B of Line 1)***
Specify second angle endpoint: ***(Pick the endpoint C of Line 2)***
Angle = 166°
Enter an option [Distance/Radius/Angle/ARea/Volume/eXit] <Angle>:

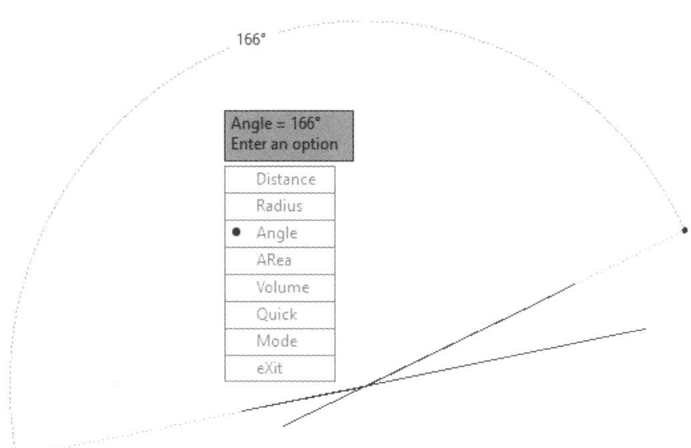

You can also measure the angle between arc endpoints. When prompted to select the object to measure the angle, simply pick the arc.

Example:

Measuring angle between arc endpoints

After selecting the arc, AutoCAD will return the information on the command line and on your screen:

Angle = 104°
*Enter an option [Distance/Radius/Angle/ARea/Volume/eXit] <Angle>: *Cancel**

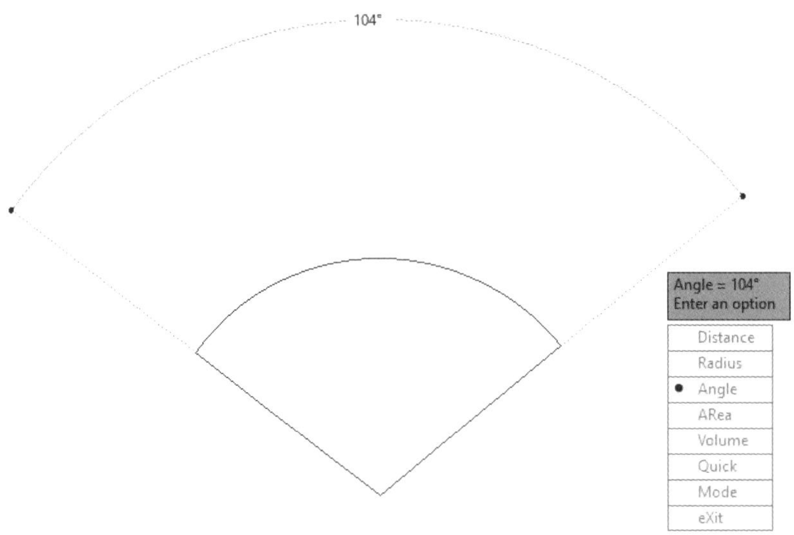

List

The List command is used to get information on an object, such as its length or location in the X-Y coordinates.

Procedure:

Pick (left click): Expand the Properties Panel of the Home Tab
Pick the **List icon** from the Inquiry toolbar.

List

Mac users: Use the pull-down **Tools, Inquiry, List**

LIST *Select objects:*
Pick the object you are interested in. The command line will continue to prompt for more objects until you press the ↵ Enter key:

Select objects:1 found
Select objects:

After you press the ↵ Enter key, the text window above the active command line will expand to provide you with the information about that object:

```
LIST
Select objects: 1 found
Select objects:
              LINE      Layer: "0"
                        Space: Model space
               Handle = 1e2
           from point, X=   0'-10"  Y=0'-9 1/8"  Z=    0'-0"
             to point, X=1'-7 7/16"  Y=0'-10 15/16"  Z=    0'-0"
        Length =0'-9 9/16",  Angle in XY Plane =     11
              Delta X =0'-9 7/16", Delta Y = 0'-1 13/16", Delta Z =    0'-0"
>_  Type a command
```

On the Mac, the command line will expand to show you the information:

```
Command: _list
Select objects: 1 found
Select objects:
      LINE     Layer: "0"
               Space: Model space
       Handle = 234
     from point, X=3'-0 7/8"  Y=-0'-3 5/16"  Z=   0'-0"
      to point, X=4'-5 3/8"  Y=0'-5 3/4"  Z=   0'-0"
    Length =1'-6 13/16",  Angle in XY Plane =    29
       Delta X =1'-4 1/2", Delta Y = 0'-9 1/8", Delta Z =   0'-0"
>_  Type a command
```

Reduce/expand command line with this icon

The information provided includes the type of object, (in this example, a line was selected), the layer that object is on, the start and end point in X & Y coordinates, the length, the angle it makes relative to the positive X-axis and the X & Y (Horizontal & Vertical) distance between the endpoints. For each object there is different information provided, depending on the type of object selected. Try this on your own and you will discover how useful this can be.

If more information is available than can be shown in the expanded text window, the active command line will prompt you to *Press ENTER to continue.*

The text window can be minimized, expanded, or closed using the icons located on the upper left.

For the Mac, the expanded command line can be reduced/expanded using the icon on the lower part of the command line. Left-click it once, and it will reduce to a single line. Left-click again, and it will expand to several lines.

Fillet – Creating Round or Sharp Corners

We have been able to make circles, lines, and construction lines. When we trim intersecting lines or construction lines, we end up with a sharp corner. There are many times that we want to make rounded corners. AutoCAD has a command just for that and it is called Fillet.

But, in addition to making rounded corners, Fillet can also make sharp corners. This doesn't seem logical at first, but it can really come in handy. The sharp-corner Fillet is created by using a radius value of 0″. One major advantage of using the Fillet command for a sharp corner is to trim or extend lines simultaneously to complete an intersection.

The Fillet command allows you to connect two objects with an arc of a specified radius. The icon is on the Modify Panel of the Home Tab.

Procedure:

Pick (left click): **Fillet icon** from the Modify Panel of the Home Tab.

The command line prompts you with the following:

Mac

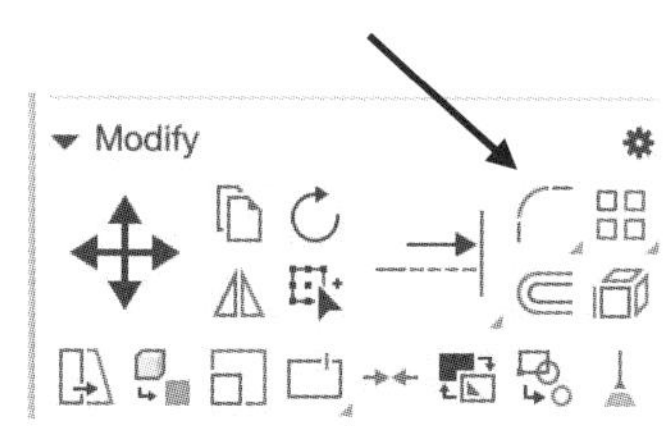

Current settings: Mode = TRIM, Radius = 0'-0"
***FILLET** Select first object or [Undo/Polyline/Radius/Trim/Multiple]:*

Note that the "Current settings" shows you what the Mode and Radius values are set to. These can be changed prior to selecting your first object. Both Radius and Trim are options shown in the square brackets that you can choose. To change the radius value, type **r↵** or pick ***Radius*** with your cursor. To change the trim value, type **t↵** or pick ***Trim*** with your cursor. If you have many fillets to create, you can choose the multiple option by typing **m↵** or pick ***Multiple*** with your cursor. If you do not choose multiple, then the fillet command will end when you complete the single fillet.

Setting the Fillet Radius

The fillet radius is the radius of the arc that connects the two objects. If you set the fillet radius to 0″, filleted objects are trimmed or extended until they intersect, but no arc is created. Whatever value you choose for the fillet radius will be the default radius value the next time you select the fillet command.

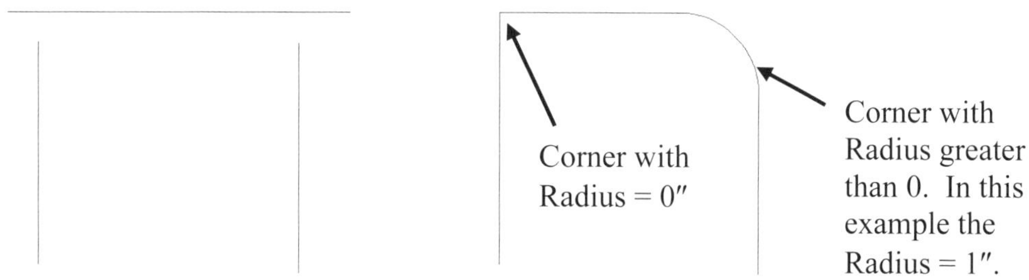

3 Lines before using Fillet

3 Lines after using Fillet

Trim Option

You can use the Trim option to specify whether the selected objects are trimmed or extended to the endpoints of the resulting arc or left unchanged. By default, all objects except circles, full ellipses, closed polylines, and splines (ellipses, polylines and splines will be discussed in a later chapter) are trimmed or extended when filleted.

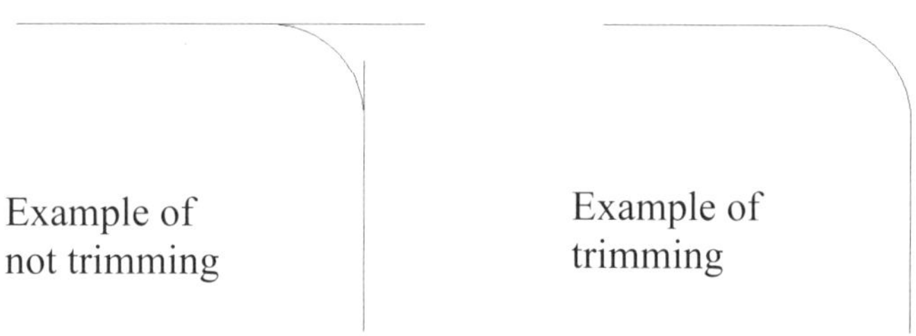

Selecting Objects to Fillet

Select the first of two objects required to define a fillet, then, select the second object. The following will result (with *Mode = TRIM*):

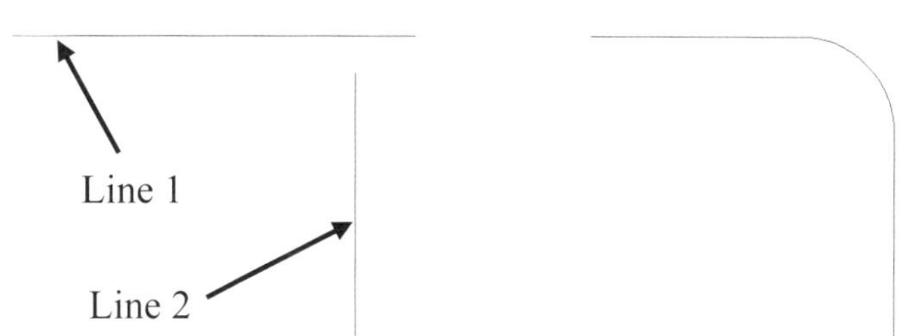

Before Fillet

After Fillet

Note that although the lines are labeled as “1” & “2”, the order selected does not matter. As you will see later, what does matter is where you pick the objects to fillet.

If you select lines, arcs, or polylines, AutoCAD extends or trims them until they intersect. Circles do not extend or trim with the fillet command.

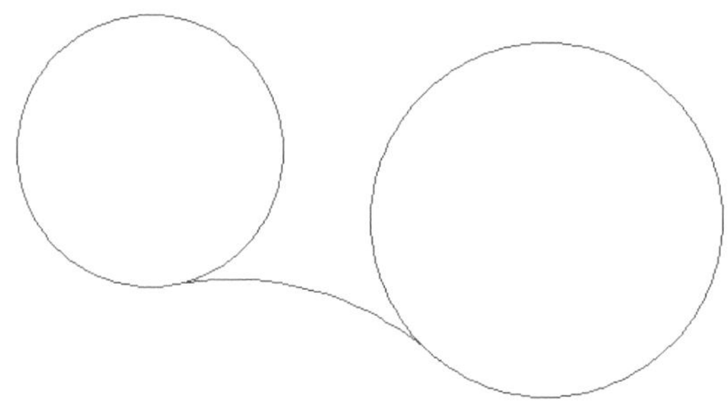

Importance of Pick Location

Depending on the locations you specify, more than one possible fillet can exist between the selected objects. Compare the selection points and resulting fillets for Lines “1” & “2”:

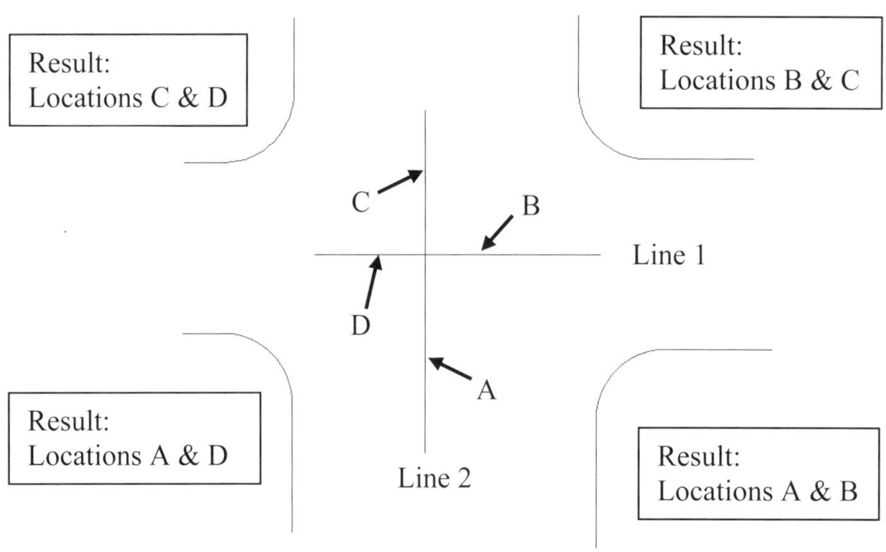

More than one fillet can exist between arcs and circles. AutoCAD chooses the fillet with endpoints closest to the points you select.

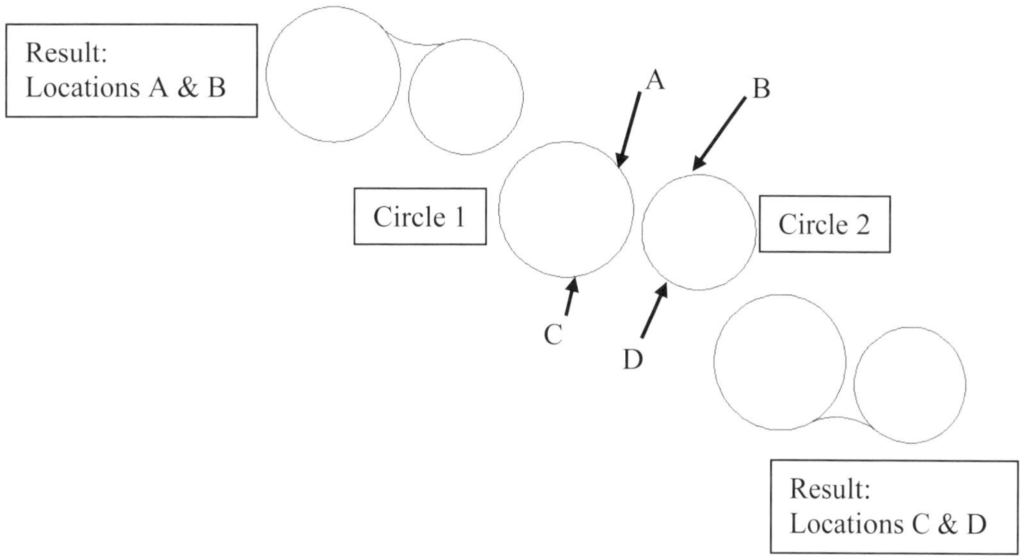

Recommendation:

Fillets are very useful for rounding inside or outside corners. With a radius value set to 0″, Fillets are extremely handy for closing a gap between two lines you want to have intersected with each other. For example, if you offset the inside wall line toward the outside to create the outside wall line, this will come up short. Extending would be difficult because the "boundary" also comes up short. Using Fillet will extend and trim both intersecting corner lines in one command.

Try it:

Let's try two examples:

1. Fillet between two lines
2. Fillet between a line and a circle

Example 1: Draw two lines anywhere on your screen. Make sure they are at least a couple inches long and are not parallel to each other:

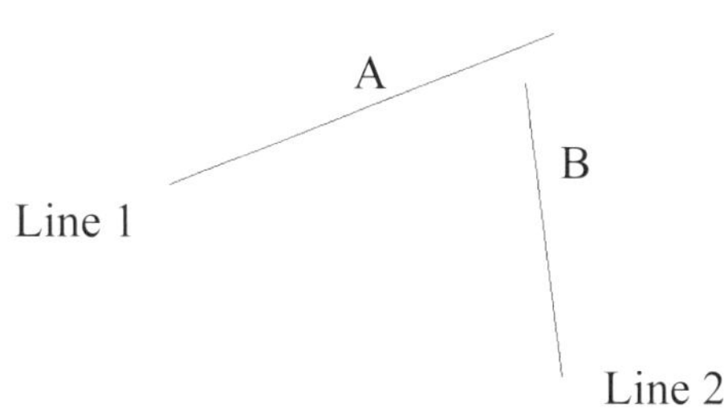

Now use the Fillet command to draw a 1″ Radius arc between them. Make sure that the Trim mode is on.

(Pick the Fillet icon)

Current settings: Mode = TRIM, Radius = 0'-0"
FILLET *Select first object or [Undo/Polyline/Radius/Trim/Multiple]:* **r↵**
(Type the letter "r" and press the ↵ Enter or pick *Radius* with your cursor)

Specify fillet radius <0'-0">: **1↵**
Select first object or [Undo/Polyline/Radius/Trim/Multiple]: ***(Pick Line 1 near location A)***
Select second object or shift-select to apply corner or [Radius]: ***(Pick Line 2 near location B)***

When you are done, your drawing will look like this:

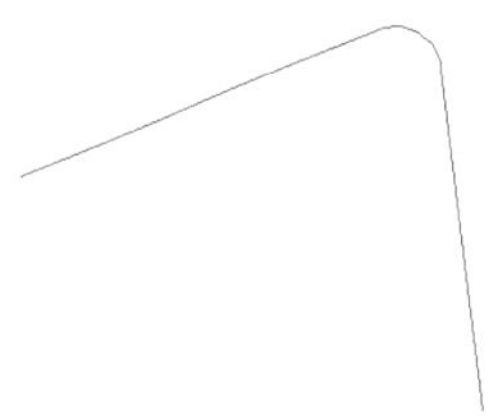

Example 2: Draw a 2″ radius circle. Draw a line from the center of the circle to several inches beyond the circle:

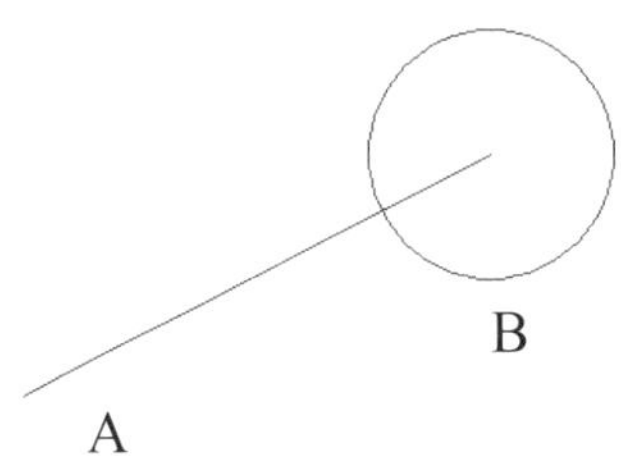

The default value for the radius is 1" because that was the value last used with this command from Example 1.

(Pick the Fillet icon)

Current settings: Mode = TRIM, Radius = 0'-1"
FILLET *Select first object or [Undo/Polyline/Radius/Trim/Multiple]:* ***(Pick the line near location A)***
Select second object or shift-select to apply corner or [Radius]: ***(Pick the circle near location B)***

When you are done, your drawing will look like this:

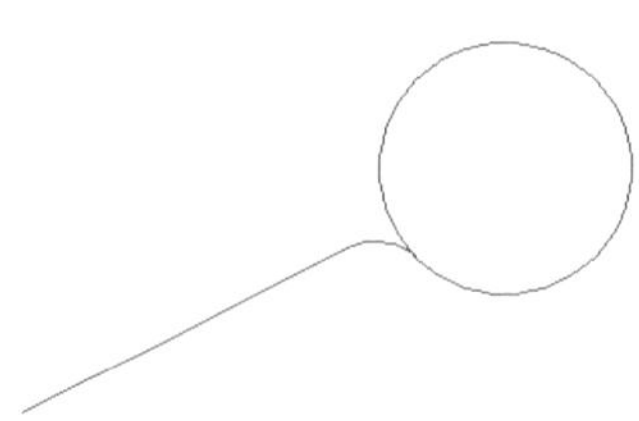

Chamfer – Creating Beveled Edges

The Chamfer command allows you to create a beveled edge of a specified angle or distance between two non-parallel lines. It is on the Modify Panel of the Home Tab. The icon is a fly-out type of icon, with fillet as the default icon on top. You must pick the black triangle to expand the fly-out to access the Chamfer icon. Once you select the Chamfer icon, it will be displayed on top.

<u>Procedure:</u>

Pick (left click): **Chamfer icon** from the Modify Panel of the Home Tab.

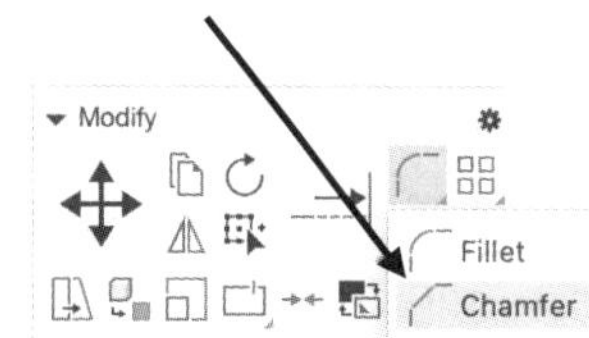

Mac

The command line prompts you with the following:

(TRIM mode) Current chamfer Dist1 = 0'-0", Dist2 = 0'-0"
CHAMFER *Select first line or [Undo/Polyline/Distance/Angle/Trim/mEthod/Multiple]:*

Note that the "Current chamfer" shows you what the Mode and Distance values are set to. These can be changed prior to selecting your first object. Both Distance and Trim are options shown in the square brackets that you can choose. To change the distance value, type **d↵** or pick ***Distance*** with your cursor. To change the trim value, type **t↵** or pick ***Trim*** with your cursor. To change the angle value, type **a↵** or pick ***Angle*** with your cursor. If you have many chamfers to create, you can choose the multiple option by typing **m↵** or picking ***Multiple*** with your cursor. If you do not choose multiple, then the chamfer command will end when you complete the single chamfer.

Setting the Chamfer Distance

The chamfer distance is the starting and ending distance from the intersection of the two lines. If you set the chamfer distance to 0″, chamfered lines are trimmed or extended until they intersect, but no chamfer is created. Whatever value you choose for the chamfer distance will be the default distance values the next time you select the chamfer command. You can also specify the chamfer angle. This option will require you to specify the distance to the first line and then the angle value.

Example of Chamfer with trim option on

Other than the fact that this command creates angled corners (as opposed to rounded corners) it is very similar to the Fillet command. The trim option can be turned on and off, and the pick location is important. It is recommended that you understand the Fillet commands first and then explore the Chamfer command on your own.

Recommendation:

Chamfers are very useful for beveling corners. With a distance value set to 0″, chamfers are extremely handy for closing a gap between two lines you want to have intersected with each other. For example, if you offset the inside wall line to the outside to create the outside wall line, this will come up short. Extending would be difficult because the "boundary" also comes up short. Using Chamfer, with a distance value of 0″, will extend and trim both intersecting corner lines in one command.

Try it:

Usually (but not always) when you want to bevel an edge, it is between two perpendicular lines. For this example, let's draw a 45° beveled edge that begins 1″ from the corner.

Draw two perpendicular lines, each at least a few inches long, anywhere on your screen:

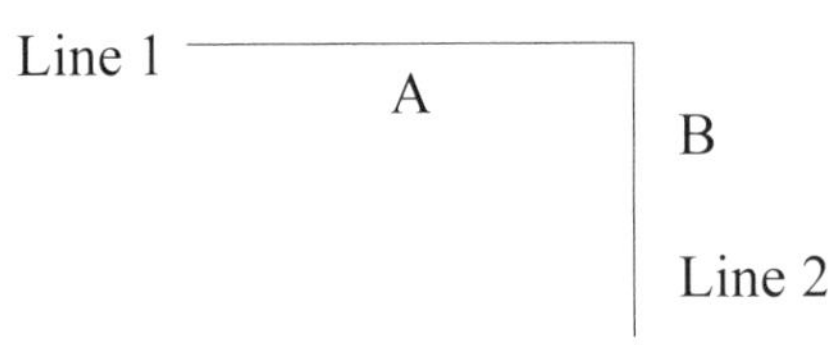

(Pick the Chamfer icon)

(TRIM mode) Current chamfer Dist1 = 0'-0", Dist2 = 0'-0"
CHAMFER Select first line or [Undo/Polyline/Distance/Angle/Trim/mEthod/Multiple]: ***a↵***
(Type the letter "a" and press the ↵ Enter or pick *Angle* with your cursor)

Specify chamfer length on the first line <0'-0">: **1↵**
Specify chamfer angle from the first line <0>: **45↵**
Select first line or [Undo/Polyline/Distance/Angle/Trim/mEthod/Multiple]: ***(Pick Line 1 near location A)***
Select second line or shift-select to apply corner: ***(Pick Line 2 near location B)***

When you are done, your drawing will look like this:

Manipulating Existing Objects

You can manipulate existing objects in the following ways:

- Move objects using the Move command.
- Make a copy of the objects to a new location using the Copy command.
- Rotate objects using the Rotate command.
- Make a mirror image of objects using the Mirror command.
- Make a rectangular or polar array – combines Move with Copy, and Rotate with Copy.

These commands are two-part commands. The first part of the command requires you to select the objects. After the objects are selected, press the ↲ Enter key to get to the second part of the command. The second part of the command is further explained for each command in this document. The command icons are located on the Modify Panel of the Home Tab.

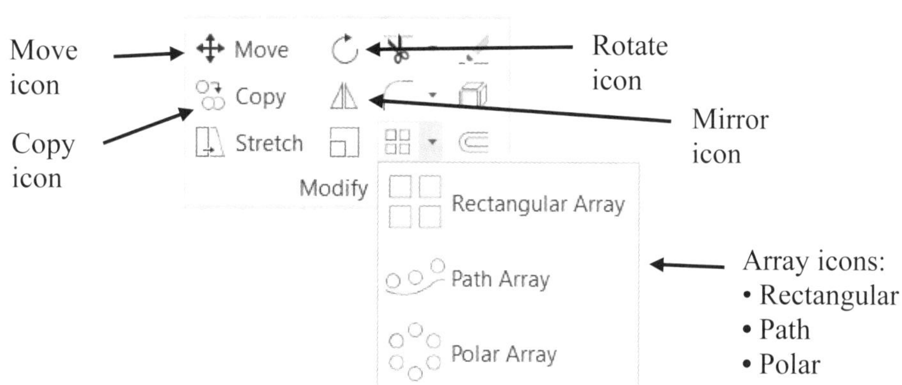

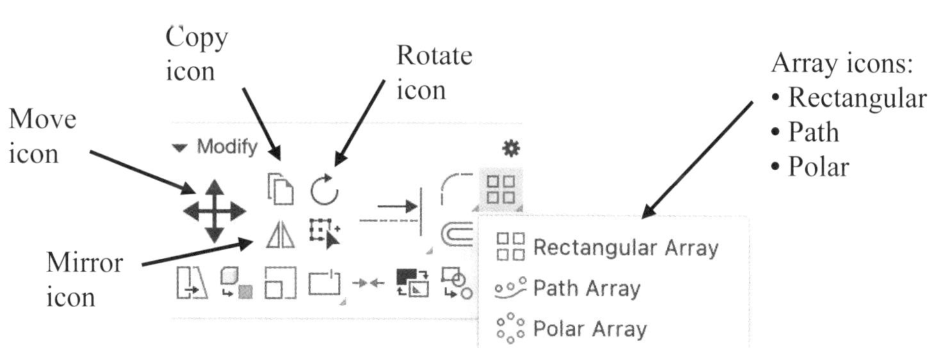

Mac

Move

Procedure:

Pick (left click): **Move icon** from the Modify Panel of the Home Tab. 

AutoCAD will prompt you to select objects, and will continue to do so until you press the ↵ Enter key.

MOVE *Select objects:* ***(Pick the objects you wish to move)***
Select objects: 1 found (You can continue selecting as many objects as you desire to move)
Select objects: ↵ (Pressing the ↵ Enter key will get you to the second part of the command)
Specify base point or [Displacement] <Displacement>: ***(Pick a point to move "From")***
Specify second point or <use first point as displacement>: ***(Pick a point to move "To")***
(AutoCAD ends the command)

Try it:

Let's move an object to a specific location on the screen. For this example, let's move a circle to the intersection of two lines.

Before beginning this example, make sure that you have Object Snap (OSNAP) turned on with Center and Intersection selected.

Draw two intersecting lines anywhere on your screen. Draw a circle off to the side of these two lines. Now use the Move command to relocate the center of the circle to the intersection of the two lines:

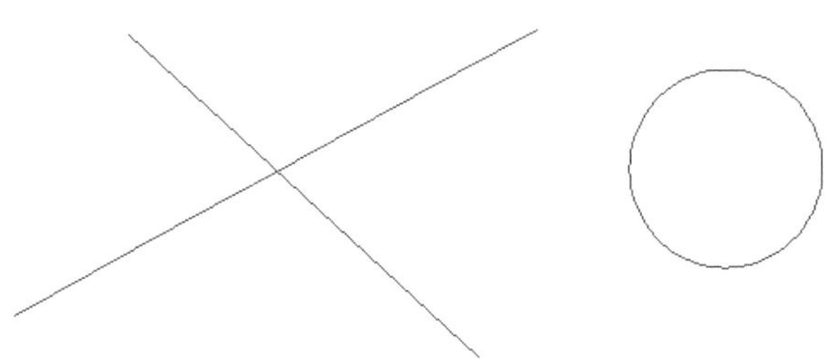

(Pick the Move icon)

MOVE *Select objects:* ***(Pick the circle)*** *1 found*
Select objects: ↵

Specify base point or [Displacement] <Displacement>: ***(Pick the center of the circle – ensure that the AutoSnap marker shows that the center of the circle was found)***

Specify second point or <use first point as displacement>: ***(Pick the intersection of the lines – ensure that the AutoSnap marker shows that the intersection was found)***

When you are done, your drawing will look like this:

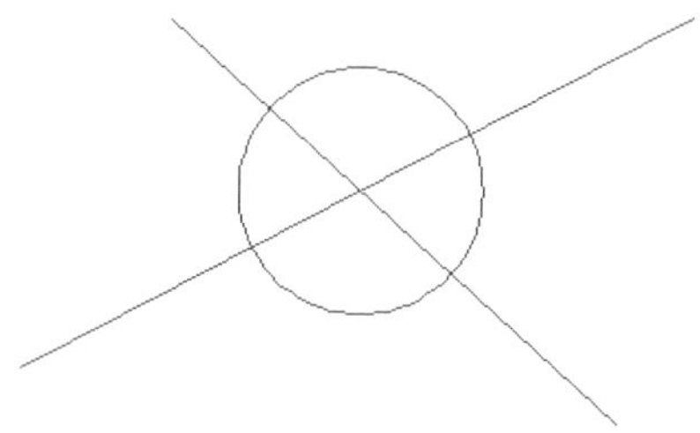

Copy

Procedure:

Pick (left click): **Copy icon** from the Modify Panel of the Home Tab. **Mac**

AutoCAD will prompt you to select objects, and will continue to do so until you press the ↵ Enter key.

COPY *Select objects:* ***(Pick the objects you wish to copy)***
Select objects: 1 found (You can continue selecting as many objects you desire to copy)
Select objects: ↵ (Pressing the ↵ Enter key will get you to the second part of the command)
Current settings: Copy mode = Multiple
Specify base point or [Displacement/mOde] <Displacement>: (***Pick a point to copy "From")***
Specify second point or [Array] <use first point as displacement>: ***(Pick a point to copy "To")***
Specify second point or [Array/Exit/Undo] <Exit>: ↵

AutoCAD allows you to continue to make multiple copies. Pressing the ↵ Enter key will end the command.

Try it:

Starting with the example from the Move command, add two more intersecting lines on your drawing:
(Make sure Object Snap is turned on with Center and Intersection selected)

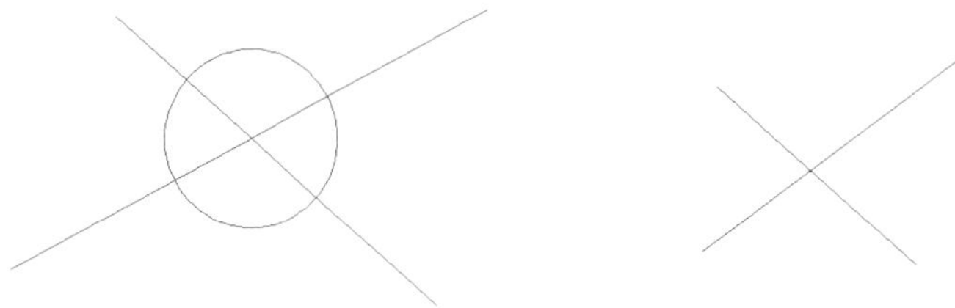

(Pick the Copy icon)

***COPY** Select objects: **(Pick the circle)** 1 found*
Select objects: ↵
Current settings: Copy mode = Multiple
*Specify base point or [Displacement/mOde] <Displacement>: **(Pick the center of the circle)***
*Specify second point or [Array] <use first point as displacement>: **(Pick the intersection of the 2 new lines)***
Specify second point or [Exit/Undo] <Exit>:↵

When you are done, your drawing will look like this:

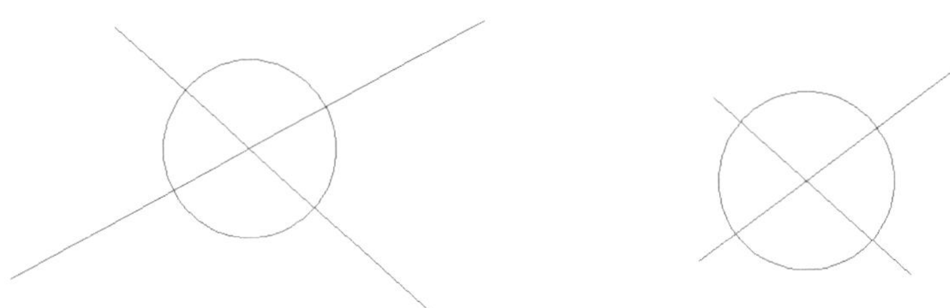

Rotate

Procedure:

Pick (left click): **Rotate icon** from the Modify Panel of the Home Tat 

AutoCAD will prompt you to select objects, and will continue to do so until you press the ↵ Enter key.

Current positive angle in UCS: ANGDIR=counterclockwise ANGBASE=0
ROTATE** Select objects: **(Pick the objects you wish to rotate)
Select objects: 1 found (You can continue selecting as many as objects you desire to rotate)

Select objects: ↵ (Pressing the ↵ Enter key will get you to the second part of the command)

Specify base point: ***(Pick a point to rotate about***)
(The objects begin to rotate with movement of the cursor)
Specify rotation angle or [Reference]: **45** ↵
(Type in a desired angle. Remember, the angle is measured in a counterclockwise direction. Alternatively, you can Pick a point to define the angle)
(AutoCAD ends the command)

Try it:

Starting with the example of the Copy command, let's rotate the right circle 90° about the left circle.

(Pick the Rotate icon)
Current positive angle in UCS: ANGDIR=counterclockwise ANGBASE=0
ROTATE *Select objects:* ***(Pick the right circle)*** *1 found*
Select objects: ↵
Specify base point: ***(Pick the center of the left circle)***
Specify rotation angle or [Copy/Reference] <0>: **90**↵

When you are done, your drawing will look like this:

Notice that we have entered a specific angle to rotate these objects. You can use the Reference option to rotate objects without entering a specific value. Instead, you select locations on the drawing as a reference for the angle.

Example:

Rotate the circle to the horizontal line:

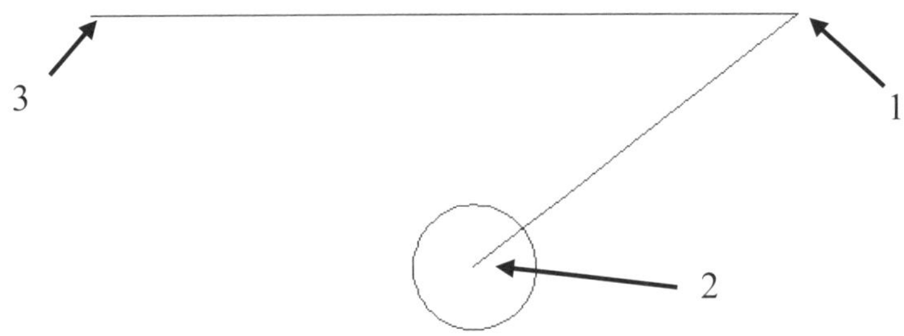

(Pick the Rotate icon)
Current positive angle in UCS: ANGDIR=counterclockwise ANGBASE=0
ROTATE** Select objects:* ***(Pick the circle) *1 found*
Select objects: ↵
Specify base point: ***(Pick point 1)***
Specify rotation angle or [Copy/Reference] <0>: **r**↵
(Type the letter "r" and press the ↵ Enter or pick *Reference* with your cursor)

Specify the reference angle <0>: ***(Pick point 1)*** *Specify second point:* ***(Pick point 2)***
Specify the new angle or [Points] <0>: ***(Pick point 3)***

The circle has rotated through an angle to match the horizontal line. By using the Reference option, we did not need to know the value of the angle.

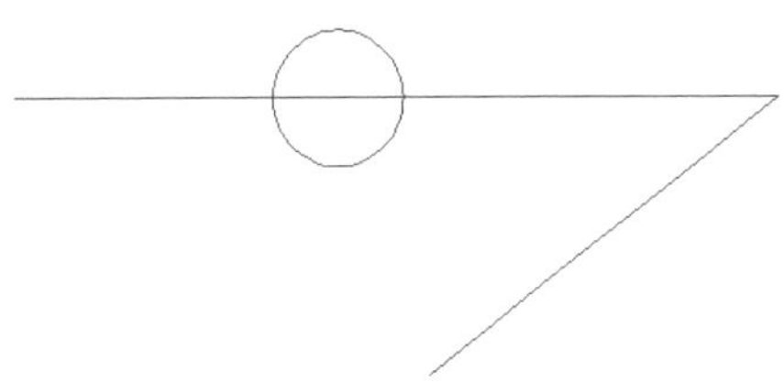

Mirror

Prior to using the Mirror command, it is a good idea to have a pre-defined line to mirror about. AutoCAD looks for two points that define a mirror line.

Procedure:

Pick (left click): **Mirror icon** from the Modify Panel of the Home Tab. 

AutoCAD will prompt you to select objects, and will continue to do so until you press the Enter ↵ key.

MIRROR Select objects: **[Pick the objects you wish to mirror]**

Select objects: 1 found	(You can continue selecting as many objects as you desire to mirror)
Select objects: ↵	(Pressing the Enter ↵ key will get you to the second part of the command)

Specify first point of mirror line:

(If you have a pre-determined line you want to mirror about, select the first endpoint of that line. A mirror image of the objects will follow your cursor until the second mirror line is defined)

Specify first point of mirror line: Specify second point of mirror line: **(Select the second endpoint of the pre-defined line)** (The mirror image will temporarily disappear)

Delete source objects? [Yes/No] <N>:

(Type "**y**" or pick ***Yes*** with your cursor if you wish to delete the original objects. Otherwise, accept the default value of "**n**" by pressing the ↵ Enter key. This will leave the original objects in place and you will have a mirrored-copy of your objects)

(AutoCAD ends the command)

Try it:

Starting with the example from the Rotate command, let's make a mirror image of what we have drawn.

Start by drawing a line that is nearly vertical towards the left side of the objects on the screen:

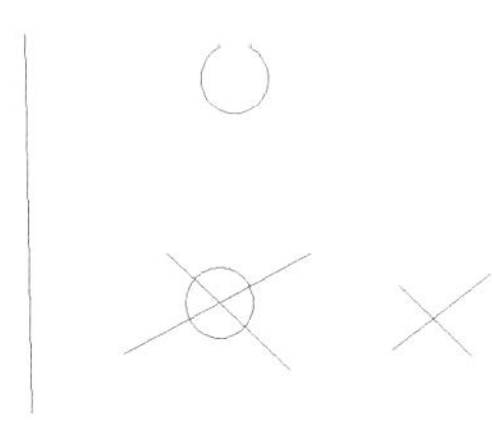

(Pick the Mirror icon)

MIRROR *Select objects:* ***(Pick the objects that are to the right of the line using a selection window)***
Specify opposite corner: 6 found
Select objects: ↵
Specify first point of mirror line: ***(Pick the endpoint of the nearly-vertical line)***
Specify second point of mirror line: ***(Pick the other endpoint of the nearly-vertical line)***
Erase source objects? [Yes/No] <N>: ↵

When you are done, your drawing will look like this:

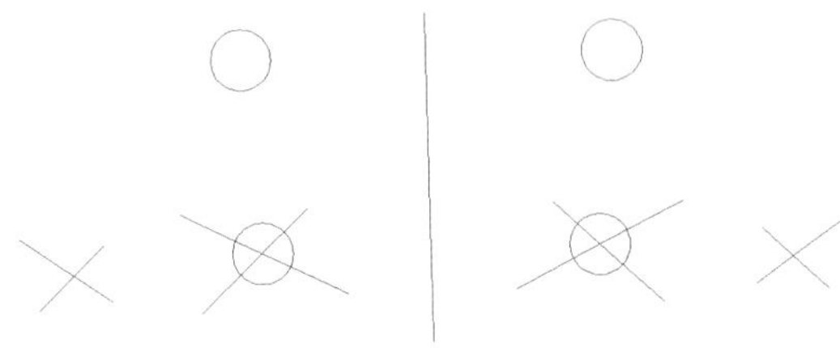

Recommendation:

These commands are very powerful and allow you to complete a drawing much faster than doing it by hand. There are additional options for these commands that are not covered here. It is left to the student to learn more about these options by exploring or using the online help. To rotate while copying, or move while copying, use the Array command.

Array Commands

The Array commands allow you to copy while rotating or moving. After the array is created, it is treated as one object. The Array command icon is a fly-out type of icon (as indicated with the black triangle in the lower right-hand corner), located on the Modify Panel of the Home Tab. There are three icons that occupy the same position on the toolbar, which are stacked on top of each other. The most recently used icon is one displayed on the top. This chapter will cover the Rectangular and Polar Array commands.

Rectangular Array

The Rectangular Array will allow you to make copies of the original object in rows and columns. The quantity of rows is the count in the vertical direction. The quantity of columns is the count in the horizontal direction

Procedure:

Pick (left click): **Rectangular Array icon** from the Modify Panel of the Home Tab.

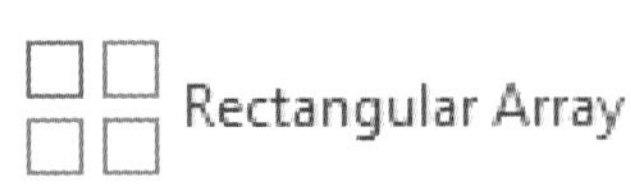

ARRAYRECT *Select objects:* ***(Pick the objects that will be used for the array)***

Select objects: 1 found (AutoCAD will allow you to continue picking objects until you press the ↵ Enter key)

Select objects: ↵

Type = Rectangular Associative = Yes
Select grip to edit array or
[ASsociative/Basepoint/COUnt/Spacing/COLumns/Rows/Levels/eXit]<eXit>:

You will get immediate visual feedback. In addition to having multiple rows and columns of the objects selected, grips will also appear. Each grip has a different function.

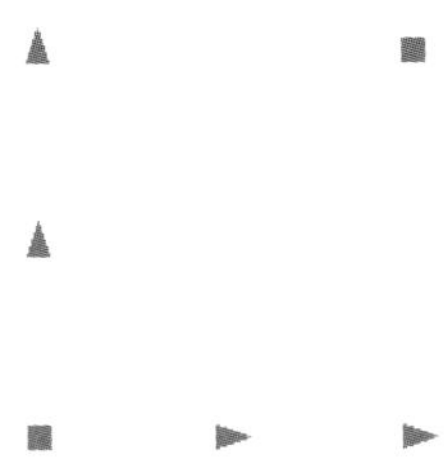

Rectangular Grips
Lower Left: Moves the entire array.
Upper Right: Adjusts row and column count

Triangular Grips
Left Column
    Top: Adjusts row count
    Bottom: Adjusts row spacing
Lower Row
    Right: Adjusts column count
    Left: Adjusts column spacing

To use the grips, Pick on the grip of your choice (left click and release). The grips will disappear. As you move the cursor to a new position, it will appear as if a line is "rubber banding" from the original grip location to the new location. This is not a line; it is a visual aid to show the old and new locations of the grip selected.
You will get visual feedback of the change you are making. When you are satisfied, left click again to choose the new grip position.

Using the grips for adjusting row and column count, as well as repositioning the array, is easy to control.

In addition to the grips, you can make changes using the Array Creation tab that automatically appears on the Ribbon:

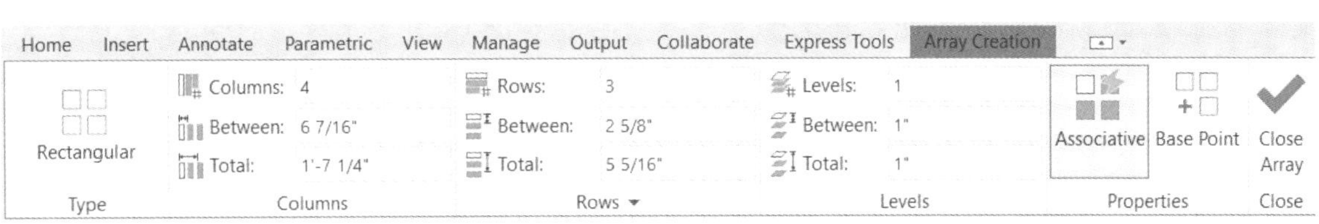

You can edit the values in the Columns and Rows panels as you desire. Because there is a physical relationship of number of columns (or rows) along with the space between, the Total distance adjusts automatically. Alternatively, you can change the Total distance and the space between adjusts automatically.

On the Mac, a Visor will appear at the top of the screen. It is similar to the Array Creation tab on the PC, but it is simplified. You can change the base point or the number of rows or columns. You can close the Visor by selecting the circled X on the right side.

Mac

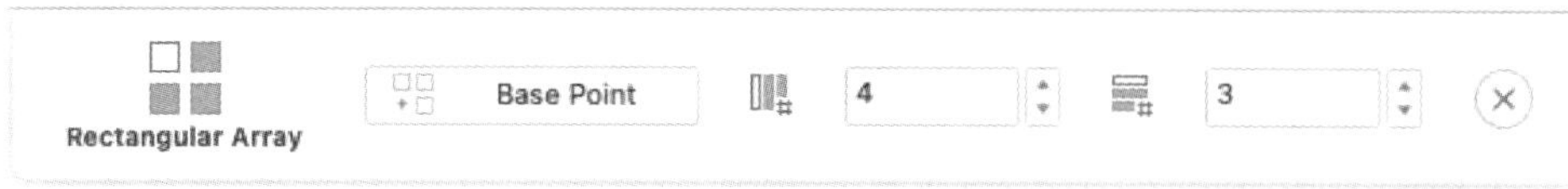

Count Option

Although the visual feedback of rows and columns comes in handy, there are occasions when you want a large enough quantity that you don't want to count them on the screen as they appear with cursor movement. Using the Count option allows you to type in the value you desire for each. After you have chosen the objects for the array, use the Count option of the command by pressing the ↵ Enter key.

Select grip to edit array or [ASsociative/Base point/COUnt/Spacing/COLumns/Rows/Levels/eXit]<eXit>: **cou↵**
(Type the letters "cou" and press the ↵ Enter or pick *COUnt* with your cursor)

Enter the number of columns or [Expression] <4>:

Enter the number of rows or [Expression] <4>: Type in a value for the number of rows (vertical direction), followed by pressing the ↵ Enter key.

Enter number of columns or [Expression] <X>:

Type in a value for the number of columns (horizontal direction), followed by pressing the ↵ Enter key.

The Rectangular Array command will then prompt for the spacing as described earlier.

Spacing Option

You will most likely want to control the spacing value. Rather than simply picking on the screen, you can specify the distance. After you have chosen the number of rows and columns, use the Spacing option of the command:
Select grip to edit array or [ASsociative/Base point/COUnt/Spacing/COLumns/Rows/Levels/eXit]<eXit>: **s↵**
(Type the letter "s" and press the ↵ Enter or pick *Spacing* with your cursor)

As an example, if we want to space our rows and columns 1" apart, we would type in the value when prompted. The prompt will include a default value in the angled brackets. This value will be different each time.

Specify the distance between columns or [Unit cell] < X-' XX">:
Type in a specified distance you want between columns, followed by pressing the ↵ Enter key.
Specify the distance between rows < X-' XX">:

Type in a specified distance you want between rows, followed by pressing the ↵ Enter key.

When you are finished specifying distances between columns and rows, the prompt will return to the original choices.

Select grip to edit array or [ASsociative/Base point/COUnt/Spacing/COLumns/Rows/Levels/eXit]<eXit>:

Try it:

Example 1: Use the command line method of changing the array.

Let's draw a 6 X 6 pattern of 1″ squares that are 1-1/8″ apart (this will put a 1/8″ gap between the squares):

First, draw the 1″ square anywhere on the screen (use the Rectangle command):

(Pick the Rectangular Array command)

ARRAYRECT *Select objects:* ***(Pick the square)***
Select objects: 1 found ↵

Type = Rectangular Associative = Yes
Select grip to edit array or [ASsociative/Base point/COUnt/Spacing/COLumns/Rows/Levels/eXit]<eXit>: **cou↵**
(Type the letters "cou" and press the ↵ Enter or pick *COUnt* with your cursor)

Enter the number of columns or [Expression] <4>: **6↵**
Enter the number of rows or [Expression] <3>: **6↵**

> As an alternative: Pick a point in a direction away from the objects until you see 6 rows and 6 columns of squares

The original prompt returns to the command line. Adjust the spacing by choosing that option:
Select grip to edit array or [ASsociative/Base point/COUnt/Spacing/COLumns/Rows/Levels/eXit]<eXit>: **s↵**
(Type the letter "s" and press the ↵ Enter or pick *Spacing* with your cursor)
Specify the distance between columns or [Unit cell] <1 1/2">: **1-1/8↵**

Specify the distance between rows <1 1/2">: **1-1/8↵**

When the original prompt returns, press the Enter ↵ key to exit the command.

Select grip to edit array or [ASsociative/Base point/COUnt/Spacing/COLumns/Rows/Levels/eXit]<eXit>: ↵

When you are done, your drawing will look like this:

Note that these 36 squares are treated as one object identified as an Array. To make these individual squares, use the Explode command.

<u>Example 2: Use the Array Creation panel (Mac Visor) on the Ribbon method of changing the array.</u>

First, draw the 1″ square anywhere on the screen (use the Rectangle command).

(Pick the Rectangular Array command)

ARRAYRECT *Select objects:* ***(Pick the square)***
Select objects: 1 found ↵

The Array Creation panel appears on the Ribbon:

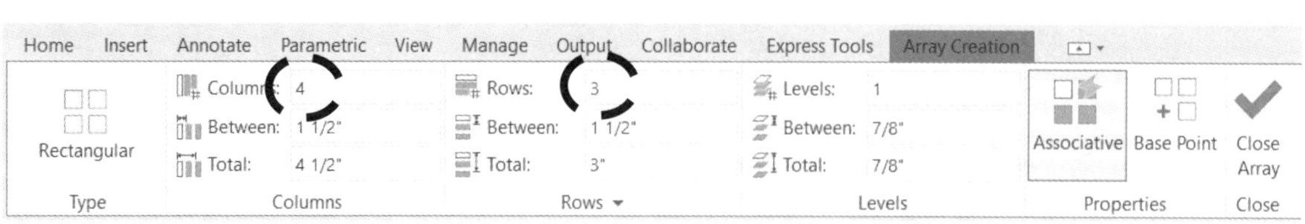

On the Mac, the Visor will appear at the top of your screen:

Mac

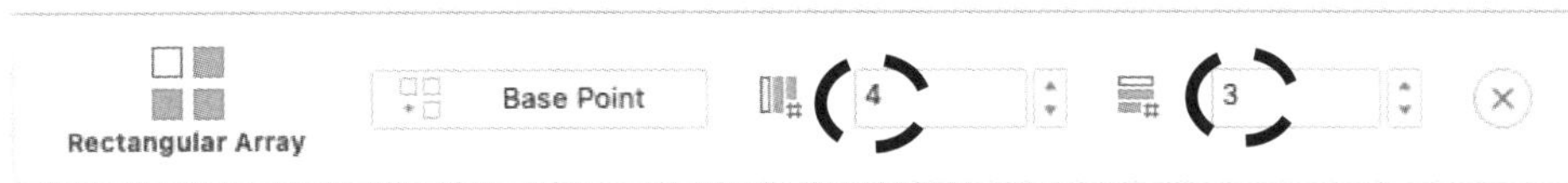

Change the values in Columns panel and the Rows panel to 6. You can click the existing value to highlight it and type the new value.

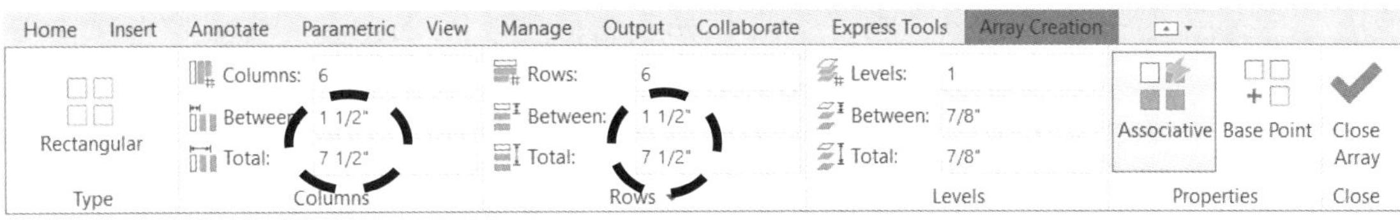

Notice that the "Total" value changes automatically because the "Between" value remains the same. Change the Between values to 1-1/8".

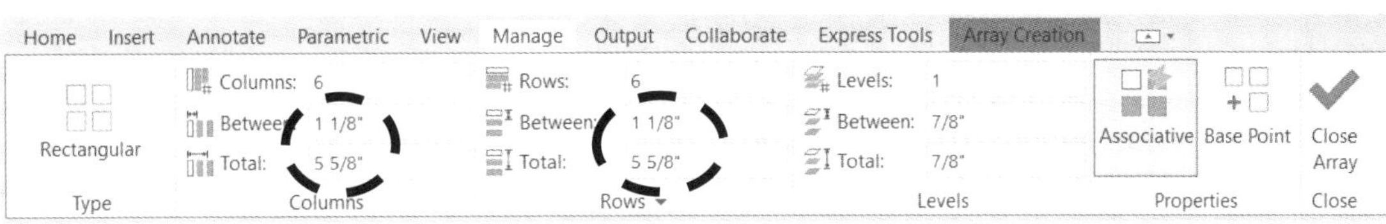

The "Total" value changes again because the Columns and Rows remain the same value, but the "Between" value changed.

On the Mac Visor, there are no "Between" or "Total" values displayed.

Mac

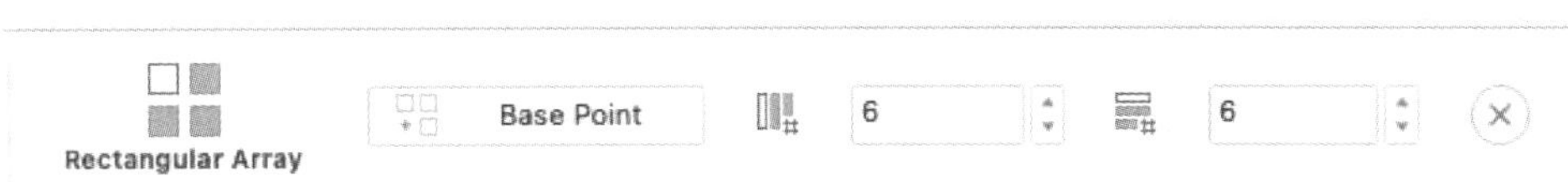

In order to control the spacing on the Mac, you must type **s**↵ in the command line and specify the spacing for both rows and columns.

End the command by picking the Close Array icon on the Array Creation panel (or the Close icon on the Mac Visor). Your final array will look exactly as it did for Example 1.

Polar Array

The Polar Array will allow you to make copies of the original object rotated about a point.

Procedure:

Pick (left click): **Polar Array icon** from the Modify Panel of the Home Tab.

ARRAYPOLAR *Select objects:* ***(Pick the objects that will be used for the array)***

Select objects: 1 found (AutoCAD will allow you to continue picking objects until you press the ↵ Enter key)

Select objects: ↵

Type = Polar Associative = Yes
Specify center point of array or [Base point/Axis of rotation]:
(Pick a point that the selected objects will rotate about)

Select grip to edit array or [ASsociative/Base point/Items/Angle between/Fill angle/ROWs/Levels/ROTate items/eXit]<eXit>:

You will get immediate visual feedback. In addition to having multiple copies of the objects selected, grips will also appear. Each grip has a different function.

Initially, you may only get a single triangular grip for angle between items.

Rectangular Grips
Normal Square: Moves the entire array.
Angled Square: Stretches the radial distance from the base point

Triangular Grips
1st - Changes the angle between items
2nd - Changes item count

After you select the first triangular grip, a second one may appear for item count.

To use the grips, Pick on the grip of your choice (left click and release). The grips will disappear. As you move the cursor to a new position, it will appear as if a line is "rubber banding" from the original grip location to the new location. This is not a line; it is visual aid to show the old and new locations of the grip selected.
You will get visual feedback of the change you are making. When you are satisfied, left click again to choose the new grip position.

In addition to the grips, you can make changes using the Array Creation tab that automatically appears on the Ribbon:

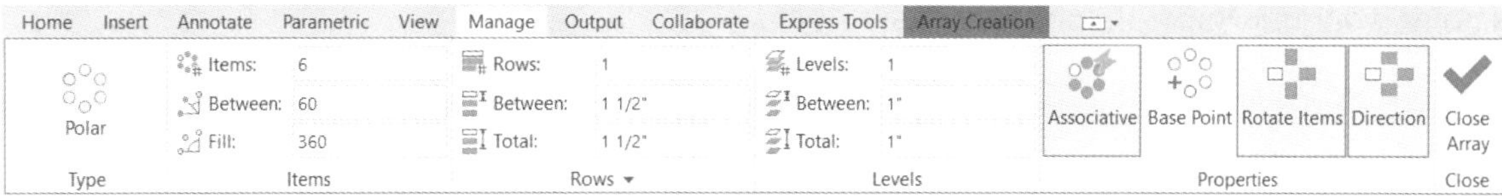

On the Mac, the Visor will appear at the top of your screen:

Mac

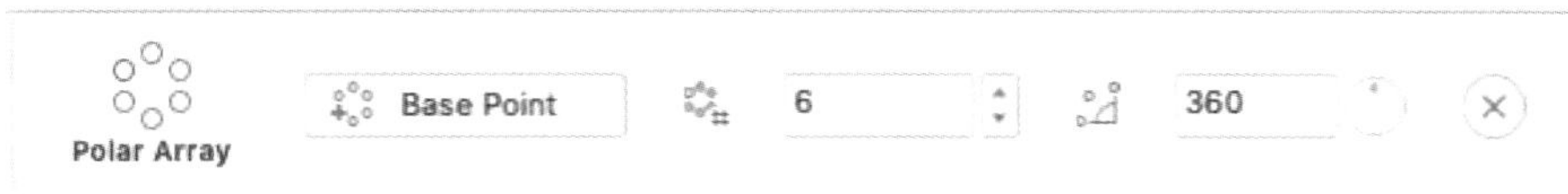

You may have a specific number of items that must fill a certain angle, or you may know the angle between items that you want. This command allows you to define the array in multiple ways. We will just cover the fill angle and the number of items.

If you want to fill a full circle, use the Fill option with an angle of 360. Note that the fill angle of 360 is the default fill angle, so you typically do not need this option if you plan to fill a full circle.

Specify the angle to fill (+=ccw, -=cw) or [EXpression] <360>:

If you know the number of items, use the Items option.

Enter number of items in array or [Expression] <X>:

Pressing the ↵ Enter key will end the command.

Try it:

Let's draw the 4 flower petals shown:

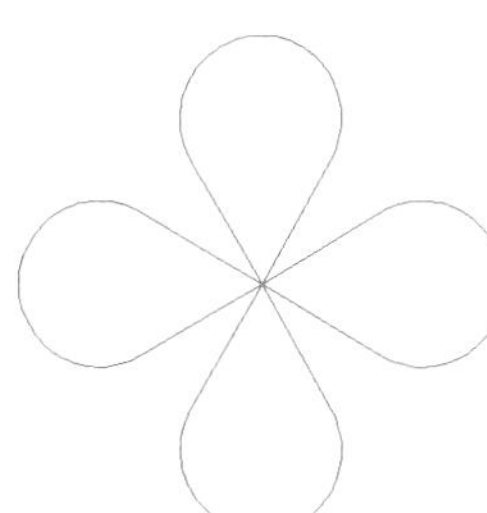

First we will draw a single flower petal, and then we will rotate and copy that petal by using the Polar Array command. The petal is a 1″ radius circle drawn at the intersection of a line and a 2″ radius circle.

Start by drawing a 2″ radius circle anywhere on your screen. Now draw a horizontal construction line through the center of the circle. At the right intersection of the construction line and the 2″ radius circle, draw a 1″ radius circle.

At this point, your drawing will look like this:

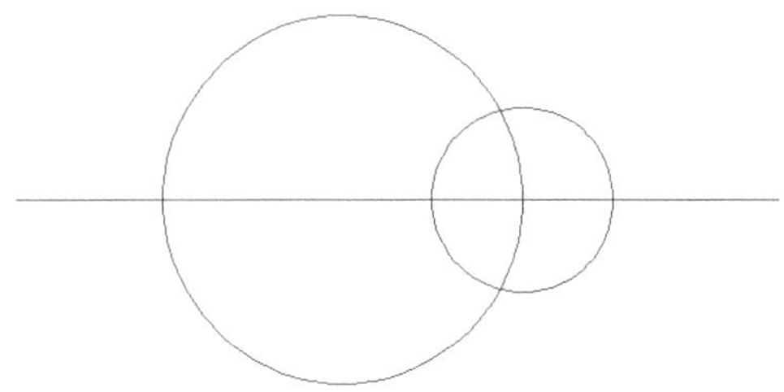

Now draw two lines that start from the center of the 2″ radius circle and ending tangent to the 1″ radius circle:

If you do not have OSNAP set to Tangent, you can type **tan↵** to snap to the tangent of the circle when the Line command is prompting for the second endpoint.

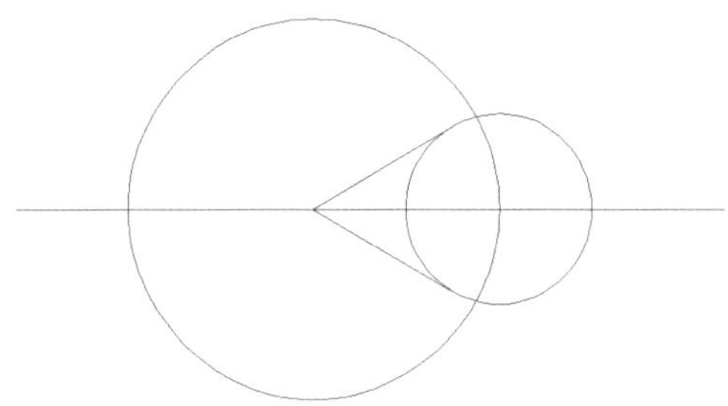

Use the Trim command to trim away the small portion of the 1″ radius circle:

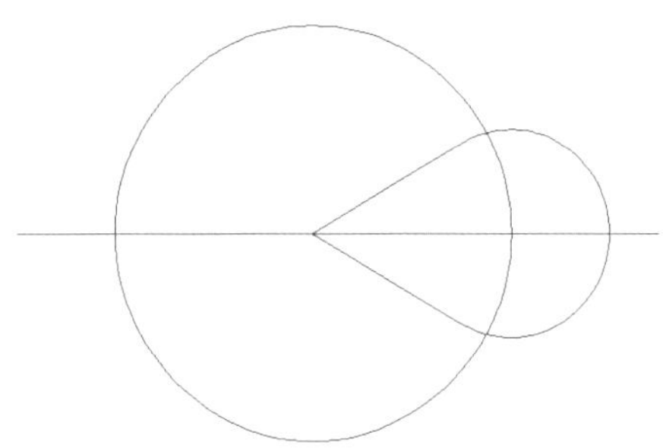

Now that we have the first petal drawn, we can use the Polar Array command to copy it around the center of the 2″ radius circle.

(Pick the Polar Array command)

ARRAYPOLAR *Select objects:*

(Pick the two lines and the semi-circle)

Select objects: 1 found
Select objects: 1 found, 2 total
Select objects: 1 found, 3 total
Select objects: ↵

Type = Polar Associative = Yes
Specify center point of array or [Base point/Axis of rotation]:

(Pick the Center of the 2″ radius circle)

Method 1: Use the command line options to change the array.

Use the Items option to specify the number of petals to be 4:

Select grip to edit array or [ASsociative/Base point/Items/Angle between/Fill angle/ROWs/Levels/ROTate items/eXit]<eXit>: **i↵**
(Type the letter "i" and press the ↵ Enter or pick *Items* with your cursor)

Enter number of items in array or [Expression] <6>: **4↵**

Method 2: Use the Array Creation panel (Mac Visor) on the Ribbon to change the array.

The Array Creation panel appears on the Ribbon:

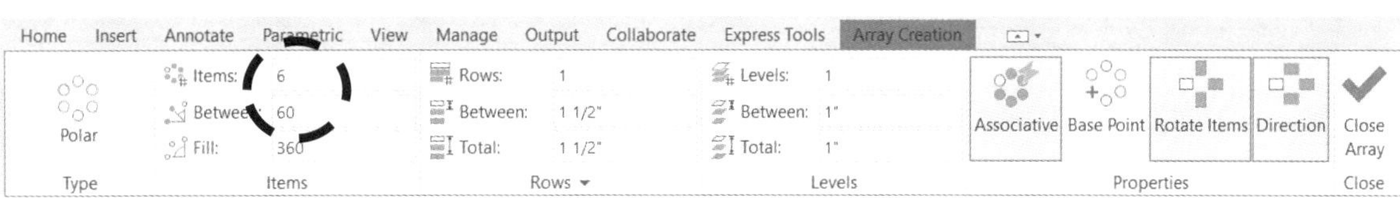

On the Mac, the Visor will appear at the top of your screen:

Mac

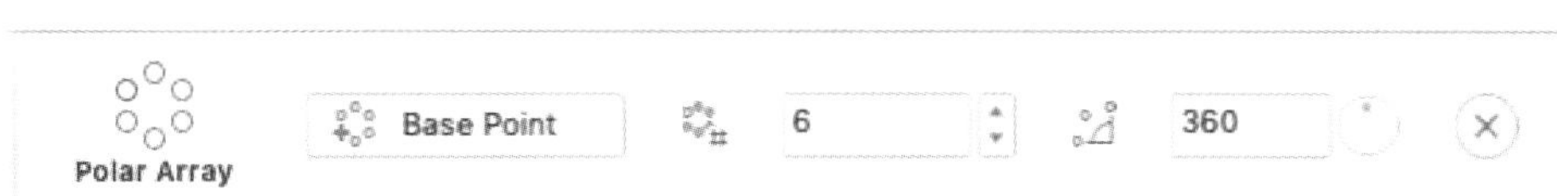

Change the values in the Item panel to 4. You can click the existing value to highlight it and type the new value.

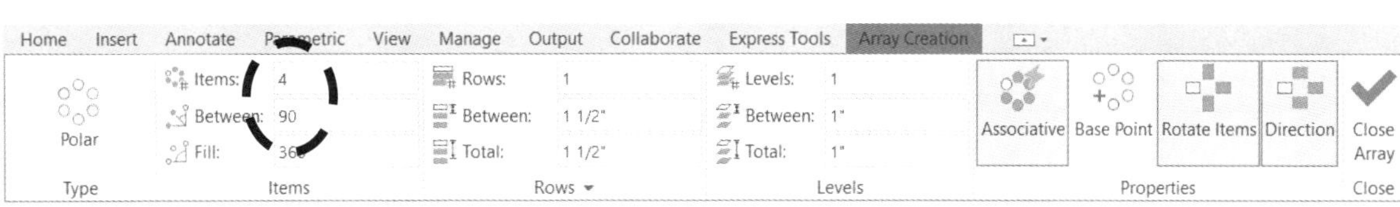

Notice the "Between" value changed to 90 because the number of items changed to 4 and the "Fill" remained at 360.

Mac

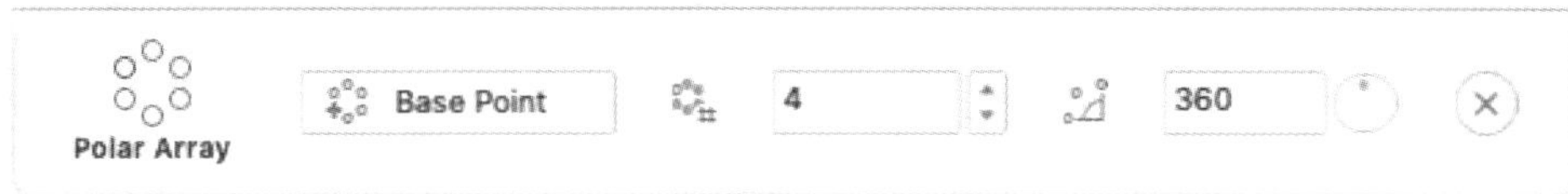

Since 360 was the default value for angle to fill, we do not need to specify the fill angle. We can exit the command by pressing the ↵ Enter key or by picking the Close Array icon on the Array Creation panel (or the Close icon on the Mac Visor).

When you are done, your drawing will look like this:

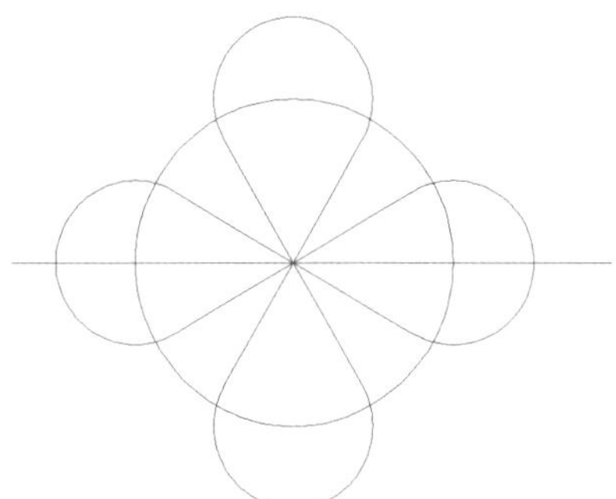

You can erase the 2″ radius circle and the construction line to get the final drawing of the flower:

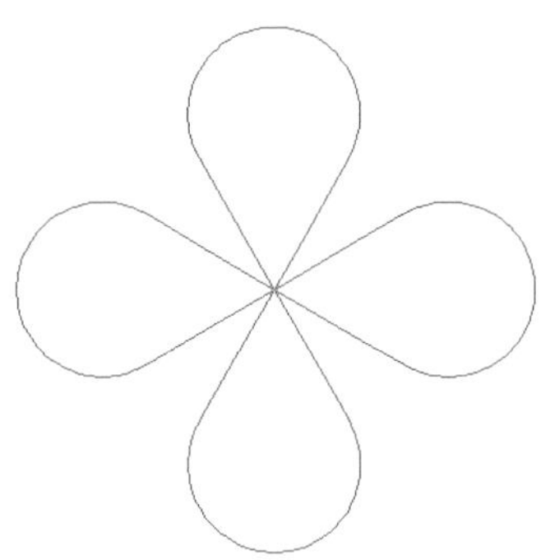

Summary

In this chapter you have learned to:

- Recognize and understand a Fly-out icon
- Measure distances between points
- Measure the radius and diameter of an arc or circle
- Measure the angle between lines
- Obtain all the information available about an object
- Move, copy, rotate, and mirror objects
- Create a rectangular pattern of objects
- Create a circular pattern of objects

Review Questions

1. What is a Fly-out style icon?

2. On the Utilities Panel, you see the Distance command but not the Angle command. Where is it and how do you get to it?

3. When using the distance command, AutoCAD will give you the distance between two points. What other information will AutoCAD provide?

4. The information about an object will show up in your command line and where else?

5. When using either the Fillet or Chamfer commands, does the order in which you pick the objects matter? Does the location matter?

6. If Fillets are used to make rounded corners, how can you use it to make a sharp corner?

7. Why would you use Fillet to make sharp corners instead of using either the Trim or Extend commands?

8. When using the Move, Copy, or Rotate commands, what is a base point that AutoCAD is prompting for?

9. Prior to using the Mirror command, what should you have prepared in advance?

10. Which commands are used for making either rectangular or circular patterns?

Exercises

1. Draw the conference room. The doors are 1-3/4" thick.

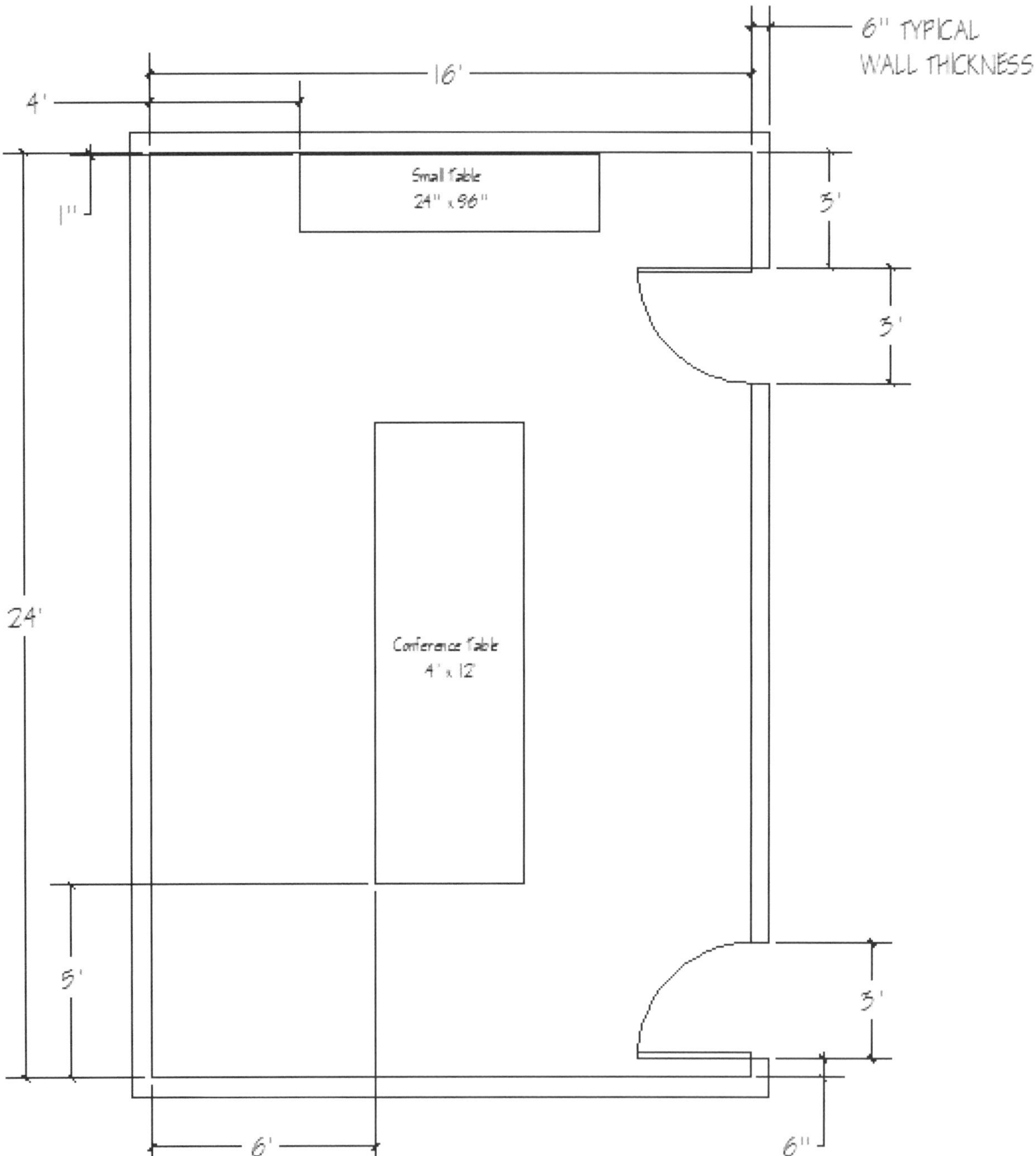

2. Draw the 3′ X 1-3/4″ door and door swing. Make mirrored-copies of the door. Copy and rotate the mirrored-copies 90°.

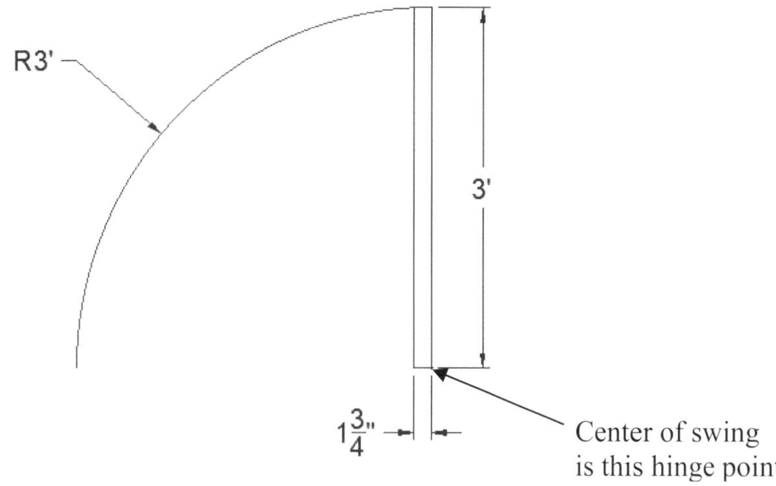

Door & Swing dimensions

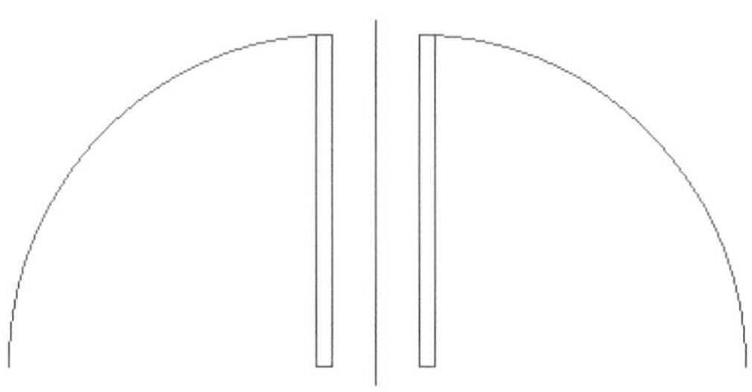

Door & Swing mirrored

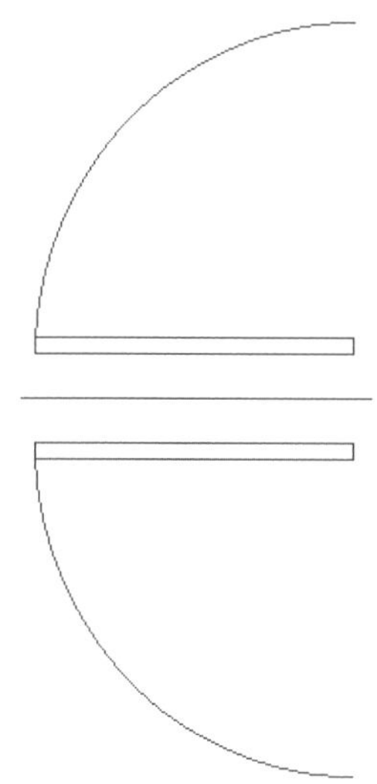

Door & Swing rotated 90° after mirroring

3. Draw the Conference Chair.

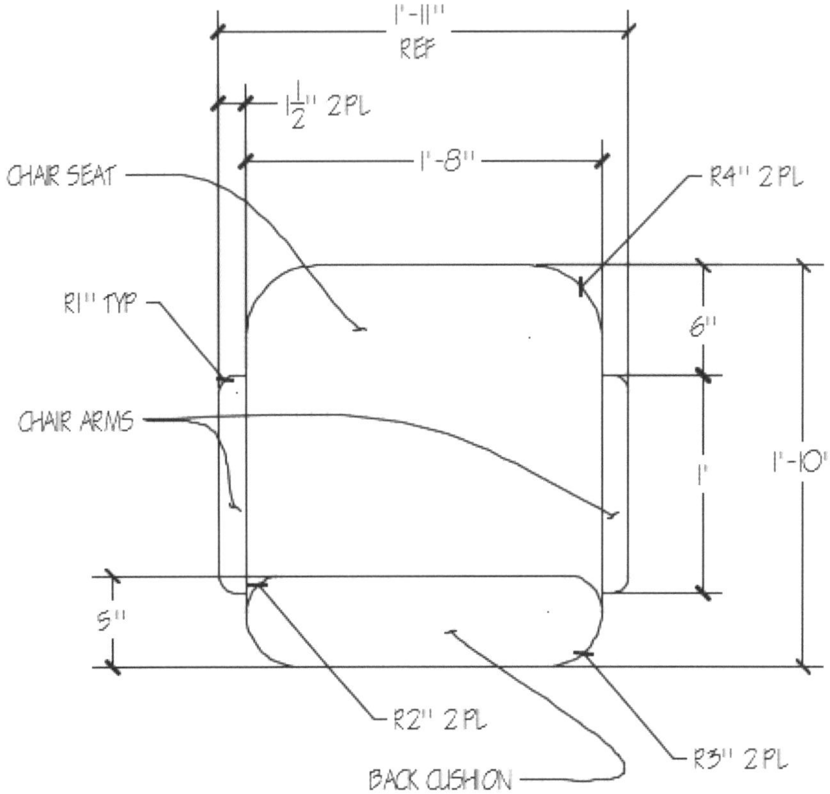

4. Draw the tile pattern. The spacing between tiles is 1/16″.

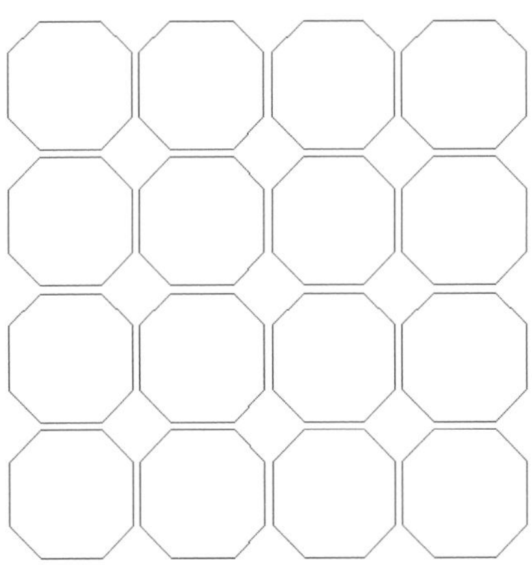

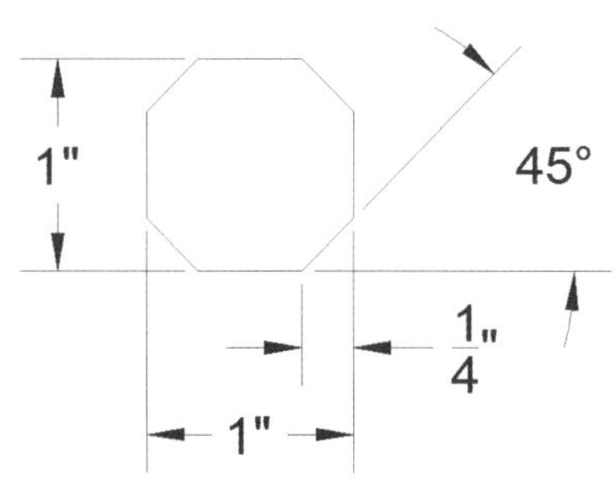

Draw the single tile shown and use a Rectangular Array with spacing set to 1-1/16″ for both columns and rows

5. Draw the Spoke Chair.

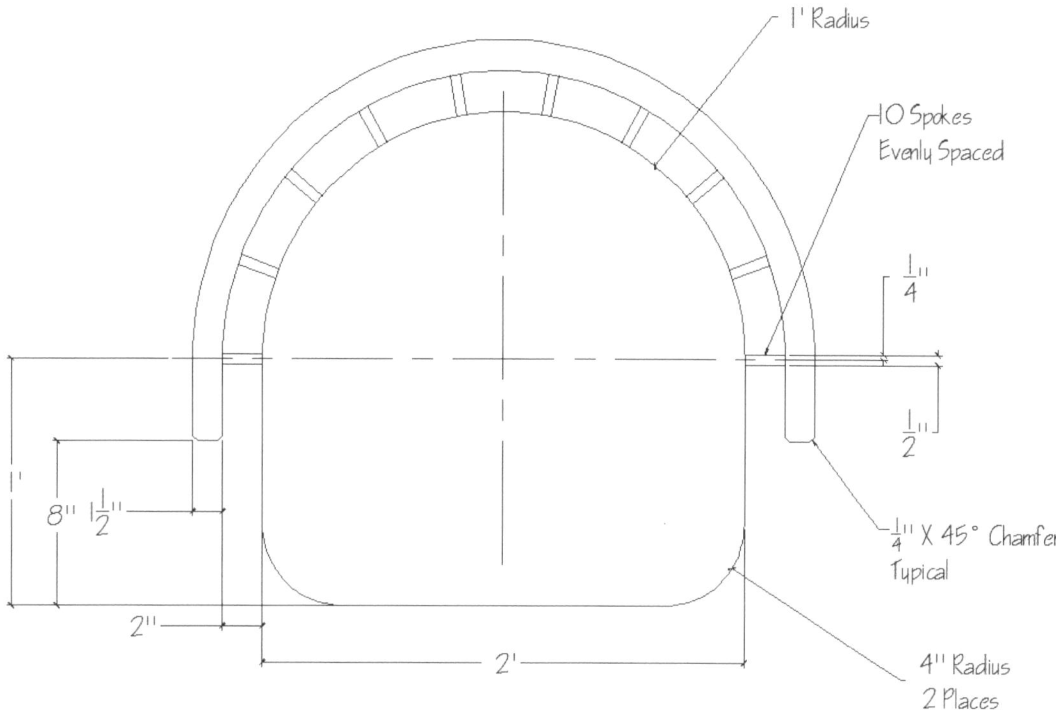

Hint: Draw 1 spoke and use the Polar Array to copy them around the chair – 10 places within 180°

6. Draw the medallion.

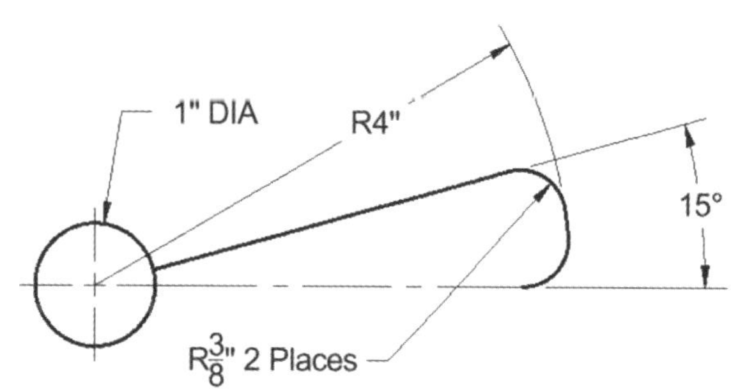

To draw the medallion, start with the drawing above. Use a Polar Array to rotate and copy the objects. Do not include the 1″ diameter circle, the centerlines nor the horizontal line when you select the objects for the array.

7. Draw the bathroom vanity.
   The knobs are 1-1/4" square and the drawer pulls are 1/2" x 5-1/2". The drawer pulls are centered on each drawer. Hints: start with a rectangle 4' x 2'10" and then explode the rectangle. Draw the knobs and drawer pulls off to the side first then make copies to position them on the vanity. Take advantage of the symmetry – draw one side and make a mirrored copy on the other side. Note: the abbreviation Typ stands for typical.

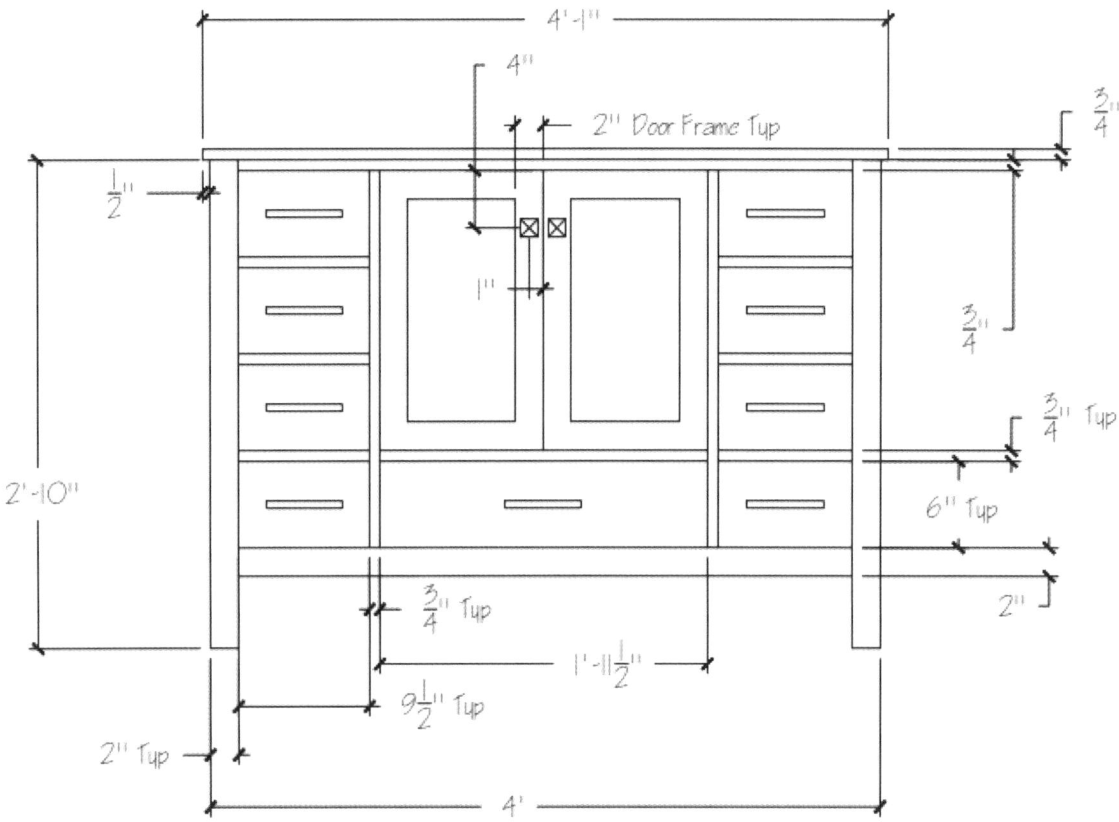

Chapter 6

Hotel Suite Project – Tutorial 2

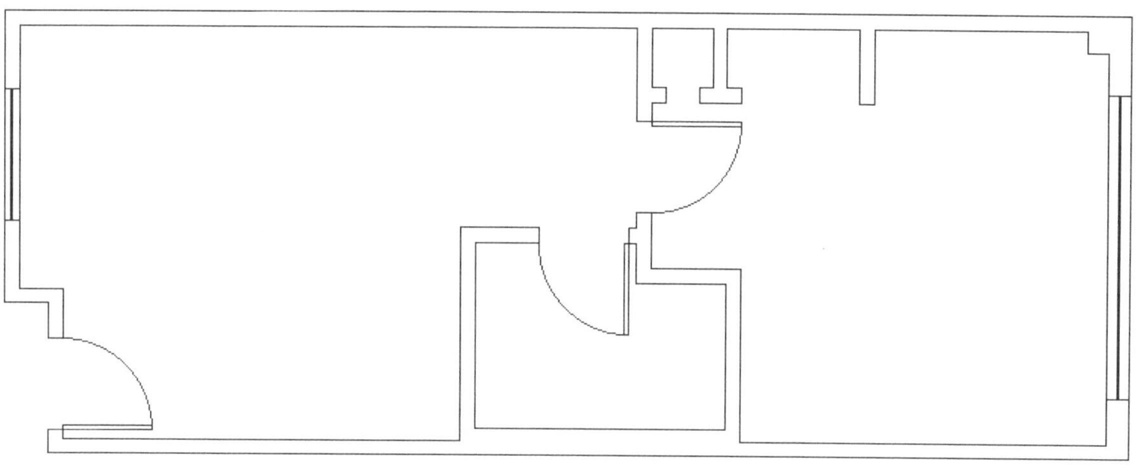

Learning Objectives:

- **To continue creating a drawing of a real-world application of AutoCAD**
  - **Create the plan view of the bathroom and closet walls of the hotel suite**
  - **Create the doors and windows of the suite**
- **To utilize and reinforce the use of the AutoCAD commands learned in the previous chapters**

This tutorial builds on Tutorial 1 found in chapter 4. We will create the bathroom and closet walls of the hotel suite. When you are finished with this tutorial, all the walls of the plan view of the hotel suite will be completed.

The drawing methods used to complete the walls are very similar to those used for tutorial 1.

Commands & Techniques:

- Opening an existing drawing
- Zoom - All
- Rectangle
- Offset
- Explode
- Construction Line – Offset & Horizontal
- Trim
- Erase
- Fillet
- Repeating commands by using the ↵ Enter key
- Object Snap – Endpoint
- Distance
- Copy
- Rotate
- Mirror
- Move
- Save

Create the Bathroom Walls

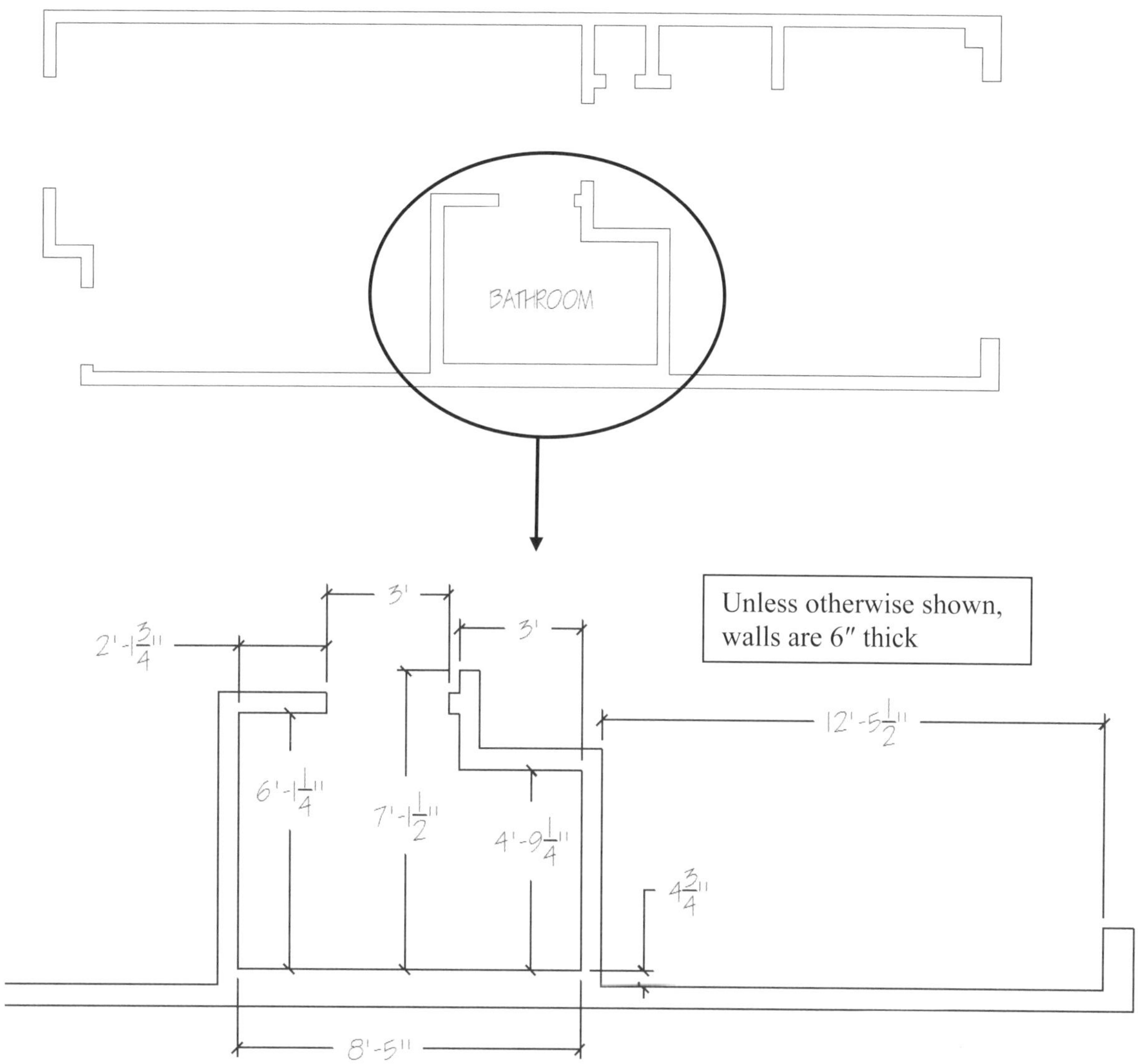

Bathroom Dimensions

- To begin, we will call up the drawing that you created in Tutorial 1.

1. Use the Open icon (or Fill pull-down menu) to open the Hotel Suite drawing

(Pick the Open icon)

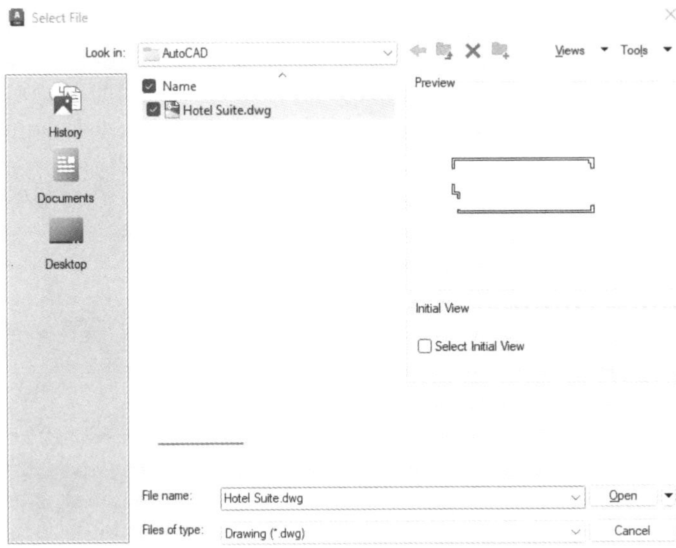

Mac

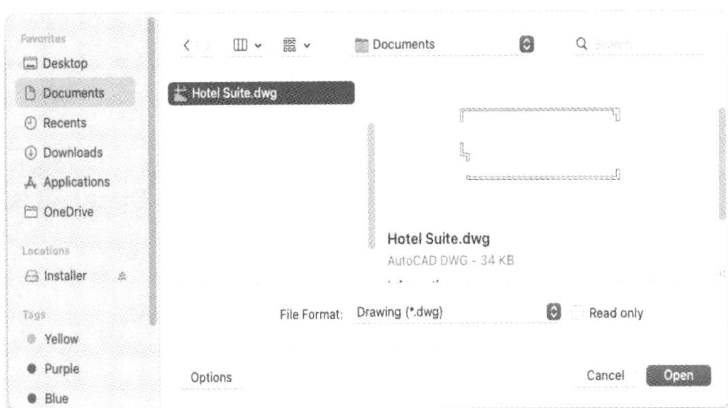

(Pick the "Hotel Suite.dwg" file icon)

The preview pane shows you a thumbnail representation of the drawing. This makes it easy to determine if you are about to open the correct drawing.

(Pick Open)

Your drawing should now appear on your computer screen. Zoom and Pan to the area of the drawing that will become the bathroom.

2. Create construction lines for the right and left vertical walls

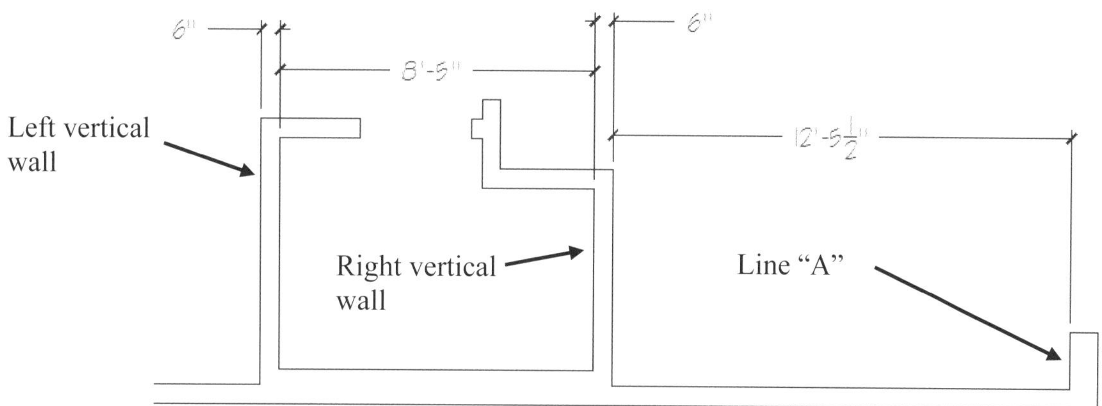

2a. Create a Construction Line Offset 12′5-1/2″ from line "A"

Use the **Construction Line** command with the **Offset** option

2b. Offset the construction line of step 2a 6″ to create the wall thickness

Use the **Offset** command.

2c. Offset the construction line of step 2b 8′5″ to create the inside left vertical wall line

Press the ↲ Enter key to repeat the **Offset** command

2d. Offset the construction line of step 2c 6″ to create the wall thickness

When you are done, your drawing should look like this

3. Create the lower horizontal wall

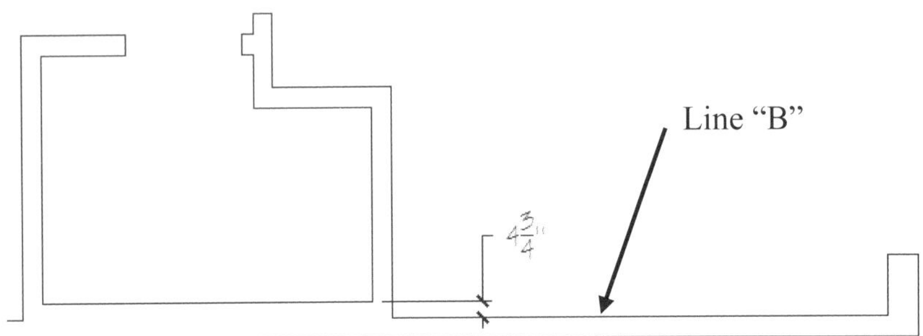

3a. Offset line “B” 4-3/4″ to create the wall thickness

3b. Use the Trim command to complete the lower horizontal wall

Take advantage of using a crossing window to select your cutting edges.

Remember, if during trimming you have extra lines as a result of the location and order in which you picked the lines to trim, use the Erase command to eliminate them.

When you are done, your drawing should look like this:

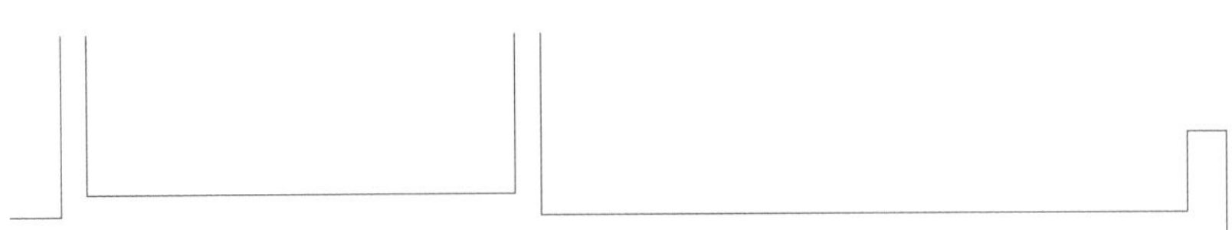

4. Create the upper left horizontal wall

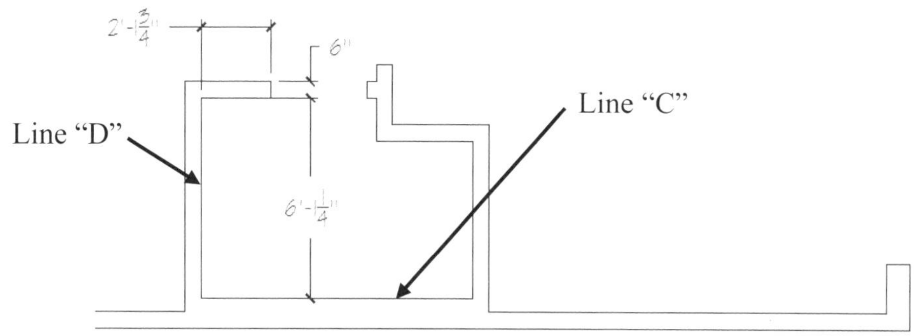

4a. Offset line "C" 6′1-1/4″ up to create the inside line of the upper left horizontal wall

4b. Offset the line created in step 4a 6″ up to create the wall thickness

4c. Offset line "D" 2′1-3/4″ to the right

So far, your drawing should look like this:

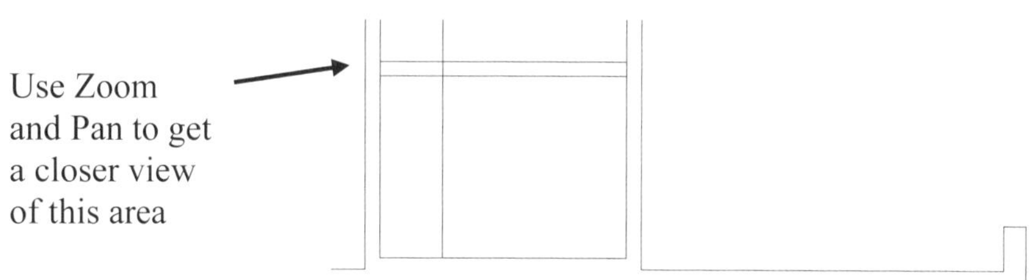

To continue on, it may be easier to complete the wall by getting a closer view. Use the wheel mouse to Zoom and Pan to do this.

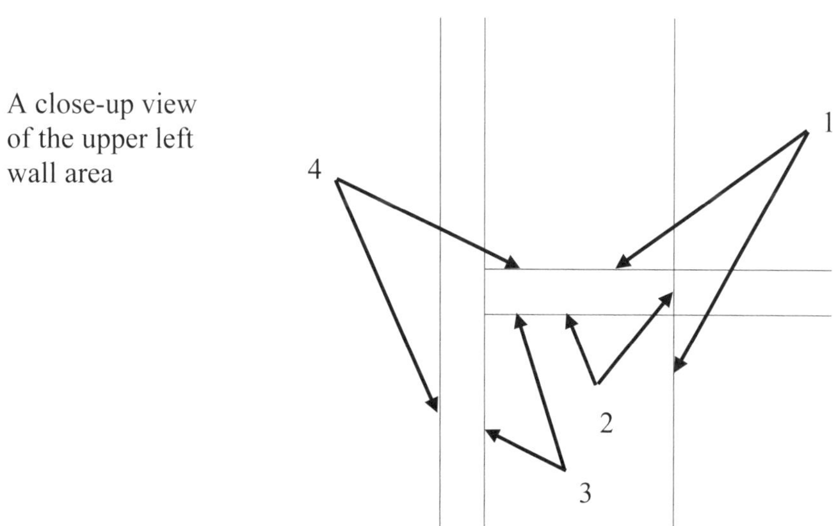

4d. Use the Fillet command to close out the wall lines

> If the Radius is not set to 0′-0″ press **r↵** or pick ***Radius*** with your cursor and change the value by typing **0↵**

(Pick the Fillet icon)

Current settings: Mode = TRIM, Radius = 0'-0"
FILLET *Select first object or [Undo/Polyline/Radius/Trim/Multiple]:*
(Pick one of the lines at location marked 1)
Select second object or shift-select to apply corner:
(Pick the other line at location marked 1)

The Fillet command will end after the second line is picked and it will trim both lines.

Both lines are trimmed and the corner is sharp

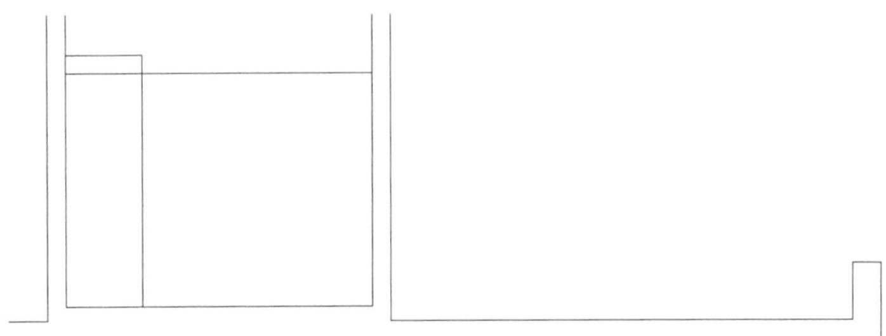

4e. Continue using the Fillet command to trim the lines at locations marked 2, 3 & 4

Remember, you can quickly repeat the Fillet command by pressing the ↵ Enter key.

Now that you have used the Trim and/or Extend commands and the Fillet command, you may notice that the Fillet command comes in very handy. I find the Fillet command to be fewer steps. The Trim command is still needed when you want to remove a mid-section of an object.

When you are done, your drawing should look like this:

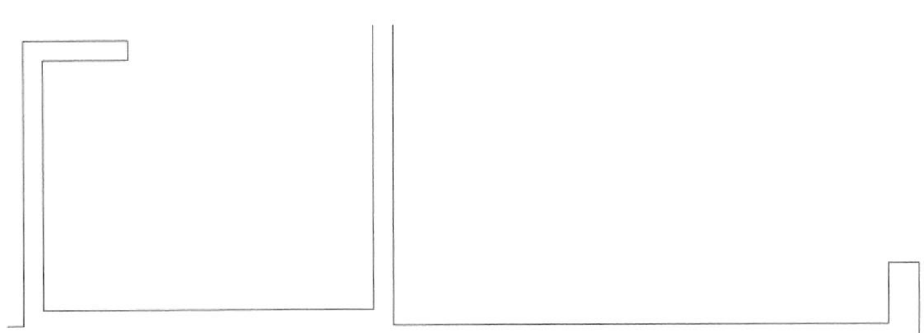

5. Create the upper right horizontal and vertical walls

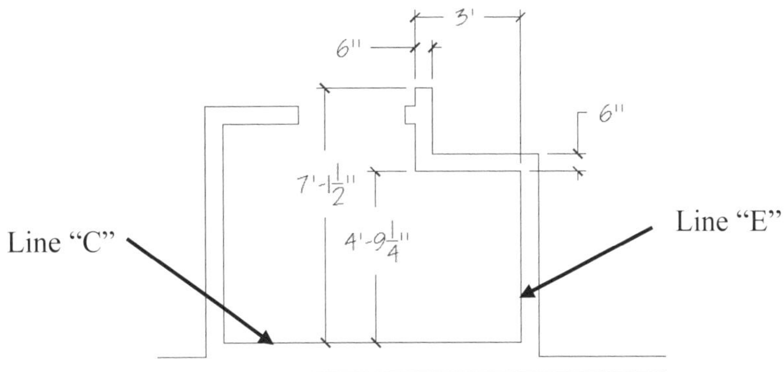

5a. Offset line "C" 4′9-1/4″ up to create the inside wall line

5b. Offset the line you created in step 5a 6″ up to create the wall thickness

5c. Offset line "E" 3′ to the left

5d. Offset the line you created in step 5c 6″ to the right to create the wall thickness

So far, your drawing should look like this:

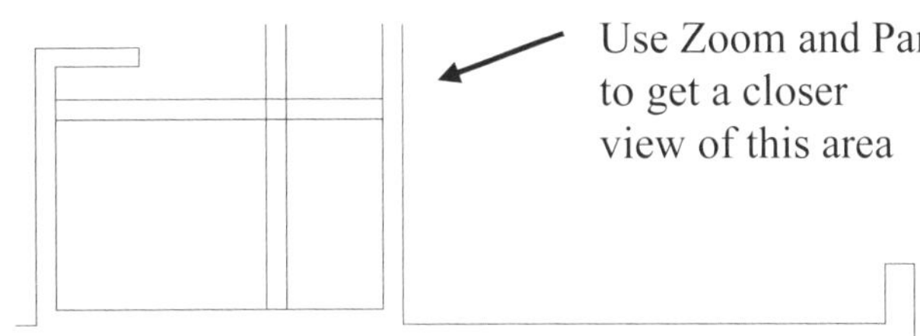

Use Zoom and Pan to get a closer view of this area

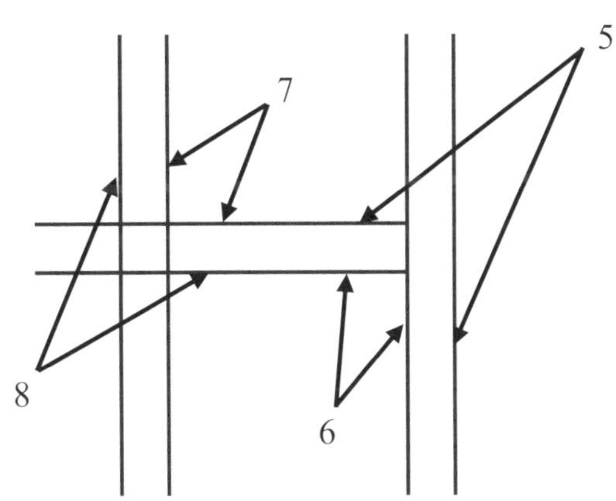

5e. Use the Fillet command to trim the lines at locations marked 5, 6, 7, & 8

When you are done, your drawing should look like this:

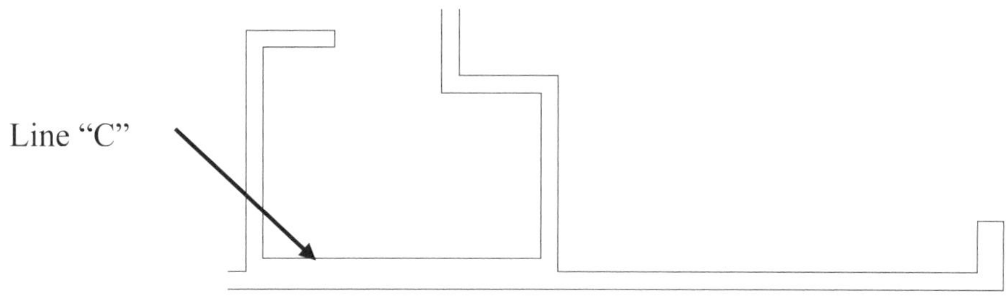

5f. Offset line "C" 7′ 1-1/2″ up

5g. Use the Fillet command to close out the corners of the wall

6. Create the door opening

For the door opening, a small piece of horizontal wall needs to be added. This is in-line with the left horizontal wall.

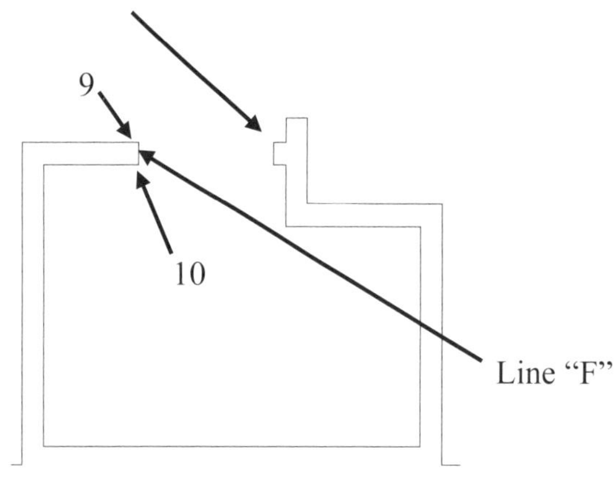

6a. Turn on Object Snap Endpoint

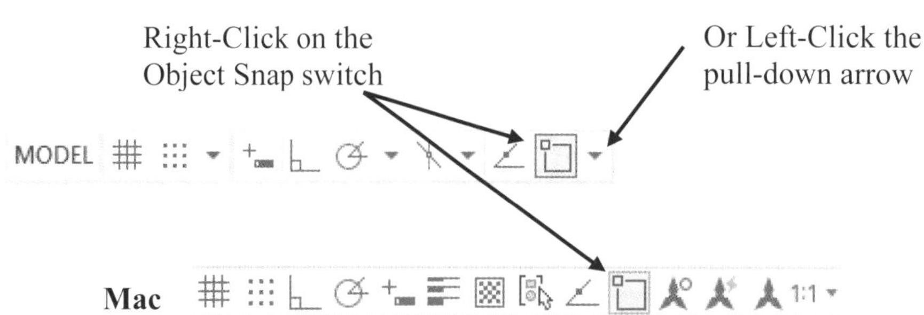

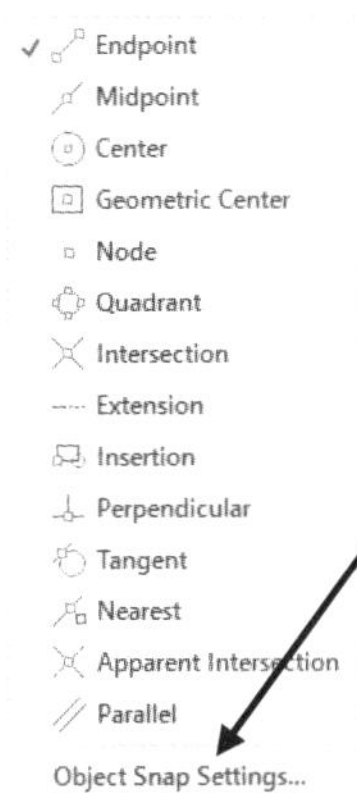

(Pick Object Snap Settings…)

Mac

(Pick Settings…)

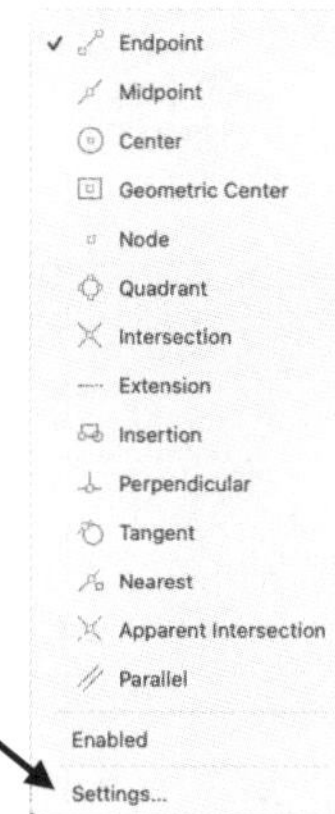

When the Drafting Settings dialog box appears, left-click the check-box next to Endpoint and Object Snap On if they are not already checked off. Pick OK to close the dialog box.

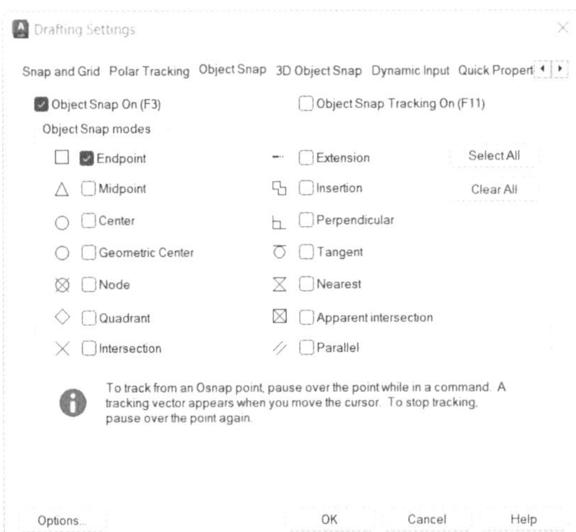

Mac

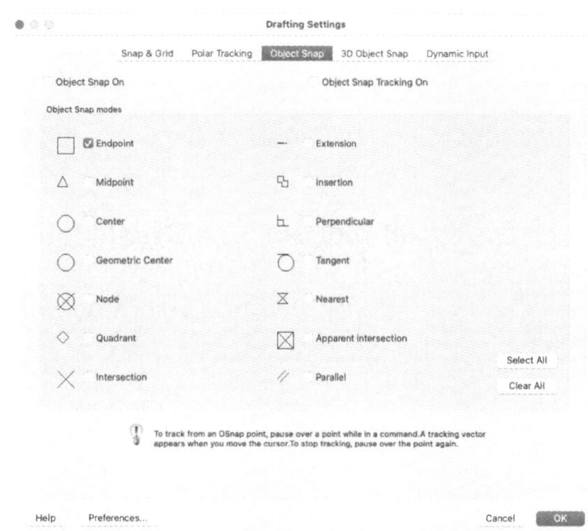

6b. Create Horizontal Construction Lines to define the right side of the door opening

(Pick the Construction Line icon)

XLINE *Specify a point or [Hor/Ver/Ang/Bisect/Offset]:* **h** ↵
Specify through point: ***(Pick the endpoint at location marked 9)***
Specify through point: ***(Pick the endpoint at location marked 10)***
Specify through point: ↵

6c. Offset line "F" 3′ to the right to define the door opening

6d. Use the Trim command to complete the opening

6e. Use the Erase command if needed to eliminate any extra lines

This now completes the bathroom portion of the floor plan.

When you are done, your drawing should look like this:

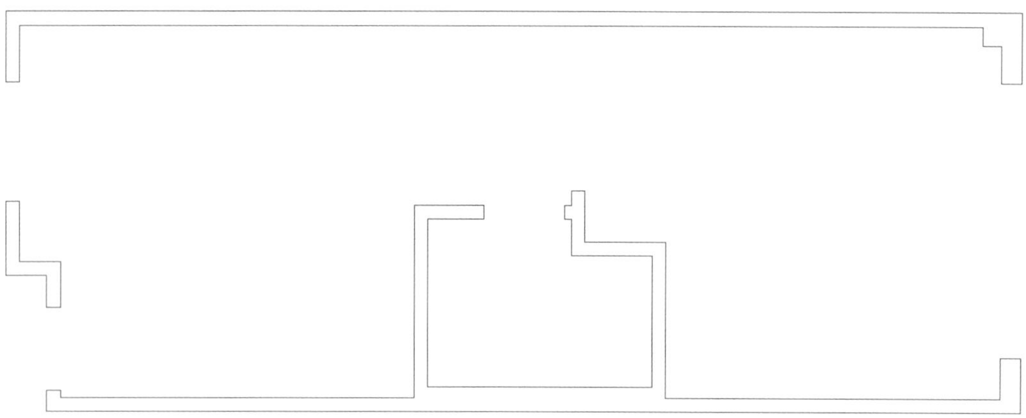

Make sure to save your drawing. Next, we will add the closet wall lines.

Create the Closet Walls

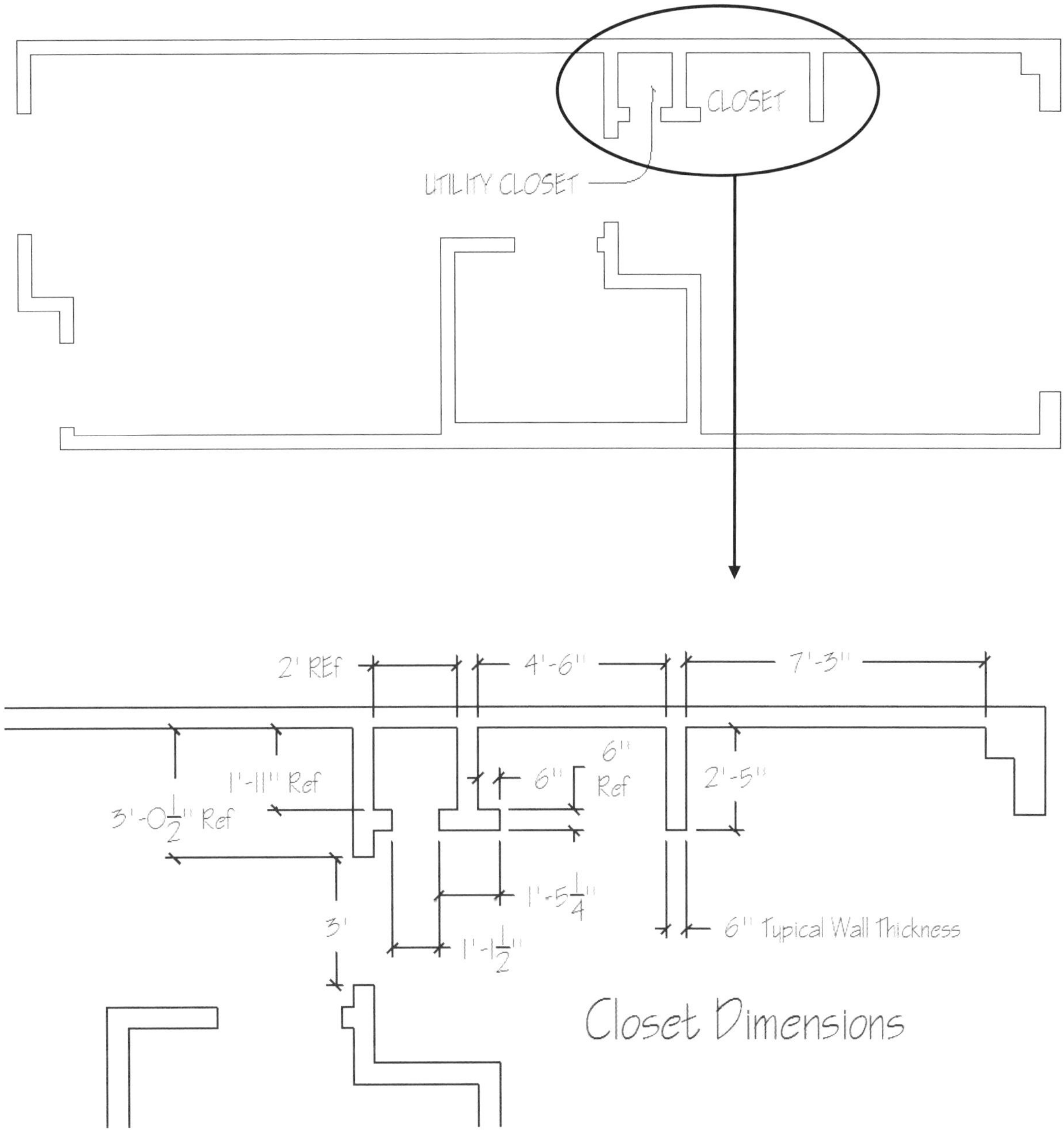

7. Create the right vertical wall of the right closet

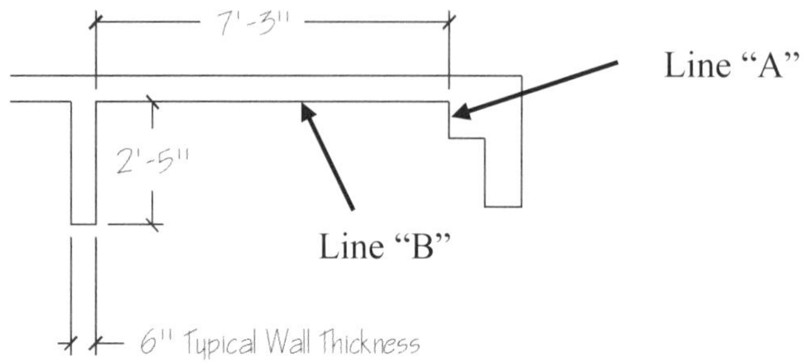

7a. Create a Construction Line Offset 7′3″ from line "A"

7b. Offset the construction line of step 7a 6″ to create the wall thickness

7c. Offset line "B" 2′5″ down to create the wall length

7d. Use the Trim command to complete the wall

When you are done, your drawing should look like this

8. Create the left wall of the right closet

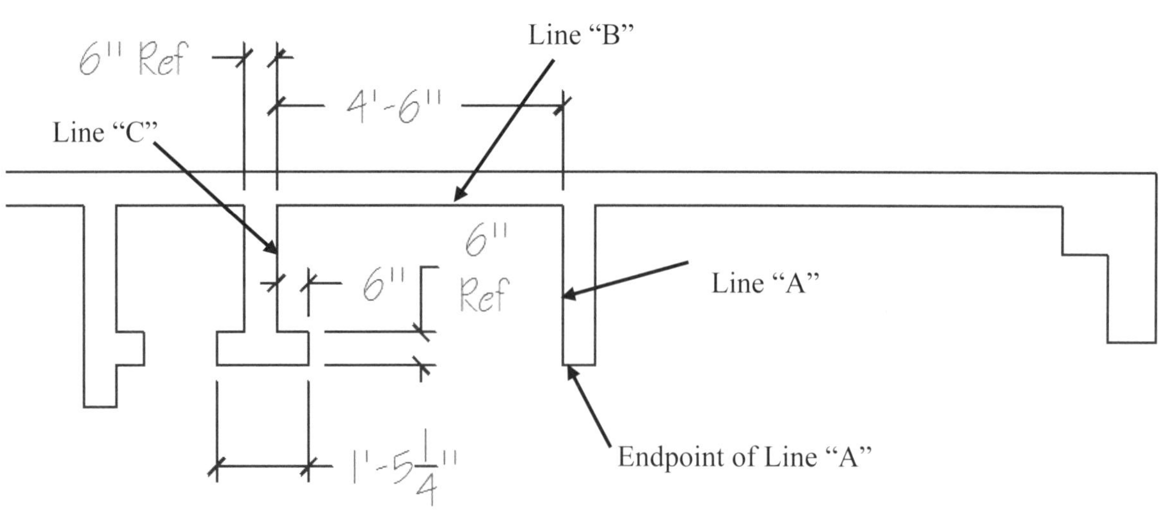

8a. Offset line "A" 4′6″ to the left

8b. Offset the line created in step 8a 6″ to the left

8c. Use the Trim command to trim line "B"

8d. Create a Horizontal Construction Line from the endpoint of line "A"

8e. Offset 6″ - the horizontal construction line upward and line "C" to the right

8f. Repeat the Offset command and Offset the vertical line created in step 8e 1′5-1/4″ to the left

8g. Use the Fillet command with a 0″ radius to finish the corners shown

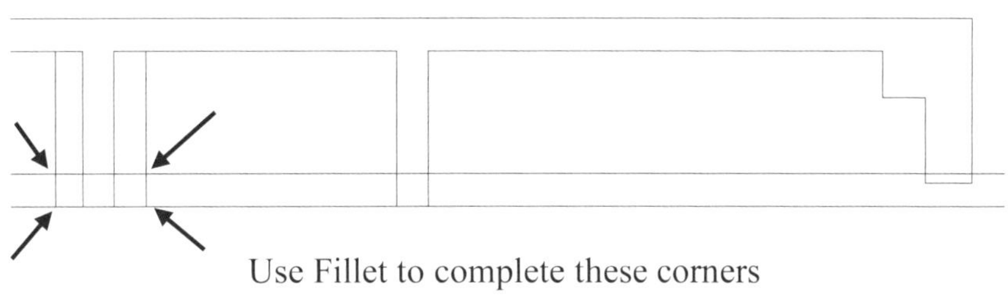

When you are done, your drawing should look like this

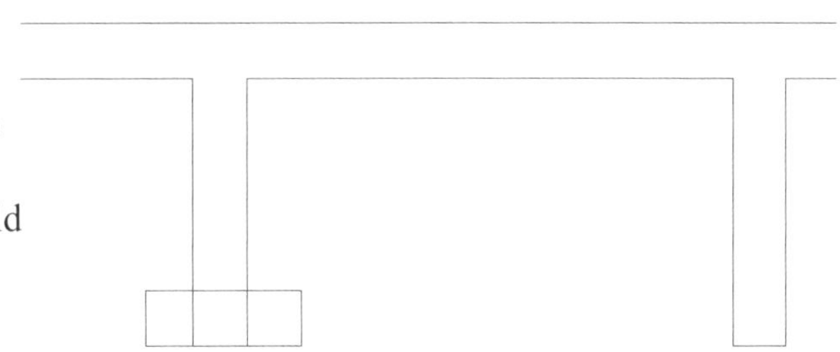

8h. Use the Trim command to clean up the remaining lines

When you are done, your drawing should look like this

9. Create the left wall of the utility closet

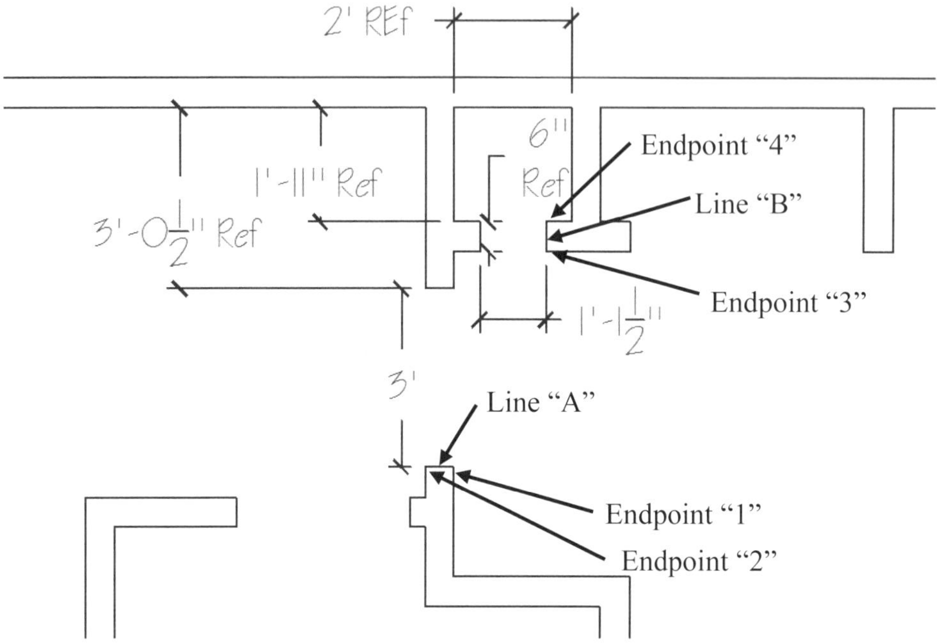

9a. Create Vertical Construction Lines passing through endpoints "1" and "2"

9b. Use the Trim command to complete the top part of the left utility closet wall

When you are done, your drawing should look like this

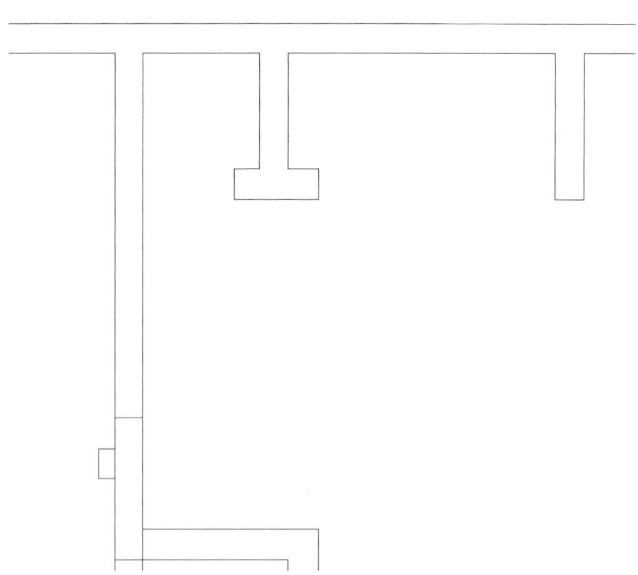

10. Create the door opening for the bedroom

10a. Offset line "A" 3′ up

10b. Use the Trim command to complete the door opening

When you are done, your drawing should look like this

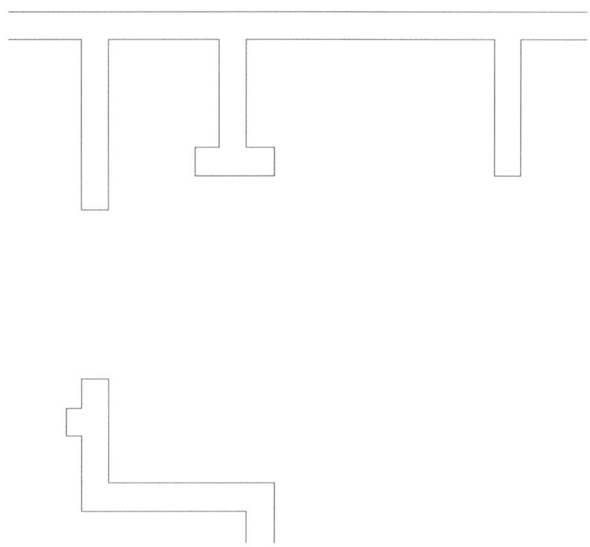

11. Finish the utility closet structure

11a. Create Horizontal Construction Lines through endpoints "3" and "4"

11b. Offset line "B" 1′1-1/2″ to the left

11c. Use the Trim command to complete the structure

When you are done, your drawing should look like this

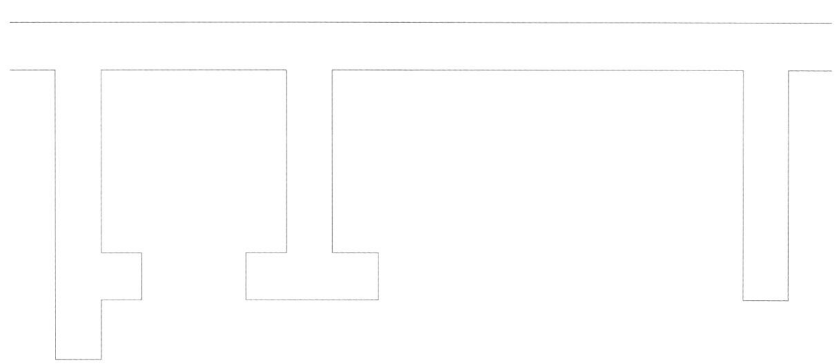

12. Confirm the reference dimensions for lines “A”, “B”, and “C”

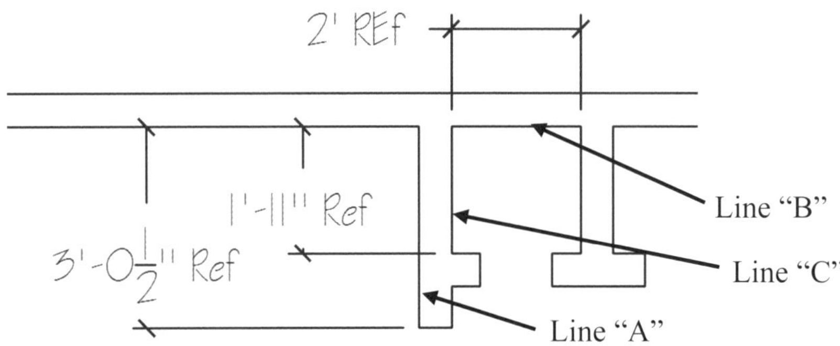

12a. Pick the Distance command from the Utilities Panel of the Home Tab

Enter an option [Distance/Radius/Angle/ARea/Volume] <Distance>: _distance
MEASUREGEOM *Specify first point:* ***(Pick one endpoint of line “A”)***
Specify second point or [Multiple points]: ***(Pick the other endpoint of line “A”)***
Distance = 3'-0 1/2", Angle in XY Plane = 90, Angle from XY Plane = 0
Delta X = 0'-0", Delta Y = -3'-0 1/2", Delta Z = 0'-0"
Enter an option [Distance/Radius/Angle/ARea/Volume/eXit] <Distance>:

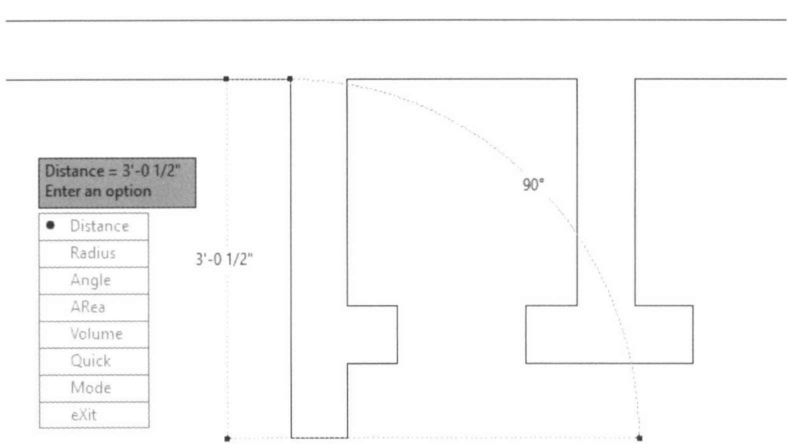

Note: You will see dimensions on your screen like this. The same info is displayed in your command line. Dynamic Input must be turned ON to see it on-screen.

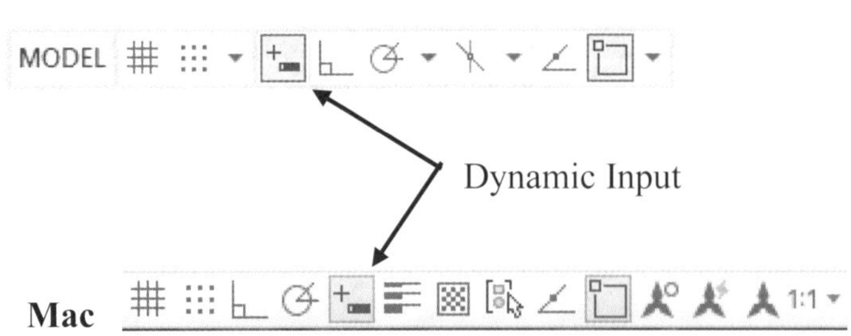

Mac

12b. Press the ↵ Enter key to repeat the Distance command

MEASUREGEOM *Specify first point:* ***(Pick an endpoint of line "B")***
Specify second point or [Multiple points]: ***(Pick the other endpoint of line "B")***
Distance = 2'-0", Angle in XY Plane = 0, Angle from XY Plane = 0
Delta X = 2'-0", Delta Y = 0'-0", Delta Z = 0'-0"
Enter an option [Distance/Radius/Angle/ARea/Volume/eXit] <Distance>:

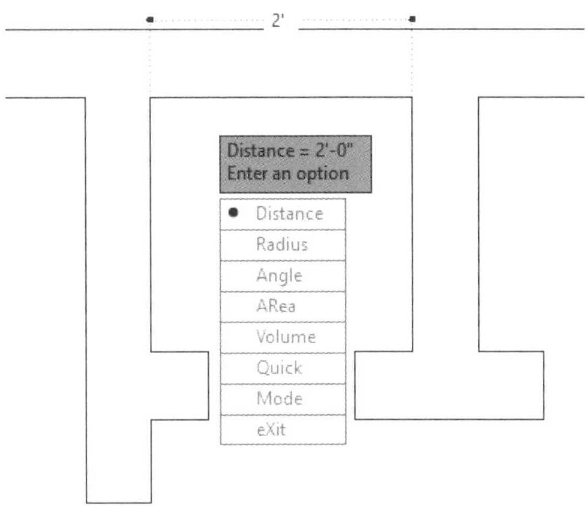

12c. Press the ↵ Enter key to repeat the Distance command

MEASUREGEOM *Specify first point:* ***(Pick and endpoint of line "C")***
Specify second point or [Multiple points]: ***(Pick the other endpoint of line "C")***
Distance = 1'-11", Angle in XY Plane = 90, Angle from XY Plane = 0
Delta X = 0'-0", Delta Y = -1'-11", Delta Z = 0'-0"
*Enter an option [Distance/Radius/Angle/ARea/Volume/eXit] <Distance>: *Cancel**
Press the Escape key to end the command

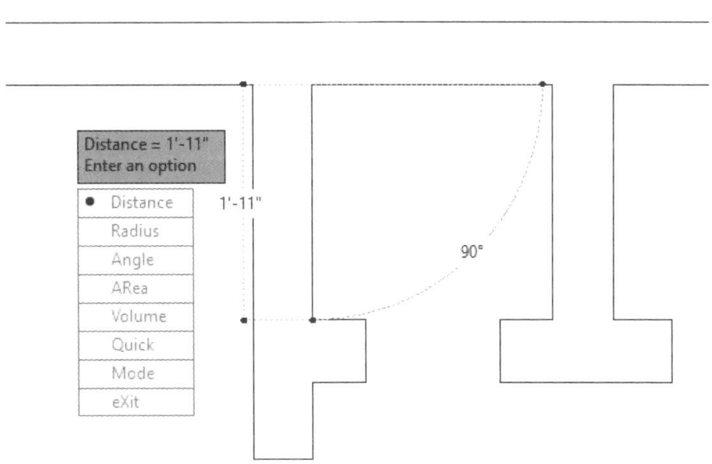

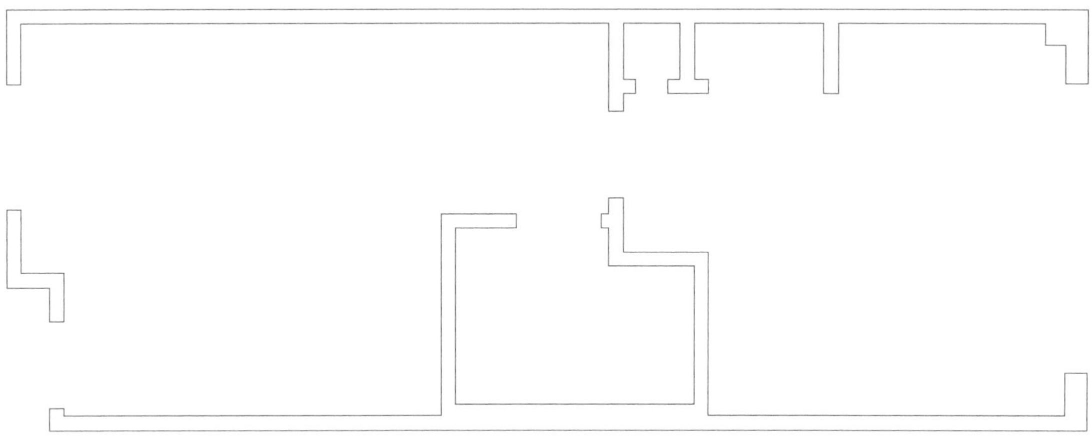

When you are done, your completed drawing will look like this

Create the Doors and Windows

The doors for this room are 1-3/4″ thick. There are three doors to the suite. We could create each door individually, but instead, we will take advantage of the Copy, Move, and Mirror commands.

The window glass is 1″ thick and is centered in the window opening. Let's complete the windows first since that is easier to do.

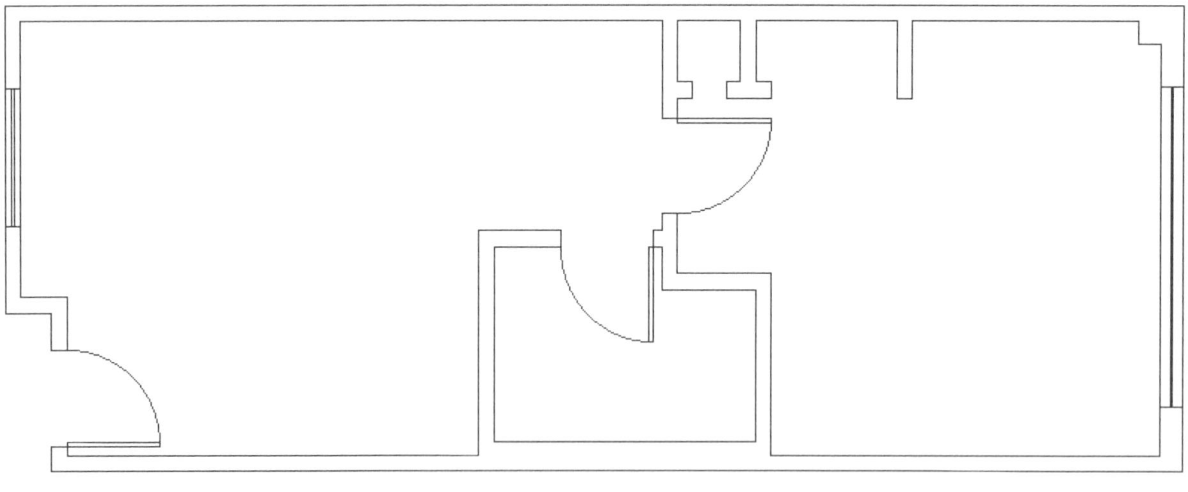

13. Create the left window

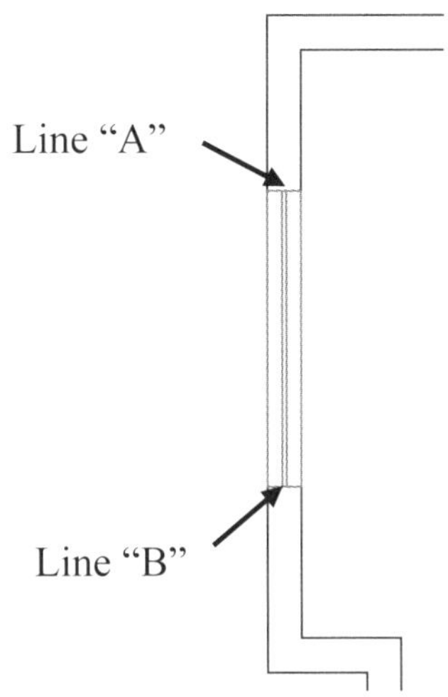

The window glass is 1″ thick and is centered in the window opening

13a. Change the Object Snap setting to ensure Midpoint is selected

13b. Use the Line command to create a line from the Midpoint of line "A" to the Midpoint of line "B"

13c. Offset the line created in step 13b 1/2″ in each direction

The window glass is 1″ thick centered in the opening. Offsetting half the thickness of the glass (in this case it is 1/2″) from the center of the window (which is what we created in step 13b) will give us the full thickness of the glass (1″).

13d. Erase the line created in step 13b

13e. Use the Line command to create 2 vertical lines – one at each endpoint of lines "A" and "B"

When you are done, your drawing should look like this

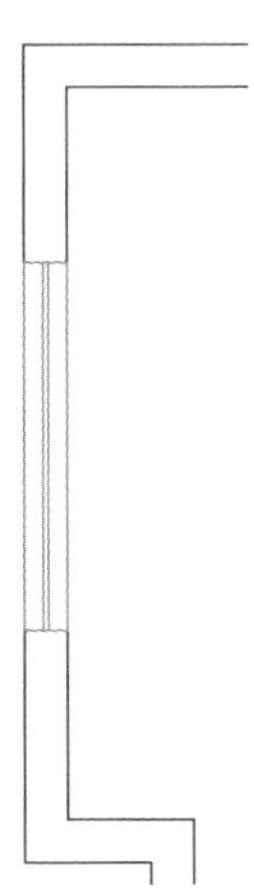

14. Create the right window

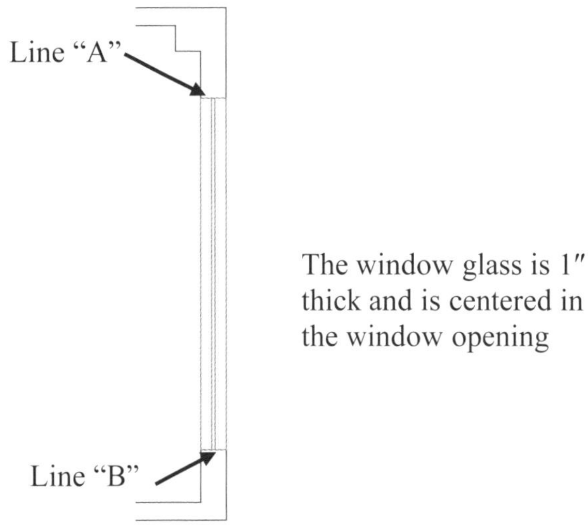

Creating this window is identical to creating the left window. Follow the steps used to create the left window to create this window.

15. Create the Entry Door

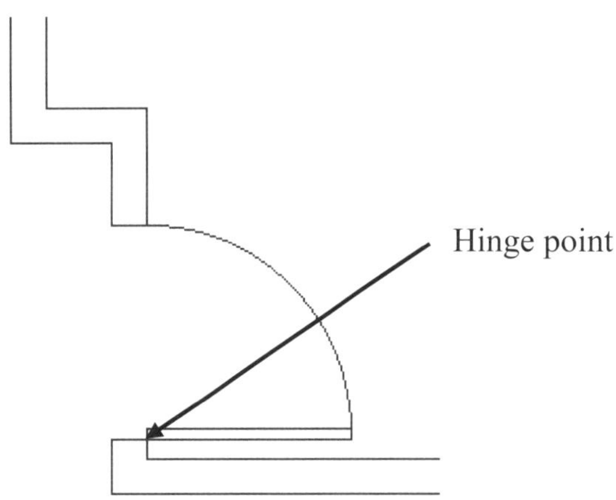

15a. Draw a 1-3/4″ x 3′ Rectangle starting at the hinge point. Pick the opposite corner to be towards the inside of the room

15b. Create a 3′ radius Circle centered on the hinge point

15c. Trim the circle to the rectangle and the corner point of the door opening

You have now completed the entry door. We will use this same door in the two remaining locations. Notice that the orientation is not identical to the entry door. We will use the Copy, Rotate, Mirror, and Move commands to complete the other doors.

16. Copy the entry door off to the side of your drawing

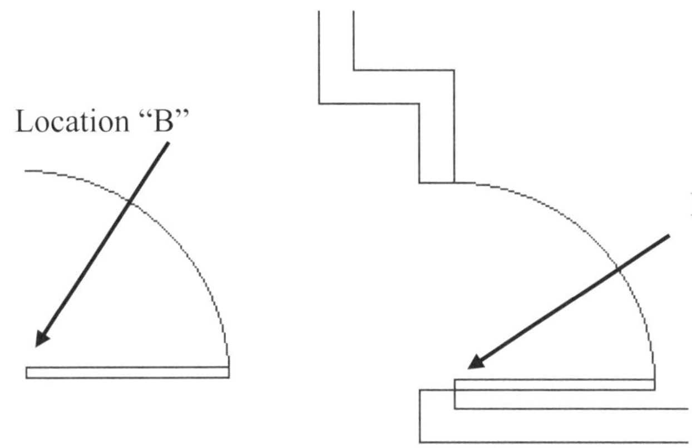

(Pick the Copy command)
COPY *Select objects:* ***(Pick the arc)****1 found*
Select objects: ***(Pick the rectangle)****1 found, 2 total*
Select objects: ↵
Current settings: Copy mode = Multiple
Specify base point or [Displacement/mOde] <Displacement>: ***(Pick a point near location "A")*** *Specify second point or <use first point as displacement>:* ***(Pick a point near location "B")***
Specify second point or [Exit/Undo] <Exit>:↵

17. Create a Mirror image of the copy you just made of the door and swing

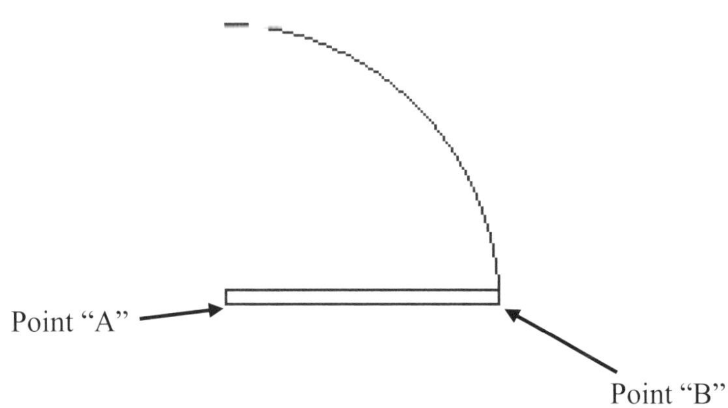

(Pick the Mirror command)
MIRROR *Select objects:* ***(Use a Selection Window to pick the door and swing objects)***
Specify opposite corner: 2 found
Select objects: ↵
Specify first point of mirror line: ***(Pick the line near point "A")***
Specify second point of mirror line: ***(Pick the line near point "B")***
Erase source objects? [Yes/No] <N>: **y**↵
(Type the letter "y" and press the ↵ Enter or pick *Yes* with your cursor)

When you are done, your drawing should look like this

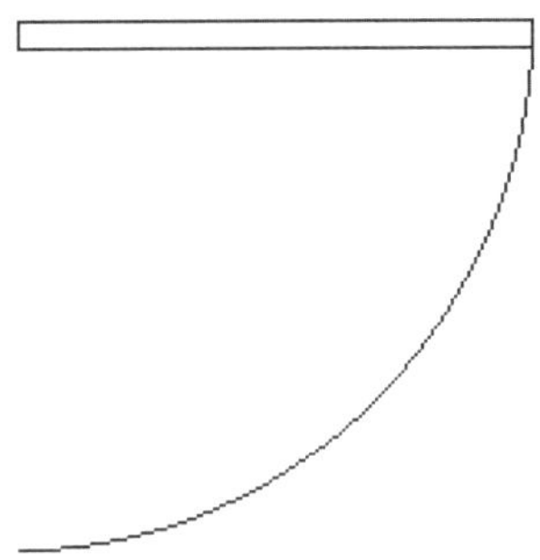

This door and swing orientation can be used for the bedroom door

18. Copy the new door and swing from step 17 to the bedroom location

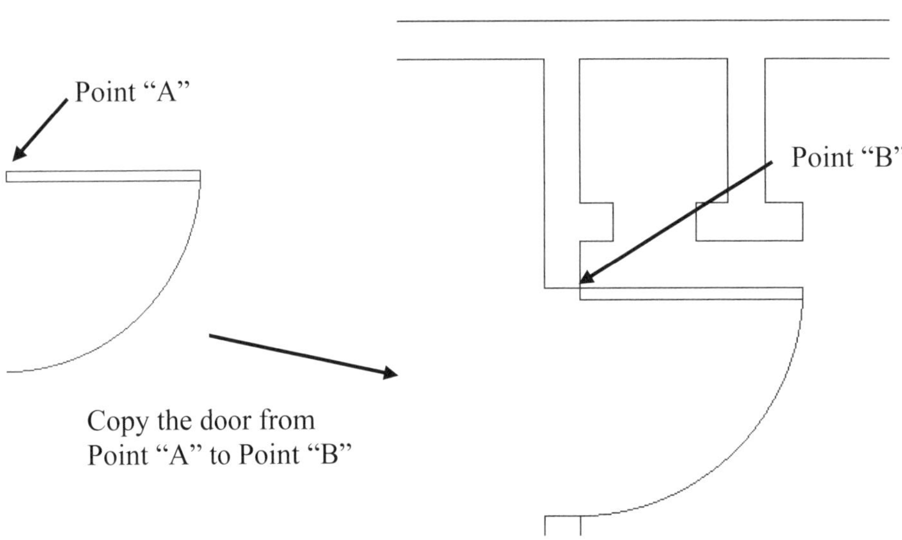

(Pick the Copy icon)
COPY *Select objects:* ***(Use a Selection Window to pick the door and swing objects)***
Specify opposite corner: 2 found
Select objects: ↵
Current settings: Copy mode = Multiple
Specify base point or [Displacement/mOde] <Displacement>: ***(Pick point "A")***
Specify second point or <use first point as displacement>: ***(Pick point "B")***
Specify second point or [Exit/Undo] <Exit>: ↵

Because we used the Copy command, we still have the door and swing off to the side of our drawing. We will now change the orientation so that it can be used for the bathroom.

19. Rotate the door and swing to get it in the correct orientation for the bathroom

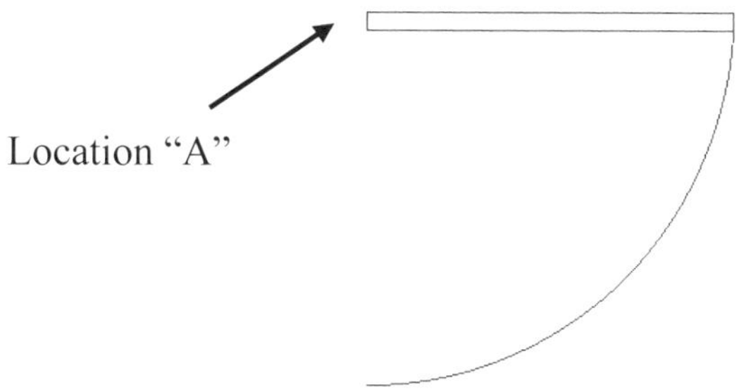

(Pick the Rotate icon)
Current positive angle in UCS: ANGDIR=counterclockwise ANGBASE=0
ROTATE *Select objects:* ***(Use a Selection Window to pick the door and swing objects)***
Specify opposite corner: 2 found
Select objects: ↵
Specify base point: ***(Pick a point near location “A”)***
Specify rotation angle or [Copy/Reference] <0>: **-90**↵

When you are done, your drawing should look like this

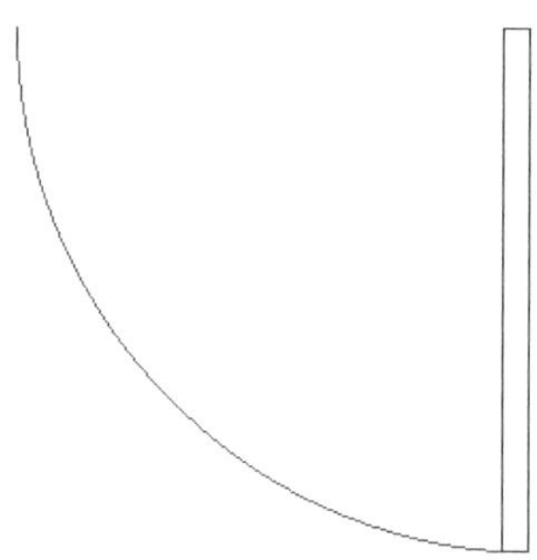

This door and swing orientation can be used for the bathroom door

20. Move the door and swing to the bathroom location

Move the door from Point “A” to Point “B”

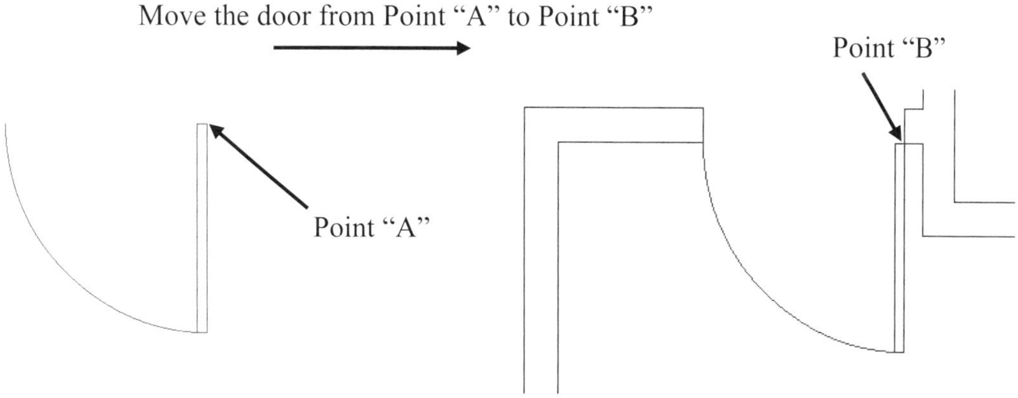

Congratulations! You have now completed the floor plan walls, doors, and windows for the hotel suite.

When you are done, your completed drawing will look like this:

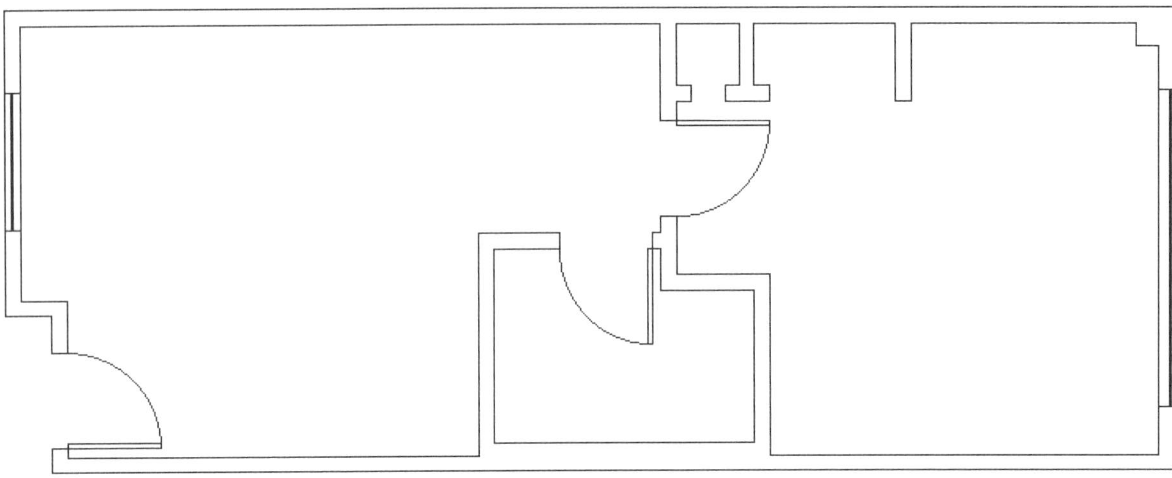

Remember to Save your drawing. We will continue building the Hotel Suite in the next Tutorial.

Chapter 7

Commands – Set 3: Laying-out Your Drawing for Printing

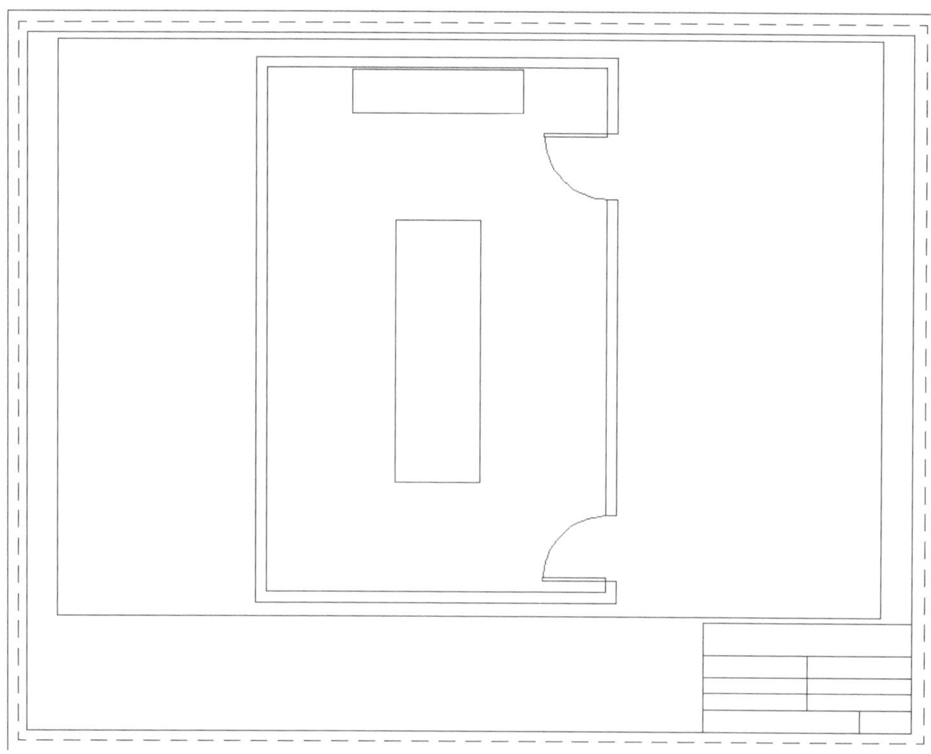

Learning Objectives:

- **Understand the difference between Model Space and Paper Space**
- **Creating Viewports on your Layout to see your Model Space objects**
- **Changing the size and location of the Viewport on your Layout**
- **Setting and Locking the Scale of the Viewport**
- **Setting up and Plotting from Paper Space**
- **Renaming, adding, and deleting Layout tabs**

Downloading Files from Publisher

There are several files available on the publisher's website that can be downloaded. Some of the files will be referenced in this text. Go to www.sdcpublications.com and select the Authors tab. Search for Muccio, Dean and click the hyperlink. Select the Books tab. Click on the book version you are using. Select the Downloads tab and then click on the Download File button. Files will appear in your Downloads folder. These may show up within a zipped folder. If so, extract all the files from the zipped folder.

Model Space & Paper Space

Model Space

All the drawing work we have been doing so far has been in the Model tab and the space we have been drawing in is called Model Space. In Model Space, the designer creates the objects full scale.

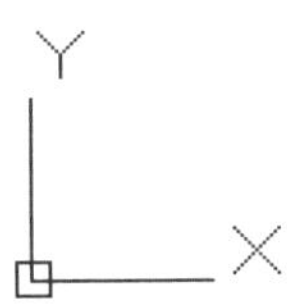

The UCS icon for Model Space is an X-Y axis

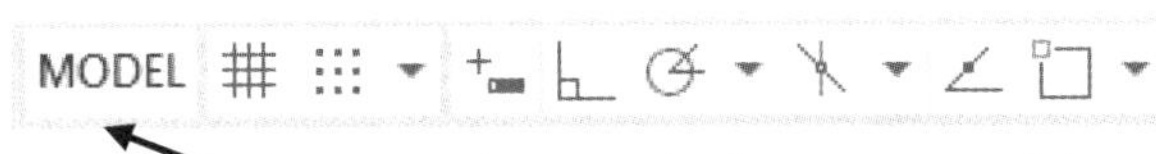

The status bar on the lower part of the screen shows the word MODEL to signify that you are working in Model Space.

On the Mac, it is an icon.

Mac

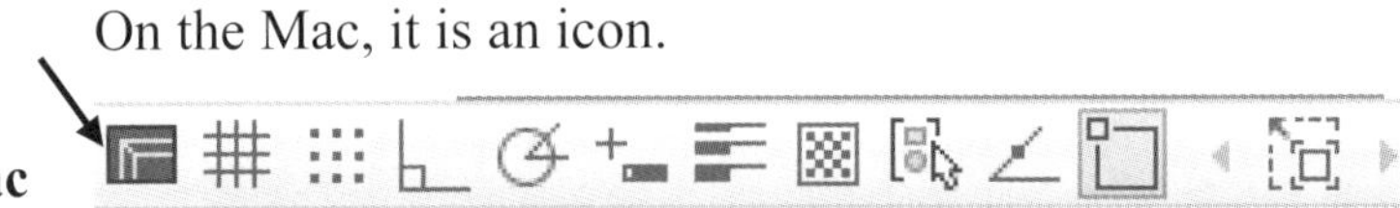

Since we need to convey the drawing to the client on a standard format and to scale, typically used is ¼″ =1′, AutoCAD allows you to do that in a Layout by using what is known as Paper Space.

On the bottom left of the AutoCAD drawing screen there are several tabs. The left-most tab is the Model tab. This is where we have been creating our objects. The other tabs are the Layout tabs. The Layout tabs are where we use Paper Space to create a finished layout of a drawing for printing.

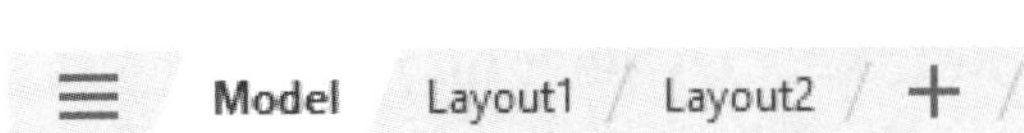

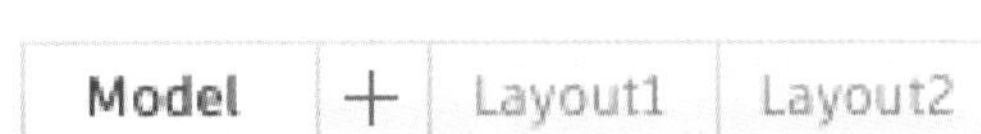

Mac

Paper Space

Paper Space can be accessed only by using a Layout. You cannot work in Paper Space on the Model tab. Paper Space is used for items such as a drawing border, title block, drawing notes, schedules, and to display different views of the model. Paper Space is scaled 1:1 to the paper you print on. As an example, if you use ¼″ high text characters in Paper Space, when you print it out, they will measure ¼″ in height.

The UCS icon for Paper Space is a triangle.

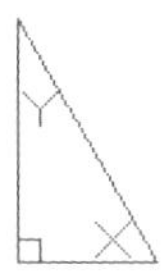

The status bar shows the word PAPER to signify that you are working in Paper Space. Clicking this icon will toggle to Model Space.

The Paper Space icon is displayed on the status bar to signify that you are working in Paper Space. Clicking this icon will toggle to Model Space.

Mac

Viewports

Viewports are used to view specific areas of the model. You can think of viewports as windows that show different views of the model. Viewports can be different sizes and shapes. The default shape is rectangular. The shape of the viewport on some of the drawing templates is a polygon (AutoCAD calls this a Polyline).

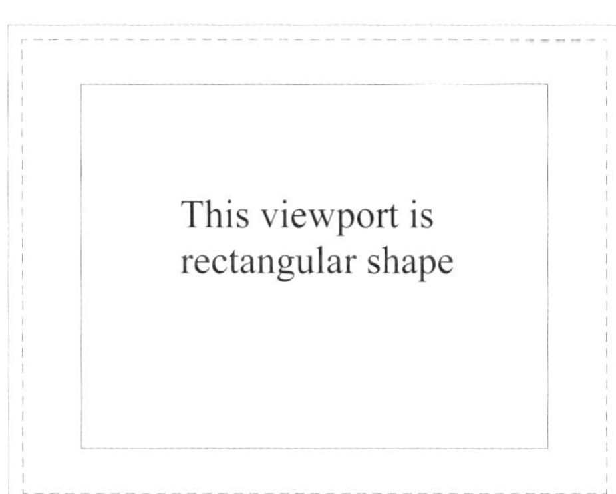

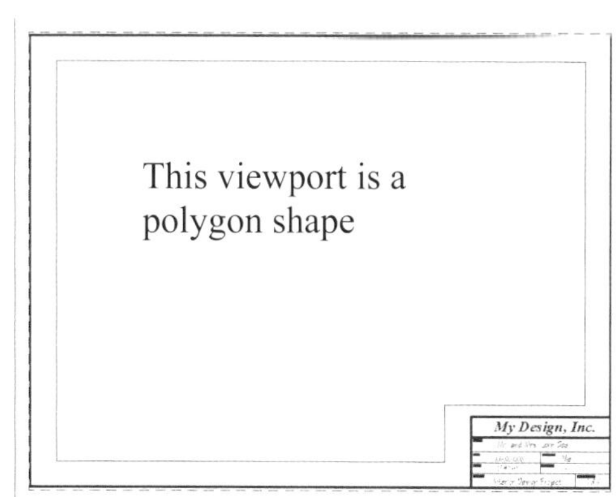

The border that defines the viewport is a Paper Space object, and can be on its own layer, have its own color, and it can be erased, re-sized, or moved just like any rectangle or polygon can.

A Layout can have more than one viewport. As an example of multiple viewports, open the file *Conference Room.dwg* that was downloaded from the publisher's website. Pick the Viewport Example Layout tab. It shows two viewports, one showing the chair, and the other showing the plant. The objects were created in Model Space in different locations on the drawing space. The viewports allow you to look at the model objects – which can be positioned in the viewport using Pan and Zoom.

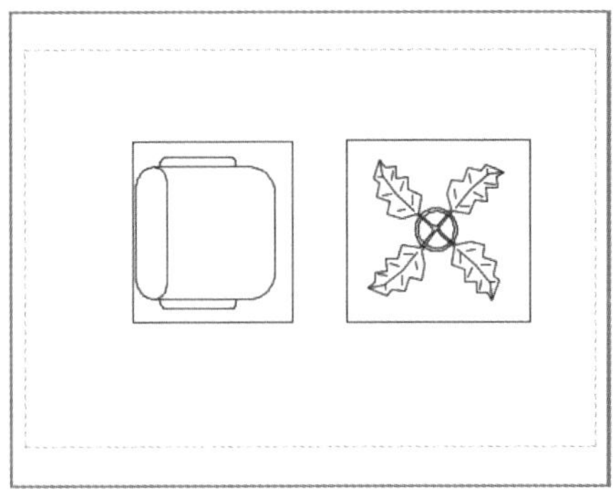

Viewports Tool

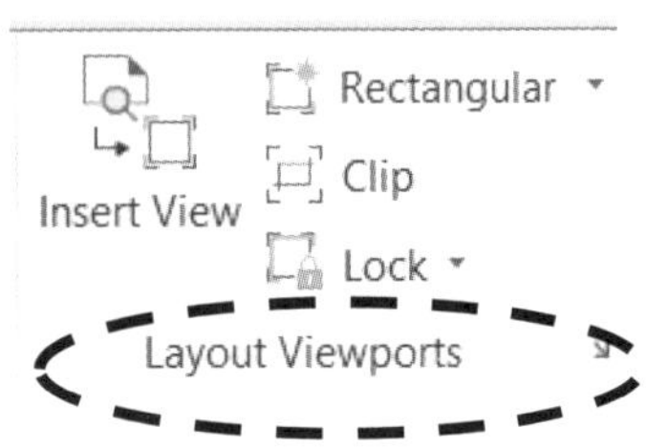

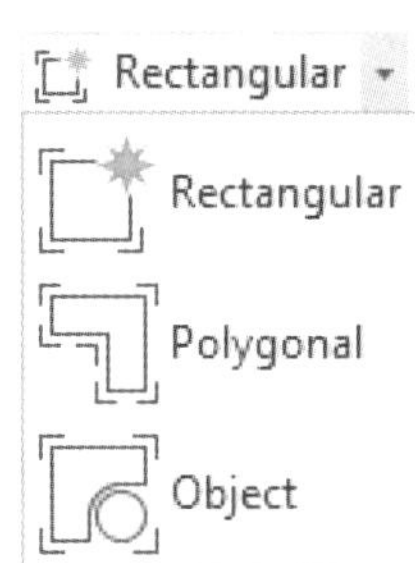

The icon is a fly-out style. The last used icon in the list will appear at the top of the list.

The Viewports tool allows you to easily create additional viewports. You can create a single viewport by selecting the Rectangular viewport icon located on the Layout Viewports Panel of the Layout Tab. The Viewport tool is only active when you are in a Layout tab.

For the Mac, use the pull-down menu View, select Viewports, then select 1 Viewport:

Mac

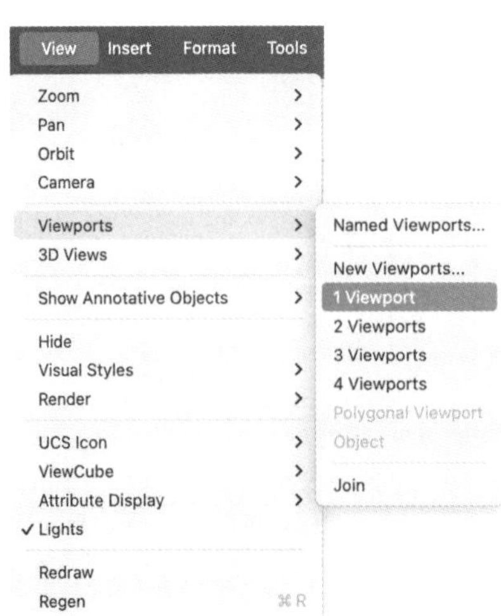

Once selected, the command line prompts you with the following:

-VPORTS *Specify corner of viewport or*
[ON/OFF/Fit/Shadeplot/Lock/Object/Polygonal/Restore/Layer/2/3/4] <Fit>:

For a simple rectangular shaped viewport, simply specify opposite corners on the Layout.

As an example, let's start with the single view drawing of the chair. Pick the "Try It" Layout to find the following:

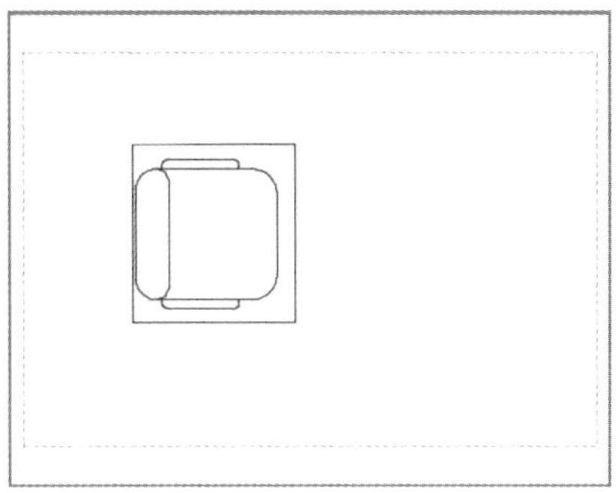

To create a second viewport, use the Rectangular Viewport icon (on the Mac, use the pull-down menu View, select Viewports, then select 1 Viewport), and select two opposite corners to define a second rectangular viewport to the right of the existing viewport:

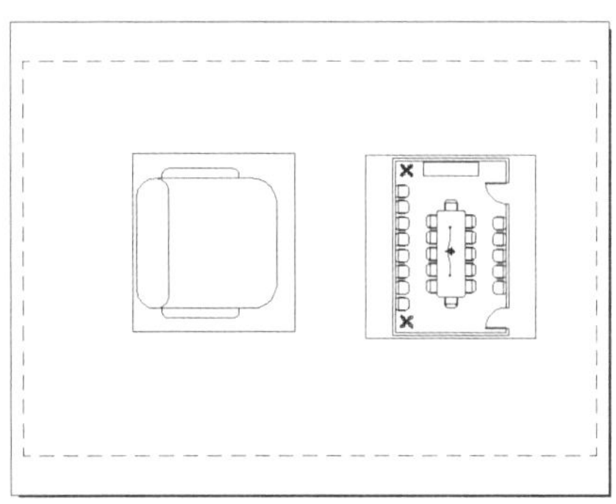

To make a viewport active, double-left-click inside it. Use Ctrl-R to toggle between viewports.

Notice that the new viewport does not show the objects of the model the way that we want it. We can now switch to Model Space by selecting the PAPER button on the status bar, so that it becomes a MODEL button. This will activate the viewport. Alternatively, you can double-left-click in the viewport to make it active.

To switch back to Paper Space, select the MODEL button on the status bar so that it becomes a PAPER button. Alternatively, you can double-left-click an empty area on the layout outside of the viewport to switch back to Paper Space.

Only one viewport can be active at a time. If the active viewport is not the one you just created, you can use Ctrl-R to toggle to this viewport and make it active.

Use the wheel mouse to Pan and Zoom to find the plant. Change the scale by using the scale on the status bar. Select a scale of 1-1/2″ = 1′.

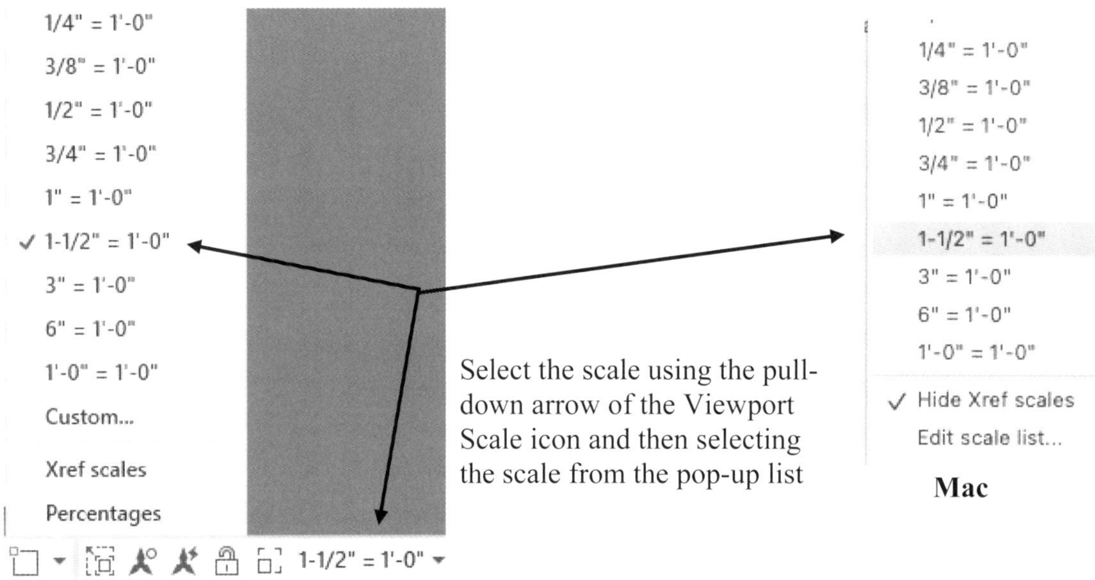

Select the scale using the pull-down arrow of the Viewport Scale icon and then selecting the scale from the pop-up list

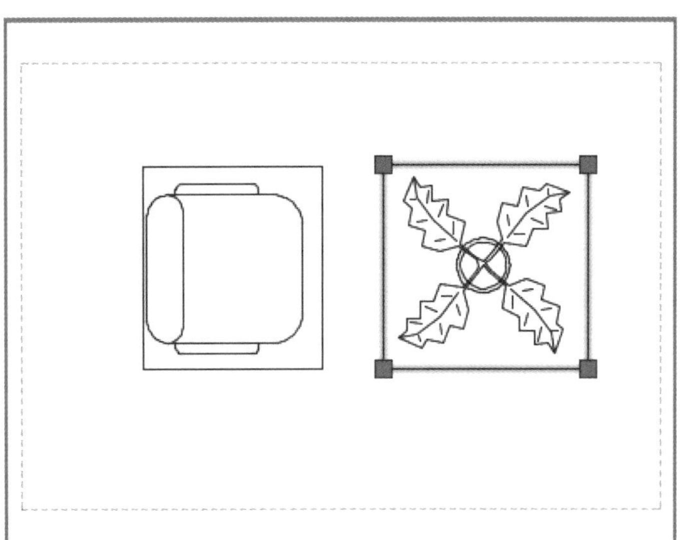

After you get the scale set, you may still have objects in the viewport that are visible that you don't want. You can re-size the viewport (in Paper Space) to show only the objects you want by using Grips.

Re-Sizing a Viewport

We had discussed Grips (those little blue squares) in a previous chapter, and we chose to use the Escape key to get rid of them. Re-sizing a Viewport is a situation where Grips come in handy. When you are in Paper Space with no active command in the Command line, pick the viewport border. The Grips will appear at each corner of the viewport. You can pick and drag a Grip and the size of the Viewport will change. It may be best to turn the OSNAP off to do this.

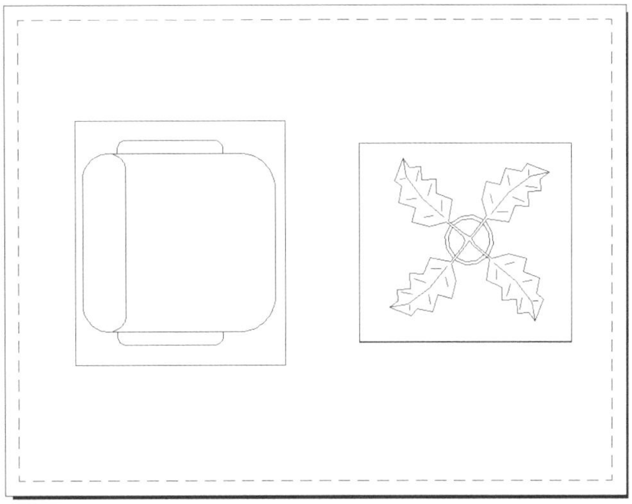

After re-sizing, the extra lines are eliminated from the view of the plant while maintaining the Viewport Scale.

Access Model Space while in a Layout

Although we have been working on our model using the Model tab, we can also work on our model in the Layout tab, as long as at least one viewport is created. While in the Layout tab, pick the PAPER button on the status bar, or double-left-click in the viewport. The text on the button will become MODEL, the UCS icon will change from a triangle to an X-Y axis, the cursor crosshairs are only visible in the active viewport, and the viewport border will thicken or highlight.

If you have more than one viewport, only one viewport border will thicken/highlight. This signifies that it is the active or current viewport. You can make a different viewport active/current by clicking in it or by holding the Ctrl key and the letter R simultaneously (Ctrl-R). Using Ctrl-R allows you to toggle between viewports.

Once the viewport is active, you can create or modify the Model Space objects, and you can Pan or Zoom to make the objects fit the viewport better.

To return to Paper Space, you can double-left-click an empty area on the layout outside a viewport. The changes you made are displayed in the viewport.

Create and Modify Model Space Objects in a Layout

Creating or modifying Model Space objects in the Layout is best done by using the Maximize Viewport button on the status bar. The maximized layout viewport expands to fill the drawing area. The center point and the layer visibility settings of the viewport are retained, and the surrounding objects are displayed.

Once you maximize the viewport, the button changes to a Minimize Viewport button. 

You can pan and zoom while you are working in Model Space, but when you restore the viewport (using the Minimize Viewport button) to return to Paper Space, the position and scale of the objects in the layout viewport are restored.

Adjust the Position and Scale of Model Space Objects in a Viewport

If you plan to adjust the position of Model Space objects within the viewport, first activate the viewport and then use the wheel mouse to Pan. The viewport border becomes thicker, and the crosshair cursor is visible in the current viewport only. All other viewports in the layout remain visible while you work.

To accurately and consistently scale each displayed view in the plotted drawing, set the scale of each viewport. You can change the view scale of the viewport using the Viewport Scale button on the Status bar. The viewport must be active before you can do this.

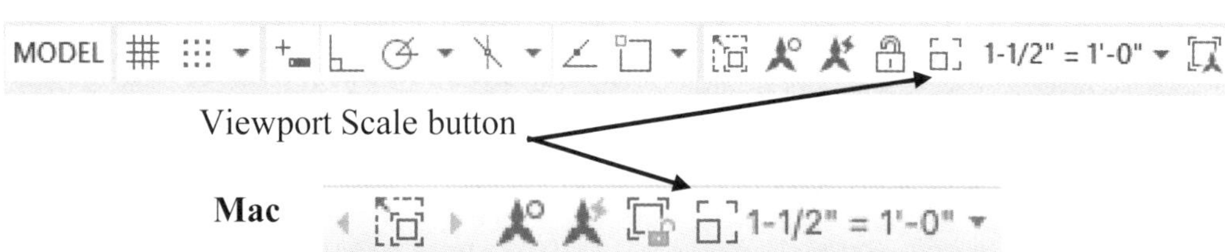

When you work in a layout, the scale factor represents a ratio between the actual size of the model displayed in the viewports and the size of the layout. Changing the scale factor can be done while in Model Space by using the Viewport Scale button. As an example, the Conference Room drawing is scaled at ¼″ =1′. This is a standard scale that was set by using the pull-down arrow on the Viewport Scale button.

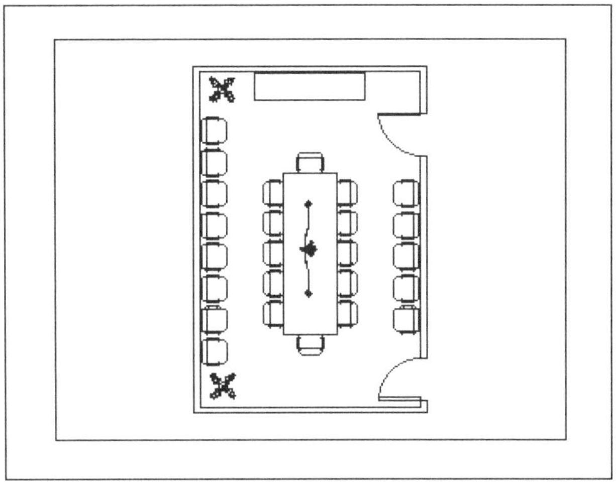

Conference Room shown at a scale of 1/4” = 1’

Note that scaling or stretching the layout viewport border, while in Paper Space, does not change the scale of the view of the model within the viewport.

Lock the Scale of Layout Viewports

Once you've set the viewport scale, if you zoom in (while still in Model Space) within the viewport, you will be changing the viewport scale at the same time. By locking the viewport scale first, you can zoom in to view different levels of detail in your viewport without altering the viewport scale.

When the scale is locked, the ZOOM command will enlarge/minimize the entire layout, not just the model within the viewport.

Scale locking will lock the scale that you set for the selected viewport. Once the scale is locked, you can continue to modify the objects in the viewport without affecting the viewport.

To lock the Viewport scale, pick the Lock/Unlock Viewport icon on the status bar:

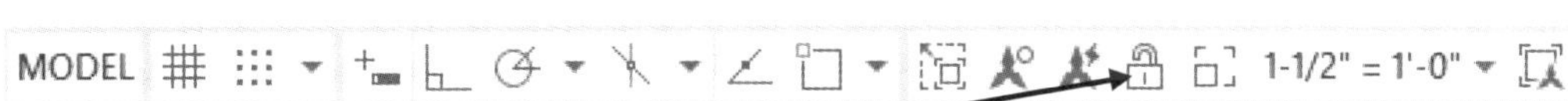

Viewport Scale Lock/Unlock icon

Mac

Once selected, the icon now appears as a closed padlock:  **Mac** 

Plotting from Paper Space

Paper Space was created to allow you to set up your drawing, which was done in real world size, for printing on selected size of paper. The paper size can be chosen from multiple standard sizes.

Plot, Plot Preview and Page Setup can be found under the Application Menu Browser

Mac

Print and Page Setup Manager can be found by using the File pull-down

If a printer or plotter is not selected for the layout, selecting Plot Preview from Application Menu Browser will result in the following message above the active command line:

Command: _PREVIEW No plotter is assigned. Use Page Setup to assign a plotter to the current Layout.

Both paper size and assigning a printer/plotter are chosen from the Page Setup Manager.

Page Setup Manager

The Page Setup Manager can be found under the Application Menu Browser and the icon can be found under the Layout Panel of the Layout Tab.

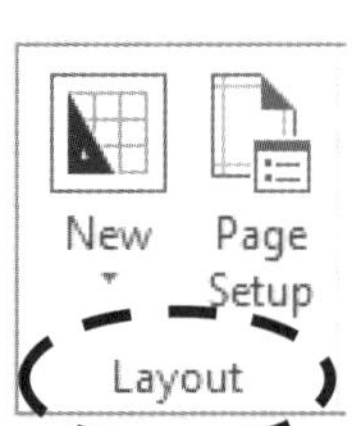

Page Setup icon

For the Mac, use the File pull-down menu and select Page Setup Manager.
When you select Page Setup the Page Setup Manager dialog box appears. Pick the Modify button. On the Mac, pick the tool to Edit.

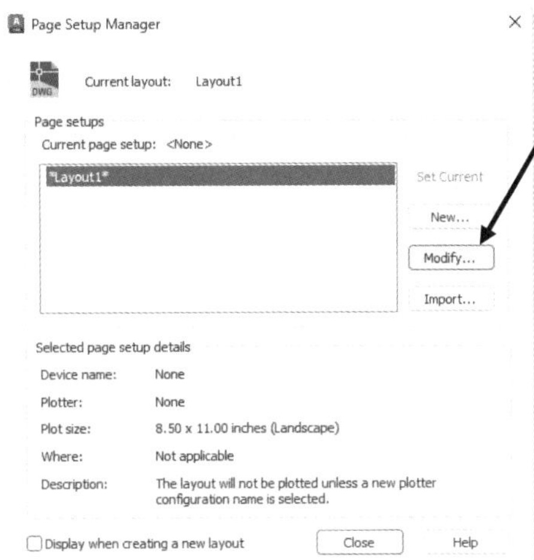

Pick the Modify button to set up the layout for printing/plotting

Mac

Pick the tool to Edit

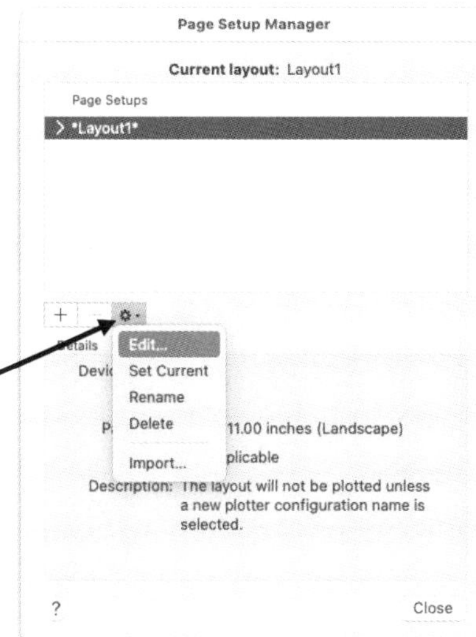

The Page Setup dialog box for the current layout will appear.

Select the Printer/plotter here

Select the paper size here

Choose the orientation here

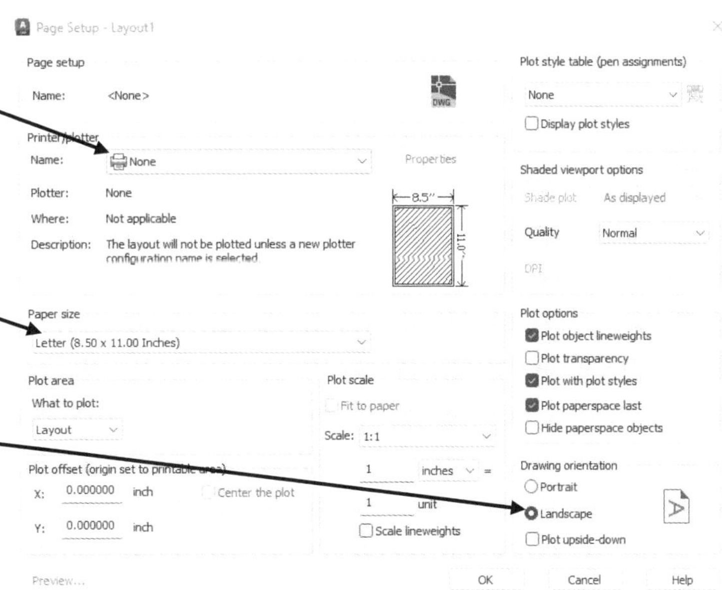

Select the Printer/plotter here

Select the paper size here

Choose the orientation here

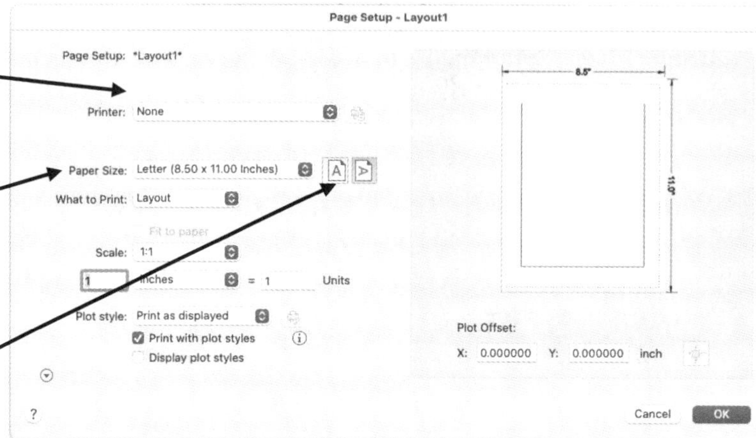

Mac

Use the pull-down arrow to select the printer you plan to use.

The choices of Printers/plotters that are available depend on what is loaded on your computer.

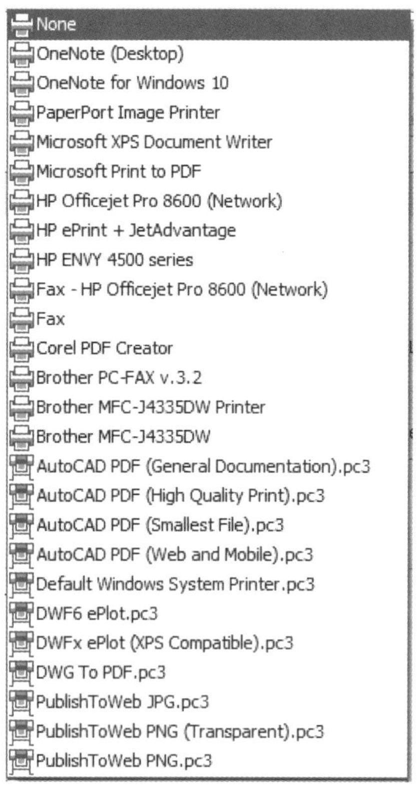

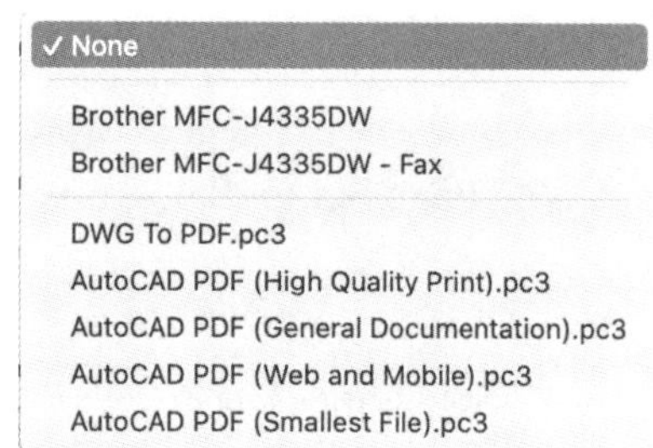

Mac

Use the pull-down arrow in the Paper size section of the dialog box to select the size of the paper to print. This will also change the size of the Layout drawing area to match.

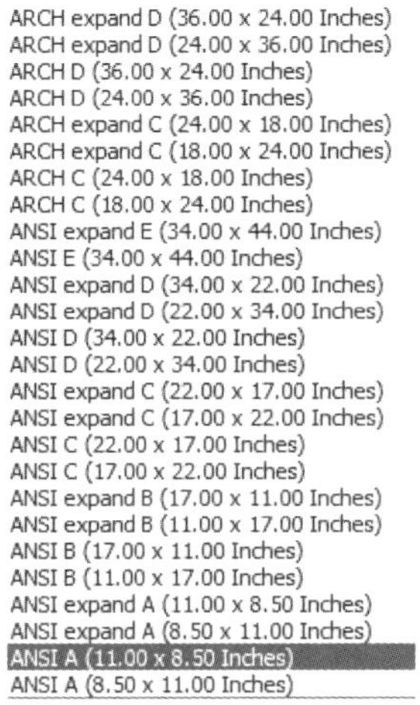

This is a partial listing of the sizes

The list of paper sizes depends on the printer/plotter selected

Mac

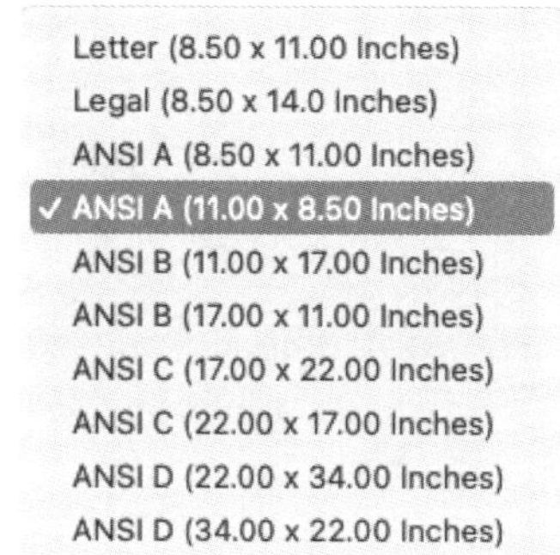

For this example, the DWG To PDF is chosen. This will create a Portable Data File (PDF) which can be viewed on any computer that has a PDF reader. If you do not have a PDF reader on your computer, you can download a free PDF reader from the Internet.

Once a Printer/plotter has been selected, the Preview button is now active. You can preview what the drawing will look like before you print it by selecting the Preview button.

To preview on the Mac, pick OK to close the Page Setup dialog box, then pick Close to exit the Page Setup Manager. Use the File pull-down menu to select Print… and the Plot dialog box will appear. Use the Preview button available in this dialog box.

Some printers have a limited print area. Although they can print on standard size paper, the actual area available for printing varies by each printer model. The actual print area will likely be smaller than the entire sheet. Adjustments can be made to your layout border in Paper Space, and additional adjustments can be made by changing the X-Y values in the Plot offset portion of the dialog box.

Additional adjustments can be made to fit your Plotter/printer by changing the X-Y values here

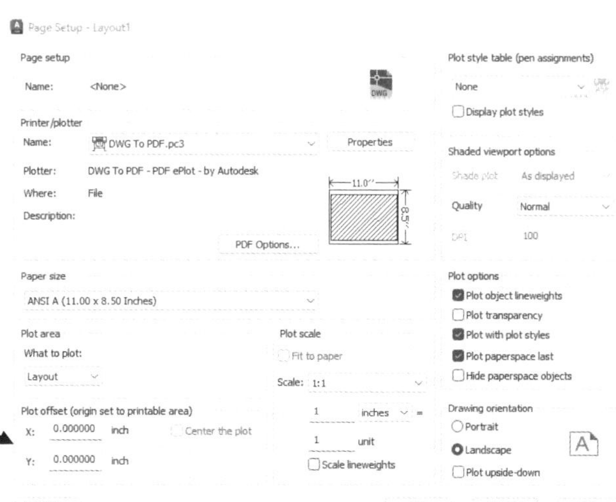

Use the Preview button to ensure satisfactory results before printing on paper

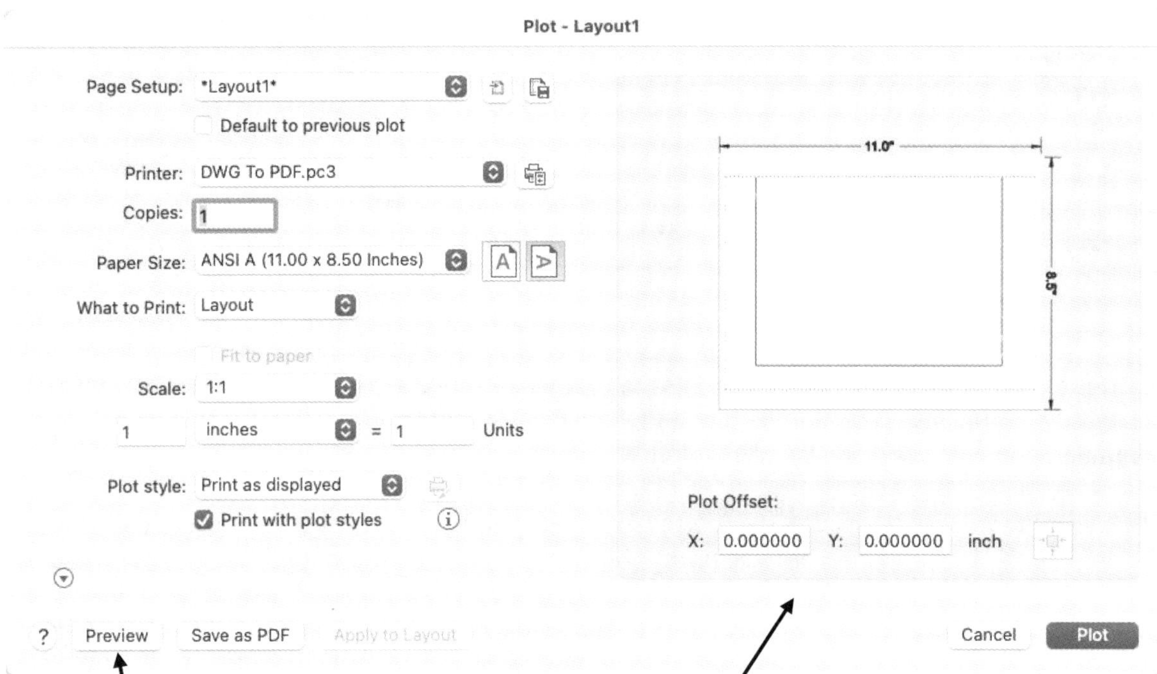

Mac

Use the Preview button to ensure satisfactory results before printing on paper

Additional adjustments can be made to fit your Plotter/printer by changing the X-Y values here

Once you select the Preview button, a preview of the drawing will appear. To return to the Page Setup dialog box, press the Escape key or the ↲ Enter key (on the Mac, use the Close button on the upper left side of the preview screen). When you are satisfied with the setup, press the OK button to exit the dialog box. Press the Close button to exit the Page Setup Manager dialog box.

Plotting/Printing Your Drawing

Use the Application Menu Browser to select Print (or Plot under the sub-menu of Print).

A Plot dialog box will appear. Additional plotting changes can be made here prior to Printing/plotting. Many choices are similar to the Plot Manager dialog box.

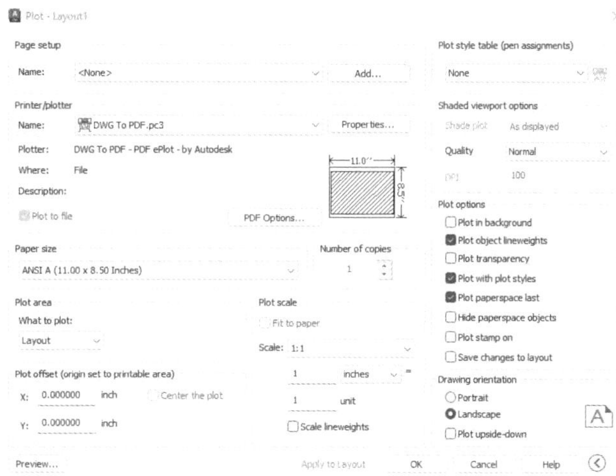

Pick the OK button (Plot button on Mac) to send the drawing to the Printer/plotter. A message balloon will appear on the lower right side of the screen (lower left for Mac) that indicates that plotting was successful.

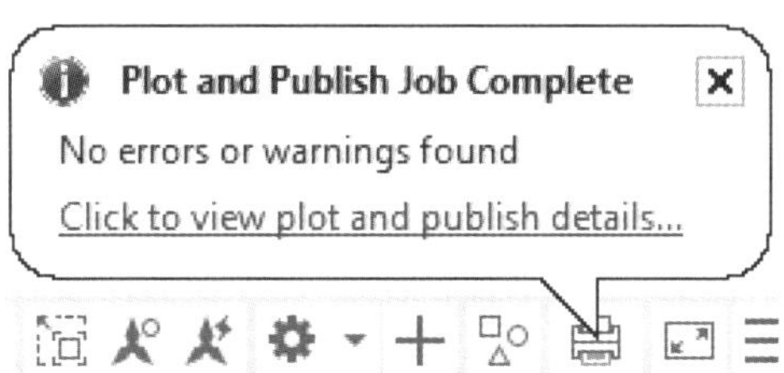

Mac

Model & Layout Tabs

Initial AutoCAD drawings have three tabs displayed at the bottom left of the screen as follows:

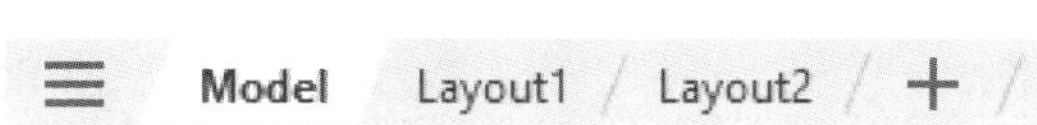

Mac

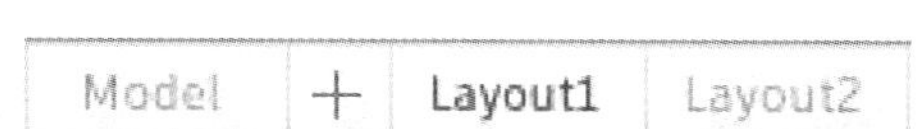

The Model tab is the one that AutoCAD defaults to. It is for Model Space objects and is the one that we have been doing all of our drawing work in. The Layout tabs display the Paper Space.

Renaming a Layout

The Layout tabs can be renamed for your convenience. A typical name that you may find would be Sheet 1 or Sheet 2, etc. Or, you could name them Floor Plan, Elevation, etc. It is up to you. The Model tab cannot be renamed.

To rename the Layout, use the following instructions:

Right-Click on the tab that you wish to rename. A dialog box of choices appears. Select Rename.

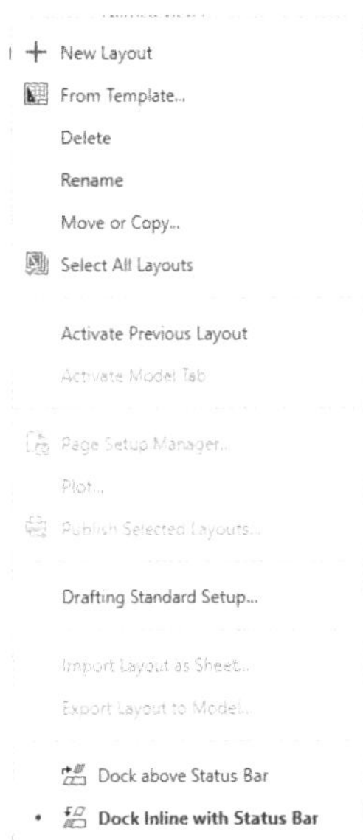

Mac

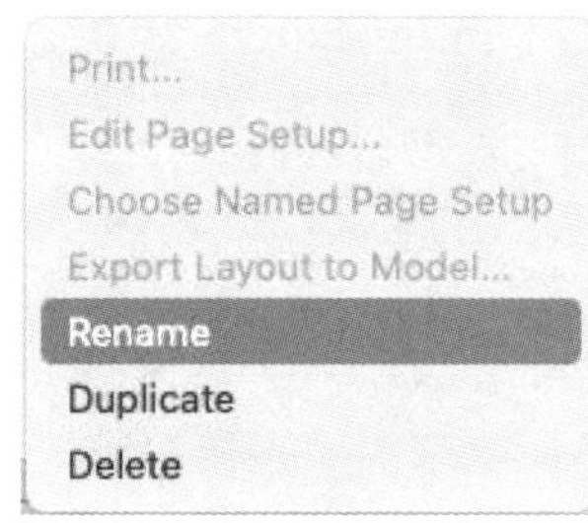

The current layout name highlights and is ready for editing. For this example, let's assume you wish to name this Sheet 1. Type Sheet 1 for the new name.

Mac

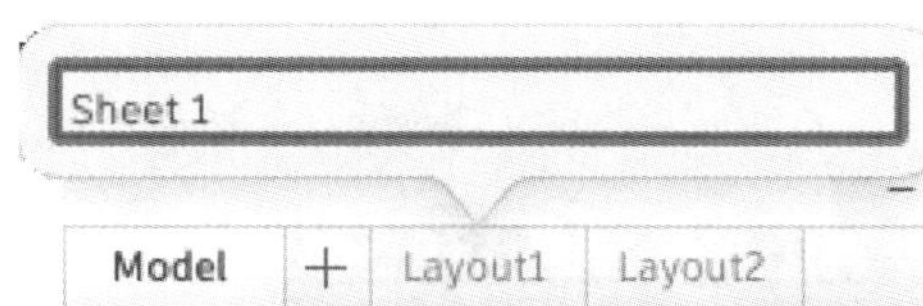

Notice that the tab has been renamed to the new name that you typed in.

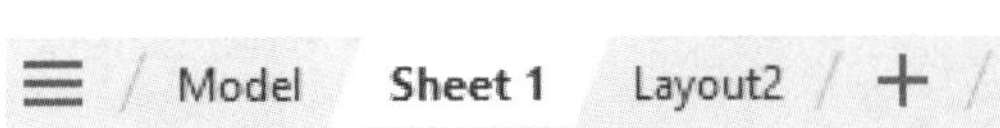

Mac

Renaming Layouts for Mac

Pick the Show Drawings & Layouts icon on the top left of the screen:

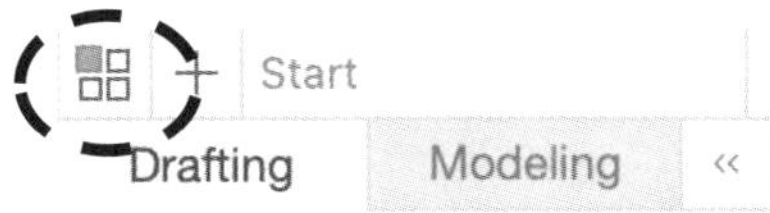

The QUICKVIEW command is entered in the command line and a preview of the Model and Layouts appears:

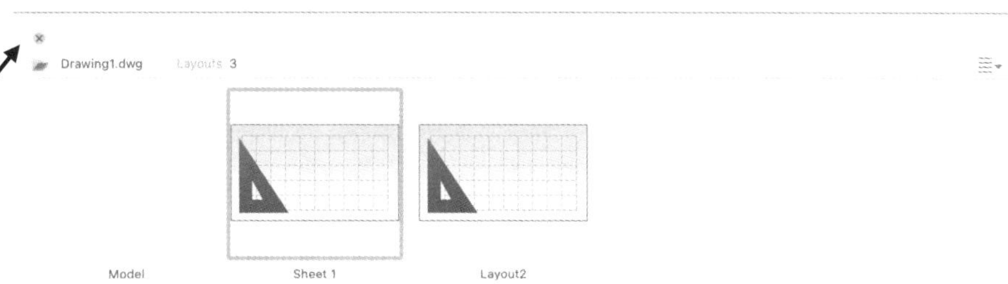

Picking the Close button will close the QUICKVIEW

Right-click on the Layout you want to rename. Select Rename.

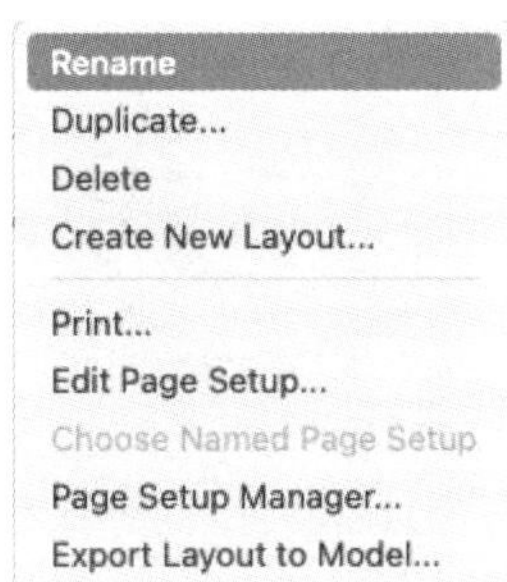

The layout name is highlighted for editing. For this example, let's assume you wish to name Layout2 as Sheet 2. Type Sheet 2 for the new name and press the ↵ Enter key. Close the QUICKVIEW by picking the close button on the upper left.

The Layout has been renamed to the new name that you typed in.

Adding a Layout

Let's assume that you already have Sheet 1 and Sheet 2 for named layouts:

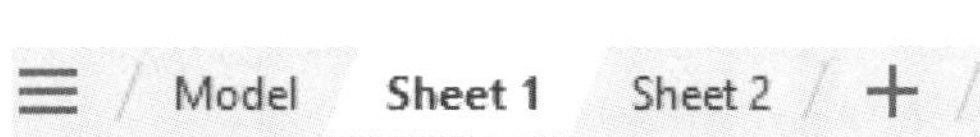

If you have a drawing that requires more than two sheets, you may wish to add another. To do that, you can click on the "+" button. However, if you want the same Paper Space objects, such as a drawing format, use the following instructions (Mac users, see the next section for instructions):

Right-Click on the Sheet 2 tab to bring up the dialog box. Pick Move or Copy… from the choices you are given.

The Move or Copy dialog box appears. Pick the (move to end) choice and put a check mark in the Create a copy check-box.

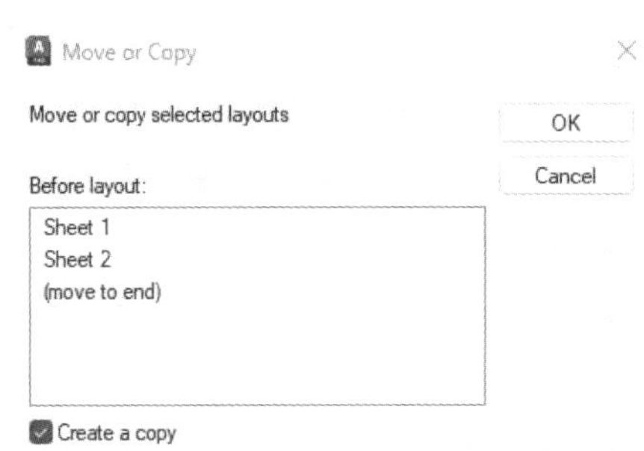

A copy of Sheet 2 is created and added to the end of the layout tab listing. AutoCAD automatically assigns the name of Sheet 2 (2) for this new layout tab.

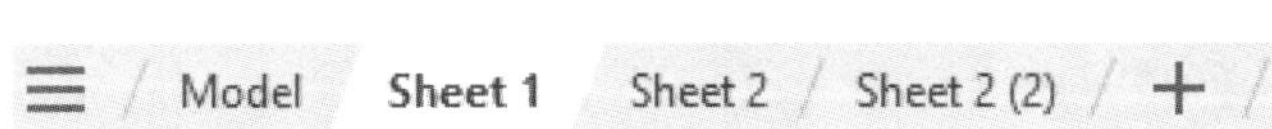

Rename this new tab to Sheet 3 using the same technique as described above for renaming layout tabs.

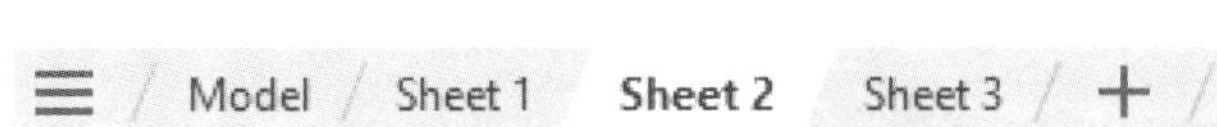

Adding a Layout for Mac

Let's assume that you already have Sheet 1 and Sheet 2 for named layouts:

If you have a drawing that requires more than two sheets, you may wish to add another layout. To do that, use the following instructions:

Pick the Show Drawings & Layouts icon on the top left of the screen to bring up the Quickview.

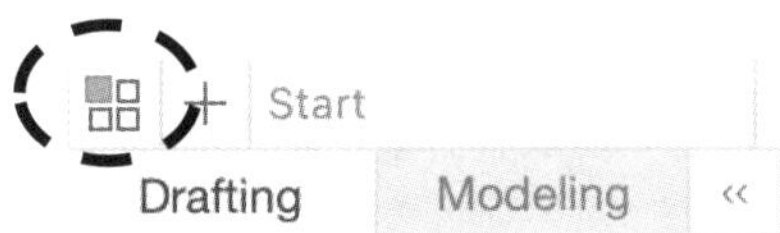

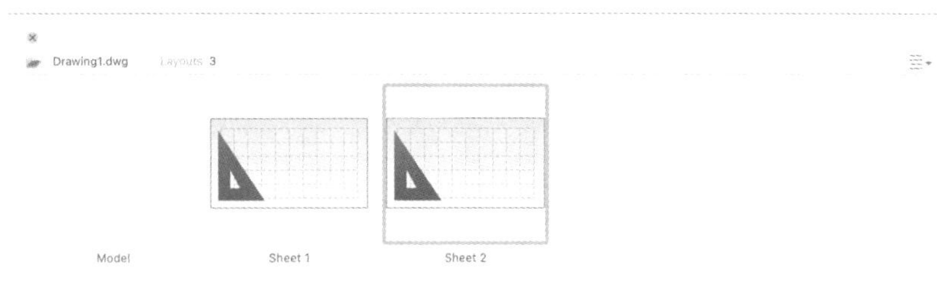

Make a duplicate of Sheet 2 in the Quickview

Right-click on the Layout you want to duplicate. In this example, Sheet 2 was selected. The mini-menu of choices will appear. Select Duplicate.

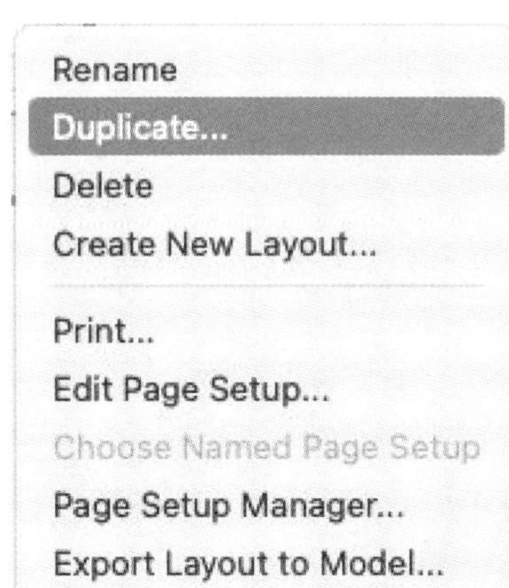

A dialog box will appear and is waiting for you to edit a new name for the new layout.

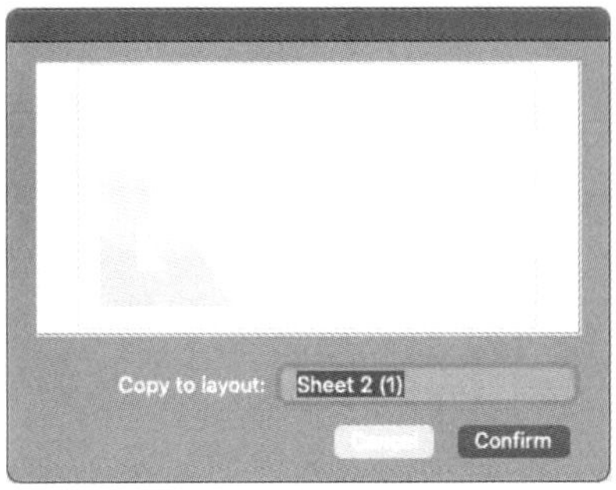

Name the new layout Sheet 3 and pick the Confirm button. Close the Quickview.

You now have 3 layouts:

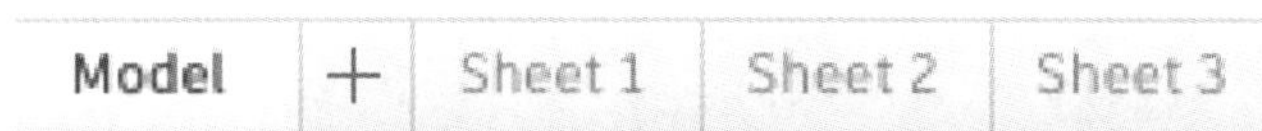

Add Layout from Template

If you want to use a standard template for your layout, or one that you created, you can add a layout tab that way as well. Mac users, see the next section for instructions.

Right-Click on a layout tab to bring up the dialog box. Pick From template…

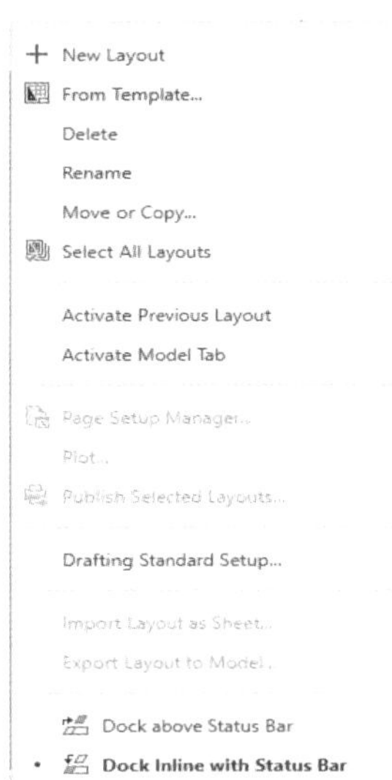

The Select Template From File dialog box appears. Pick the Tutorial-iArch template and pick Open:

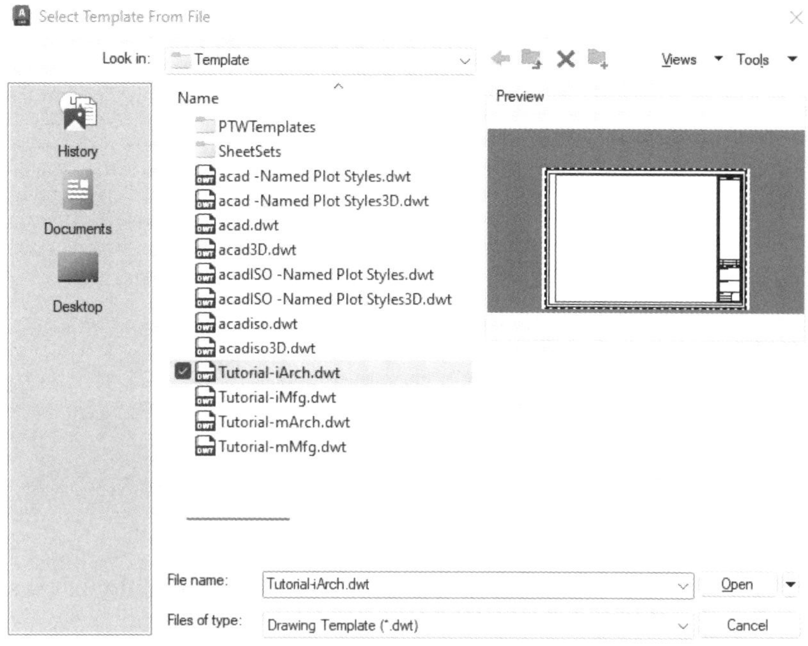

The Insert Layouts dialog will appear. For this template, only one layout style will appear. Pick the OK button.

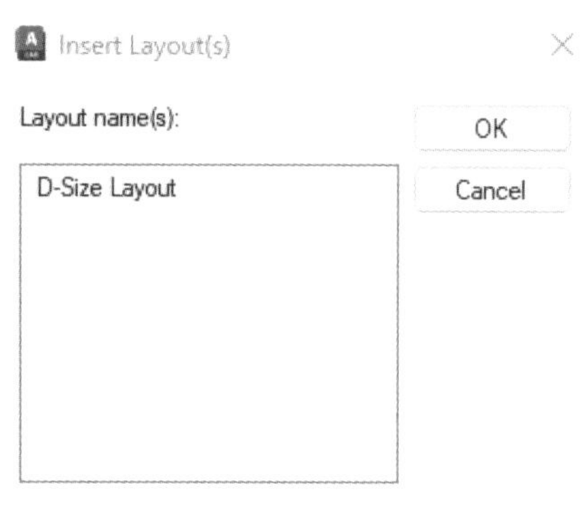

A new tab is created and the default name is D-Size Layout. This can be renamed.

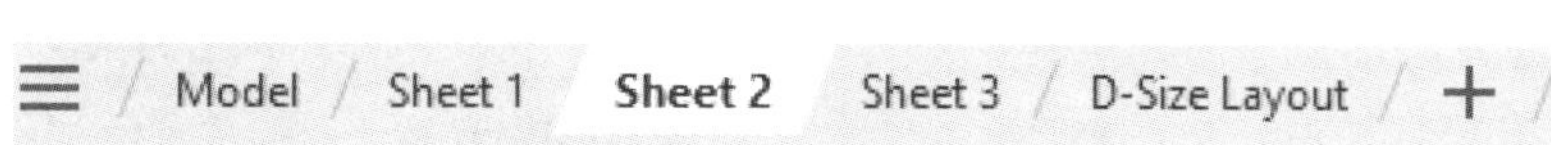

This layout is an architectural drawing format with the titleblock along the right side and has a single viewport that has a pre-set, locked scale of 1/4″=1′. This can be changed to whatever you desire.

If you want to change anything on this template for future use, you may want to do that starting with a blank drawing and renaming the template.

This template is a 24″ x 36″ size. This would represent a standard size for an architectural firm, but for most people, printing this at home may not be practical. You may be able to find a local print shop that could print your PDF file of your drawing for you on large paper.

Add Layout from Template for Mac

Pick the Show Drawings & Layouts icon on the top left of the screen to bring up the Quickview. Pick the icon on the upper right of the Quickview to bring up a mini-menu of choices. Pick the New Layout From Template choice.

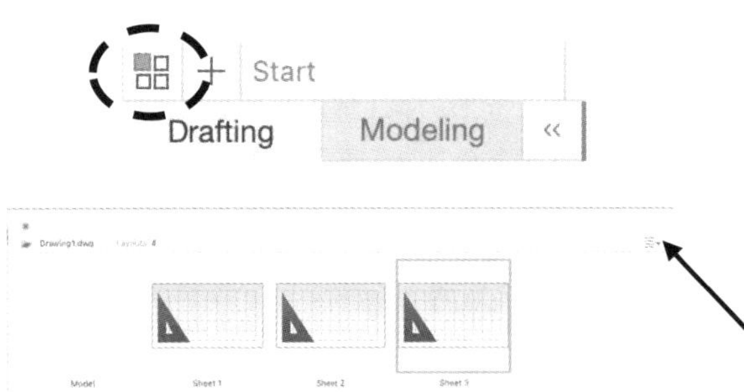

Pick this pull-down icon to bring up mini-menu of choices.

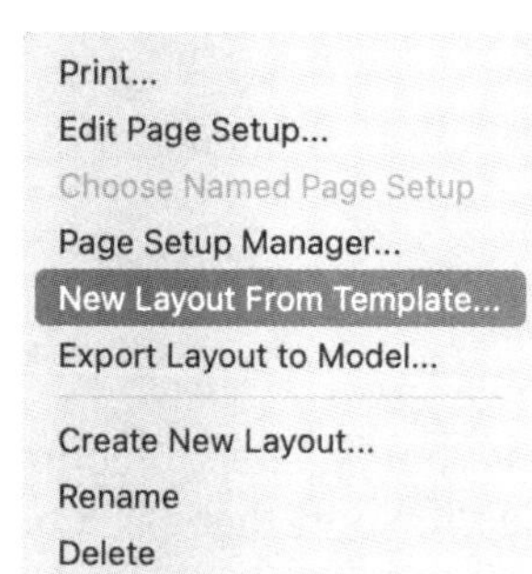

Pick New Layout From Template

A Select Template dialog box will appear. Pick the Tutorial-iArch template and pick Open:

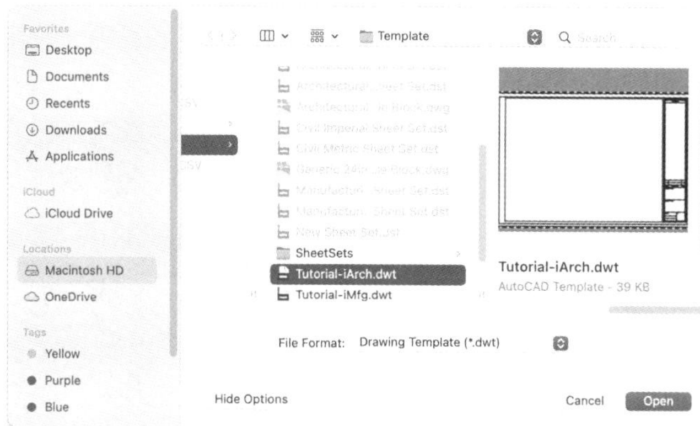

The Insert Layouts dialog will appear. For this template, only one layout style will appear. Pick the Insert button.

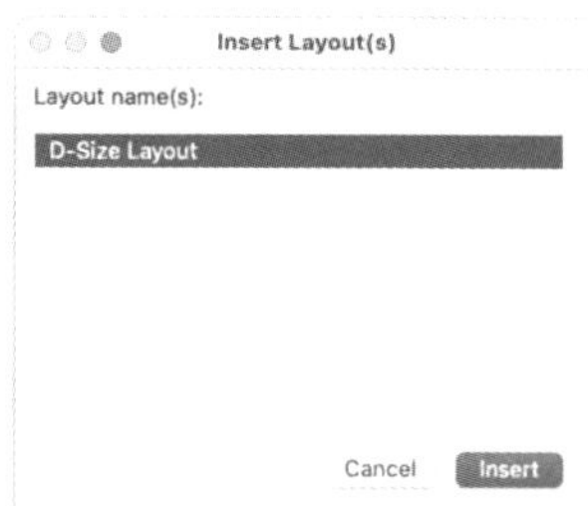

The new layout is added to your list of layouts. You can rename this layout.

Deleting Layouts

To delete a Layout, use the following instructions:

Right-Click on the Layout tab you wish to delete (for Mac, you can also do this in Quickview). A dialog box appears. Pick Delete from your given choices.

Mac

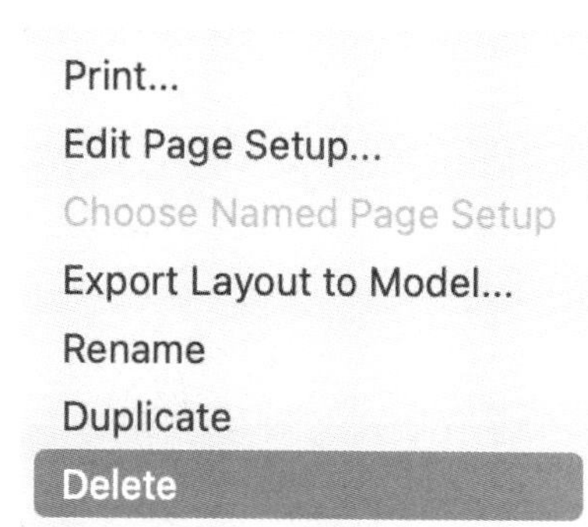

A warning dialog box appears. This dialog box warns you that by taking this action, the layout will be permanently deleted. Pick the OK button.

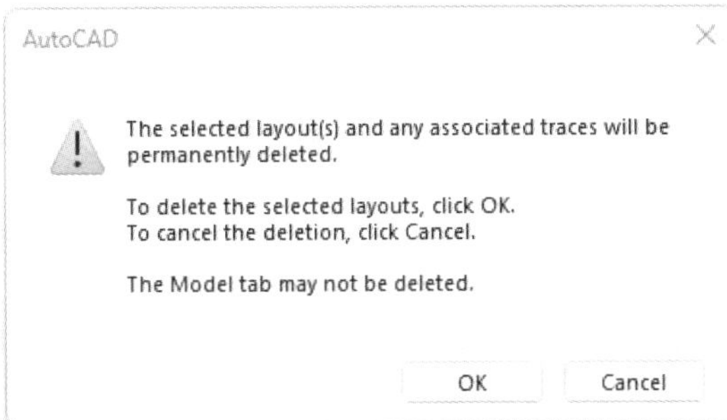

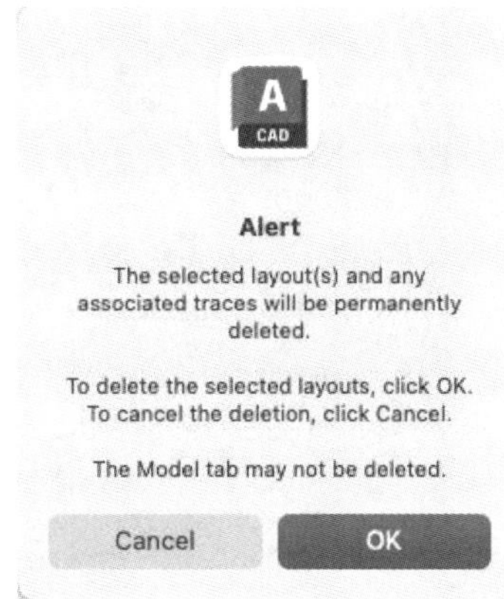

Mac

Your selected layout is now deleted and no longer appears as a tab on the lower part of your screen (or in the list of layouts on the Mac).

Summary

In this chapter you have learned to:

- Understand the concept of Model Space and Paper Space
- Create a viewport using the Viewport toolbar
- Re-size a viewport
- Set and lock the scale of the viewport
- Set up for plotting using Page Setup Manager
- Plot your drawing from Paper Space
- Rename Layout tabs
- Add or delete Layout tabs

Review Questions

1. Why does AutoCAD have both Model Space and Paper Space?

2. What is the difference between Model Space and Paper Space?

3. What is a Layout?

4. What is an easy way to change the size/shape of a Viewport?

5. What is the advantage of using Paper Space?

6. Does changing the scale of the Viewport change the size of the objects themselves?

7. To print your drawing, what do you need to do first to set it up for printing?

8. The AutoCAD default template provides two Layout tabs named Layout 1 and Layout 2. How can you add more Layout tabs and rename them?

9. Why can't you delete the Model tab?

10. Why can't you access Paper Space from the Model tab?

Exercises

1. Starting with the Conference Room of Chapter 5 Exercise 1 (or a different drawing you have created already), create a Title Block on Layout 1 Tab in Paper Space. You may need to Zoom and Pan the view of the conference room off to the side to improve your visibility.

While in Model Space, Pan and Zoom your view of the conference room to the side so that you can draw the Title Block with better visibility. After you do this, make sure to switch to Paper Space before drawing the Title Block

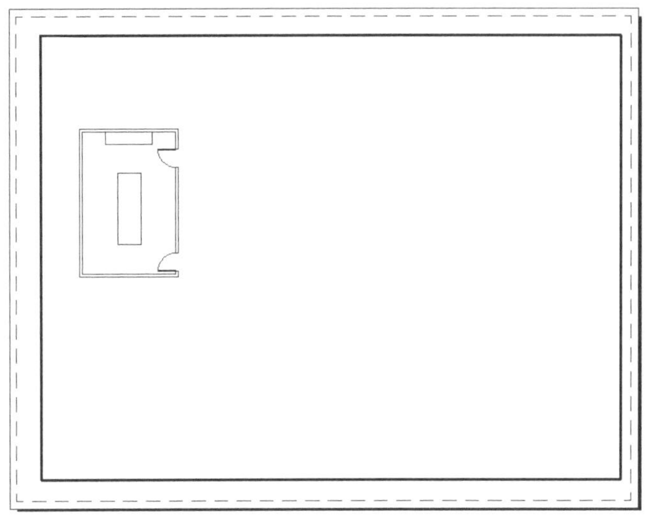

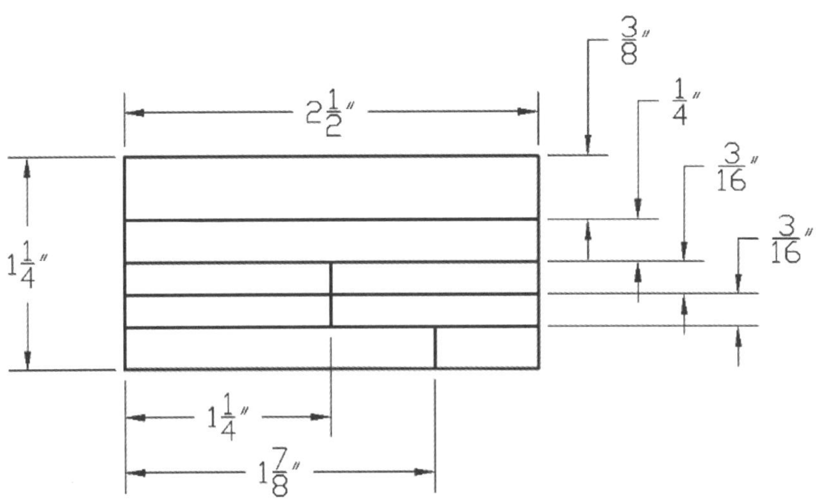

Title Block Dimensions

2. In Paper Space, add to Exercise 1 by drawing a 10-1/4″ x 7-3/4″ border. Position the border so that it fits well on the layout. Move the Title Block to the lower right-hand corner. Use Grips to re-size the Viewport so it does not cross the Title Block. Rename the Layout Tab as "Sheet 1".

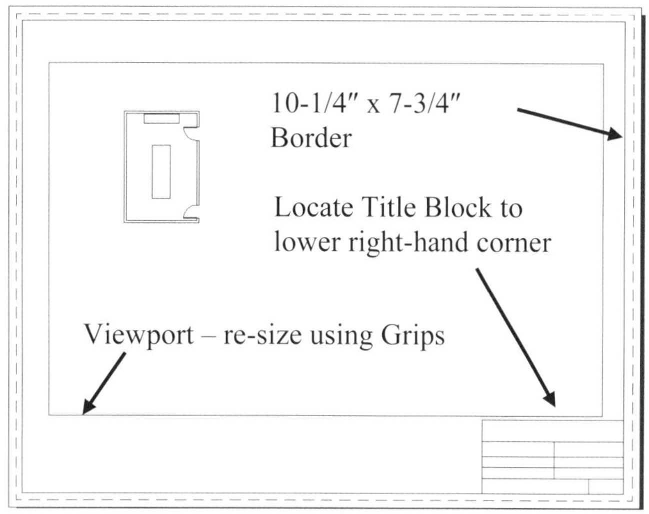

3. After you complete Exercise 2, switch back to Model Space to set the scale and place the view of the conference room properly on the drawing format. Set and Lock the Viewport Scale to ¼″ = 1′. You may have to re-size the viewport again to make sure the entire conference room is in the viewport.

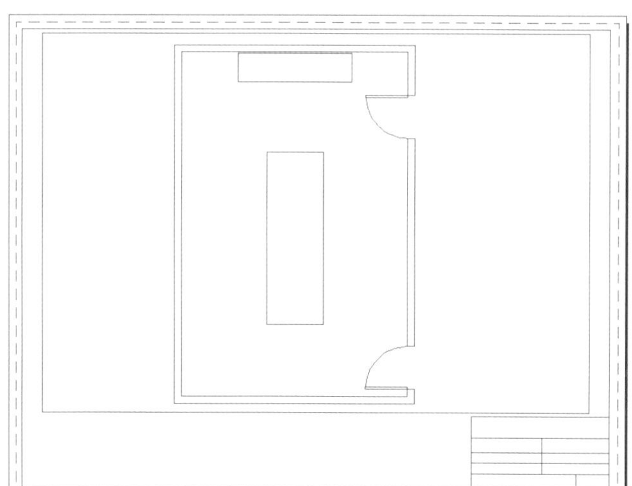

4. After completing Exercise 3, set up and plot the conference room drawing. Use the Page Setup Manager to select the proper paper size for your printer. Use the Preview button to ensure that your drawing will plot correctly for your printer. Make size adjustments using plot offset and make a print of your drawing.

Chapter 8
Hotel Suite Project – Tutorial 3

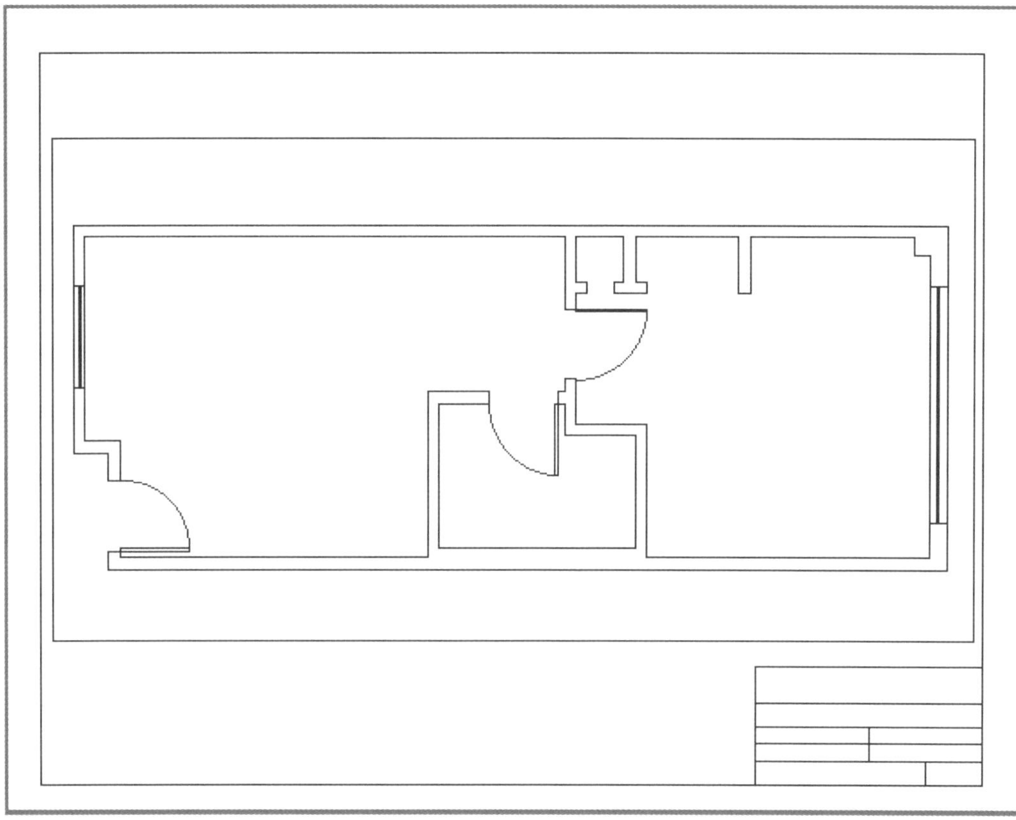

Learning Objectives:

- **To continue creating a drawing of a real-world application of AutoCAD**
    - **Create a layout for plotting the plan view of the hotel suite at a standard scale**
    - **Create a drawing border and titleblock for the layout**
    - **Set up and plot the layout**
    - **Create a drawing template**
- **To utilize and reinforce the use of the AutoCAD commands learned in the previous chapters**

This tutorial builds on Tutorial 2 found in chapter 6. We will use Paper Space for a layout of the model created; set and lock the scale of the drawing; create a drawing border and titleblock; and set up and plot the layout. When you are finished with this tutorial, you will have a scaled printout of the floor plan.

The following commands and techniques will be used:

Commands & Techniques:

- Opening an existing drawing
- Zoom
- Pan
- Toggle Paper/Model Space
- Viewport Scale
- Viewport Lock/Unlock
- Grips - Stretching
- Page Setup Manager
- Printing
- Rectangle
- Move
- Construction Line
- Offset
- Renaming a Layout Tab
- Save
- Save as…

Create a Layout for Plotting

Before beginning, open the Hotel Suite drawing that you updated in Tutorial 2.

1. View the Layout to see how the drawing will look when printed:

Pick the Layout1 tab:

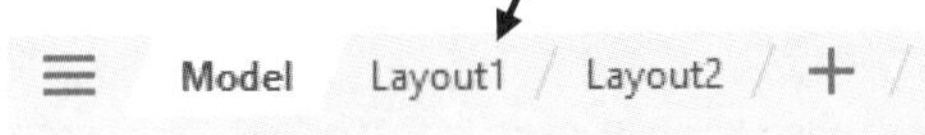

Mac

AutoCAD will bring you to the Paper Space of Layout1.

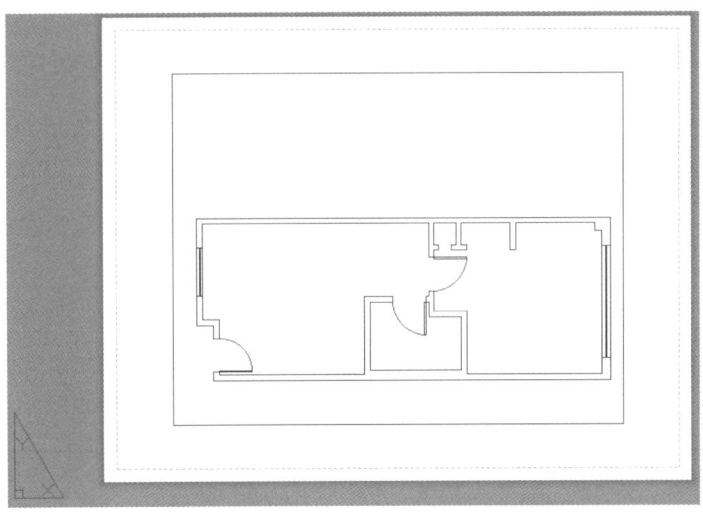

When in the Paper Space mode of Layout1, your drawing screen will look similar to that shown above. Notice the UCS icon is a triangle shape. This is how it appears when you are in the Paper Space mode.

Depending on where you drew the hotel suite relative to the drawing area, the hotel suite may not appear exactly as shown here.

2. Switch from Paper Space mode to Model Space mode:

(Pick the PAPER toggle) near the bottom of your screen (on the Mac it is an icon):

Mac

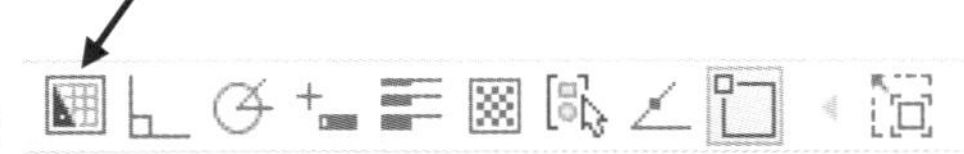

Once you pick the toggle, it will switch from Paper Space mode to Model Space mode, and the toggle will display the word MODEL. On the Mac it will display the Model Space icon.

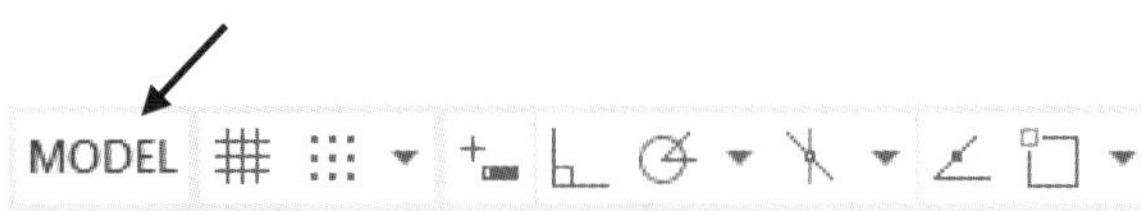

Mac

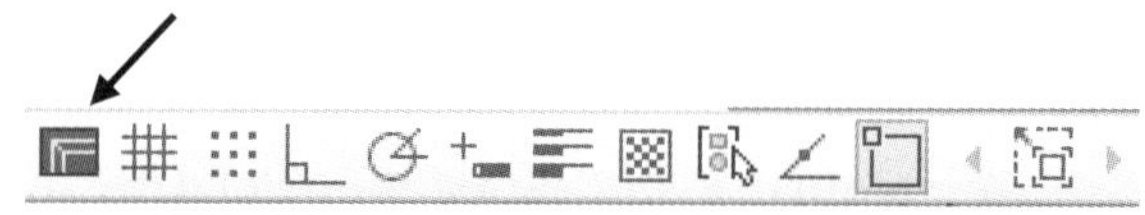

In addition, the outline of the Viewport becomes highlighted, and the Model Space UCS icon appears inside the Viewport. This is shown in the following figure.

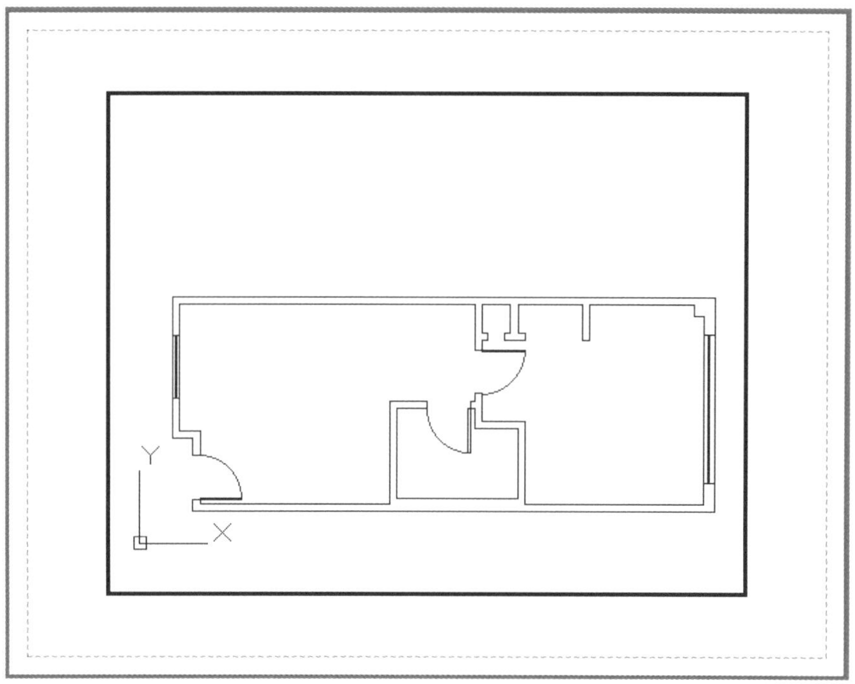

If you desire, you can turn off the UCS icon and the Navigation Cube. Refer to Chapter 1 for instructions to turn these off.

3. Pan and Zoom the model to fit on the layout:

Using your mouse wheel, relocate and size the model so that it fits on the layout. Note that the default layout size is 8-1/2″ x 11″ for a standard paper printer.

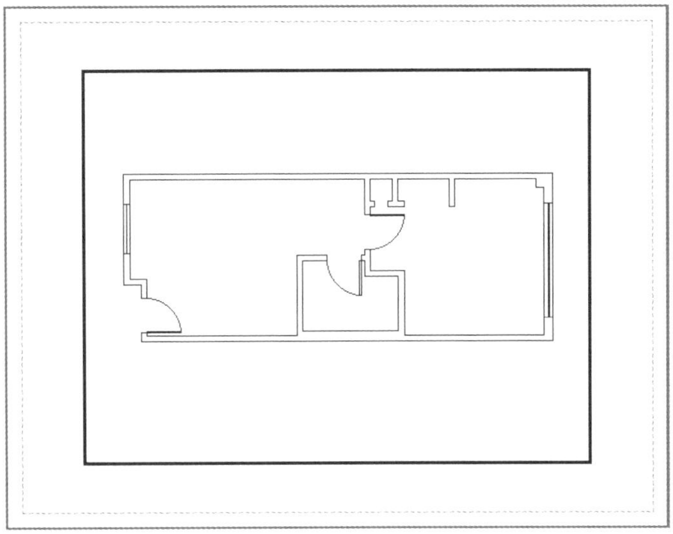

When you print your drawing, you want to be able to print it at a standard scale. When we used the zoom and pan commands to change the way the model was displayed on the layout, we did not set it to any specific scale factor. Let's try the scale factor of ¼″ = 1′, which is typical for Interior Design. Sometimes, another standard scale may be required. This would depend on the size of the room, and the size of the paper you want to plot it on. In this case ¼" = 1' did not work with this Viewport size; however, 3/16" = 1' did. If we want ¼" =1' to be the scale factor, we will need to resize the Viewport.

4. Set and lock the scale of the drawing relative to the paper:

(Pick the Viewport Scale icon) at the bottom right side of the screen. Then select the 1/4″=1′ scale:

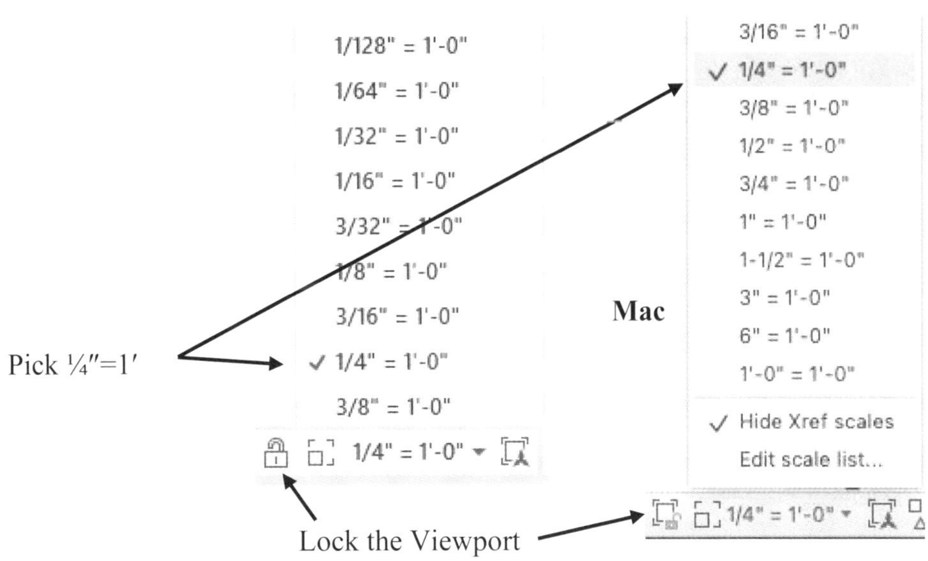

The scale of your drawing should now be ¼″=1′ relative to the paper. You may have noticed a slight change in the size of the drawing on your layout.

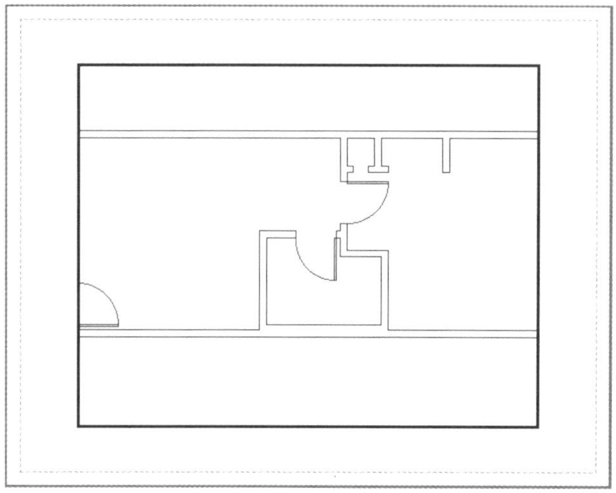

(Pick the Lock/Unlock Viewport icon) to lock the display.

Any time that you attempt to zoom when the viewport scale is locked, the following message will appear above the active command line:

Viewport is view-locked. Switching to Paper space.
Switching back to Model space.

(Pick the Model toggle) to switch back to Paper Space. (On the Mac, double-click outside the Viewport on blank area to switch back to Paper Space.)

(Pick the Viewport border) to get Grips. Use the Grips to re-size the Viewport and fit the entire floor plan on the paper. Press the Esc key to get rid of the grips.

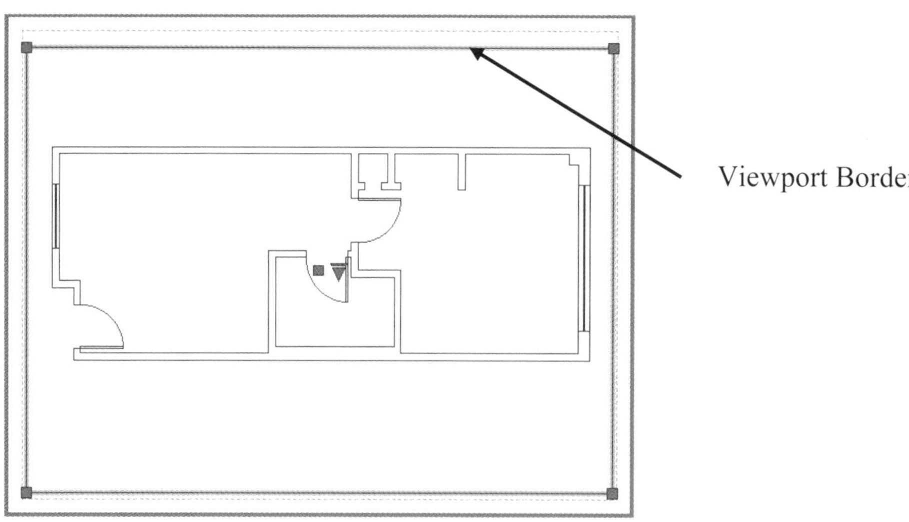

5. Select the printer and plot:

(Pick the Page Setup icon on the Layout Panel of the blue Layout Tab on the Ribbon)
(On the Mac, Pick Page Setup Manager from the File pull-down menu)

The Page Setup Manager dialog box will appear.

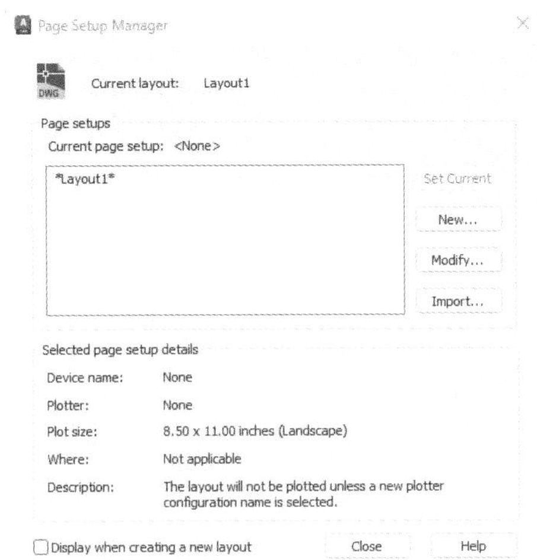

(Pick the Modify… button)

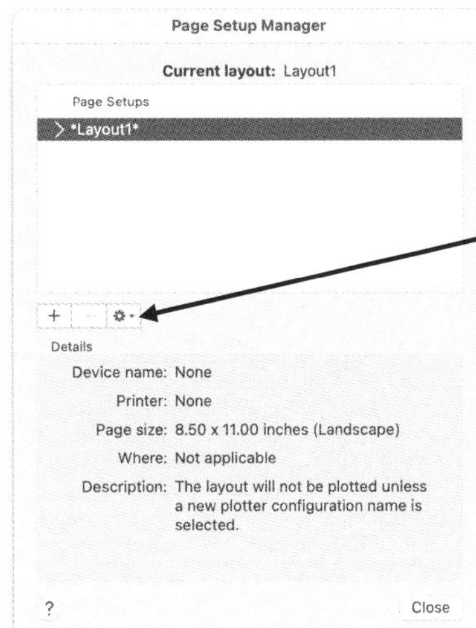

(Pick the tool to Edit and select Edit…)

Mac

The Page Setup dialog box will appear.

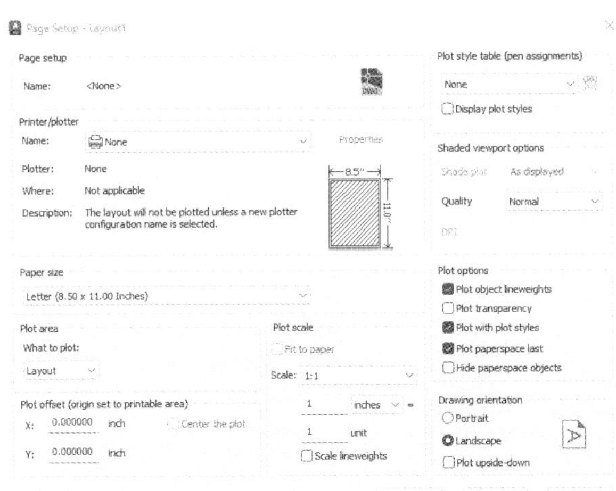

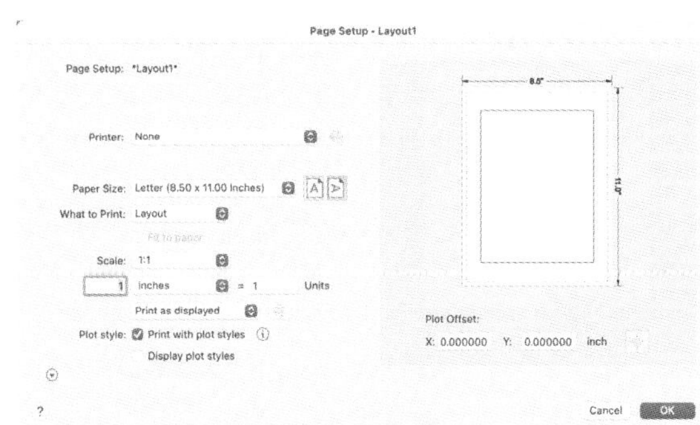

Mac

(Use the pull-down arrow to select the printer)

You must have a printer connected to print. It may have defaulted to "None". Use the pull-down arrow to select a printer.

Once a printer is selected, several items that were grayed-out are now available. In this example, a DWG to PDF was chosen as the printer, and ANSI A (11.00 x 8.50 Inches) was chosen for the Paper Size:

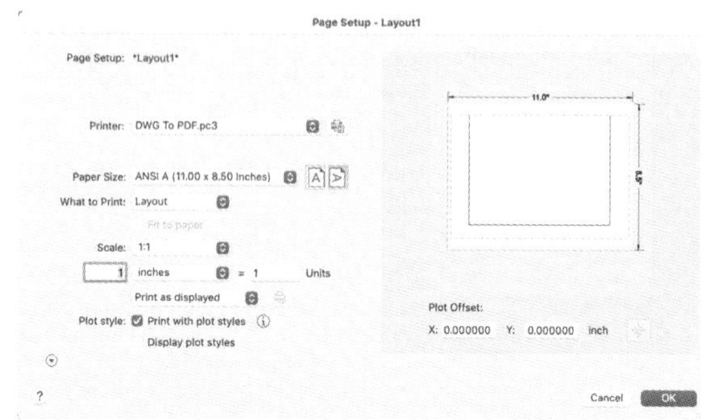

Mac

- The pull-down for Paper size is all the available sizes for your chosen printer.
- The Plot scale section will allow you to fit your print to the size of the paper or select a specific scale.
- You can preview your plot by selecting the preview button.

If you are satisfied, close the Preview, Pick OK to close the Page Setup, and close the Page Setup Manager dialog box. If you are satisfied, use the Application Menu Browser (File pull-down on Mac) to select Print (or Plot under the sub-menu of Print). Pick OK in the Plot dialog box.

A display showing the progress of your plotting will appear. After it is complete, a notification balloon will appear at the bottom of your screen.

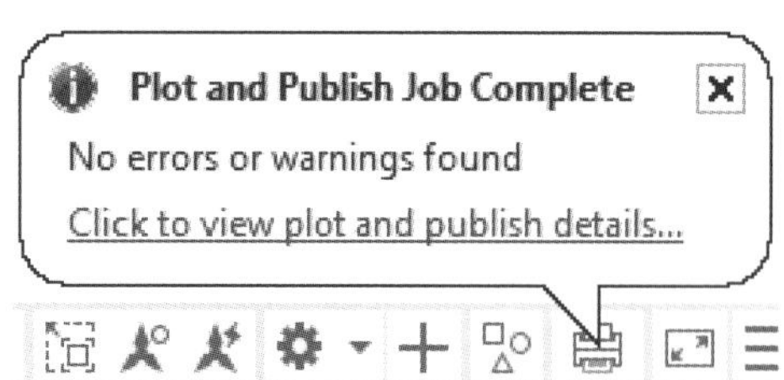

Mac

Create a Drawing Format

If you want to make your drawing look even more professional, you can add a Title Block and Border to create a drawing Format. Remember, these are drawn as Paper Space objects.

For the 8-1/2″ x 11″ paper, let's create the same Title Block and Border that was done for one of the Exercises of Chapter 7. The dimensions of the border are 7-3/4″ x 10-1/4″ and the dimensions for the Title Block are shown below:

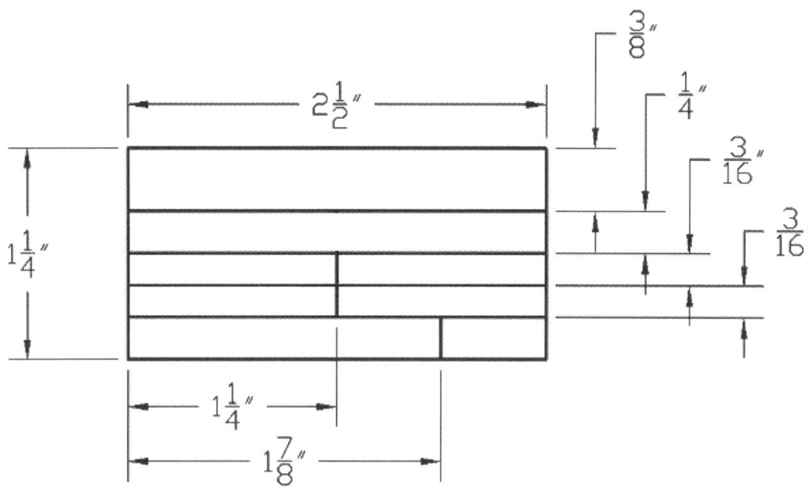

Title Block Dimensions

6. **Create the drawing format in Paper Space.** ***(Pick the Model toggle or double-click outside the Viewport)*** **to change to Paper Space.**

   6a. Draw a rectangle 10-1/4″ in the Horizontal direction and 7-3/4″ in the Vertical direction to create the border around the paper

   6b. Use the Move command to locate the rectangle for best fit on the layout

   6c. Draw the 2-1/2″ x 1-1/4″ rectangle in the lower right corner of the border

   6d. Use Grips to adjust the size of the Viewport to clear the Title Block

   6e. Offset the top horizontal line of the Title Block 3/8″ down

   6f. Offset the new line from step 6e 1/4″ down

   6g. Offset the new line from step 6f 3/16″ down

   6h. Offset the new line from step 6g 3/16″ down

6i. Offset the left vertical line of the Title Block 1-1/4″ to the right

6j. Offset the left vertical line of the Title Block 1-7/8″ to the right

6k. Trim the vertical lines as shown in the Title Block dimensions

7. Rename the Layout

Let's rename our Layout from "Layout 1" to "Plan View".

7a. Right-click on the Layout 1 tab and pick Rename from the list of choices (on the Mac, an alternate method is to bring up the Quickview, right click on Layout1 and pick Rename from mini-menu)

Mac

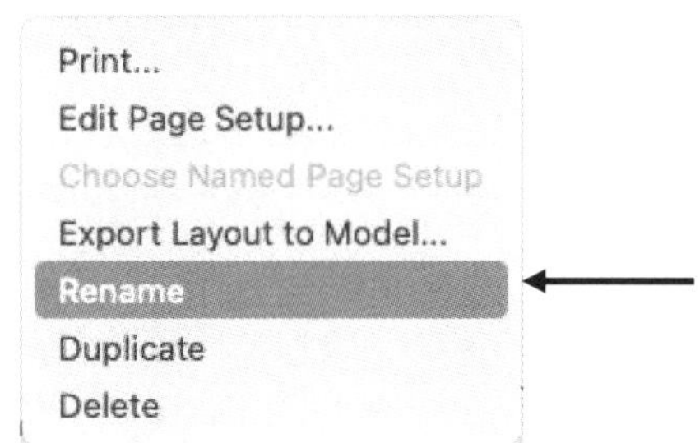

7b. Type the words "Plan View" in place of the Layout 1

Mac

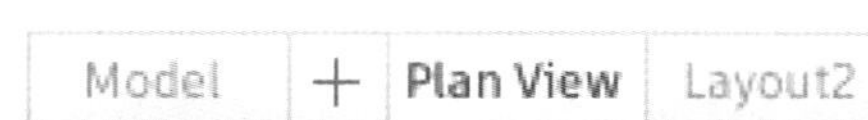

8. Pick Plot (or Print for Mac) from the File pull-down menu and plot your drawing.

Your final plot of the drawing will look like this:

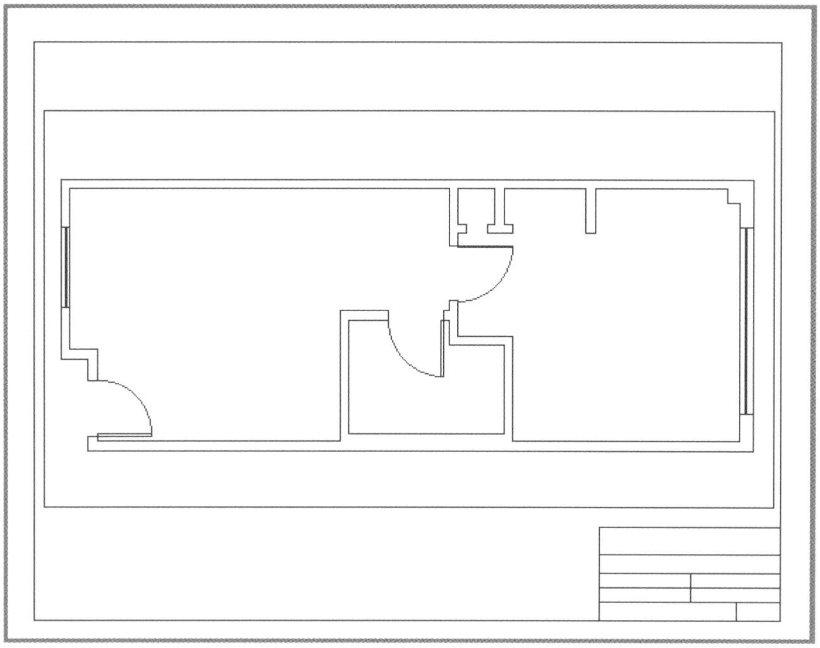

9. Save your drawing.

Create a Template Drawing

Now that we have a drawing with architectural units, and a drawing format with title block, we can save this as a template for future use. We will need to erase all the objects in Model Space so we can have a blank drawing.

10. Create the template drawing.

10a. Pick the Model tab. On the Mac, pick Model from the Model/Layout list.

10b. Zoom to "All" to be able to capture everything on the Model Space.

10c. Using either a Crossing Window or a Selection Window, erase all the objects in the Model Space.

10d. Pick File, Save As…, to save the drawing as a template. Under "File of type", pick AutoCAD Drawing Template (*.dwt). AutoCAD will automatically choose the Template folder as the "Save in" location. Name your template "Interior Design". Pick Save.

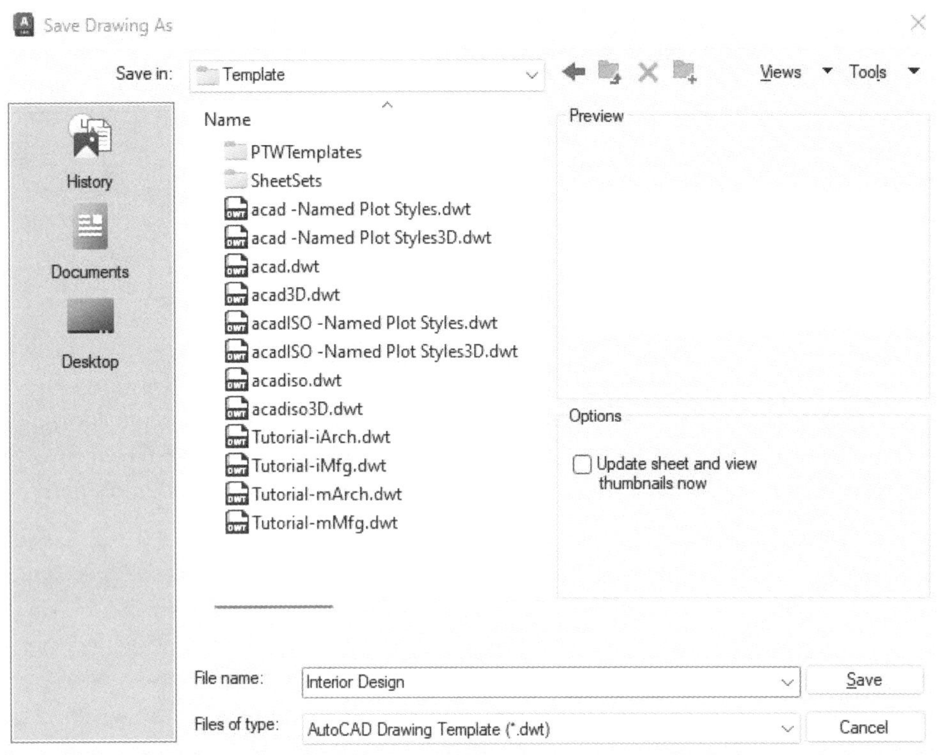

10e. A template Options dialog box will appear. On the Mac, the Command line will prompt for this information. If you desire, you may type in additional information for the description here. Otherwise, pick OK to close it out. On the Mac, press the ↵ Enter key to step through the prompts.

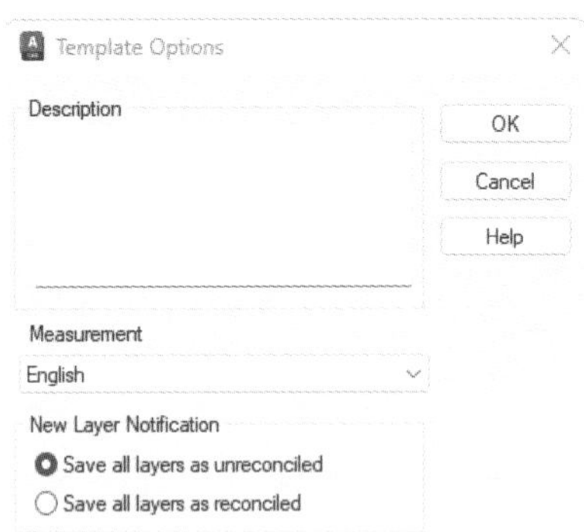

Now that you have saved this as a drawing template, you can use this when starting a new drawing. We can customize this template further as we desire.

Congratulations! You have now completed Tutorial 3.

Chapter 9

Commands – Set 4: Re-Using Objects and Getting Organized

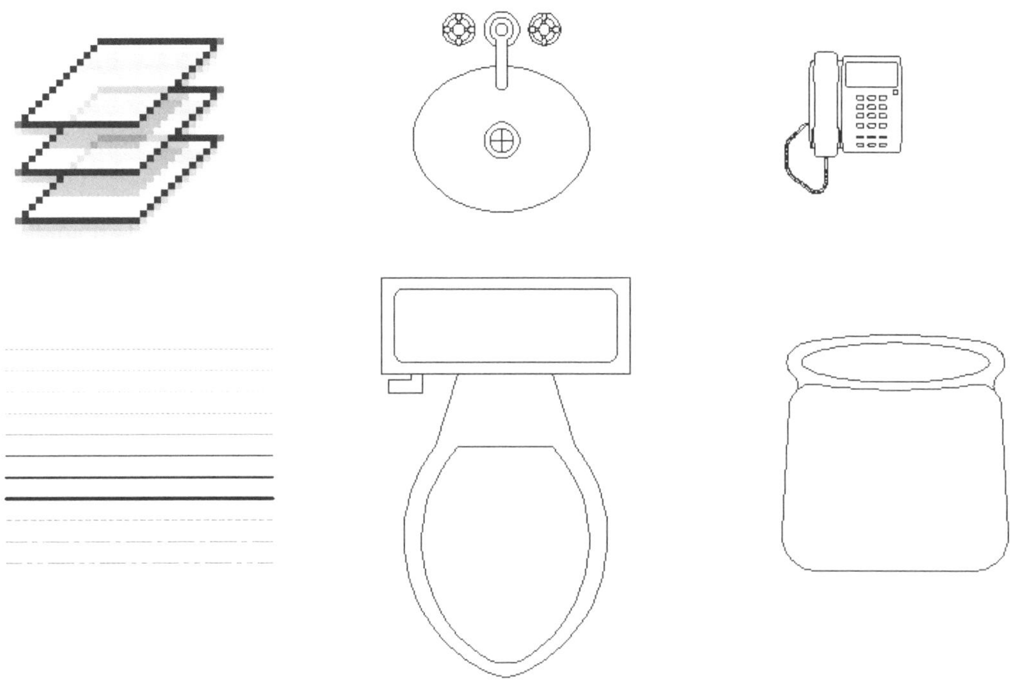

Learning Objectives:

- **Creating and Using Blocks**
- **Using Design Center to bring Blocks in from other drawings**
- **Using other drawings as External References**
- **Creating and using Layers**
- **Changing Properties**
- **Setting Color, Line Type, and Lineweights**

Everything we have done so far, we have had to create ourselves. A big advantage of using AutoCAD is that you only need to create something once. You can then use what you created multiple times throughout your drawing, and for other drawings as well. In fact, you can use groups of objects (Blocks) that someone else created, which can save you time. In this chapter we will see the major advantage that this has over drawing by hand.

Blocks – Treating Multiple Objects as One

AutoCAD allows you to group objects together and treat them as one object. The name of this grouping is a Block. This is very useful for many Interior Design objects, such as furniture, fixtures, doors, windows, etc.

Making Blocks

The Create Block command allows you to associate multiple objects so that they are treated as a single object. The icon is on the Block Panel of the Home Tab and also on the Block Definition Panel of the Insert Tab. On the Block Definition Panel, the icon is a fly-out type of icon, with Create Block as the default icon on top. If you use the fly-out to select Write Block, that icon would then appear on top.

Procedure:

Pick (left click): **Create Block icon** from the Block Panel of the Home Tab.
(As an alternative, use the Block Definition Panel of the Insert Tab)

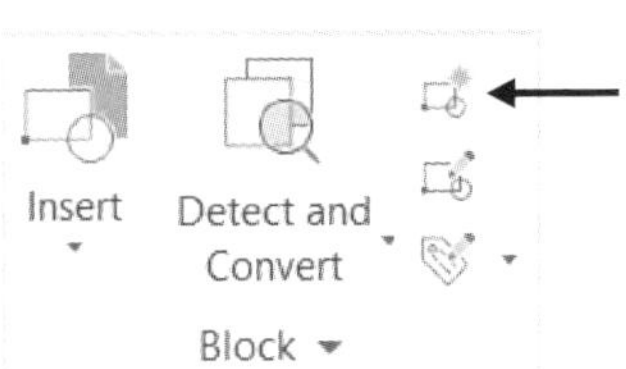

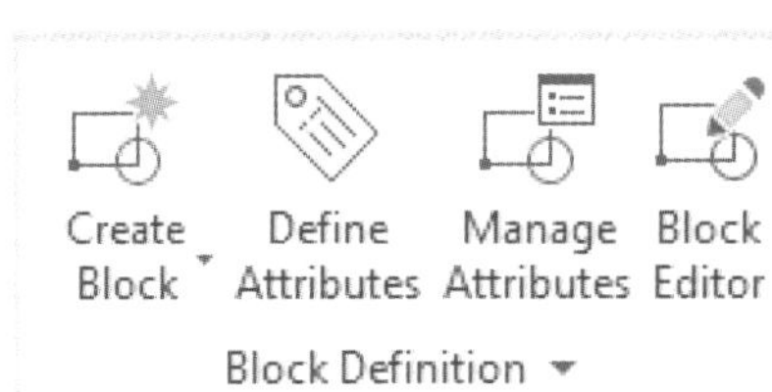

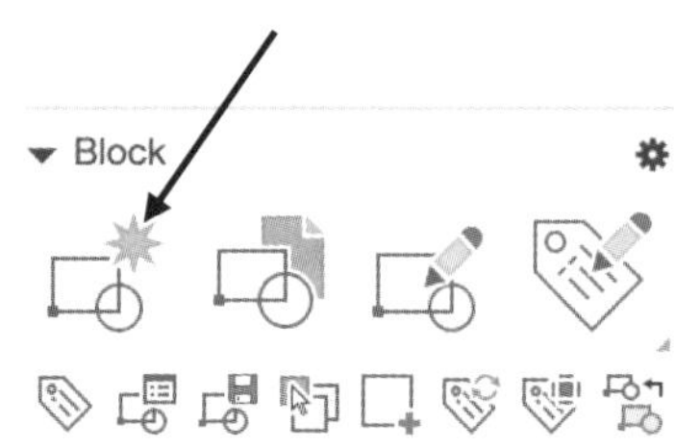

Mac

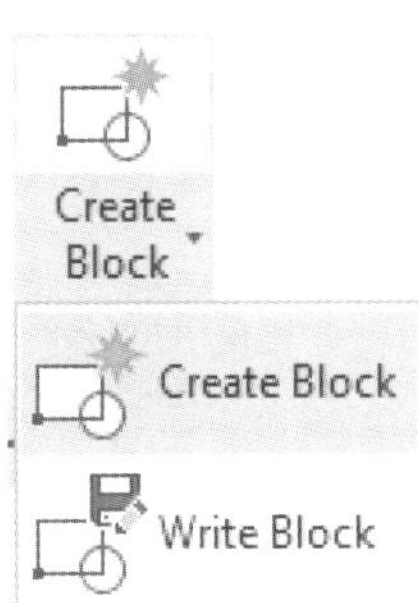

This is a fly-out style icon. If Write Block appears on top, click the black triangle to expose the Create Block icon

The Block Definition dialog box will appear. This is where you specify the name of your block, the objects that it will consist of, and the insertion base point:

On the Mac, the Define Block dialog box will appear:

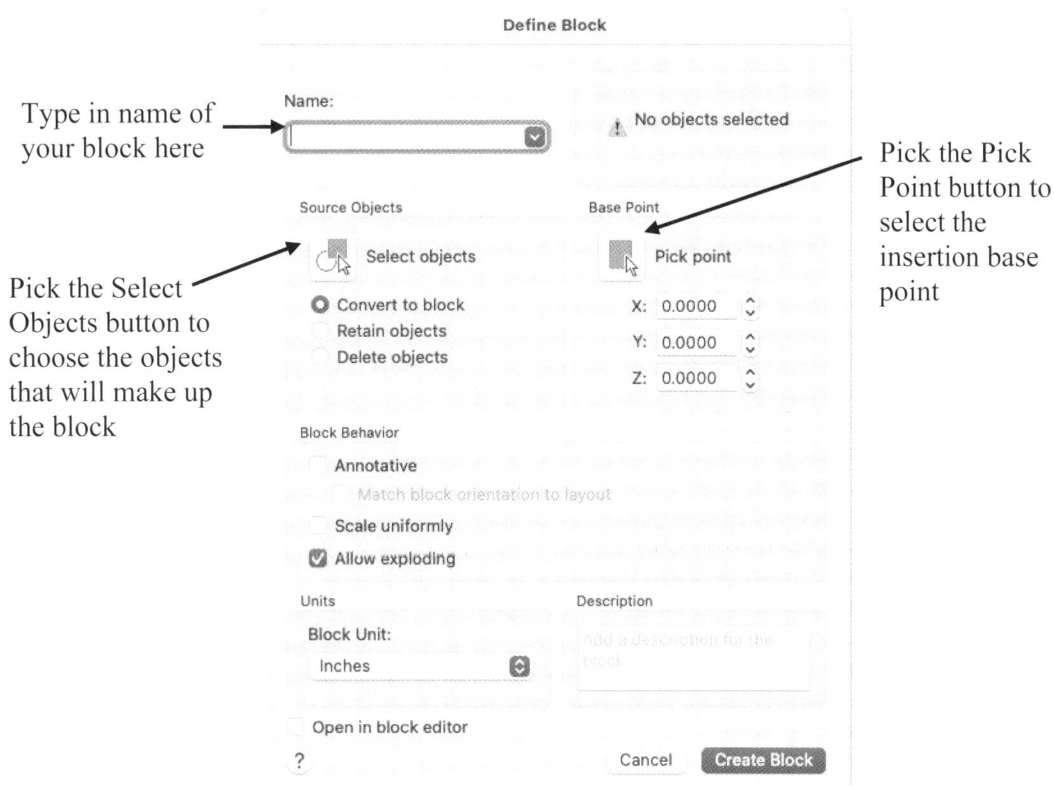

As an example, open the *Telephone.dwg* from the files you downloaded from the publisher website, and select the Create Block icon. This is an example of multiple objects that should be treated as a single item in your drawing.

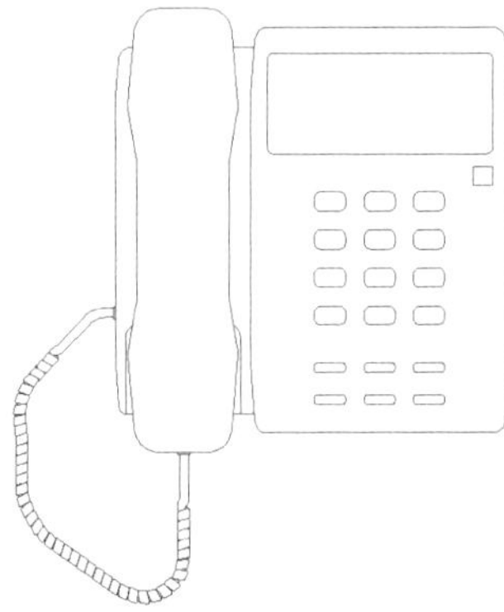

We will type in the name “Telephone” for the name of the block.

We need to select the objects that make up the block. Pick the Select Objects button in the dialog box. The dialog box will disappear, and the command line will prompt you to select the objects. Use a Selection Window to select all the objects that make up the telephone.

BLOCK *Select objects:*
Select objects: Specify opposite corner: 747 found
Select objects: ↵

Once all the objects are selected, press the ↵ Enter key.

The dialog box will reappear on your screen. A small image of the selected objects will appear in the dialog box.

We need to select the Base Point of the block. This is the point that will become the origin of the block. Select the Pick point button in the dialog box. The command line will prompt you to select the insertion base point.

Specify insertion base point:
Pick any object on the telephone as your base point. As soon as you pick the point, the dialog box will reappear. Base point X and Y values may be different than yours, depending on which point was selected.

Mac

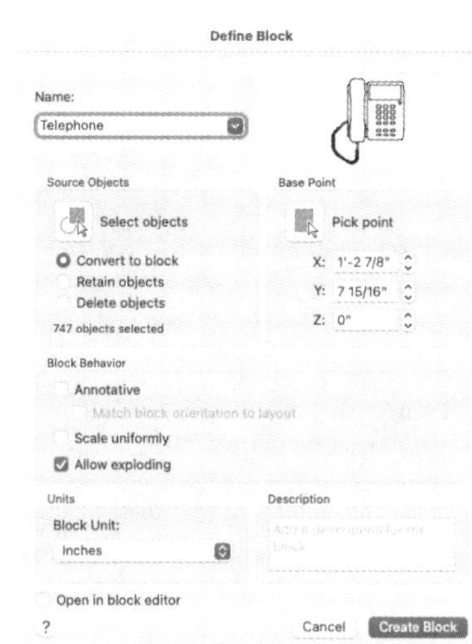

Pick the OK button (Create Block button on Mac) to exit the dialog box, and the Block command will exit automatically.

You have now created a block of the telephone. Since we left the radio button selected to "Convert to block", the existing objects that make up the telephone are now joined as a block. You can confirm this with the List command.

LIST *Select objects: 1 found*

Select objects: ↵

BLOCK REFERENCE Layer: "0"
Space: Model space
Handle = af2
Block Name: "Telephone"
at point, X=1'-2 3/4" Y=0'-7 11/16" Z=   0'-0"
X scale factor: 1.0000
Y scale factor: 1.0000
rotation angle: 0
Z scale factor: 1.0000
InsUnits: Inches
Unit conversion: 1.0000
Scale uniformly: No
Allow exploding: Yes

> Your X and Y values may be different than shown here; it is dependent on where you selected your Pick Point. Also, your Handle name may be different than shown. The Handle name is how AutoCAD tracks each object – nothing for us to worry about.

Inserting Blocks

The Insert Block command allows you to insert Blocks into your drawing. These can be blocks that were created within the drawing, or the complete insertion of an external drawing. The icon is on the Block Panel of the Home and Insert Tabs.

Procedure:

Pick (left click): **Insert Block icon** from the Block Panel of the Home Tab.
(As an alternative use the Block Panel of the Insert Tab.)

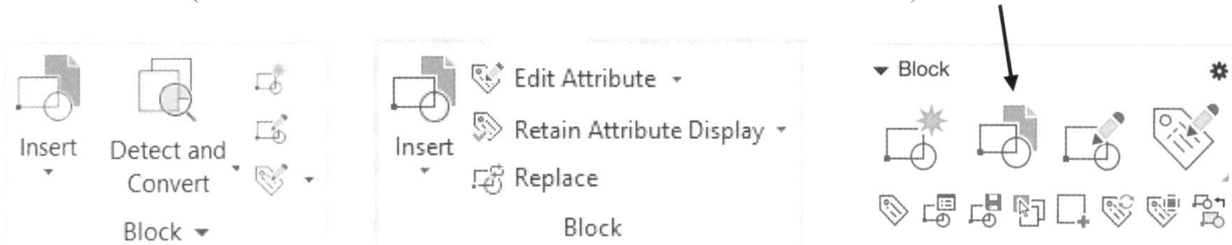

Mac

Icons of available blocks will appear when you pick Insert.

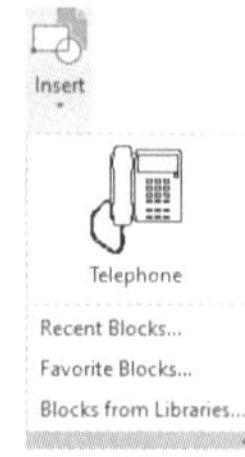

After picking the icon of the telephone, the block will appear on the screen and will follow your cursor. You can place the block in the drawing by left-clicking.

If you want to select a specific Block from a drawing other than the current drawing, pick "Blocks from Libraries…". The first time you select this, a Select Drawing File dialog box will appear. Scroll to select the file that contains the block and pick Open. For example, pick Plant.dwg from the downloads file. A new Blocks palette will appear. You can choose the entire drawing or just the block. Once you select the block, it will appear on the screen and will follow your cursor. You can place the block in the drawing by left-clicking. When you are done, close the Blocks palette.

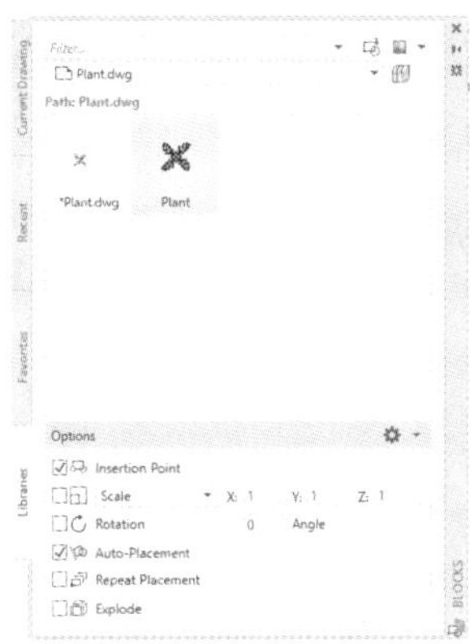

Inserting Blocks on Mac

On the Mac, the Blocks Palette will appear. This is where you select the block to insert into your drawing. In this example, the Telephone is the only block available. Right-click on the block you want and select Insert in Drawing from the menu. Alternatively, double-click on the block icon.

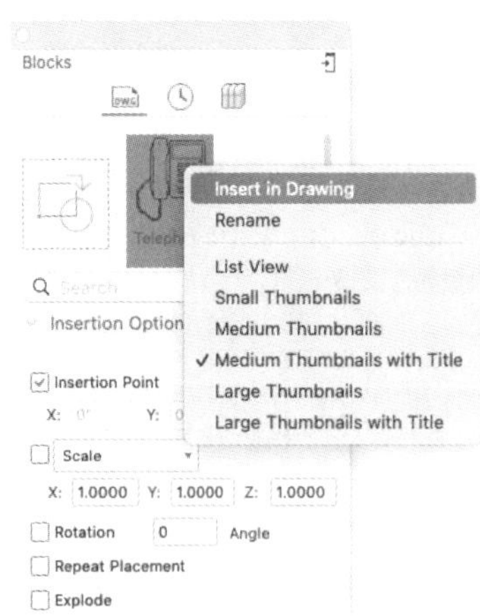

An image of your block will follow your cursor, and the command line will prompt you to specify the location for the block:

INSERT *Specify insertion point or [Basepoint/Scale/X/Y/Z/Rotate]:* **Pick a location on your screen to insert the block.**

The block will appear on your drawing and the command will end.

On the Mac, if you select the Plus button  to browse available drawings. The Select Drawing File dialog box will appear. This is very similar to an Open File dialog box. Using this browse method will insert an entire drawing into your current drawing. It will not limit it to just a specific Block from that drawing. You can try this on your own.

AutoCAD also has the Design Center feature that allows you to pick blocks from other drawings. For Mac users, the Content Palette is used instead.

Design Center

The Design Center feature of AutoCAD allows you to use items that were created on other drawings and bring them into your current drawings. It is especially useful for Blocks but can also be used for other things such as Dimension Styles, Layers, Text Styles, Layouts, etc. Although Design Center is not available on the Mac, you can bring Blocks in using the Blocks Palette instead. See those instructions for more info.

You can bring up the Design Center palette by selecting the Design Center icon, located on the Palettes Panel of the View Tab.

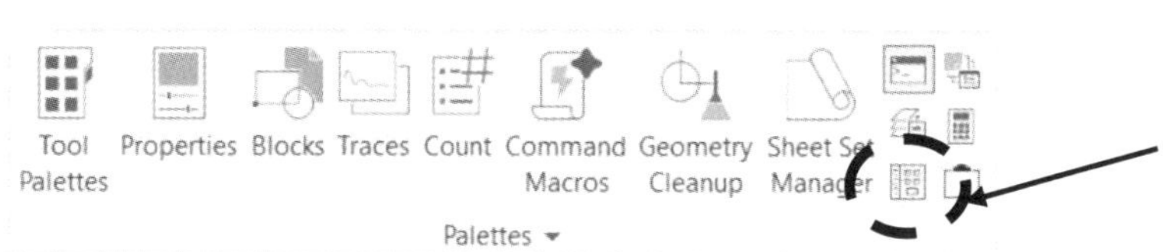

Once you select the icon, the Design Center palette will appear on your screen:

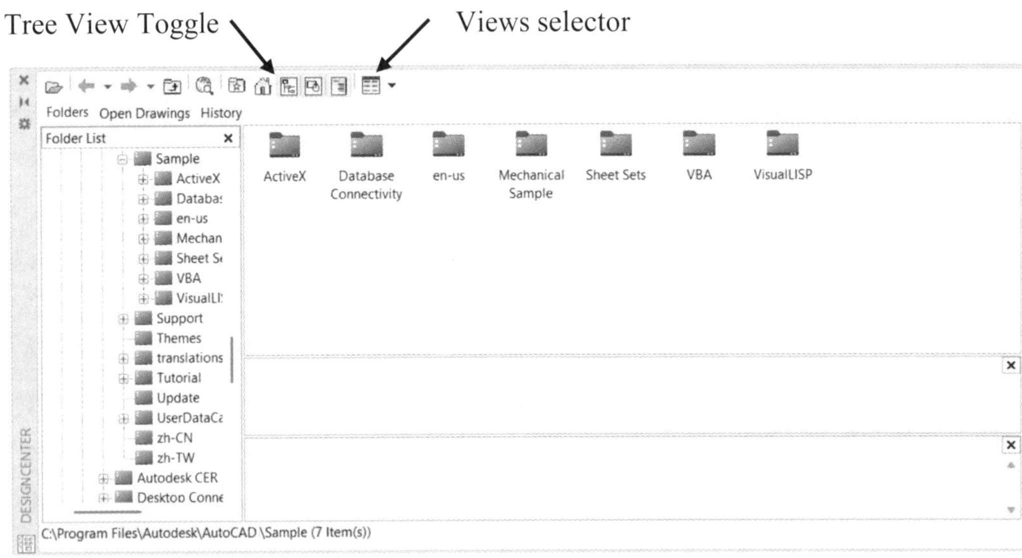

The left side of the palette shows a Tree View or hierarchy of folders that are on your computer. The right side of the palette shows the contents of the selected folder or file. If the Tree View is not displayed, pick the Tree View Toggle at the top of the palette to bring it up.

When you initially bring up the Design Center, AutoCAD may open the folder within the AutoCAD program to the Samples that were provided with the program. Use the Tree on the left side to select the folder you want. Using the Views selector icon can control the method by which the contents are displayed. In this example, the display is using Large icons and the folder is Sample.

Pick the "+" plus icon that is to the left of the "en-us" folder. Another level of folders will appear in the tree. Pick the "+" plus icon that is to the left of the "DesignCenter" folder. The next level of contents that appears will be icons of AutoCAD drawings. Pick the icon for "Home – Space Planner.dwg". The categories of contents contained in that drawing will be displayed on the right side of the palette. This display will be typical for any drawing.

Note that the entire palette size and the size of the Folder List section can be changed. Use your cursor at the edge of the border for each section and then click and drag to resize. Use the slide bars on the folder list to better see the contents as needed.

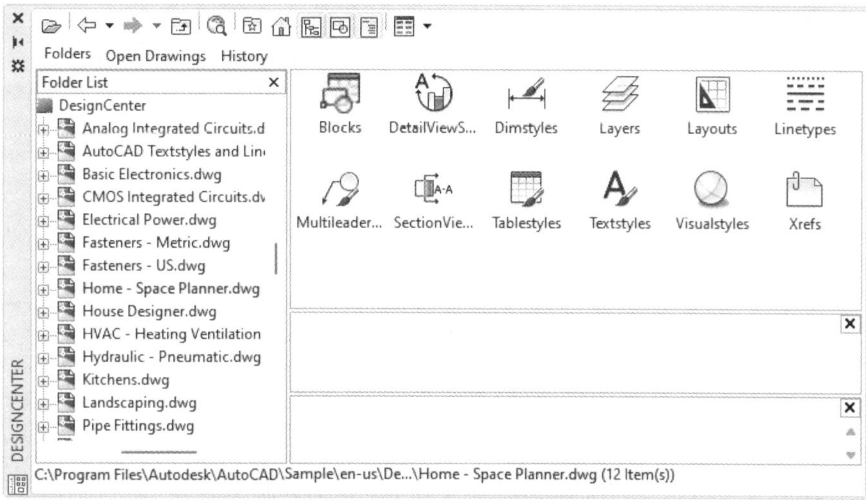

The first time you use Design Center, it will open to the Sample folder that came with the AutoCAD program. Once you start opening contents in that folder, or any other folder, the Design Center palette will open to the folder you last left open. If you want to always be able to open to a specific folder, you can set that folder as a "home" folder by right-clicking on the folder and choosing "Set as Home". In this example, let's choose the folder "DesignCenter" as the home folder:

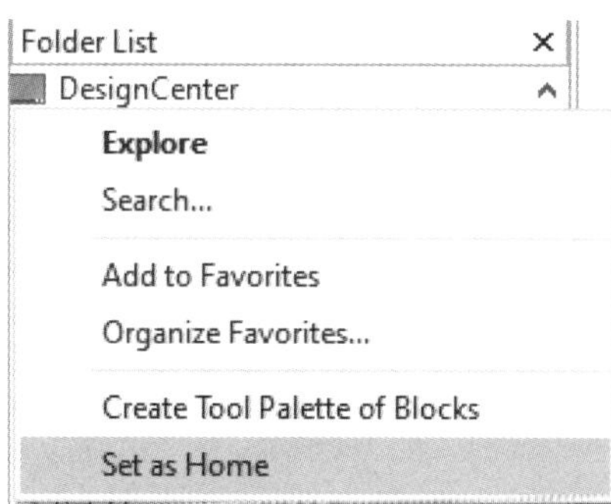

If you always want the Design Center to open a specific folder when you first bring it up, you can right-click on that folder and select "Set as Home" from the shortcut menu. In addition, if there are multiple folders that you want to access frequently, you can right click on each folder (one at a time) and select "Add to Favorites" from the shortcut menu. You can then find them in the Favorites folder at the top of the Design Center Palette: 

Using Design Center

The following examples assume that you currently have a drawing open and you wish to bring in items from existing drawings. It also assumes that you have already opened the Design Center palette and selected the drawing of your choice.

Bring Blocks into Your Drawing

Blocks that were previously created, other than those in the drawing you are currently working on, are easy to bring into your drawing by using the Design Center.

1. Double-click the Blocks icon on the right side of the Design Center palette. The alternative is to expand the drawing by picking on the "+" in front of that drawing on the left side of the Design Center palette and then single-click the Blocks icon.
2. The right side of the Design Center palette now displays all the blocks contained in the drawing. Click on the block of your choice and drag it into your drawing by holding the left mouse button. When you are satisfied with the location, release the left mouse button.
3. An alternate method is to double-click on the block of your choice and follow the instructions of the Insert dialog box that appears. A checkmark next to Specify On-screen followed by selecting the OK button will allow you to locate the block in the drawing with your mouse (without holding the mouse button). When you are satisfied with the location, left-click.

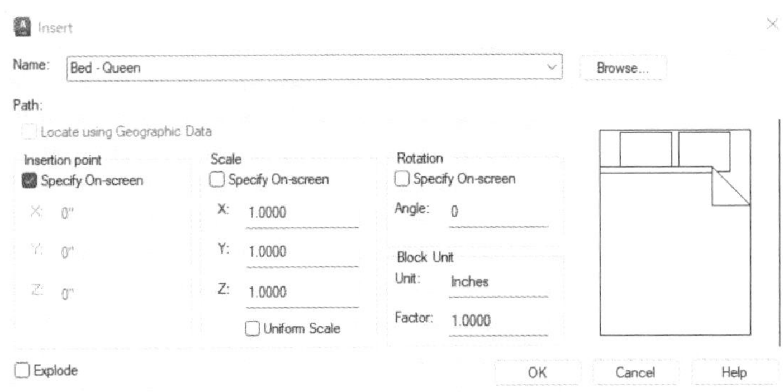

Double-clicking the block will bring up the Insert dialog box

Bring Styles, etc. into Your Drawing

Bringing other items, such as Dimension Styles, Text Styles, Layers, Layouts, etc. are done in the same manner as bringing Blocks into your drawing. The only difference is that it may not be as obvious that it was brought into the drawing. You can use the Styles toolbar to verify that the Dimension Styles, Text Styles, and Table Styles were brought in. Use the Layers Manager to verify that Layers were brought in, etc.

Blocks Palette for Mac

Although Design Center is not available, Mac users can use the Blocks Palette instead. The Blocks Palette is available by using the Window pull-down and selecting Blocks, or by picking the icon in the Block Tool Group.

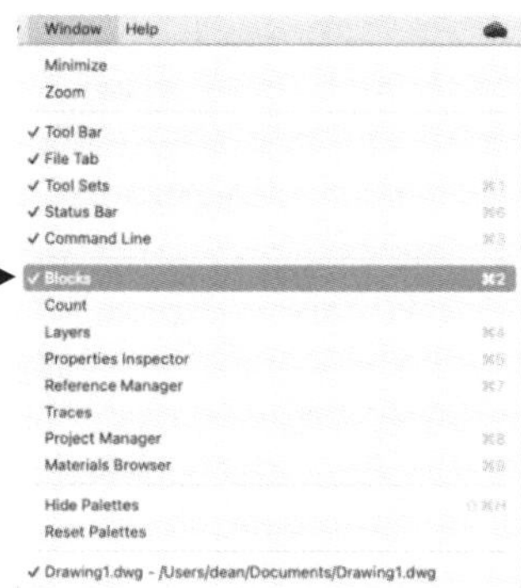

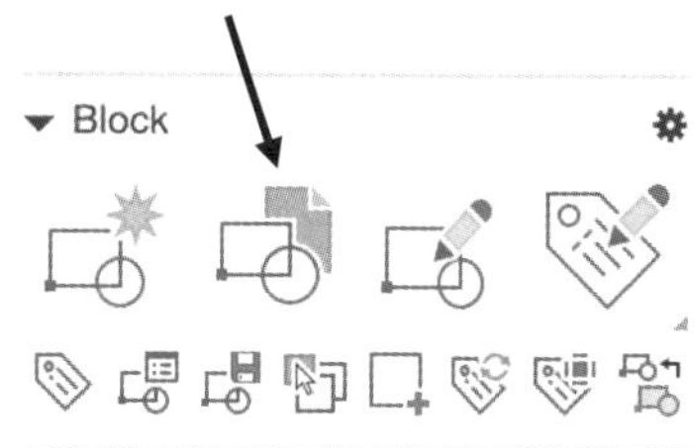

When selected, the Blocks Palette will appear on your screen. If it is docked, you can expand it or undock it. You will use Libraries to manage content. To do that, pick the Libraries icon, then use the pull-down arrow to choose the library.

Pick the Libraries icon to display the available libraries.

Use the pull-down arrow to choose from the available libraries

Palettes can be docked or floating by selecting this switch

Pick the File Navigation icon to add libraries and content to your library of blocks

Adding Block Libraries for Mac

After you pick the File Navigation icon, a file manager dialog box appears. Navigate through your documents or cloud service to find a file that contains blocks or a folder that contains drawing files.

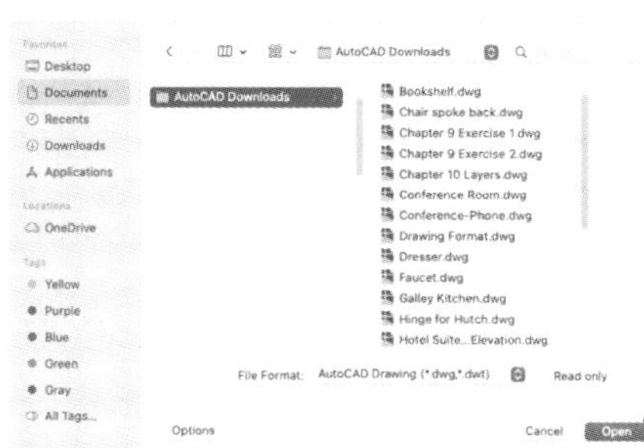

After selecting the file or folder, Pick Open to add your library

After selecting the Open button, a new Library is added. As an example of a file, the Hotel Suite Blocks drawing was added. Available blocks can be displayed as thumbnails or a list.

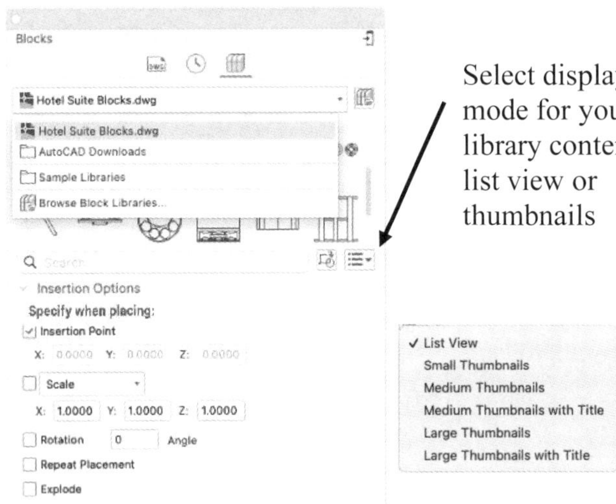

Select display mode for your library content – list view or thumbnails

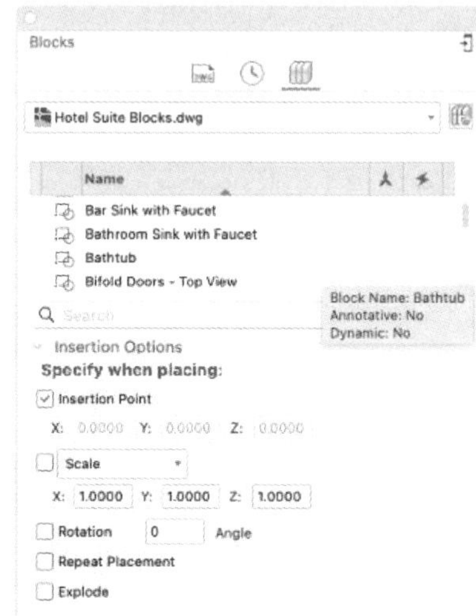

Available Blocks Shown as Thumbnails

Available Blocks Shown as a List

You can also select a folder that contains drawing files. As an example of a folder, the AutoCAD Downloads folder from the publisher's site was selected. Once the folder is in your library, you can select the folder to see which drawings are in it. You can select one of the drawings to explore which blocks are available. Because the Hotel Suite Blocks drawing was within that folder, that drawing was selected.

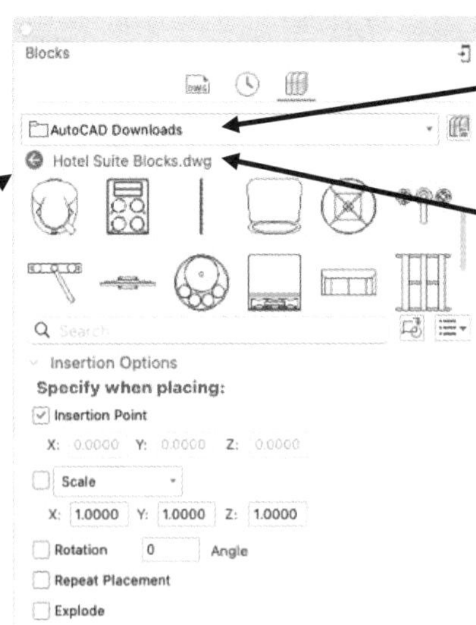

The folder selected is displayed here

The drawing selected is displayed here

To return to the folder contents, select the back button

Bring Blocks into the Drawing on Mac

With the Blocks Palette open, use the pull-down arrow to select the library. Select the Hotel Suite Blocks library that you just created. The blocks will now appear in your content palette.

There are several insertion options:

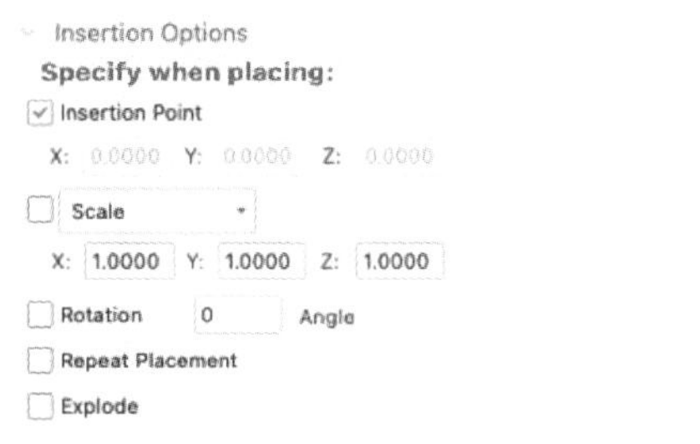

You can specify an exact location using X-Y, you can specify a rotation angle, repeat the placement, or even explode the block during insertion. For now, just leave the Insertion Point option checked.

To bring in a block, pick and drag it into your drawing, or double-click on it. If you have difficulty with this, you can right-click on the block and select "Insert in Drawing" from the options given. You can then place the block in your drawing by selecting a location in your drawing with your cursor.

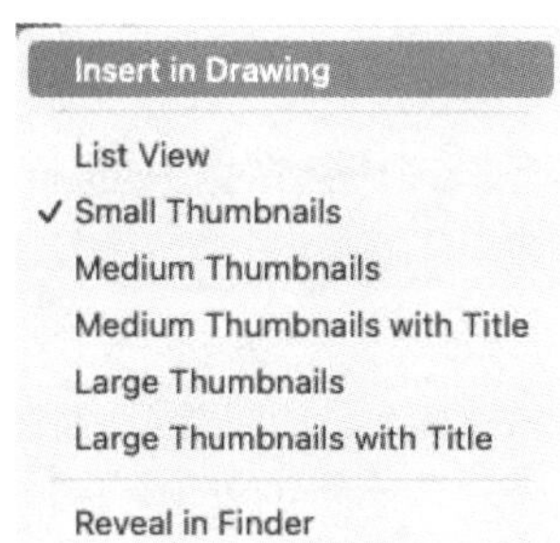

When inserting, an option to rename the block becomes available if the block already exists on the drawing:

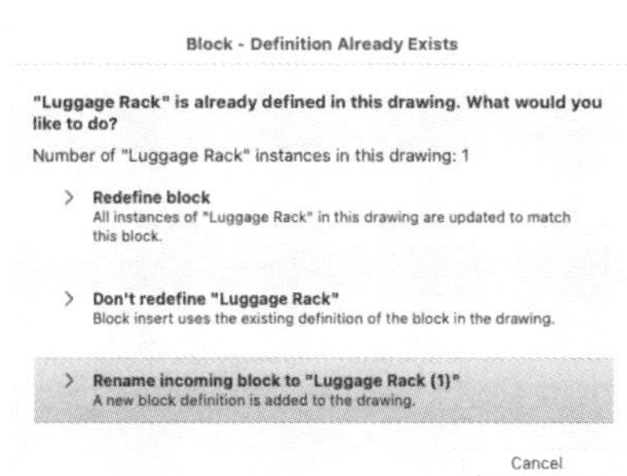

This may not appear when using the pick and drag method of inserting the block

Renaming helps to avoid duplication of the block definition.

Xrefs

An alternative to importing information directly to and making it part of your drawing would be to bring it in as reference material. It will be visible to you without actually making it part of your drawing and you can use object snaps to create your design around it. This comes in handy if you are working with an architect, and there are several architectural design iterations being made at the same time you are completing your interior design. Periodic updates can be made to the reference material to ensure you have the latest version. The AutoCAD function to accomplish the use of external references is Xref.

Attaching a drawing as a Reference

Procedure:

Pick (left click): **Attach icon** from the Reference Panel of the Insert Tab.

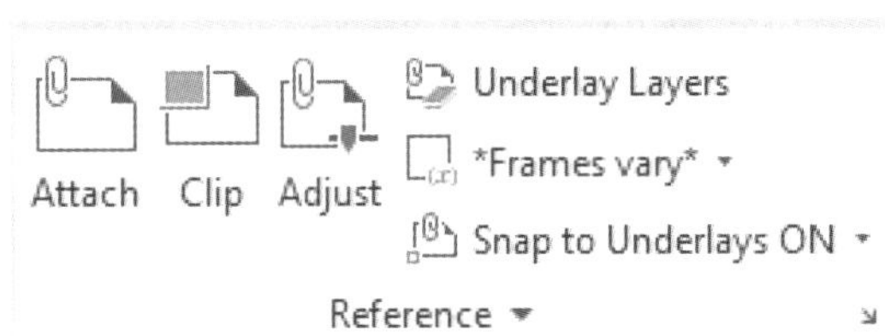

For Mac: Use pull-down menu **Insert** and select **DWG Reference…**

Mac:

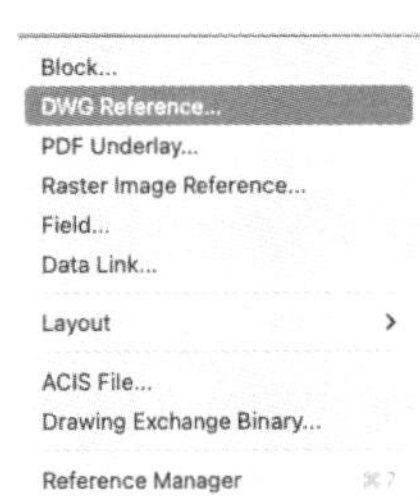

The Select Reference File dialog box will appear. This is where you specify the drawing you want to use as a reference. Pick the Browse button to find that drawing, pick the drawing, and pick the Open button. The reference drawing can be located on your own computer drive or on a shared drive (cloud). Make sure the file type is DWG.

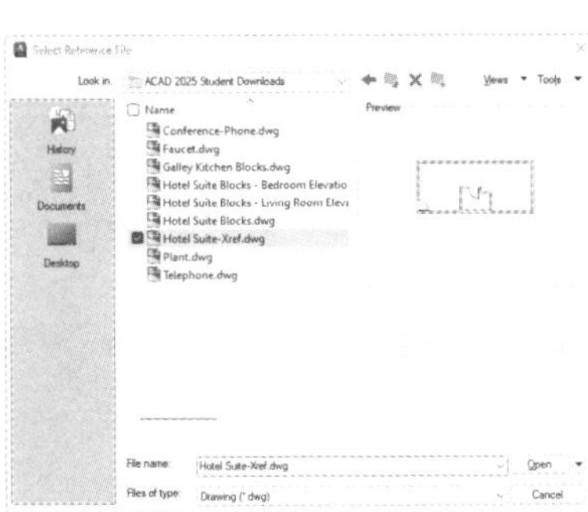

Mac:

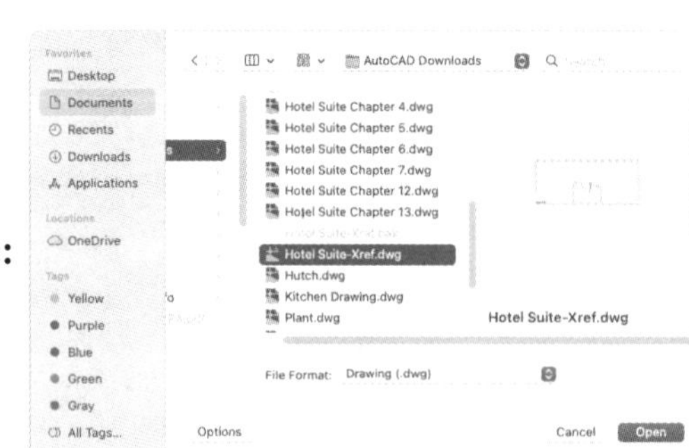

Once you pick Open, the Attach External Reference dialog box will appear.

Mac:

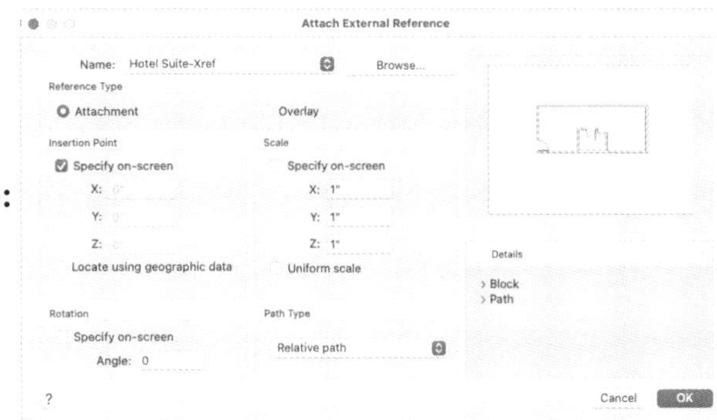

You can designate the reference as either an attachment to the drawing or as an overlay. As an overlay, you will only get the drawing you select as the reference, and it will not include any references that may be embedded within that drawing. If you want the drawing, including all the references that are attached to it, then select the reference type to be an Attachment.

Within the dialog box you can also show the reference at a scale or at an angle. You also have the option of specifying the insertion point on-screen. These choices are all similar to the Insert Block dialog box.

<u>Example:</u>

During the development of the hotel suite, you are focusing on options for the layout of the bathroom. You attach the latest floor plan from the architect to a new drawing and concentrate only on that portion of the floor plan.

Select Hotel Suite-Xref.dwg from the downloaded files from the publisher.

For this example, the reference will be designated as an attachment and the option of specifying the insertion point on screen are selected. Pick OK after the options are chosen.

The command line will show the path to where the file can be found and will prompt you for the insertion point:

ATTACH _attach
Attach Xref "Hotel Suite-Xref": C:\My Documents\AutoCAD downloads\Hotel Suite-Xref.dwg
"Hotel Suite-Xref" loaded.

***ATTACH** Specify insertion point or [Scale/X/Y/Z/Rotate/PScale/PX/PY/PZ/PRotate]*

(Pick a location on the screen to locate the reference drawing)

The reference drawing will appear on your screen, but it will be grayed-out because it is there only for reference.

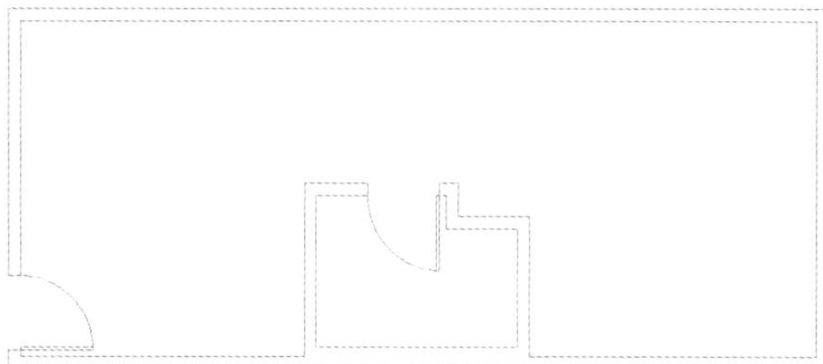

Because you only want to focus on a specific area, you can use the Clip option to only show that portion of the reference. The icon can be found on the Reference Panel of the Insert Tab.

Clipping the visible area of a Reference

Procedure:

Pick (left click): **CLIP icon** from the Reference Panel of the Insert Tab.

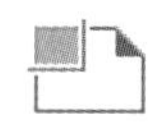

For Mac: Type **CLIP** in the command line

CLIP *Select Object to clip:* ***(Pick anywhere on the attached drawing)***
Select Object to clip: 1 found
Enter clipping option
[ON/OFF/Clipdepth/Delete/generate Polyline/New boundary] <New>:↵

(We are creating a new clipped area, accept the default option)

Outside mode - Objects outside boundary will be hidden.
Specify clipping boundary or select invert option:
[Select polyline/Polygonal/Rectangular/Invert clip] <Rectangular>: ↵

(We want the clipped area to be rectangular shaped, accept the default option)

Specify first corner: ***(Pick a location on the screen)***

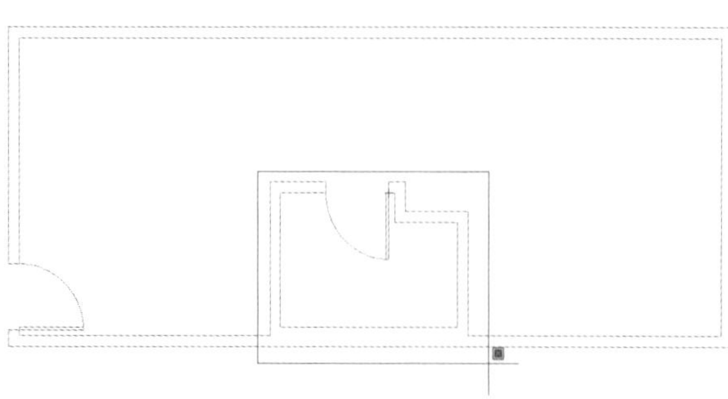

Specify opposite corner: ***(Pick the final location to define the rectangular boundary)***

After the Clip command is complete, your reference will only display the area you designated, and your drawing will look like this:

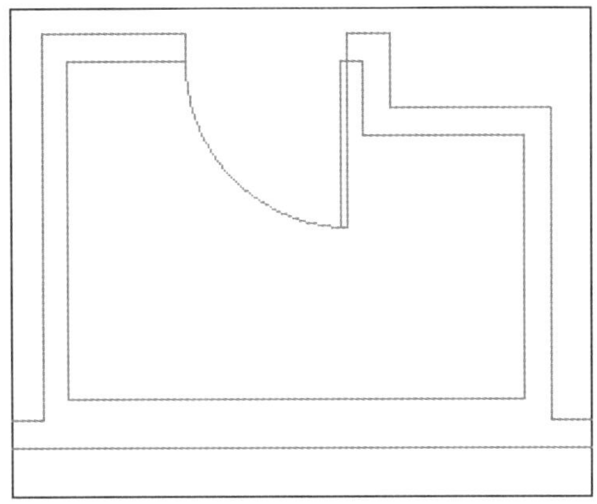

Try it:

Starting with the previous example of the clipped reference showing the bathroom, use Design Center (Blocks Palette for Mac) to insert blocks for the toilet, sink with faucet, tub, and shower head from the Hotel Suite Blocks drawing that you downloaded from the publisher's web site. Just place these off to the side for now.

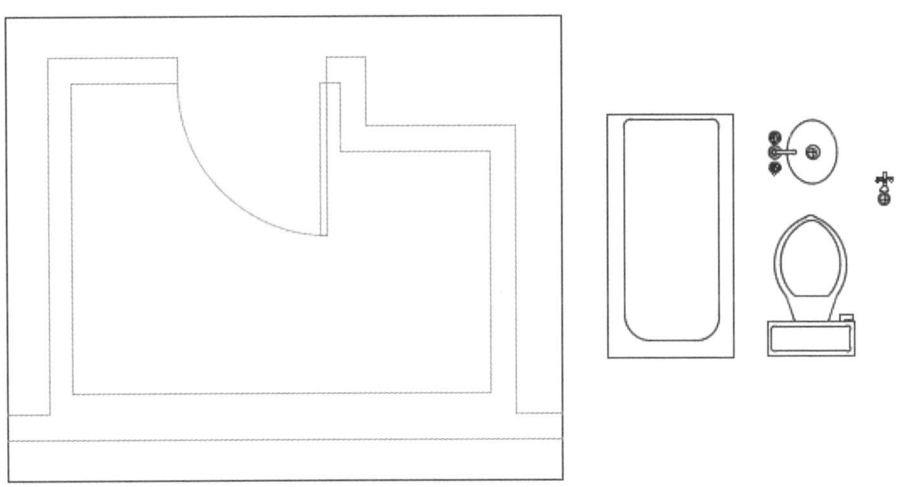

With the blocks inserted in the drawing and the clipped Xref attachment of the bathroom, arrange the blocks in the bathroom by using the move and rotate commands as needed to the positions shown:

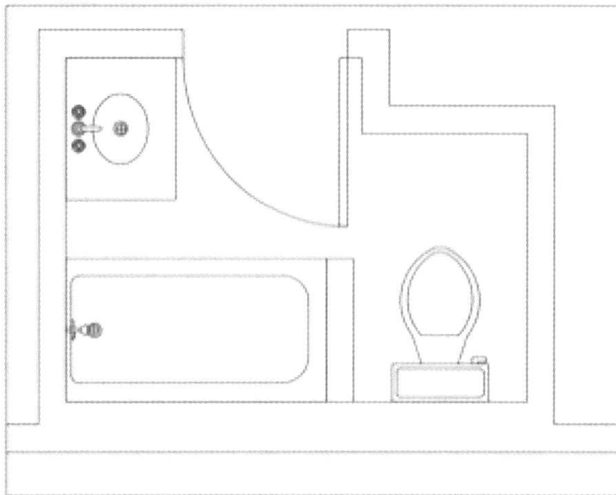

With this bathroom layout, a 24-inch deep by 30-inch-wide vanity is used, a 6-inch-thick dividing wall is added between the tub and the toilet, and the toilet is centered between the walls. One thought you may have is that perhaps the empty space in front of the toilet can be used for shelving and the space adjacent to the sink can be used for a trash can. You propose this design to the team, and it is accepted.

Editing a Reference

Because this design requires the addition of a wall, this feature needs to be added to the architect's drawing – which you are currently using as a reference. You can simply add that feature directly to the reference by using the Edit Reference command. This command can be found by expanding the Reference Panel of the Insert Tab, or by double left-clicking anywhere on the reference drawing:

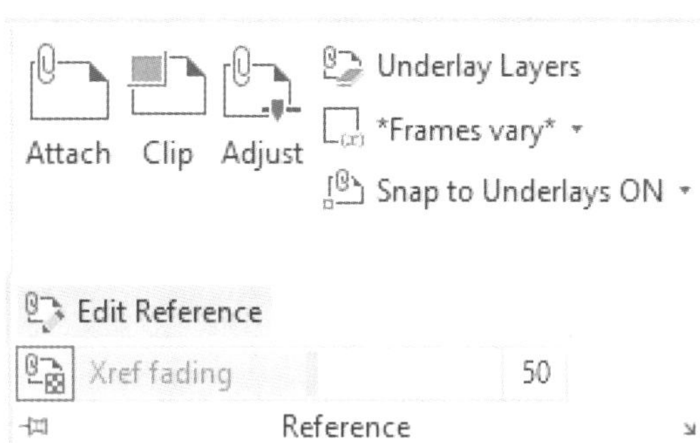

Procedure:

Pick (left click): **Edit Reference icon** from the Reference Panel of the Insert Tab. 

REFEDIT *Select reference:* ***(Pick anywhere on the attached drawing)***

Mac: Double left-click on the reference drawing

A Reference Edit dialog box will appear. Pick the OK button (Edit for Mac):

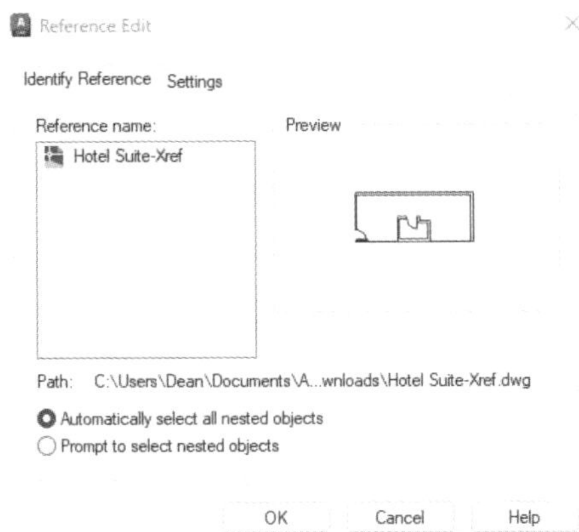

Mac:

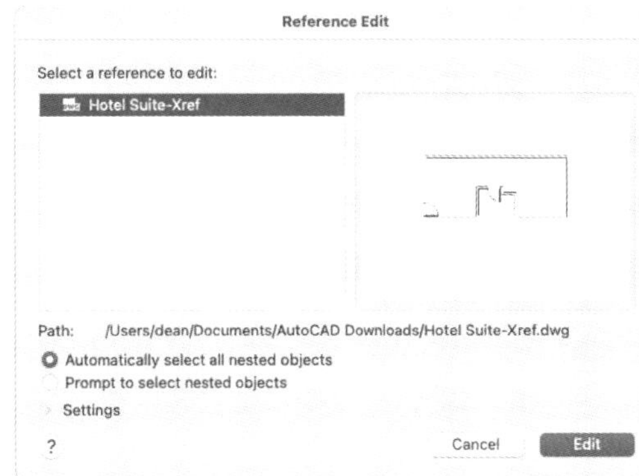

If you are editing a reference that was from a previous released version of AutoCAD, a warning dialog box will appear stating that the reference drawing will be updated to the current release drawing format. Pick OK.

An Edit Reference Panel will appear on the ribbon (Visor for Mac) and the command line will prompt you with the following:

Use REFCLOSE or the Refedit toolbar to end reference editing session.
*** Automatic save disabled during reference editing ***

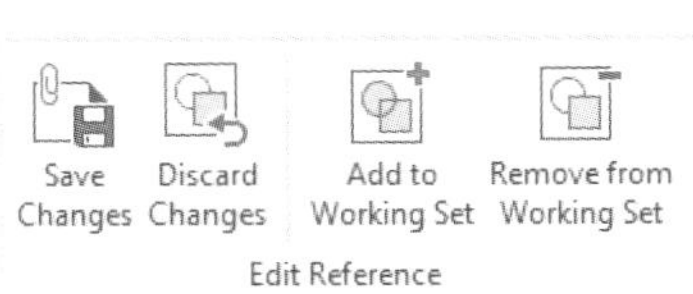

Mac:

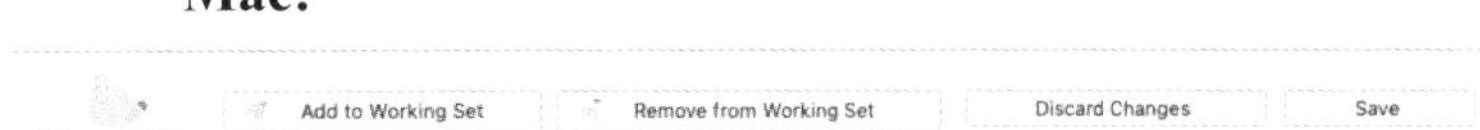

Pick (left click): **Add to Working Set icon**. 

Mac: 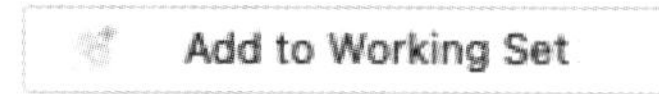

REFSET *Transfer objects between the RefEdit working set and host drawing...*
Enter an option [Add/Remove] <Add>: _add
Select objects: ***(Pick the three lines of the new wall)*** *1 found*
Select objects: 1 found, 2 total
Select objects: 1 found, 3 total
Select objects: ↵
3 Added to working set

Use the trim command to trim the intersection of the new wall with the original wall.

Pick the Save Changes icon from the Edit Reference toolbar (Save icon on Mac). A warning dialog box will appear that will allow you to confirm the save or cancel. Pick the OK button to save the changes (Save button on Mac).

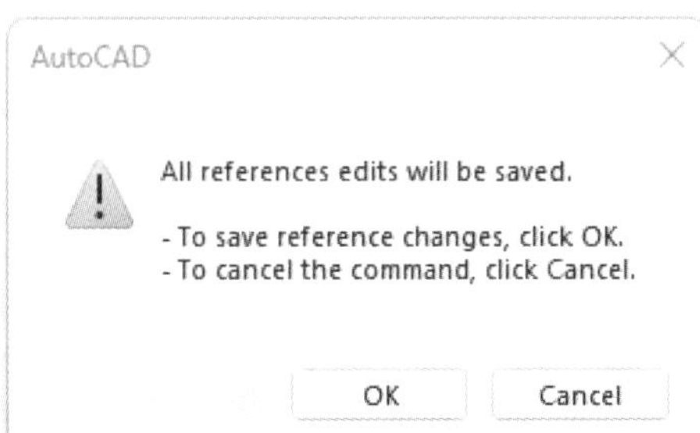

Mac: 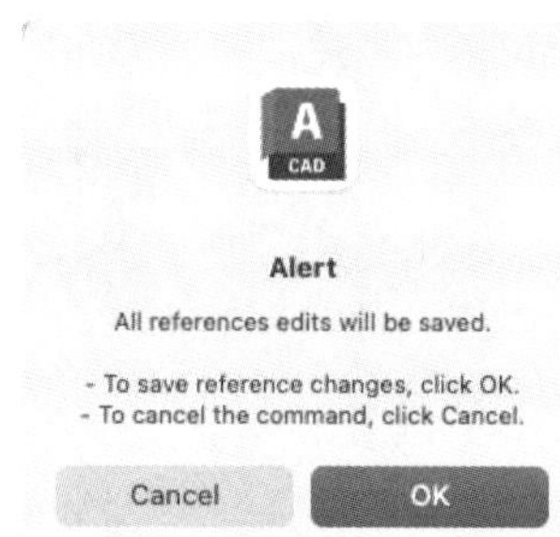

The changes you have made will now be part of the reference drawing. You can confirm this by opening the Hotel Suite-Xref drawing. Notice the new wall will appear on the drawing:

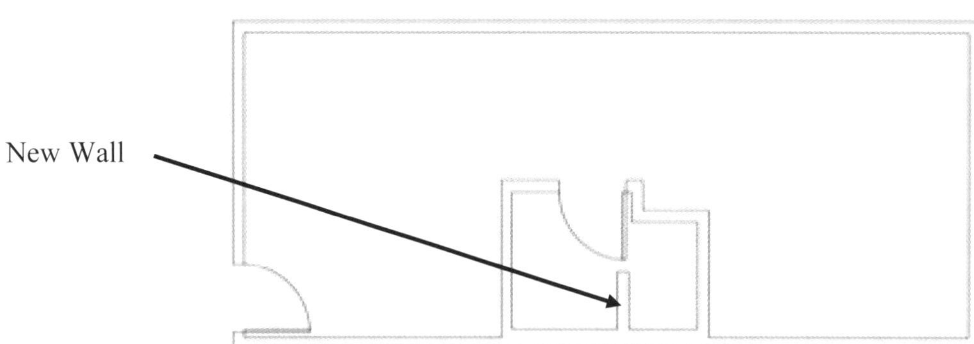

After you have confirmed this change, close the Hotel Suite-Xref drawing.

External Reference Manager – Reload and Detach

You can see which attachments are on your drawing by selecting the downward arrow on the Reference Panel. For the Mac, use the pull-down menu Insert and select Reference Manager. The External References Manager will appear:

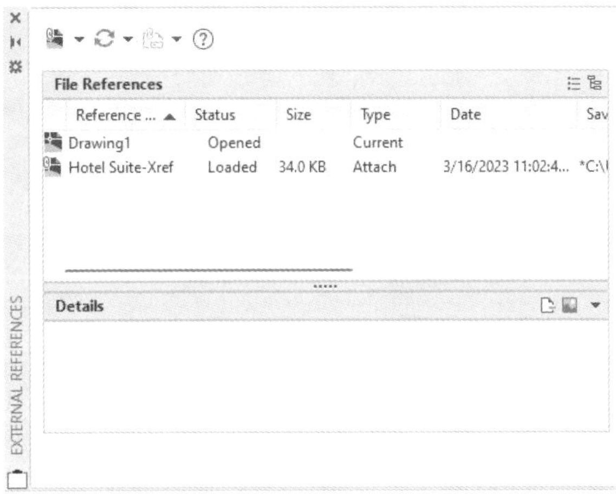

Mac:

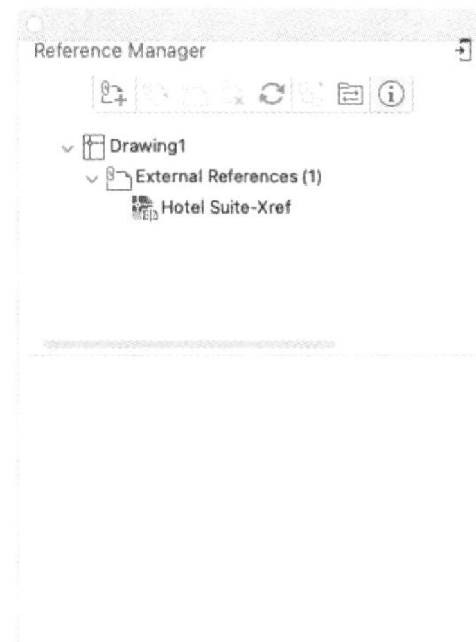

There are advantages to using Xrefs. It will provide a warning to you whenever the reference has changed:

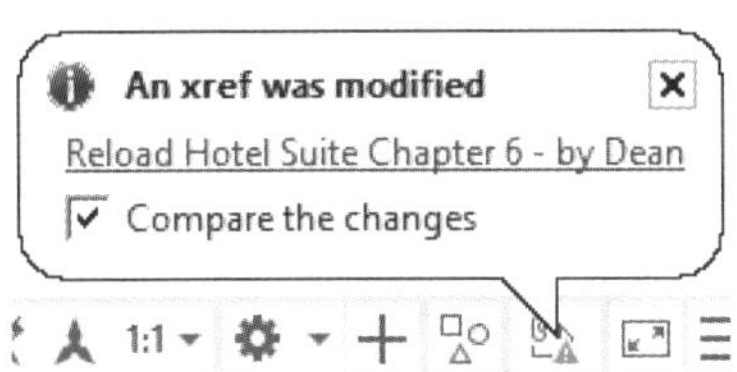

Mac:

When a reference has been modified, you can update that reference on your drawing by reloading it. To reload the reference in this example, right-click on the Hotel Suite-Xref in the External Reference Manager and then select Reload from the choices given.

Mac:

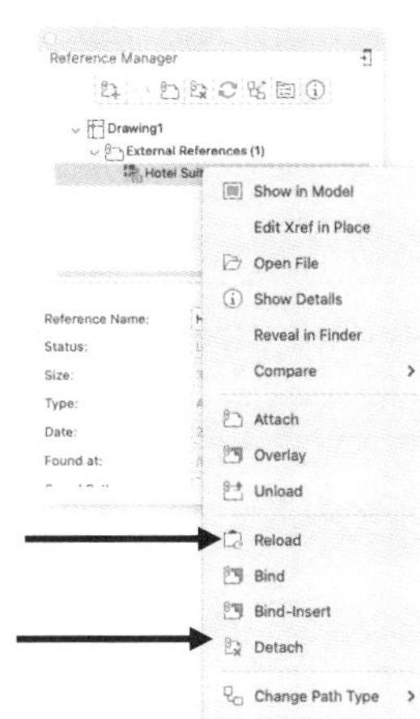

Because AutoCAD is looking in a specific location to find the reference, that reference drawing needs to remain there for AutoCAD to find it. If it is moved to a different memory location on your computer or the shared drive that the team is using, that linkage will be lost. You can browse to find the new location, but it is good practice to leave it in the same location. This is not a bad thing but something that you will need to pay attention to.

You can remove references from your drawing by detaching them. It is recommended that you detach them rather than erase them to completely remove anything from the reference.

To detach the reference, right-click on the Hotel Suite-Xref in the External Reference Manager and then select Detach from the choices given. Click Yes in the pop-up to confirm.

When you are done, close the External Reference Manager.

Layers

Layers are available in AutoCAD. Layers can be thought of as see-through sheets that are stacked on top of each other. You can use layers to organize and manage your objects. You can make specific layers invisible by turning them off or freezing them. You can lock any layer so that any objects on that layer cannot be changed. Some design teams require you to follow specific naming conventions for your layers, and other teams do not. If you are working independently, as the designer, it is your choice how you use and name layers. You can add any number of layers. Once layers are created, and you no longer need them, they can also be deleted. You cannot delete Layer 0. It is the default layer for AutoCAD drawings. If you insert dimensions, or bring items in using Design Center, AutoCAD may create a layer named Defpoints. You cannot delete this layer either – just ignore it. The Layers Panel is on the Home Tab:

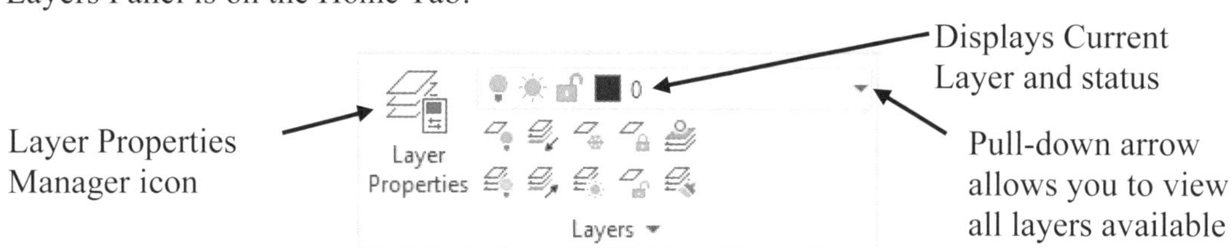

For the Mac, the Layers Palette may already be docked. If it is not already visible, use the Window pull-down menu to turn on the Layers Palette.

Mac

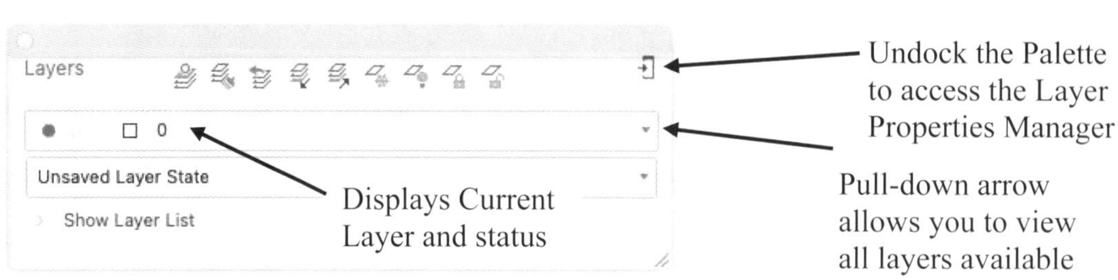

Layer Properties Manager

When you select the Layer Properties Manager icon, a dialog box will appear. For the Mac, select the Show Layer List arrow to expand the Layers Palette.

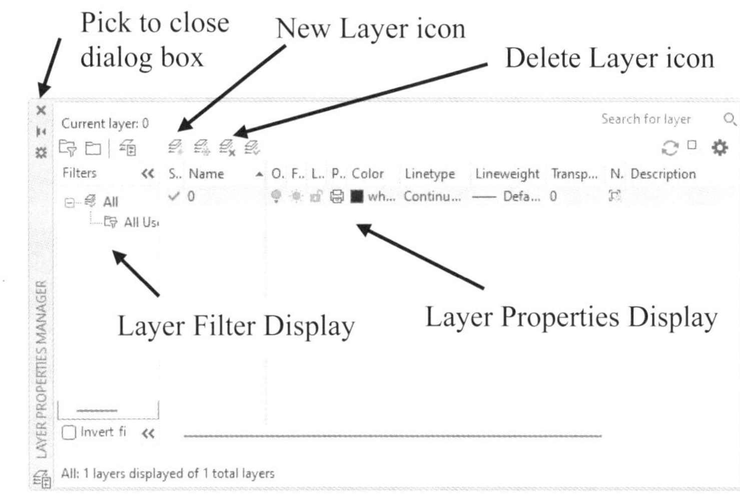

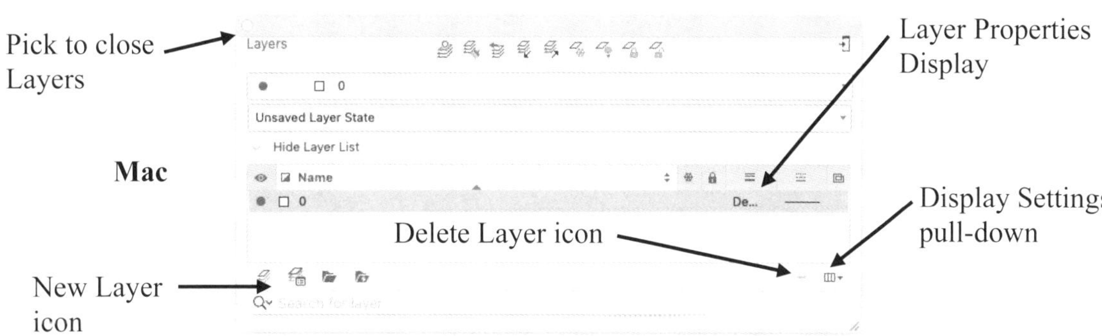

Notice that the dialog box has two sides: the Layer Filter and the Layer Properties. We will not be using Filters, so these instructions will be limited to Layer Properties.

The dialog box shown has Layer 0. We will use this dialog box to create new layers and define properties for those layers. When done, pick the "X" to close the dialog box.

Creating a New Layer

Pick the New Layer icon. A new row appears on the list. This represents the new layer and is automatically given a default name of Layer1, which is highlighted and ready for editing. As an example, let's name this layer Existing Structure. Simply type that in place of Layer1.

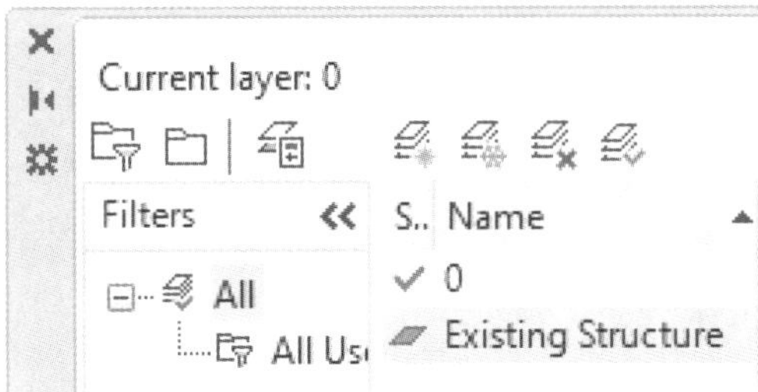

Mac

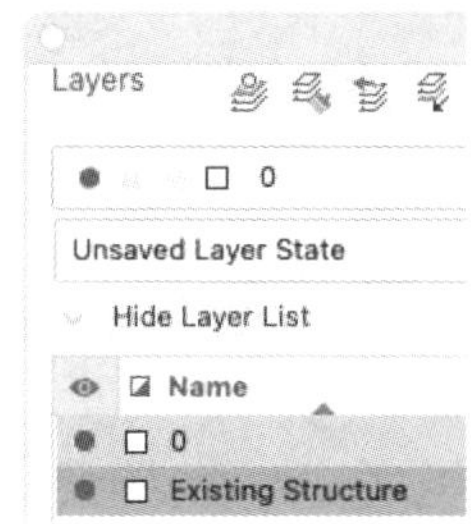

For the Mac, columns can be added to or removed from the Palette using the pull-down arrow for Display Settings and selecting the View Options. When an item is displayed, a checkmark will appear next to it. Uncheck any item to remove it from the Palette. Notice the change in the Layers Palette. When done, make sure Status is checked.

Mac

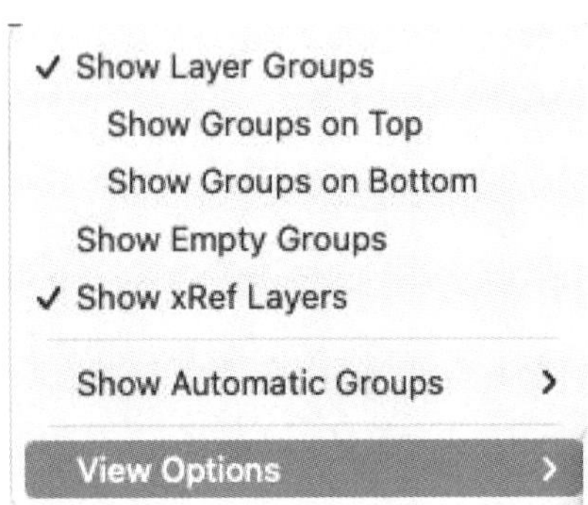

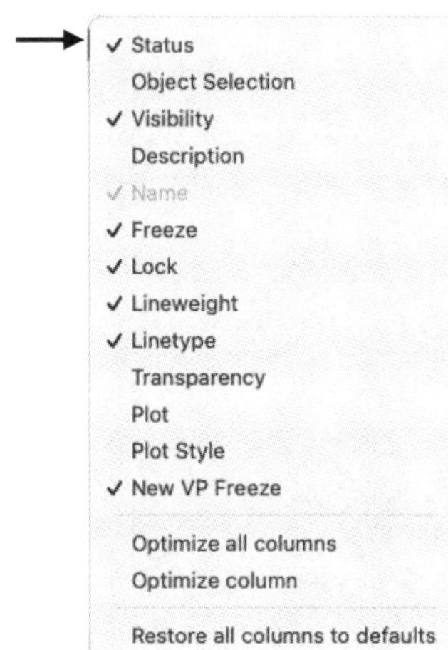

There are several columns in the Layer Properties display. The width of the columns can be adjusted by moving your cursor to the line separating the column names and dragging. Double-clicking will adjust the column to minimum width and still allow the word to fit.

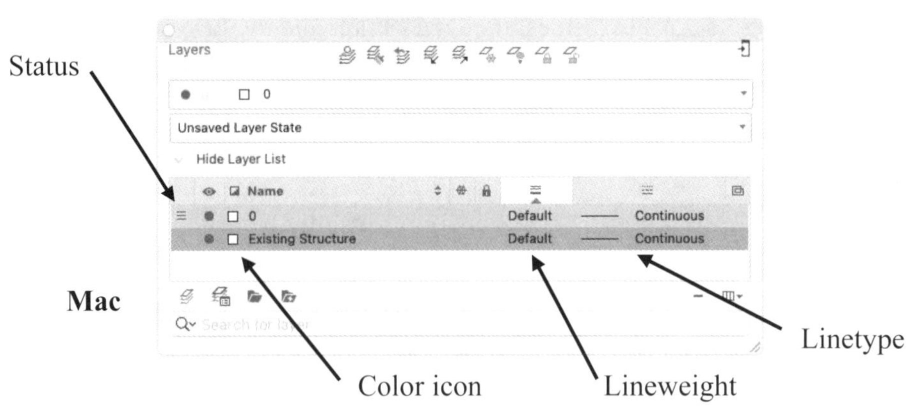

Visibility of Layers

Layers can be turned on or off, frozen or thawed, and locked or unlocked, by picking the relative icon in each column. These icons change as each option is selected:

Icon | Meaning

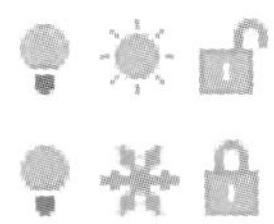

On, Thawed, Unlocked

Off, Frozen, Locked

Mac

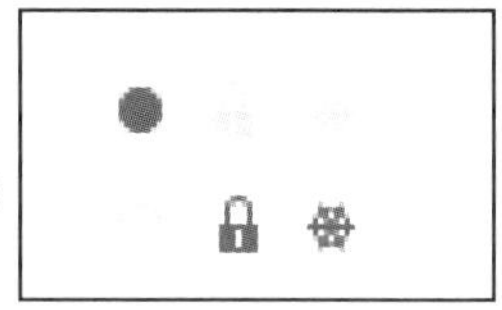

On, Unlocked, Thawed

Off, Locked, Frozen

For the Mac, to Freeze a layer, pick in the column displays the snowflake. A snowflake displayed in the column for that layer indicates that it is frozen. To lock a layer, pick in the column that shows the lock. A lock is displayed in the column for that layer to indicate that it is locked. To thaw or unlock the layer, pick the icon in the column for that layer and the icon will no longer be visible.

When a layer is turned off or frozen, the objects on that layer become invisible. The difference between the two is subtle – the drawing is regenerated when you thaw a frozen layer, but it is not when you turn a layer back on that was off. The typical designer doesn't care about this subtlety. These differences are not important.
What is important is this: when in a Layout, freezing a layer in the "current viewport" is the best way to control visibility – especially for printing. If you turn a layer off, it is invisible in all viewports; this is usually not what is desired. This difference comes in handy when you have multiple viewports or multiple Layouts.

When a layer is Locked, it remains visible, but you cannot change or delete any of the objects that reside on that layer. This is a good tool for preserving objects, such as those on layers provided by the architect. You use this feature when you don't want to risk changing objects that were provided by others on your design team.

For the new layer we just created, we will leave the icons On, Thawed, and Unlocked.

Assigning a Color to the Layer

To change the color of a layer, pick the color icon in the Color column. When you pick it, the Select Color dialog box will appear. On the Mac, several standard colors appear along with "Select Color" choice. Picking Select Color will show the Select Color dialog box (Color Palette on Mac).

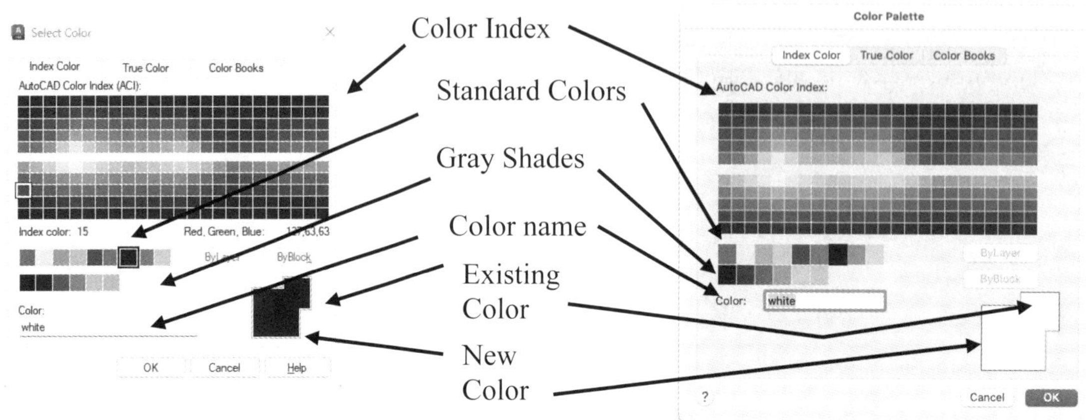

Mac

There are three tabs to choose your color: Index Color, True Color, and Color Books. The index color is shown above and has pre-defined standard colors and numbered colors. The other tabs are illustrated below:

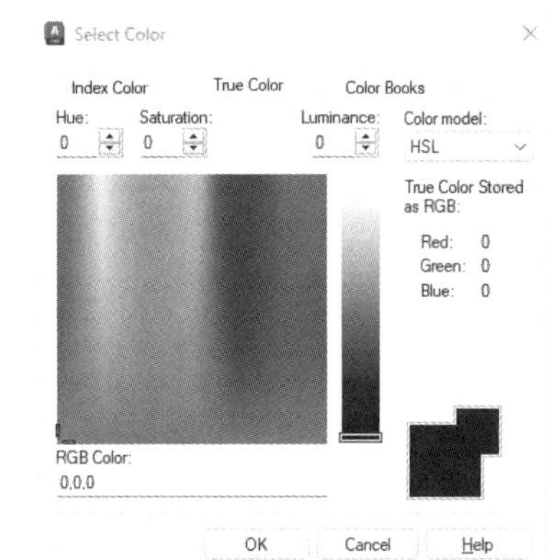

Mac

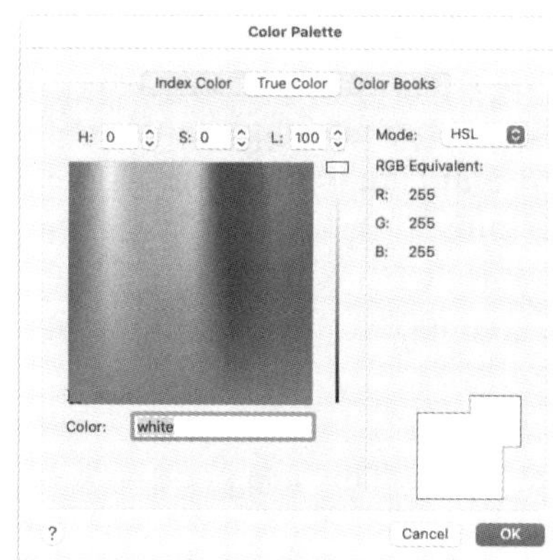

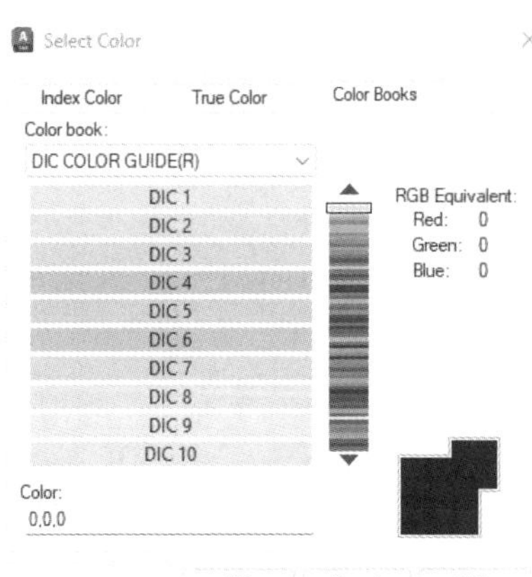

Mac

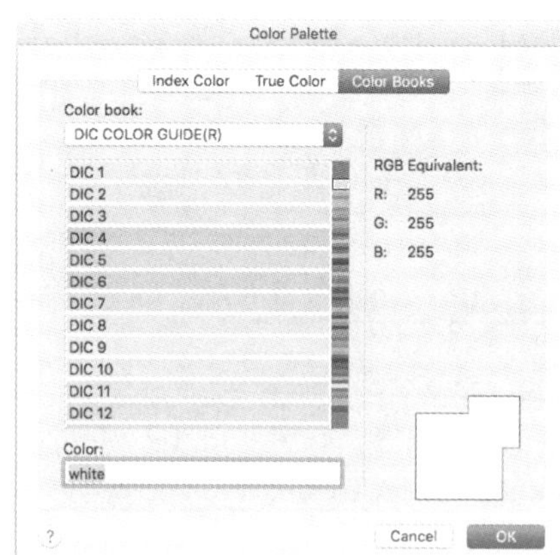

Under the Color Books tab, there is a pull-down arrow that you can use to select from a variety of available color books, including Pantone colors.
Choose the color you desire for your layer then pick the OK button to exit the dialog box.

Assigning a Linetype to the Layer

To change the Linetype of a layer, pick the word in the Linetype column (in this case the word is Continuous). When you pick it, the Select Linetype dialog box will appear. On the Mac, select Manage to get the dialog box to appear.

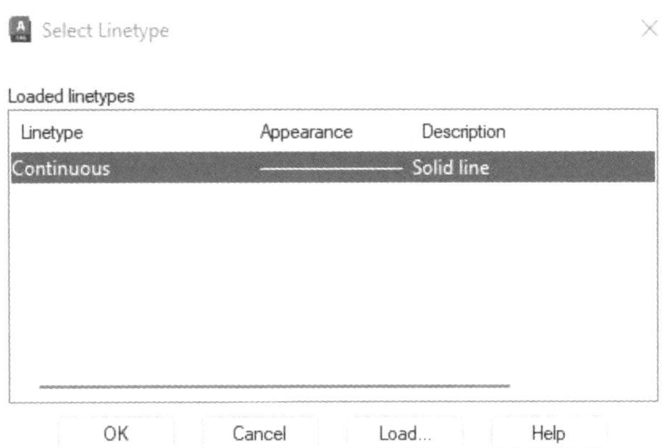

Mac

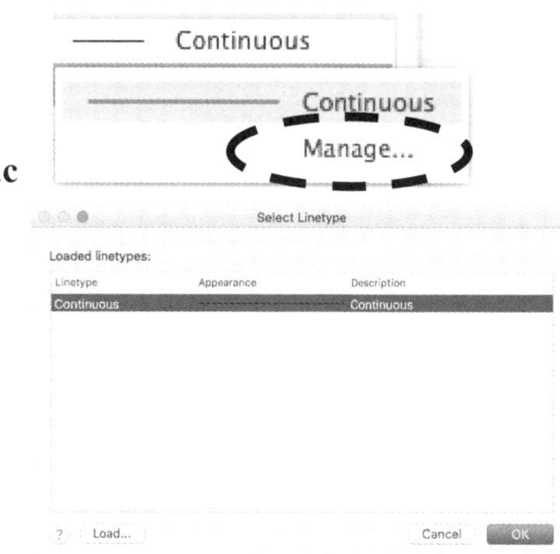

There are a number of different line types to choose from in AutoCAD; however, they may not be loaded in your drawing yet. These are stored in a common AutoCAD program file in order to minimize the amount of memory each drawing will require.
As an example, suppose we wish to change the Linetype to a hidden line. Since that is not available in the Select Linetype dialog box, we will have to load it. Pick the Load… button. The Load or Reload Linetypes dialog box will appear.

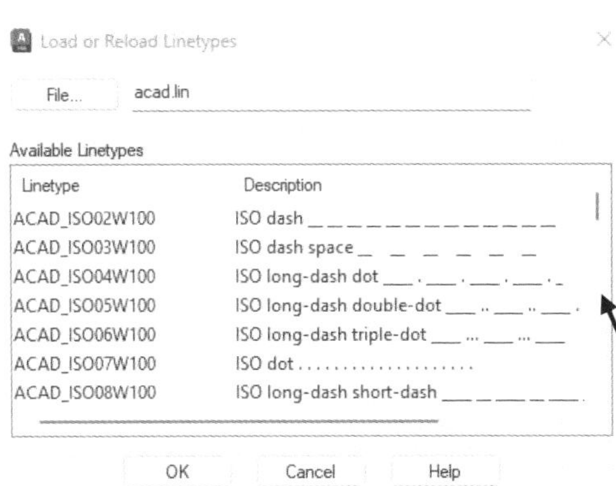

Mac

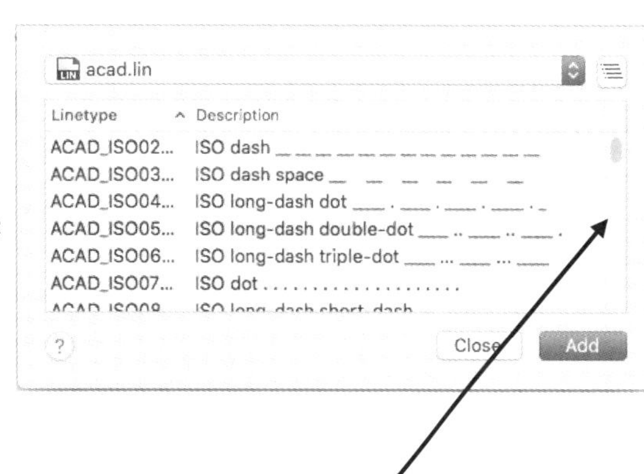

Scroll down the list to find the Linetype you desire

Scroll down the list until you find Hidden. Pick on the word Hidden and that Linetype will be highlighted. Then pick the OK button (Add on Mac) to exit the dialog box and return to Select Linetype dialog box. In that dialog box, the Hidden Linetype is now available as a Linetype choice.

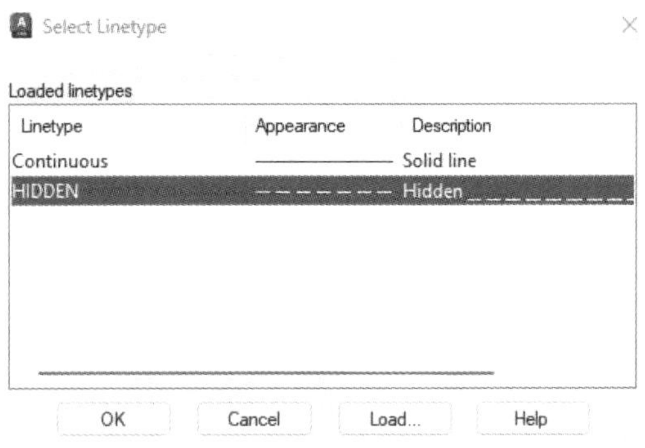

Mac

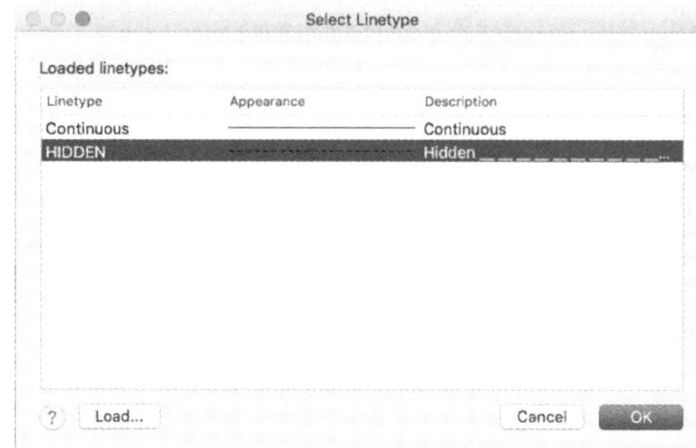

Pick the HIDDEN Linetype to select it, and then pick the OK button to exit the dialog box and return to the Layer Properties Manager dialog box.

Pick to close dialog box

Mac

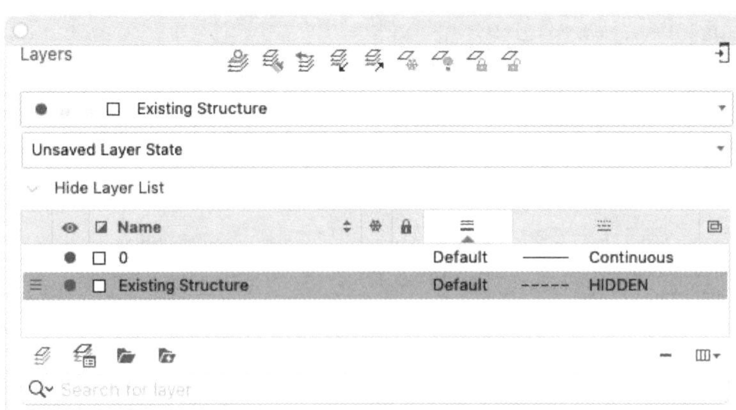

When you are done, you can close the Layer Properties Manager.

Linetype Scale

Each linetype is defined as a specific size. For a hidden line, AutoCAD defines the length of the dash, and the length of the space between dashes. With large drawings used in interior design, the hidden line may actually appear as a solid line. To correct the visibility of the hidden line, you can change the linetype scale. To change the scale of all Linetypes in your drawing, you need to type in the command "ltscale" on the command line:

Example:

Shown here is a countertop with three cabinets underneath. The lines of the cabinets should be dashed because they are hidden lines. We can create those lines on a layer with the linetype of hidden. However, because of the size of the object, it is difficult to distinguish that these are dashed lines.

We can correct this by typing the LTSCALE command. The value of the scale factor can be determined by trial and error.

ltscale↵

LTSCALE *Enter new linetype scale factor <1.0000>:* **10↵**

Regenerating model.

The following shows the results of using the scale factor of 10:

As you can see, the appearance of the hidden lines is much better.

Using the LTSCALE command globally changes the scale factor of all Linetypes on your drawing. This may not always be desirable. If you also have centerlines on your drawing, applying the same scale factor may not be desired. In that case, you can use the Properties palette to change the linetype scale of an individual object selected.

Current Layer

The Current Layer is the layer that objects will reside on as you draw. There are a number of ways to make a layer the Current Layer. While still in the Layer Properties Manager, you can highlight the layer and pick the Set Current icon. When a layer is the current layer, the green check mark is shown in the Status column for that layer.

The Layers Panel on the Home Tab will now show the layer you selected as the Current Layer.

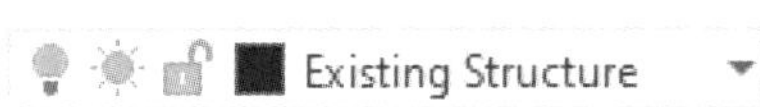

On the Mac, instead of a green checkmark, the current layer is shown in the status column with this icon:

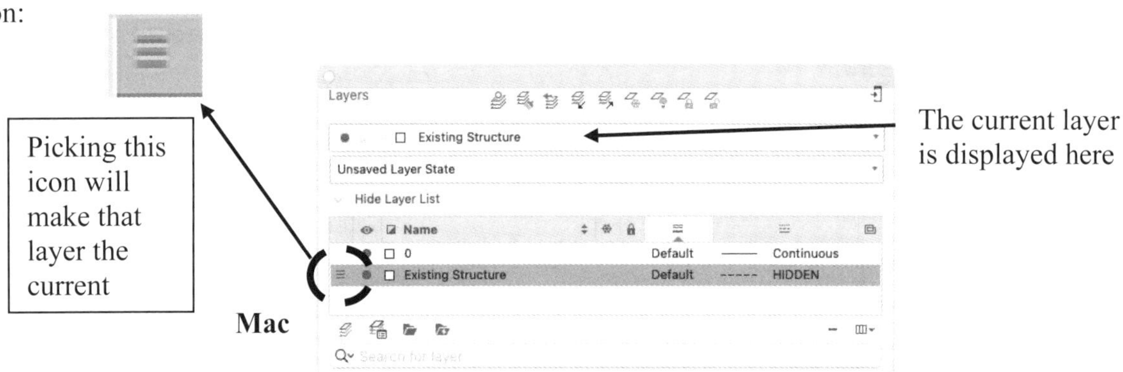

Using the Layers toolbar, you can change the Current Layer by using the pull-down arrow and picking the layer. As an example, let's make layer 0 the Current Layer:

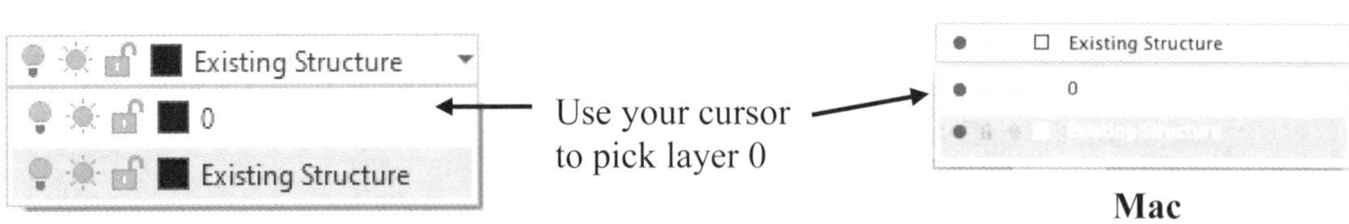

Layer 0 is now displayed as the Current Layer:

Mac

You can also use the Make Current icon. With nothing in the command line, select an object. The blue grips will display, and the Layers toolbar will show the name of the layer that the object is on.

As an example, suppose there are two circles on the drawing. One circle is on layer 0, and the other is on layer Existing Structure. Regardless of the current layer displayed, when an object is selected, the name of the layer that it resides on will be displayed in the Layer toolbar:

Picking the Make Current icon makes the Layer that the selected object is on the Current Layer.

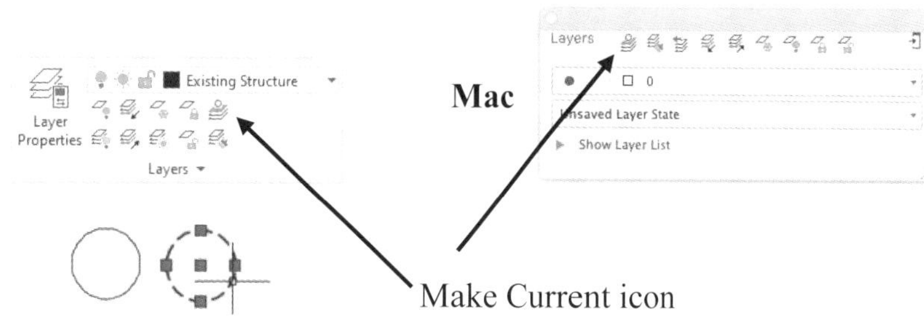

Lineweight

Typically, the object lines for your designs should be thicker than the dimension lines. That makes it easier to distinguish the items of interest. AutoCAD has a feature that allows you to control and view the Lineweight. This can be done for individual objects or for any object drawn on a layer that has the Lineweight defined. This is very similar to assigning colors or linetype.

Before setting the Lineweight, make sure the unit that you select for Lineweight is Inches and not Millimeters. To ensure that you have the correct units, use the pull-down arrow of the Lineweight section of the Properties Panel of the Home Tab and pick Lineweight Settings…

On the Mac, use the pull-down menu Format, and select Lineweight…

The Lineweight Settings dialog box will appear. Ensure that the radio button in front of Inches is selected and the check box for Display Lineweight is checked (PC only). When you are done, pick the OK button to close the dialog box.

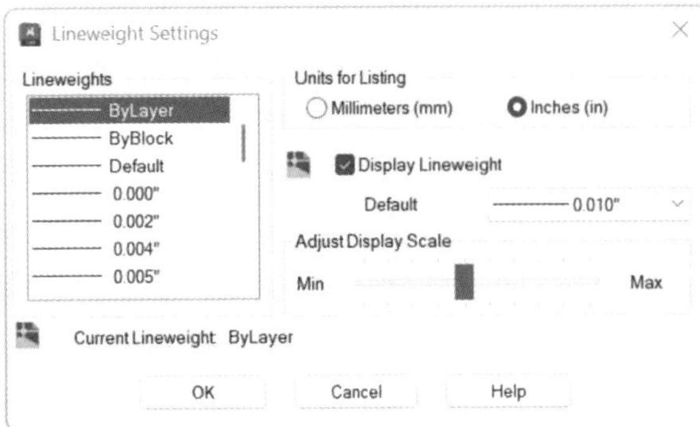

Mac

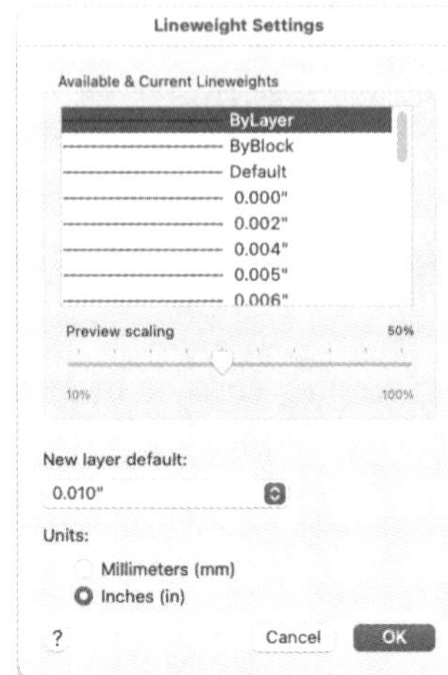

To change the Lineweight of all objects on a specific layer, use the Layer Properties icon to bring up the Layer Properties Manager dialog box. On the Mac, display the Layers Palette.

In this example, we will change the Lineweight of layer Existing Structure to a thicker value than the default value. The default value of Lineweight is set at .25 mm (which is approximately .010 inches). We will choose .020″ (.50 mm) to make the lines twice as thick.

In the Layers Palette, pick on the word Default under the Lineweight column of the layer Existing Structure. A Lineweight dialog box will appear. Scroll down the list of available Lineweights and pick .020″. If you prefer to work in millimeters, pick .50 mm to achieve the thickness. When you are done, pick the OK button to close the dialog box (except for Mac).

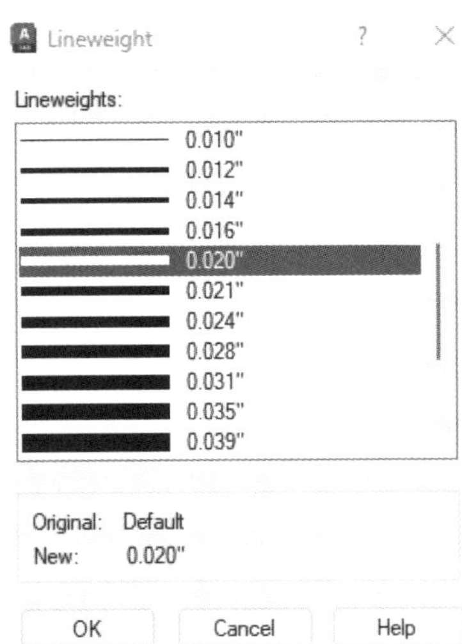

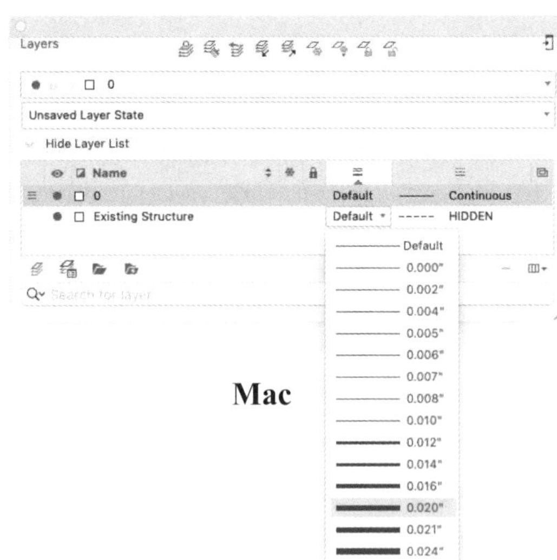

Mac

Notice that the new value of the Lineweight for the layer Existing Structure is displayed in the Layer Properties Manager dialog box. Pick the X in the upper left corner to close the dialog box.

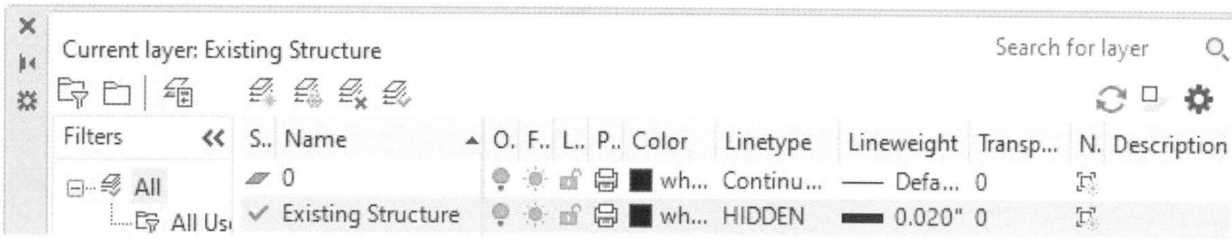

Mac

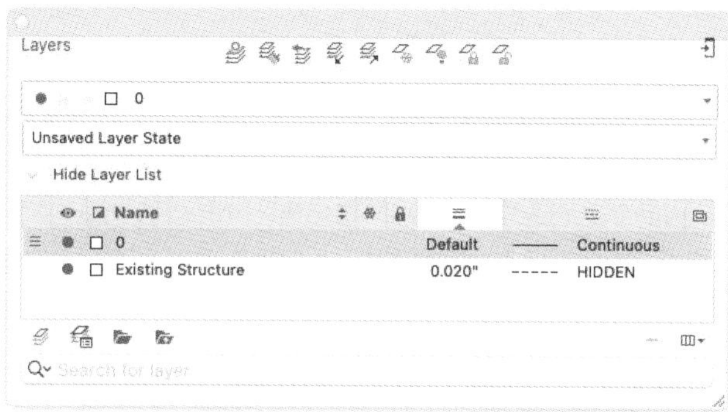

When in a Layout, the visibility of the thicker lines will not appear on the screen unless you use the check box in the Lineweight Settings dialog box. You can also toggle the Show/Hide Lineweight switch on the status bar. If it is not on the status bar, add it using the customization switch.

Show/Hide Lineweight
Toggle Switch

This is an example of the visibility of the lineweight. The object lines are twice as thick as the dimension lines.

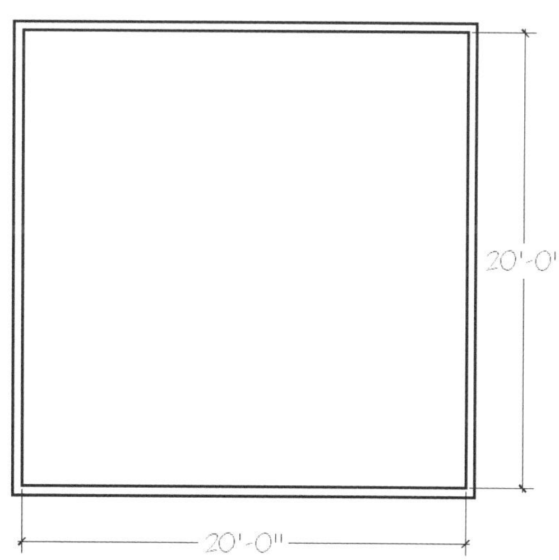

Properties

The Properties Panel is on the Home Tab. Pick on the downward arrow to expand the panel.

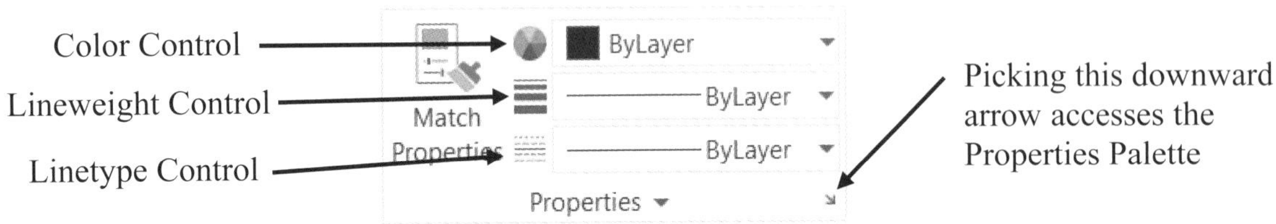

All three controls have ByLayer and ByBlock as selection options. The default is ByLayer, which means that the values that were set for that Layer will be used for the objects drawn. ByBlock allows you to retain the properties of the Blocks inserted. You can use these controls to change the properties of individual objects instead of having the entire layer with the object properties. Simply select the object, and then use the pull-down arrow to change to the desired property.
For the Mac, there is no Properties Panel. Use the Properties Inspector Palette instead. This is explained in the next section.

Changing Object Properties

You can change the properties of objects using the Properties Palette. The Properties Palette is accessed by picking the downward arrow on the lower right of the Properties Panel. On the Mac, use the Window pull-down menu to turn on Properties Inspector. When you select this, the Properties palette will appear:

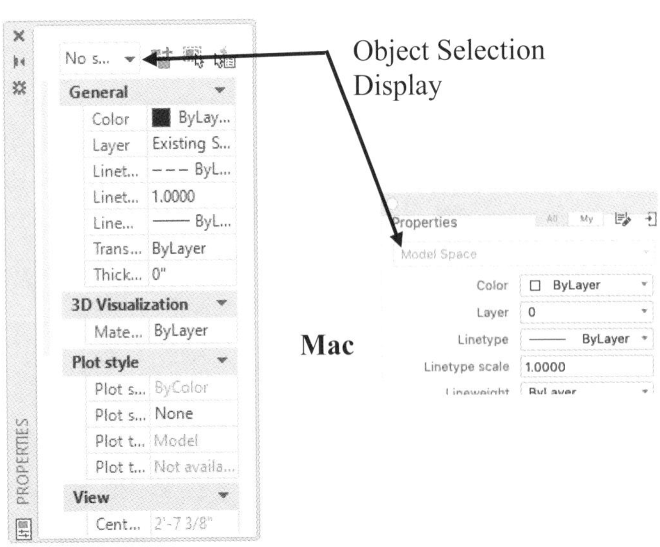

Using the Properties dialog box allows you to change properties for selected objects. You can change any of the items that are shown in the dialog box. For example, if you want to change the color of an item, pick on Color, and the entire section is highlighted, and a pull-down arrow appears. Use the pull-down arrow to select the color. When you are done, close the dialog box. Use the escape key to remove the grips from the selected objects.

Example:

Suppose we had a circle located on the center of the countertop of the previous example, with lines drawn and the Linetypes of the lines set to "center". With the current LTSCALE factor of 10, the centerlines of the circle will appear as follows:

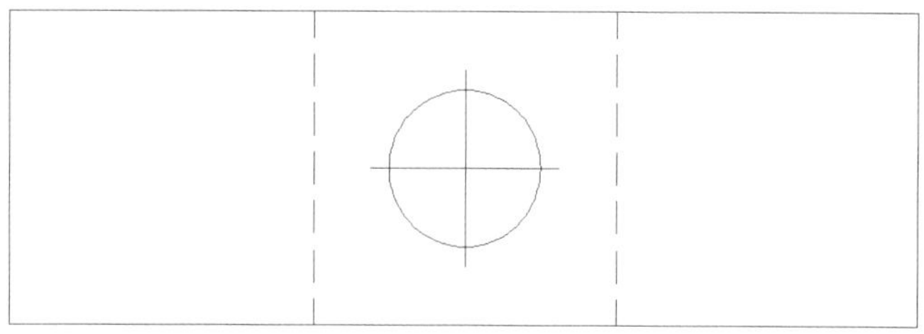

As you can see, they do not properly appear as centerlines. Since we like the scale factor we have chosen for the hidden lines, we do not want to globally change that factor by using the LTSCALE command. Instead, we can use the Properties palette, select the centerlines, and change the Linetype scale factor for those lines.

Here we can see that the two centerlines were selected and the Properties palette Linetype scale portion was also selected. We can simply type in a new scale factor for the centerlines. In this case, a scale factor of .5 seems to work best. Choosing .5 would have been the same as a global scale factor of 5 since a global scale factor of 10 is already applied (.5 x 10 = 5).

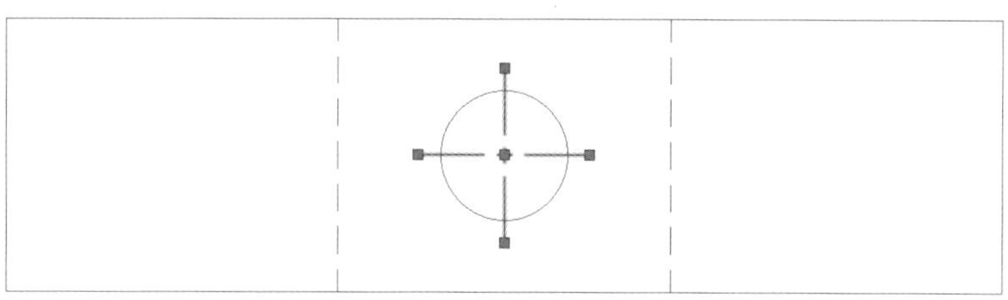

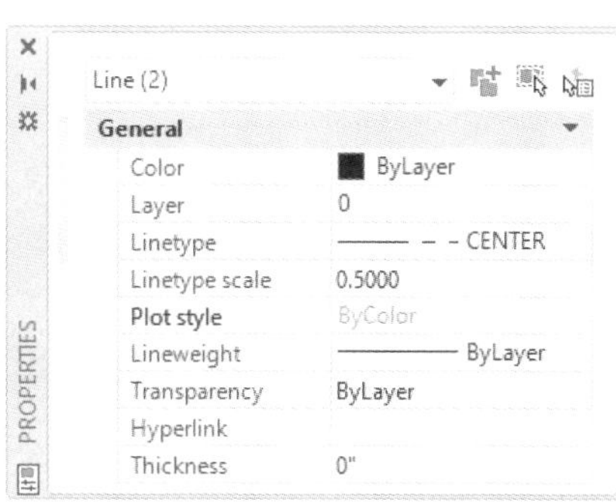

Mac

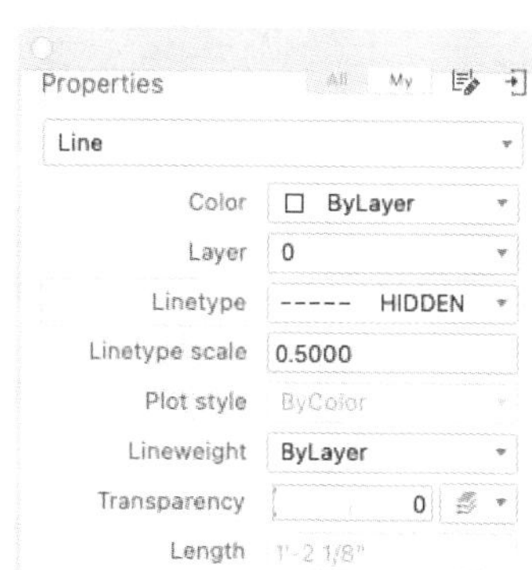

After you apply the scale factor to the centerlines, the drawing will look like this:

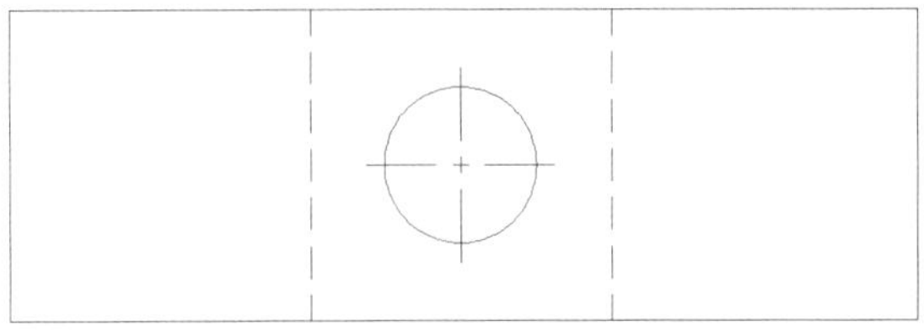

Match Properties

The Match Properties command allows you to easily copy the properties of an existing item. This would include all properties such as the layer it is on, color, linetype, lineweight, etc. After selecting the command, the object that has the properties you want must be selected first. This is called the source object. Then, the object that you want to change is selected. This is called the destination object.

Procedure:

Pick (left-click): **Match Properties icon** from the Properties Panel of the Home Tab. 

Mac users: Pick the **Match Properties icon** from the toolbar above the drawing space.

Current active settings: Color Layer Ltype Ltscale Lineweight Transparency Thickness PlotStyle Dim Text Hatch Polyline Viewport Table Material Multileader Center object
MATCHPROP *Select source object:*

Pick the object that has the properties that you want to copy.

After selecting the source object, the command line prompts you with the following:

Select destination object(s) or [Settings]:

Select the object you want to change.

Select destination object(s) or [Settings]: ↵

Pressing the ↵ Enter key will exit the command.

The destination object now has the same properties as the source object.

Purge

If you created, or imported, blocks, layers, etc. that you are no longer using in your drawing, you may no longer want them to be part of your drawing. The way to eliminate items that you don't need because they are not being used is to use the Purge command.

Procedure:

Pick (left click): **Purge icon** from the Cleanup Panel of the Manage Tab 
(As an alternative, pick the **Application Menu Browser,** select **Drawing Utilities,** and select **Purge)**

Mac users: Pick the **Purge icon** from the toolbar above the drawing space.

A dialog box will appear:

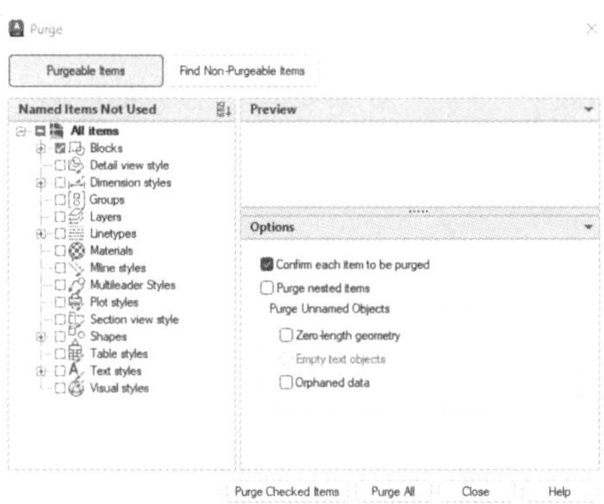

Mac

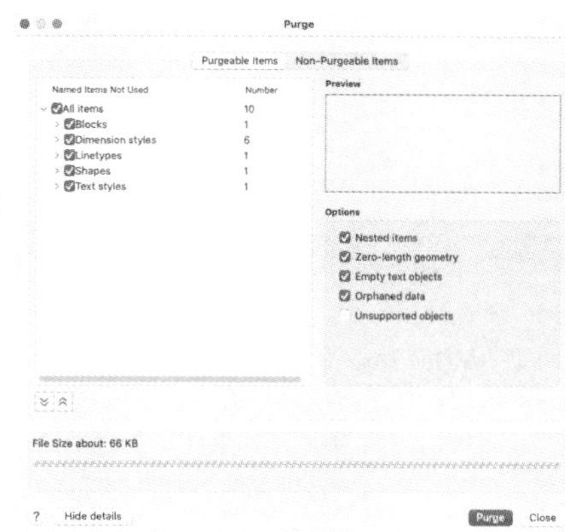

You can check off items you want to purge, then pick the Purge Checked Items button (Purge button on Mac). If you just want to clean up the drawing entirely of unused items, click on the Purge All button (PC only). After selecting the Purge All button, a confirmation dialog box will appear:

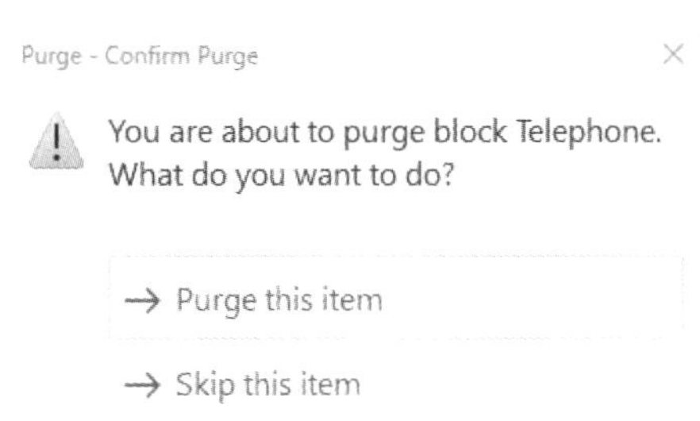

Dialog box when Purge Checked Items button is selected

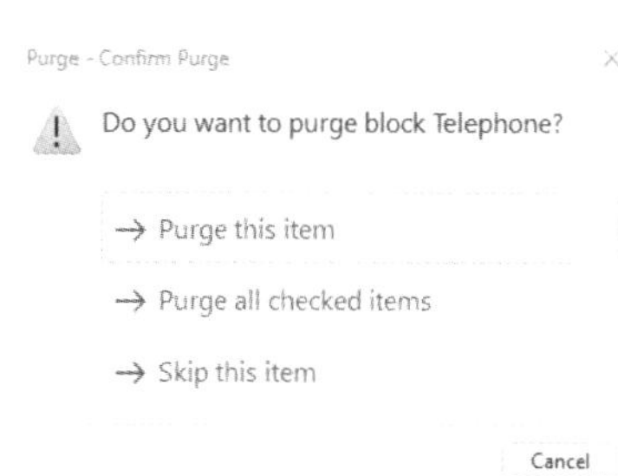

Dialog box when Purge All button is selected

You can select to purge the item (or purge all checked items), or skip purging the item. When all items that can be purged have been confirmed, pick the Close button to exit the Purge dialog box.

Summary

In this chapter you have learned to:

- Group objects together to become a block
- Insert blocks that exist within the drawing or entire files from outside the drawing
- Use Design Center to bring blocks in from other drawings
- Use Xref to bring in reference material to use but not be part of your drawing
- Create new layers
- Load new Linetypes
- Rename and define properties – Color, Linetype, Lineweight – for layers
- Change properties of individual objects
- Copy the properties of an object using Match Properties
- Clean-up your drawing by purging unused items

Review Questions

1. What is a grouping of objects called in AutoCAD?
2. What method is used to bring Blocks in from other drawings?
3. What other things besides Blocks can be brought into your drawing using Design Center?
4. What is the AutoCAD name for a solid line type?
5. How do you change a line from solid to hidden?
6. What are Layers and how are they used?
7. How do you change an object line thickness and display it on your screen?
8. What are object properties and how are they changed?
9. How do you correct the visibility of a hidden line if it still appears solid?
10. Why is freezing a layer in the "current viewport" more useful than turning a layer off?

Exercises

1. Open the Conference Room from exercise 1 of chapter 5. Use the Insert Block command to import the Conference Chair you created from exercise 3 of chapter 5. Use the copy and move commands to locate the chairs in the conference room.

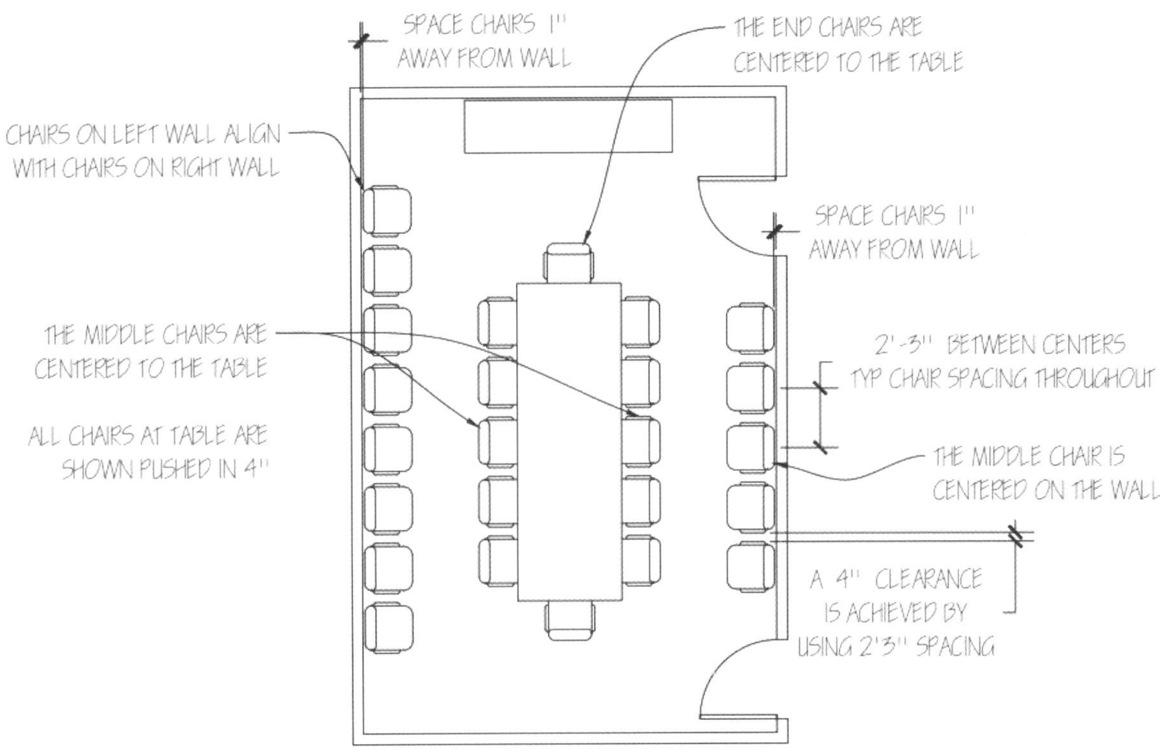

2. Download the Plant and Conference Phone drawings from the publisher's web site. Use Design Center to put two plants and the conference phone into the conference room drawing as shown:

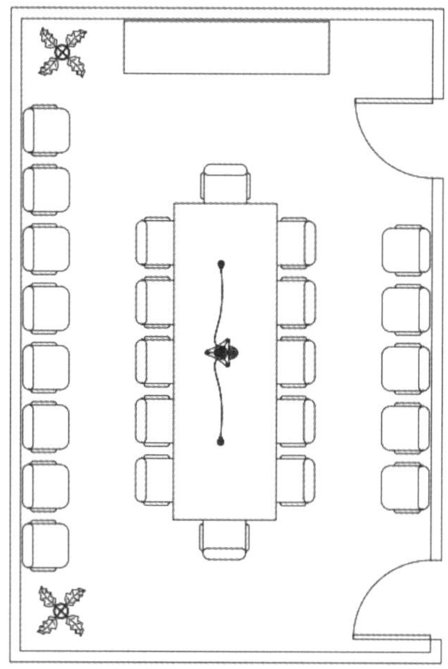

3. Continue building on Exercise 2 by creating layers "Furniture", "Misc" and "Structure". Assign properties to those layers as shown. After the layers are created, change the layer that the walls and doors are on from "0" to "Structure"; tables and chairs from "0" to "Furniture"; and the plants and conference phone from "0" to "Misc".

Name	Color	Lineweight
Furniture	magenta	0.012"
Misc	green	Default
Structure	blue	0.012"

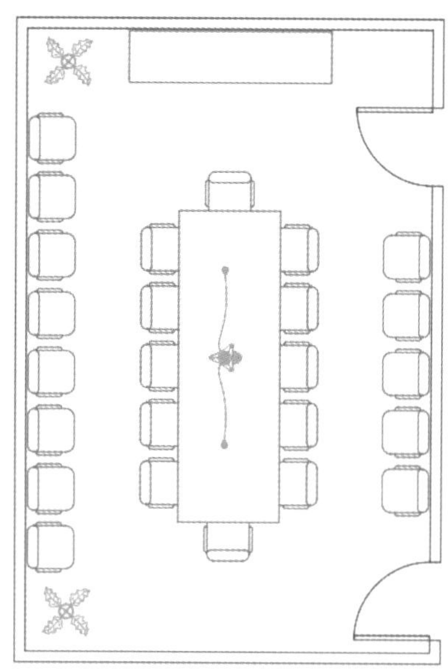

4. Draw the Galley Kitchen. Use Design Center to insert the Range, Refrigerator, and Sink. These are provided with the AutoCAD program and are also available on the publisher's web site. Create layers "Structure", "Appliances", "Plumbing", and "Cabinets". Place the objects on their corresponding layer. Because the hidden lines of the base cabinets align with the wall cabinets, these need to be separate lines. Note that the countertop depth is shown as the same depth as the base cabinets for simplicity.

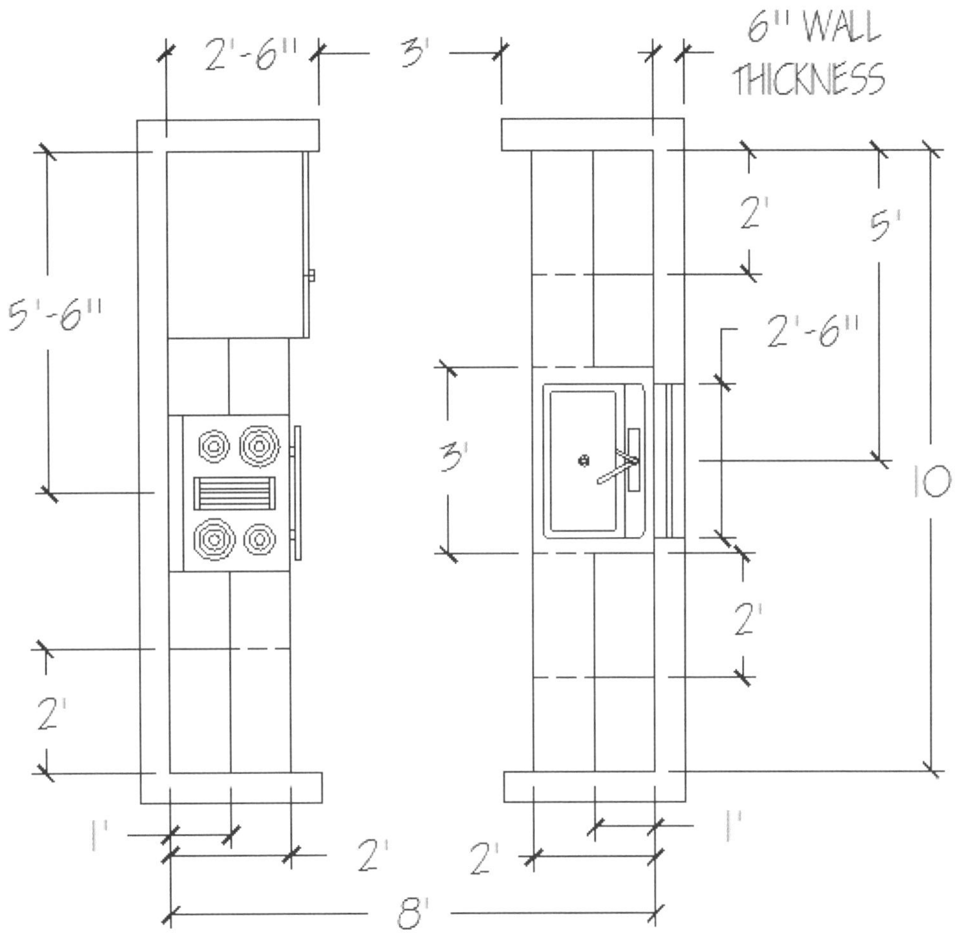

5. The design team for the hotel suite agreed to eliminate the tub/shower and replace it with just a shower with a glass door. They also agreed to enlarge it slightly – 8 inches into the bedroom and some small amount into the hallway direction as well. In addition, instead of swing doors, they opted for pocket doors.

   Create a new drawing for the bathroom shown below. Download the *Hotel Suite-Xref* drawing and insert it as an Xref into your bathroom drawing. Use the blocks from the *Hotel Suite Blocks* drawing. Draw any new walls as 6" thick. Edit the Xref and add just the wall changes (including pocket doors) to the Working Set and save them. When completed, you will have completed the bathroom drawing and the revised *Hotel Suite-Xref* drawing.

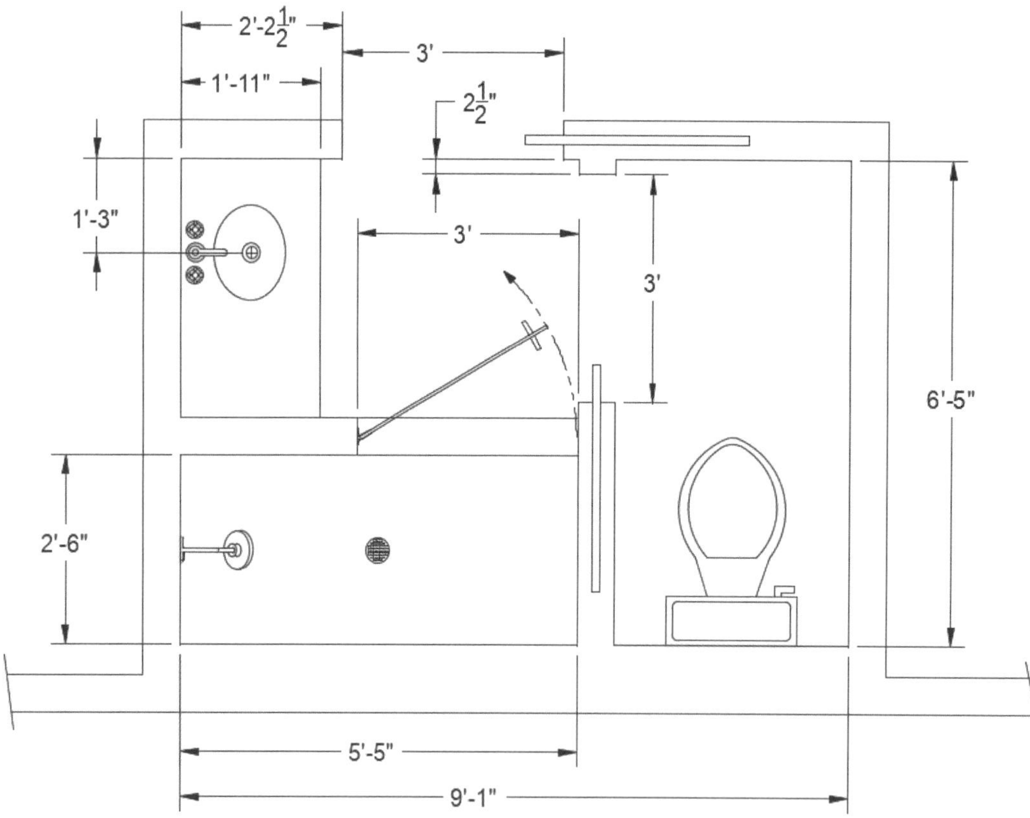

Chapter 10

Hotel Suite Project – Tutorial 4

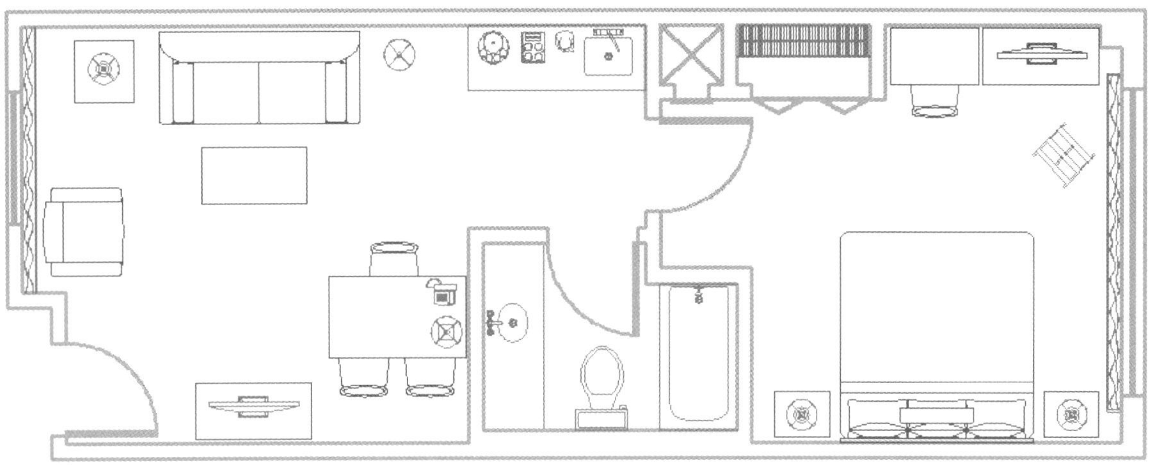

Learning Objectives:

- **To continue creating a drawing of a real-world application of AutoCAD**
    - **Use Design Center to insert furniture Blocks into the plan view**
    - **Create and use Layers**
    - **Change object Properties**
- **To utilize and reinforce the use of the AutoCAD commands learned in the previous chapters**
- **Update the Template drawing**

This tutorial builds on Tutorial 3 found in chapter 8. In this tutorial, we will put the furniture into our floor plan of the Hotel Suite. In addition, we will create and use layers. We will start with the simple rectangular shapes first. Rather than bring these in as Blocks, we will create them. When you are finished with this tutorial, all the furniture in the plan view of the hotel suite will be completed.

In addition, we will update our template drawing to include Layers and Lineweights.

Commands & Techniques:

- Opening an existing drawing
- Zoom
- Pan
- Offset
- Fillet
- Trim
- Rectangle
- Copy
- Line
- Move
- Erase
- Design Center
- Rotate
- Explode
- Move
- Layers
- Properties
- Save

Placing Furniture on the Floor Plan

Before beginning, open the Hotel Suite drawing that you updated in Tutorial 3.

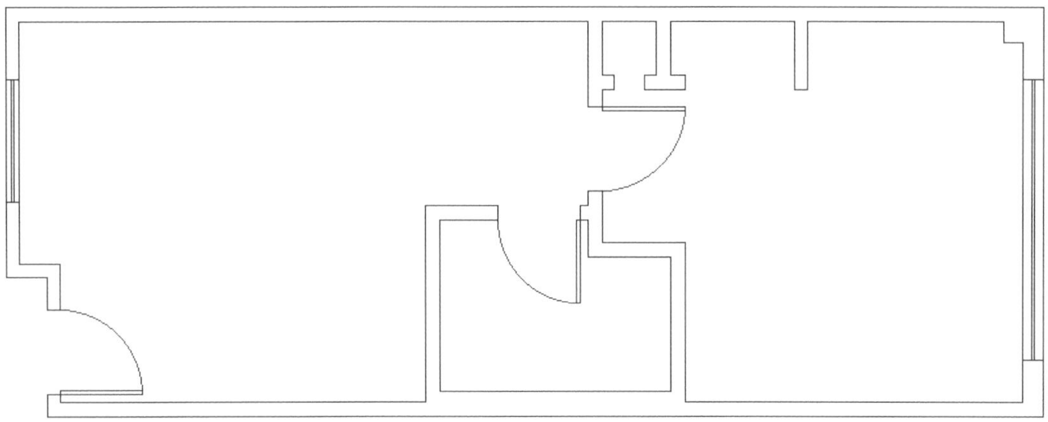

Many of the items of furniture, miscellaneous, etc. are already pre-drawn and have been provided for you in the form of Blocks. However, for the simple items that are rectangular shaped, we will draw those ourselves. The following drawing shows all the rectangular shapes we will draw.

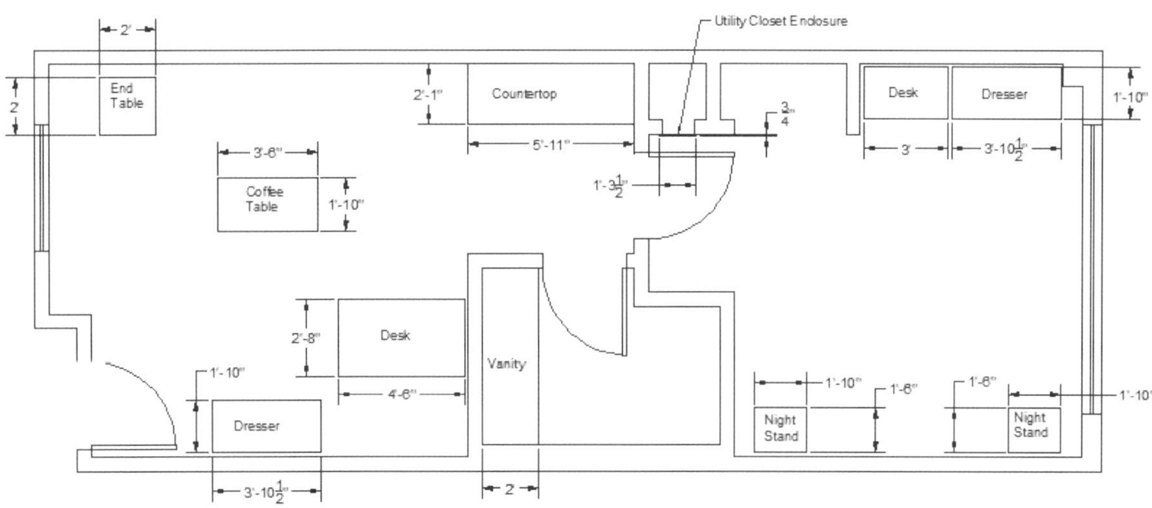

Let's start with the Living Room area and Bathroom. Although a drawing is provided, a listing of items and their sizes are as follows:

End Table:	2′ x 2′
Coffee Table:	3′6″ x 1′10″
Countertop:	5′11″ x 2′1″
Desk:	4′6″ x 2′ 8″
Dresser:	3′10-1/2″ x 1′10″
Vanity:	2′ x wall-to-wall

The vanity in the bathroom is the full length between the walls. The countertop is nestled in the corner of the living room. Both of these pieces are permanently located in place. Since furniture is movable, all pieces are located approximately as shown.

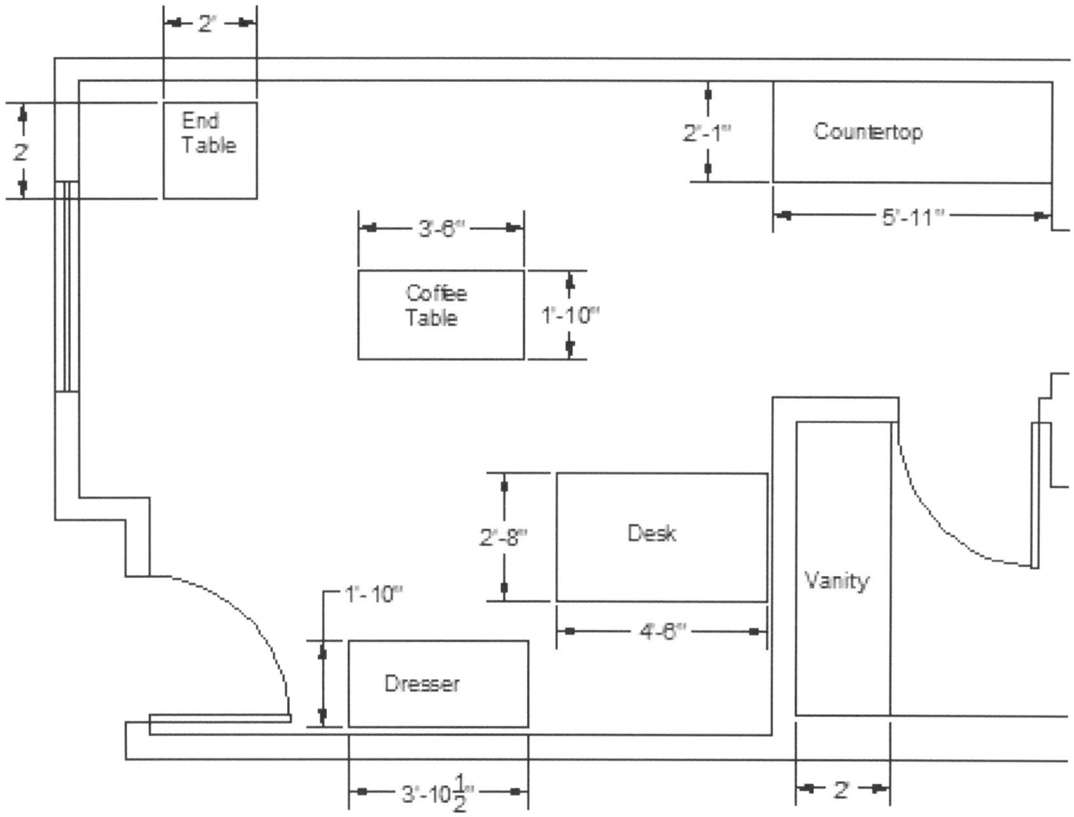

1. **Offset the left bathroom wall 2′ to create the vanity.**

2. **Offset the upper right living room wall lines 5′11″ to the left and 2′1″ down.**

3. **Use either the Fillet or Trim command to complete the countertop.**

4. **Use the Rectangle command to create the End Table, Coffee Table, Desk, and Dresser.**

   - Use the dimensions and drawing to create and locate these items on the plan view.

Now we will create the rectangular shapes in the Bedroom. Although a drawing is provided, a listing of items and their sizes are as follows:

Night Stand:	1′10″ x 1′6″
Desk:	3′ x 1′10″
Dresser:	3′10-1/2″ x 1′10″ (Same as the one in the living room)
Utility Enclosure:	1′3-1/2″ x 3/4"

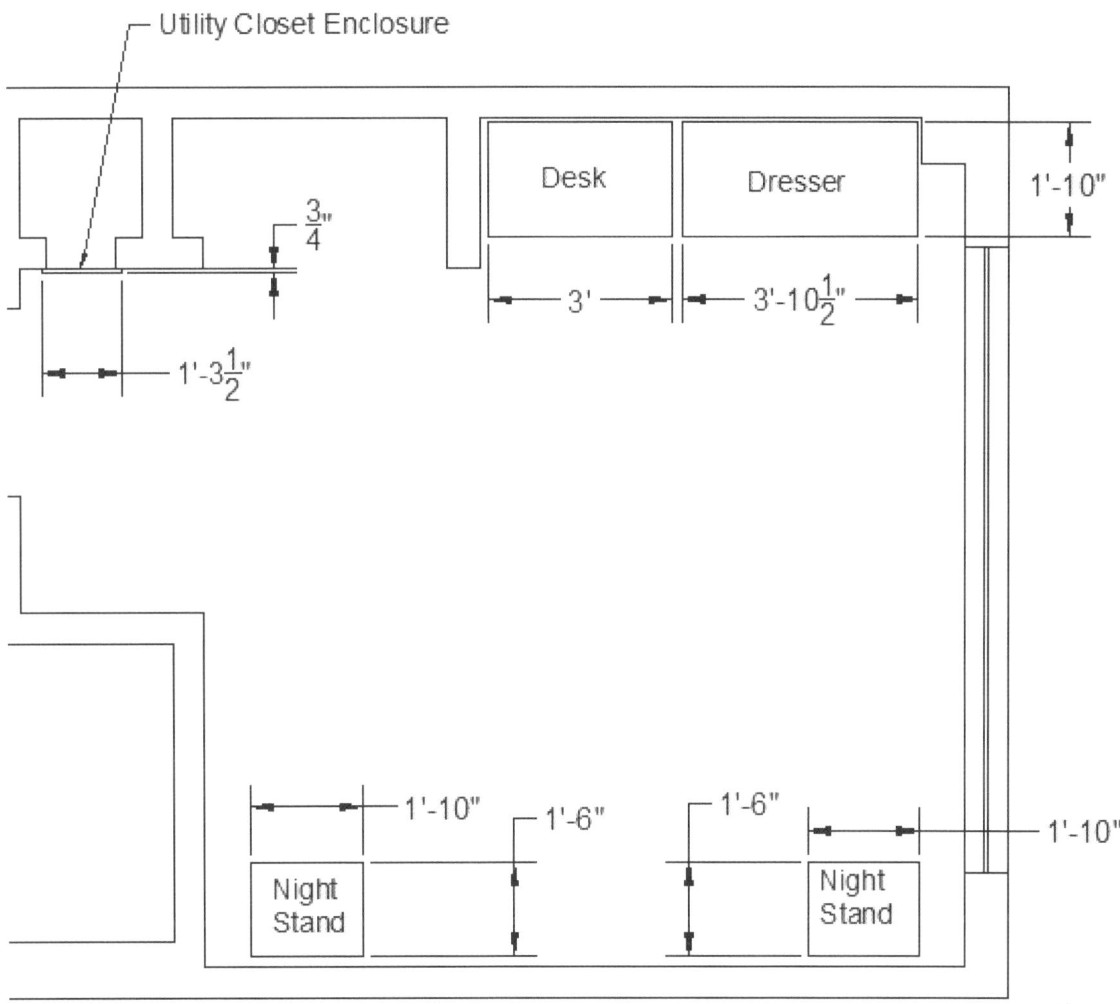

5. Use the Rectangle command to create the Desk and one Night Stand.

- Use the dimensions and drawing to create and locate these items on the plan view.

6. Use the Copy command to create a second Night Stand.

7. Use the Copy command to duplicate the dresser created for the living room and locate it in the bedroom to the approximate location shown.

The Utility Closet Enclosure is centered in the opening. In order to get the enclosure located where we want it, we will first create it in the middle of the room, then move it to the center of the opening. To find the center of the opening, we will draw a line across the opening.

8. Use the Rectangle command to draw the Utility Closet Enclosure in the middle of the bedroom.

9. Use the Line command to draw a line across the opening of the utility closet between points "A" & "B".

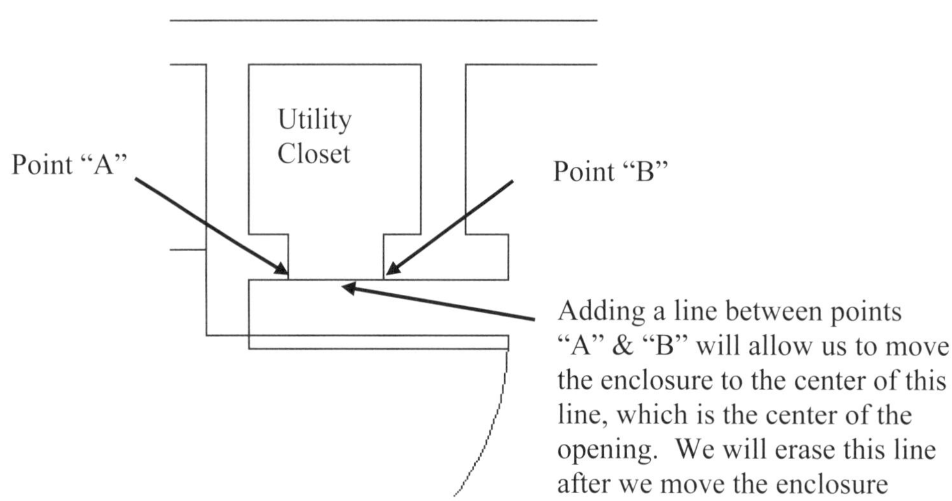

We will now relocate the Utility Closet Enclosure (the rectangle created in step 8) to the center of the opening. We will use Snap to Midpoint to find the middle of the top line of the rectangle, and the middle of the line created in step 9. Prior to moving on to step 10, make sure Object Snap (OSNAP) is turned on and Midpoint is selected. As an alternative, you can use the Snap to Midpoint icon of the Object Snap toolbar twice during the Move command.

10. Use the Move command to relocate the rectangle created in step 8 to the center of the line created in step 9.

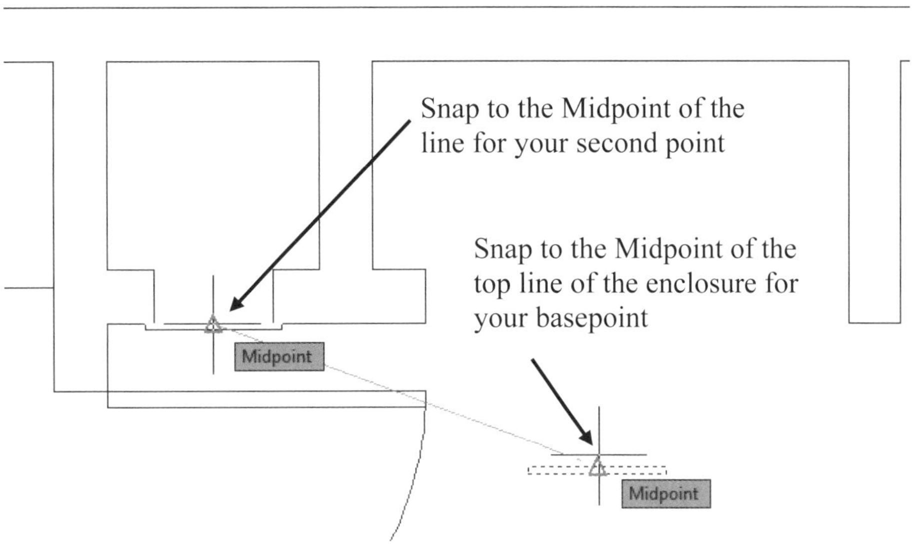

11. Erase the line that was created in step 9. Use a Selection Window (Left-to-Right) to pick just the line and not the rectangle.

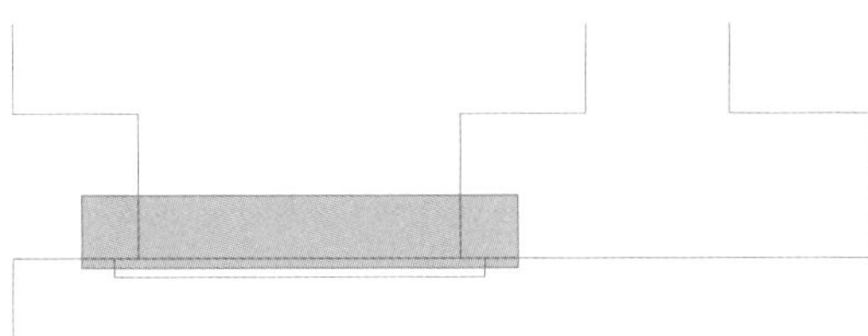

When you are done, your completed drawing will look like this:

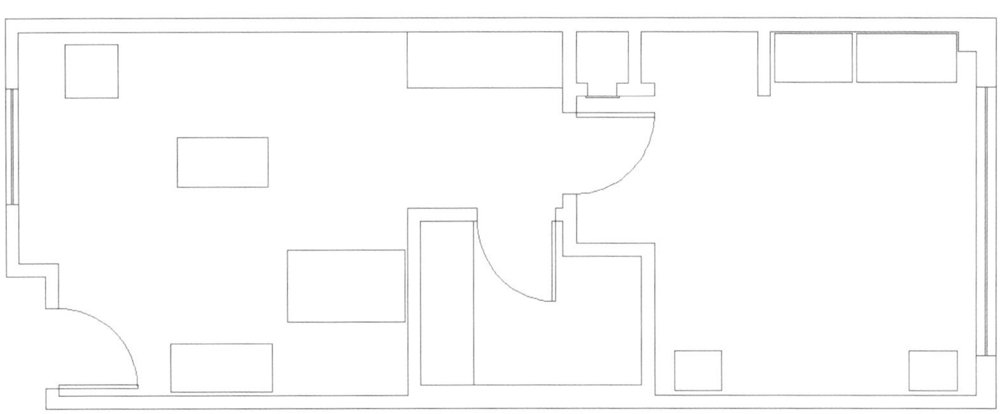

Now that we have all the rectangular shapes created, we will use Design Center to bring in the blocks for the furniture, fixtures, etc.

Adding the Blocks to the Drawing

Prior to bringing the blocks in, you must have the Hotel Suite Blocks drawing that you can download from the publisher's website.

The Blocks that we are going to use for the Plan View are shown below:

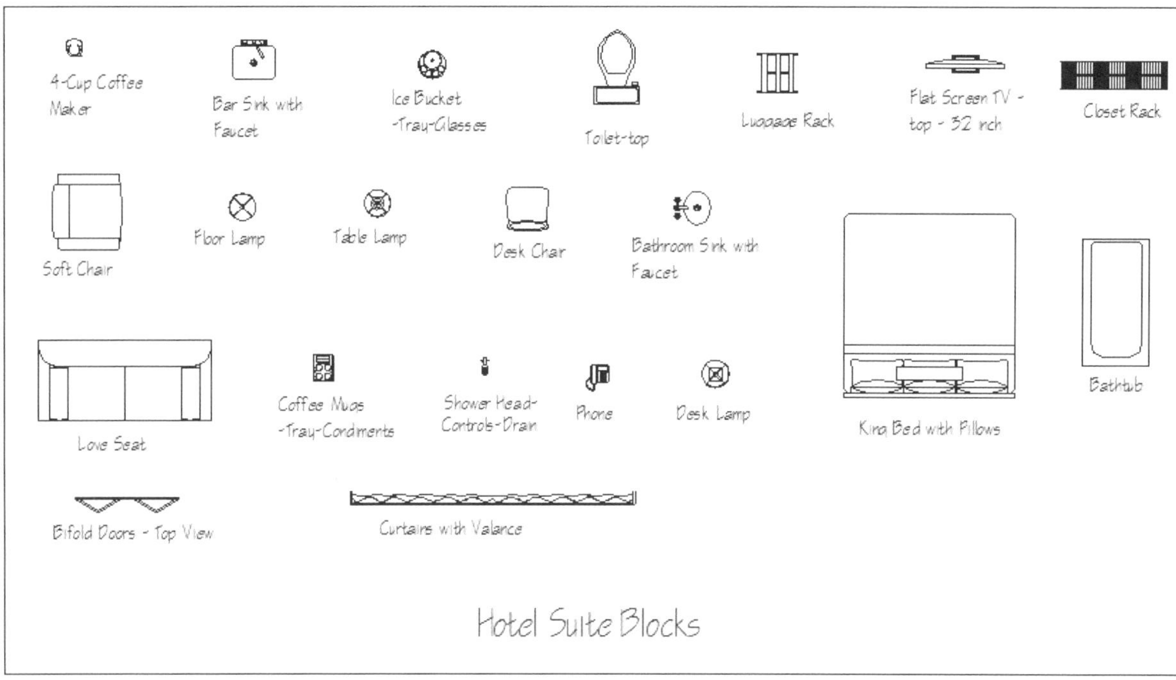

Adding Blocks to the Bedroom

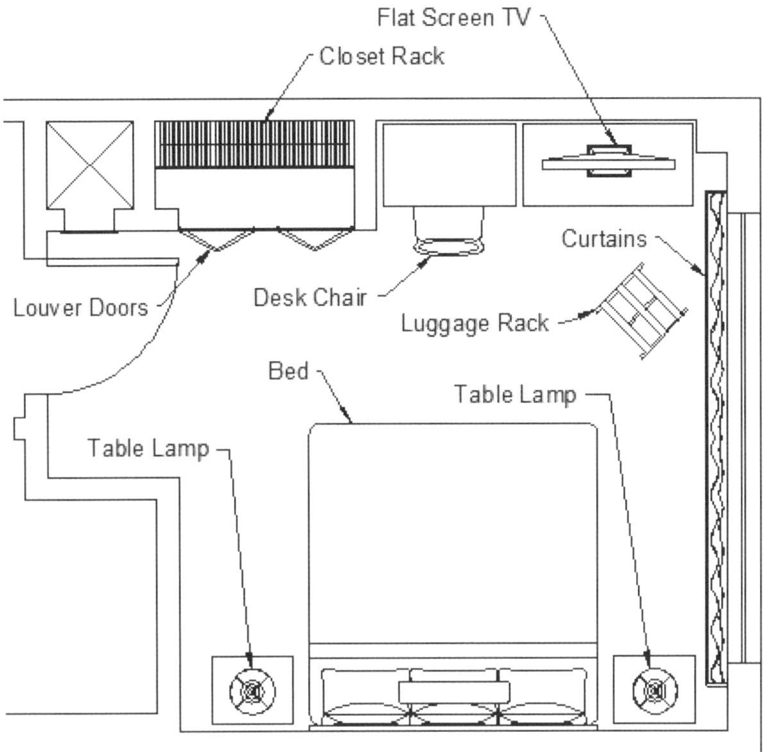

12. Use Design Center to bring in the Blocks for the Bedroom. (PC Only)

(Pick the Design Center icon)

The Design Center Palette will appear on your screen. Using the Tree View on the left side of the Design Center Palette, find the Hotel Suite Blocks drawing.

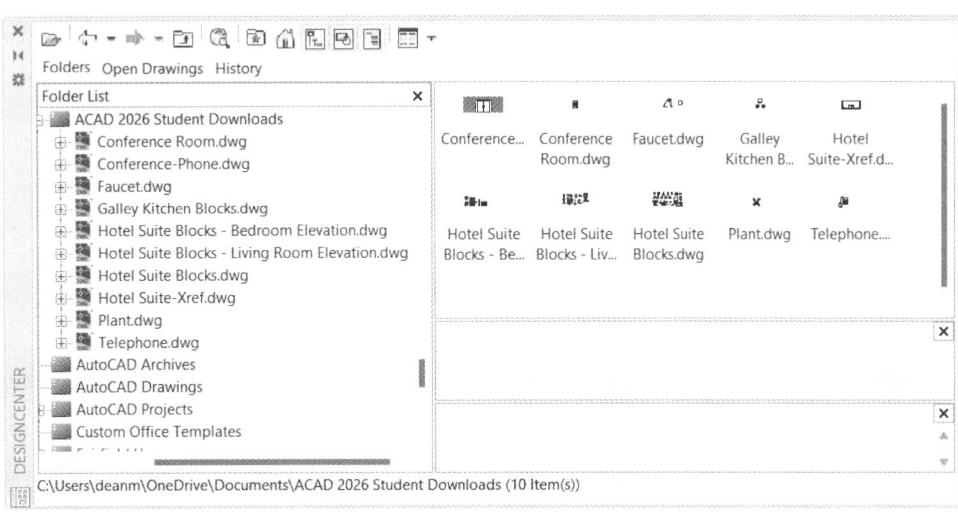

Once you select the Hotel Suite Block drawing, the right side of the Design Center Palette will look like this:

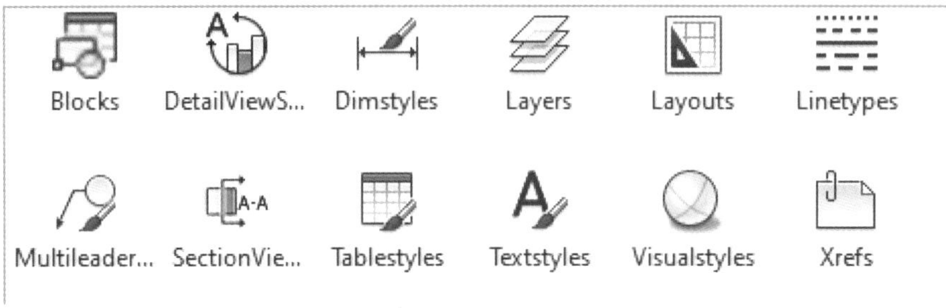

(Double-click the Blocks icon in the Design Center Palette)

The right side of the palette will now show the small icons representing the blocks.

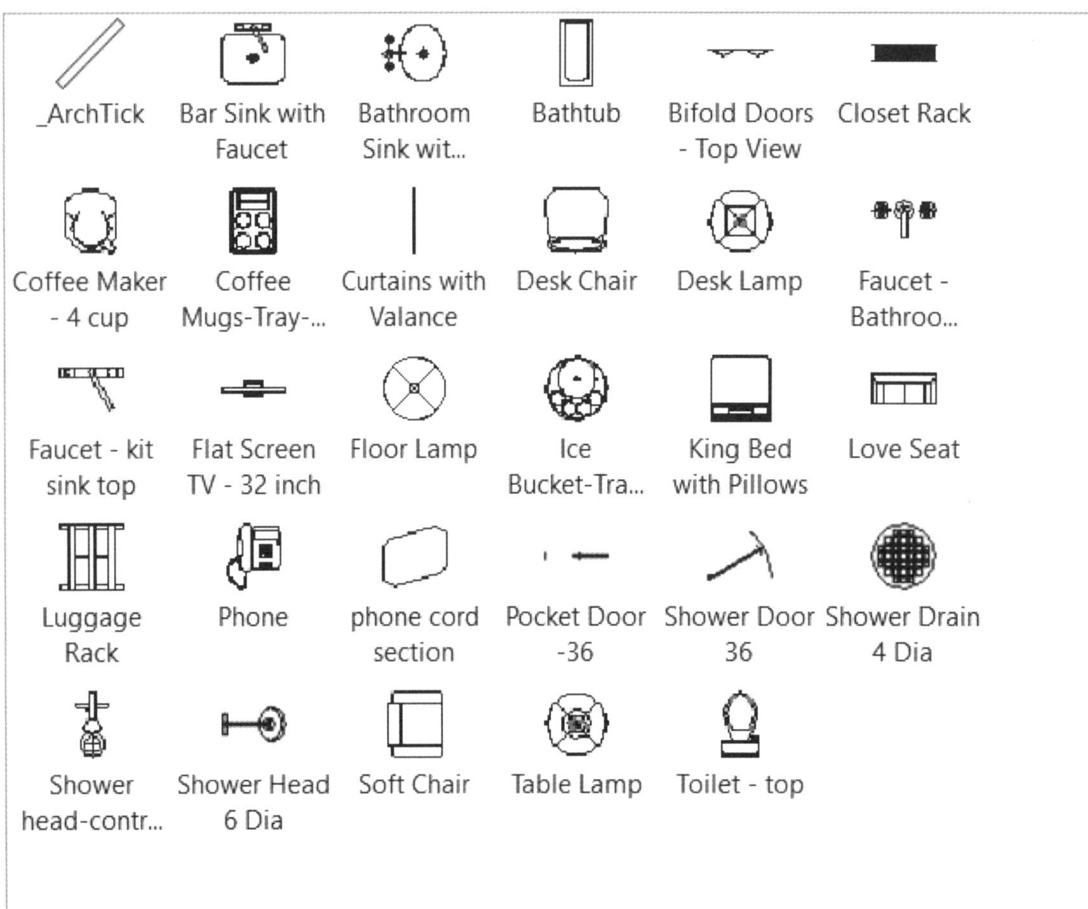

Let's move the bed into the drawing:

(Pick & Drag the icon of the King Bed with Pillows into the Bedroom)

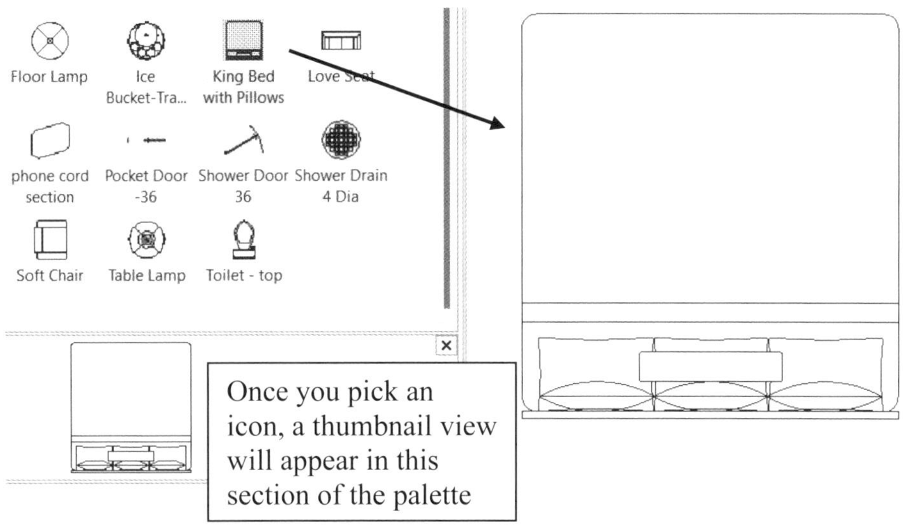

Pick the icon of the bed and drag it into a clear area of your drawing

(Pick the X in the upper corner of the palette to close it)

12. Use Blocks Palette to bring in the Blocks for the Bedroom. (Mac Only)

Use the Window pull-down and select Blocks, or pick the icon in the Block Tool Panel to display the Blocks Palette.

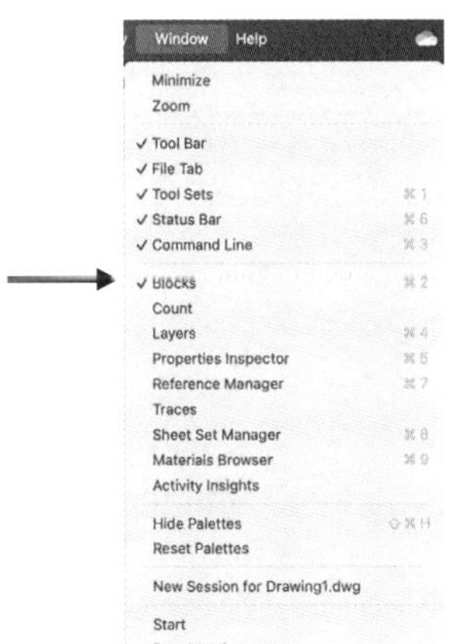

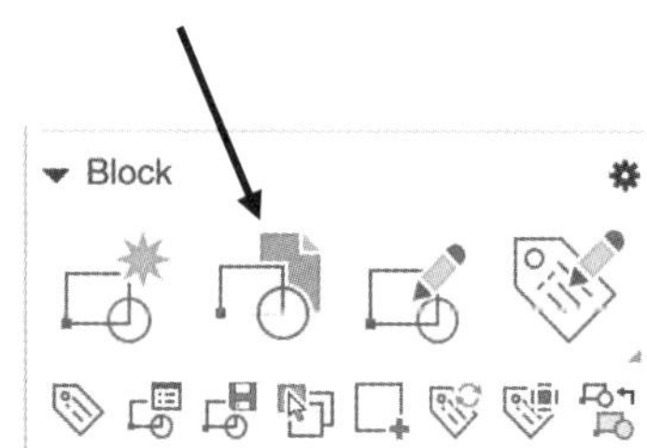

After the Blocks Palette appears, pick the Libraries icon (if it is not already selected) to view the available content. Use the pull-down arrow to choose the Hotel Suite drawing. If it is not already available, you can search for it by either picking the File Navigation icon or selecting Browse Block Libraries… from the pull-down list.

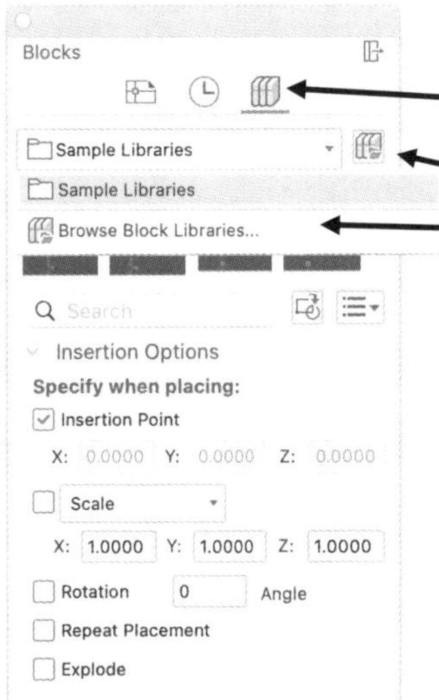

Pick the Libraries icon to view available

Pick the File Navigation icon or select Browse Block Libraries… from the pull-down choices

After you pick the File Navigation icon (or selected Browse Block Libraries…), a file manager dialog box appears. Navigate through your documents or cloud service to find a file that contains the Hotel Suite blocks or the entire folder that contains that drawing file.

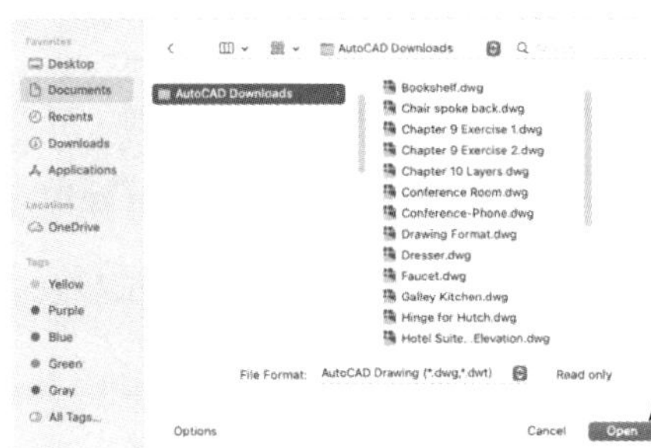

After selecting the file or folder, Pick Open to add your library

Let's move the bed into the drawing. Use the scroll bar to find the icon of the bed. Click and drag the bed into the drawing.

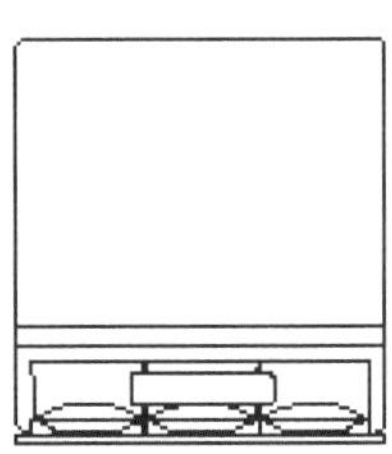

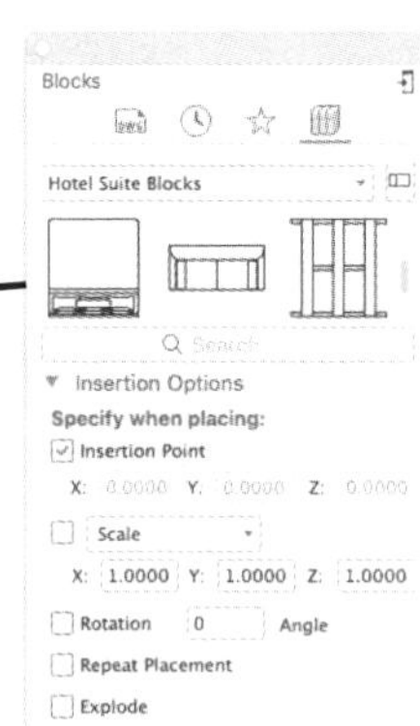

Scroll to find the icon of the bed

Pick the icon of the bed and drag it into a clear area of your drawing

We will now locate the bed to the correct location in the room using the Move command. We want the bed to be located so that it is centered and against the wall. This will be easy to do since we can use Snap to Midpoint just like we did for the Utility Closet Enclosure.

13. Use the Move command and move the block of the bed.

Remember, because the bed is a block, it is treated as a single object. However, we can still use Snap to Midpoint of the lower horizontal line of the bed as the basepoint. We will then use the midpoint of the lower wall line for the second point.

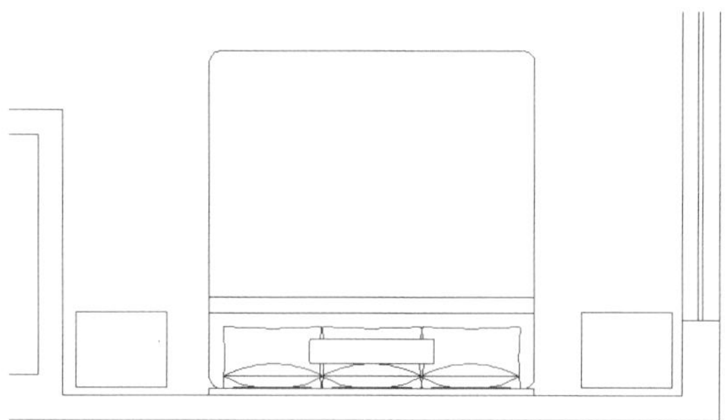

14. Continue using the Design Center (or Blocks Palette on the Mac) to bring in additional blocks to complete the bedroom.

-You can bring the blocks in to the side of the Hotel Suite, and then use the Move command to locate them in the room. Use the same technique used to locate the Utility Closet Enclosure for the Closet Doors, Closet Rack, and the Curtains.

15. Use the Rotate command to rotate the Luggage Rack 45°.

16. Move the Desk Chair under the desk. Explode the Desk Chair and use the Trim and Erase commands to show that the chair is under the desk.

17. Use the Line command to draw lines corner-to-corner inside the Utility Closet.

When you are done, your drawing will look like this:

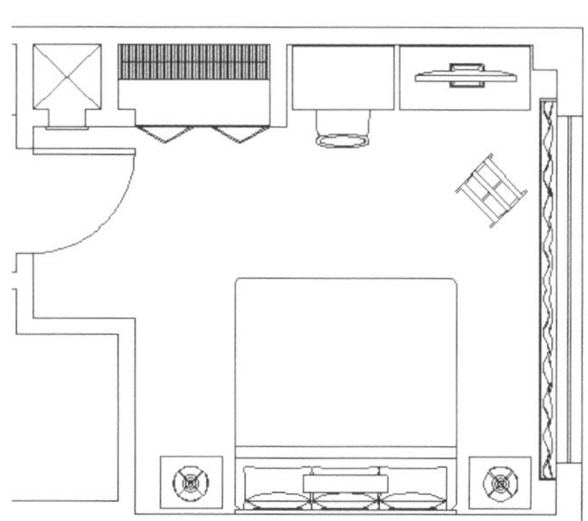

Adding Blocks to the Bathroom

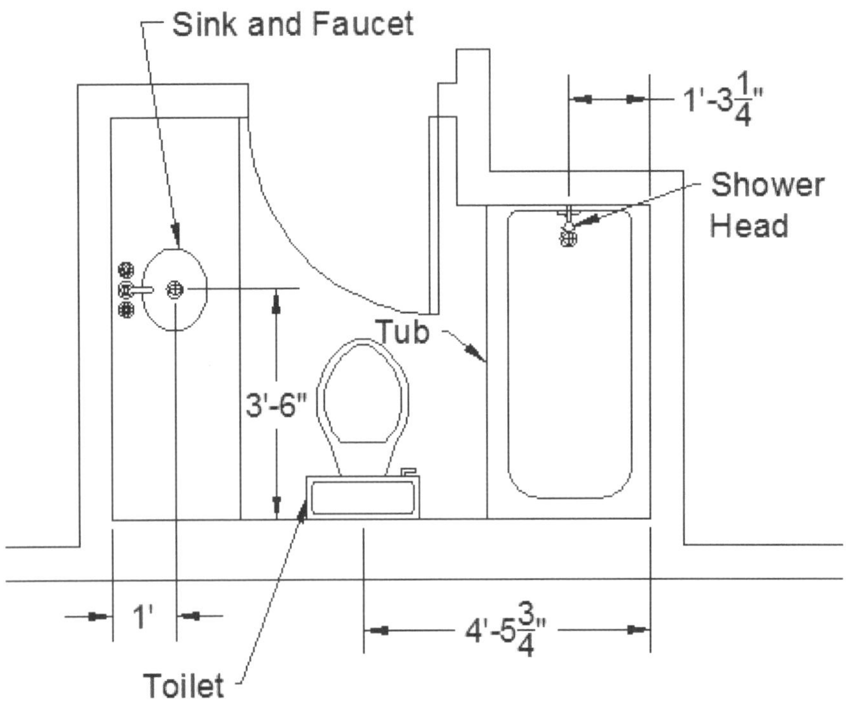

18. Use Design Center (or Blocks Palette on the Mac) to bring in the Blocks for the Bathroom.

19. Use the Move command to move the Tub to the lower right hand corner.

20. Offset the right wall 1′3-1/4″ to the left.

21. Use the Move command to move the Shower Head into position.

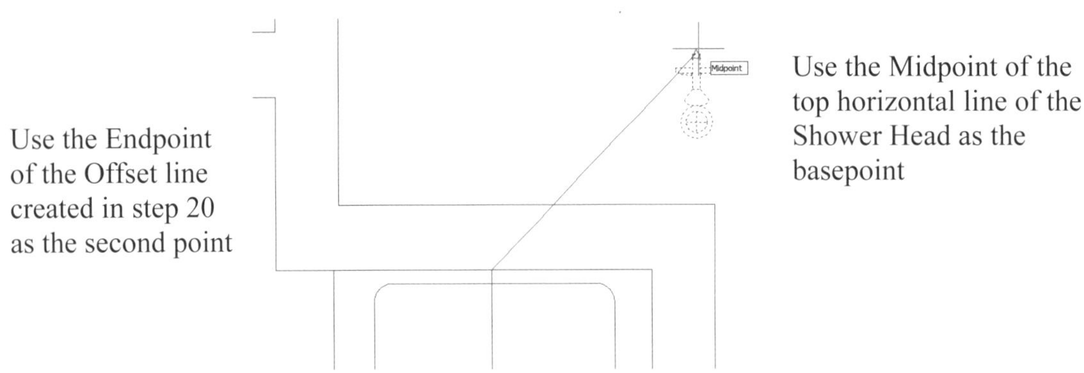

22. Erase the Offset line that was created in step 20.

23. Offset the right wall 4′5-3/4″ to the left.

24. Use the Move command to move the Toilet into position.

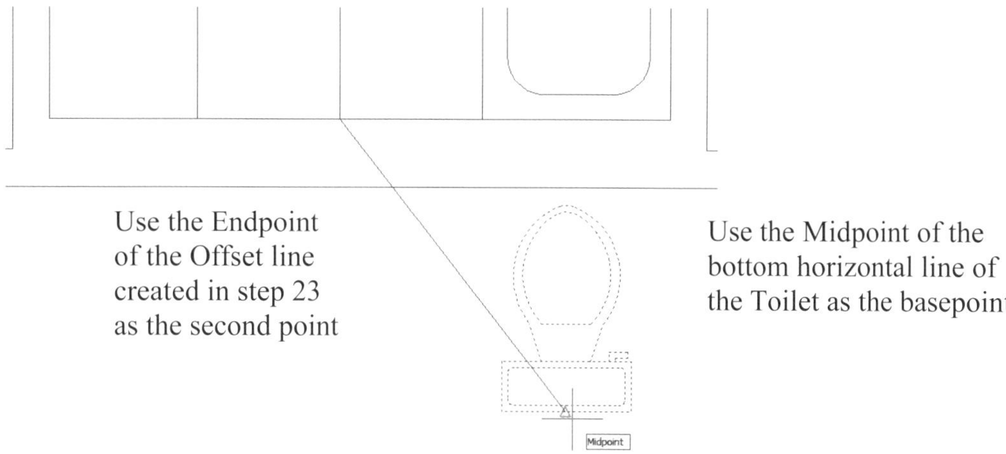

25. Erase the Offset line that was created in step 23.

26. Offset the left wall 1′ to the right and the lower wall 3′6″ up.

27. Use the Move command to move the Sink into position.

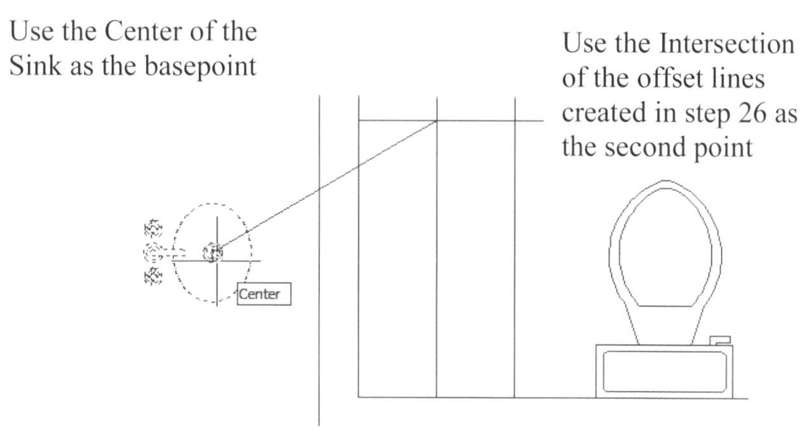

28. Erase the Offset lines that were created in step 26.

When you are done, your drawing will look like this:

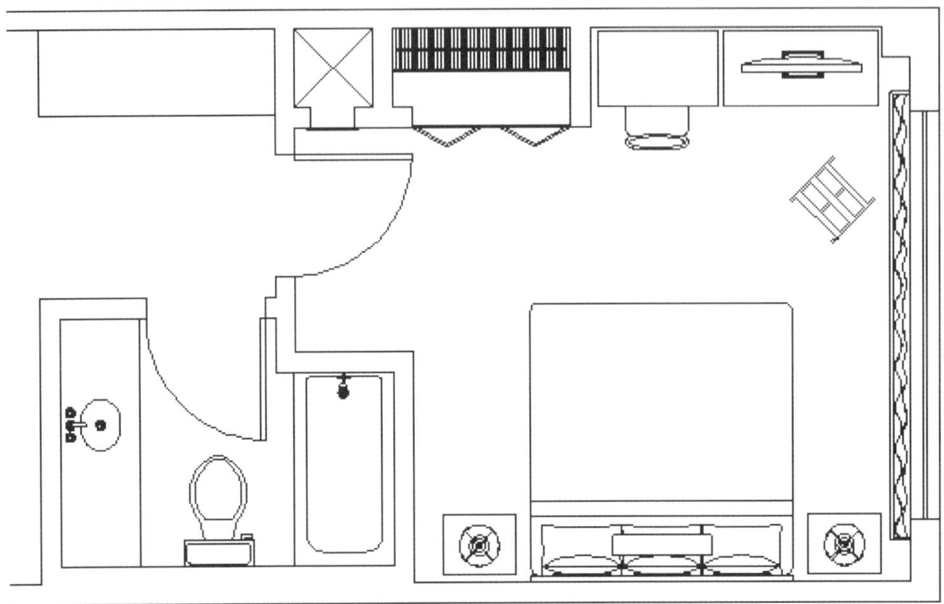

Adding Blocks to the Living Room

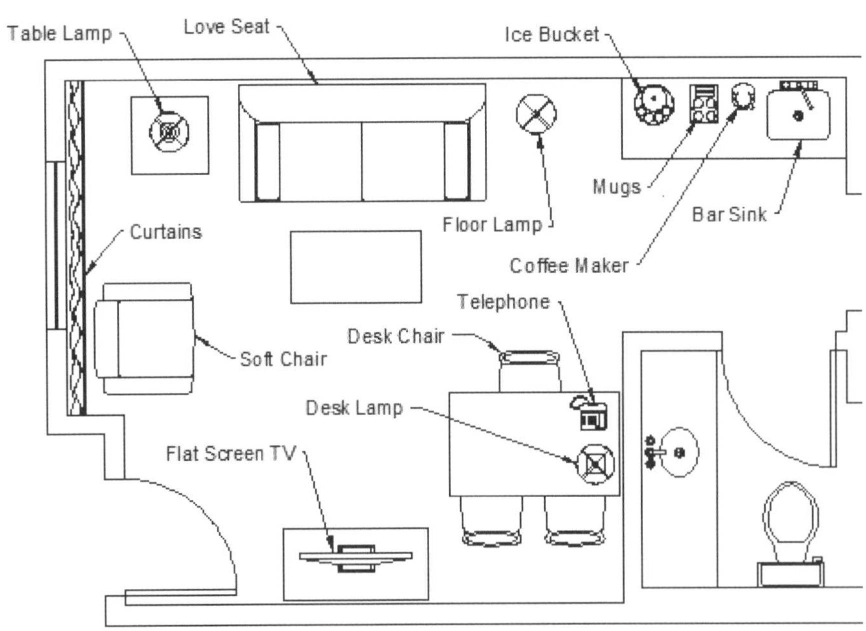

29. Use Design Center (or Blocks Palette on the Mac) to bring in the Blocks for the Living Room.

We need to locate the Bar Sink on the countertop. The Bar Sink is located as shown:

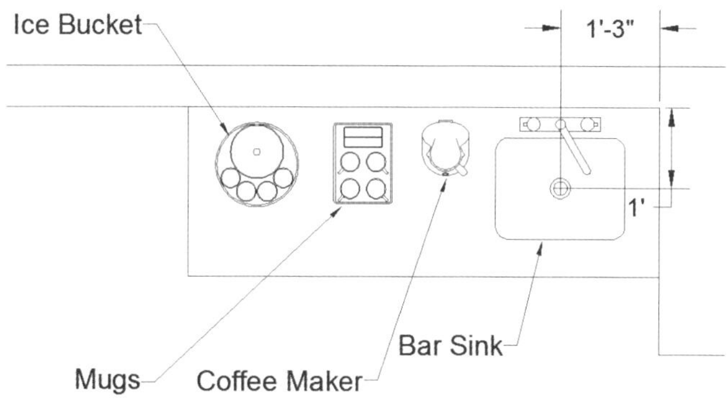

30. Offset the upper right wall line 1′3″ to the left and the upper wall line 1′ down.

31. Use the Move command to move the Bar Sink into position.

Use the Center of the Bar Sink as the basepoint

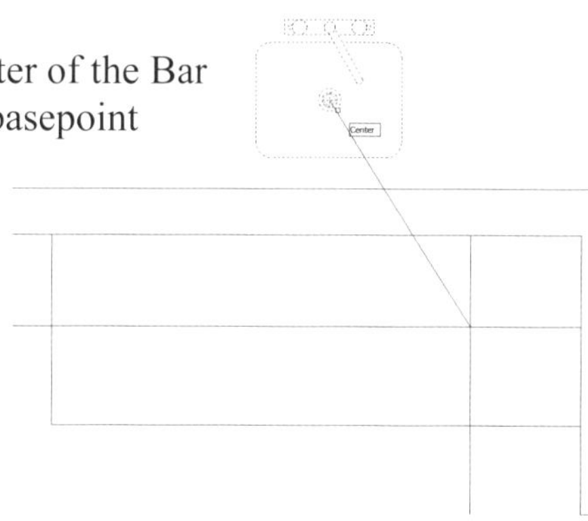

Use the Intersection of the offset lines created in step 30 as the second point

32. Erase the Offset lines that were created in step 30.

33. Use the Copy command to create 2 more Desk Chairs.

34. Continue to use the Move command to locate all the other items in the Living Room except for the Curtain.

35. Use the Rotate command to rotate the Flat Screen TV, one of the Desk Chairs, and the Curtains 180°. Rotate the Telephone -90°.

- Note that the Curtains should still be off to the side of your drawing.

36. Use the Move command to move the Curtains into position.

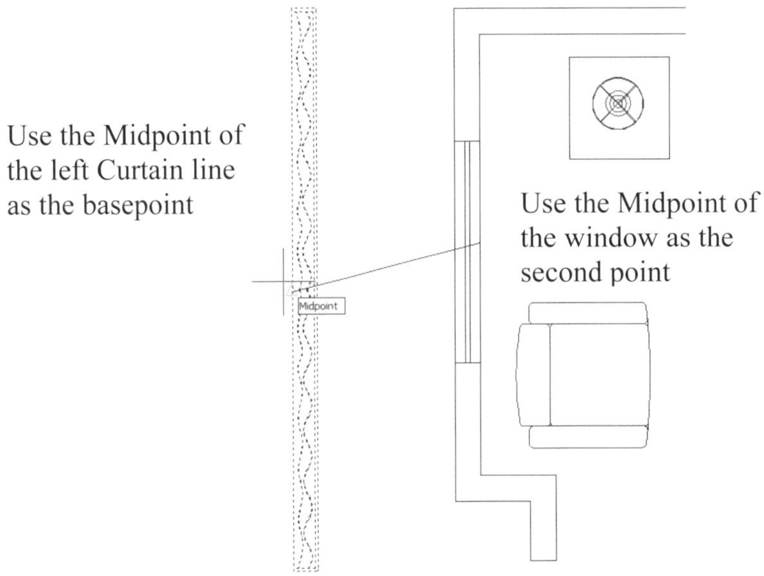

37. Explode the Curtain block and use the Trim and Erase commands to complete the Living Room window treatment.

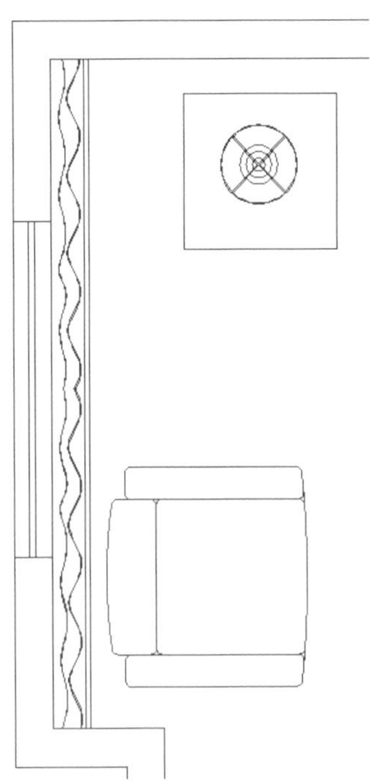

You are now done inserting all the Blocks onto the Plan View. Save your drawing.

When you are done, your drawing will look like this:

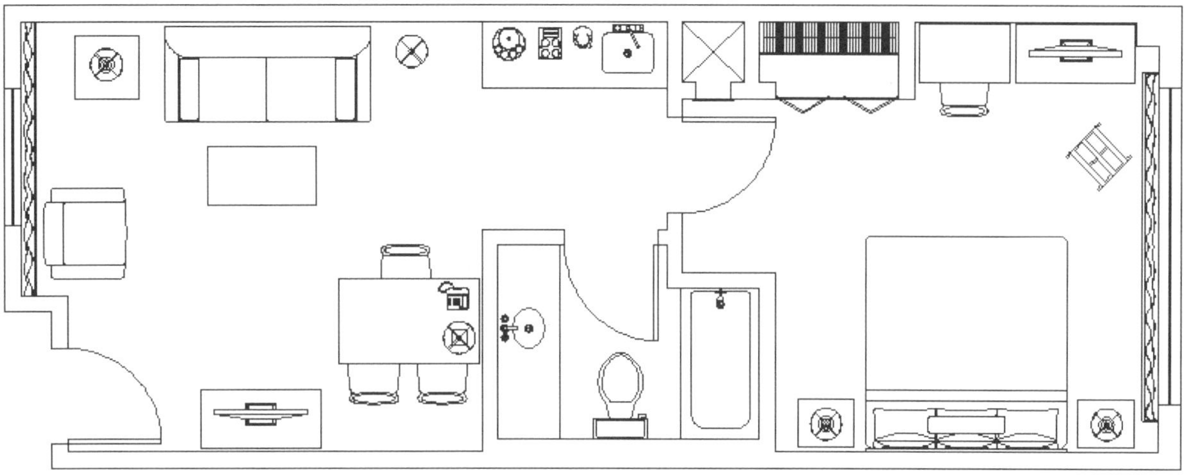

Creating Layers

Now that we have the Floor Plan completed, we can create layers and move the objects to the new layers. This will allow us to show only the items that we want to see. For this tutorial, we will create layers "Format", "Viewport", "Structure", "Furniture", "Plumbing", "Lighting", and "Misc". We will assign colors and lineweights to each layer.

38. Bring up the Layer Properties Manager. The icon is on the Layers Panel of the Home Tab.

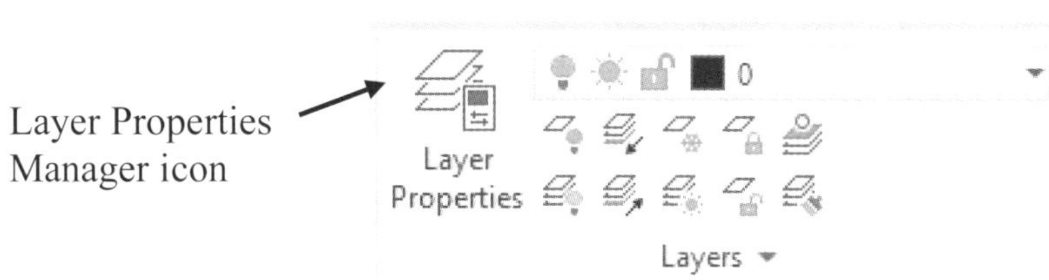

(Pick Layer Properties Manager icon)

The Layer Properties Manager dialog box will appear.

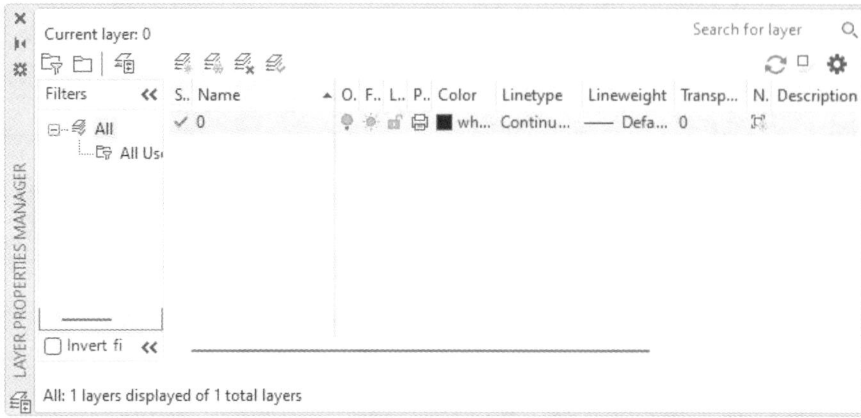

For the Mac, undock the Layers Palette icon. If it is not already visible, use the Window pull-down menu to turn on the Layers Palette and undock it if required.

Mac

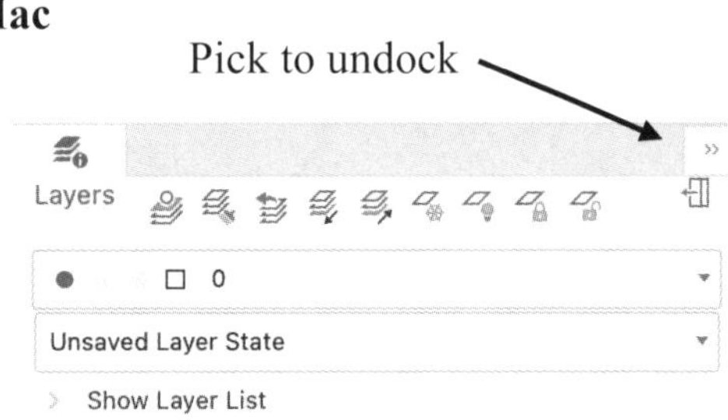

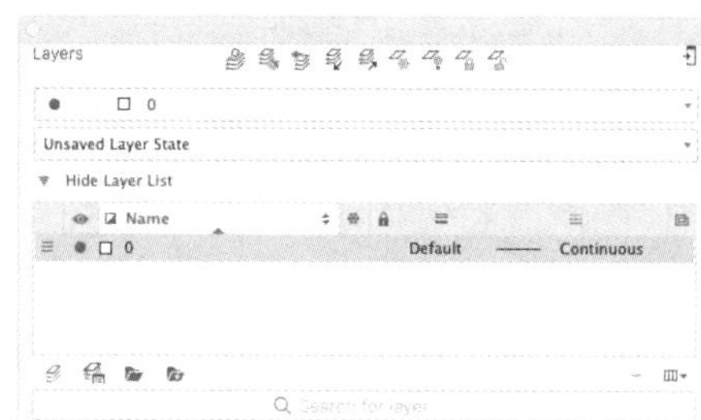

39. Add new layers and name them as shown:

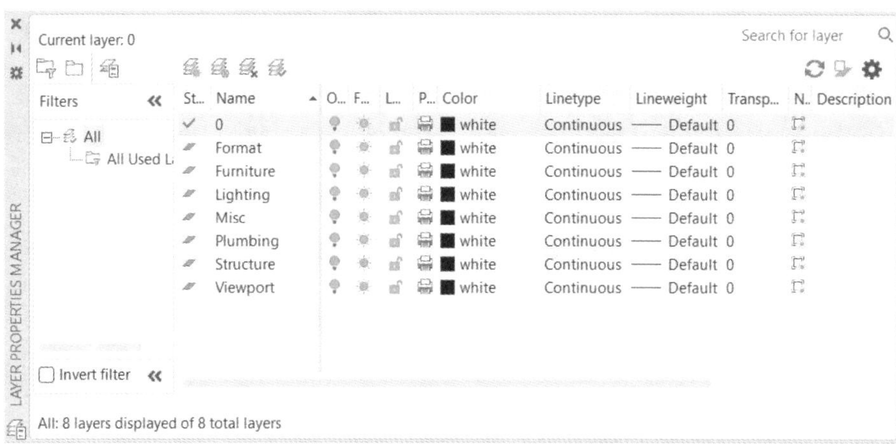

40. Using the Standard colors, change the color of layer "Furniture" to blue; layer "Lighting" to yellow; layer "Misc" to red; layer "Plumbing" to magenta; layer "Structure" to green; and layer Viewport to cyan. Layer "Format" will remain white. In addition, change the Lineweight of layer "Format" to .020″ (.50mm); layer "Structure" to .012″ (.30mm); layers "Furniture", "Lighting", "Plumbing", and "Misc" to .010″ (.25mm).

When you are done, your Layer Properties Manager dialog box will look like this:

(Pick the "X" in the upper LH corner of the dialog box to close it)

On the Mac, the Layers Palette will look like this:

Mac

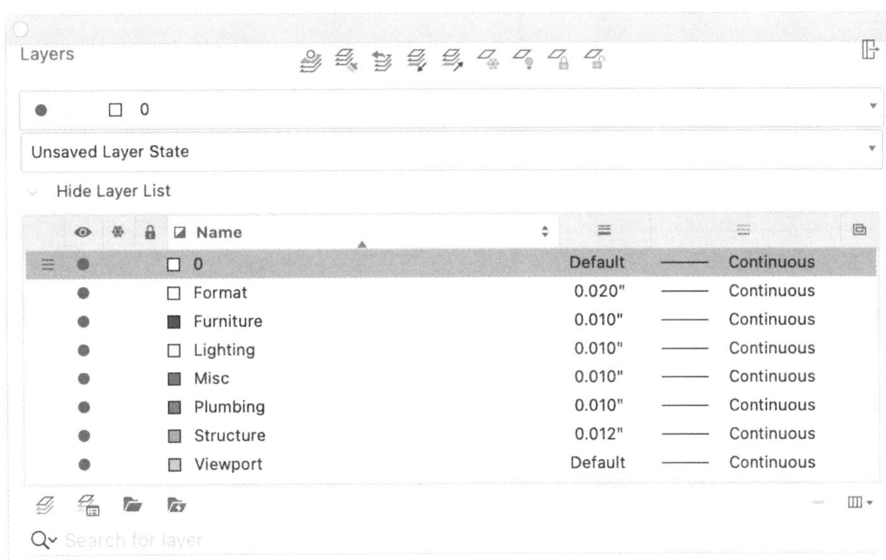

41. Use the Properties Palette (Properties Inspector on the Mac) to change the layer for the walls, doors, and windows.

(Pick the downward arrow on the Properties Panel of the Home Tab to access the Properties Palette)

Pick this downward arrow

(On the Mac, use the Window pull-down menu and select Properties Inspector)

The Properties palette will appear (on the Mac, the Properties Inspector will appear):

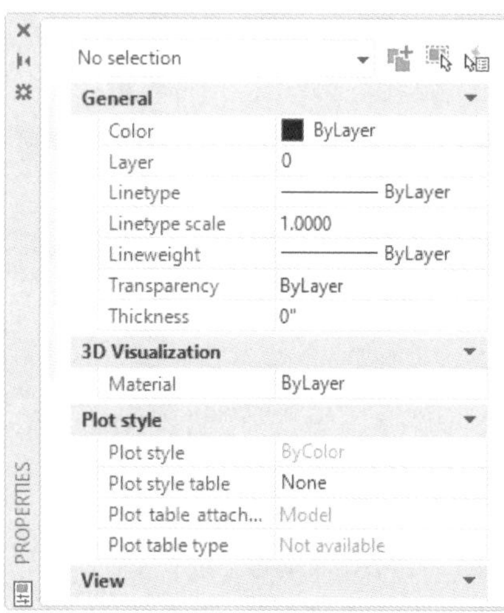

Mac

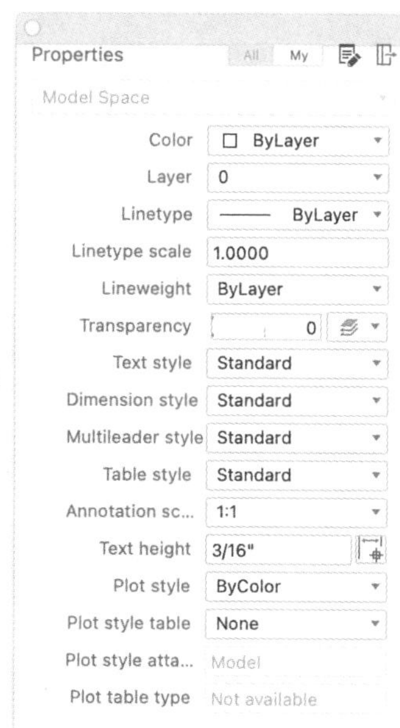

(Pick all the objects that make up the walls, doors, and windows)

It is not necessary to select all the objects at once – you can repeat the process until all objects that belong on this layer have been changed. You can pick anywhere in the drawing space and press the Esc key to eliminate the selection set. This is helpful if you do not pick all the items at once.

After you begin to select the objects do the following:

(Pick Layer and use the pull-down arrow to select layer "Structure")

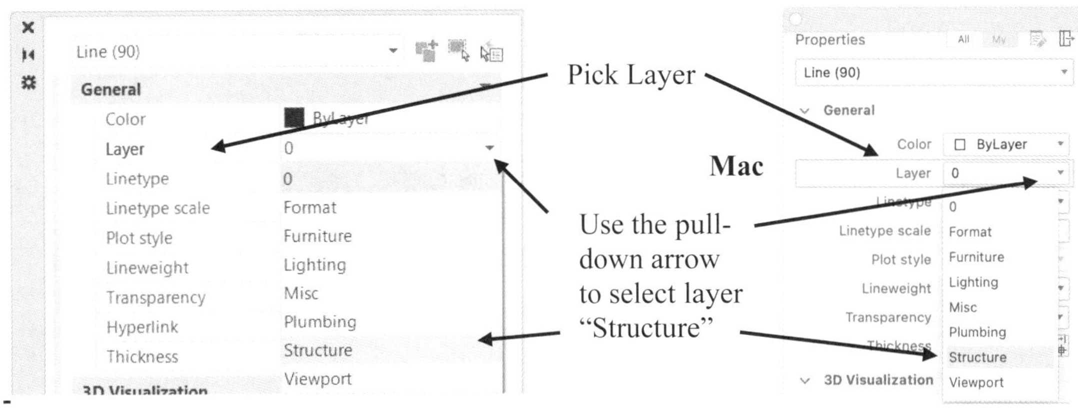

42. Close the Properties Palette (Properties Inspector on Mac) and press the Esc key.

When you are done, your drawing will look like this:

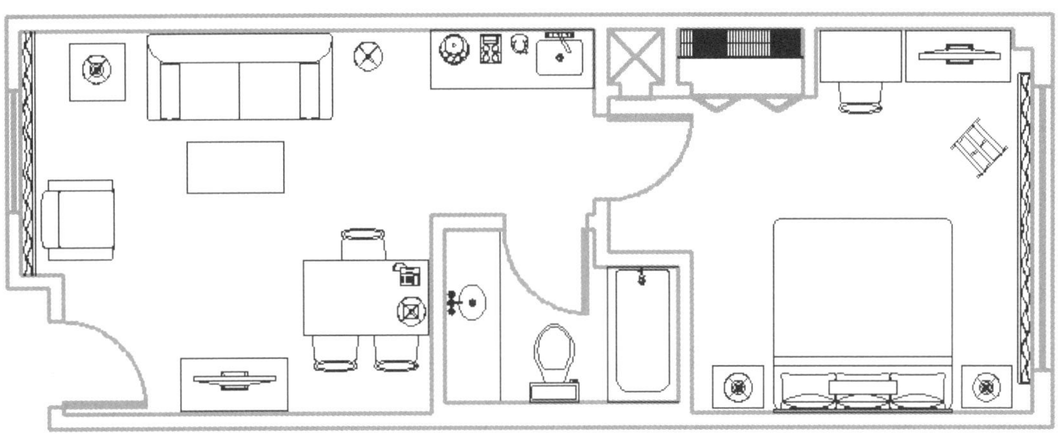

43. Use the pull-down arrow in the Layers toolbar to turn layer “Structure” off.

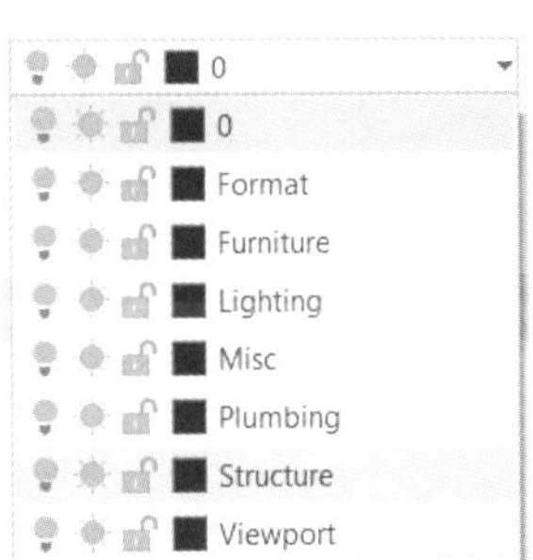

After turning the layer off, pick anywhere in the drawing space to close out this pull-down.

Mac

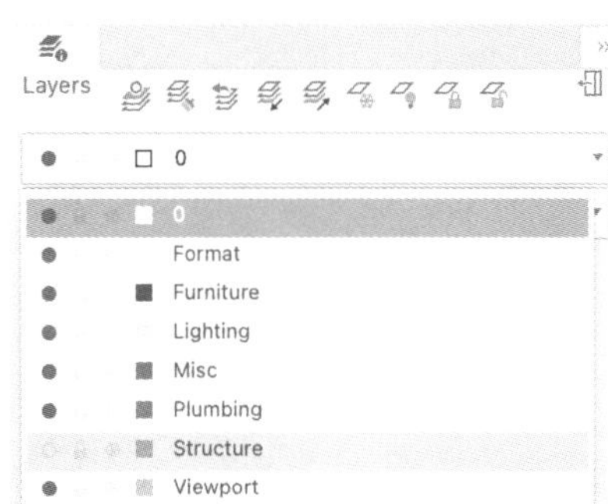

With layer “Structure” turned off, it is easier to select the other objects to change their layer.

44. Repeat the process described in steps 41 & 42 to change the layer for the furniture, plumbing, lighting, and miscellaneous items. Turn all layers back on when done.

You can turn layers on and off as desired to help facilitate selecting the objects.

When you are done, your drawing will look like this:

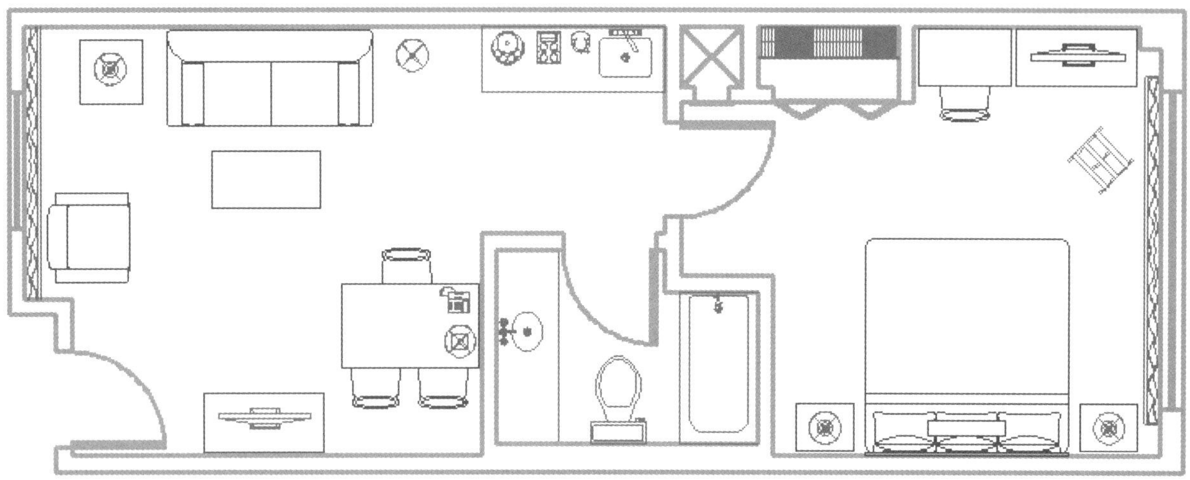

45. Pick the Plan View Layout and switch to Paper Space.

46. Use a Selection Window or a Crossing Window to select the drawing format with the titleblock. The grips will appear. Use the pull-down arrow on the Layers toolbar and pick layer Format. This changes all the selected objects to layer Format. Use the Escape key to eliminate the grips.

47. Pick the viewport border. Use the pull-down arrow on the Layers toolbar and pick layer Viewport. This changes the viewport border to layer Viewport. Use the Escape key to eliminate the grips.

Congratulations! Save your drawing – we will continue to build on this in the next tutorial.

Add Layers to Template

For PC users, let's take advantage of the layers we created in this tutorial and build them into our drawing template. For Mac users, skip steps 49 and 50, and instead create the layers that we just created in this tutorial.

48. Start a new drawing using the Interior Design drawing template that was created in Chapter 8.

49. Open Design Center and find the Hotel Suite drawing you just saved. Highlight Layers in the Tree View. The preview pane shows all the layers that were created for the Hotel Suite.

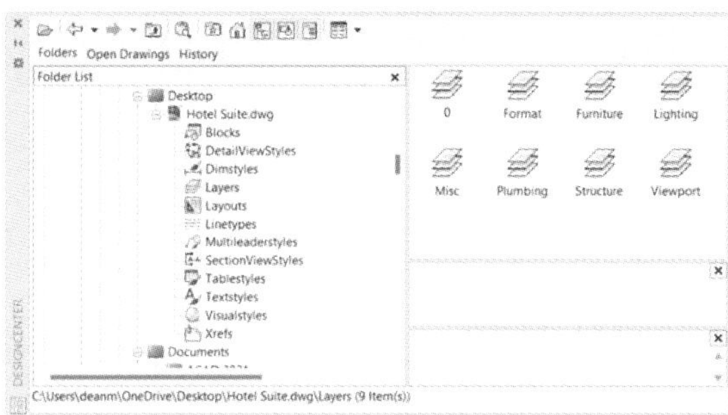

50. Either double-left-click or click-and-drag each layer (except layer 0) into your drawing. When you are done, close the Design Center.

51. Verify that the layers came in by opening the Layer Manager.

52. Pick the Plan View tab and switch to Paper Space.

53. Use a Selection Window or a Crossing Window to select the drawing format with the titleblock. The grips will appear. Use the pull-down arrow on the Layers toolbar and pick layer Format. This changes all the selected objects to layer Format. Use the Escape key to eliminate the grips. Repeat this method to change the viewport border to layer Viewport.

54. Over-write the existing template: Pick File, Save As… and picking the Interior Design template to save the changes to the template. You will get a warning that it already exists. Pick Yes. Pick OK for Template Options.

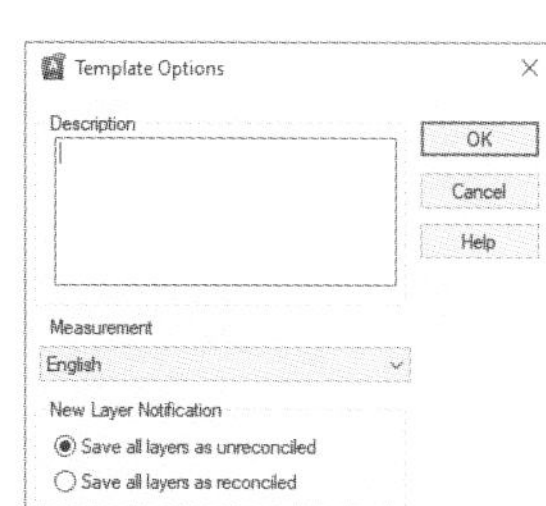

Congratulations! You have now updated the Interior Design template drawing to include layers.

Chapter 11

Commands – Set 5: Annotating Your Drawing

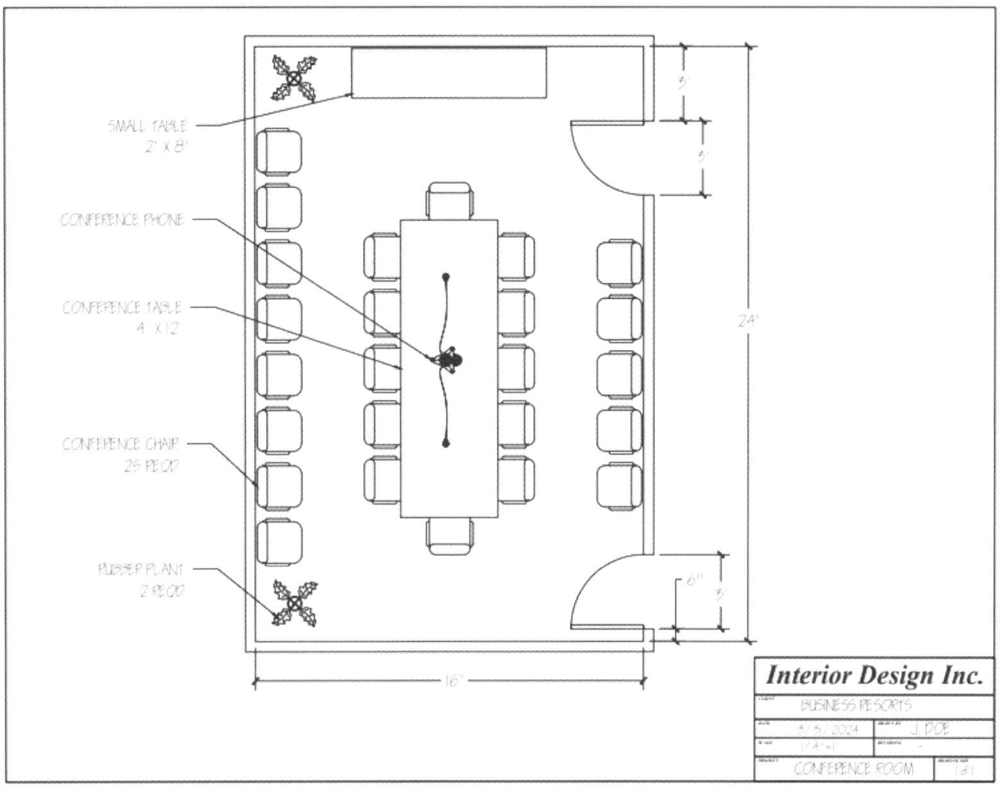

Learning Objectives:

- **Creating a style and using Text**
- **Creating a style and using Dimensions**
- **Creating labels with the Multileader command**

We can now create accurate drawings. However, this alone is not enough to convey the information when you want to explain your design to a client or to a contractor. All drawings will need text and dimensions to identify what is drawn as well as the size and location of objects.

In this chapter, we will cover Text, Dimensions, and Multileader. The Multileader is the AutoCAD name for a label.

Text

Putting text in your drawings is essential to identify items you have drawn or for notes you wish to make. It is recommended that the text is inserted in your Layout. Text can be a Model Space object or a Paper Space object. When inserting Model Space text in a Layout, it is best to use Annotative Style text so that the text will be scaled to the Viewport scale. Make sure the Viewport scale is set and locked before inserting the Annotative Style text.

AutoCAD allows you to have Single Line text, or Multiline text. There is a default font available, but for Interior Design, a popular font is City Blueprint. We can create a custom Text Style and we will define the font.

Text Style

To begin, expand the Annotation Panel of the Home Tab, and pick the Text Style icon:

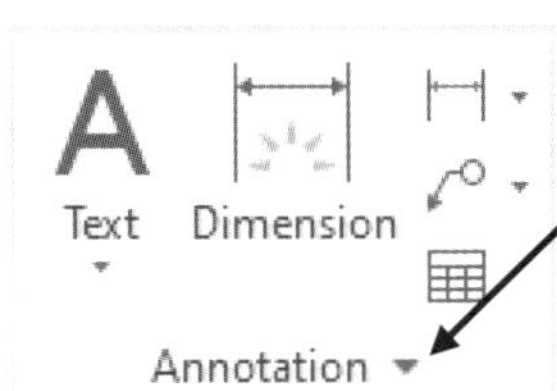

Use Pull-down arrow to expand

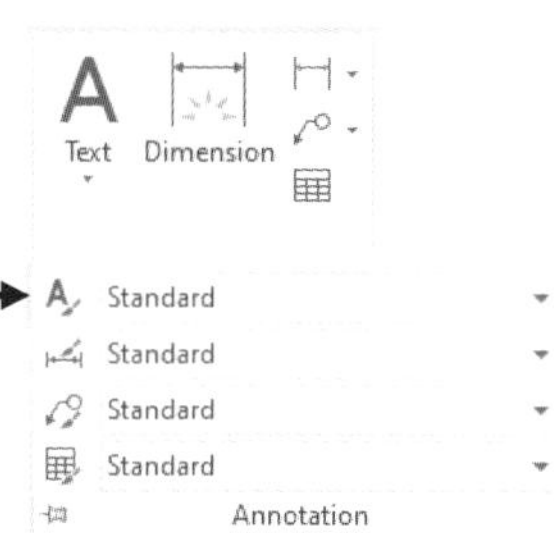

As an alternative, pick the downward arrow of the Text Panel of the Annotate Tab:

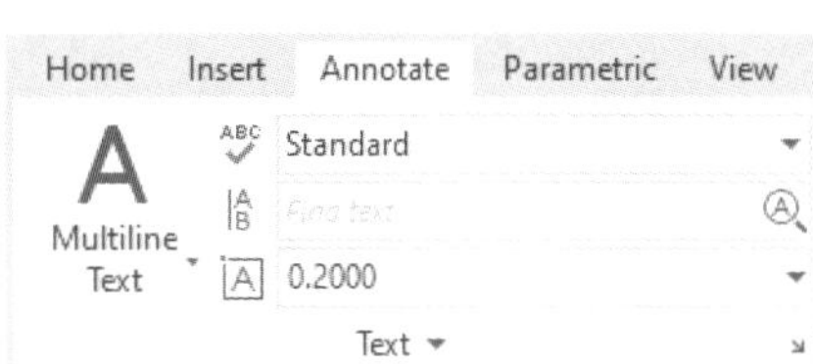

Pick the downward arrow

Mac

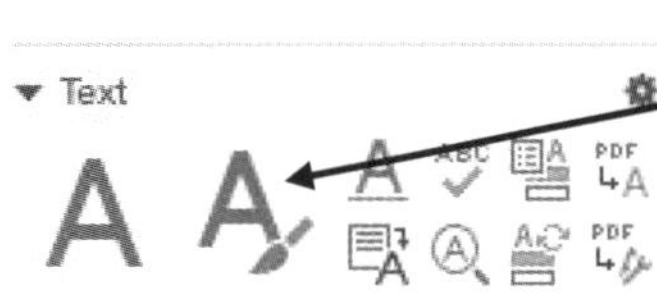

Pick the Text Style icon on the Text toolbar

After selecting either the Text Style icon on the Annotation Panel of the Home Tab, or the downward arrow of the Text Panel of the Annotate Tab, (or Text Style from Format pull-down on the Mac), the Text Style dialog box appears. We will create a new style by picking the New button (or the "+" button on the Mac).

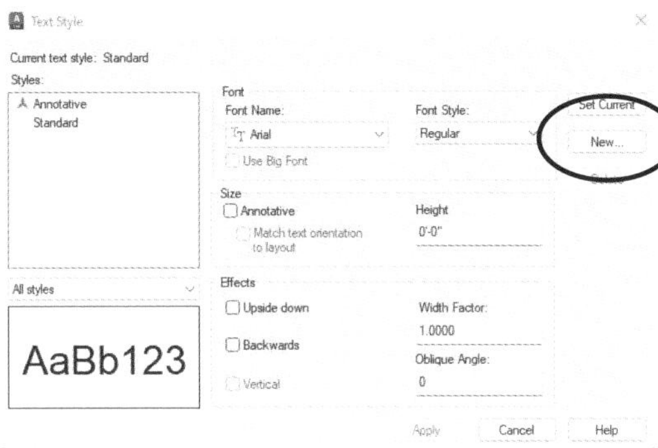

Mac

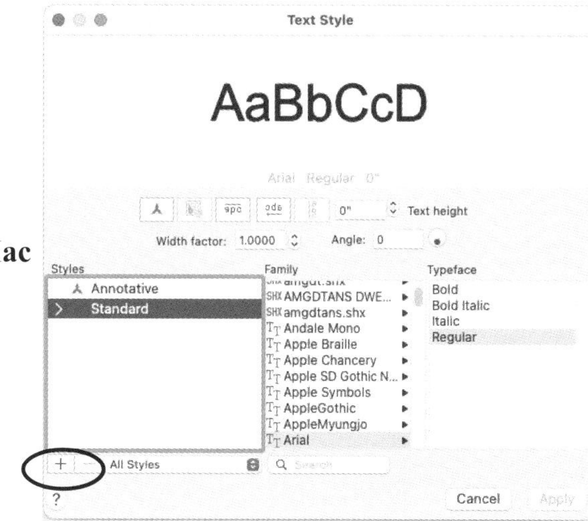

On the PC, a New Text Style dialog box appears with a default "style1" name, which is ready for editing to a name of your choosing. Let's choose "Notes". Type that in, and then pick OK.

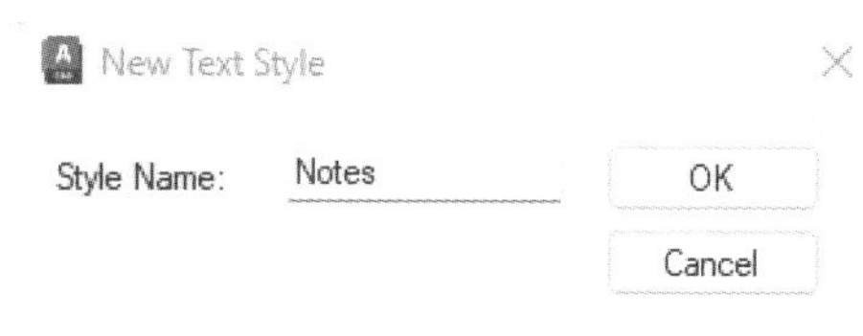

Use the pull-down selection under "Font Name:" to select CityBlueprint as the font. Once you pick the font, the Preview pane shows what the font looks like. Check off "Annotative" under the "Size" portion of the dialog box. Annotative text allows you to scale the text to your layout so that you do not have to have multiple text styles at different heights. Set the "Paper Text Height" to 1/8″. If you leave the Paper Text Height at 0″ you will be prompted to specify the text height while you are inserting the text. You can explore this on your own. When done, Pick the Apply button then Pick the Close button.

If you leave the height at 0″ AutoCAD will prompt you for text height while placing text in your drawing. You can check out the difference by inserting Standard style Text and the 1/8″ Notes style just created.

On the Mac, a new style will appear in the Styles section of the dialog box with a default "style1" name, which is ready for editing to a name of your choosing. Type "Notes". In the Family section of the dialog box, select CityBlueprint as the font. Pick the Annotative icon and change the Text height to 1/8″. The preview pane shows the new style. Pick Apply to save changes.

Mac

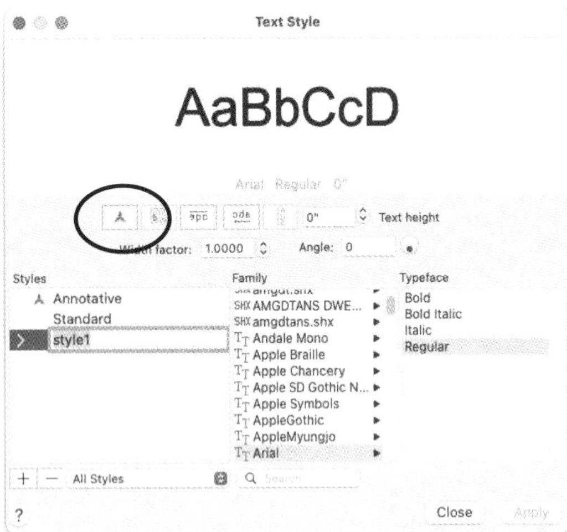

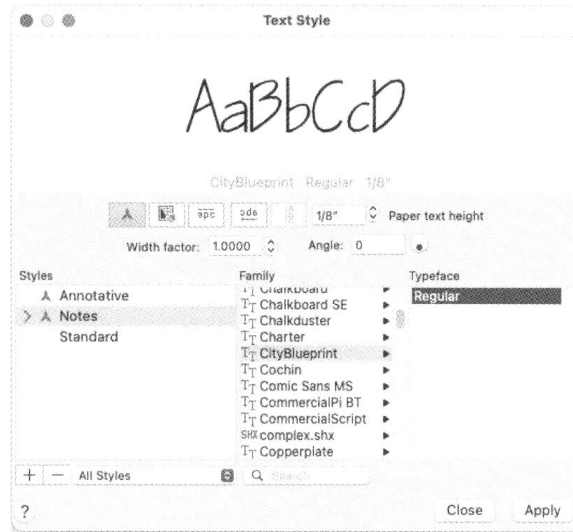

For future use, let's create a second Text Style. Create the new text style by starting with Standard and name it Titleblock. Select the font (Family on the Mac) as Times New Roman and the font style (Typeface on the Mac) as Bold Italic. Leave the text height as 0″. Do not check Annotative because this text will be inserted as a Paper Space object. Pick the Apply button.

When done, your dialog box will look like the following:

Mac

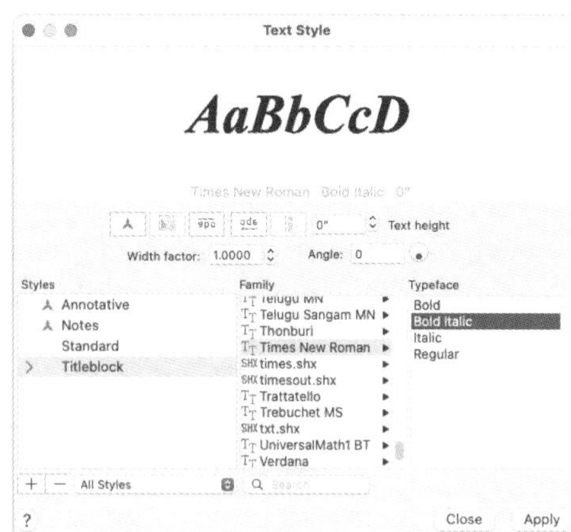

Select the Notes style and pick the Set Current button. On the Mac, right click on the Notes style and pick Set Current. Pick the Close button to exit the dialog box.

In the Text Panel, the current style is the one that is displayed. Ensure that the new style of Notes is the current style before you begin to use text. If it is not, use the pull-down arrow to choose it.

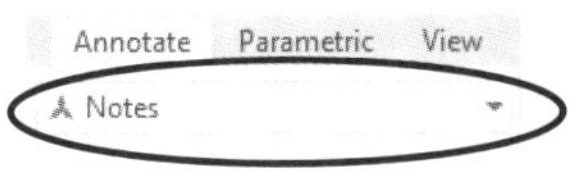

Annotate Tab

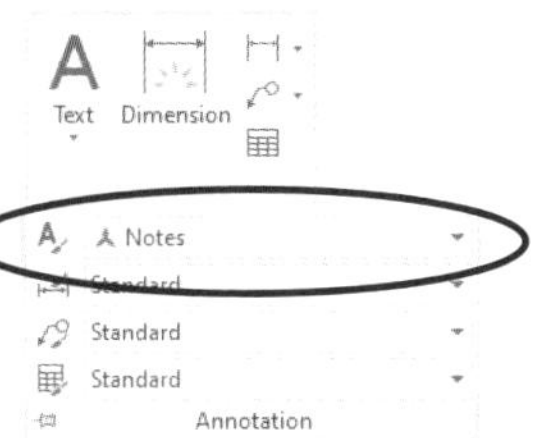

Home Tab

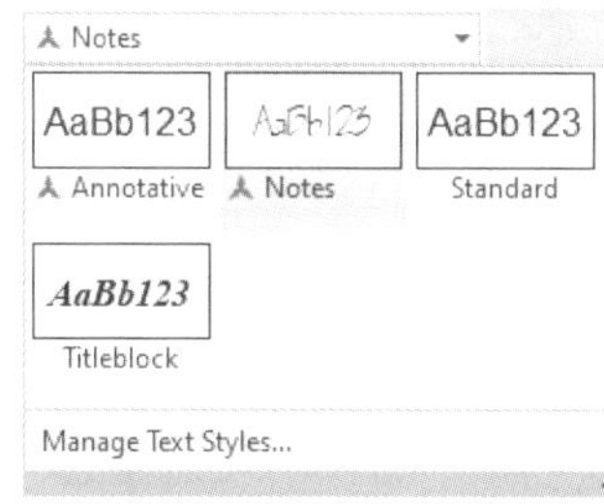

Use pull-down to choose Notes

Multiline Text

You can create multiple lines of text in a defined area. Before entering or importing text, you specify opposite corners of a text bounding box that defines the width of the paragraphs in the multiline text object. The length of the multiline text object depends on the amount of text, not the length of the bounding box. You can use grips to move or rotate a multiline text object.

Ensure you are in Model Space in a Layout and the Viewport scale is set and locked before you begin to insert Annotative Style text. The following procedure describes the Notes Style text inserted in Model Space with the Viewport scale set and locked to ¼″ = 1′.

Procedure:

Pick (left click): **Multiline Text icon** from the Annotation Panel of the Home Tab.
(As an alternative, use the Text Panel of the Annotate Tab)

Mac users: Pick the icon on the Text Toolbar

The command line prompts you with the following:

Current text style: "Notes" Text height: 6" Annotative: Yes

MTEXT *Specify first corner:* ***(Pick on your screen for first corner of bounding box)***

Specify opposite corner or [Height/Justify/Line spacing/Rotation/Style/Width/Columns]: ***(Pick on your screen for the second corner of bounding box)***

Notice that the Text Height is 6″. We had defined the height to be 1/8″, but because of the scale factor of ¼″ = 1′, the Model Space height needs to be 6″ to show up as 1/8″ on the Layout.

After you define the bounding box for the text, a Text Editor Tab appears on your ribbon (on the Mac, a Text Editor Visor appears at the top of the screen) and a ruler appears above the bounding box you defined on your drawing screen:

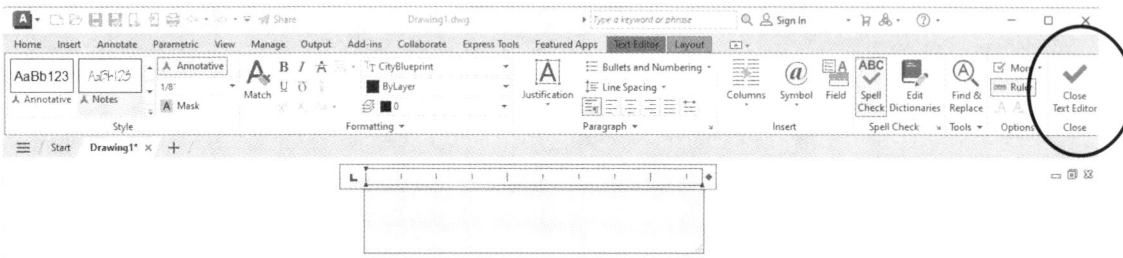

Mac

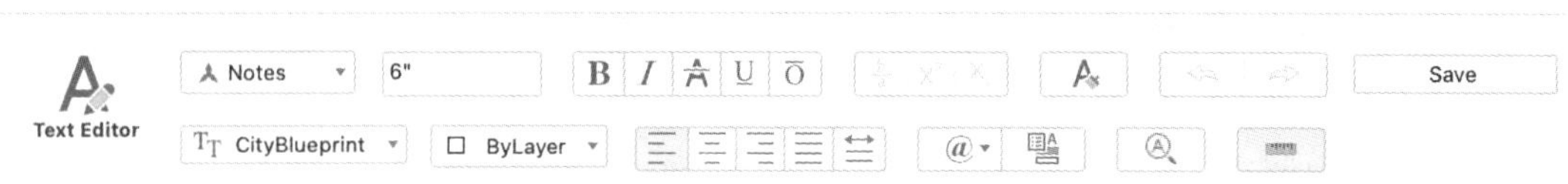

Type in the text you want in the bounding box. When you are done, pick Close Text Editor icon on the Text Editor Tab of the Ribbon. On the Mac, pick the Save button on the Text Editor Visor.

Multiline text is useful for large amounts of text that is cut/pasted from a document. In addition, you have many options at your disposal with this command such as controlling formatting, special symbols, creating columns of text, etc. Otherwise, use Single Line Text.

Single Line Text

We will use the Single Line Text icon on the Annotate Panel of the Home Tab (or use the Text Panel of the Annotate Tab):

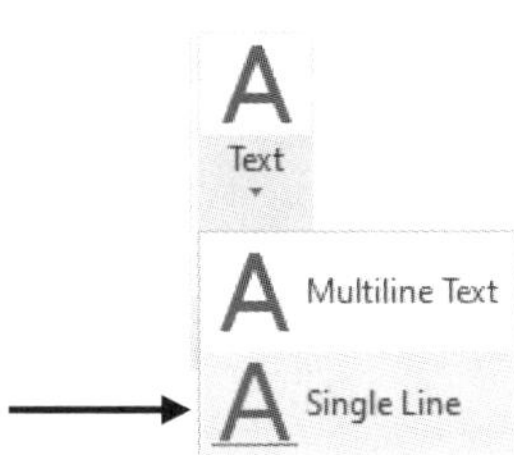

The Text icon is a fly-out. Once you pick Single Line Text as your command, on the PC, it will remain visible, and Multiline Text will be hidden.

Mac

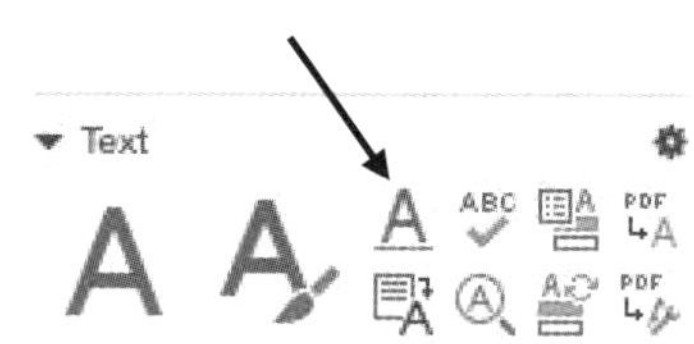

Procedure:

Pick (left click): **Single Line Text icon** from the Annotation Panel of the Home Tab. 
(As an alternative, use the Text Panel of the Annotate Tab)

The command line prompts you with the following:

Current text style: "Notes" Text height: 0'-6" Annotative: Yes Justify: Left

TEXT *Specify start point of text or [Justify/Style]:* ***(Pick a point on the drawing to place the text)***

Specify rotation angle of text <0>: ↵ **Press the ↵ Enter key to accept the default angle. Key in your text. Your text will appear on the drawing.**

AutoCAD allows additional lines of text; you press the ↵ Enter key to start the next line of text. When you are done entering text, **Press the ↵ Enter key.**

If you only want a single line of text, press the ↵ Enter key twice to exit the command.

Note that if you were to place Annotative text onto your drawing while in the Model tab a dialog box will appear the first time you attempt to do this:

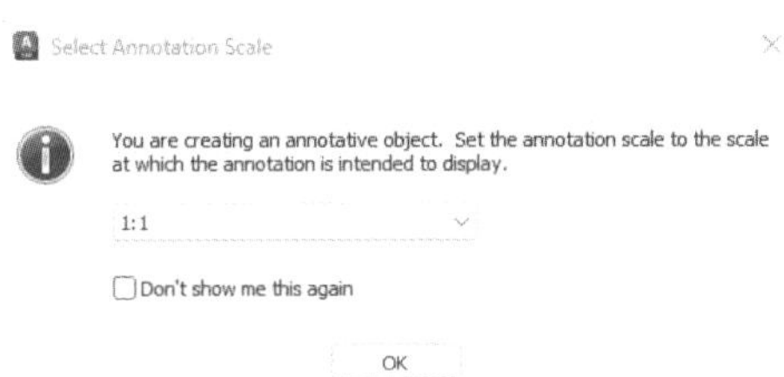

Mac

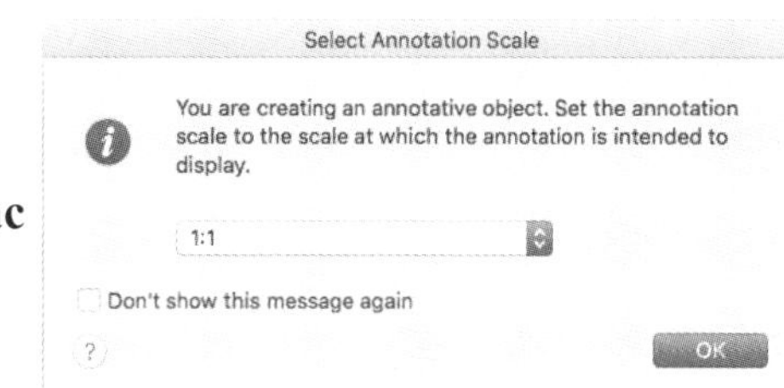

Using Annotative text is best done while you are working in a Layout in Model Space. Most times when you wish to apply text to your drawing, you want to apply it when you are laying out your drawing for printing.

Prior to using Annotative text, set and lock the scale of your Model Space relative to the Paper Space. AutoCAD will automatically scale the text for you.

AutoCAD does the scaling for you with Annotative text. If you are using a scale of ¼″=1′, your text height would have to be 48 times bigger to appear on the drawing. <u>Do the math:</u> ¼″=1′ is the same as ¼″ = 12″ (the units need to be in inches for the math to work). Multiply both sides by 4 (to get rid of the fraction), you get 1″=48″. This means that to get a line of text to appear 3/16″ high on a drawing with a scale factor of ¼″=1′, the text would have to be drawn in the full-scale model 9″ high (3/16 x 48 =9).

As you can see, it is certainly convenient for AutoCAD to do the math for us when it comes to getting the text to appear at the correct height on our layout.

<u>Editing Text</u>

For text that is already on your drawing that you wish to edit, you can double-click on it and it will allow you to edit it. Different text editing features are available depending on whether it is Single Line Text or Multiline Text.

Editing Single Line Text

After double-clicking the text, the command line will show the command, ***TEXTEDIT,*** and the text that you double-clicked will highlight and allow you to begin editing. You can click within the text for specific character changes, or while the entire line of text is highlighted, you can type new text to completely replace it. The delete key on the keyboard can be used to delete characters as desired. Highlighting text and then typing will overwrite the text that was highlighted. After you finish editing, press the ↵ Enter key twice to exit the command.

Editing Multiline Text

After double-clicking the text, the command line will show the command, ***MTEDIT_mtedit,*** and the Text Editor Tab (or Visor) will appear on the ribbon (at the top of the screen). This is the same Text Editor that appeared when you were creating Multiline text. Editing of Multiline text is done in the same manner as single line text. When you are done, pick Close Text Editor icon (or Save on the Mac) on the Text Editor Tab of the Ribbon (or Text Editor Visor on the Mac).

Relocating text

To relocate text on your drawing, it is easily done using grips with the Object Snap feature turned off. Simply pick the text to get the grip, and then pick the grip and move the text to the new location.

Special Characters

There are times when you need to insert a special character or symbol into your Single Line of text. Probably the most commonly used one would be the degree symbol "°".

You can insert a special character while inserting or editing text by keying in the correct code.

The following codes result in special characters:

Code	Resulting Character	Character Name
%%d	°	Degree Symbol
%%p	±	Plus/Minus Symbol
%%c	∅	Diameter Symbol

Example:

Typing: "Door swings through 120%%d", results in "Door swings through 120°".

For Multiline text, you can add symbols and special characters directly from a list of choices. The list is found by using the Symbol icon, which is on the Insert Panel of the Text Editor Tab.

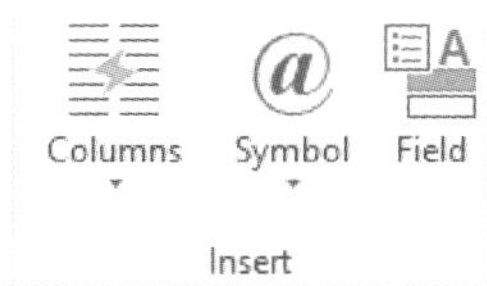

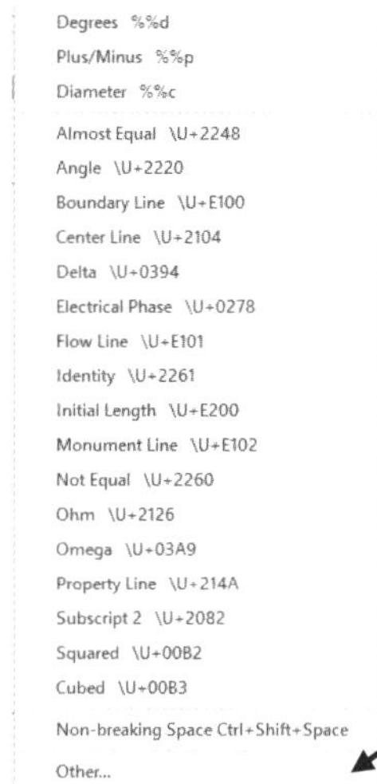

A listing of symbol choices will appear

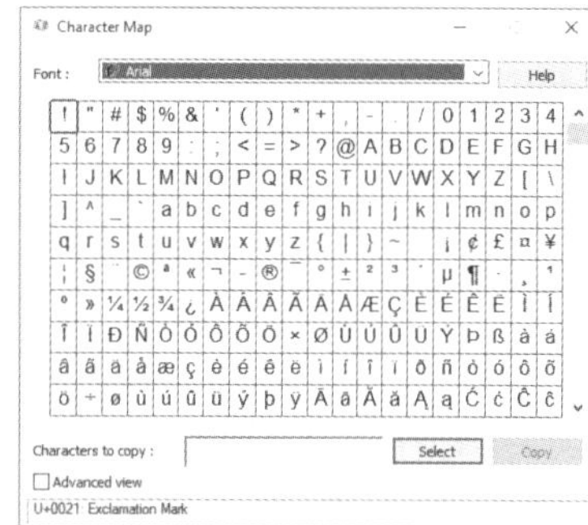

Picking Other… will bring up the Character Map. This will give many additional choices.

Mac

Expand the Character Viewer for additional choices

Scaling Text

For non-Annotative style text only, the text height can be changed using Scale Text on the PC only (Mac users can change the scale of text using the Properties Inspector). Pick the icon then pick the text you want to scale. The Scale Text icon is found by expanding the Text Panel of the Annotate Tab.

Procedure:

Pick (left click): **Scale Text icon** from the Text Panel of the Annotate Tab. 

The command line prompts you with the following:

SCALETEXT *Select objects:* ***(Pick the text)***
Select objects: 1 found ↵
Enter a base point option for scaling
[Existing/Left/Center/Middle/Right/TL/TC/TR/ML/MC/MR/BL/BC/BR] <Existing>: ↵
Specify new model height or [Paper height/Match object/Scale factor] <3/16">: **3/8** ↵
1 objects changed

You cannot change the scale of Annotative text. If you tried, your command line will advise:

1 annotative objects ignored

Dimensions

It is important to use dimensions in your drawing to describe the size and placement of items. AutoCAD has a variety of dimensions available that can be customized. There are several types of dimensions: linear, aligned, radial, diameter, angular, etc. A standard style is available as the default style. This style is more suitable for engineering than it is for Interior Design. We will create a unique style that is better suited for use in Interior Design.

Dimension Style

To create a unique dimension style, expand the Annotation Panel of the Home Tab, and pick the Dimension Style icon.

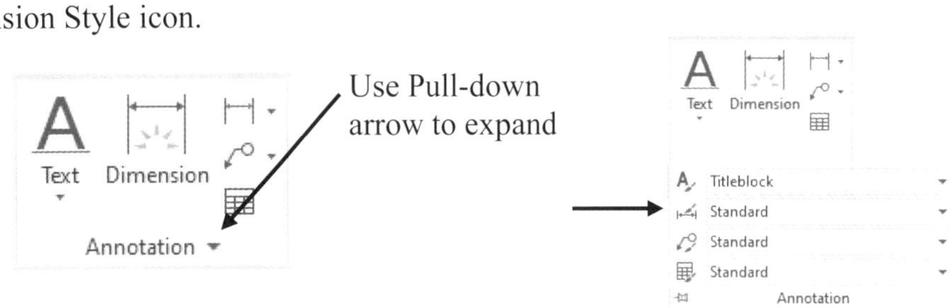

As an alternative, pick the downward arrow of the Dimensions Panel of the Annotate Tab:

Mac

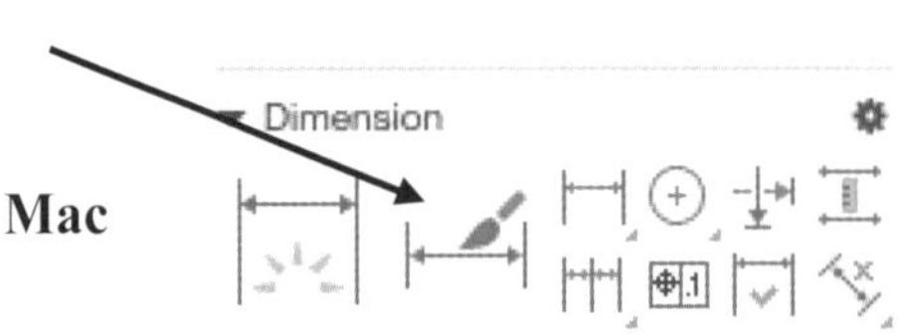

The Dimension Style Manager dialog box will appear.

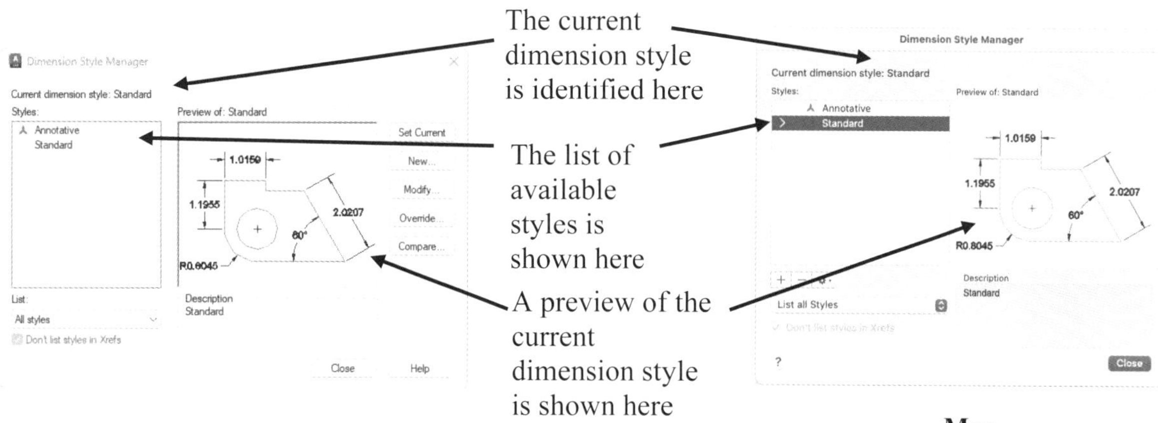

Mac

To create a new dimension style, pick the New… button (or the "+" button on the Mac). A new dialog box will appear. Under New Style Name, the text "Copy of Standard" is highlighted and ready for editing. Let's name the new style Interior Design. Also, check-off Annotative.

Mac

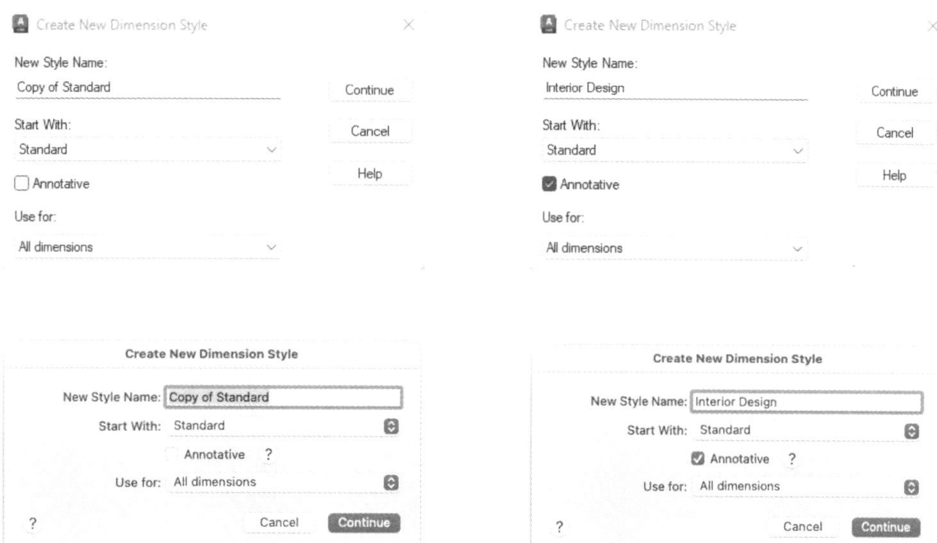

After changing the name, pick the Continue button. A New Dimension Style dialog box will appear. There are seven tabs to choose in this dialog box. Pick the Primary Units tab (if it is not the currently displayed tab). It is here that we will change to architectural units by using the pull-down arrow of Unit format under the Linear Dimensions section on the left side of the dialog box.

Make the following change:

- Change Unit Format to Architectural.

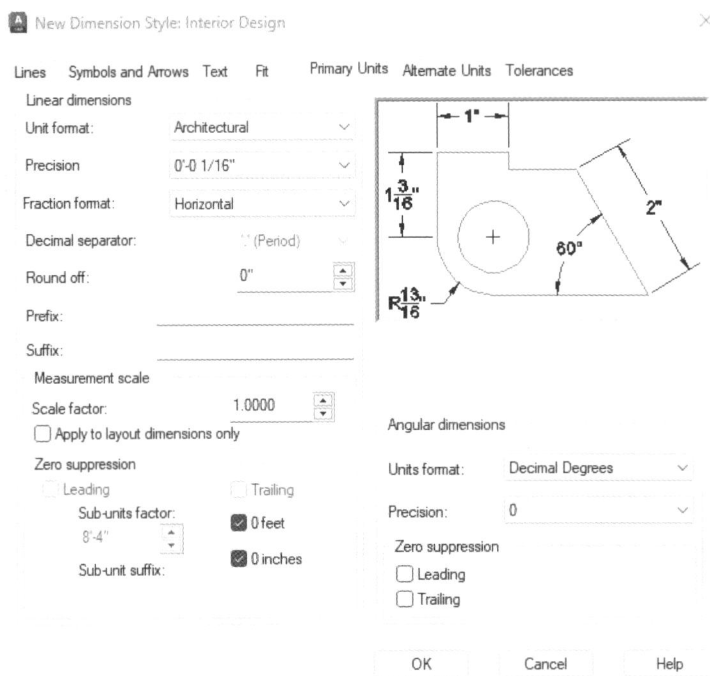

Mac

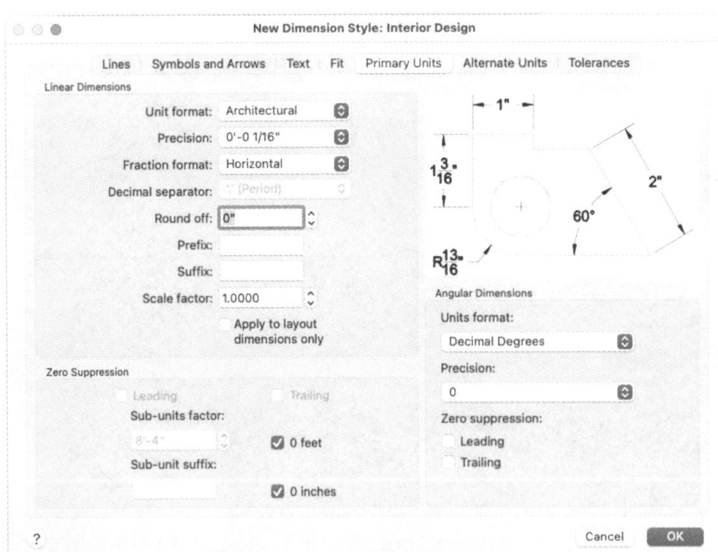

Notice the preview pane shows how the dimensions will appear. That is all we will change in the Primary Units tab. We will leave the Angular dimensions as Decimal Degrees with a zero precision.

Next, pick the Lines tab. It is here we can control the dimension lines and extension lines.

Make the following changes (if these values are not already there):

- Change the value of Baseline spacing to 3/8.
- Change the value of Extend beyond dim lines to 1/8.
- Change the value of Offset from origin to 1/8.

When done, your dialog box should look like this:

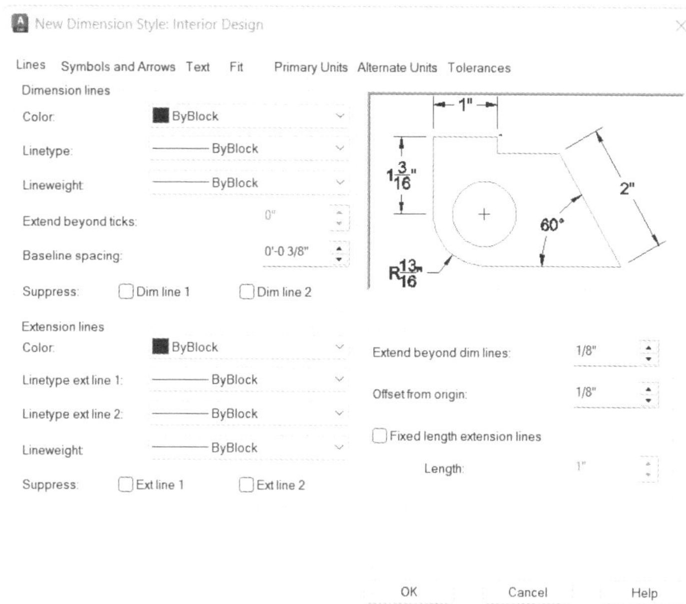

Mac

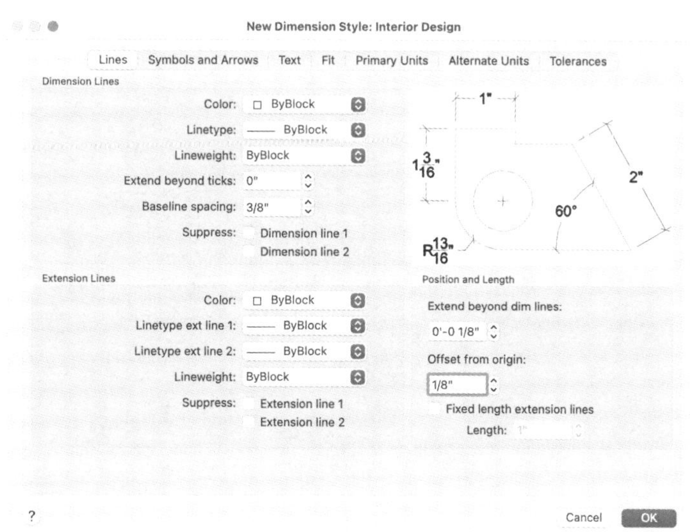

Now, pick the Symbols and Arrows tab. It is here we will control the style and size of the arrowheads.

Make the following changes under the Arrowheads portion of the dialog box:

- Change the arrow style to Oblique under both First and Second.
- Change the Arrow size to 1/8.

When done, your dialog box should look like this:

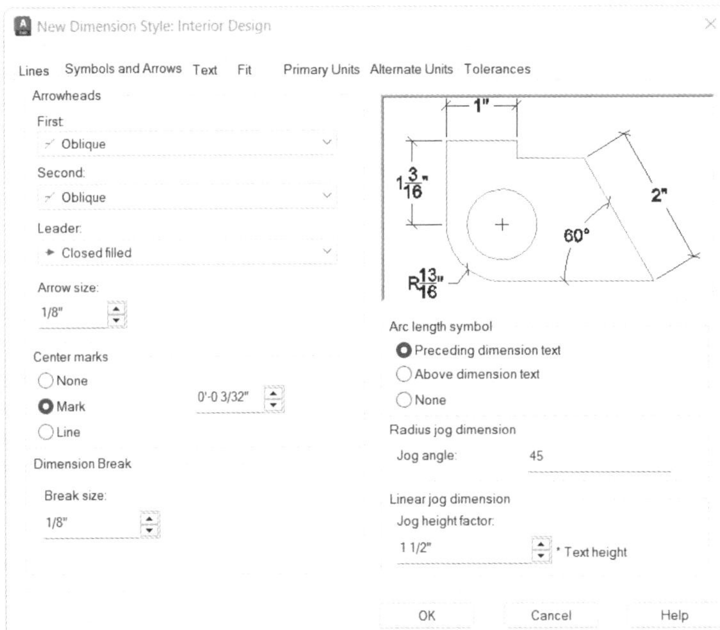

Mac

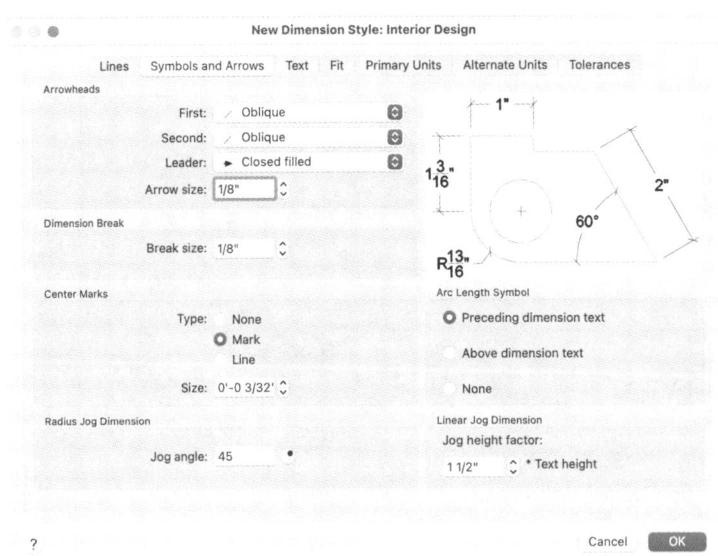

Pick the Text tab. We will change the appearance and placement of the text. For the alignment, we will leave the default value of Horizontal.

In the Text Appearance portion of the dialog box, make the following changes:

- Change the Text height to 1/8 (Mac only – do this before changing style)
- Change the Text style to Notes (if you have not already created this style, you must create that first before this can be done)

When done, your dialog box should look like this:

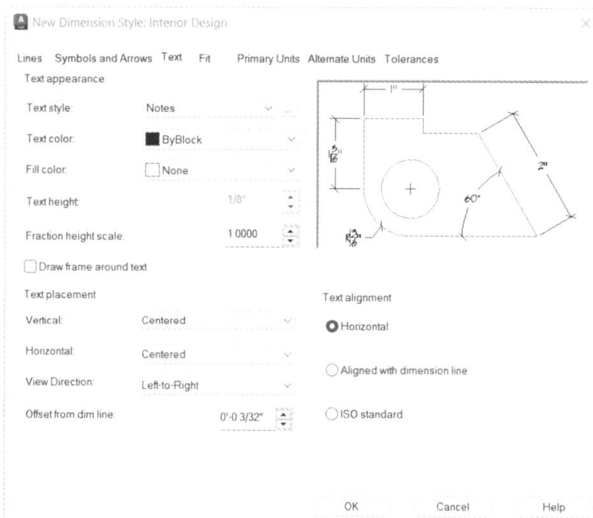

Note that the Text height becomes grayed-out because the Text style of Notes already has a Text height value of 1/8″

Mac

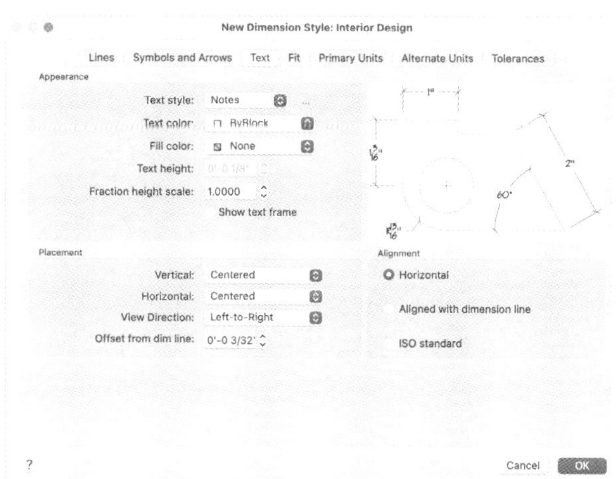

Next, pick the Fit tab. We will change the Scale and Fine Tuning and leave the Options and Placement at the default values.

In the Scale for dimension features portion, Annotative should already be checked because we checked Annotative when we began creating this Dimension Style. If you didn't do that, you can check it off here.

In the Fine Tuning portion, pick the check boxes for both items available. This will allow us to place the dimension text where we want it (instead of AutoCAD automatically placing it) and it will draw the dimension lines between extension lines (primarily handy for radius and diameter dimensions).

When you are done making these changes, your dialog box will look like this:

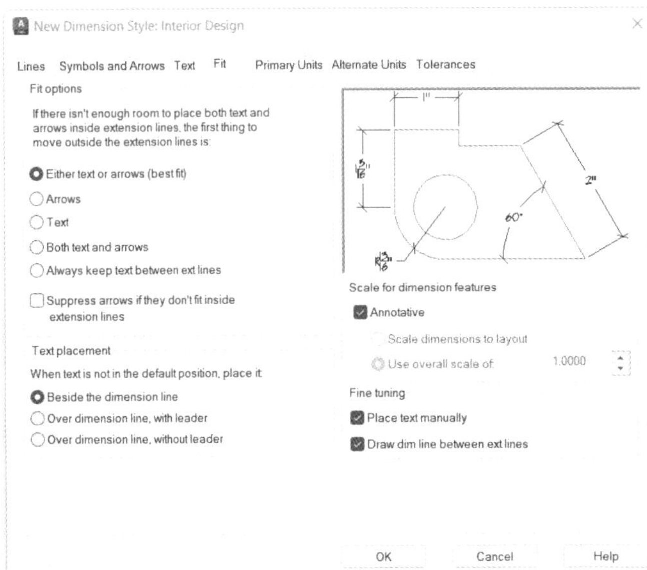

Mac

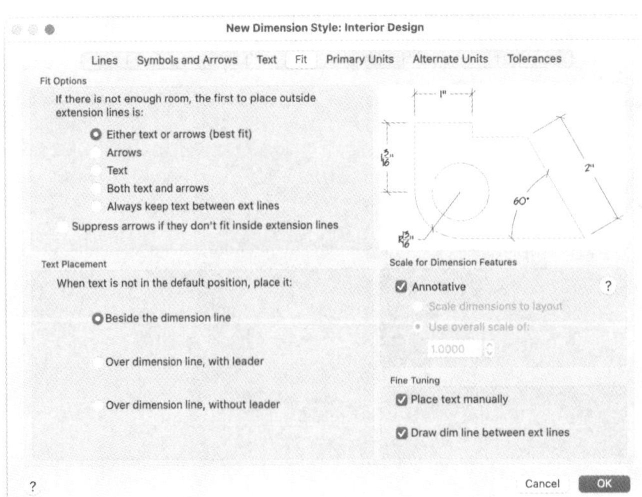

Since these are the only changes that we plan to make for our new dimension style, pick the OK button to exit the dialog box. AutoCAD will return you to the Dimension Style Manager dialog box.

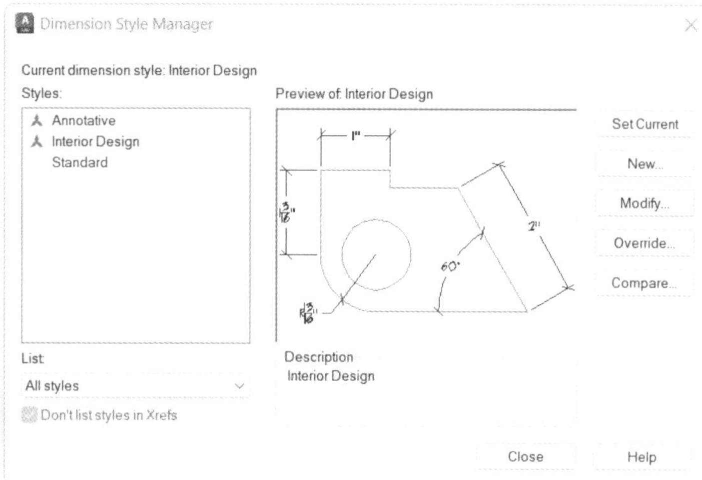

Mac

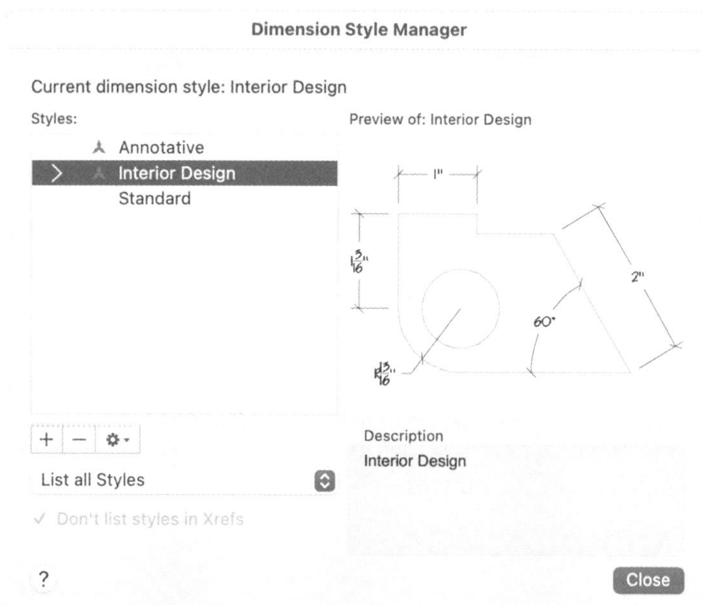

Ensure that Interior Design is the current dimension style. If it is not, pick it to highlight it (on the left side of the dialog box), and then pick the Set Current button. When done, pick the Close button to exit the dialog box.

Using Dimensions

It is important to use dimensions in your drawing to describe the size and placement of items. There are several types of dimensions: linear, aligned, angular, radius, diameter, etc. Icons for each type are available by using the fly-out icon in either the Annotation Panel of the Home Tab, or the Dimension Panel of the Annotate Tab. You can access those dimensions by using the pull-down menu Dimension. On the Mac, click and hold the Linear Dimension icon to expose the other dimension icons.

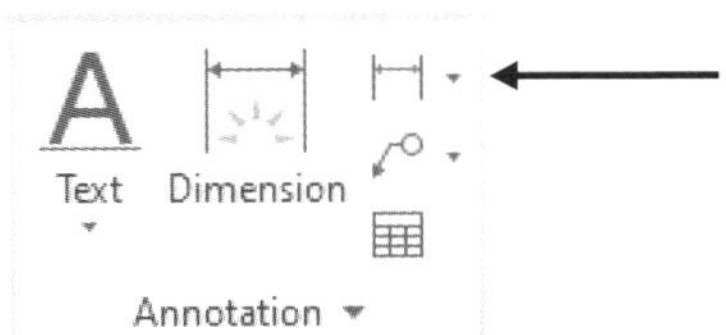

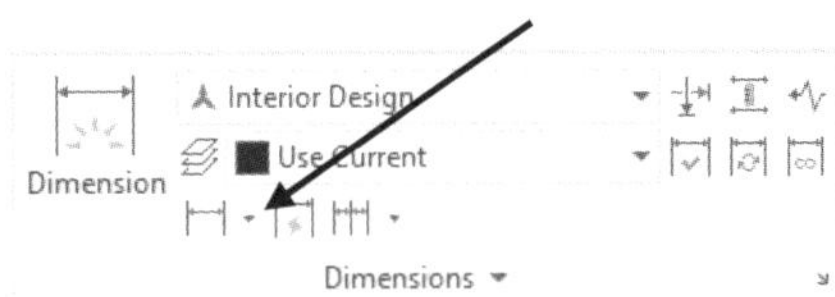

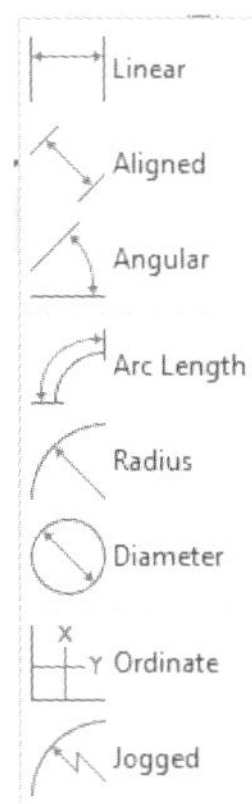

Mac

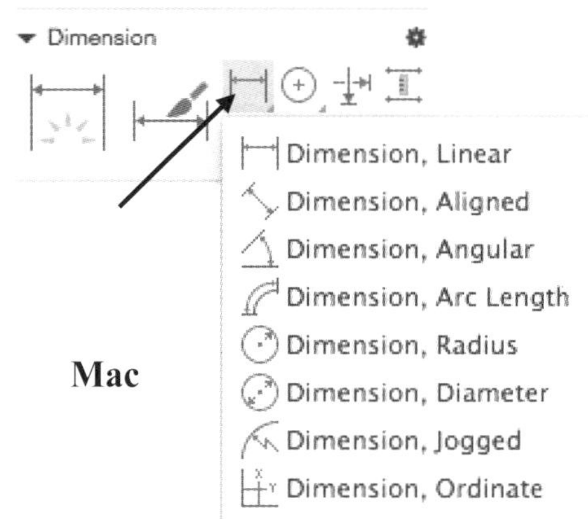

You have just created a new dimension style. These instructions will show you how to use the various dimension icons.

As an example of using dimensions, open the file *Faucet.dwg* that was downloaded from the publisher website. We will dimension the faucet.

Before beginning to use the dimensions, ensure that OSNAP is turned on and the settings are logical for what you plan to select (example: Endpoint, or Intersection). The faucet drawing already has the Text and Dimension styles we just created. Make sure that Interior Design is the Current style.

Pick the Faucet Layout before you begin to insert dimensions. While in the Layout, change from Paper Space to Model Space. Because the scale is already set and locked to 6″=1′, the Annotative style will automatically adjust the size of the dimensions accordingly.

Linear Dimension

Linear dimensions are used to define the horizontal or vertical distances.

Procedure:

Pick (left click): **Linear Dimension icon** from the Annotation Panel of the Home Tab.
(As an alternative, use the Dimension Panel of the Annotate Tab)

The command line prompts you with the following:

DIMLINEAR Specify first extension line origin or <select object>: **(Pick endpoint A)**

Specify second extension line origin: ***(Pick endpoint B)***

Specify dimension line location or
[Mtext/Text/Angle/Horizontal/Vertical/Rotated]: ***(Pick a location for the dimension text)***

Dimension text = 1 1/4"

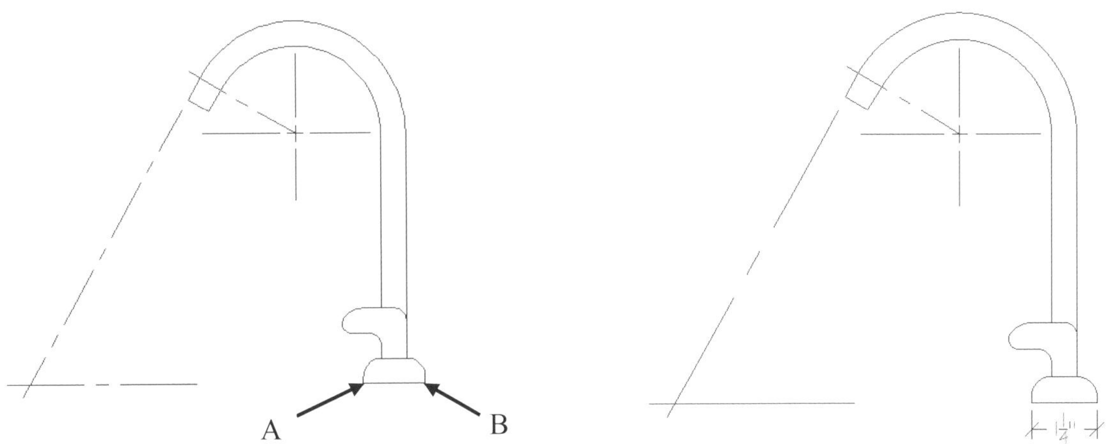

Result

Aligned Dimension

Procedure:

Pick (left click): **Aligned Dimension icon** from the Annotation Panel of the Home Tab.
(As an alternative, use the Dimension Panel of the Annotate Tab)

The command line prompts you with the following:

DIMALIGNED *Specify first extension line origin or <select object>:* ***(Pick intersection point C)***
Specify second extension line origin: ***(Pick endpoint D)***

Specify dimension line location or
[Mtext/Text/Angle]: ***(Pick a location for the dimension text)***

Dimension text = 1/2"

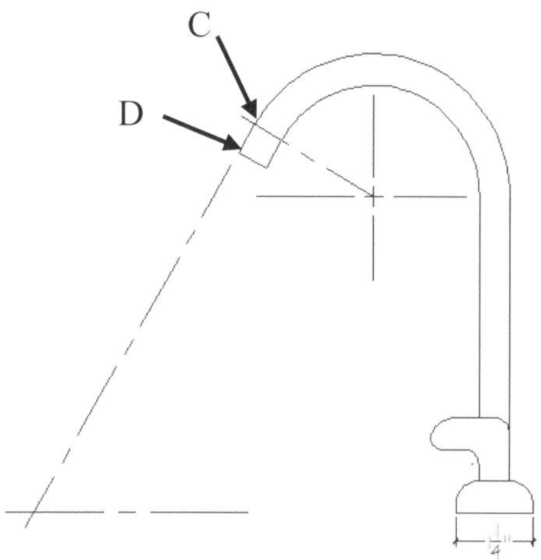

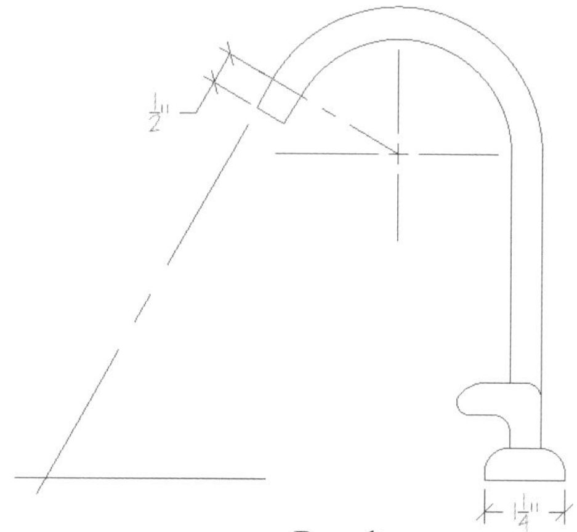

Result

Radius Dimension

Procedure:

Pick (left click): **Radius Dimension icon** from the Annotation Panel of the Home Tab.
(As an alternative, use the Dimension Panel of the Annotate Tab)

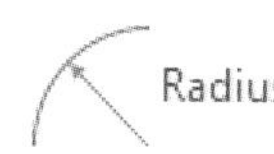

The command line prompts you with the following:

DIMRADIUS *Select arc or circle:* ***(Pick arc E)***

Dimension text = 1 3/4"
Specify dimension line location or [Mtext/Text/Angle]: ***(Pick a location for the dimension text)***

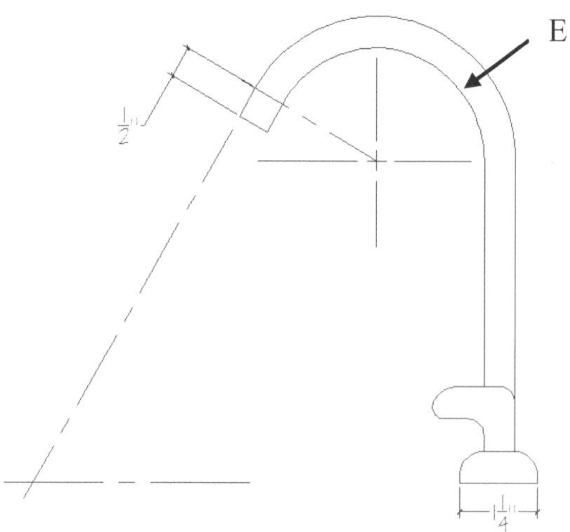

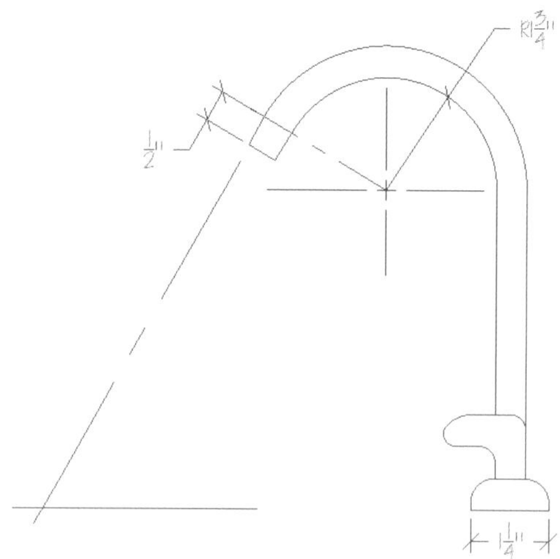

Result

Angular Dimension

Procedure:

Pick (left click): **Angular Dimension icon** from the Annotation Panel of the Home Tab.
(As an alternative, use the Dimension Panel of the Annotate Tab)

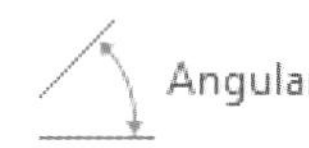

The command line prompts you with the following:

DIMANGULAR *Select arc, circle, line, or <specify vertex>:* ***(Pick line F)***

Select second line: ***(Pick line G)***

Specify dimension arc line location or [Mtext/Text/Angle]: ***(Pick a location for the dimension text)***

Dimension text = 60

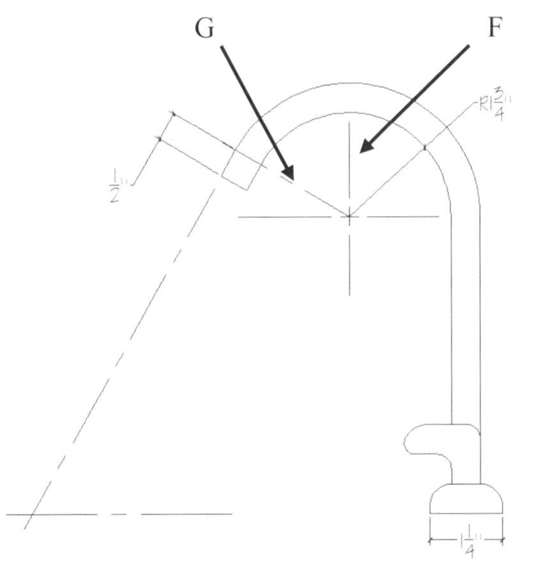

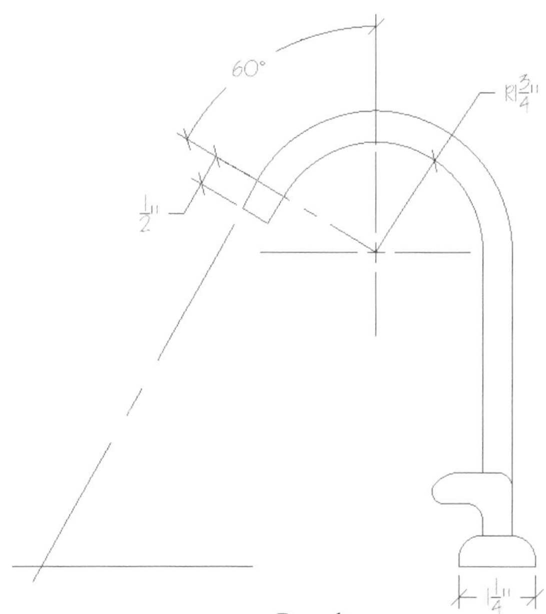

Result

Diameter Dimension

As an example, for this dimension type, we will use a simple 4″ diameter circle, which can be found on the Circle Layout tab. This layout has a scale of 1:1.

Procedure:

Pick (left click): **Diameter Dimension icon** from the Annotation Panel of the Home Tab. 

(As an alternative, use the Dimension Panel of the Annotate Tab)
The command line prompts you with the following:

DIMDIAMETER *Select arc or circle:* ***(Pick the circle)***

Dimension text = 4"
Specify dimension line location or [Mtext/Text/Angle]: ***(Pick a location for the dimension text)***

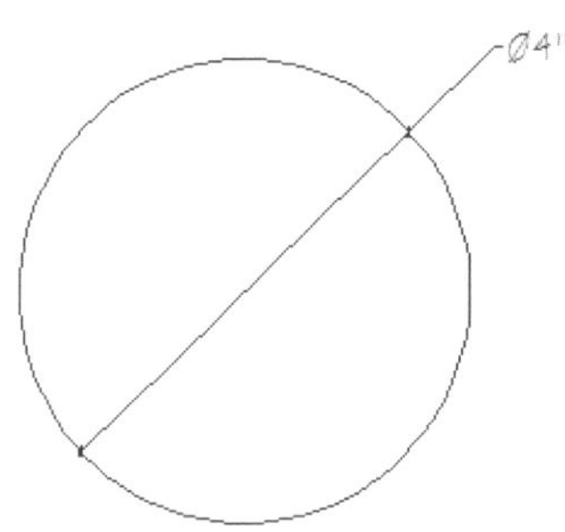

The default setting for AutoCAD diameter dimension is to use the diameter symbol: ∅.

We can change that by modifying the existing style. Pick the Dimension Style icon. When the Dimension Style Manager dialog box appears, select the New button.

In the Create New Dimension Style dialog box, use the pull-down arrow under Use for: to select the Diameter dimensions, then pick the Continue button.

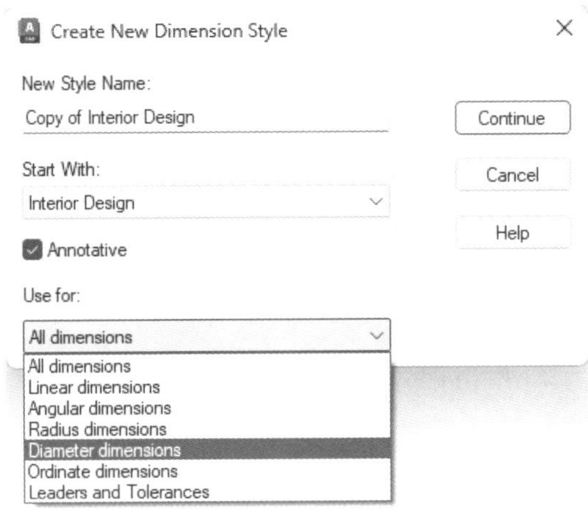

Mac

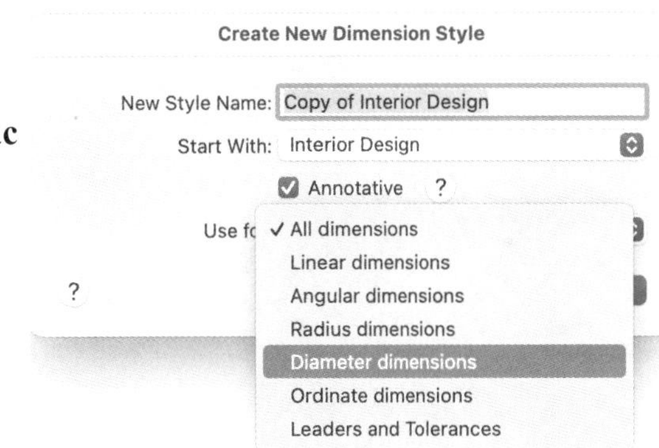

When the New Dimension Style dialog box appears, select the Primary Units tab.

Change the Prefix text by typing a space (you won't be able to see it). Change the Suffix text by typing a space and the word DIA. Notice how it changes in the preview pane. Pick the OK button when you are done.

Mac

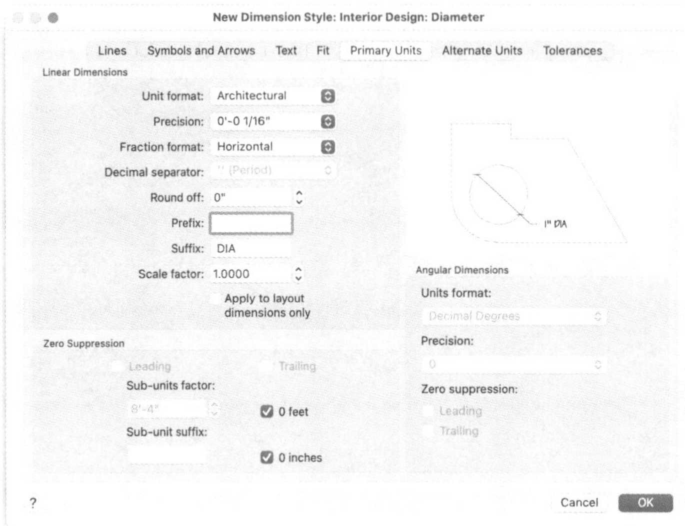

AutoCAD returns to the Dimension Style Manager dialog box. Notice that the new diameter style that was just created is a subset of the dimension style Interior Design.

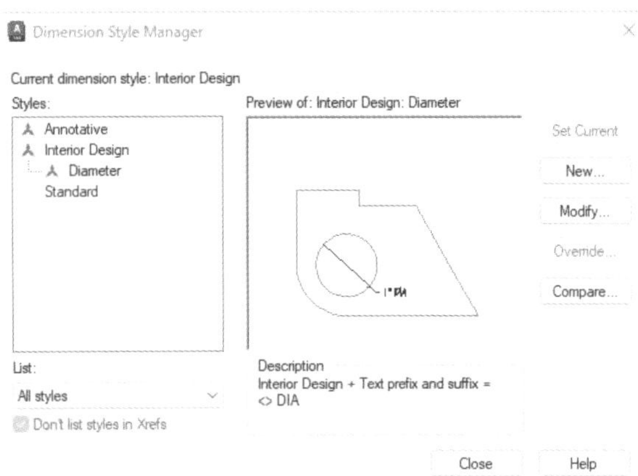

Mac

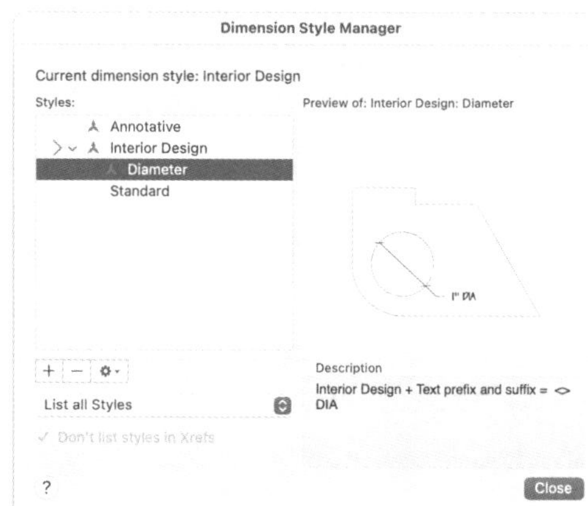

Now when a diameter dimension is created using the style Interior Design, the diameter dimension will look like this:

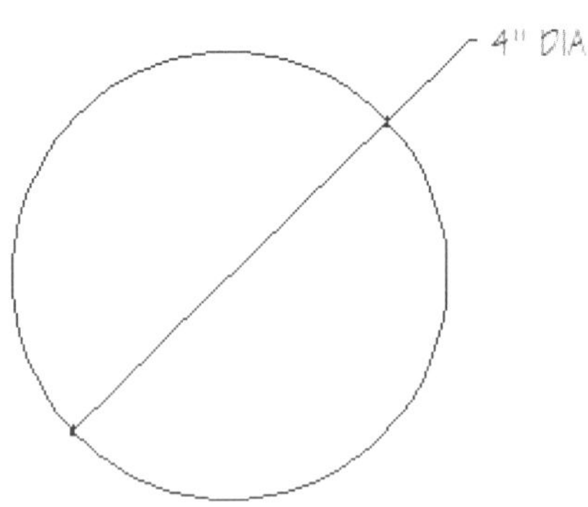

Modifying Existing Dimensions

There are times when dimensions share the same extension lines. Rather than create a unique style with the dimension line suppressed, this can be accomplished by using the Properties Palette (Properties Inspector on the Mac and picking All). In the Properties Palette/Inspector, after the dimension is selected, either extension line 1 or 2 or both can be turned off.

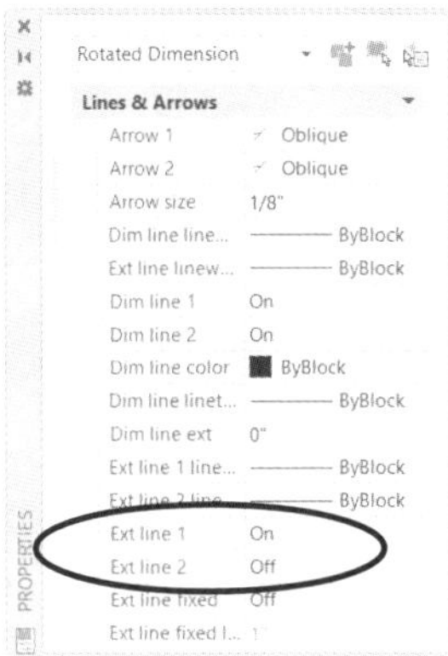

Mac

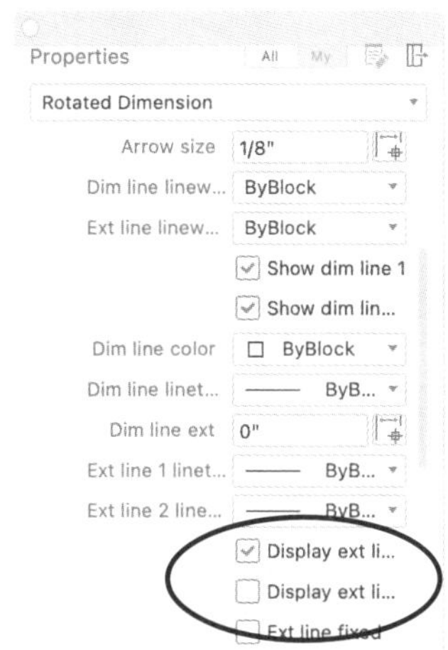

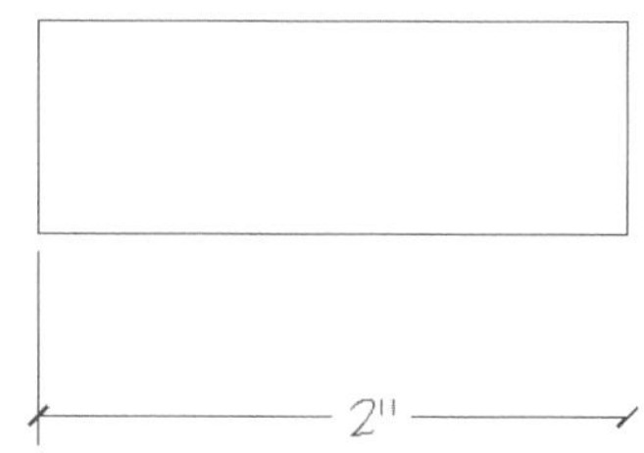

This example shows the Properties Palette/Inspector was used to turn Ext line 2 off.

Multileader

To label items on your drawing, use a Multileader. The Multileader can have an arrow with line and text. You can create a unique Multileader style in a similar way that we created a unique dimension style.

Multileader Style

To create a unique Multileader style, expand the Annotation Panel of the Home Tab, and pick the Multileader Style icon.

Mac users: Pick the Multileader style icon from the Leader Toolbar

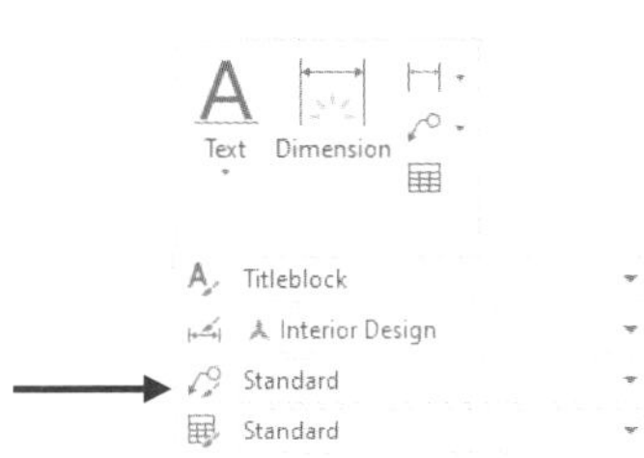

Mac

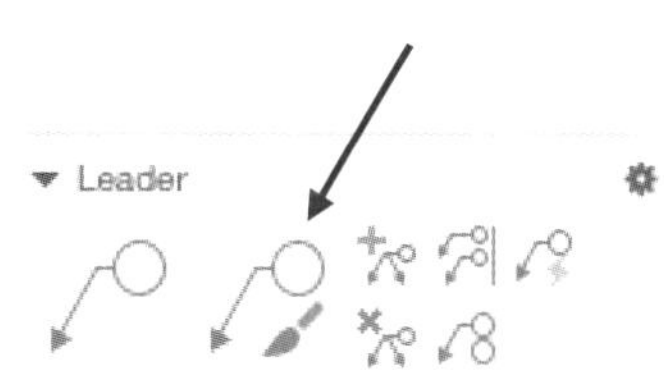

As an alternative, pick the downward arrow of the Leaders Panel of the Annotate Tab:

The Multileader Style Manager dialog box will appear.

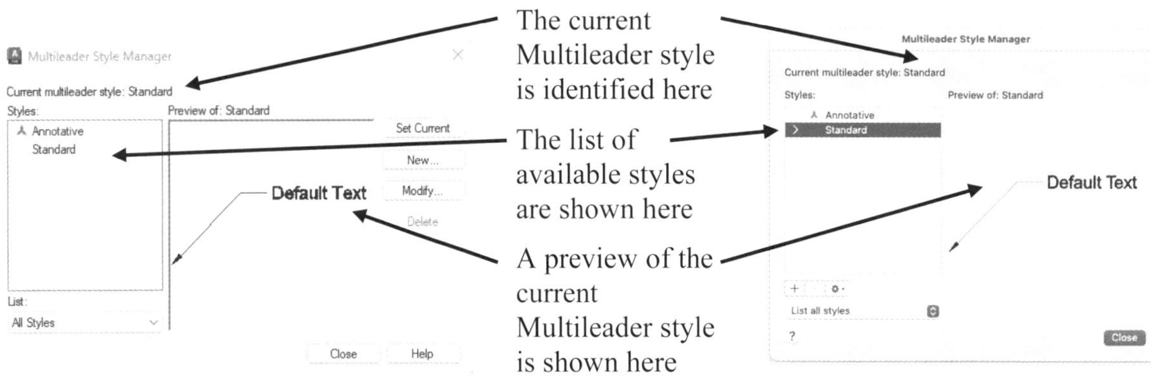

Mac

To create a new Multileader style, pick the New… button (or the "+" button on the Mac). A new dialog box will appear. Under New Style Name, the text "Copy of Standard" is highlighted and ready for editing. Let's name the new style Label. Also, check-off Annotative. Pick the Continue button when done.

Mac

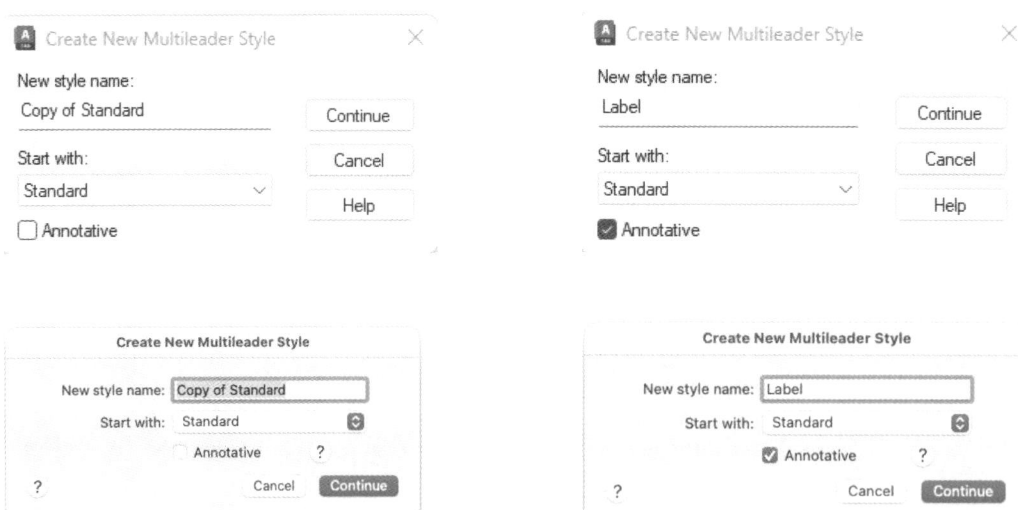

A Modify Multileader Style dialog box will appear. This is where you will make the setting changes. There are three tabs to choose from. Pick the Content tab.

Make the following changes under the Content tab:

- Change the Text height to 1/8 (Mac only – do this before changing style)
- Change the Text style to Notes (as created in previous chapter)

When done, your dialog box should look like this:

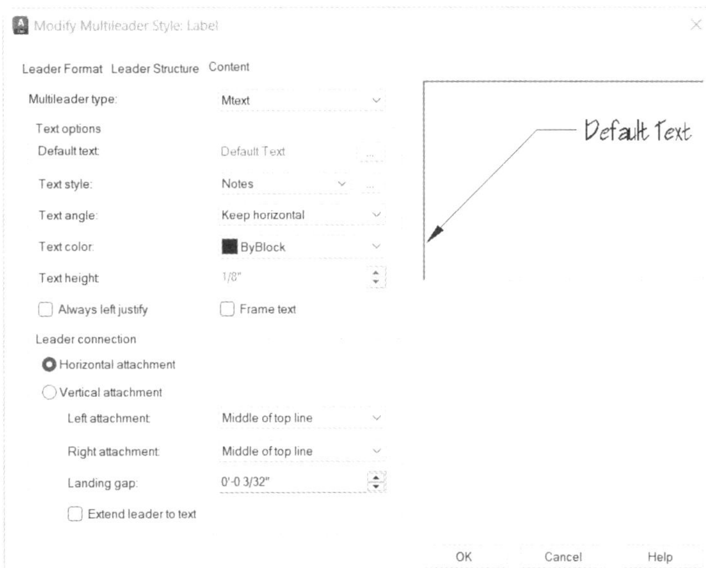

Mac

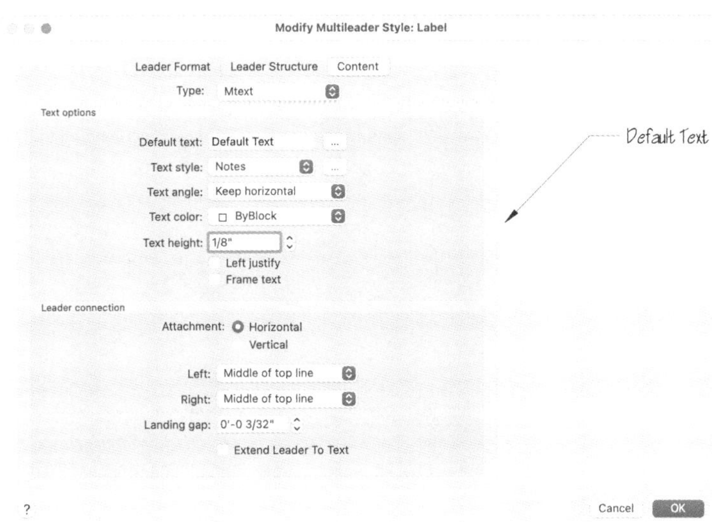

Pick the Leader Format tab. This is where the style of leader (straight or spline), and the choice of multiple arrowheads are made.

The following shows the difference between a Straight Leader and a Spline Leader:

For this style, we will leave the Type as Straight.

The multiple arrowhead choices are found by using the pull-down arrow in the Arrowhead section of the dialog box:

For this style, we will leave the Arrowhead Symbol as Closed filled.

Make the following changes under the Leader Format tab:

- Change the Arrowhead Size to 1/4.

When done, your dialog box should look like this:

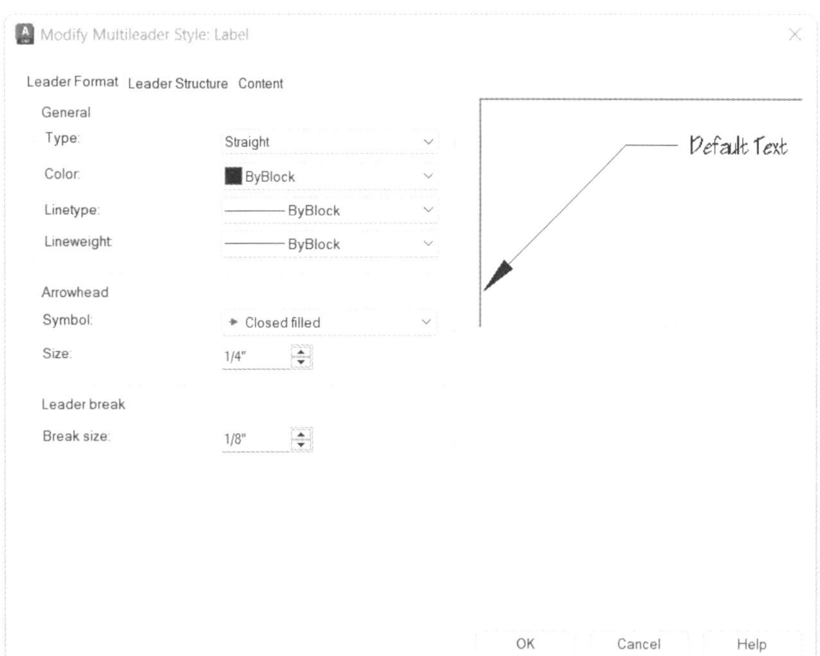

Mac

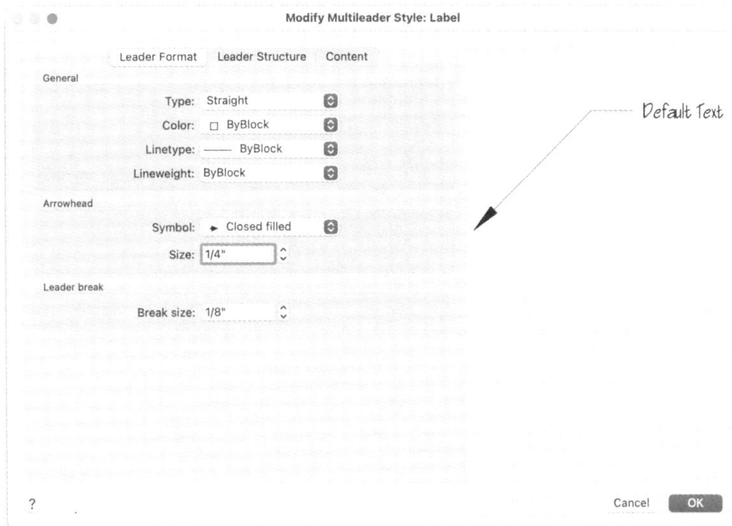

Pick the Leader Structure tab. Each line segment can be constrained as you desire.

Make the following changes under the Leader Structure tab:

- Change the landing distance to 1/4.

If you forgot to set the Scale to Annotative when creating this style, you can set it here while in the dialog box.

When done, your dialog box should look like this:

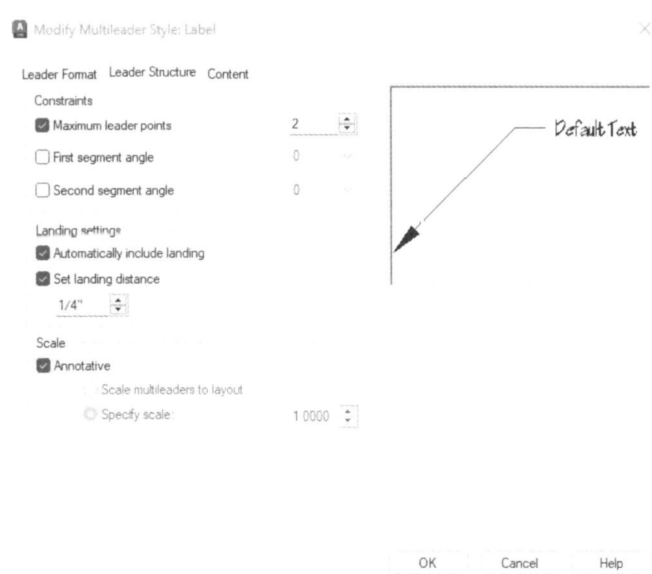

Mac

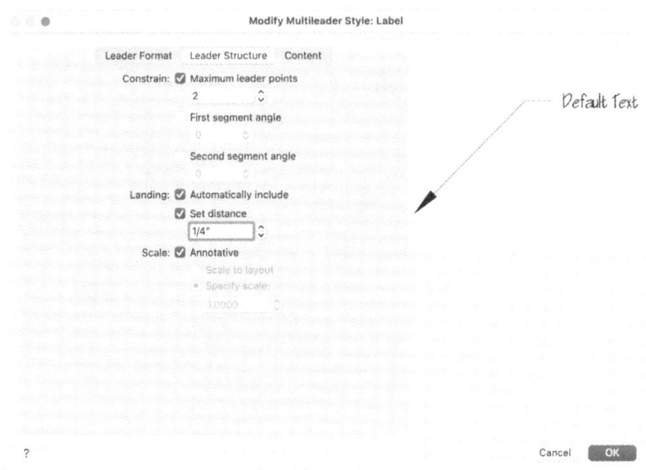

Note that if you desire, you can change the Maximum number of leader points. Below is an example of 3 leader points:

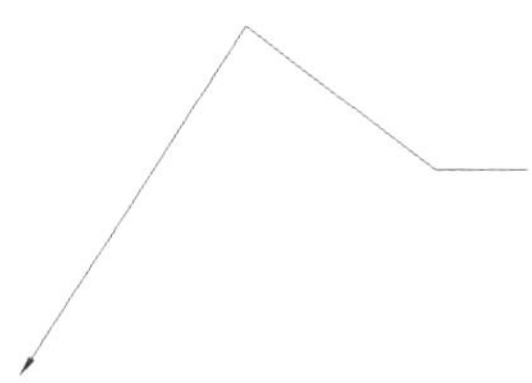

Pick OK to exit the dialog box. On the Mac, right click on Label and select Set Current. Pick Close to exit the Multileader Style Manager dialog box.

The current style should now be set to Label:

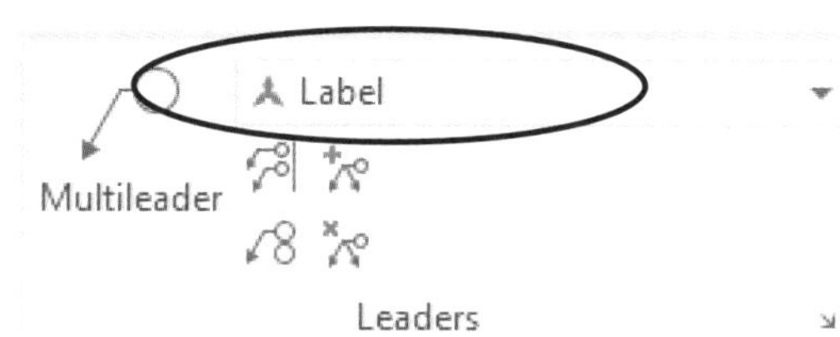

Inserting a Multileader on Your Drawing

Procedure:

Pick (left click): **Multileader icon** from the Annotation Panel of the Home Tab.
(As an alternative, use the Leaders Panel of the Annotate Tab)

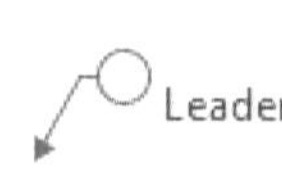

The command line prompts you with the following:
MLEADER *Specify leader arrowhead location or [leader Landing first/Content first/Options] <Options>:* **(Pick the object that you are adding a label to. This will be the Arrow end of the first segment. This may be an endpoint or midpoint, or somewhere close to the object with OSNAP off)**

Specify leader landing location: **(Pick a location for the end of the arrow)**

As soon as you pick the leader landing location, the Text Editor Panel will appear on the ribbon. Also, a flashing I-bar will appear near the leader landing. This is where you type in the information for your Multileader (label).

(Key in the desired text.)

When you are done typing in the text, pick the Close Text Editor icon on the Text Editor Panel. This will close the dialog box and exit the command.

As an example, let's assume we are labeling a coffee table. When done, your Multileader should look like this:

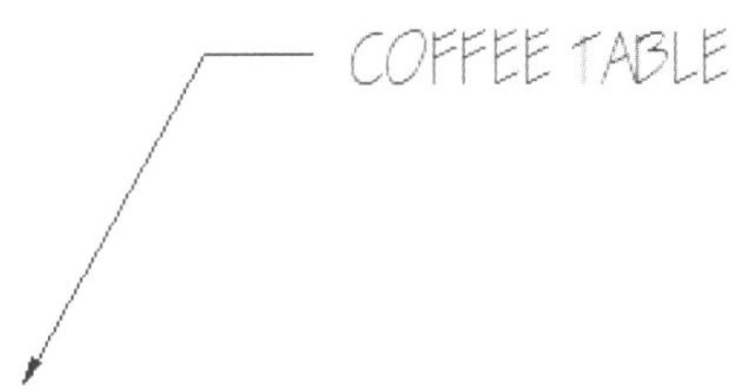

Summary

In this chapter you have learned to:

- Create different styles of text
- Create a style for dimensions that is suitable for interior design
- Use various types of dimensions, including linear, aligned, radial and angular
- Modify existing dimensions
- Create a label style for Multileader
- Use Multileaders for labeling objects

Review Questions

1. What does "Annotative" style mean?
2. What does "current style" mean?
3. What does a text height of 0″ mean?
4. What are the differences between Single Line Text and Multiline Text?
5. What is an easy way to relocate text on your drawing?
6. After text is already on the drawing, how can you change its size?
7. What is the difference between a dimension line and an extension line?
8. What is an easy method to turn a dimension extension line off?
9. How do you change the default diameter symbol?
10. What is a Spline Leader?

Exercises

1. Draw the bookshelf. Use the 8-1/2″ x 11″ layout to set and lock the scale to 1″ = 1′. Create layers "Object", "Viewport", and "Dimension and Text". Set the Lineweight of layer Object to .012″ . Place the viewport border on layer Viewport and Freeze the layer. The bookshelf is drawn on layer Object. Use the dimension, text, and multileader styles created in this chapter. The dimensions and multileaders must be Model Space objects and placed on the Dimensions and Text layer. The text items are Paper Space objects and belong on Dimensions and Text layer.

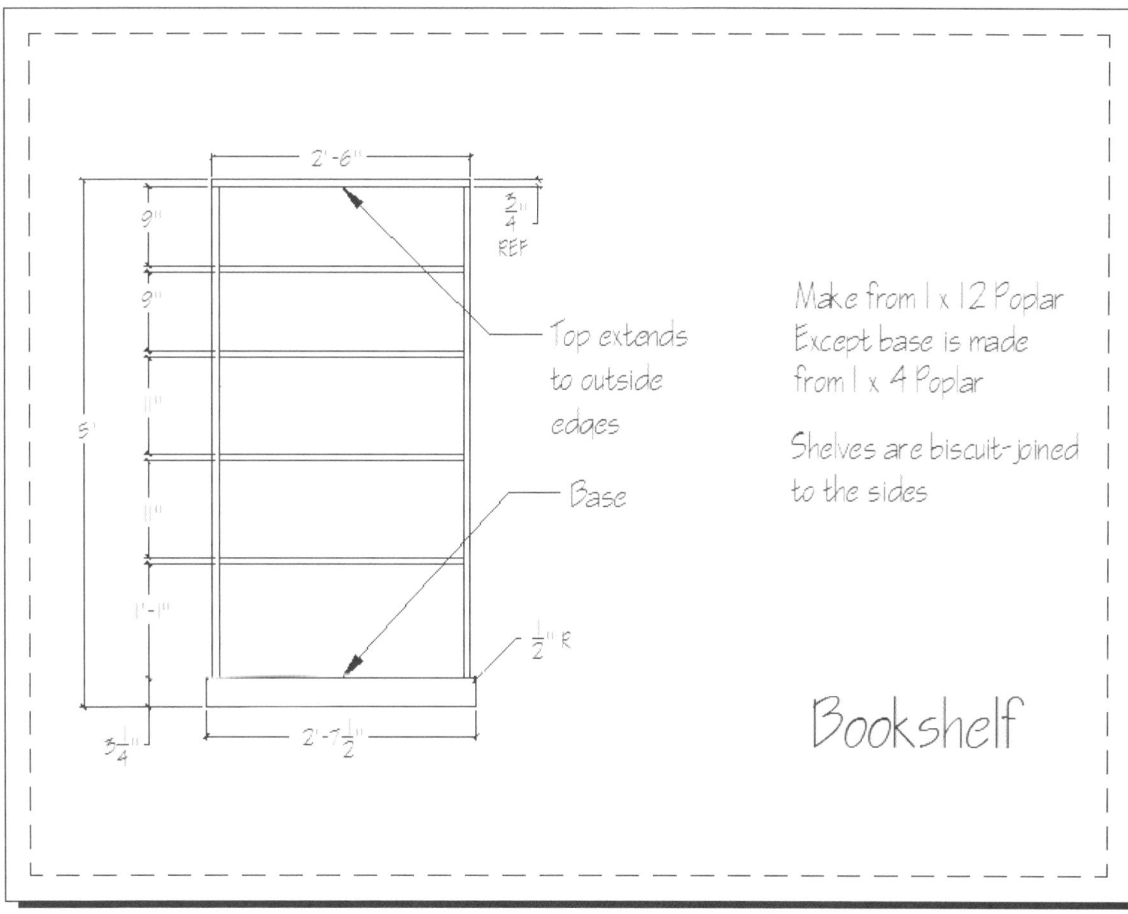

2. Draw the Hinge and Screw Detail. Use Paper Space with two viewports – one for the hinge, the other for the screw detail. Set the scale for the hinge viewport to 1:1 and the screw detail to 4:1. Dimension the hinge and the screw detail – make sure to use the annotative dimension style you created in this chapter. Change the properties of the screw slot dimension precision to 1/32.

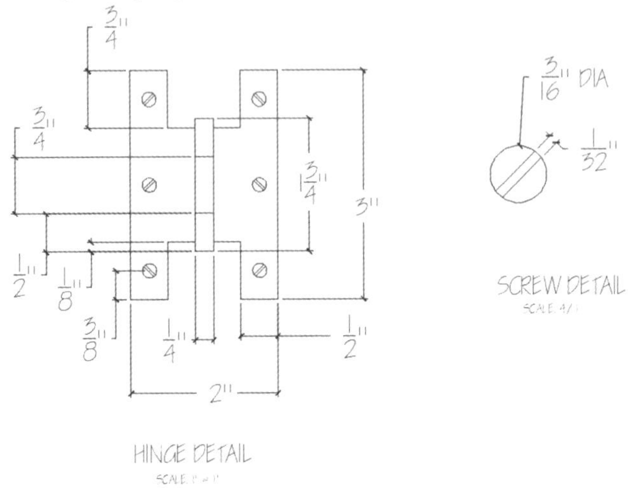

3. Draw the country hutch. Use the drawing format sheet, layers, dimensions, text, multileaders, and create viewports and layouts.
The hutch drawing details are on the following three drawing sheets:
(Hint for side view: draw the arcs as circles, draw a line tangent to the circles for the angled line (use Snap-to-Tangent), and trim the circles so they become arcs).

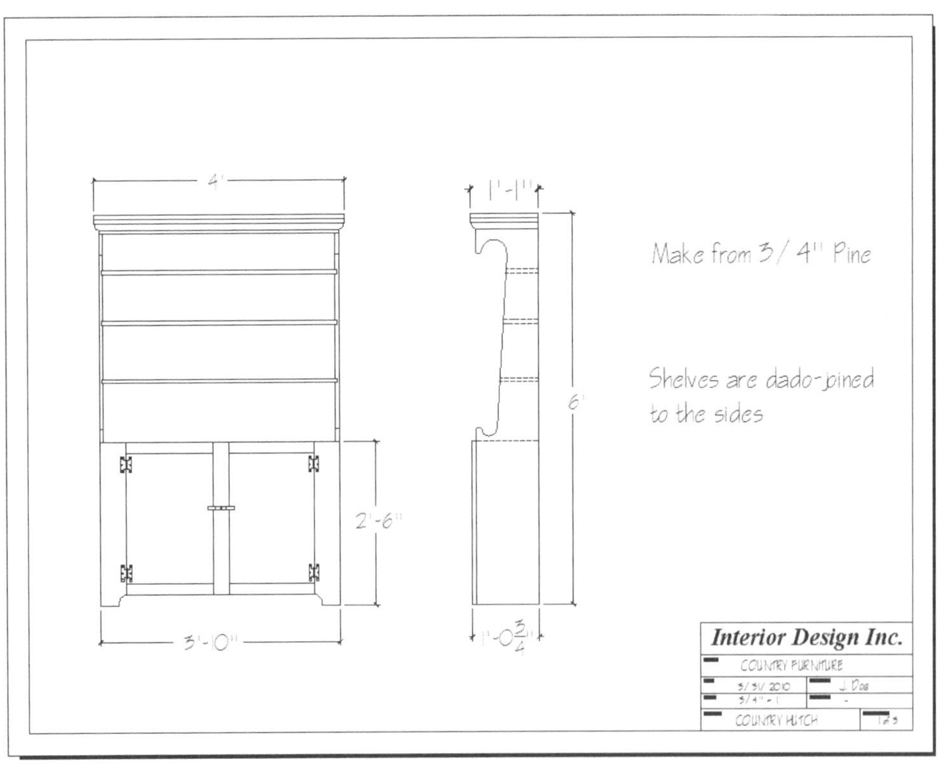

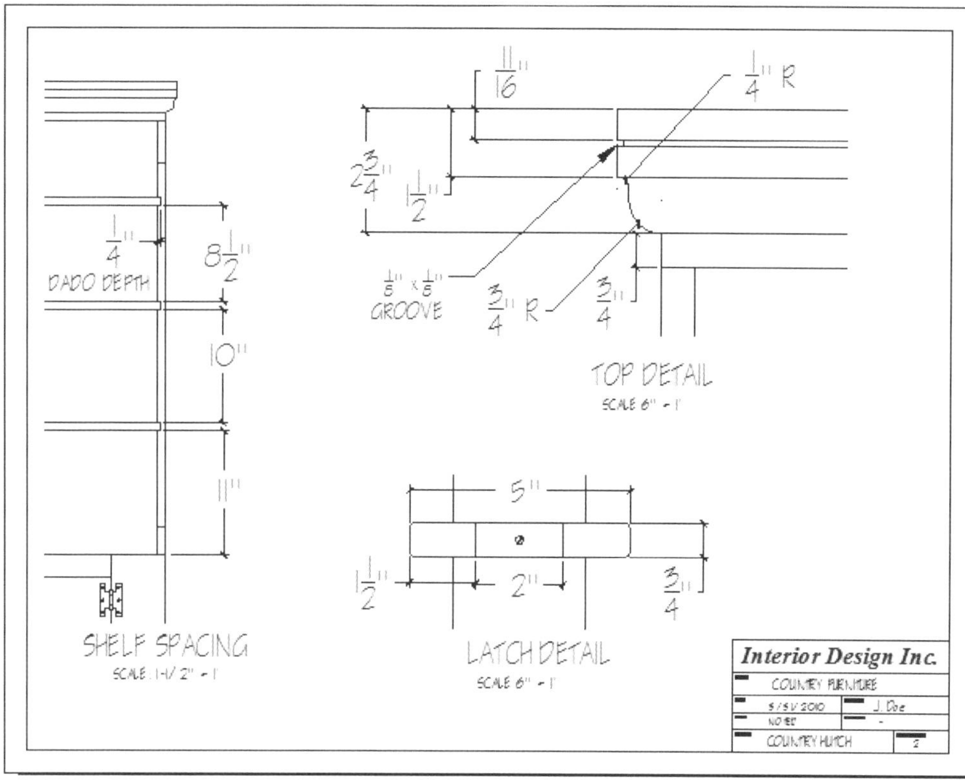
SHELF SPACING
SCALE: 1-1/2" = 1'
DADO DEPTH
TOP DETAIL
SCALE 6" = 1'
GROOVE
LATCH DETAIL
SCALE 6" = 1'
Interior Design Inc.
COUNTRY FURNITURE
J. Doe
COUNTRY HUTCH

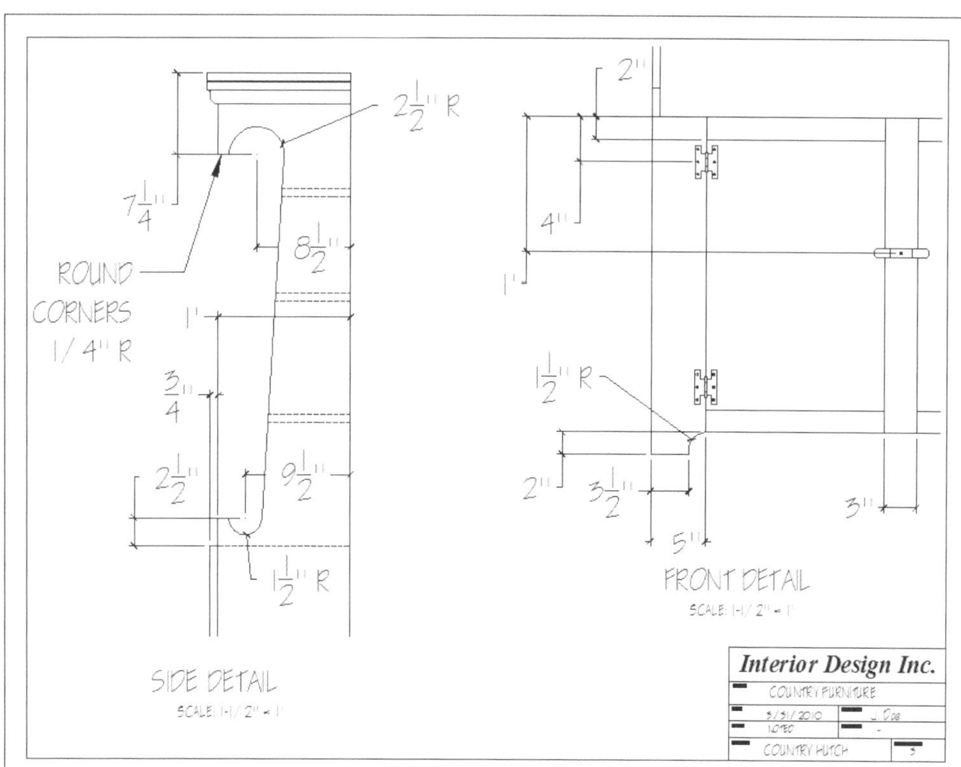
ROUND CORNERS 1/4" R
SIDE DETAIL
SCALE: 1-1/2" = 1'
FRONT DETAIL
SCALE: 1-1/2" = 1'
Interior Design Inc.
COUNTRY FURNITURE
J. Doe
COUNTRY HUTCH

Chapter 12
Hotel Suite Project – Tutorial 5

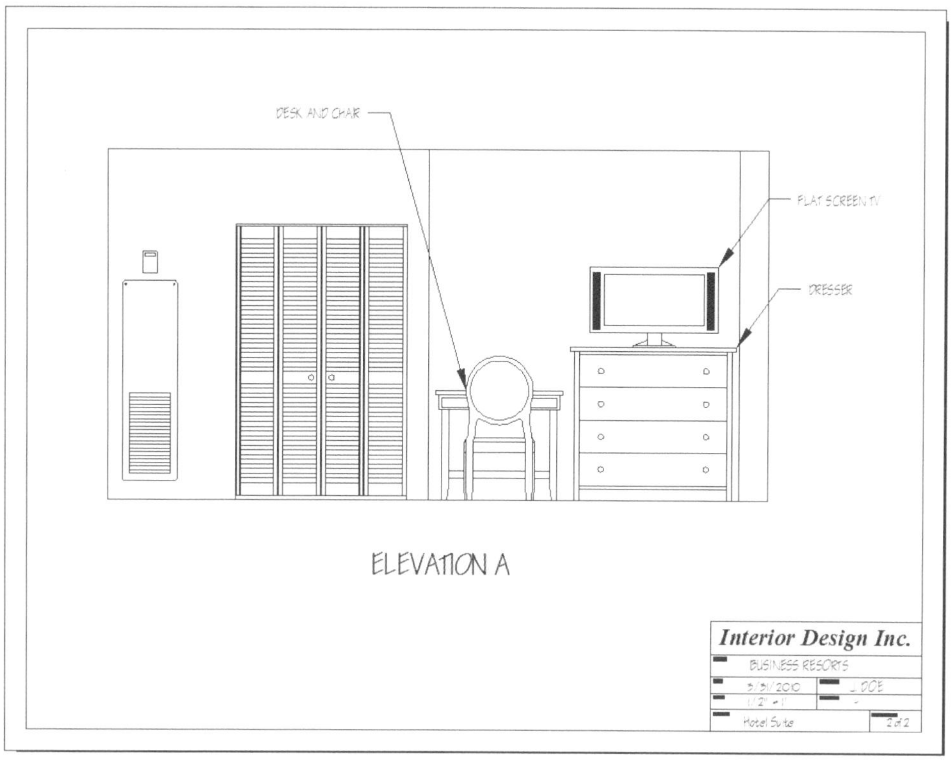

Learning Objectives:

- **To continue creating a drawing of a real-world application of AutoCAD**
  - **Create an elevation view**
  - **Annotate with Text, Dimensions, and Multileader**
  - **Create multiple layouts**
- **To utilize and reinforce the use of the AutoCAD commands learned in the previous chapters**
- **Update the Template drawing**

This tutorial builds on Tutorial 4 found in chapter 10. In this tutorial, we will create an elevation view of the bedroom. We will also create additional layers and annotate the drawing. When you are finished with this tutorial, the bedroom elevation will be completed, and you will have dimensions, labels, and text on your printable 8-1/2″x 11″ sheets.

In addition, we will update our template drawing to include Text, Dimension, and Multileader styles.

Commands & Techniques:

- Opening an existing drawing
- Zoom
- Pan
- Construction Line
- Trim
- Design Center
- Line
- Object Snap
- Move
- Erase
- Offset
- Fillet
- Text Style
- Single Line Text
- Grips
- Create new Layout
- Dimension
- Multiline Text
- Multileader
- Save

Create an Elevation View

Before beginning, open the Hotel Suite drawing that you updated in Tutorial 4. Note, for this tutorial, the author has changed the colors of the layers back to white and hidden the lineweights to make it easier to see in the textbook. Make sure layer "Structure" is the current layer.

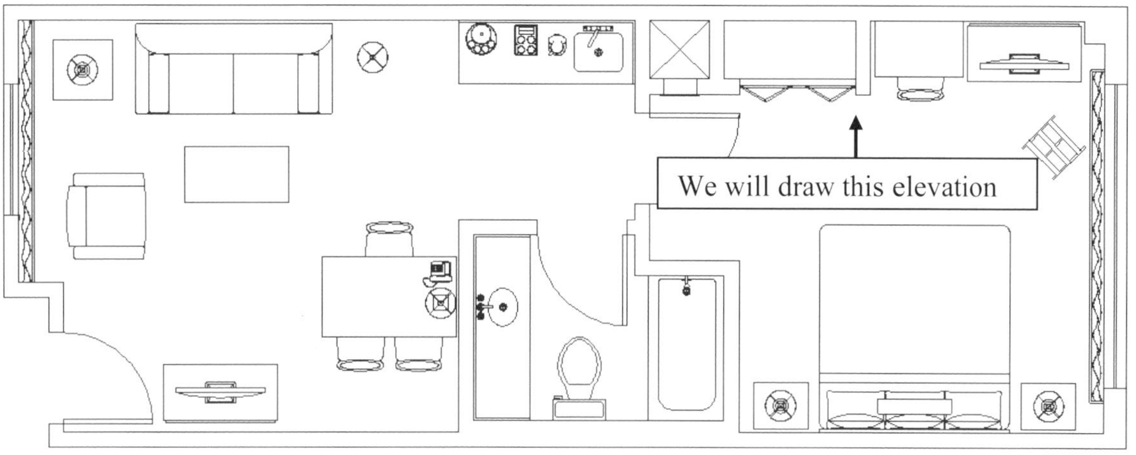

We will draw the elevation view of the bedroom as shown above. As you already know from drawing elevation views by hand, the best way to start the new view is to project from the plan view. In AutoCAD, the projection lines will be construction lines.

1. Create vertical construction lines to project below the plan view.

You do not need to project all the lines. In fact, for the utility closet, it is best to project the midpoint instead of the endpoints because the access panel will cover the opening. The same is recommended for aligning the furniture – project the midpoints of the desk and dresser instead of the endpoints.

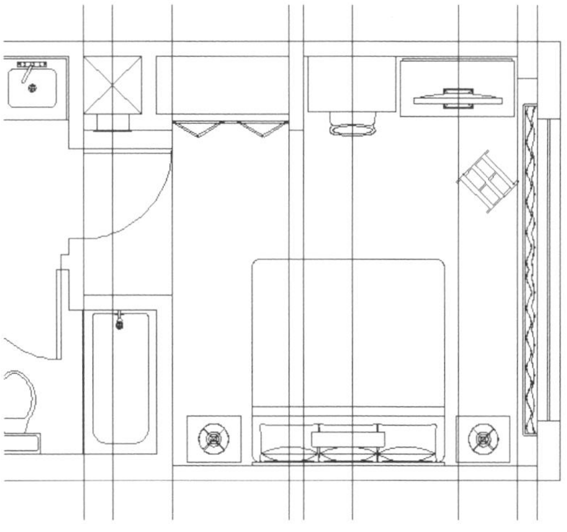

Vertical construction lines are used to project either endpoints or midpoints (as appropriate) from the plan view into the elevation view.

We will build the elevation view directly below the plan view. Leave some space between the plan and elevation views. It is important to note that the ceiling height is 8′.

2. Create a horizontal construction line a reasonable distance below the plan view.

This horizontal construction line will represent the ceiling of the room in the elevation view.

3. Offset the horizontal construction line 8′ down.

This offset construction line will represent the floor of the room in the elevation view.

4. Use the Trim command to trim all the construction lines.

After trimming, your drawing will look like this:

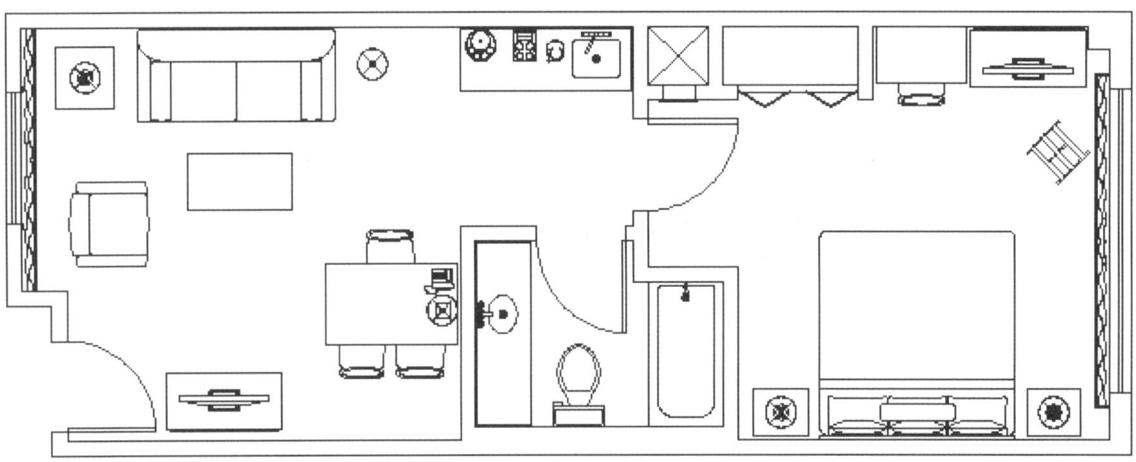

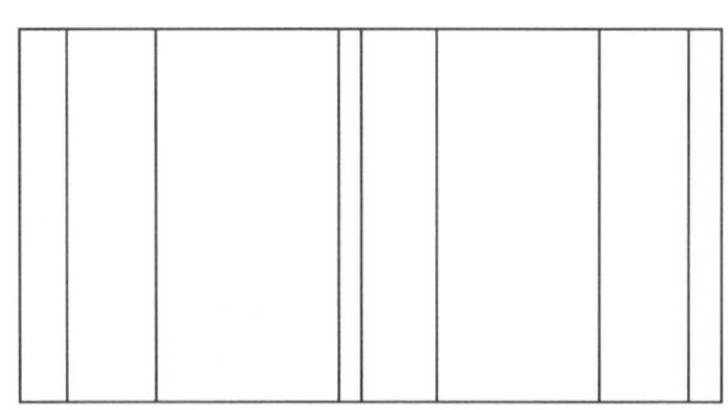

Adding the Blocks to the Drawing

Prior to inserting the block, you must have the Hotel Suite Blocks – Bedroom Elevation drawing that you can download from the publisher's web site.

The Blocks that we are going to use for the bedroom elevation view are shown below:

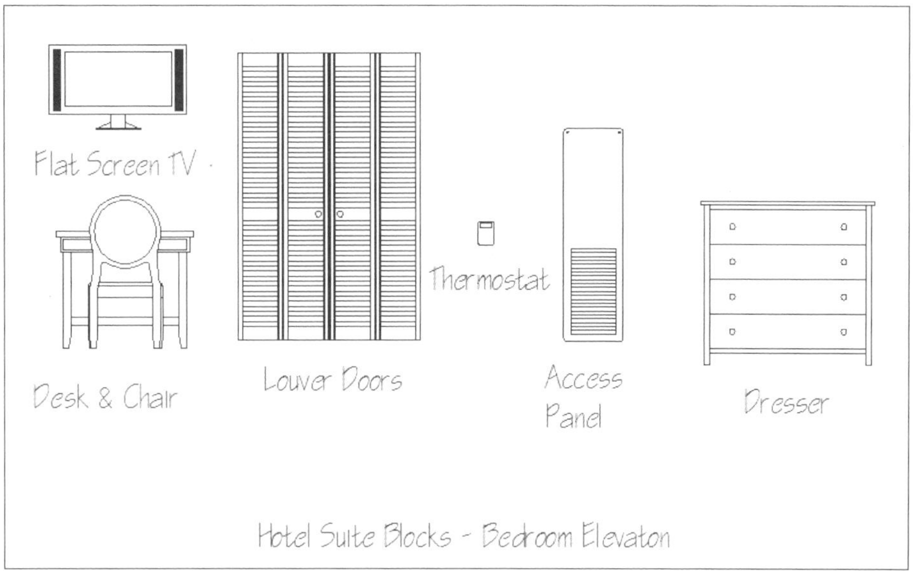

Mac Users: **Add a new Blocks Library and add the Bedroom Elevation blocks to it.**

Adding Blocks to the Bedroom Elevation

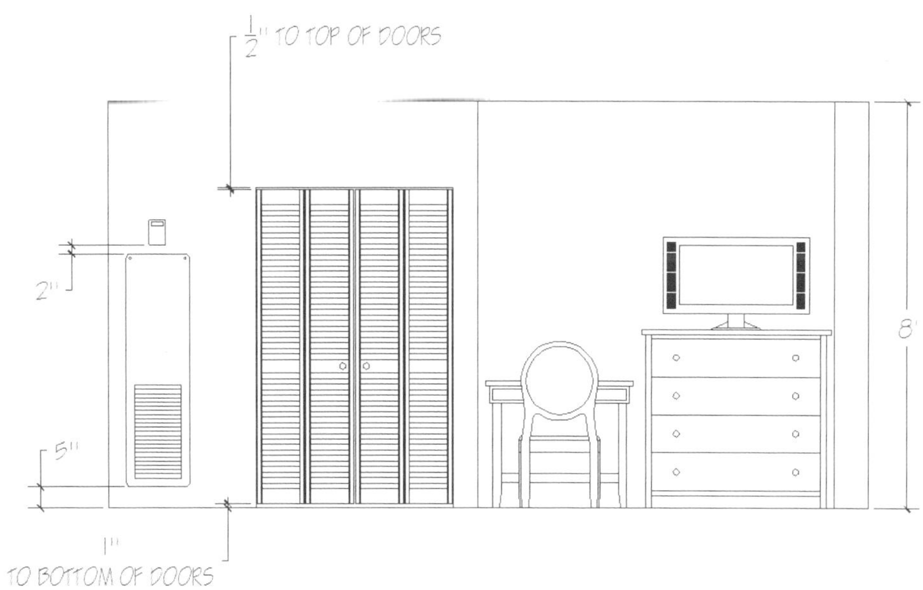

Let's insert the blocks one at a time. **Before inserting the furniture blocks, make sure layer "Furniture" is the current layer.**

5. Use Design Center (or Blocks Palette on the Mac) to insert the Dresser block.

6. Use the Line command to draw a line between the legs of the dresser.

Because the dresser needs to be aligned with the projection line, we need to locate the center. The reason for adding a line between the legs of the dresser is because the dresser must set on the floor.

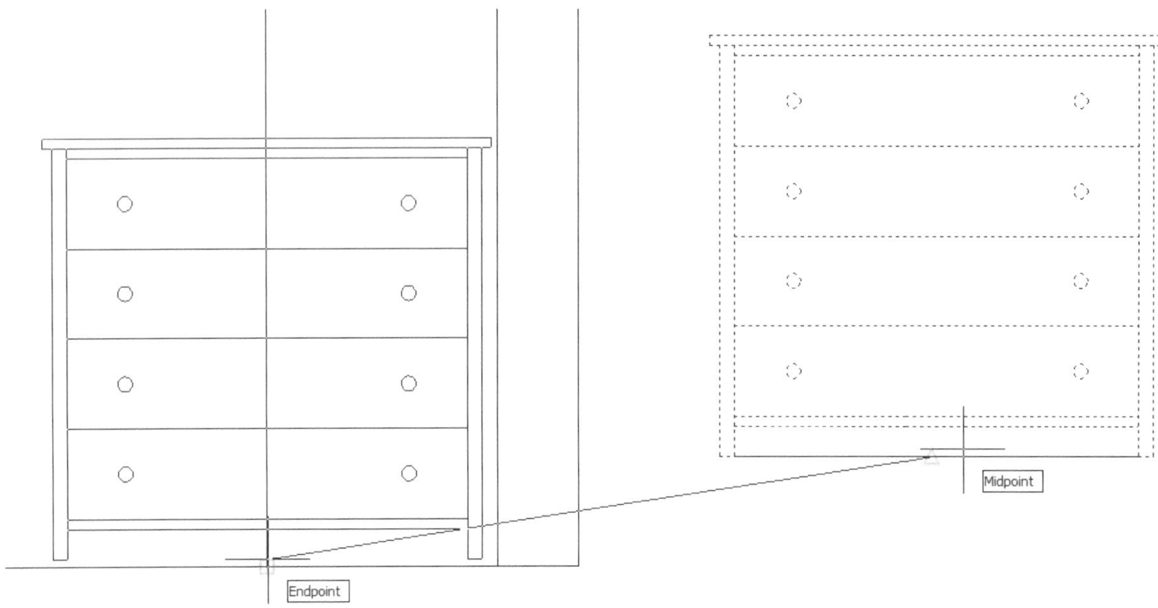

7. Use the Move command to relocate the dresser from the midpoint of the line created in step 6 to the endpoint of the projection line.

Pick only the Dresser block, not the line.

8. Use the Erase command to erase the line created in step 6 and the projection line.

When you are done, your elevation view will look like this:

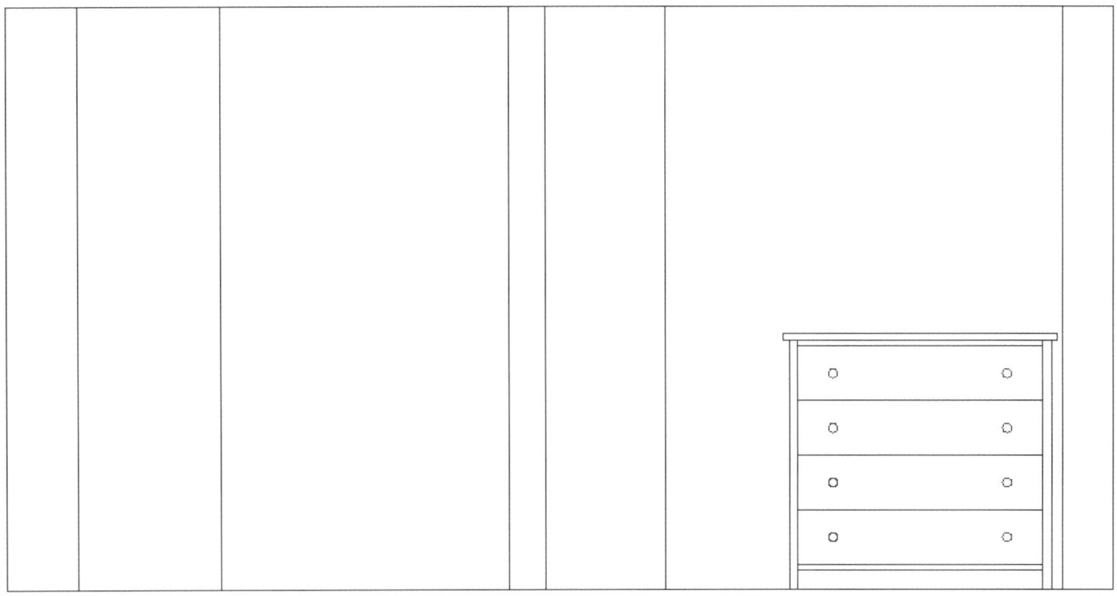

9. Use Design Center (or Blocks Palette on the Mac) to insert the Desk & Chair block.

10. Use the Line command to draw a line between the legs of the desk.

Because the desk needs to be aligned with the projection line, we need to locate the center. The reason for adding a line between the legs of the desk is because the desk must set on the floor.

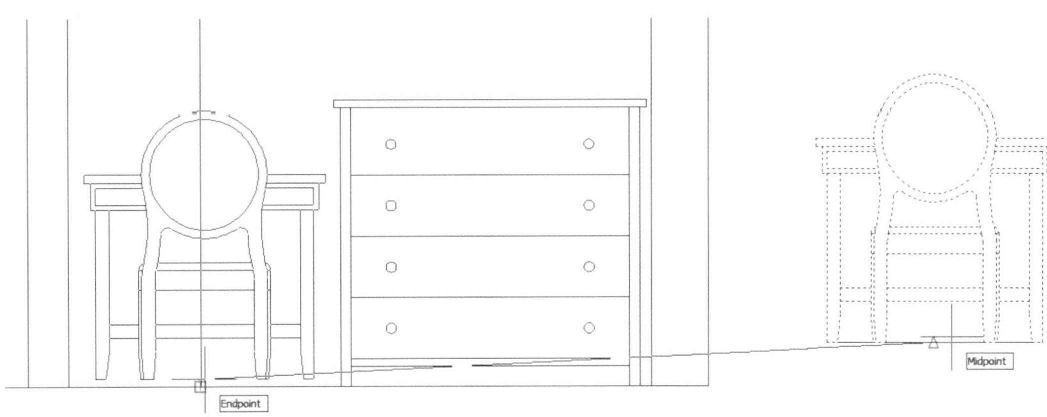

11. Use the Move command to relocate the desk from the midpoint of the line created in step 10 to the endpoint of the projection line.

Pick only the Desk & Chair block, not the line.

12. Use the Erase command to erase the line created in step 10 and the projection line.

When you are done, your elevation view will look like this:

The bottom of the louver doors is 1″ above the floor to provide adequate clearance for opening and closing. Before we bring in the block for the doors, we will create the location off the floor. **In addition, we will change the current layer to "Structure".**

13. Offset the floor 1″ upward.

14. Trim the offset line between the door opening.

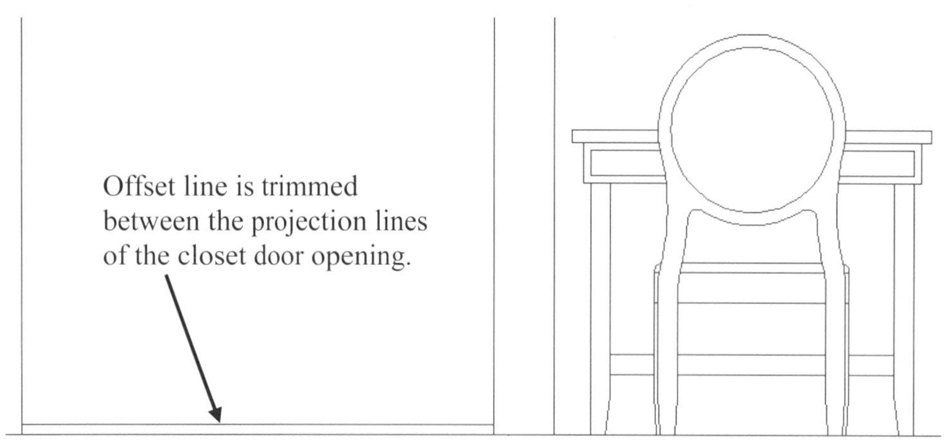

15. Use Design Center (or Blocks Palette on the Mac) to insert the Louver Doors block.

16. Use the Line command to draw a line at the bottom and between the two middle doors.

Because the doors must be centered in the opening and above the floor, we need to locate the center.

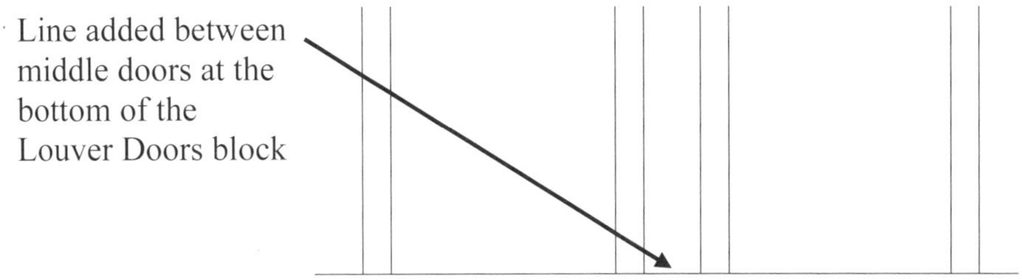

17. Use the Move command to relocate the doors from the midpoint of the line created in step 16 to the midpoint of the line created in step 14.

Pick only the Louver Doors block, not the line.

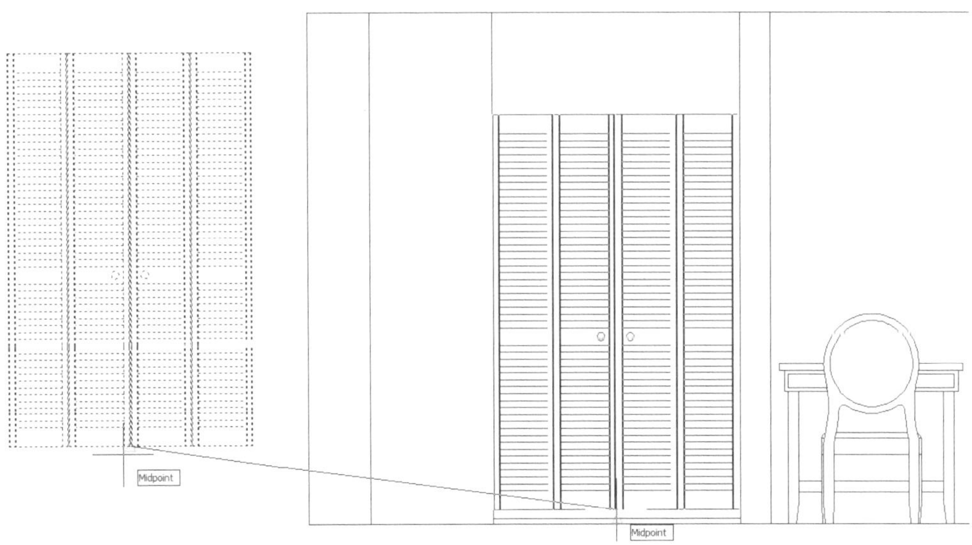

18. Use the Erase command to erase the lines created in steps 14 and 16.

When you are done, your elevation view will look like this:

There is a 1/2″ clearance at the top of the louver doors. We will draw that in next.

19. Create a horizontal construction line at the top of the louver doors.

Snap to any endpoint of the lines at the top of the louver doors.

20. Offset the construction line 1/2″ upward.

21. Erase the construction line created in step 19.

22. Use the Fillet command with a radius of 0″ to close out the projection lines and the offset construction line.

When you are done, the top of the louver door opening will look like this:

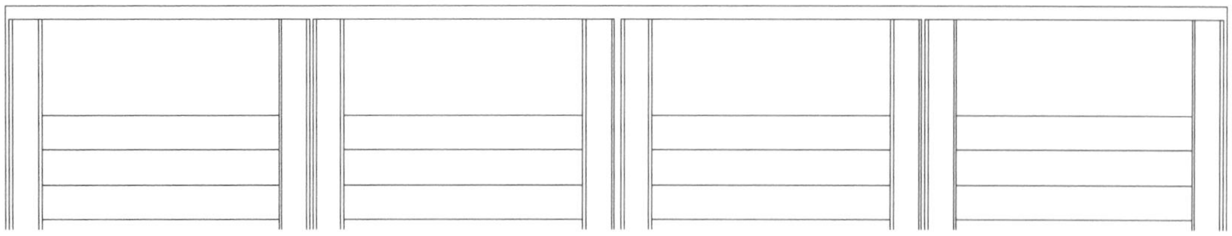

23. Use Design Center (or Blocks Palette on the Mac) to insert the Access Panel block.

Because the bottom of the access panel is 5″ off the floor, we will need to create an offset line from the floor.

24. Use the Offset command to offset the floor 5″ upward.

25. Use the Move command to relocate the Access Panel.

Snap to the Midpoint of the bottom horizontal line of the access panel and to the intersection of the projection line and the offset line created in step 24.

26. Use the Erase command to erase the line created in step 24.

For now, we will keep the projection line. We will need it to locate the thermostat.

When you are done, your elevation view will look like this:

27. Use Design Center (or Blocks Palette on the Mac) to insert the Thermostat block.

The thermostat is located on the same centerline as the access panel and the bottom of the thermostat is 2″ above the access panel. We will need to create a line offset 2″ above the top of the access panel.

28. Create a horizontal construction line at the top of the access panel.

29. Offset the construction line 2″ upward.

30. Erase the construction line created in step 28.

31. Use the Move command to relocate the Thermostat.

Snap to the Midpoint of the bottom of the thermostat to the Intersection of the construction line of step 29 and the projection line.

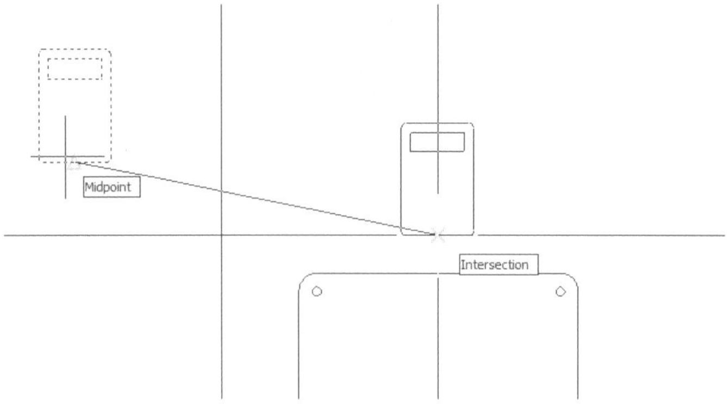

32. Use the Erase command to erase the projection line and the line created in step 29.

When you are done, your elevation view will look like this:

Before we insert the Flat Screen TV block, change the current layer to "Misc".

33. Use the Design Center (or Blocks Palette on the Mac) to insert the Flat Screen TV block.

34. Use the Move command to relocate the TV to the top of the dresser.

Snap to the Midpoint of the bottom of the TV to the Midpoint of the top of the dresser.

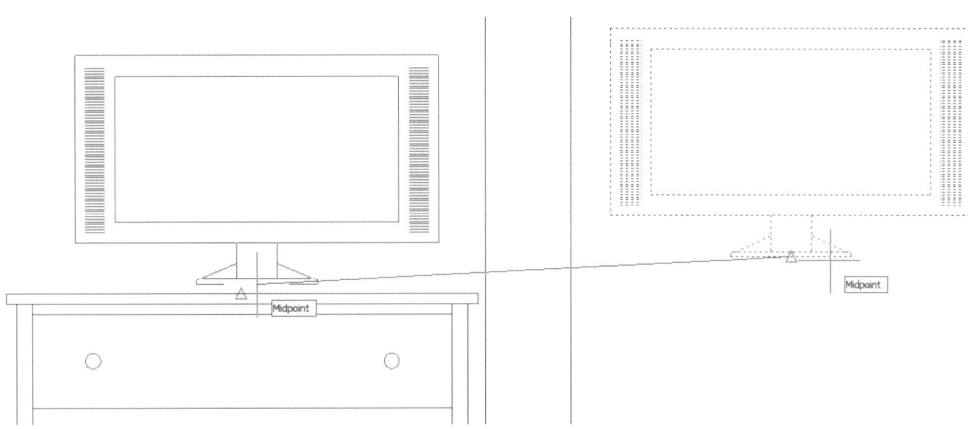

When you are done, your elevation view will look like this:

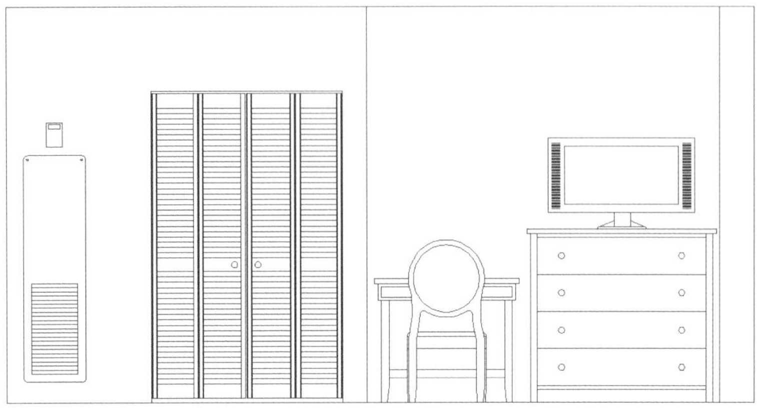

Lay out the Drawing

Before we begin a layout of the bedroom elevation, we should fill out the titleblock that was created for the Plan View layout tab in Tutorial 4.

35. Create text styles so that we can fill in the titleblock.

(Pick the Text Styles icon. On the Mac, use the Format pull-down and select "Text Style…")

The Text Style dialog box appears.

(Pick the New button. On the Mac, pick the "+" button)

The New Text Style dialog box appears (PC only). Name the new style "Titleblock".

36. Select the font of Times New Roman for the Font Name (Family on the Mac) and Bold Italic for the Font Style.

We will leave the Height at 0″ so that we can key in the value as we place the text on the drawing.

37. While still in the Text Style dialog box, we will create an additional style and name it "Notes". The new style will have the following properties:

Font: CityBlueprint
Annotative: yes – place a check mark in the box
Text Height: 1/8″

38. While in the Plan View layout, place Single Line text in the titleblock as shown:

Make sure you are in Paper Space before you attempt to insert text.

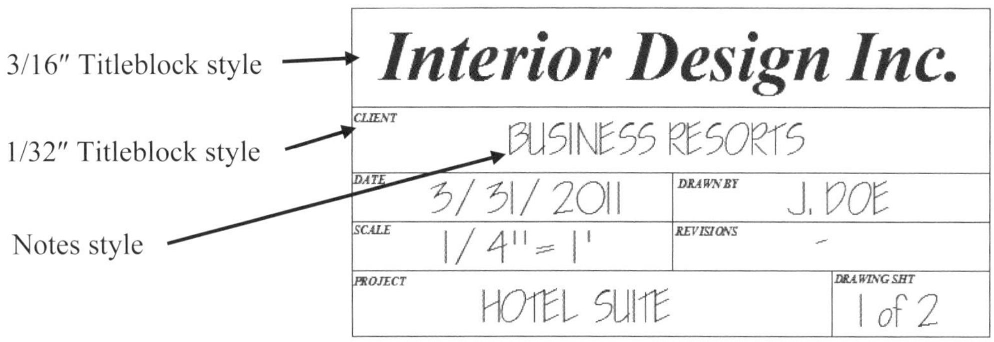

38a. Use the pull-down arrow on the Text Style portion of the Annotation Panel of the Home Tab to make Titleblock the current style. On the Mac, use the Format pull-down and select "Text Style…". When the dialog box appears, right-click on Titleblock, pick Set Current, and Close the dialog box.

38b. Use the Single Line Text command on the Annotation Panel of the Home Tab to insert the company name in the titleblock.

(Pick the Single Line Text icon)

Current text style: "Titleblock" Text height: 0'-0 3/16" Annotative: Yes

TEXT *Specify start point of text or [Justify/Style]:* ***(Pick a location in the titleblock)***
Specify height <0'-0 3/16">: ↵
Specify rotation angle of text <0>:↵
Key in the text "Interior Design Inc." and press the ↵ Enter key twice to exit the command.

38c. Use Single Line Text to insert the remaining titleblock text which is all capital letters.

Press the ↵ Enter key to repeat the single line text command.

Current text style: "Titleblock" Text height: 0'-0 3/16" Annotative: Yes

TEXT *Specify start point of text or [Justify/Style]:* ***(Pick a location in the titleblock)***
Specify height <0'-0 3/16">: **1/32** ↵
Specify rotation angle of text <0>: ↵

Key in the text to fill in the remainder of the titleblock. Press the ↵ Enter key twice to exit the command.

38d. Use the pull-down arrow in the Text Style section of the Annotation Panel of the Home Tab to change the current Text Style to Notes. On the Mac, use the Text Toolbar to select Text Style icon. When the dialog box appears, right-click on Notes, pick Set Current, and Close the dialog box.

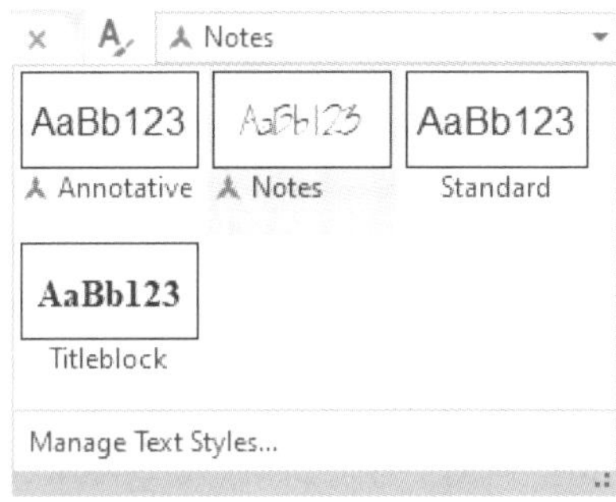

38e. Complete the titleblock.

The text you placed in the titleblock may not be placed exactly where you want it. Use grips to relocate the text. Turn off Object Snap before moving the text around.

38f. Change the layer that the titleblock and format border rectangle are on to layer "Format".

Now that we have the titleblock in the Plan View layout filled out, we can create another layout for the bedroom elevation view.

39. Create a layout for the bedroom elevation view.

(PC): ***Right-click the Plan View tab, Pick "Move or Copy…"***
After the Move or Copy dialog box appears:

- ***Pick in the check box to "Create a copy"***
- ***Pick "(move to end)"***
- ***Pick the OK button when you are done.***

(Mac): ***Pick the Show Drawings & Layouts icon on the Status Bar to bring up the Quickview***
After the preview of the Model and Layouts appears:

- ***Right-click on the Plan View Layout***
- ***Select Duplicate from the mini-menu of choices***

After the dialog box appears, edit a new name for the new layout

- ***Type: "Bedroom Elevation" and Pick Confirm***
- ***Close the Quickview and go to Step 41.***

40. Rename the new layout to "Bedroom Elevation".

41. While in the Bedroom Elevation layout, switch to Model Space.

42. Unlock the viewport scale and pan the view of your model so that you center the bedroom elevation. Change the scale to 1/2″ = 1′, and lock the viewport scale.

If the plan view is still showing in the viewport, switch back to Paper Space and re-size the viewport so that only the bedroom elevation view is showing. Leave enough empty space around it to allow for dimensions and text.

43. Switch back to Paper Space and edit the scale and sheet number in the titleblock.

The text for scale should read: 1/2″ = 1′
The text for the sheet number should read: 2 of 2

(Double-click on the text to edit)

DDEDIT *Select an annotation object or [Undo]:* ***(Pick the text and edit it)*** ↵
Select an annotation object or [Undo]:↵

44. Delete the Layout 2 tab.

You will now have two layouts – Plan View and Bedroom Elevation.

Your Plan View layout will look like this:

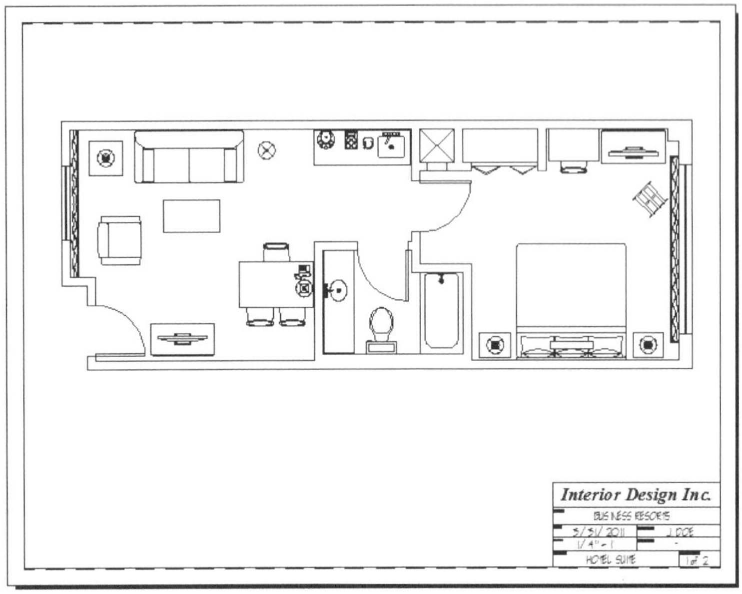

Your Bedroom Elevation layout will look like this:

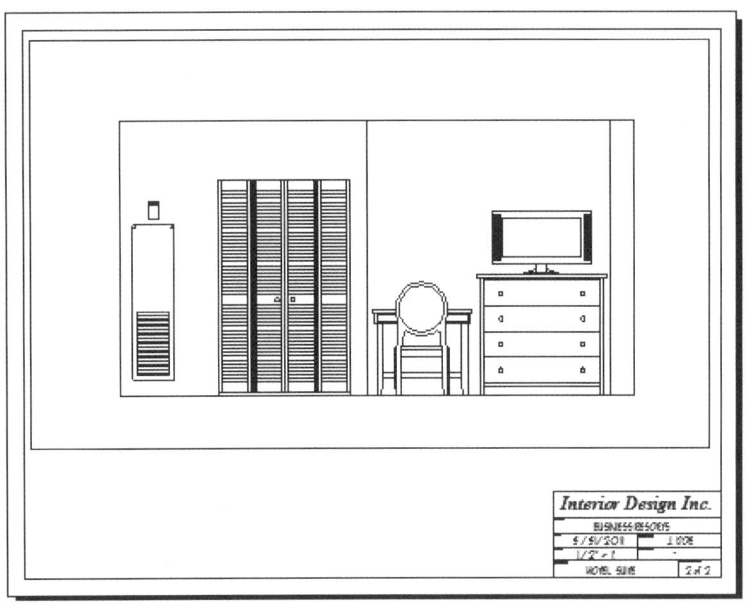

Notice that the viewport border is visible. When you print your drawing, it is not desirable to have the viewport border on the printout. We cannot delete it because it will leave us with a blank drawing. To get around this, we can create a unique layer and we can freeze the layer from visibility.

45. For each layout, if it is not already done, change the layer that the viewport is currently on, to layer Viewport.

46. For each layout, use the pull-down arrow on the Layers Panel of the Home Tab to freeze layer Viewport. On the Mac, show the Layer List in the Layers Palette and pick in the VP Freeze column for layer Viewport.

You must be in Paper Space before you freeze layer Viewport.

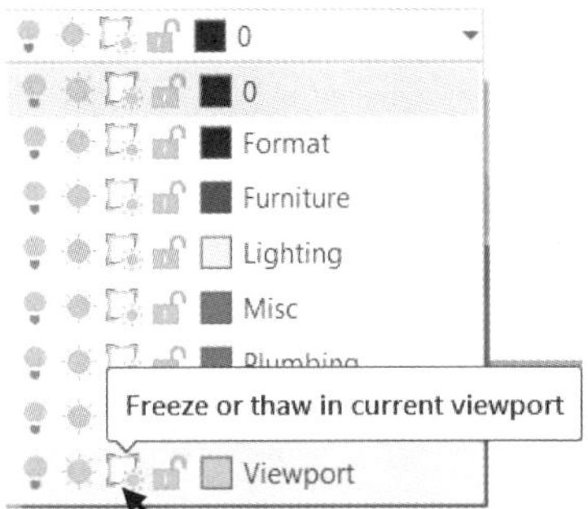

(Pick the Freeze or thaw in current viewport icon for layer Viewport)

Mac

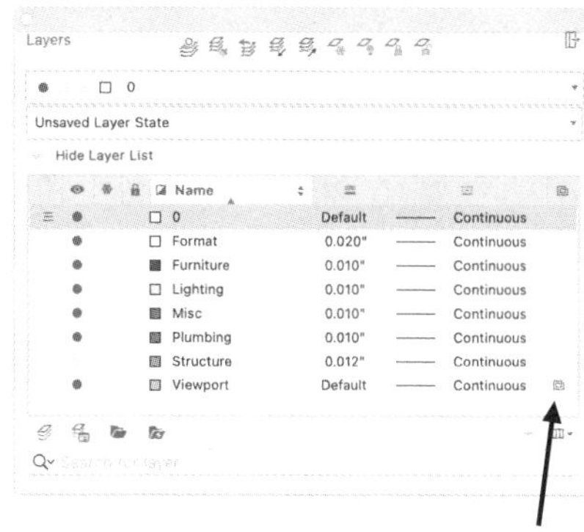

(Pick in the New VP Freeze column of layer Viewport)

Annotating the Drawing

We are done setting up the drawing layouts. We can now annotate the drawing with dimensions and labels. First, we will need to create styles for both Dimensions and Multileader. We will use the same styles that we created in chapter 11. The steps to creating those styles will not be repeated here. Please refer to that chapter to create the styles. Otherwise, import them using Design Center (PC only).

Before you begin, create a new layer and name it "Dimensions and Text", and make it current.

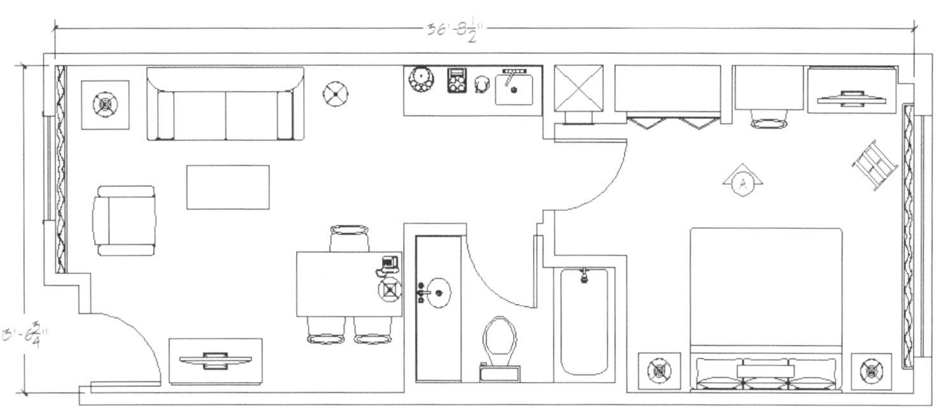

47. Add two linear dimensions to the plan view.

Make sure you are in the Plan View layout and working in Model Space with Object Snap set to Endpoint.

(Pick the Linear icon on the Annotation Panel of the Home Tab. On the Mac, pick the icon from the Annotation Tool Set)

DIMLINEAR *Specify first extension line origin or <select object>:*
(Pick one of the endpoints for the horizontal dimension at the top of the drawing)

Specify second extension line origin:
(Pick the other endpoint for the horizontal dimension)

Specify dimension line location or
[Mtext/Text/Angle/Horizontal/Vertical/Rotated]: ***(Pick a location for the dimension text)***
Dimension text = 36'-8 1/2"

Press the ↵ Enter key to repeat the command.

DIMLINEAR *Specify first extension line origin or <select object>:*
(Pick one of the endpoints for the vertical dimension at the side of the drawing)

Specify second extension line origin:
(Pick the other endpoint for the vertical dimension)

Specify dimension line location or
[Mtext/Text/Angle/Horizontal/Vertical/Rotated]: ***(Pick a location for the dimension text)***
Dimension text = 13'-6 3/4"

Creating a View Symbol Block

The symbol can be created as a triangle that surrounds a 1/4″ diameter circle.

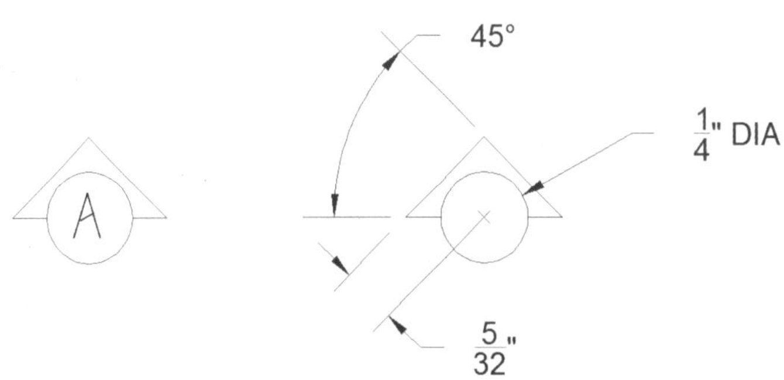

We will create a view symbol as a Model Space object and convert it to an annotative style Block. Because we are making it annotative, it will take on the correct scale on your layout.

48. Create the view symbol:

48a. Select the Model tab and zoom in on a blank area of your drawing.

48b. Draw a circle that is 1/4″ diameter.

48c. Draw a horizontal construction line through the center of the circle.

48d. Draw two angled construction lines through the center of the circle: one at 45° and one at -45 °.

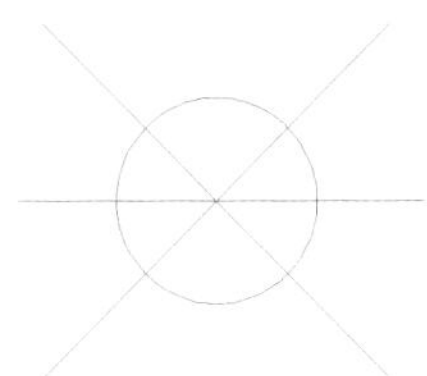

48e. Offset the angled construction lines 5/32″ up.

48f. Erase the original angled construction lines created in step 48d.

48g. Trim the construction lines.

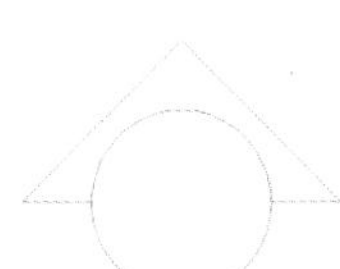

48h. Use Single Line Text to insert the symbol text. Turn off Object Snap and use grips to position the text where it looks best.

Make sure text style is set to Notes.

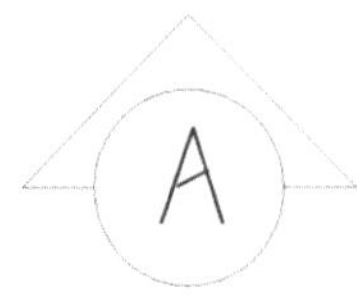

48i. Create a Block of the view symbol. Select Annotative in the Block Definition dialog box. Turn Object Snap back on and select the center of the circle as the Base point. Type the name "View Symbol". Pick Delete in the Objects section of the dialog box.

49. Add the View Symbol Block to the Bedroom in the Plan View layout as a Model Space object.

Because the View Symbol was created as an Annotative Block, it will scale automatically to the scale of the Viewport.

50. Add Multiline Text to the Plan View layout as a Paper Space object.

Using 1/4″ Bold letters, type the words "PLAN VIEW".

51. Add labels, as Model Space objects, to the elevation view by using Multileader.

Because the Label style Multileader was created as an Annotative style, it will scale automatically to the scale of the Viewport.

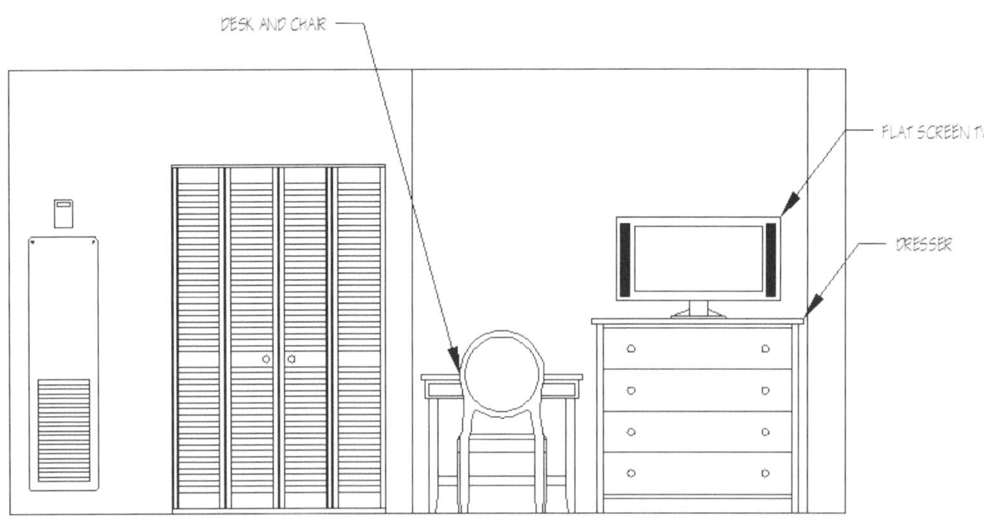

52. Add Multiline Text to the Bedroom Elevation layout as a Paper Space object.

Using 1/4″ Bold letters, type the words “ELEVATION A”.

Congratulations! You have now completed all the tutorials. Be sure to save your drawing.

Your two drawing sheets will now look like this:

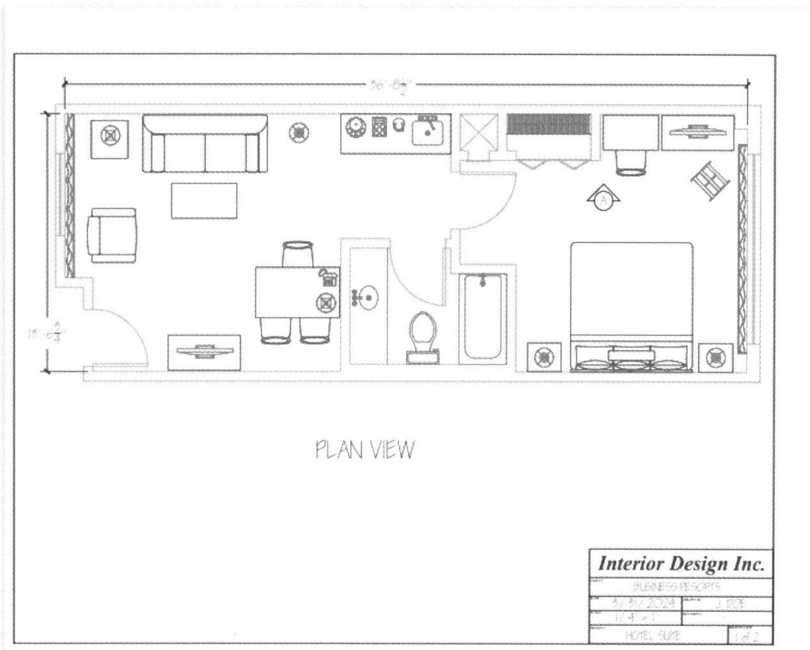

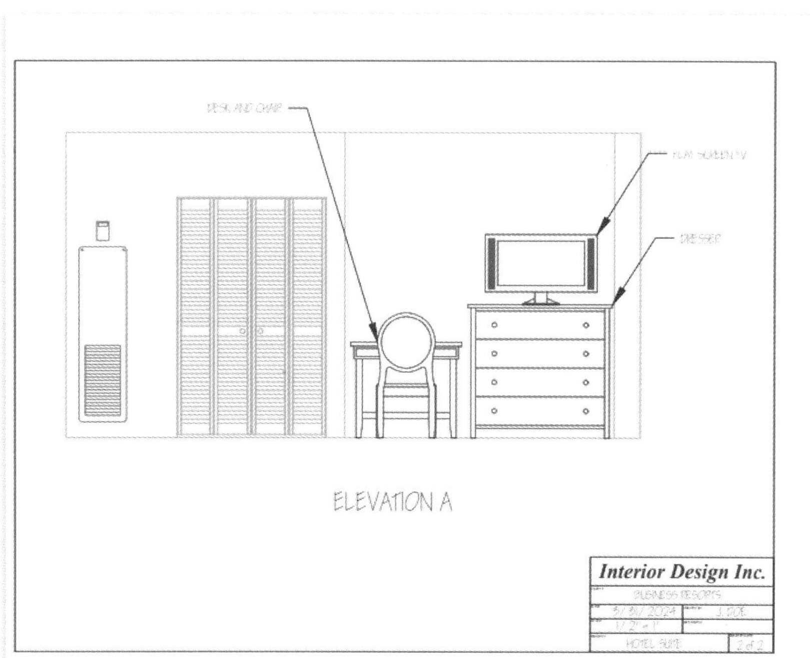

Add a Block and Text, Dimension, and Multileader Styles to Template

PC users, take advantage of the various styles and the Block we created in this tutorial and build them into our drawing template. Mac users: Manually add to your template.

53. Start a new drawing using the Interior Design drawing template that was updated in Chapter 10.

54. Open Design Center Palette and find the Hotel Suite drawing you just saved.

54a. Highlight Textstyles in the Tree View. The preview pane shows all the text styles that were created for the Hotel Suite, in addition to Standard and Annotative. Double-left-click or click-and-drag the "Notes", and "Titleblock" styles to bring them into the template.

54b. Highlight Dimstyles in the Tree View. The preview pane shows all the Dimension styles that were created for the Hotel Suite, in addition to Standard and Annotative. Double-left-click or click-and-drag the "Interior Design" as well as the sub-set to "Interior Design" style, to bring them into the template.

54c. Highlight Multileaderstyles in the Tree View. The preview pane shows all the Multileader styles that were created for the Hotel Suite, in addition to Standard and Annotative. Double-left-click or click-and-drag the "Label" style, to bring it into the template.

54d. Highlight Blocks in the Tree View. The preview pane shows all the Blocks that are part of the Hotel Suite. Double-left-click the View Symbol. Pick Cancel in the Insert Block dialog box. This method places the Block definition into the drawing without placing the Block in the drawing space.

54e. Close the Design Center Palette.

55. Fill in the Titleblock with text of your choosing, similar to what was done in this tutorial.

56. Use Save As… and save the template as "Interior Design". Make sure the File Type is .dwt. Pick Yes to the warning and OK to the Template Option dialog boxes.

Congratulations! You have now updated the Interior Design template drawing to include a filled-in Titleblock, Text, Dimension, and Multileader styles in addition to the View Pointer Block!

Chapter 13

Commands – Set 6: Creating and Editing Schedules

Paint Schedule			
Room	Walls	Ceiling	Trim & Doors
Dining Room	California Paints Tomahawk Red, 7856A Latex, Eggshell Finish	Glidden Paints Ceiling White, GC3070 Latex	Benjamin Moore Navajo White, N31973 Acrylic, Eggshell Finish
Living Room	Behr Paints Forest Green Latex, Eggshell Finish	Glidden Paints Ceiling White, GC3070 Latex	Benjamin Moore Navajo White, N31973 Acrylic, Eggshell Finish

Learning Objectives:

- **Creating a style for your Schedule using Table Style**
- **Use the Table feature to create a Schedule**
- **Edit an existing Table**

Tables – Creating a Schedule

You can create a schedule by using the AutoCAD Table command. Tables can have any number of rows and columns that you define. Defining a Table Style allows you to customize how the table will look.

Creating a Table Style

To begin, expand the Annotation Panel of the Home Tab, and pick the Table Style icon:

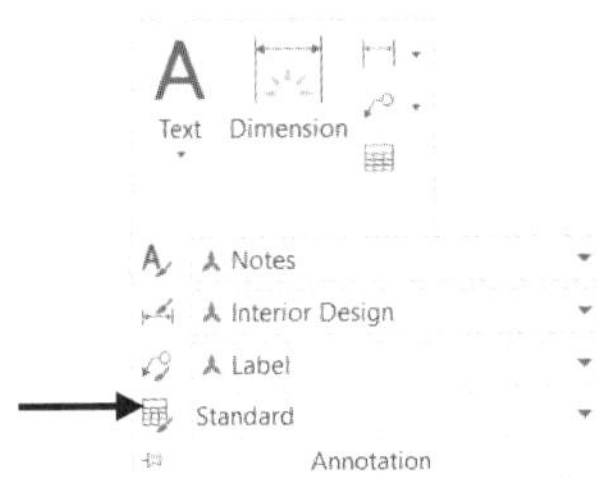

As an alternative, select the Table Icon of the Tables Panel of the Annotate Tab, then pick the downward arrow:

Pick the
downward arrow

Mac

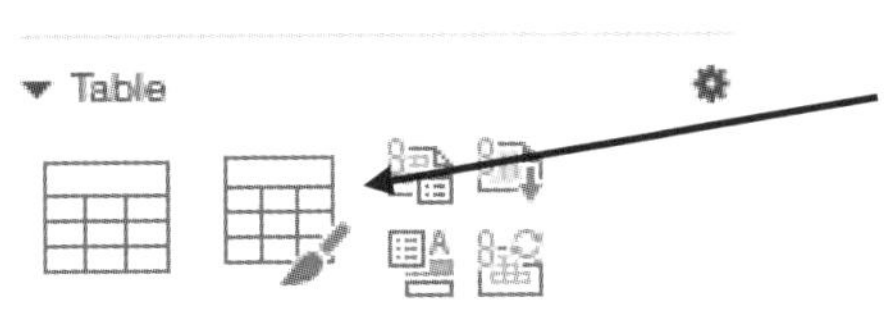

Pick the Table Style icon
on the Table toolbar

After selecting either the Table Style icon on the Annotation Panel of the Home Tab, or the downward arrow of the Tables Panel of the Annotate Tab, the Table Style dialog box appears.

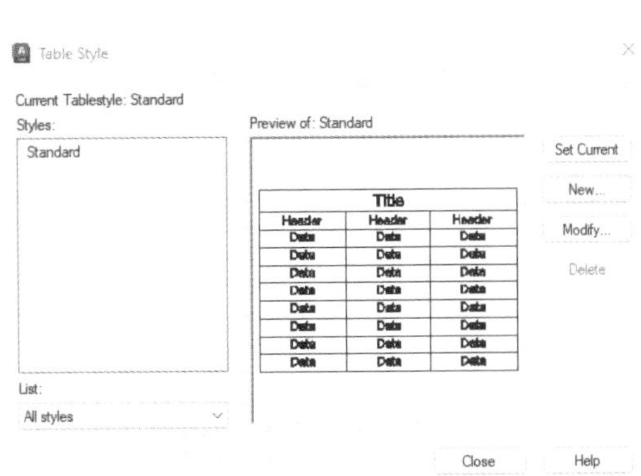

Mac

To create a new table style, pick the New… button (or the "+" button on the Mac). A new dialog box will appear. Under the New Style Name, the text "Copy of Standard" is highlighted and ready for editing. Let's name the new style Schedule.

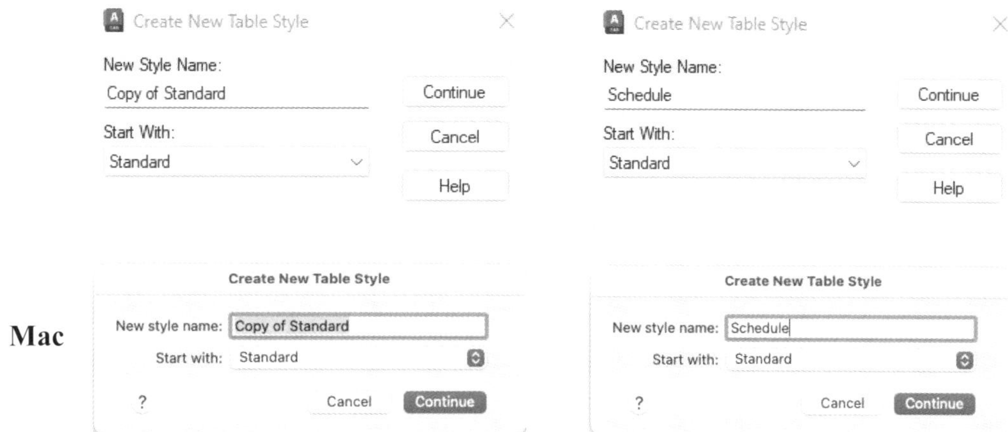

Pick the Continue button. Another dialog box will appear. This dialog box will allow you to define several features for your Table Style. There are three sections to the table: Title, Header, and Data. This is illustrated in the preview pane. Properties for each section are controlled using the choices within each of the three tabs.

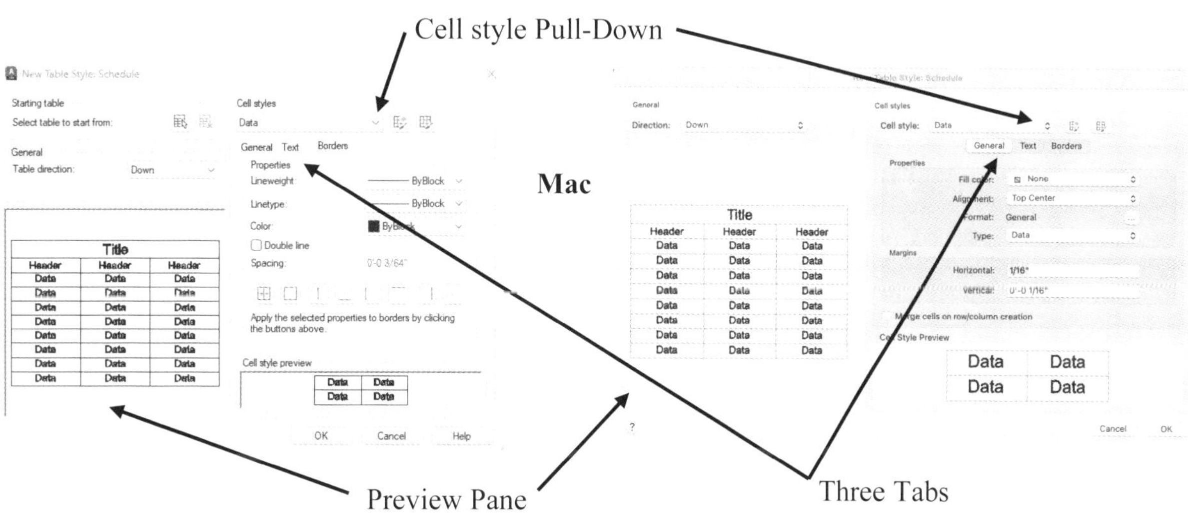

Each section can have its own properties for Alignment and Color, Text Style, and Border style. Each section is selected by using the pull-down under Cell styles. Once selected, the properties for that section are controlled using the tabs General, Text, and Borders.

Prior to choosing the style of text for each section, we need to have a style already defined. Previously, we created a style and named it Notes. We also set the text height for Notes to 1/8″.

Notice that the Title text height is larger than the Header and Data text heights. By setting the text height in Text Style, we are not able to change that height to a larger size for the Title section. That is why we created the second style: Titleblock.

Table Title

Use the pull-down to select Title under Cell styles.

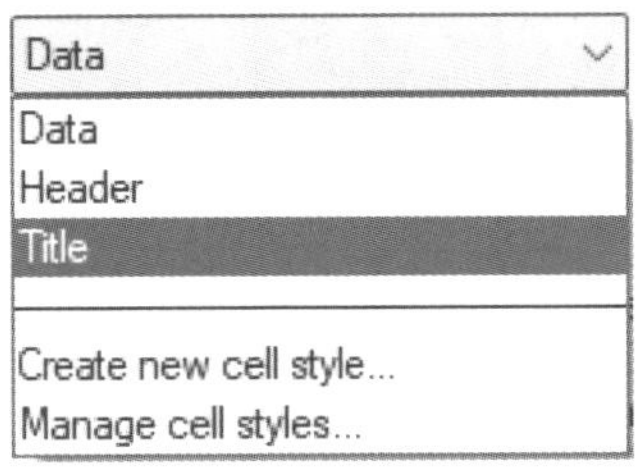

Mac

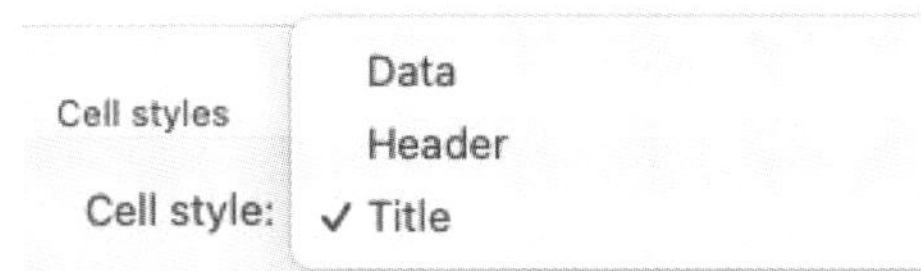

We will not make any changes under the General tab.
Pick the Text tab and make the following changes:

- Change the Text style to Titleblock.
- Set the Text height to 1/4 ″.

When done your changes are reflected in the preview panes and your dialog box will now look like the following:

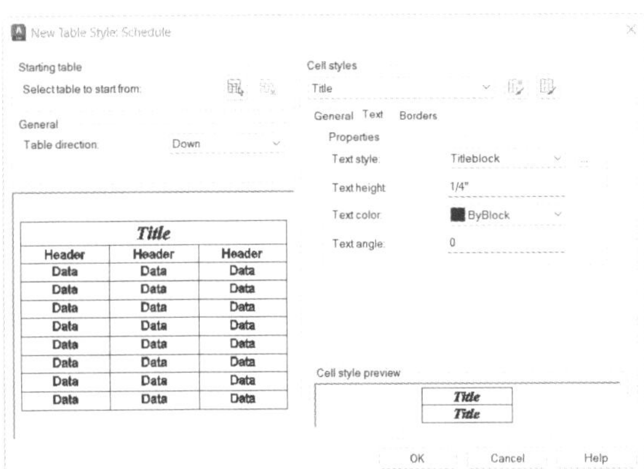

Mac

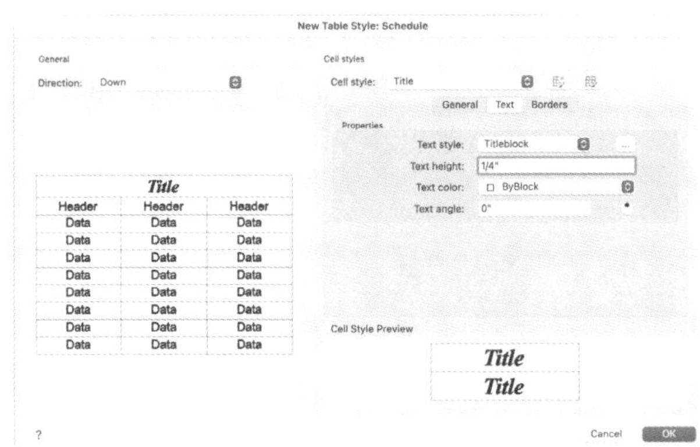

Pick the Borders tab and make the following change:

- Pick the left-most button for the grid border.

When done, your dialog box will now look like the following:

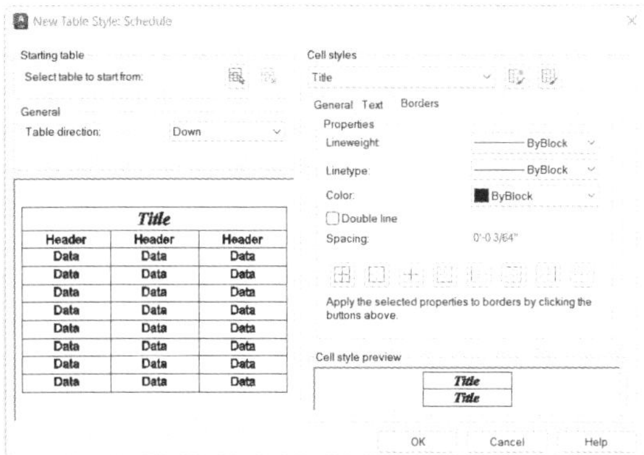

Mac

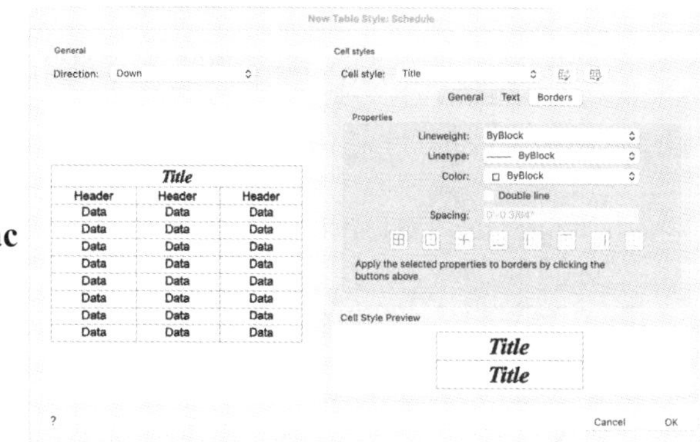

Table Header

Use the pull-down to select Header under Cell styles.

Pick the Text tab and make the following change:

- Change the Text style to Notes.

When done, the dialog box will now look like the following:

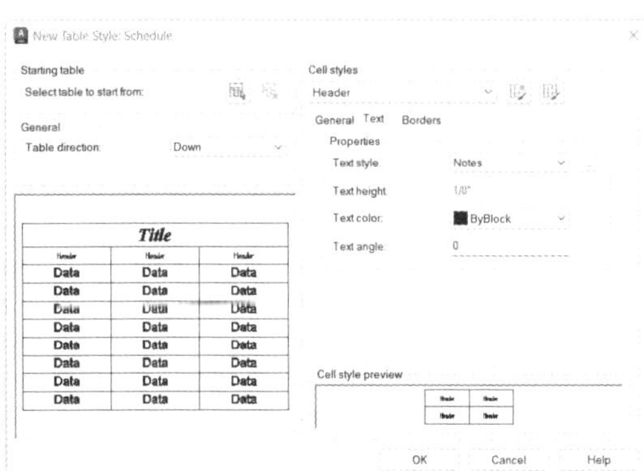

Mac

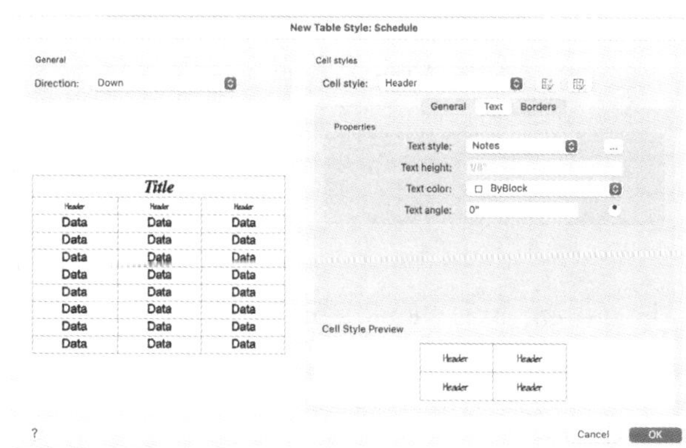

Pick the Borders tab and make the same changes for Header as you did for the Title style:

- Pick the left-most button for the grid border.

Table Data

Use the pull-down to select Data under Cell styles.

Pick the Text tab and make the same change for Data that you made for the Header style:

- Change the Text style to Notes.

Pick the Borders tab and make the same changes for Data as you did for both the Header and Title styles:

- Pick the left-most button for the grid border.

The table style of Schedule is now complete. Pick the OK button to exit the New Table Style dialog box and return to the Table Style dialog box. Pick the Schedule Style on the left side of the dialog box, and then pick the Set Current button to make it the current style. Pick the Close button to exit the dialog box.

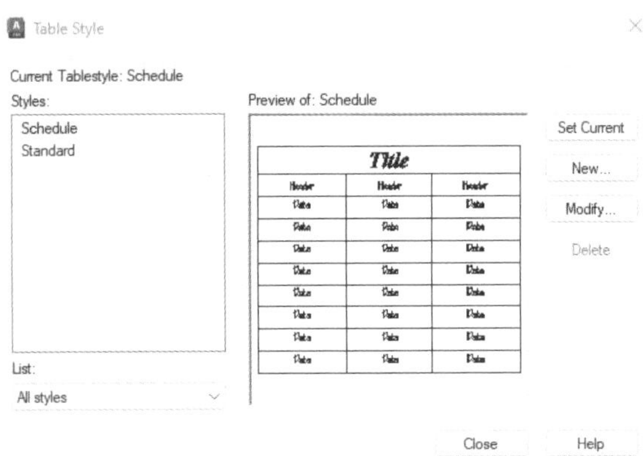

Mac

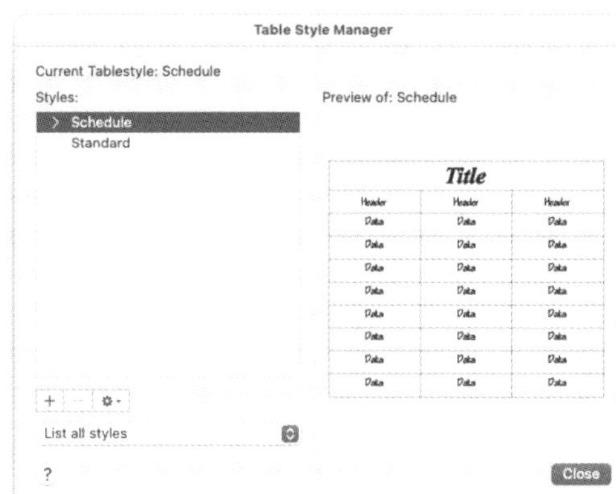

The current style should now be set to Schedule:

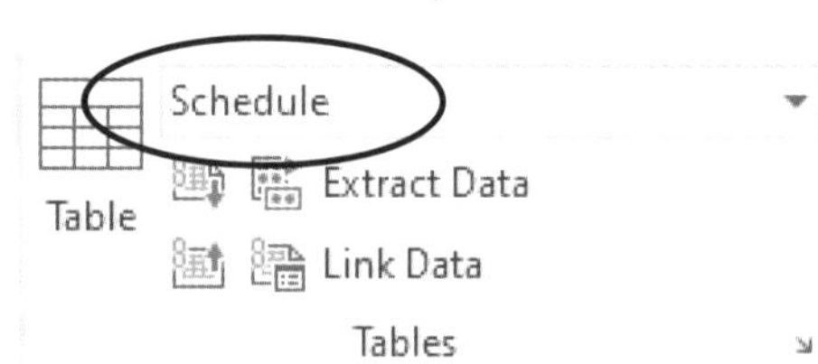

Inserting Tables on the Drawing

To insert a table on the drawing, it is best done on the Layout tab in Paper Space.

Procedure:

Pick (left click): **Table icon** from the Annotation Panel of the Home Tab. 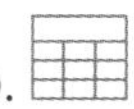
(As an alternative, use the Tables Panel of the Annotate Tab.)

Mac Users: the icon is on the Table Tool Panel

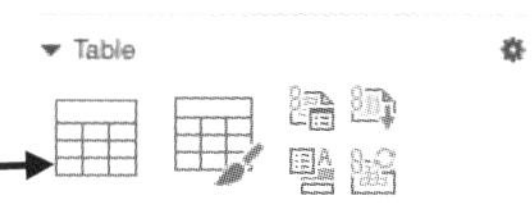

The Insert Table dialog box will appear. In this dialog box, the number of rows and columns can be specified, as well as the height and width of the rows and columns. For this example, change the number of columns to 3. Pick the OK button to insert the table.

Mac

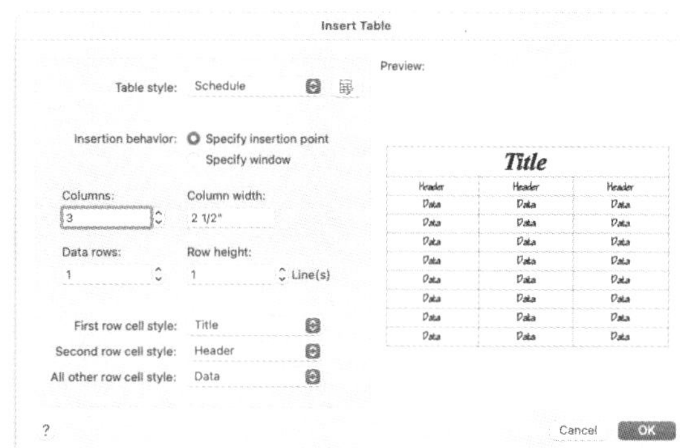

An image of the table will appear on the screen and will follow the cursor. Left-click to place the table in a desired location on the drawing sheet.

A Text Editor Tab will appear on the ribbon (Text Editor Visor on the Mac), and a blank table will appear on the drawing space.

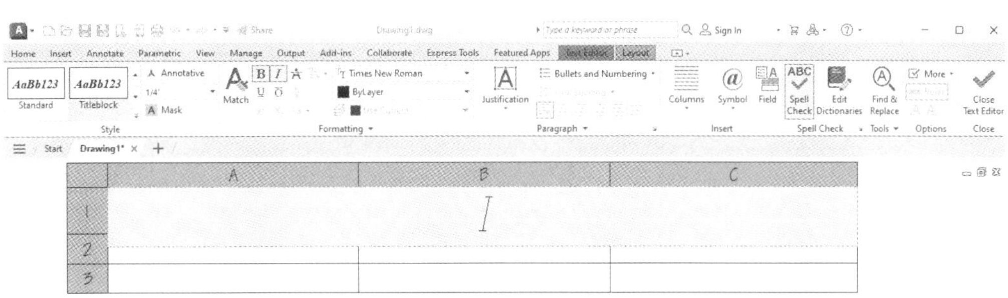

Mac

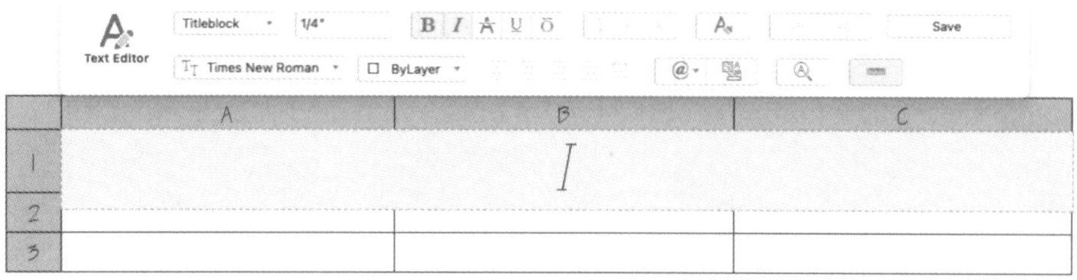

The cell that you will add text to will be highlighted. Enter the text as desired.

- To add lines of text within a cell, hold down the ALT key (Option key on the Mac) and press the Enter ↵ Key.
- To move to the next cell, use the Tab key.

Try it:

We will create a schedule on the Layout 1 tab. The schedule will be a Paper Space object. Before we insert the Table, erase the viewport that is on Layout 1 – we will not need to see any part of our Model, so we won't need any viewports.

Let's create the following paint schedule:

Paint Schedule		
Walls	Ceiling	Trim & Doors
California Paints Tomahawk Red, 7856A Latex, Eggshell Finish	Glidden Paints Ceiling White, GC3070 Latex	Benjamin Moore Navajo White, N31973 Acrylic, Eggshell Finish

1. For the Title section, Pick the Underline button on the Formatting Panel of the Text Editor (because Titleblock style was created as Bold Italic, those are already highlighted):

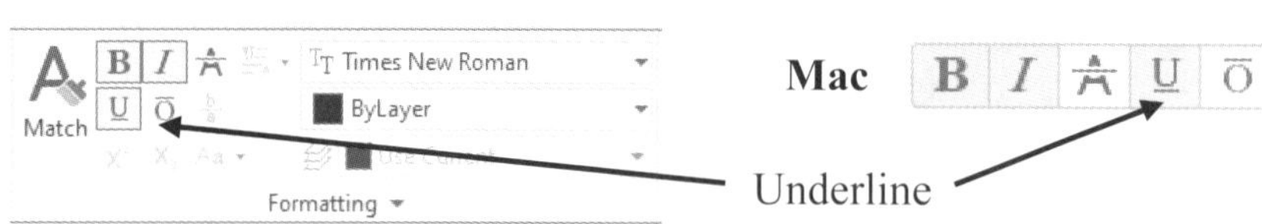

2. Type the words: **Paint Schedule**

3. Press the Tab key to move to the next cell. This is the Header cell for the 1st column.

4. Pick the Underline button.

5. Type the word: Walls

6. Press the Tab key to move to the next cell. This is the Header cell for the 2nd column.

7. Fill in the remaining Header cells. You will need to pick the Underline button for each Header cell. Use the tab key to change cells. After the last Header cell, the tab key will move you to the 1st column of the Data cell.

8. Type the words: California Paints

9. Hold the ALT key down (Option key on the Mac) and press the ↵ Enter Key. This allows you to create another line of text within the same cell. Type the text. Repeat this for the third line of text.

10. Press the tab key to move to the next Data cell. Continue entering the information for all the cells.

11. Pick the Close Text Editor button (Save button on the Mac) to exit the command and complete the table.

Editing an Existing Table

If you simply want to add text to an existing cell, double-left-click inside the cell. The cell will highlight, and the Text Editor will appear. All methods used to enter information to the table are the same as when the table was initially created.

To edit an existing table, such as adding rows or columns, pick in a cell (single left click). The Table Cell Tab appears on the ribbon. It is here where you can make changes to the cells.

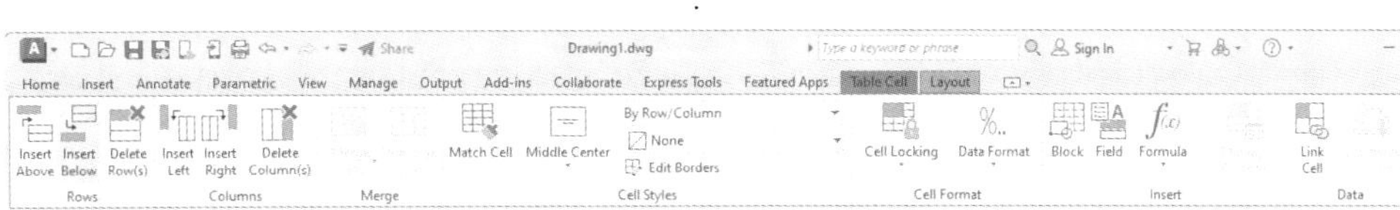

Mac

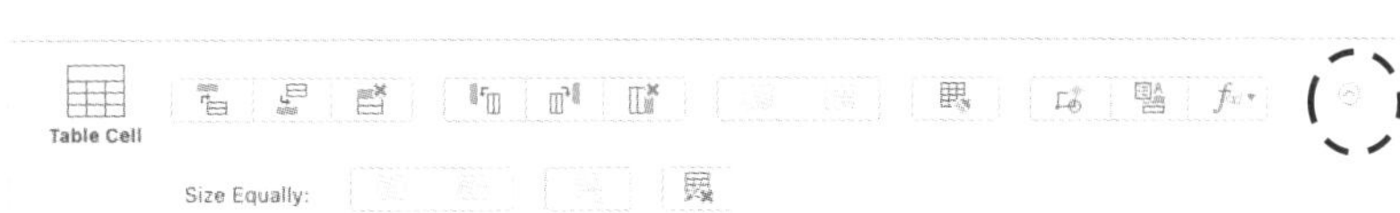

Shown expanded

Try it:

Let's modify the Paint Schedule we just created by adding another column to identify the room that the paint scheme applies to:

1. ***(Pick a cell in Column A of the Paint Schedule to make the Table Cell Tab appear)***
2. ***(Pick Insert Left from the Columns Panel)***

A new column will appear to the left of the column labeled Walls.

1. ***(Pick a cell in Row 3 of the Paint Schedule)***
2. ***(Pick Insert Below from the Rows Panel)***

A new row will appear below the bottom row of the schedule.

Paint Schedule			
	Walls	Ceiling	Trim & Doors
	California Paints Tomahawk Red, 7866A Latex, Eggshell Finish	Glidden Paints Ceiling White, GC3070 Latex	Benjamin Moore Navajo White, N31973 Acrylic, Eggshell Finish

Let's title the new column as "Room". For the first row this will be for the "Dining Room". For the second row, this will be for the "Living Room". Remember to double-left click to edit the cells. For the living room we will keep the ceiling and trim and doors the same as the dining room, but we will make the walls a Behr Paints, Forest Green, Latex, Eggshell Finish. You can copy the cells for the ceiling and door paint colors by single clicking the cell that has the info, right click and select copy, and then single click the cell you want to add the information to and right click and select paste.

When you are done, your schedule will look like this:

Paint Schedule			
Room	Walls	Ceiling	Trim & Doors
Dining Room	California Paints Tomahawk Red, 7866A Latex, Eggshell Finish	Glidden Paints Ceiling White, GC3070 Latex	Benjamin Moore Navajo White, N31973 Acrylic, Eggshell Finish
Living Room	Behr Paints Forest Green Latex, Eggshell Finish	Glidden Paints Ceiling White, GC3070 Latex	Benjamin Moore Navajo White, N31973 Acrylic, Eggshell Finish

Notice that the columns are wider than they need to be. We can change the column widths and row heights by using grips. You can get the grips by using a single left-click on any cell. Turning Object Snap off first will make resizing easier.

Let's reduce the size of the first column:

(Pick in the cell that has the word <u>Room</u>)

	A	B	C	D
1	**Paint Schedule**			
2	Room	Walls	Ceiling	Trim & Doors
3	Dining Room	California Paints Tomahawk Red, 7856A Latex, Eggshell Finish	Glidden Paints Ceiling White, GC3070 Latex	Benjamin Moore Navajo White, N31973 Acrylic, Eggshell Finish
4	Living Room	Behr Paints Forest Green Latex, Eggshell Finish	Glidden Paints Ceiling White, GC3070 Latex	Benjamin Moore Navajo White, N31973 Acrylic, Eggshell Finish

(Pick the right grip and drag it left to reduce the column width. Press the Esc key when done.)

When you are done, your Paint Schedule will look like this:

Paint Schedule			
Room	Walls	Ceiling	Trim & Doors
Dining Room	California Paints Tomahawk Red, 7856A Latex, Eggshell Finish	Glidden Paints Ceiling White, GC3070 Latex	Benjamin Moore Navajo White, N31973 Acrylic, Eggshell Finish
Living Room	Behr Paints Forest Green Latex, Eggshell Finish	Glidden Paints Ceiling White, GC3070 Latex	Benjamin Moore Navajo White, N31973 Acrylic, Eggshell Finish

You can continue to re-size each column and row until you are satisfied.

Paint Schedule			
Room	Walls	Ceiling	Trim & Doors
Dining Room	California Paints Tomahawk Red, 7856A Latex, Eggshell Finish	Glidden Paints Ceiling White, GC3070 Latex	Benjamin Moore Navajo White, N31973 Acrylic, Eggshell Finish
Living Room	Behr Paints Forest Green Latex, Eggshell Finish	Glidden Paints Ceiling White, GC3070 Latex	Benjamin Moore Navajo White, N31973 Acrylic, Eggshell Finish

If you want to reposition the schedule to fit better on your layout, you can use the Move command. The Table is treated as a single object.

Summary

In this chapter you have learned to:

- Create a Table Style
- Create a schedule using the Table command
- Add and Edit Text for a Table
- Modify an existing Table by adding and re-sizing columns or rows

Review Questions

1. What does AutoCAD call Schedules?
2. Why is it better to make a schedule in Paper Space than Model Space?
3. Where can you find the Table Style icon?
4. Which toolbar has the Table command icon?
5. To edit text on an existing Table, how do you get the text editor?
6. How do you add a row or a column to an existing Table?
7. How do you change the size of a column or row in a Table?

Exercises

1. Create the following Door and Hardware Schedule in Paper Space:

Door & Hardware Schedule		
Location	Door Style	Hardware
Entrance	Jeld-Wen Prehung Solid Core Molded 6-Panel 2'6"	Stanley Hardware Square Privacy Mortise Bolt
Living Room to Study	Jeld-Wen Pocket Solid Core Molded Smooth 2'6"	Stanley Hardware Rectangular Flush Pull
Closet	Jeld-Wen Prehung Solid Core Molded 6-Panel 2'	Stanley Hardware Square Privacy Bolt

2. Update your drawing template from Chapter 12 by adding the “Schedule” table style to it.

Chapter 14
Commands – Set 7: Creating Curves and Rendering

Learning Objectives:

- Creating curved shapes using Arc, Polyline, and Spline
- Creating an Ellipse
- Using Hatch for sections and to fill shapes and Section Views
- Using Gradient Hatch to render your drawing

Up to this point, we have focused primarily on straight-line shapes. This covers the majority of items we will draw, walls, doors, windows, etc. There are many times that we will need to draw curved shapes. This is especially true for items such as curtains, bedding, upholstery, etc.

Although AutoCAD is a drafting program, not a drawing program, it has the ability to draw curved shapes. This will take some practice, but once you get used to it, it is easy to do.

Arc

The Arc command creates an arc. There are multiple ways to create an arc. We have used the Circle command with trimming in the previous chapters. Although that may not have been the most efficient method, it was intuitive and straightforward. This section will only cover one method of creating arcs. It is left to the student to explore other methods.

The method covered here is the 3-point arc. This is an arc that is created by picking 3 points. The arc created will have the first and last point picked as the endpoints. The second point picked will define the amount of curvature the arc will have. This type of arc comes in handy when you are working a design where you want to have a curvature bounded by a fixed distance.

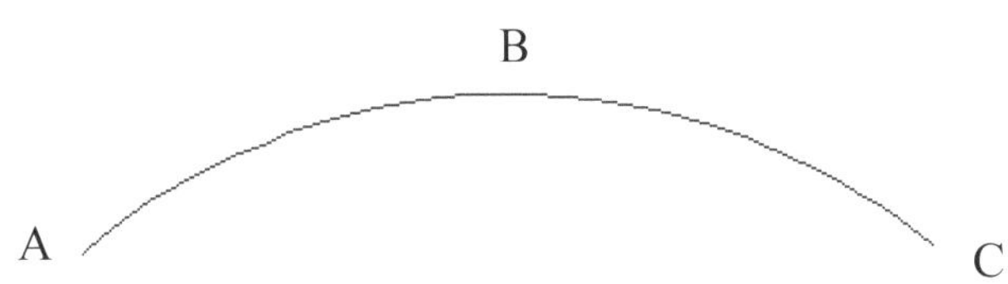

Procedure:

Pick (left click): **Arc icon** from the Draw Panel of the Home Tab.

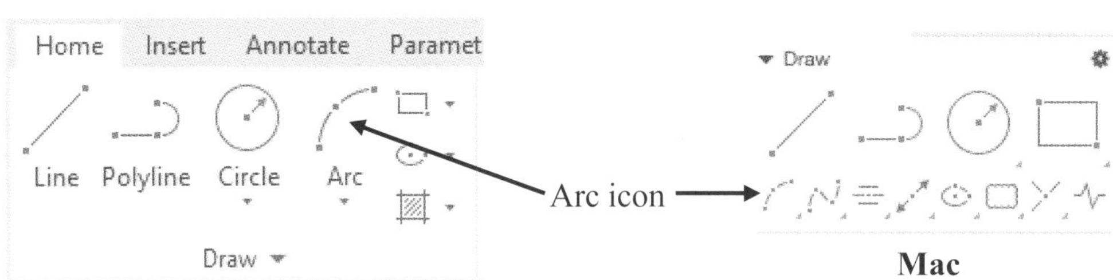

The command line prompts you with the following:

ARC *Specify start point of arc or [Center]* ***(Pick the first endpoint of the arc – Point "A")***
Specify second point of arc or [Center/End]: ***(Pick the second point which defines the curvature – Point "B")***
Specify end point of arc: ***(Pick the third point which is the endpoint of the arc – Point "C")***

Once the arc is created, AutoCAD automatically ends the command.

Try it:

As an example, let's draw an arc that is the shape for the top of a cabinet door. Before beginning, make sure that you have the Object Snap turned on with Endpoint and Midpoint selected.

This is the cabinet door before the arc is created:

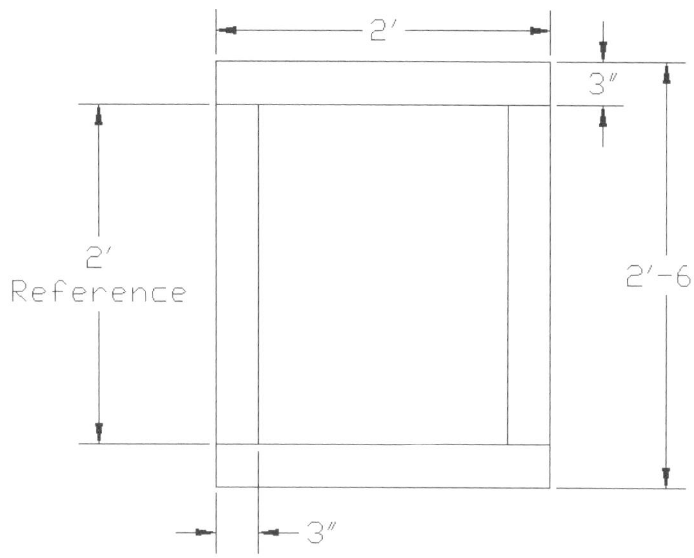

To create an arc that curves within a 1″ distance from the bottom of the top frame, let's first Explode the top rectangle (if you had created it as a rectangle).

Use the Offset command and offset the bottom line of the top frame up 1″.

(Pick the Arc icon)

ARC *Specify start point of arc or [Center]:* ***(Pick endpoint 1)***
Specify second point of arc or [Center/End]: ***(Pick the midpoint of the offset line)***
Specify end point of arc: ***(Pick endpoint 2)***

The command is completed and an arc is drawn. Use the Erase command to eliminate the offsite line.

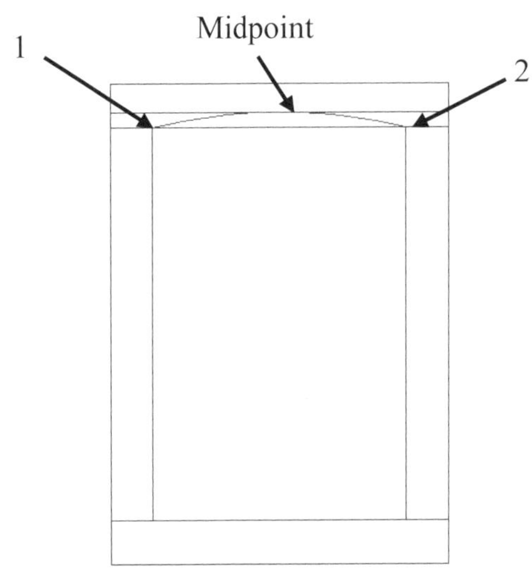

When you are done, the cabinet door will look like this:

Ellipse

The Ellipse command creates an ellipse. An ellipse looks similar to an oval, but it is a unique shape. An elliptical shape is how an object with a circular shape appears when it is viewed at an angle. Sometimes the elliptical shape is used for a table, a mirror, or as an architectural feature such as windows or archways.
An ellipse can be created in multiple ways. It is defined with a major and a minor axis. The default method of creating an ellipse using the icon is to define the two end points of the first axis plus the distance for the second axis.

Prior to creating the ellipse, it is easier to define the boundary of the ellipse by using a rectangle. Make sure the size of the rectangle is the size that you want the ellipse to be. In addition, make sure you have your object snap setting to Midpoint.

Example:

Let's draw the elliptical shape of the coffee table shown:

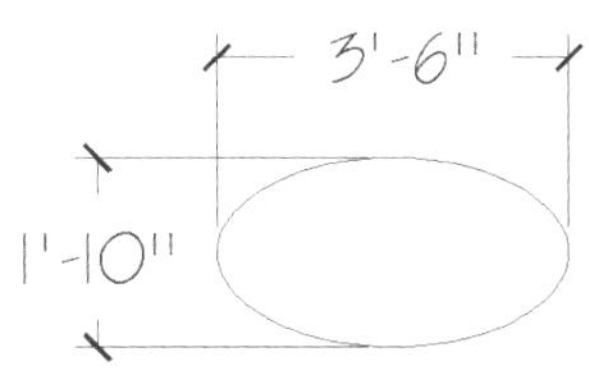

First, start with a rectangle that has the same dimensions as those shown for the ellipse:

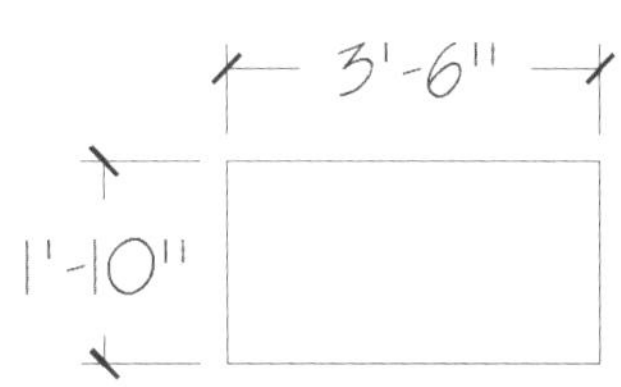

Procedure:

Pick (left click): **Ellipse icon fly-out** from the Draw Panel of the Home Tab. Pick **Axis, End icon.**

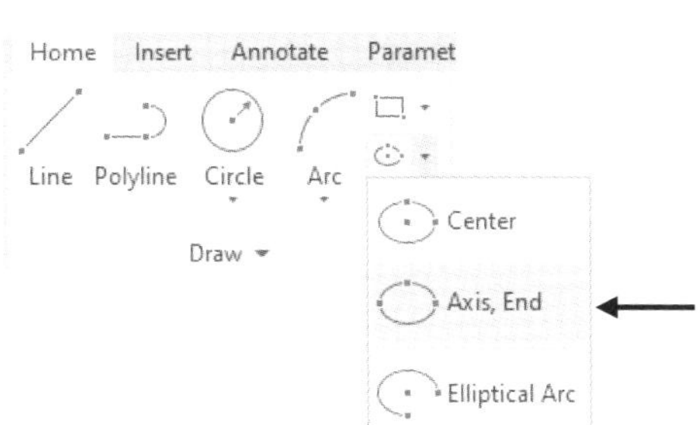

Mac

The command line prompts you with the following:

ELLIPSE *Specify axis endpoint of ellipse or [Arc/Center]:* ***(Pick the midpoint of the first line)***

Specify other endpoint of axis: ***(Pick the midpoint of the line opposite the first line)***

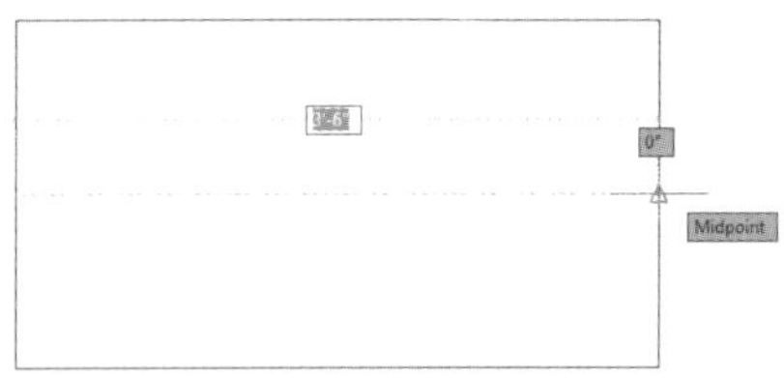

Specify distance to other axis or [Rotation]: ***(Pick the midpoint of either of the two remaining lines)***

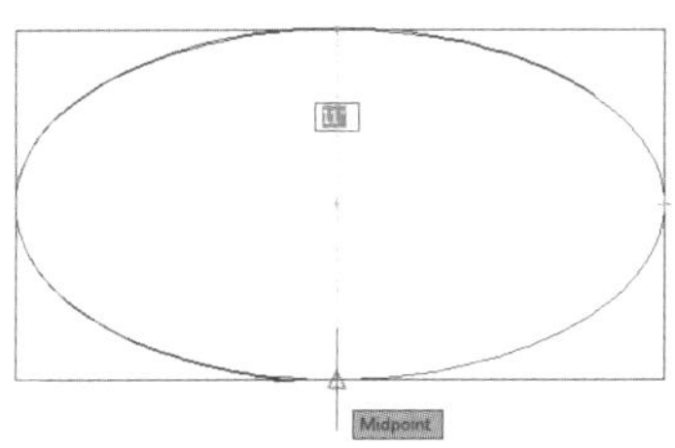

Once the ellipse is drawn, use the Erase command to erase the rectangle. The result will be an ellipse to the exact dimensions as shown:

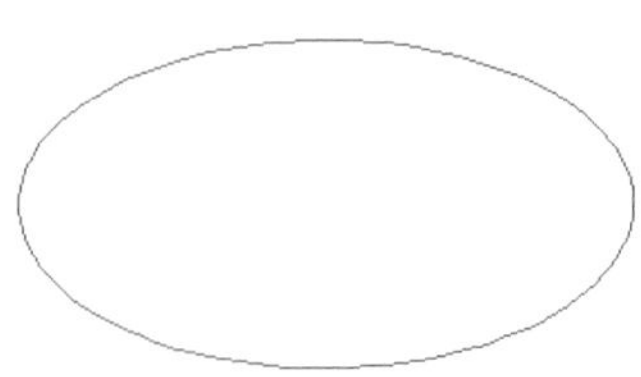

Polyline

Another command that allows you more freedom to draw curved shapes is Polyline. This command allows you to draw straight lines and arcs in a free form (as well as with precision).

For fun, let's draw a heart shape. Let's do this in a free form without worry of a specific size, and we can approximate the shape. Note, however, that the heart shape is symmetrical. We can take advantage of that fact by drawing only half the heart shape and then mirroring that about the line of symmetry.

First, draw the vertical line that we will use to mirror about. Use the construction line, with vertical as the option, to draw a vertical line somewhere on the screen. Once that is done, we can draw the shape of the half-heart. It is recommended that you turn off Object Snap so that you have better control. We will intentionally draw the half-heart crossing the construction line.

Polyline:

The Polyline command is located on the Draw Panel of the Home Tab.

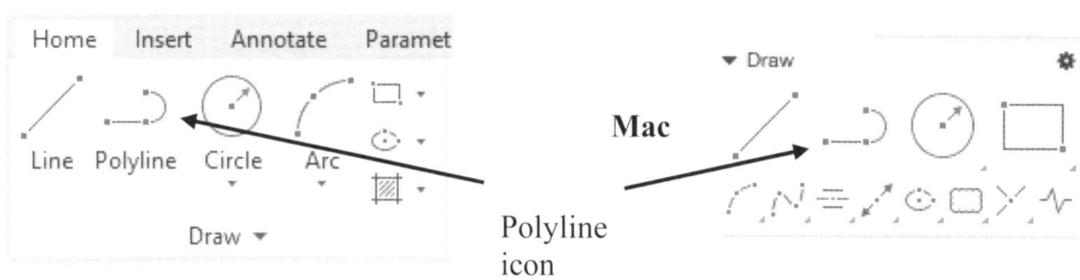

Procedure:

Pick (left click): **Polyline icon** from the Draw Panel of the Home Tab.

The command line prompts you with the following:

PLINE *Specify start point:* ***(Pick a location on the left side of the vertical construction line)***

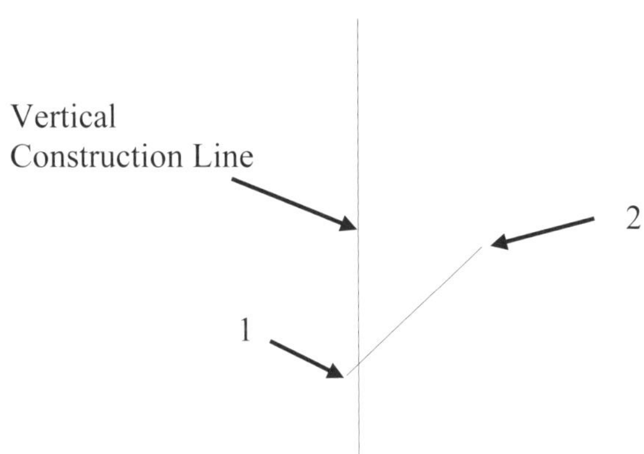

The polyline will rubber-band to follow your cursor. As you pick the second point, the polyline will be a point-to-point line.

Current line-width is 0'-0"

Specify next point or [Arc/Halfwidth/Length/Undo/Width]: ***(Pick the second point, up and to the right of the first point)***

Specify next point or [Arc/Close/Halfwidth/Length/Undo/Width]: **a** ↵

An arc will begin to be drawn. The radius and endpoint of the arc will change as it rubber-bands with your cursor movement.

Specify endpoint of arc or

[Angle/CEnter/CLose/Direction/Halfwidth/Line/Radius/Second pt/Undo/Width]: ***(Pick a location on the opposite side of the construction line to form the rounded part of the half-heart)***

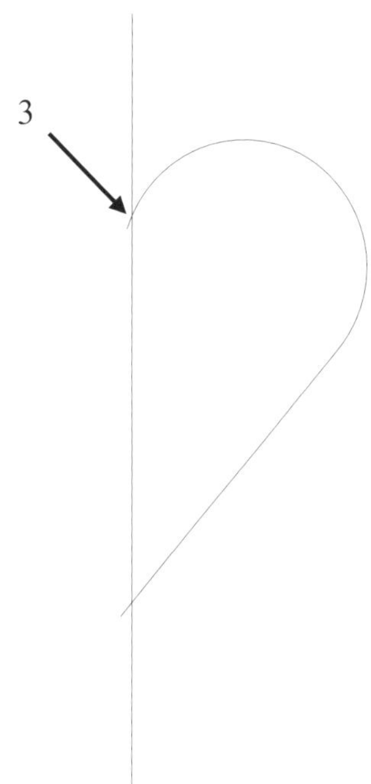

Specify endpoint of arc or

[Angle/CEnter/CLose/Direction/Halfwidth/Line/Radius/Second pt/Undo/Width]: ↵

Pressing the ↵ Enter key will exit the command.

Use the Trim command to trim the half-heart to the Construction Line.

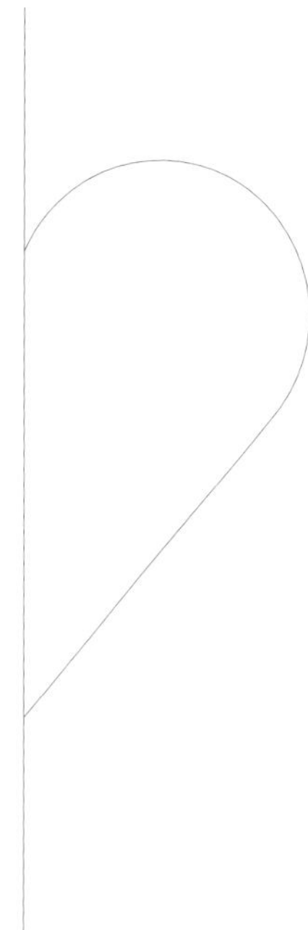

Use the Mirror command to mirror and copy the half-heart shape to become a complete heart shape. Erase the vertical construction line.

Try using the Polyline for any other shapes you would like. If you want to change its shape, use the grips. For multiple hearts, try the Array command. Have fun with it!

Spline

A command that is especially handy for free-form drawing is the Spline command. The spline is drawn by picking multiple points on the drawing. As you pick those points, the shape will rubber-band with your cursor. To end the command, press the ↵ Enter key.

There are two types of splines available: Fit and CV. This chapter will only discuss the Fit version. The Spline commands are located on the expanded Draw Panel of the Home Tab.

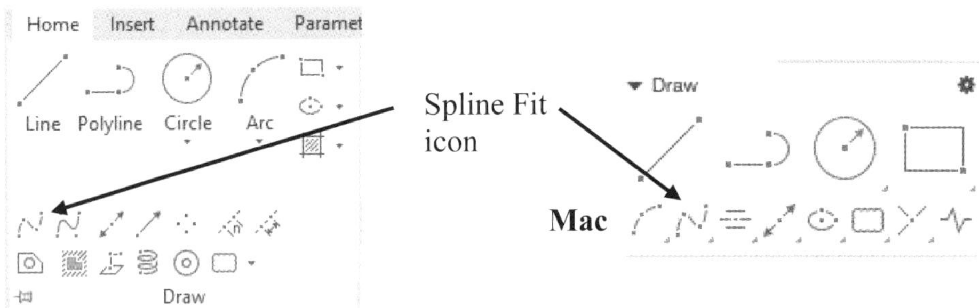

Procedure:

Pick (left click): **Spline Fit icon** from the Draw Panel of the Home Tab.

The command line prompts you with the following:

Current settings: Method=Fit   Knots=Chord
SPLINE *Specify first point or [Method/Knots/Object]:* ***(Pick a point on the screen)***
Enter next point or [start Tangency/toLerance]: ***(Pick a point on the screen)***
Enter next point or [end Tangency/toLerance/Undo]: ***(Pick a point on the screen)***
Enter next point or [end Tangency/toLerance/Undo/Close]: ***(Pick a point on the screen)***
Enter next point or [end Tangency/toLerance/Undo/Close]: ***(Pick a point on the screen)***
Enter next point or [end Tangency/toLerance/Undo/Close]: ↵

Pressing the ↵ Enter key will exit the command.

Resulting Spline shape

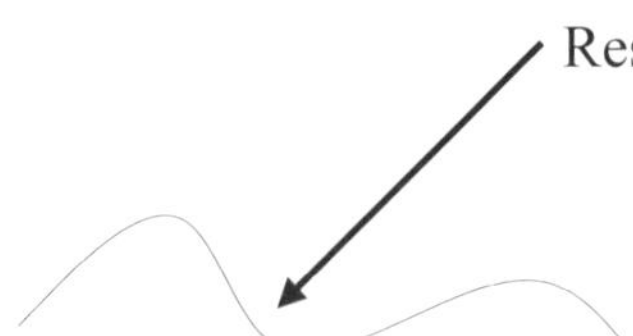

Try it:

As an example, let's draw a spiral shape with a horizontal line:

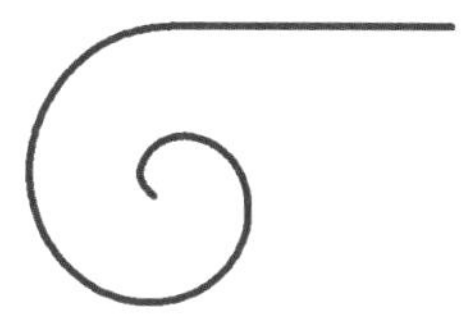

The spiral shape is drawn using the Spline command. It could be done free-hand, or for more control, by using a technique of concentric circles and lines clocked around the circle to define the points of the spline.

Before beginning, ensure that Object Snap is turned on with Center and Intersection options selected.

Draw a 1/8" radius circle and offset it by 1/8", toward the outside, 11 times. The largest circle will be 1-1/2" radius.

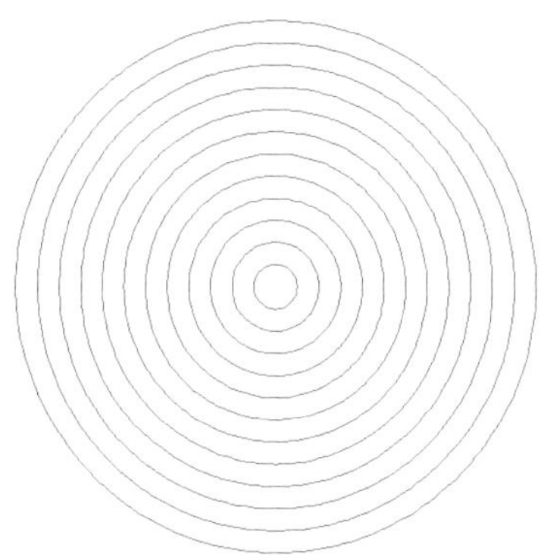

Concentric circles 1/8" apart. Smallest radius is 1/8" and the largest radius is 1-1/2"

Draw a vertical line from the center of the circles to the top quadrant of the largest circle. You may need to use the Object Snap override of Snap to Quadrant from the Object Snap toolbar.
Use the Polar Array command to rotate and copy the line 8 times within 360º.

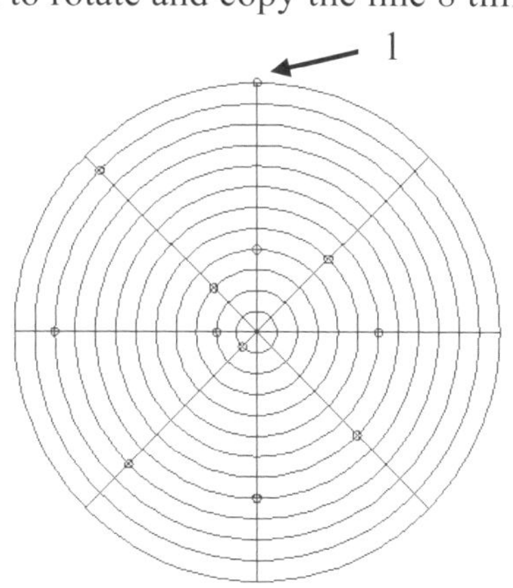

Starting at point 1, use the Spline command and pick the points of intersection of the lines and circles so that each point gets progressively closer to the center.

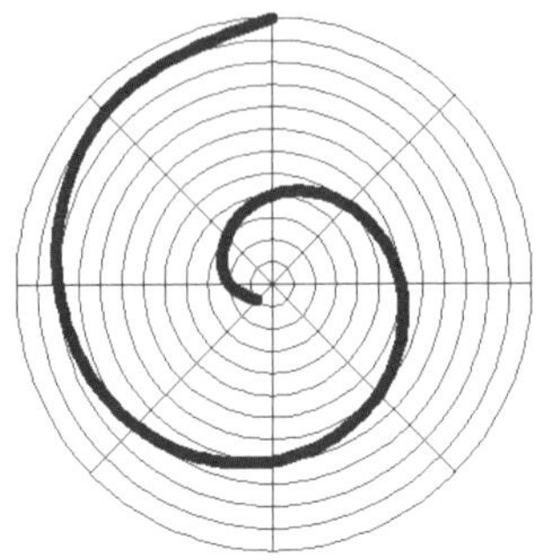

This spline was drawn at a thicker Lineweight than the circles and lines to make it easier to distinguish it.

Now that the spline is drawn, you can erase the circles and lines. An easy way to do that is to move the spline to a different location and then use a selection window to erase.

The next thing we want is a line that is tangent to the spline. Use the line command with Snap to Tangent as an Object Snap override.

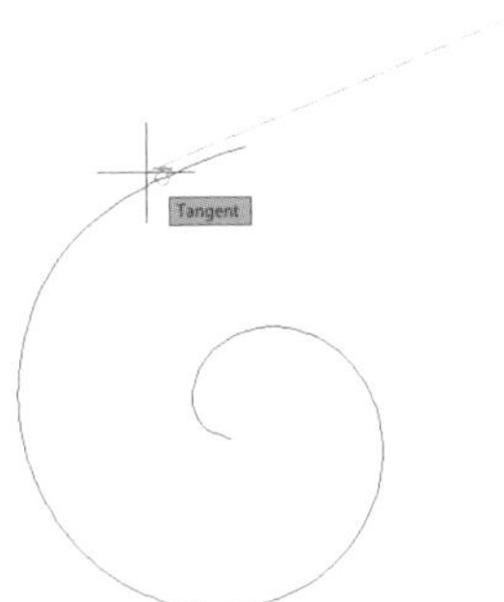

Pick the first point of the line above and to the right of the spline. The second point of the line should snap to the tangent point of the spline.

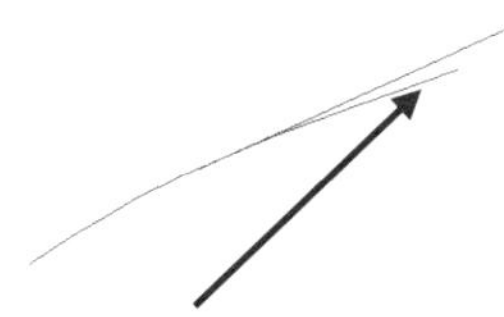

Use the trim command to trim any excess portion of the spline

We do not know the angle of the line, but we want to control the line and spiral orientation. For this example, we will rotate the spline and line together so that the line is horizontal. We will use the Reference option of the Rotate command.

To use the Reference option, we will need to draw a horizontal line through the endpoint of the angled line first. It may be necessary to trim the line so that you will have an endpoint to select.

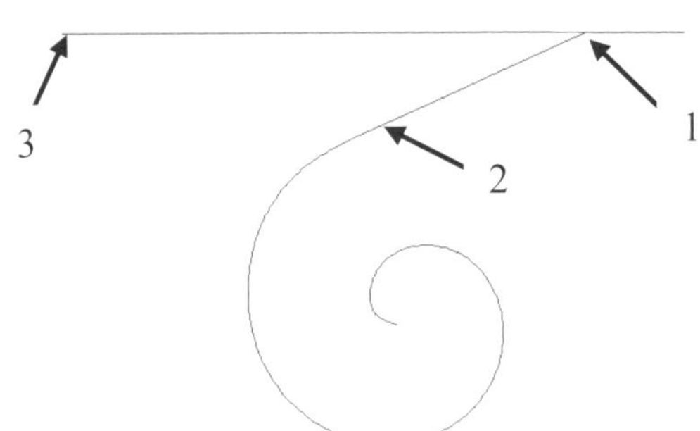

Use the Rotate command to rotate the spline and the line.

Current positive angle in UCS: ANGDIR=counterclockwise ANGBASE=0
ROTATE *Select objects:* ***(Pick the spline and line you want to rotate)***
Specify opposite corner: 2 found
Select objects: ↵
Specify base point: ***(Pick point 1)***
Specify rotation angle or [Copy/Reference] <0>: **r↵**
Specify the reference angle <0>: ***(Pick point 1)*** *Specify second point:* ***(Pick point 2)***
Specify the new angle or [Points] <0>: ***(Pick point 3)***

The spline and line have now rotated so that the line is horizontal.

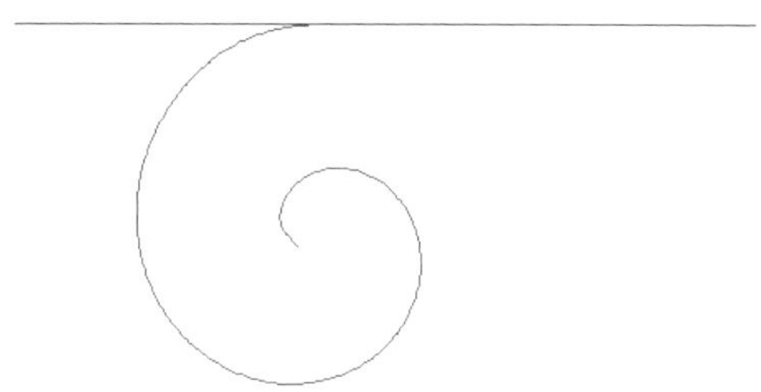

Erase the extra line that we created to use as a reference for rotation. Since this was some amount of work to create this shape, it would be a good idea to save it as a Block for future use.

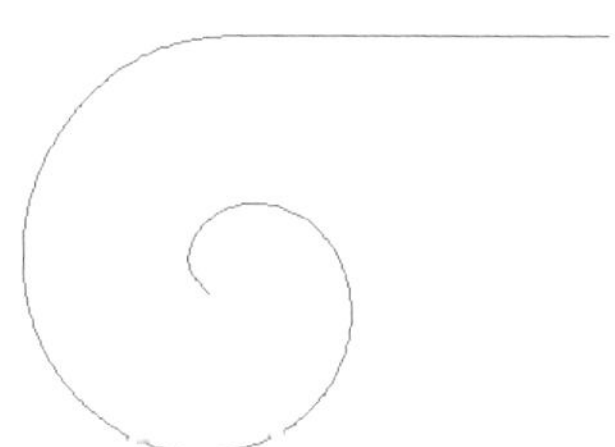

You can try different size circles and a different number of lines to pick the intersections, and you will get different shaped spirals.

Spiral created using 12 lines

Spiral created using 1/16" offset circles

Hatch

Hatch is used to fill an enclosed area with either a pattern or a solid color. It can be most useful for section views or for the solid fill color of walls for a plan view.

Procedure:

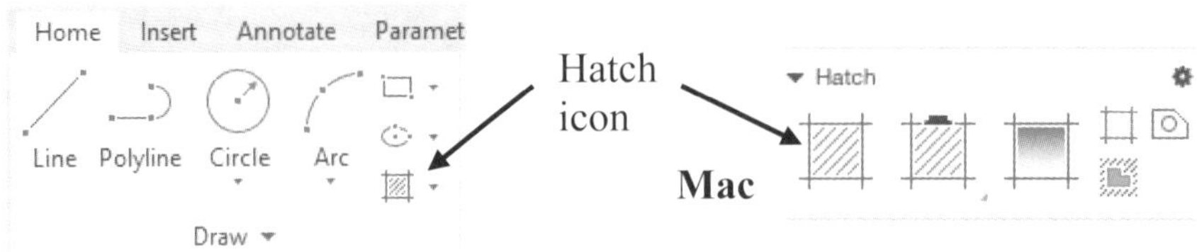

Pick (left click): **Hatch icon** from the Draw Panel of the Home Tab. 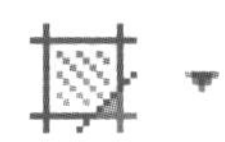

The Hatch Creation Tab will appear on the ribbon:

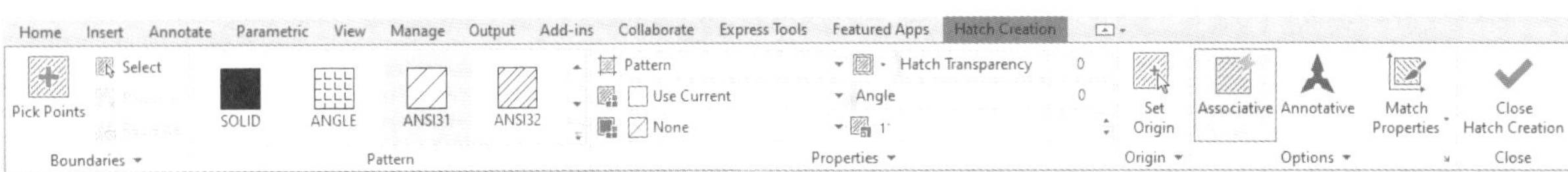

On the Mac, a Hatch Creation Visor will appear at the top of the screen:

Various patterns or solid colors are available. In addition, a two-color gradient style hatch is available. User defined is also available, but that will not be covered in this text.

Prior to selecting the enclosed area to fill with a Hatch, choose the type you want by using the double pull-down selection on the Pattern Panel. On the Mac, use the pull-down arrow of the pattern swatch.

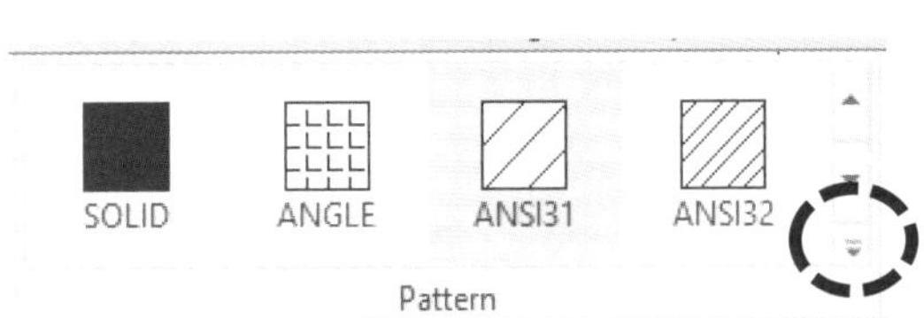

Once you choose the type, a preview of the pattern is highlighted on the Pattern Panel. You can change the pattern by expanding the Pattern Panel. On the Mac, Pick Open Library.

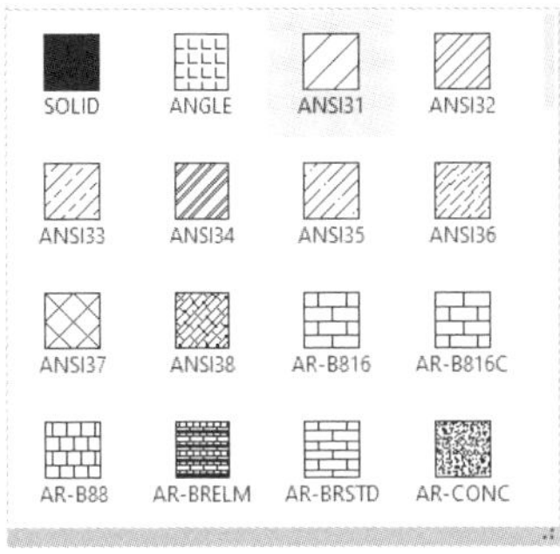

Use the slide bar to preview more hatch patterns

Mac

You can also choose the color of your hatch pattern. Choose the color you want by using the pull-down arrow for the color selection of the Properties Panel. On the Mac, pick the color swatch. If you pick Select Colors… the Select Color dialog box will appear. This will provide the same color options available to you as when choosing a color for Layers or when using the Properties tool.

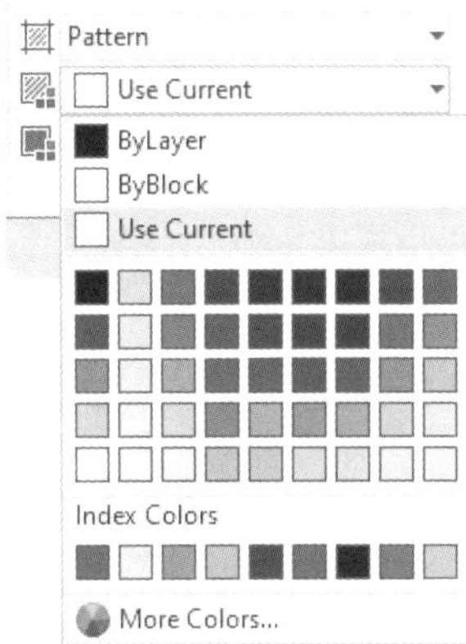

Mac

Define the boundaries of the hatch by either picking a point in the bounded area or by selecting objects that define the boundary. Using the Pick Points method is preferred but requires the boundary to be completely closed.

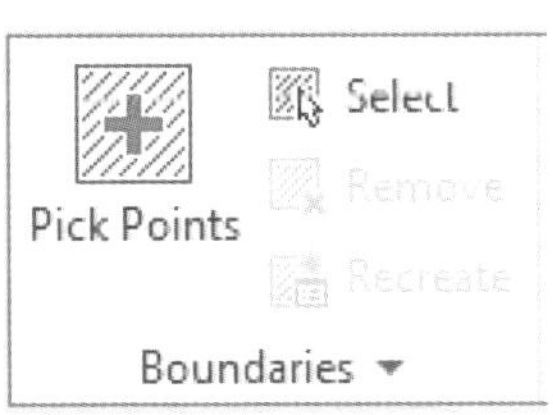

Mac

Using the Annotative option is similar to using Annotative Text and Dimensions – The scale of the Hatch pattern will coordinate with the scale of the Paper. On the Mac, you can change Hatch to Annotative by using the Properties Inspector. Use Match Properties to copy the hatch pattern of existing hatch.

Mac

Example:

Let’s use a solid color Hatch to fill in the walls of the conference room:

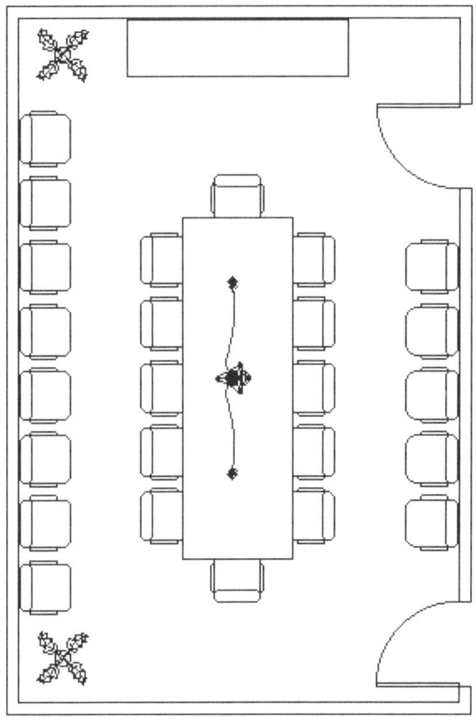

Choose Solid by using the pull-down arrow on the Properties Panel of the Hatch Creation Tab (On the Mac, use the pull-down arrow of the pattern swatch):

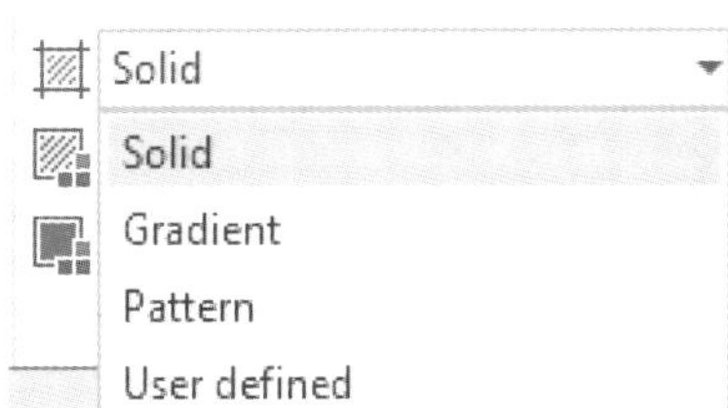

Mac

The Solid preview is highlighted in the Pattern Panel of the Hatch Creation Tab (Visor on Mac):

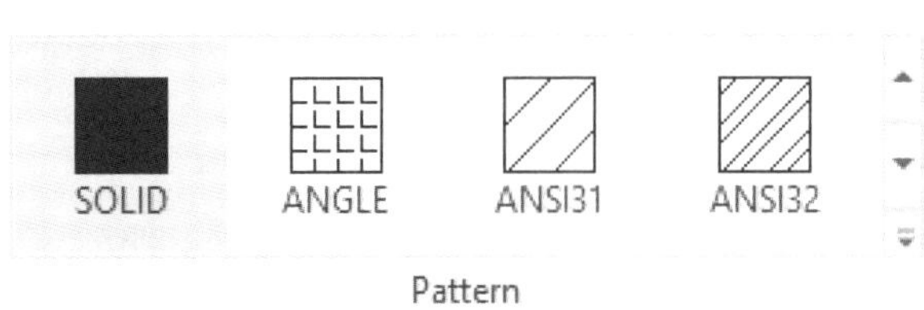

Mac

Use the pull-down arrow for the Hatch Color (on the Mac, pick the color swatch) and choose ByLayer. The color of the Hatch will be the same color as the Layer that it is created in.

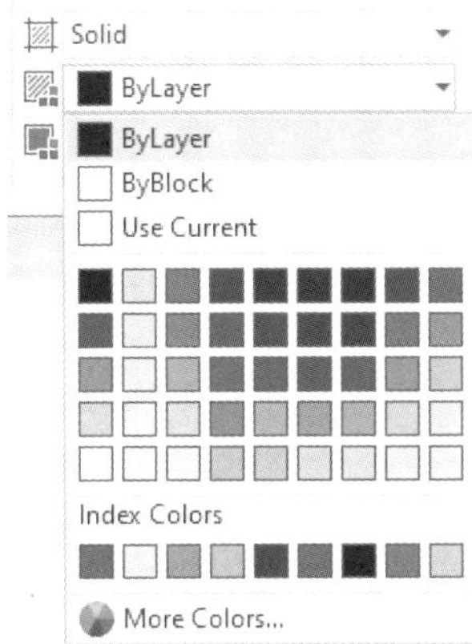

Mac

Choose the Pick Points button on the Boundaries Panel of the Hatch Creation Tab to select the area that will define the Hatch boundary.

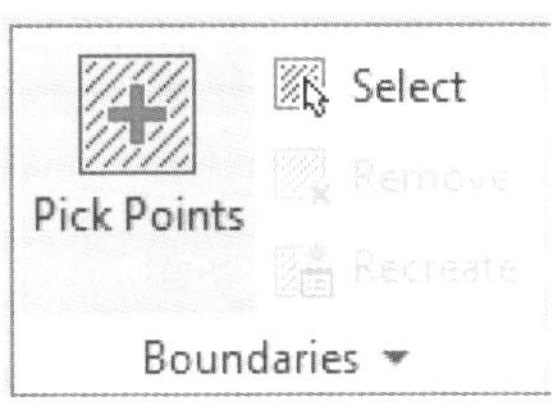

Mac

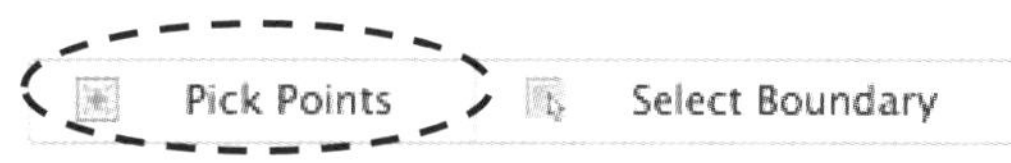

Pick a point within the parallel lines that define the walls.

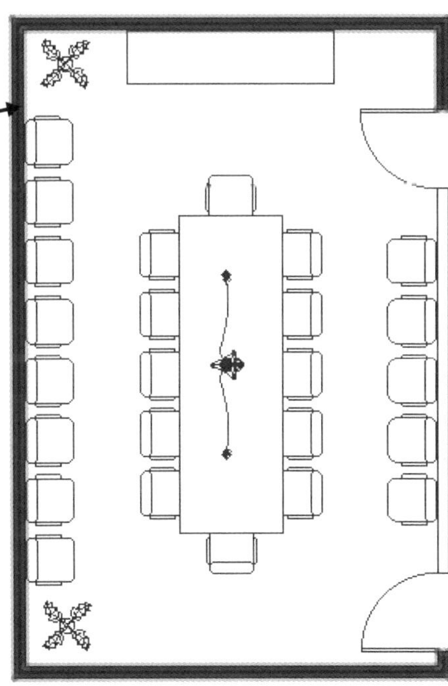

Note that this wall is separate and must also be chosen as a boundary. This can be done now or can be done at a later time. For this example, choose it now.

Your command line will display the following:
HATCH *Pick internal point or [Select objects/Draw/Undo/seTtings]:*
(Pick a point within the walls to define the boundary)

> Note: Be patient while AutoCAD searches for the boundary. At first, it may not appear that anything happened after you picked a point.

If the boundary is not well defined, or not completely displayed on your screen while you are selecting it, the following error message will appear:

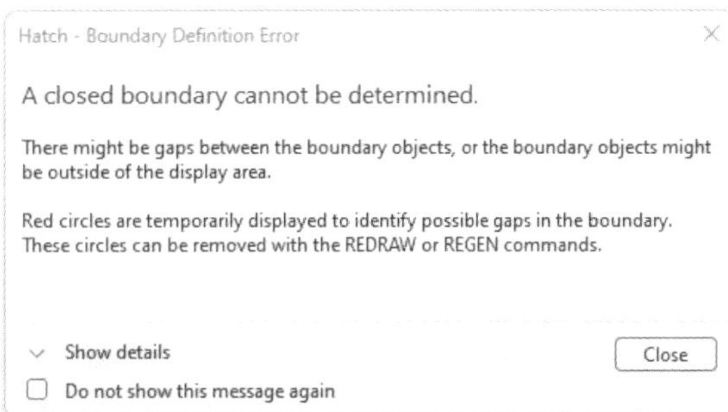

Mac

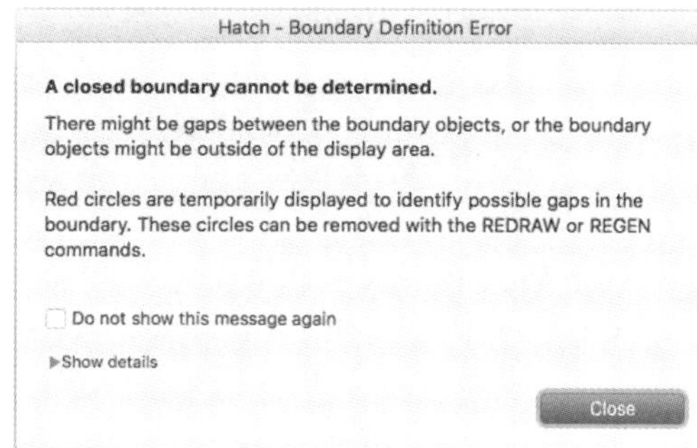

If you get this error message, try to fix the problem via one of the suggested methods given in the error message under the Show details pull-down.

In addition to the error message, AutoCAD will display small circles showing you the location of the boundary gap. If you hover your cursor over them, no tool tip will appear. If you try to erase them, they will not be selected. To eliminate them, type the following in the command line:

Command: ***REGEN*** ↵
Regenerating model.

> **REGEN** command will also smooth the display of curves that may appear as lines.

The graphics will regenerate, and the boundary circles will be eliminated.

If there are no issues with the boundary, the command line will display the following:

Selecting everything visible...
Analyzing the selected data...
Analyzing internal islands...
Pick internal point or [Select objects/seTtings]:

Since the walls are well defined (no gaps where endpoints of each line should connect) the boundary is displayed with dotted lines. AutoCAD allows you to define additional boundaries.

Choose a point within the right wall as well. Press the ↵ Enter Key. Your Hatch will appear on your drawing while you select the boundaries.

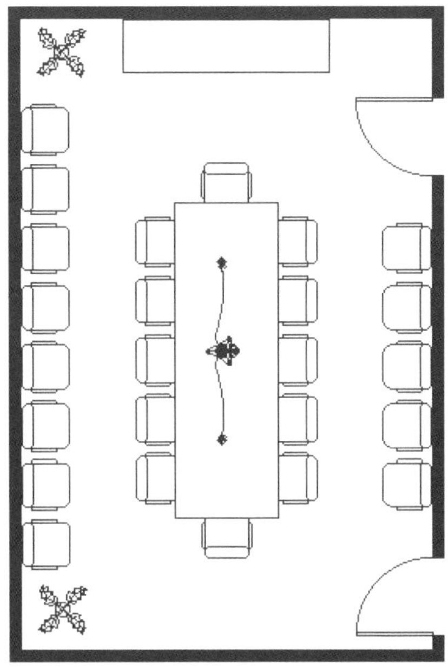

Press the ↵ Enter Key to accept the Hatch pattern. This will end the command.

Section Views

You can use Hatch for section views. The following is an example of a section view showing a detail of wall cabinets and moulding interface with the ceiling:

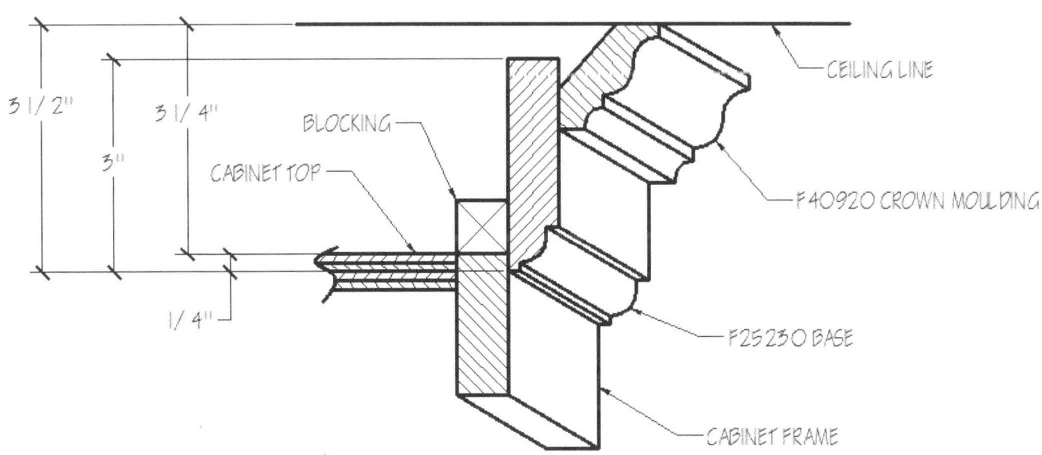

MOULDING DETAIL

In this example, the hatch pattern selected was ANSI 31. The angle of the pattern alternated between 0º and 90º.

The trick to making the detail have a "3D" look is to use the true cross-section shape of the moulding and adding 30º angled lines to it. Copy the cross-section shape to the opposite end of the angled lines and it becomes a faked 3D view.

Although the faked 3D view is not technically accurate, it helps provide a very good visual to both the client and the carpenter to be able to understand how things go together.

Rendering

You can use Hatch to render your 2-D drawings. You can accomplish this by using the Gradient Hatch.

Gradient Hatch

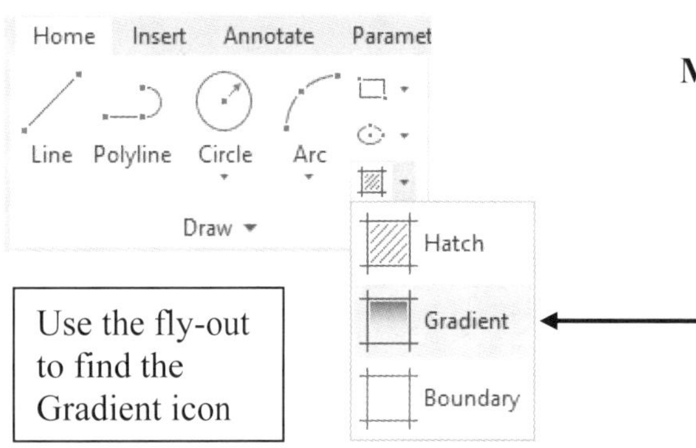

Mac

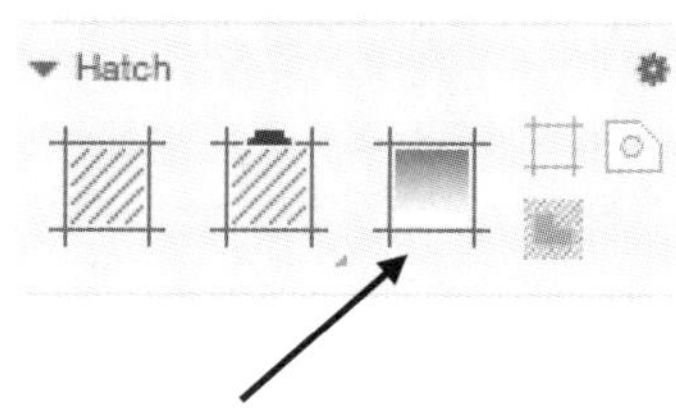

Pick (left click): **Gradient icon** from the Draw Panel of the Home Tab.

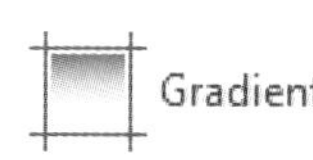

On the Mac, Pick the Hatch command first, then use the pull-down from the Visor to select Gradient.

Note that you can also get to this using the Hatch icon and then selecting Gradient using the pull-down arrow for Hatch Type on the Properties Panel of the Hatch Creation Tab.

The Panel on the Hatch Creation Tab will change to provide gradient tools:

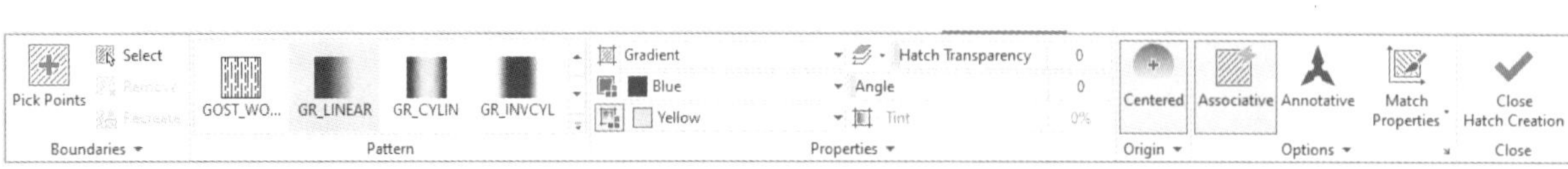

On the Mac, the Visor will change and provide Gradient Hatch tools:

Mac

The various styles available can be selected using the pull-down of the Pattern Panel. On the Mac, the Hatch Library dialog box will appear. These are shown below along with the full names of each pattern shown in the text box:

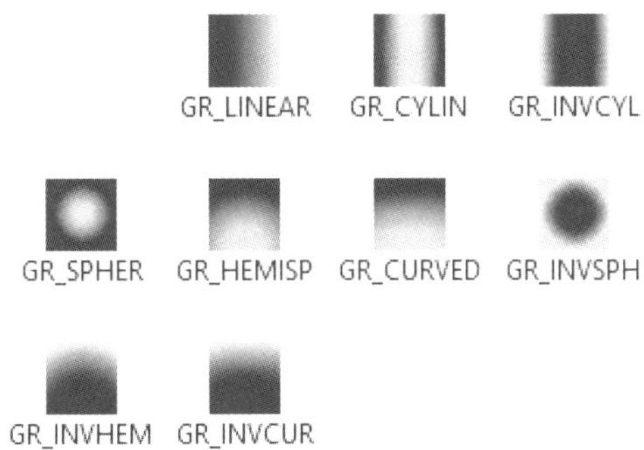

Linear
Cylindrical
Inverted cylindrical
Spherical
Hemispherical
Curved
Inverted spherical
Inverted hemispherical
Inverted curved

Mac

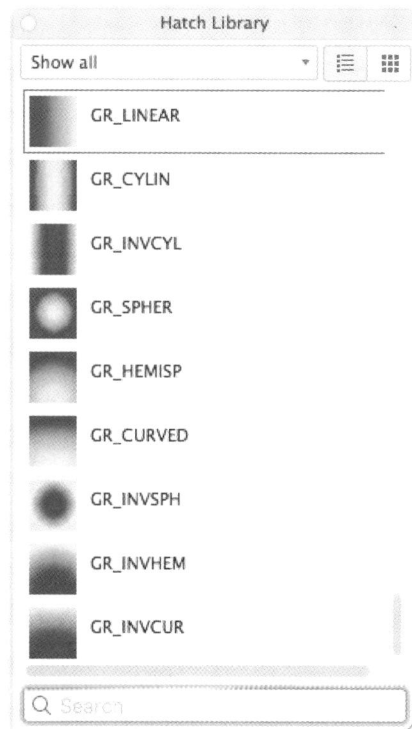

Gradient works the same as a solid Hatch except that it has two color choices. This allows you to simulate lighting conditions. To create a good visual rendering of your drawing will take practice and patience. It is likely that you may not be satisfied with the color or style the first time you place the Gradient Hatch on the drawing. This does not mean you need to erase it and try again. Instead, it is better to use the Properties Palette/Inspector to make the changes once the Gradient Hatch is on the drawing.

Another technique that can be employed is to cover small areas at a time. This is especially true when you want to have different effects for different parts of a piece of furniture or areas of a room.

Example:

Let's render the dresser that we created as homework in Chapter 3.

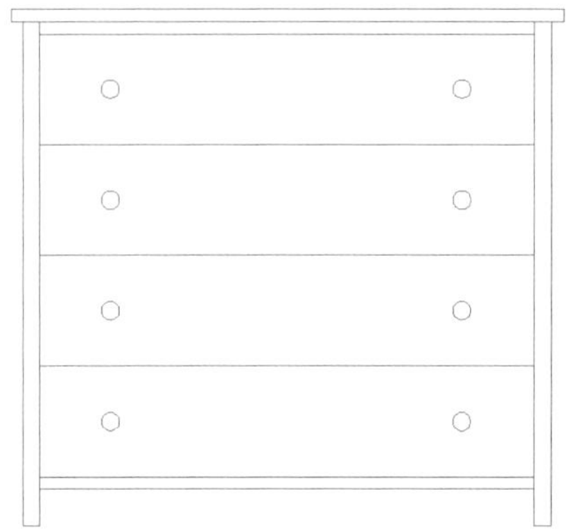

Notice that there are multiple segments that make up the dresser: knobs, drawer fronts, and vertical/horizontal structure. We can add Gradient Hatch to each portion separately.
The following is an example of adding 90° Cylindrical style Gradient Hatch to all the sections (except the knobs) at once:

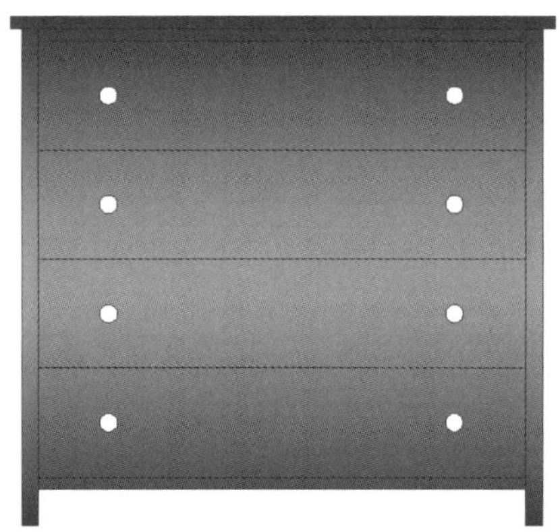

If we choose each section individually, using the same style we will obtain the following effects:

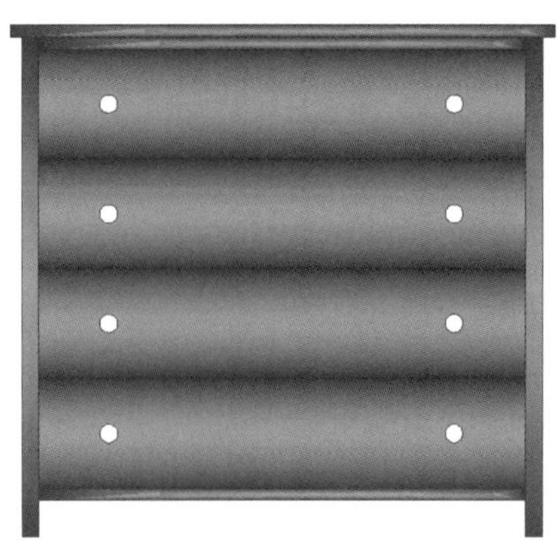

If you are not happy with the color or style, you can easily change them by using the Properties Palette. Let's change the vertical legs of the dresser to a linear style with the lighter portion toward the inside. For the left leg, this is a Gradient Angle of 0°, and for the right leg, it is 180°.

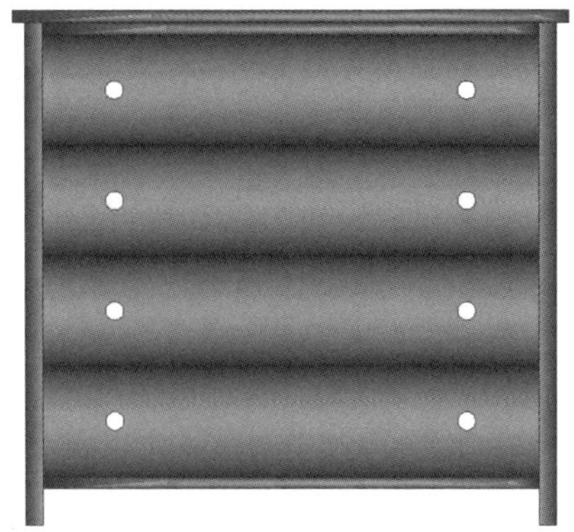

After selecting a Gradient Hatch, the Gradient Hatch Tab/Visor will allow you to change various features. The features that are most commonly changed for Gradient Hatch are Color 1, Color 2, and Gradient Angle.

Another technique that can be applied is to divide up the area that you wish to add the Gradient Hatch. As an example, let's say that you have a lamp next to a wall. The color will be lighter nearest the lamp as a result of the intensity of the light in close proximity to the lamp. Let's explore this with two floor lamps. Each lamp will have an effect on the appearance of the wall color.

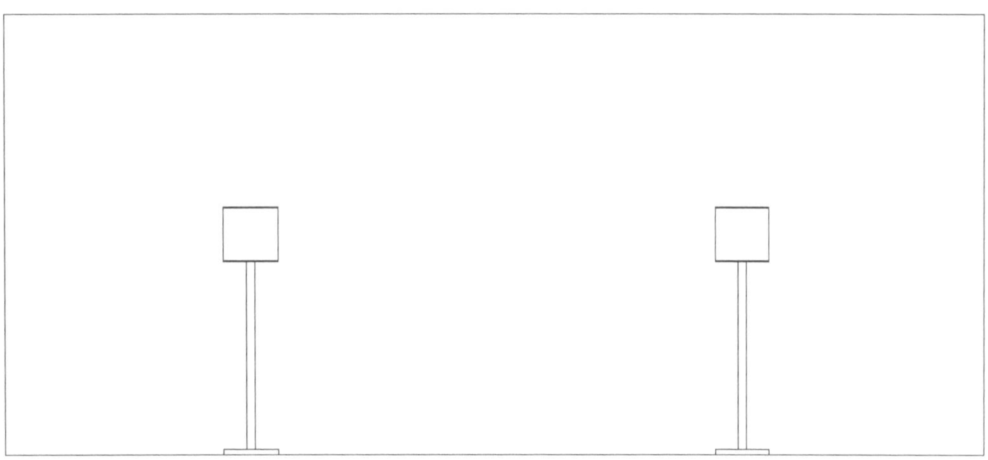

Using Cylindrical style for the wall will not provide the effect we are looking for:

Notice that the Cylindrical style would make it appear as though the light was centered on the wall. One way around this problem is to divide the room into sections. We can draw a vertical line from each floor lamp and another centered in the room to divide it into reasonable sections.

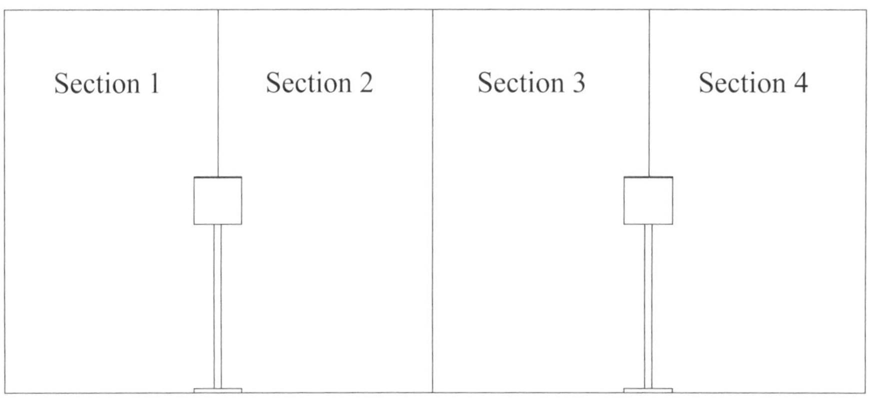

With the room divided into sections, we can add Gradient Hatch to each section. The following shows the result of using Linear style with sections 1 and 3 set at a Gradient Angle of 0° and sections 2 and 4 set at a Gradient Angle of 180°. The lines used to divide the wall have been erased.

It may not produce perfect results, but it certainly provides for a much more realistic appearance.

Summary

In this chapter you have learned to:

- Draw a 3-point Arc
- Create an Ellipse using a rectangle to define the boundaries
- Use a Polyline to draw continuous lines and arcs
- Draw a free-form curve using Spline
- Use Hatch to fill an area with a solid color or other pre-defined patterns
- Render your drawing using Gradient Hatch – Filling an area with two-color solid hatch
- Use various techniques to improve the appearance of your rendered drawing

Review Questions

1. Why would you use an Arc instead of a Circle?
2. How is an Ellipse defined?
3. What situation would you use a Polyline?
4. Why would you use a Spline instead of a Polyline?
5. If your Hatch does not appear the right size, what can you do about it?
6. What can you do if you get an error message while trying to insert Hatch?
7. How is Gradient different than Hatch?
8. How many different styles of Gradient Hatch are there available?
9. If you are not satisfied with the Gradient Hatch you put in, how can you change it without re-creating it?
10. For Gradient Hatch for a locally lit area, what technique can you use to get an improved appearance?

Exercises

1. Add to the drawing that you created through Tutorial 5 by using solid Hatch for the walls in the Plan View. Choose whichever color you desire. In addition, edit the view symbol to add solid hatch and add a view symbol for Elevation B. Change the coffee table from a rectangular shape to an elliptical shape.

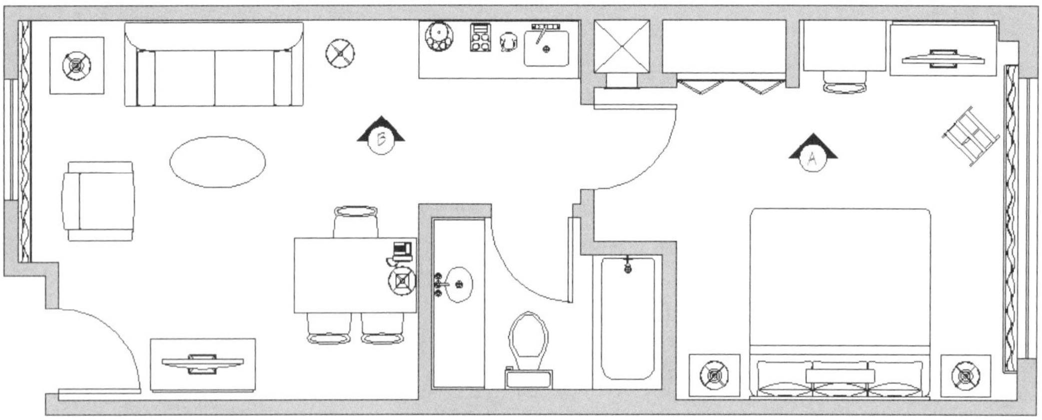

2. Download the Hotel Suite Living Room Elevation Blocks from the publisher's web site. Create Elevation B from the Plan View. Create a Layout tab for Elevation B. Set and lock the scale to a standard scale value. Complete the titleblock and annotate your drawing as desired. Note that the bar countertop overhangs 1" and a filler board is needed between the sink cabinet and the wall.

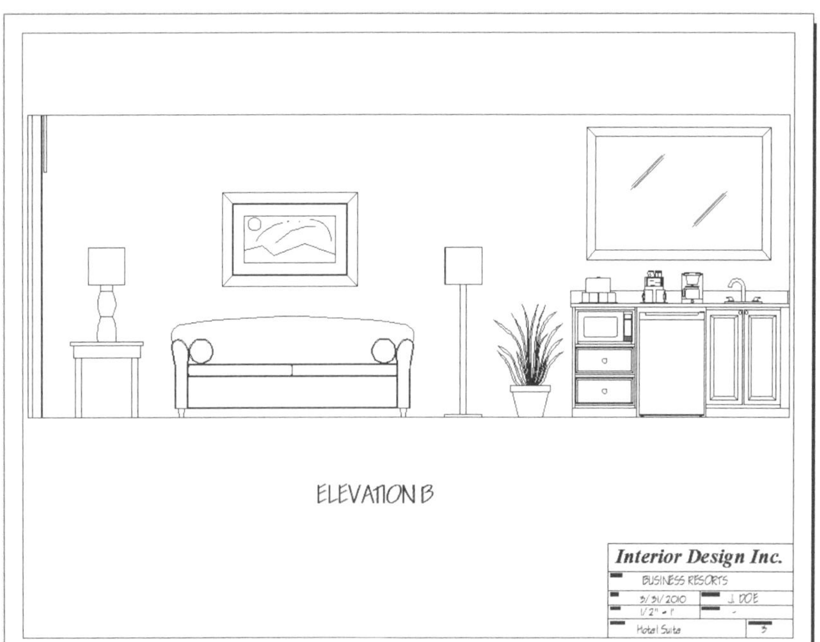

3. Create the Radiator Cover. Use NET3 style Hatch with a scale of 6 for the screen. Use a 3-point arc to create the curved top of each side.

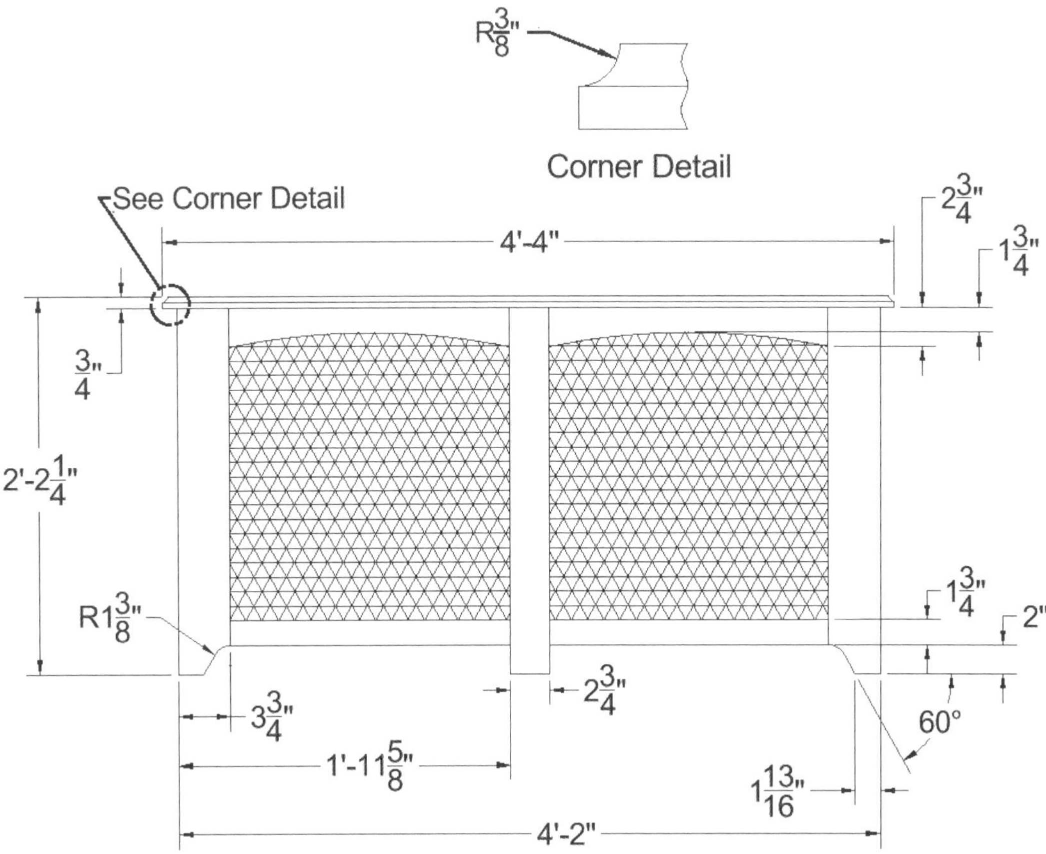

4. Create the cross-section of the radiator cover. The screen is 1/16" thick. Use Hatch and annotate your drawing as shown.

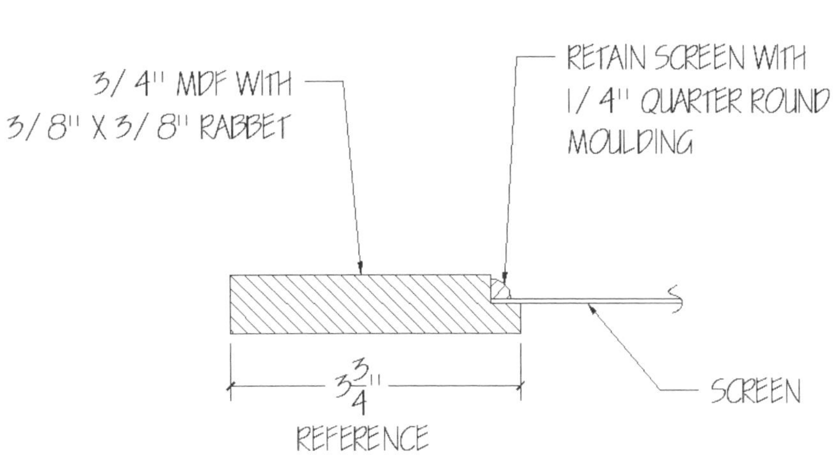

5. Create the wrought iron wall hanging. Use a Spline or Polyline to create one of the shaped ends. Use the Mirror command as well as the Array command to complete the design.

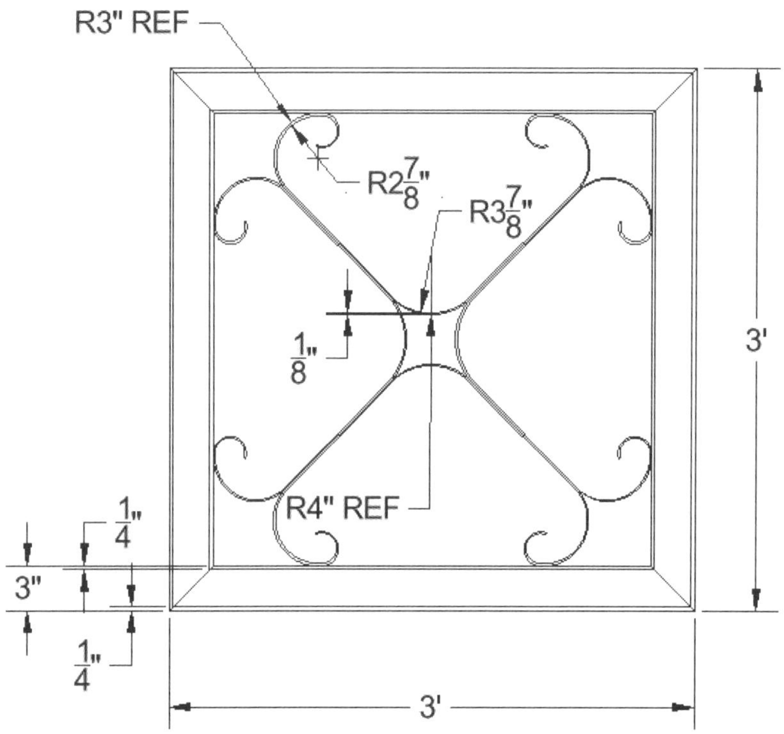

6. Render Elevation B by using both Hatch and Gradient Hatch.

7. Create the moulding detail that was shown as an example in this chapter.

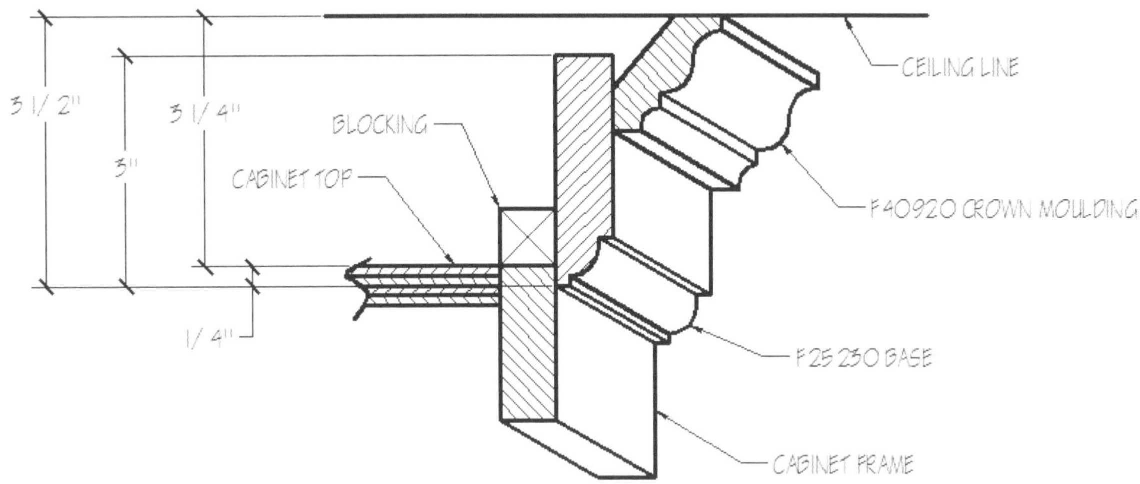

MOULDING DETAIL

The cabinet frame is 3/4" x 2" with 1/2" plywood top (each ply is drawn 1/8" thick). The Blocking is 3/4" x 3/4". Use the following dimensions for the crown moulding, and the base moulding:

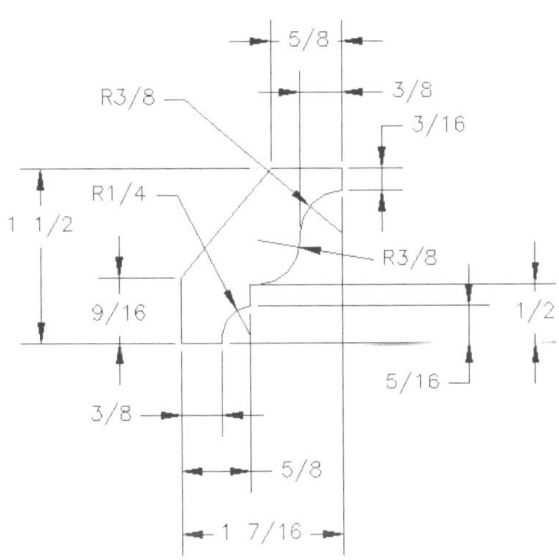

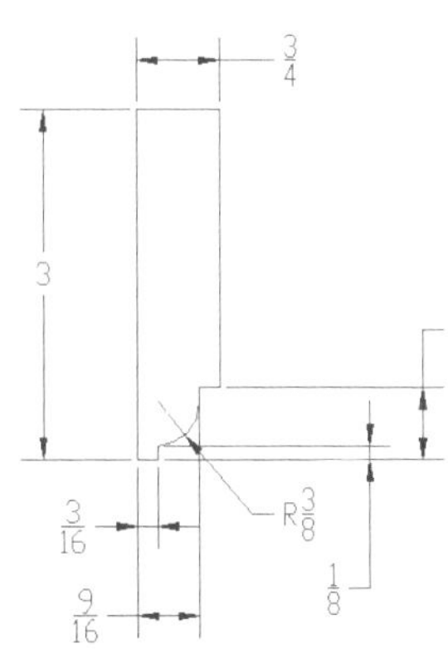

To create the appearance of 3D, draw 30º angled lines (use construction lines with angle -30º). Trim the construction lines a reasonable distance away. Copy the profile of the moulding to opposite end of the construction line. Trim the remaining lines as needed.

Chapter 15
Miscellaneous – Techniques, Commands, and Options

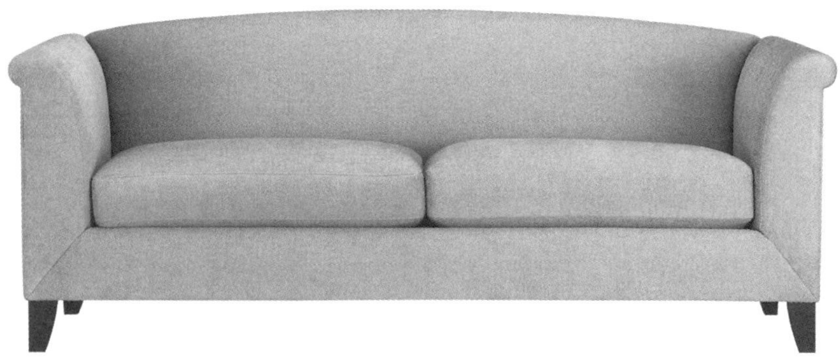

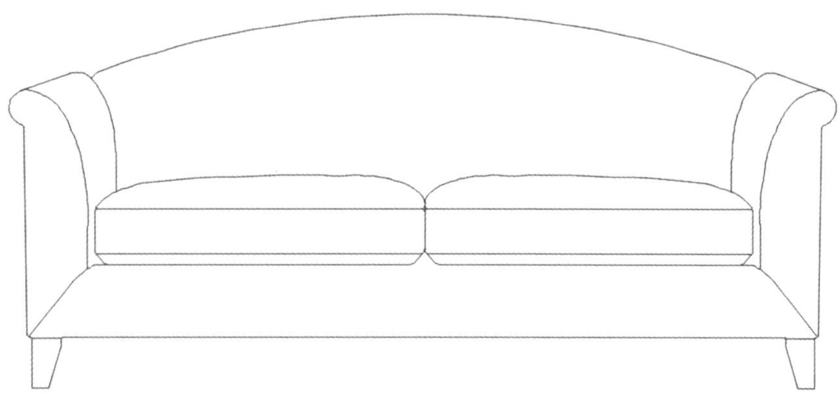

Learning Objectives:

- **Improve drawing techniques**
- **Use several new commands**
- **Explore additional command options**
- **Trace objects and correct the scale**
- **Customize User Interface**

Up to this point, we have learned enough of the AutoCAD program to be able to be productive and create our interior designs. This chapter provides some review of what we already know and consolidates them into helpful hints. In addition, there are some occasionally used commands that are explored, as well as some additional options for commands we have already learned. For the most part, you could get by without knowing the commands and options covered in this chapter and you would still be very productive. However, it is certainly worth exploring these since they can come in handy.

Helpful Hints

The following helpful hints summarize what you already know.

1. When you first begin a new drawing, make sure the units are properly set.

2. As you are about to start drawing, look at what you need to draw with an eye toward the best approach to drawing. Ask yourself if you should use lines, rectangles or construction lines.

3. AutoCAD offers multiple ways of doing the same thing. Icons, pull down menus, typing commands, and shortcuts are available. At first this can be confusing and overwhelming. Please do not let this discourage you. Use whichever method you are most comfortable with.

4. Try not to get overwhelmed by the X-Y coordinate system. Try to avoid it by using Construction Lines instead of Lines. Use the Line command when there are two specific points to snap the end points. Use the Offset and Trim commands to clean up the Construction Lines. The extra steps will go faster with more practice. In fact, you will likely get so fast that thinking of the exact X-Y value would take twice as long.

5. Any time you need to start a line or other object a specific distance away from another line, use the Offset command (or Construction Line/Offset) to find an intersection point. Use the Object Snap/Intersection setting to find your start point. After you are done, simply erase the construction line. This can also be done by using Circles for construction purposes and erasing them when you are done.

6. I find the Grid/Snap to be a hindrance; I do not use them and did not cover it in this text. Instead, I make extensive use of Object Snaps.

7. Use the Fillet command with a radius of zero to trim/extend lines simultaneously, such as a corner for an outside line for a wall.

8. When using a fly-out style icon, such as Measure Geometry (Distance), remember that the icon displayed was the last one used. So, if the last measurement made was Angle, and now you want to measure a Distance, move the cursor over the Angle fly-out icon, press and hold the left mouse button. The remaining icons "fly-out". While still holding the left mouse button, move your cursor down to the Distance icon and then release the left mouse button.

9. An alternate method of moving around the drawing instead of the Zoom or Pan command is to use the wheel on the mouse. Rolling the wheel forward and backward will Zoom in and out of the drawing. Pressing the wheel down and dragging will allow you to Pan around your drawing. For zooming the entire drawing, double-click the mouse wheel.

Finding the Center of a Rectangle

There are times when you need to locate the center of a rectangle. As an example, if you are creating a reflected ceiling plan, you may want to locate a fixture in the middle of the room. If you have a rectangular room, it is easy to find the center.

If you were drawing this by hand, you would likely draw two diagonal lines from corner to opposite corner to form an "X". The intersection of the lines would be the exact center of the rectangle.

With AutoCAD, you do not need to draw two lines. You can take advantage of the Snap to Midpoint feature and just draw one line between opposite corners. Of course, when you are done, simply erase the diagonal line.

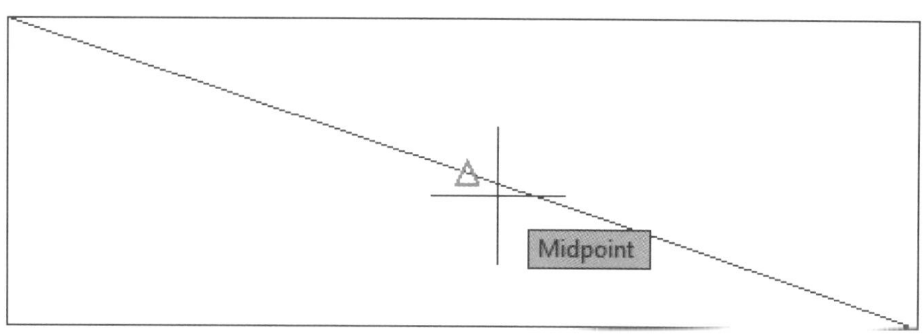

Divide

There are times when it is desired to divide an object into equal segments. Typically, this would be a line or a circle. However, AutoCAD will allow you to divide other objects as well. AutoCAD will divide the object in equal perimeter true distance.

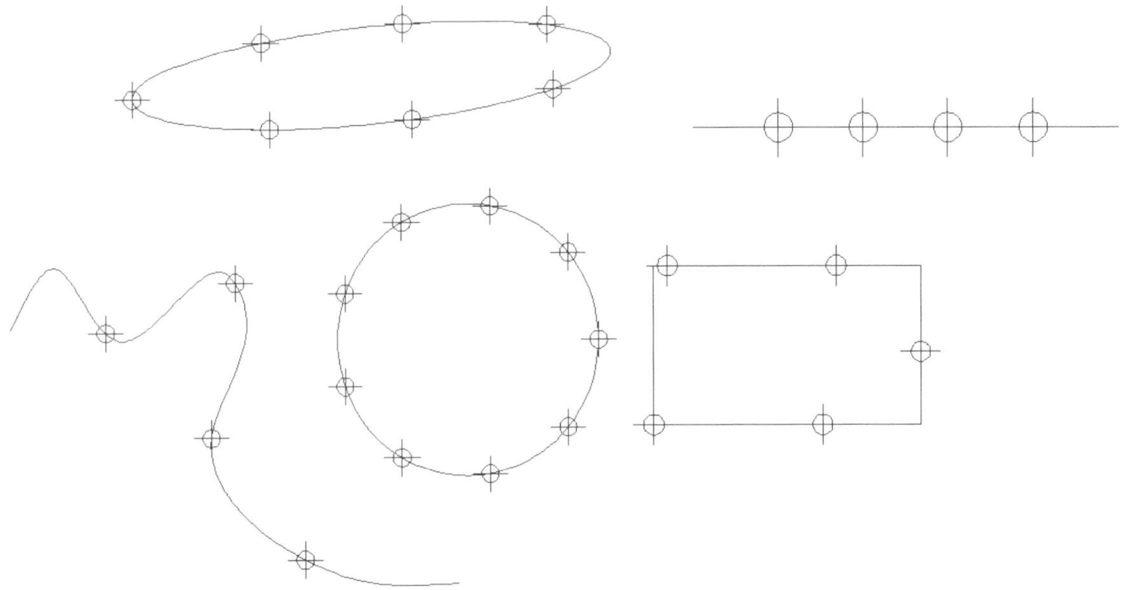

Before using the Divide command, set the Point Style. To set the Point Style, use the pull-down arrow to expand the Utilities Panel of the Home Tab and select Point Style. On the Mac, use the Format pull-down menu and select Point Style. The Point Style dialog box appears. Choose a style, set the desired size, and then pick OK.

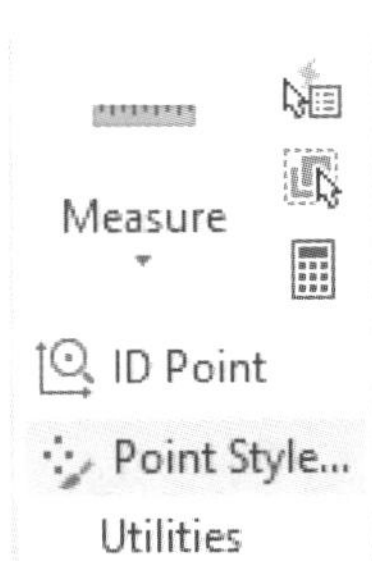

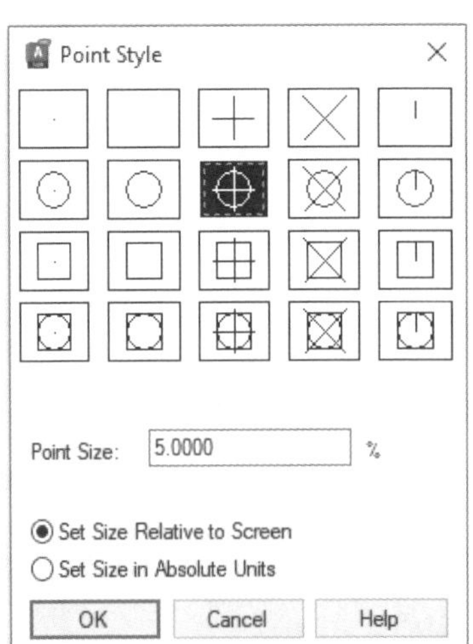

Mac

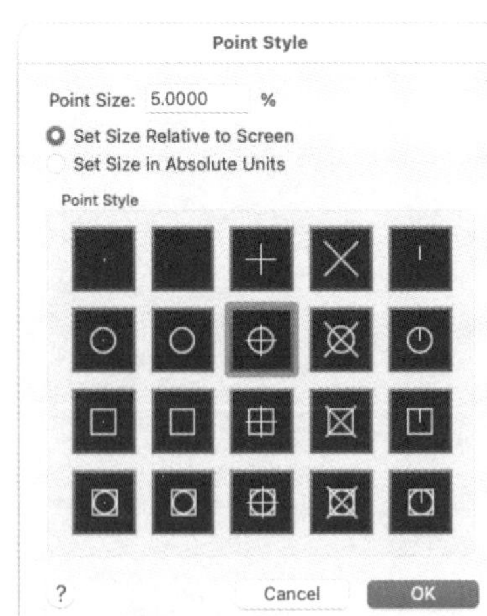

Procedure:

Type: **div↵** in the command line

The command line prompts you with the following:

DIVIDE *Select object to divide:* ***(Pick the object that you want to divide)***
Enter the number of segments or [Block]: **Type a number and then press the ↵ Enter key**

AutoCAD ends the command.

In order to snap to a point, set Snap to Node on. AutoCAD refers to points as nodes.

Try it:

After you set the Point Style using the Format pull-down menu, draw a line that is arbitrarily long at any angle on your screen:

Use the Divide command to divide the line into 5 equal segments. When you are done, your drawing will look like this:

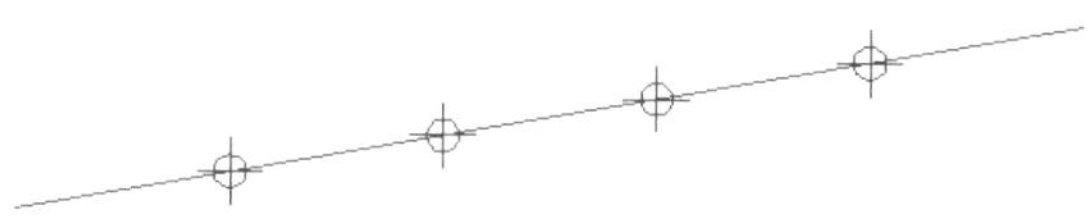

Let's draw vertical construction lines through the points that were just created. Make sure Snap to Node is selected in the Object Snap setting. Now use the Construction Line icon and choose the Vertical option. Pick each point for the vertical construction line to snap to. When you are done, your drawing will look like this:

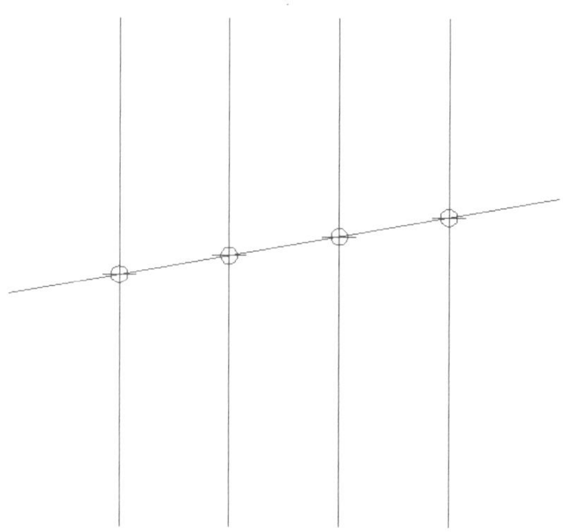

Break & Break at Point

There are times when it is desired to split a line, arc, etc. into two segments. This can be accomplished by using either the Break command or the Break at Point command. These are both located on the Modify Panel of the Home Tab.

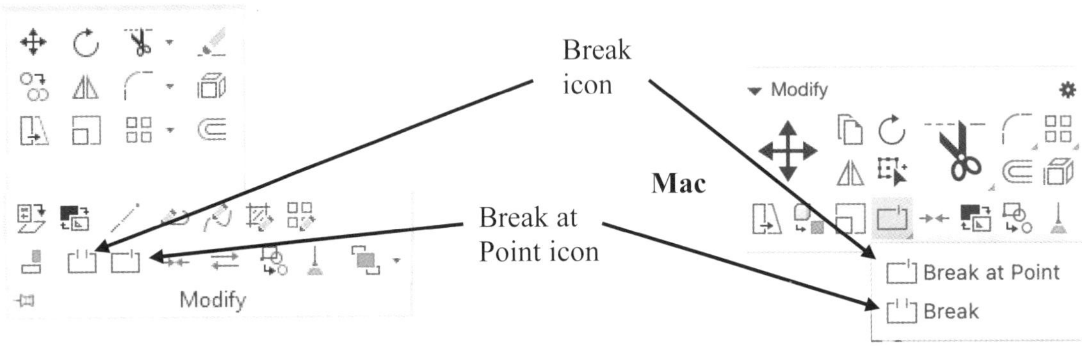

The Break command will break the object into two segments and trim away a portion of the object that you selected. The amount that is trimmed away is dependent on where the object was selected and the location picked for the break point.

Let's use a line as an example of the Break command.

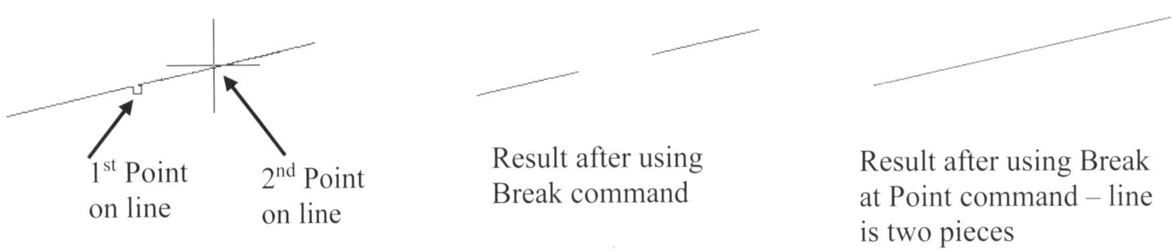

Procedure:

Pick (left click): **Break icon** [or **Break at Point icon**] from the Modify toolbar.

BREAK *Select object:* ***(Pick the line)***
Specify second break point or [First point]: ***(Pick a point on the line)***
AutoCAD ends the command.

The Break at Point command is the same as the Break command except AutoCAD automatically selects the First point option for you. This option means that the first point selected for the break will be defined by picking a location rather than the location at which the object was selected. The second point selected will automatically be chosen as the first point. The break will not be obvious because no gap will be shown. You can make the Break command work like the Break at Point command by typing "@" followed by the ↵ Enter key.

Polygon

When you need to create a multi-sided shape, such as a triangle (3 sides), hexagon (6 sides), octagon (8 sides), etc., AutoCAD provides an easy way to create it using the Polygon command. Multi-sided shapes are called polygons.

The Polygon command icon is found on the Draw Panel of the Home Tab. It is combined with the Rectangle icon and is accessed using the fly-out triangle. As with all fly-out type icons, whichever one was used last appears on the top.

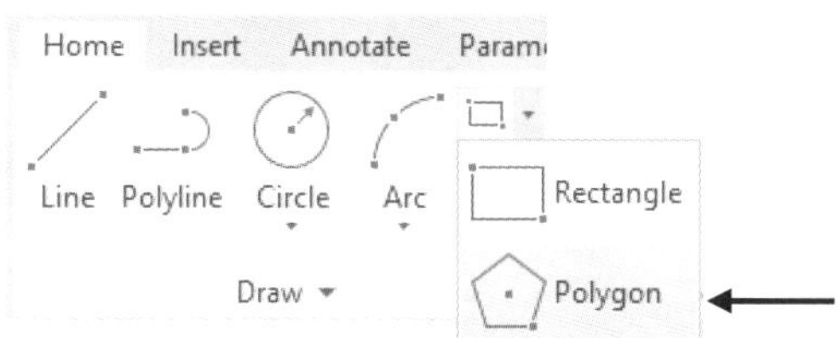

Mac

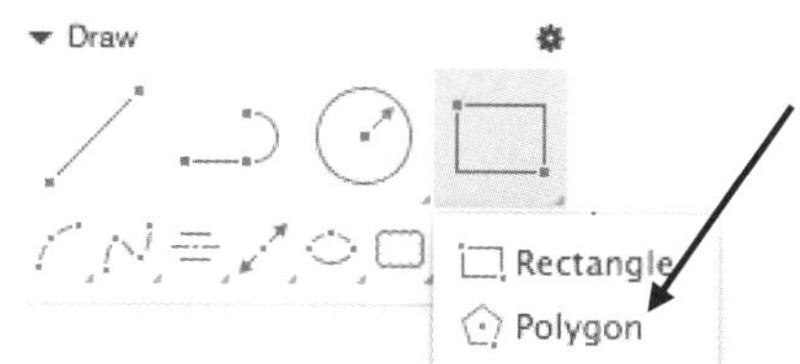

Polygon shapes have flat sides and sharp corners and are created around a circle. You can choose whether the polygon is "inscribed" or "circumscribed" around the circle. If the size of the polygon needs to fit inside the circle, you want an "inscribed" polygon. If it fits around the outside of the circle, you want a "circumscribed" polygon. One easy way to choose is if you know the distance to the flats, you want a circumscribed; and if you know the distance to the sharp corners, you want an inscribed. It may be easiest to draw the circle first and have Object Snap set to find the Center and Quadrant.

<u>Procedure:</u>

Pick (left-click): **Polygon icon** from the Draw Toolbar.

POLYGON *Enter number of sides <6>:* ***(Type the value for number of sides)*** **8↵**
Specify center of polygon or [Edge]: ***(Pick the center of the circle) (or pick anywhere on screen)***
Enter an option [Inscribed in circle Circumscribed about circle] <I>: **C↵**
Specify radius of circle: ***(Pick a quadrant of the circle) (or type the value for the radius)***

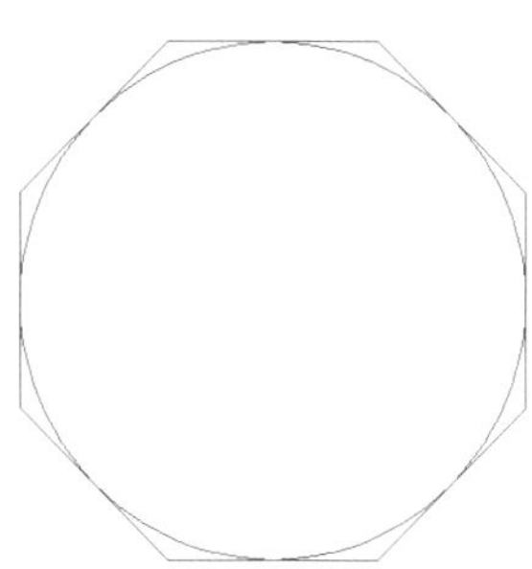

After the quadrant is selected (or radius value given), the polygon is drawn and the command ends.

Stretch

You can change the shape of an object by using the Stretch command. You can make several objects longer or shorter in one direction. An example would be if you wanted to modify the size of a room. This could be handled using the Move command and then trimming/extending the remaining objects to match. You need to exercise caution when using stretch because the objects could easily become distorted. It is important to have set up the base and target points to stretch from and to. The icon is on the Modify Panel of the Home Tab.

Mac

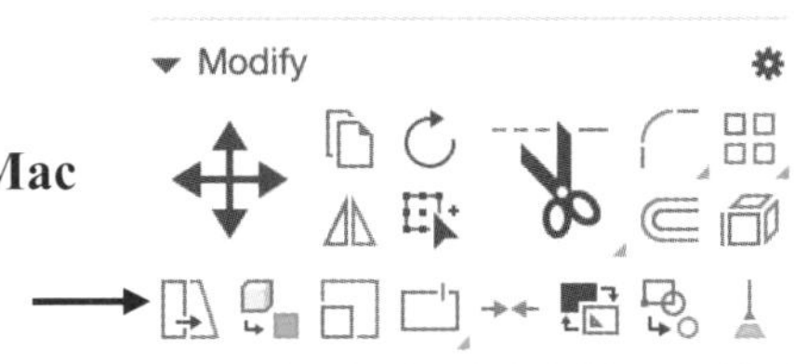

Example:

Below is an 8′ x 10′ room. The client desires to change the 8′ direction to 12′.

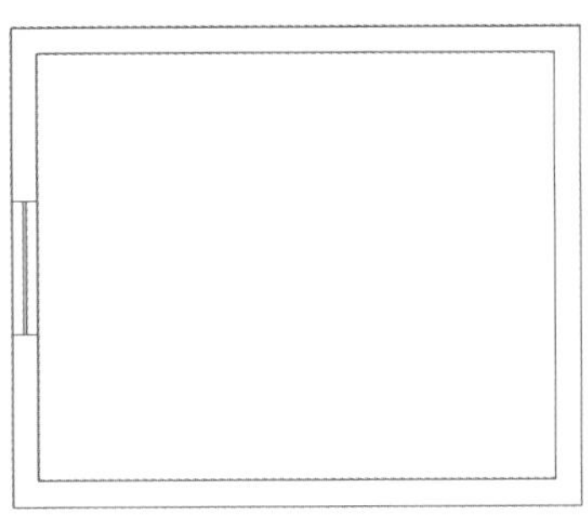

8′

10′

Existing Room

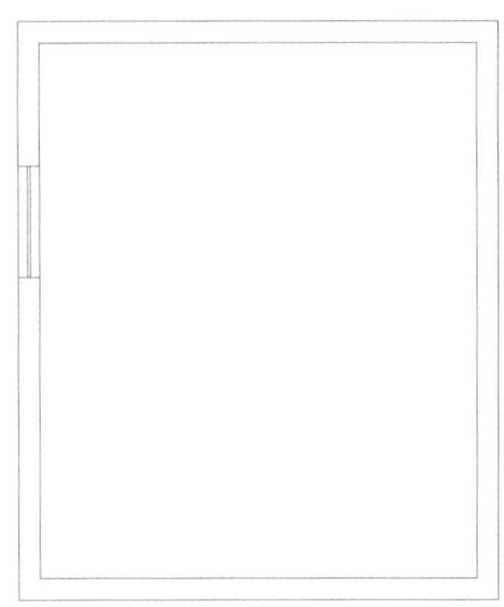

12′

10′

Desired Room

In order to use the Stretch command, offset the top horizontal line 4′ down. This will allow us to use Snap to Endpoint for the base and target points.

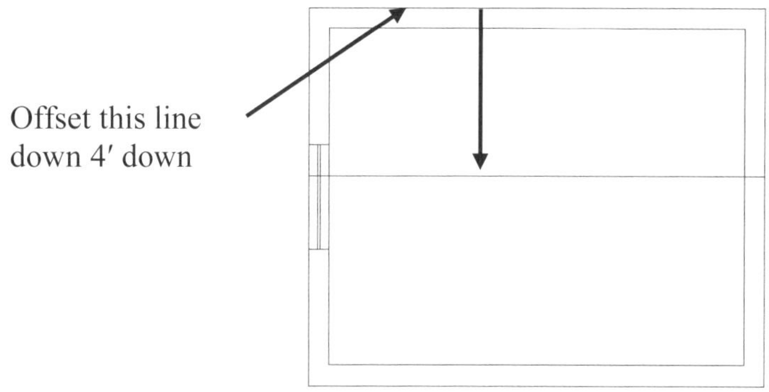

Procedure:

Pick (left click): **Stretch icon** from the Modify Panel of the Home Tab.

STRETCH *Select Objects:*
Use a crossing window to select the 4 vertical lines and the bottom horizontal lines:

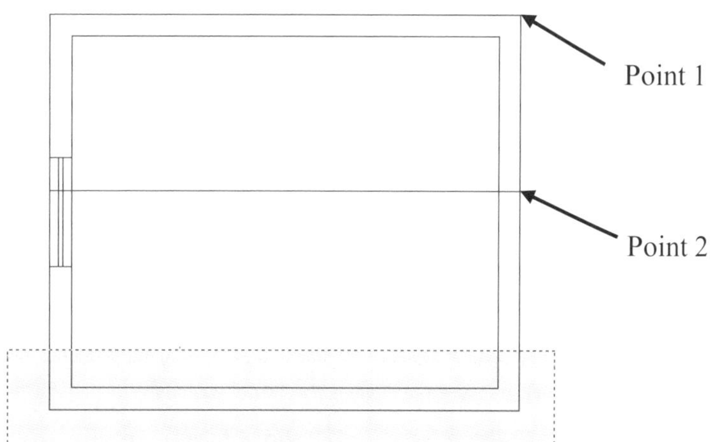

Since no more objects are to be selected, press the ↵ Enter key. This will bring us to the second part of the command.

Specify base point or [Displacement] <Displacement>: ***(Pick Point 1)***
Specify second point or <use first point as displacement>: ***(Pick Point 2)***

The result of the Stretch command looks like this:

Without good base and target points, the room could end up distorted:

It is because of this that you need to exercise caution and set things up first to avoid having this happen.

Scale

The Scale command allows you to change the size of the selected object in both directions. The object can either be enlarged or reduced depending on the scale factor you key in. If the scale factor is greater than 1, the object will be enlarged. If it is less than 1, it will be reduced.

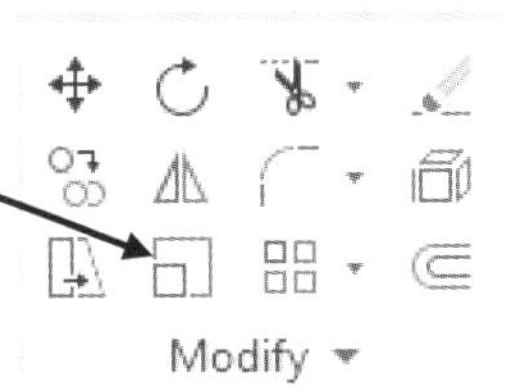

Mac

Example:

Let's enlarge a 1′ radius circle. We want the circle to be twice as big as it is, so the scale factor will be 2.

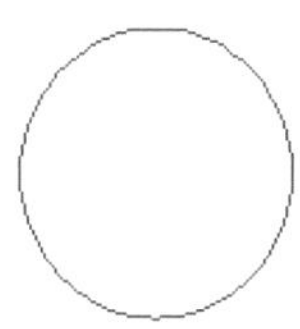

Procedure:

Pick (left click): **Scale icon** from the Modify toolbar.

SCALE *Select objects.* ***(Pick the circle)*** *1 found*
Select objects: ↵
Specify base point: ***(Pick the center of the circle)***
Specify scale factor or [Copy/Reference]: **2**↵

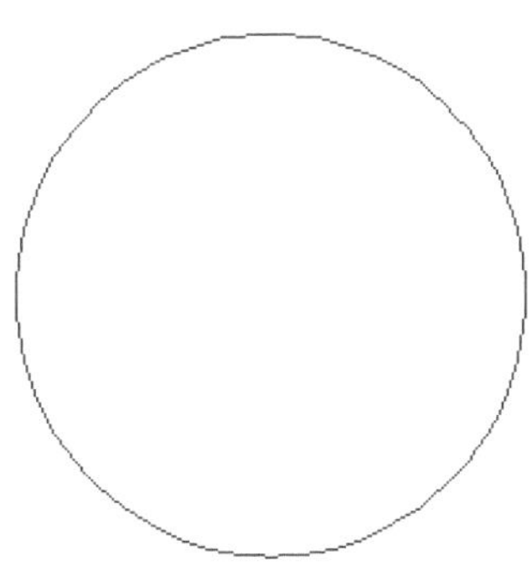

The result is a circle with a 2′ radius (2 x 1′ = 2′)

Reference Option

This option allows you to key in the final size you want and uses existing measurements to automatically calculate the scale factor for you.

Example:

Change the size of the 2′5-1/4" square to 3′x3′.

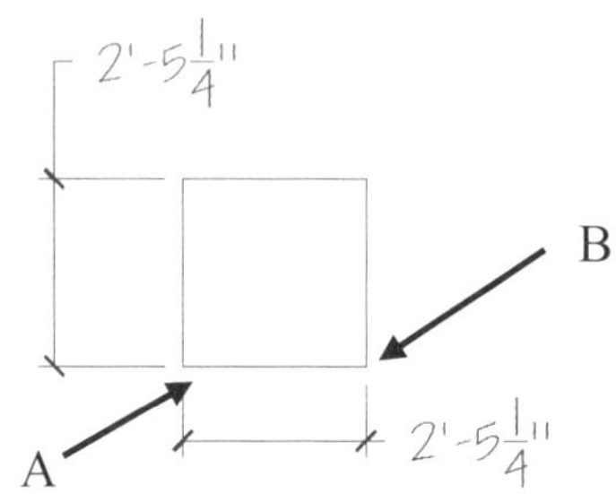

Procedure:

Pick (left click): **Scale icon** from the Modify toolbar.

SCALE *Select objects:* ***(Pick the square)*** *1 found*
Select objects: ↵
Specify base point: ***(Pick point "A")***
Specify scale factor or [Copy/Reference]: **r**↵
Specify reference length <0'-1">: ***(Pick point "A")*** *Specify second point:* ***(Pick point "B")***
Specify new length or [Points] <0'-1">: **3′**↵

The square has now changed to the size that you want.

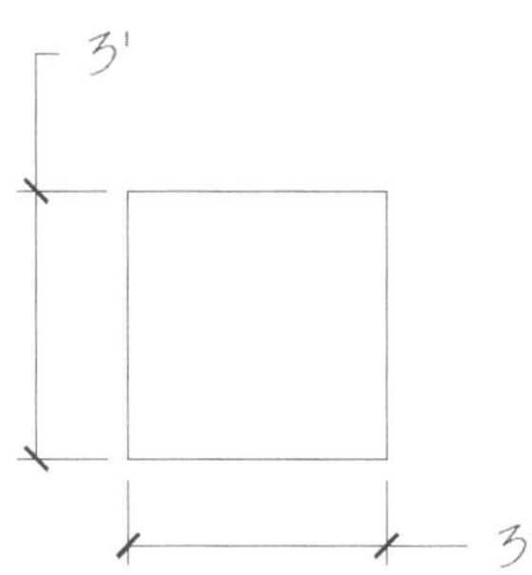

Cut (or Copy)/Paste – Using the Clipboard

Changing Objects from Model Space to Paper Space

You can easily move an object that you created in Model Space to Paper Space by using a cutting and pasting technique. For example, let's say you have created the Titleblock, in Model Space, shown below:

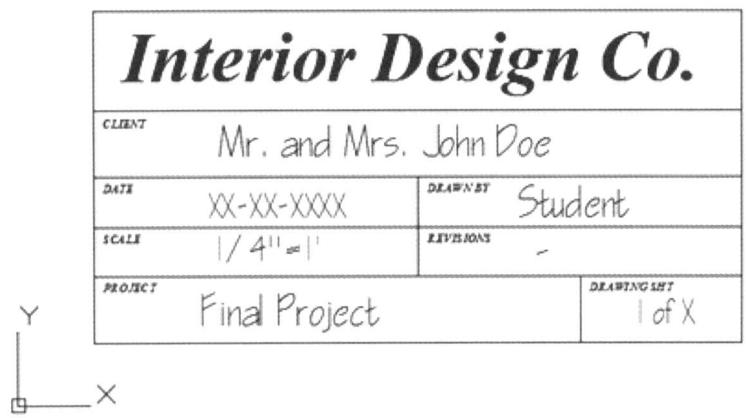

In order to get it out of model space and into paper space, use the following instructions:

Procedure:

1. Pick the Cut icon from the Clipboard Panel of the Home Tab. On the Mac, use the Edit pull-down menu and select Cut. Use a Selection Window (or a Crossing Window) to select all the objects. Press the ↵ Enter key.

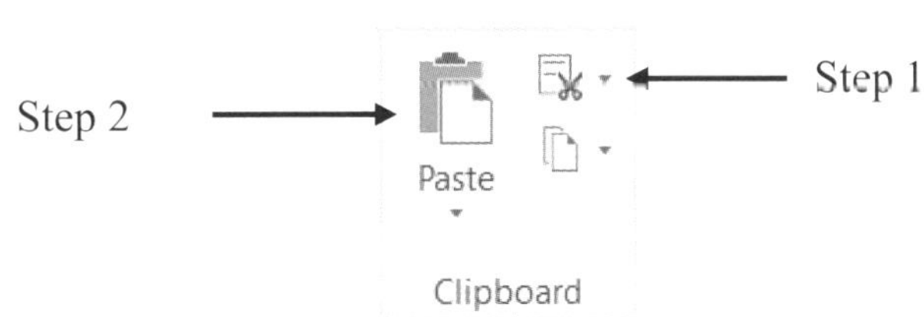

2. Pick one of the Layout tabs.

3. Pick the Paste icon from the Clipboard Panel of the Home Tab. On the Mac, use the Edit pull-down menu and select Paste.

4. An image of the Titleblock will follow your cursor. Pick on the screen to finish pasting the Titleblock in Paper Space.

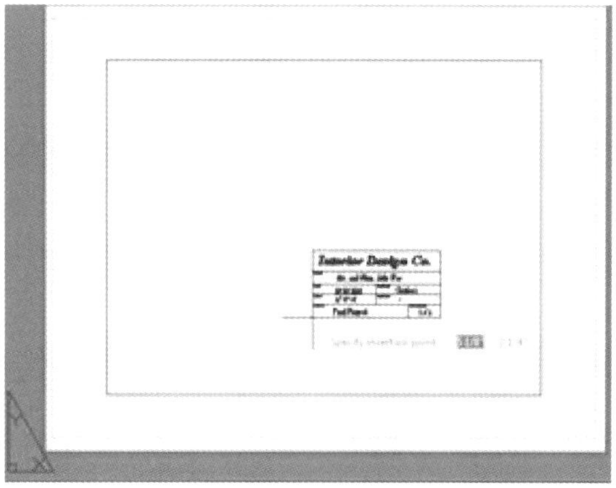

Now that the Titleblock is a Paper Space object, use the move command to re-locate it on your layout.

This same cut/paste or copy/paste technique can also be used when you want objects from another drawing that are not already defined as blocks to be brought into your drawing. You must have both drawings open to do this. Mac users: use the pull-down menu Window to switch between drawings. PC users: use the Switch Windows icon on the User Interface Panel of the View Tab to toggle between open drawings.

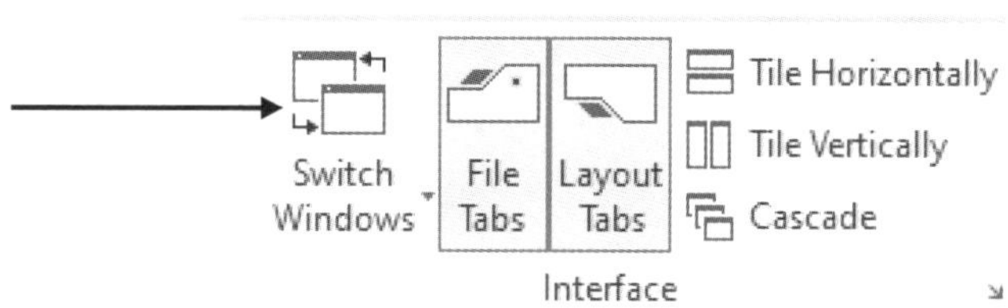

Tracing Pictures

There are times when certain pieces of furniture, such as upholstered furniture, would be needed on your drawing. Since these typically have many curves, it is difficult to simply measure and draw using lines and trimming, etc.

One technique that can be used is to cut/paste a digital picture into the AutoCAD drawing screen. You can use a photograph of the furniture or you could cut a picture from an internet catalog. It is best to get a picture looking straight on at the furniture instead of at an angle.

The following example uses a picture of a sofa cut from the internet:

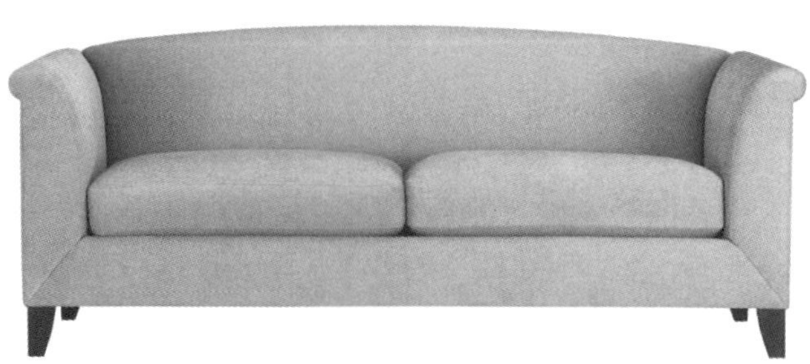

Procedure:

1. Find a picture on the internet that you want to trace. For this example, we will use the sofa.
2. Right-click on the picture in the advertisement and save it as a picture. Open the picture and select Copy to copy the image. This will copy the picture of the sofa onto the clipboard.
3. Switch from the internet browser to AutoCAD.
4. Use the Paste icon from the Clipboard Panel of the Home Tab. On the Mac, use the Edit pull-down menu and select Paste.
5. A rectangular shape will follow your cursor. Pick a location on the drawing screen to paste the picture into your drawing. Press the ↵ Enter key to accept the default scale and again to accept the default angle. The image of the sofa, with a rectangle outlining the boundary of the image, will appear.

Now that we have an image of the sofa on our drawing, we can trace it. It is a good idea to create a new layer for our tracing so that we can turn the image on and off to monitor our tracing progress. In addition, we can also use a contrasting color and a thick lineweight.

Let's start with some easy shapes to trace first, such as straight-lines sections like the legs.

6. Use the Zoom command to zoom in on a leg. Pick the Line command and insert lines to trace the shape of the leg.

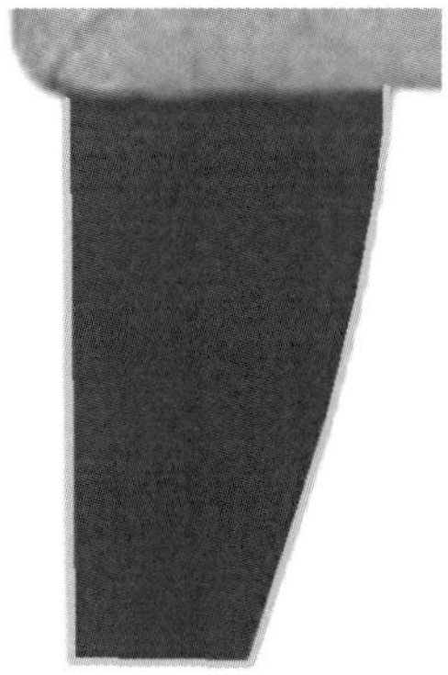

A contrasting color, thick line is used to trace the outline of the leg. Zoom in to get as close as possible for a more accurate trace. Use the wheel mouse to zoom in and out and pan to different locations.

Continue tracing the straight-line sections in a similar manner. For the curved shapes, we can use splines.

7. Zoom in on a curved shape and pick the Spline command to insert a spline.

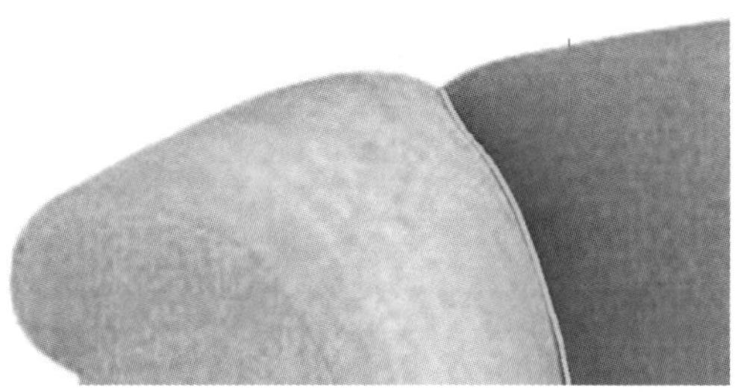

Continue tracing the curved shapes in a similar manner. For certain curves that are meant to be arcs, you can use the Circle or Arc commands instead of the Spline command. An arc may be most appropriate to use for the back of the sofa. It is your choice.

8. Turn off the layer that had the image pasted to it. What remains is the tracing that you just completed. If you notice any areas you may have missed, you can turn the layer back on and finish the tracing. Be sure to turn the image layer back off when done making corrections.

When you are done, your drawing will look like this:

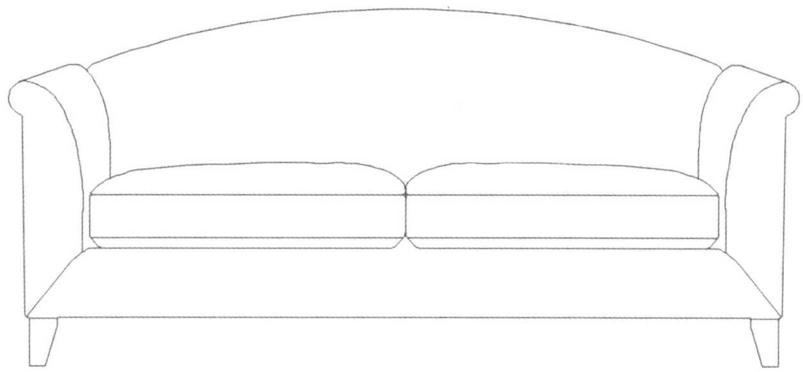

As a pictorial representation of the sofa, the tracing looks great! However, since we are very concerned about proper size, we will need to adjust the size of the tracing using the Scale command.

Measure the height and width of the sofa and compare those dimensions to the advertised size. The advertised dimensions for this sofa are 80"W x 35" H.

The measured values for our tracing are not what we want. It will vary depending on how large the image was when you pasted it to your drawing. My measurements are 154′11-3/8" W x 62′3-11/16"H:

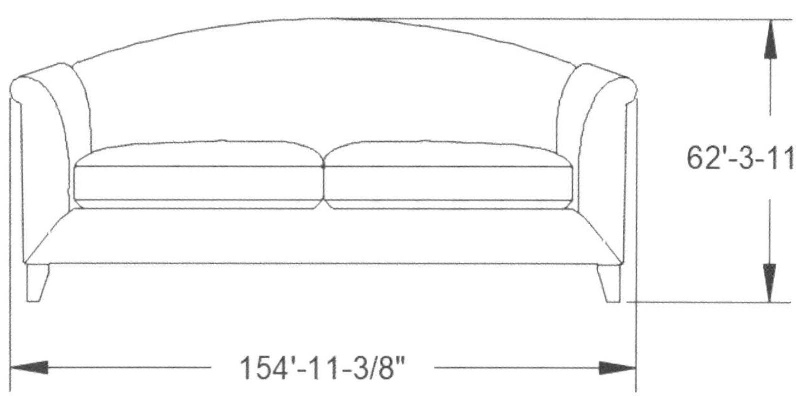

9. To correct for the width, use the Reference option of the Scale command described earlier in this chapter.

After we scale this, the new dimensions are now 80"W x 32-3/16"H. It does not measure to the exact height we wanted because the picture was taken at a slight angle.

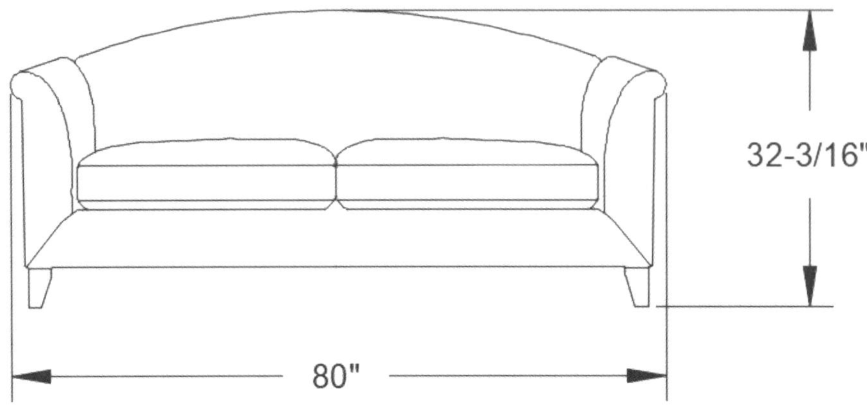

To correct for the 2-13/16" height difference, we need to be a little creative. We can use the Stretch command and change the height in sections that will not be too noticeable. We can share the distance in two areas by making the cushions a little thicker and the legs a little longer. If we make the legs 1-1/4" longer, then we would need to make the cushions 1-9/16" thicker (2-13/16" - 1-1/4" = 1-9/16"). Let's try this combination and see what the results look like.

10. Draw a vertical and horizontal construction line on the drawing. These can be anywhere on your drawing. Offset the horizontal construction line 1-14". We will use the intersections for our stretch distance and direction.

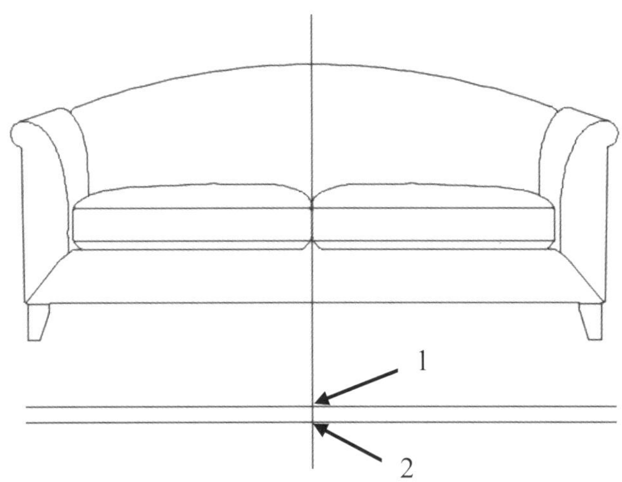

11. Pick the Stretch command and use a Crossing Window to select the legs. Pick intersection 1 as the Base "from" point and location 2 as the "to" point.
12. Erase one of the horizontal construction lines. Offset the remaining horizontal construction line 1-9/16".
13. Pick the Stretch command and use a Crossing Window to select the lower section of the sofa thru the mid-section of the cushions. Pick intersection 1 as the Base "from" point and location 2 as the "to" point.

When we are done, the sofa will now be the correct dimensions. The increased leg and cushion heights are not too noticeable. If you don't like the look of thicker cushions, try stretching other portions instead. The key is to get the correct height and be satisfied with the look.

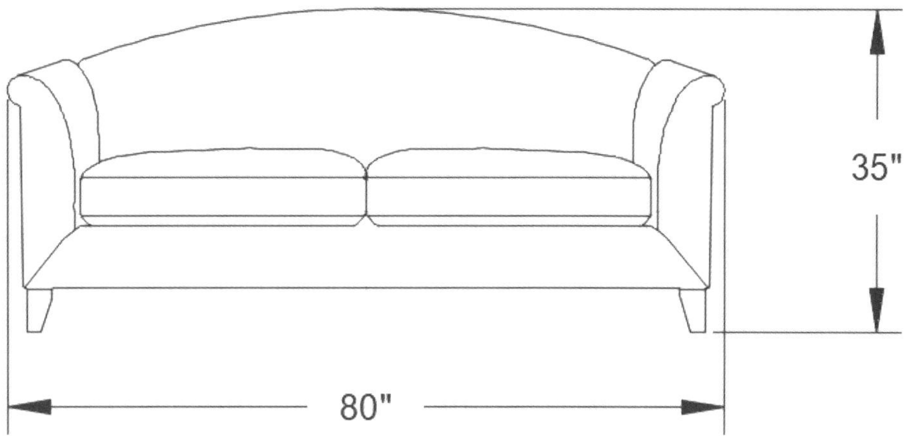

Circle Options

In Chapter 2, we learned the basic concept of the Circle command. We were able to define the circle by specifying the center point and either the radius or diameter. This is not the only way to create a circle.

AutoCAD offers many options of specifying a circle. These options are shown in the square brackets of the circle command prompt: *[3P/2P/Ttr (tan tan radius)].* The following describes each of those options.

Define the Circle with 3 points

This option allows you to define a circle using 3 points that lie on the circumference of the circle.

To use this option after selecting the Circle icon, type **3p↵**

CIRCLE *Specify center point for circle or [3P/2P/Ttr (tan tan radius)]:* **3p↵**

The command line prompts you to specify the points on the circle:

Specify first point on circle: **(Pick a point on the screen)**
Specify second point on circle: **(Pick a point on the screen)**
Specify third point on circle: **(Pick a point on the screen)**

This can come in very handy for a situation where you want a circle (or an arc after trimming the circle) to be between 3 lines and you don't know (or care) what the diameter of the circle will be. Use Snap to Tangent as you pick each of the three lines.

Example:

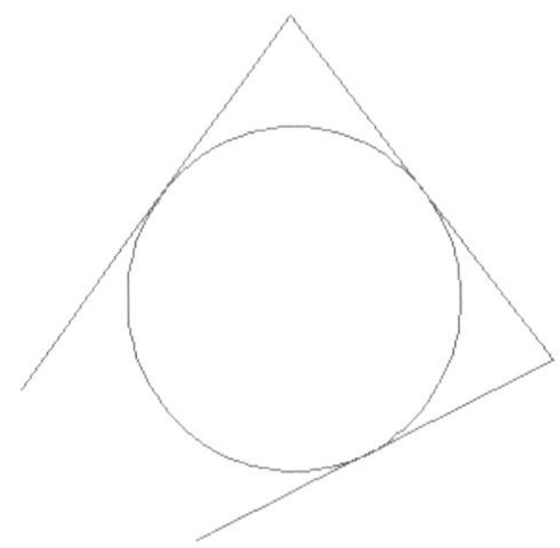

Using the 3-point option for creating a circle comes in handy when you want a circle to be nested between three lines. You must use Snap to Tangent when selecting the lines.

Define the Circle with 2 points

This option allows you to define a circle by using 2 points that define the endpoints of the diameter of the circle.

To use this option after selecting the Circle icon, type **2p↵**

CIRCLE *Specify center point for circle or [3P/2P/Ttr (tan tan radius)]:* **2p↵**

The command line prompts you to specify the points on the circle:

Specify first end point of circle's diameter: **(Pick a point on the screen)**
Specify second end point of circle's diameter: **(Pick a point on the screen)**

This could be useful in a situation such as drawing piping on an upholstered chair or a full bullnose for the edge of a countertop. After drawing the circle, it can be trimmed and you would now have a semi-circle.

Example:

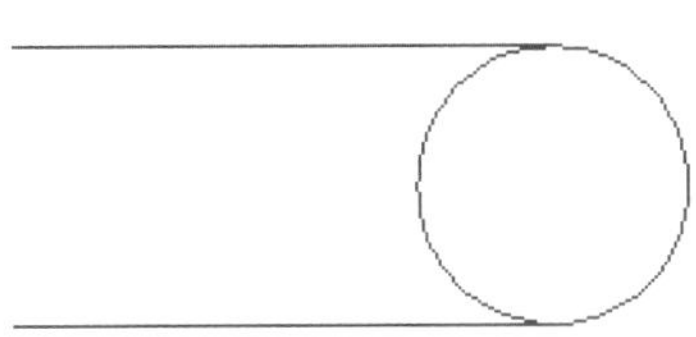

2-point circle drawn using the endpoints of two parallel lines

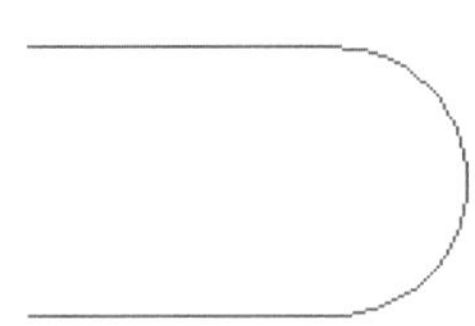

The same 2-point circle can be trimmed resulting in a semi-circle

Tan Tan Radius

This option allows you to define a circle that is tangent to two objects of a specific radius. The two objects can be circles, arcs, lines, or combinations of two of these object types. The radius specified must be large enough to be tangent to the two objects.

To use this option you must already have two objects that you plan to have the circle be tangent to. After selecting the Circle icon, type **t↵**

CIRCLE *Specify center point for circle or [3P/2P/Ttr (tan tan radius)]:* **t↵**

Specify point on object for first tangent of circle: **(Pick one of the objects)**
Specify point on object for second tangent of circle: **(Pick the second object)**
Specify radius of circle: **1↵**
If the radius that you specify is smaller than is physically possible to also be tangent to the two objects, AutoCAD will provide you with the following message in the command line and end the circle command:

Circle does not exist.

This can come in handy when you want to draw circles between two arcs/circles, or lines/circles, etc.

Example:

Varying diameter round objects, such as oranges, in a glass container: These make contact with each other or the container at two points.

Rectangle Options

In Chapter 3, we learned the basic concept of the Rectangle command. We were able to define the rectangle by specifying one corner point, specifying the distance in both the horizontal and vertical directions, and the location of the opposite corner. This method provided a rectangle with square corners.

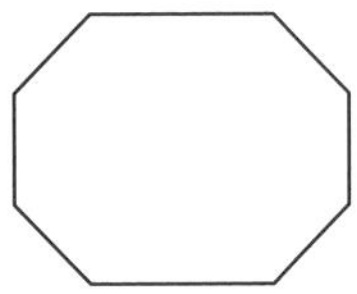

Chamfered corner rectangle

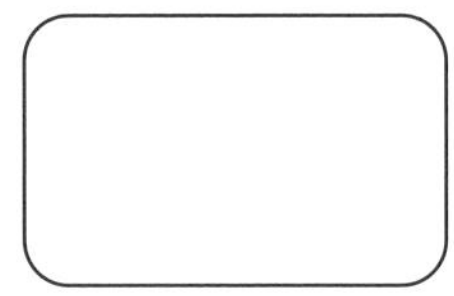

Filleted corner rectangle

Chamfered Corner Rectangle

For rectangles with chamfered corners:
Specify first corner point or [Chamfer/Elevation/Fillet/Thickness/Width]:

Type "**c**" and then press the ↵ Enter key.

Specify first chamfer distance for rectangles <X'-X">:

Type in the chamfer value then press the ↵ Enter key.

Specify second chamfer distance for rectangles <X'-X">:

Type in the chamfer value then press the ↵ Enter key. Note that both first and second values should be the same for a 45° chamfer.

After the chamfer values have been keyed in, AutoCAD prompts for the location of the corner points of the rectangle as described before.

Filleted Corner Rectangle

For rectangles with filleted corners:

Specify fillet radius for rectangles <X'-X">:

Type in the fillet radius value then press the enter key.

After the fillet value has been keyed in, AutoCAD prompts for the location of the corner points of the rectangle as described before.

Offset Options

In Chapter 3, we learned the basic concept of the Offset command. We were able to offset lines, circles, or rectangles by specifying a distance first, and then selecting the object and direction to offset. This method is most commonly used because you usually know the distance you desire to offset. In some instances, you may wish to offset to a specific location without knowing the distance.

AutoCAD Calculates Distance

You can specify a distance by picking two points on the drawing. AutoCAD will automatically calculate the distance between points and will use that value for the offset distance. The points chosen can be any arbitrary points, snapping to grid points, or snapping to specific parts of objects (such as endpoints of a line).

After picking the first point, the command line prompts you with the following:

Specify offset distance or [Through] <X'-XX>: Specify second point:

After you pick the second point the remainder of the prompts are the same as what you learned in Chapter 3.

Through Option

Use this option if you don't know the distance you plan to offset. First, the object is selected, and then the distance is defined by picking in the drawing. Typically, you would choose an end point or intersection, or some specific location for the offset value.

Specify offset distance or [Through/Erase/Layer] <Through>: **t↵**
Select object to offset or <exit>:
Specify through point:
You can select a through point or move your cursor in the direction you want to offset and key in a value for a distance to offset.

AutoCAD will continue to prompt for more objects to offset:
Select object to offset or <exit>:

To exit the command, press the ↵ Enter key or press the Esc key.

Drafting Settings

We have only taken advantage of a few Drafting Setting features: Object Snap and Show/Hide Lineweights. There are other settings that you may have a preference to use. A very brief description of some of these will be given here. Since you already know about Object Snap, it will not be described here. If you are interested in exploring these, or others, any further, the best way is to try them and to also check the Help menu.

Access to Drafting Settings is obtained by using the toggle icons on the Status Bar.

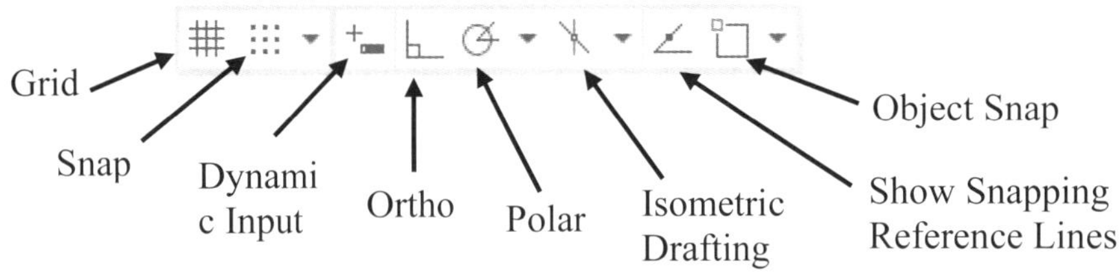

Changing any settings for any of the drafting features is accomplished by bringing up the Drafting Settings dialog box. This is accomplished by using the pull-down arrow of Snap, Polar, or Object Snap, and selecting Settings. For example, the pull-down arrow for Snap will show the following:

After right-clicking a toggle icon, select Settings…

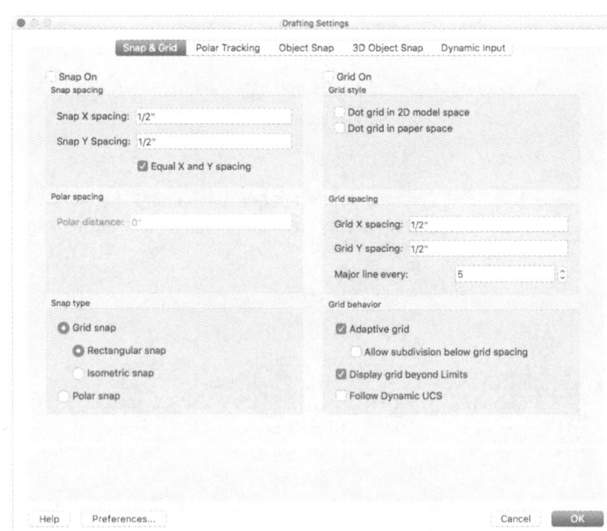

Mac

There are several tabs across the top of the dialog box. Use these to change settings.

Snap and Grid

You can use a grid and allow your cursor to snap to the grid when you make your drawing. The grid and snap settings are to the nearest increment that you choose. One reason for not using it is because real-world dimensions never fall exactly on a grid. However, it may come in handy to use as a guide for furniture placement. The best way to get familiar with the grid and snap feature is to try it.

Ortho and Polar

Ortho restricts you to horizontal (0°) and vertical (90°) directions only. This could be used on occasion when you prefer to insert a line instead of a construction line for either a horizontal or vertical direction.

Polar is similar to Ortho except it allows you to have more than 0° and 90° increments.

Try it:

Draw a 2′ x 4′ rectangle using the Line command with the Ortho and Polar buttons turned on.

Pick the first point of the line and move the cursor to the right. The line will be drawn and held in a horizontal orientation. The dynamic input will display how long the line is while you are drawing. Simply type 4′ followed by the ↵ Enter key, and it will automatically set the length of the horizontal line to 4′.

Next, move the cursor upward and a second line will be drawn and held in a vertical orientation. Again, the dynamic input will display how long the line is while you are drawing. Simply type 2′ followed by the ↵ Enter key, and it will automatically set the length of the vertical line to 2′.

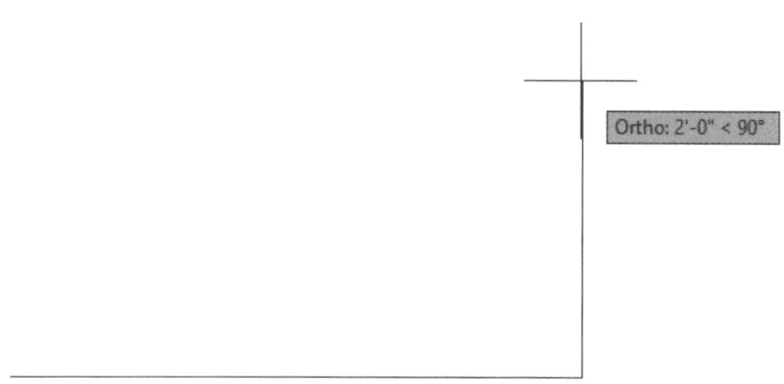

Continue this way but close the last point by selecting the end point of the first line. When you are done, you will have the 2′ x 4′ rectangle.

Super Hatch

The Super Hatch command allows you to create your own "hatch" pattern. Although it will appear as a hatch, AutoCAD will recognize it as a block. The Super Hatch command can be found on the Express Tools tab of the Ribbon. On the Mac it can be found on the Hatch Panel.

Procedure:

Pick (left click): **Super Hatch icon** from the Draw panel of the Express Tools Tab.

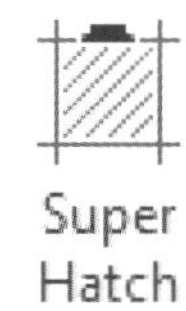

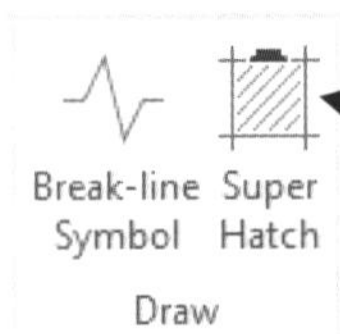

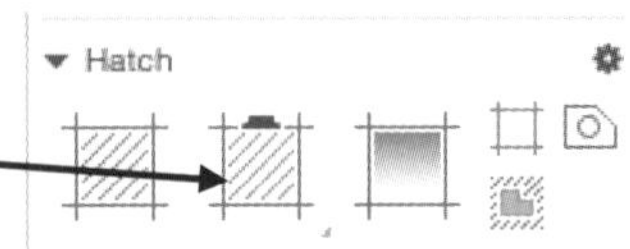

Mac

On the PC a SuperHatch dialog box will appear. Several Pattern Type options are available. This text will cover the Block option. For the Mac, the SuperHatch icon is a Fly-out. The options can be chosen using the Fly-out.

Mac

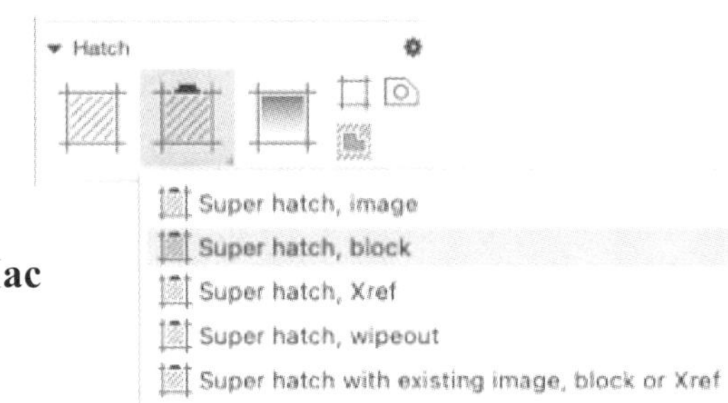

To use the Super Hatch with the block option, a block must already exist. If one does not exist, then you should create it first. For this example, a block of a heart shape was used. The boundary used was a simple rectangle.

Pick the Block option. A SuperHatch Insert dialog box will appear:

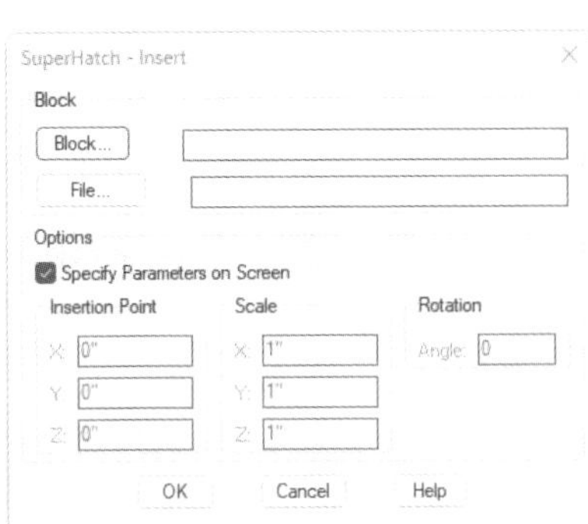

Mac

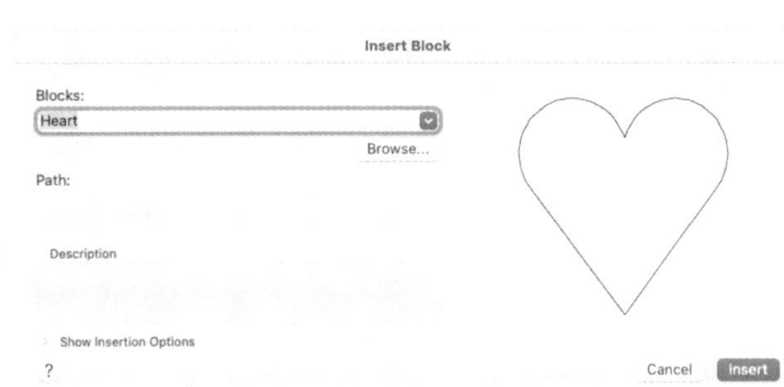

Under the Block section of the dialog box, an existing block may already be showing. If this is not the block you want, or if no block is showing, pick the Block button (pull-down arrow on Mac). On the PC, the Defined Blocks dialog box will appear with a list of all the blocks currently available in the drawing. On the Mac, the existing blocks will appear as soon as you pick on the pull-down arrow.

In this example, the Heart Block was selected

Pick the block that you want and then pick the OK button. The selected block name will now appear in the SuperHatch Insert dialog box. Leave the option to Specify Parameters on Screen checked and pick the OK button (Insert Button on the Mac) to exit the dialog box.

The command line prompts you with the following:

Command: _superhatch HEART
Units: Inches Conversion: 0'-1"
Specify insertion point or [Basepoint/Scale/X/Y/Z/Rotate/Explode/REpeat]:

Pick a point inside your hatch boundary

> The location of the insertion point you pick determines the starting point for the pattern.

Enter X scale factor, specify opposite corner, or [Corner/XYZ] <1>: ↵
Enter Y scale factor <use X scale factor>: ↵
Specify rotation angle <0>: ↵

Is the placement of this BLOCK acceptable? {Yes/No] <Yes>: ↵
Select a window around the block to define column and row tile distances.
Current rectangle modes: Width=0'-7 3/16"
Specify block [Extents] First corner <magenta rectang>: ↵
Current rectangle modes: Width=0'-7 3/16"
Selecting visible objects for boundary detection...Done.
Specify an option [Advanced options] <Internal point>:

> Accept all the default options

Pick a point inside your hatch boundary

The hatch boundary will be highlighted after you pick a point inside it.

Press the **Enter ↵ key** to accept the boundary and complete the command.

The selected boundary will fill with the Super Hatch of the Heart Block:

This command works well with a simple boundary. However, when a boundary has islands inside it that the hatch must work around, the result may be less than desired.

Overkill

There are occasions when you have a line overlapping another line and you want to delete the extra line. Although hard to detect on your screen, the section that is overlapping will appear darker. Another issue that you may run into is when a line is in multiple segments, and you really wanted a single line. Both issues are addressed using the Overkill command. It will allow you to delete any extra line or combine multiple segments into one line.

Procedure:

Pick (left click): **Overkill icon** from the Modify Panel of the Home tab 

PC: As an alternative, use the Cleanup Panel of the Manage Tab

OVERKILL *Select objects: Specify opposite corner: 2 found*
Select objects: ↵

An example of 2 overlapping lines (or two connected line segments) using a Selection Window to select the lines

A dialog box will appear:

Overlapping lines:

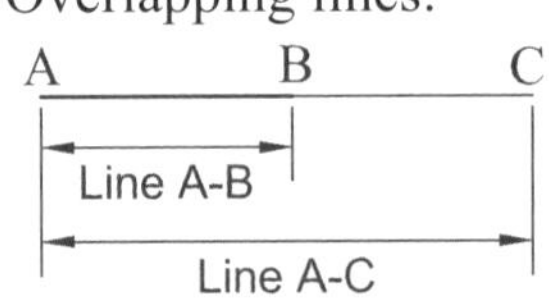

Line A-B will be deleted

Connected line segments:

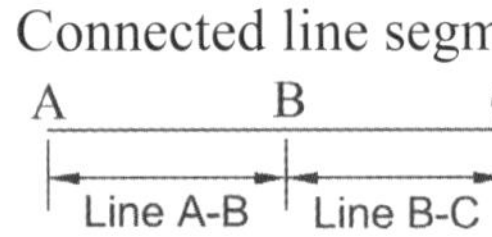

Lines will join to become a single line A-C

Pick OK to end the command
0 duplicate(s) deleted
1 overlapping object(s) or segment(s) deleted

Design Center and Mac Work-Around

Design Center

Chapter 9 introduced Design Center relative to bringing Blocks into your drawing from other drawings. In that chapter, it was briefly discussed that other items such as Dimension Styles, Text Styles, Layers, Layouts, etc. can also be brought into your drawing from other drawings. Only Blocks and Layouts had been covered before introducing the Design Center. Additional topics such as Text Styles, Dimension Styles, Multileader Styles, and Table Styles were not covered until later chapters.

An example of how this feature comes in handy is if you start a new drawing, perhaps the bookshelf of Chapter 11 Exercise 1, but you do not start with your template. After you finish drawing your objects, you want to add text and dimensions but realize that the styles you spent time creating aren't available within the drawing. Your template has all the Text Styles, Dimension Styles, etc. that you created as you went through the tutorials. You can use Design Center to bring in what you need from your template, or from any drawing you wish.

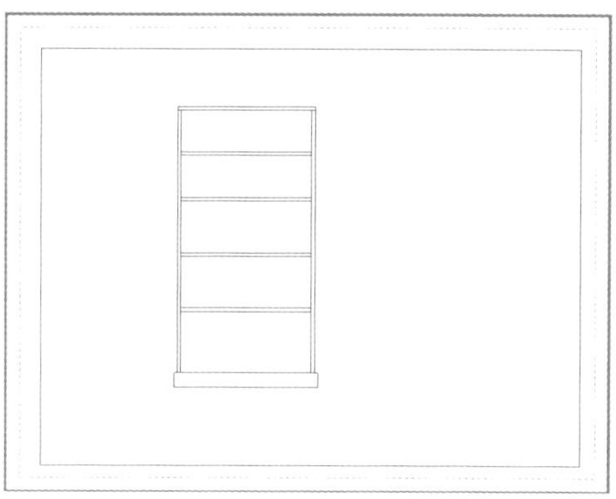

You can bring in Styles, etc. from another drawing or template by using Design Center. This will save you from re-creating items you already created in the past.

In the Palettes section of the View Tab on the Ribbon, select the Design Center icon to open the Design Center Palette. Navigate through the Folder List to find your Interior Design Template.

You created the Interior Design.dwt when you worked through the Hotel Suite Tutorials

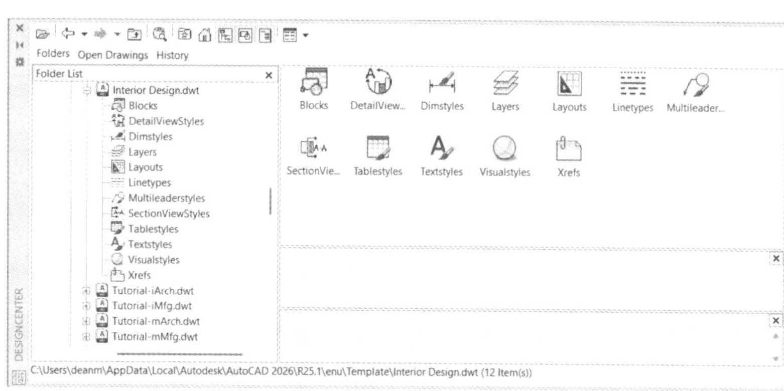

To select the Textstyle to bring in, either double click the icon on the right side of the Palette, or single click from the Folder List on the left side. The available Textstyles will be shown on the right side.

If you want to bring the Notes Textstyle in, you can either double click on the icon or click and drag the icon into your drawing. When you use the click and drag method, your cursor will be shown as an arrow with a small square on the lower right of it. Once you see that, you can let go of the mouse button. Your command line will give you the following feedback:

Textstyle(s) added. Duplicate definitions will be ignored.

You can expand the Annotation panel to verify that the Notes Text Style was brought in.

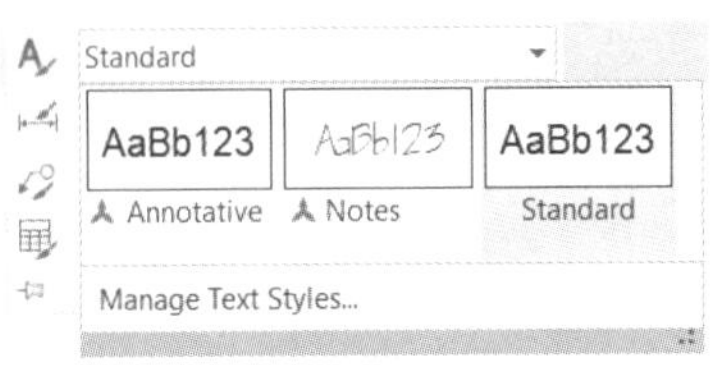

You can repeat these steps for the Dimension Style as well. To select the Dimension Style to bring in, single click Dimstyles from the Folder List on the left side. The available Dimension Styles will be shown on the right side.

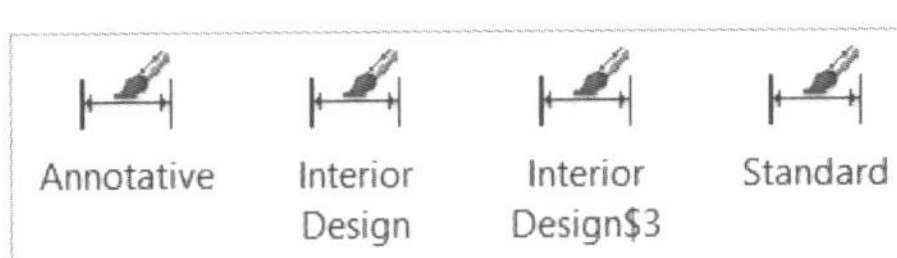

Notice that there are two Interior Design styles we can choose from. The style "Interior Design$3" is the subset of the "Interior Design" style that we created for the Diameter dimension. If we only bring in "Interior Design", then that subset will not come in. We need to bring both in by click and drag method, or by double clicking. You can confirm that they came in:

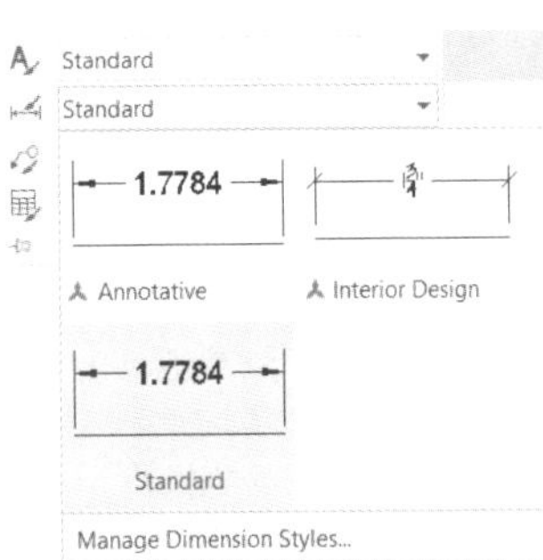

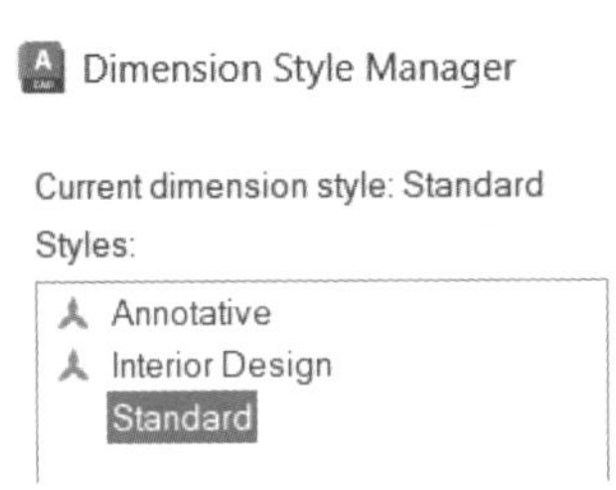

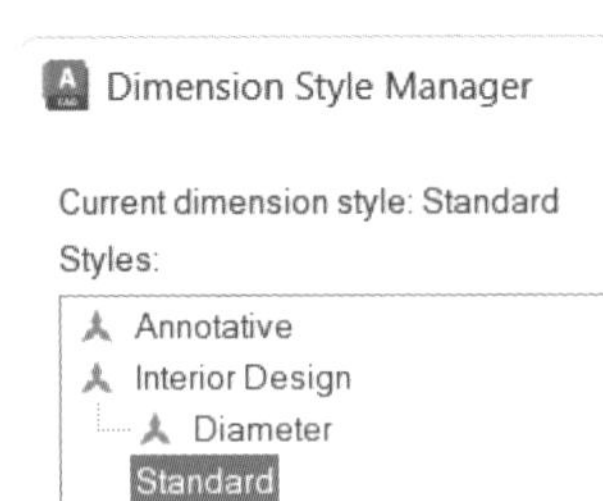

Bringing in "Interior Design$3" will bring in the subset for Diameter dimensions

Multileaders and Table Styles are brought into your drawing with Design Center in a similar manner as Textstyles and Dimension Styles. This bookshelf example does not use a Table, but it does use Multileaders. Bring in the Multileader style "Label".

If you choose to bring in the Layout that has the drawing format that you had created for the template, the method is similar. Select the Layouts icon from the Folder List and the available Layouts will be displayed on the right side of the Palette. Double click or click and drag the Plan View layout into your drawing. Notice that a new layout tab has been added to your drawing and it is named Plan View.

In addition to the Plan View layout being added, everything that supports that layout came in with it. The Textstyle used for the titleblock was Titleblock. In addition, layers Format and Viewport came in as well. You can confirm that these came in with the layout:

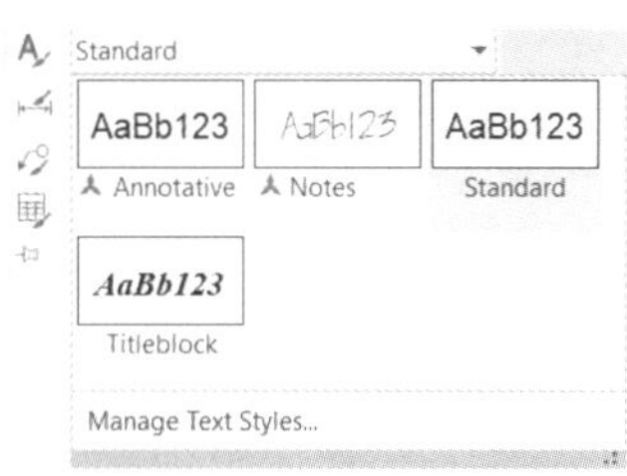

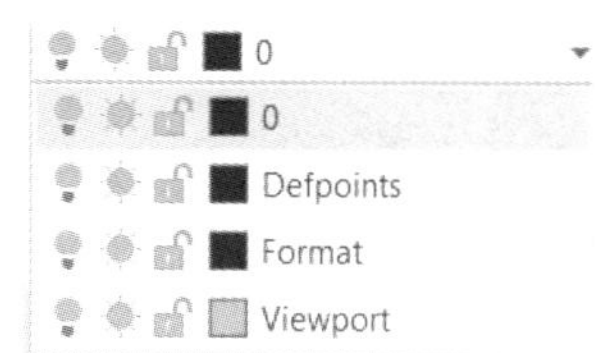

Knowing that other items will come in with the layout, it is recommended that you bring in the layout first and check what was brought in before bringing in anything else. It may save you some time. Even if you don't want that layout as part of your new drawing, bring it in anyway, then delete it. All the items that supported that layer remain with your drawing.

Work-Around for Mac

If you want to bring the layouts in, you can by following the instructions found in chapter 7.

Note, however, that only the items that support the layout come in. There may be additional items in that drawing that were not in the layout, such as Table Styles or Multileader Styles. In that case, you can bring in the entire template drawing using the Blocks Palette.

Click and drag the drawing icon into your drawing to bring everything in from that drawing, except the layouts.

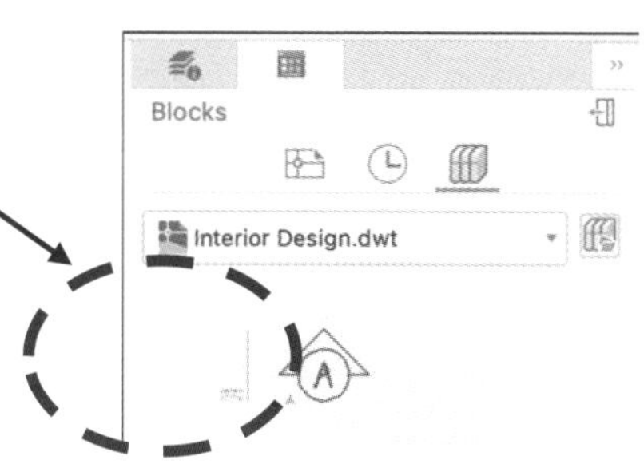

If there are any objects in the Model Space of the drawing you bring in, they will come in as a block. If you don't want those objects, then simply erase them.

Customize User Interface - PC

You may find that the default Panels and Tabs are not efficiently designed for the way you like to do your work. If you like to use the Construction Line command frequently, you may find it cumbersome to not have that command displayed on the top of the Draw Panel. Fortunately, AutoCAD allows you to customize the workspace.

The Customize User Interface command can be found on the Customization Panel of the Manage tab. It can also be found by expanding the Workspace Switching icon on the lower right of the screen and selecting Customize...

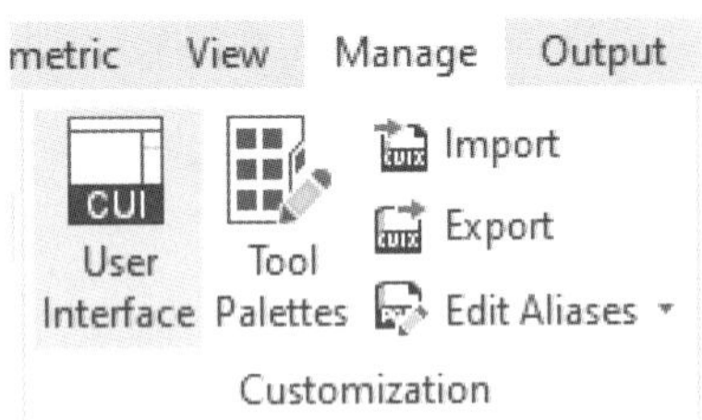

Workspace Switching

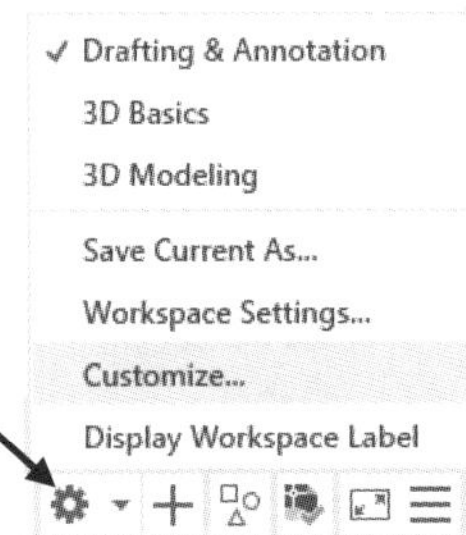

When you pick the CUI tool, the Customize User Interface dialog box will appear. Right-click Workspaces and select New Workspace.

A new Workspace1 will appear, ready for editing. Rename this to Interior Design.

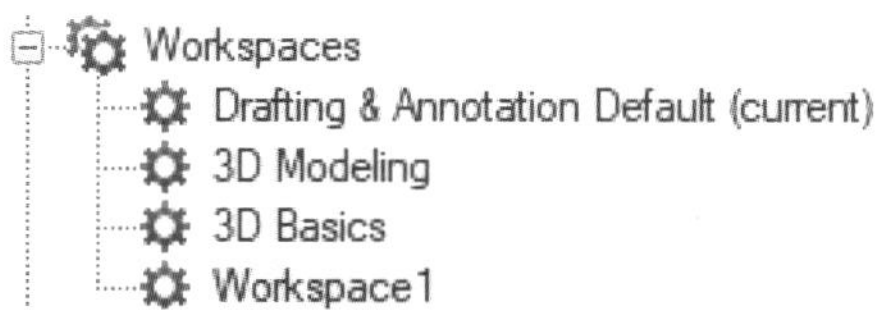

Expand the tree items below Ribbon and below Tabs on the upper left portion of the dialog box. Pick the Customize Workspace button on the upper right portion of the dialog box.

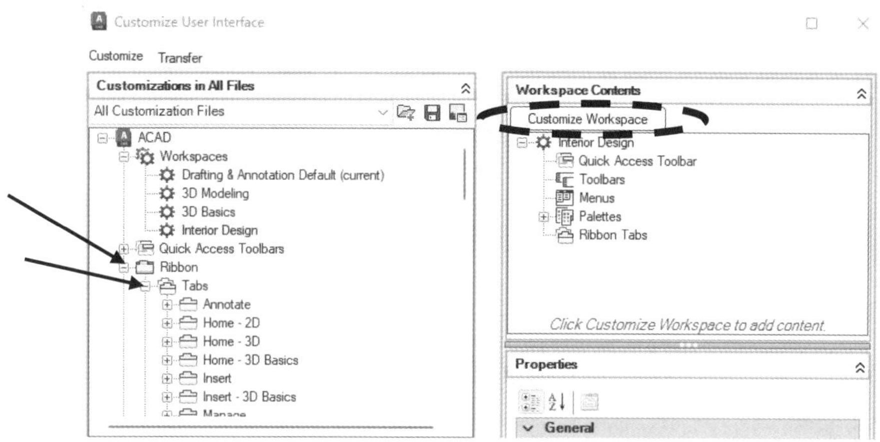

After you pick the Customize Workspace button, it will change to a Done button. Choose which Panels you want for the new Workspace by placing a check-mark next to them. The items you select will appear on the upper right portion of the dialog box.

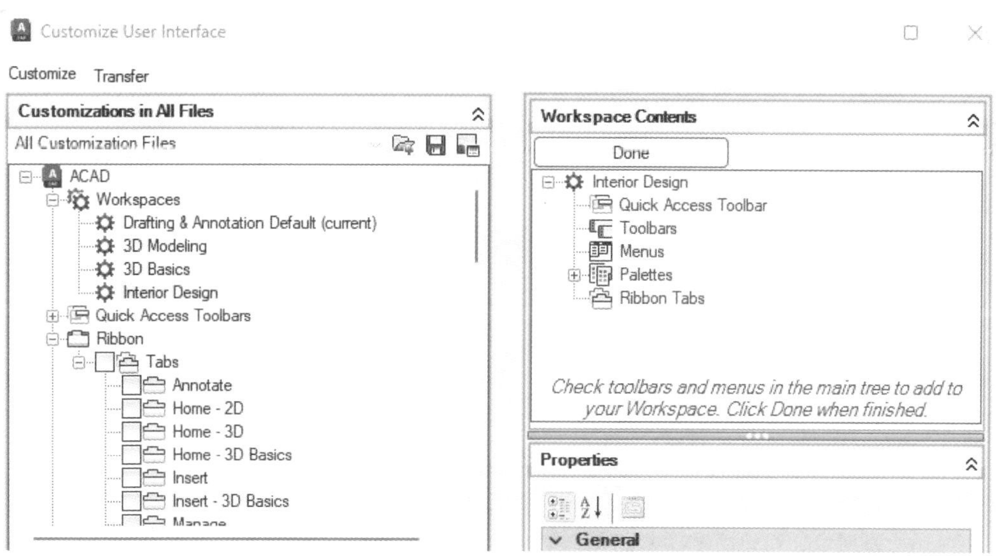

Select Home 2D on the left panel and it will appear in the right panel. Expand it and scroll down the list in the tree to find Home 2D Draw and select it and pick the Done button.

You can change the content of a Panel. Expand Panels from the tree in the upper left portion of the dialog box. You will need to scroll down to find it.

Scroll down the tree under Panels and select Home 2D-Draw. By selecting the Home 2D-Draw, a Panel Preview will appear on the upper right portion of the dialog box.

In the tree on the left portion, Expand the Home 2D-Draw. There are three rows for the 2D Draw panel. Expand the first two.

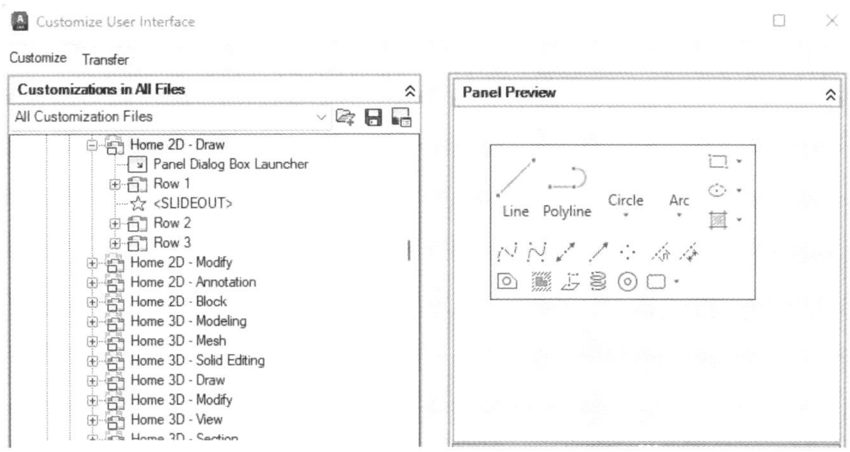

We will move the Construction Line from the second row to the first row above the Line command by picking and dragging. A drag bar will be displayed and will follow your cursor as you move.

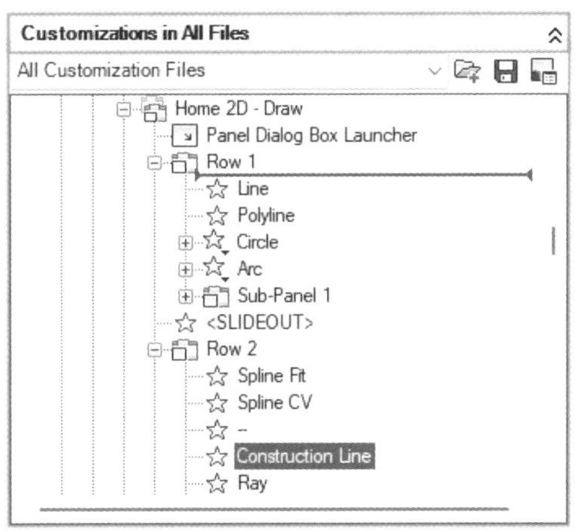

After you release the mouse button, the Panel Preview will update. Notice that the icon for Construction Line is small in comparison to the others in the first row. We can change the appearance by using the Properties section in the lower right portion of the dialog box.

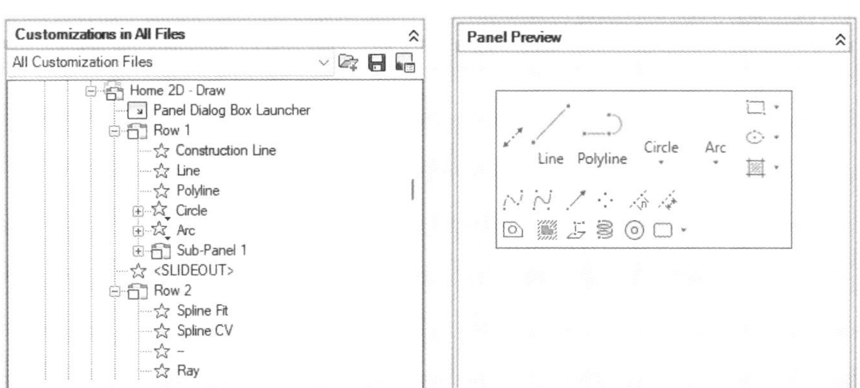

We can change the button style of the Construction Line. Select the Construction Line Button in the Panel Preview. Click on Button Style under Appearance in the Properties section and then use the pull-down arrow to select Large with Text (Vertical).

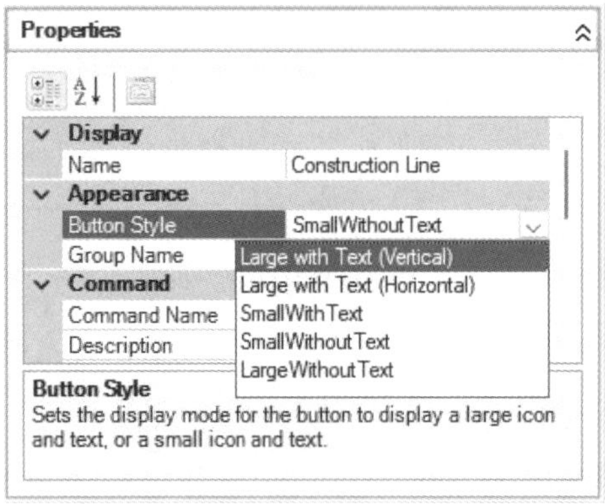

After you select this style, the Panel Preview will update to show the larger icon for the Construction Line.

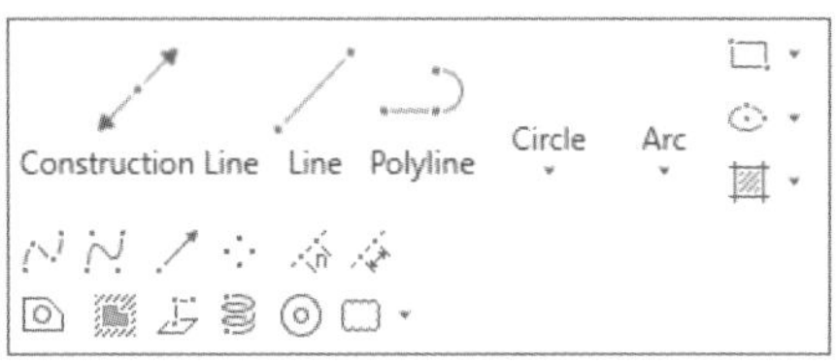

As an alternative, you may want to change all the icons to a smaller size without text to save space on your Panel. Make it however you like – this is customizing for your use!

When you are done, be sure to select Apply and OK buttons to close the dialog box.

Now that you have created a new Workspace, you will need to select it to use it. Pick the Workspace Switching icon. Interior Design is now available. Select it and your screen will change to your new customized workspace.

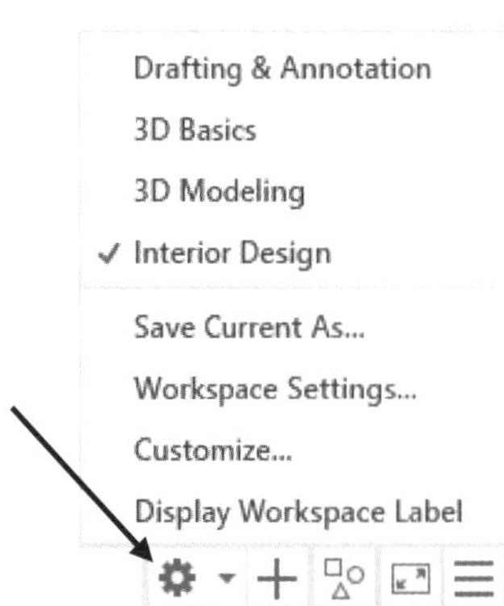

Congratulations! You are now ready to become a valuable and productive AutoCAD designer.

Customize User Interface - Mac

You may find that the default Tool Panels are not efficiently designed for the way you like to do your work. If you like to use the Measure command frequently, you may find it cumbersome to use the Tools pull-down menu. Fortunately, AutoCAD allows you to customize the workspace.

You can add a new Tool Panel for Measure by selecting the "+" at the bottom of the Tool Sets:

Pick to create
a new Panel

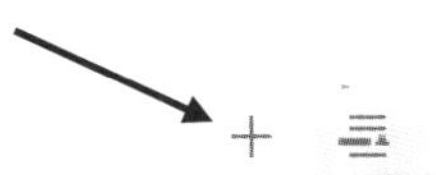

Once you select it, a New Panel dialog box will appear.

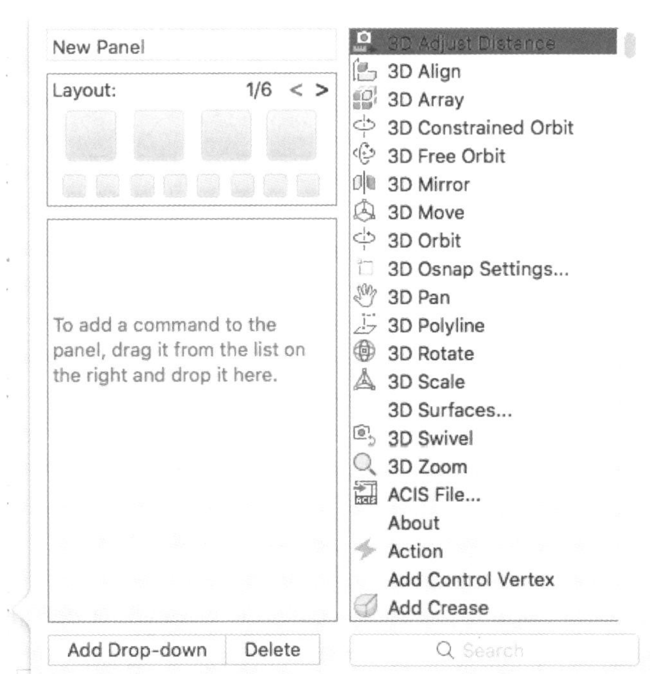

Change the name of the New Panel to "Measure". The right side of the dialog box shows available commands. Use the scroll bar to find the Distance commands. Click and drag "Measure Distance", "Measure Angle", Measure Radius", and "Measure Area" from the right side of the panel to the left side.

When you are done, your New Panel dialog box will look like this:

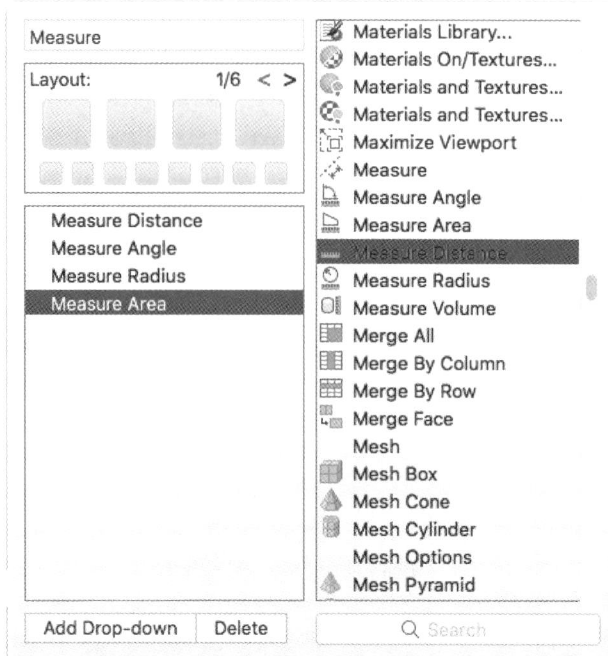

After you have completed this task, click anywhere in the drawing space and the new Measure panel will be available in your Tool Set.

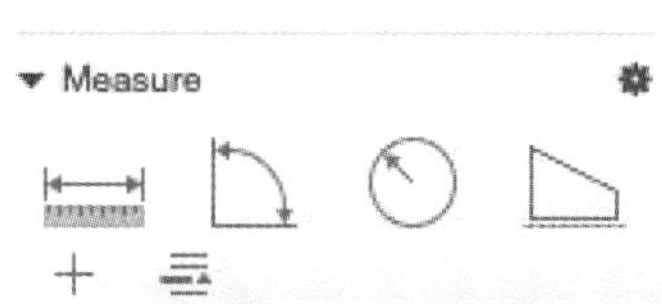

You can reorder each Tool Panel to your liking. To do this, pick the Reorder icon at the bottom of the Tool Set.

Pick this icon to reorder panels

A Reorder dialog box will appear. Click and drag each item to place them in the order you prefer.

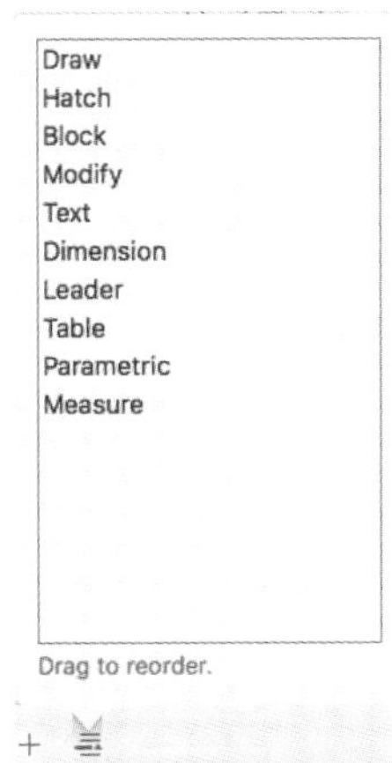

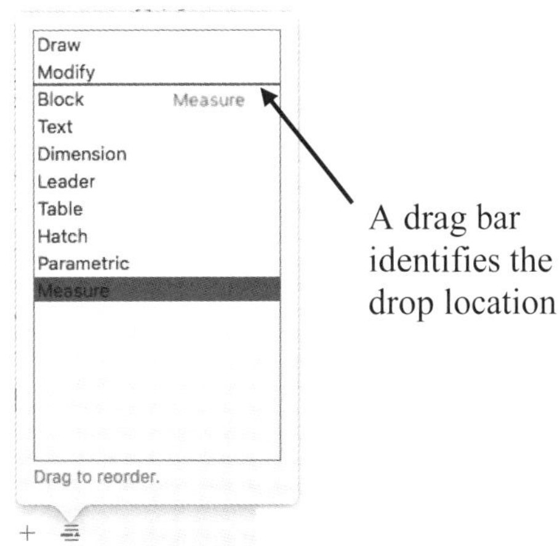

When you are done, your Tool Set will appear the way you want it to.

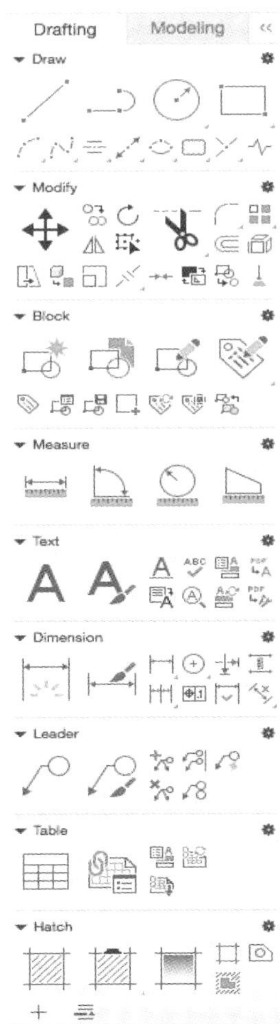

Congratulations! You are now ready to become a valuable and productive AutoCAD designer.

Exercises

1. Download the Wingback Chair from the publisher's website. Paste it into AutoCAD and trace it using splines. Adjust the scale so that it is 27 inches wide when done. Save it as a block.

   Hint: The picture is not perfectly centered, so you can use a centerline and trace half and then use the mirror command to complete the chair.

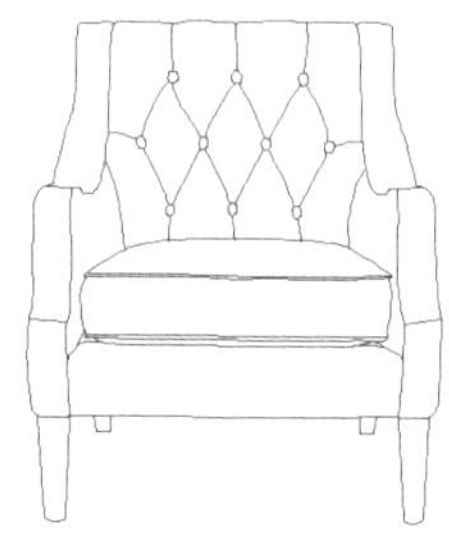

2. Take a picture, or copy a picture off the internet, of something you would like to trace. Trace the object and save it as a block.

Index

D

E

F

G

H

I

L

M

N

O

P

U

V

W

X

Z